Design and Implementation of the MTX Operating System

K. C. Wang

Design and Implementation of the MTX Operating System

 Springer

K. C. Wang
School of Electrical Engineering
and Computer Science
Washington State University
Pullman
Washington
USA

ISBN 978-3-319-36811-5 ISBN 978-3-319-17575-1 (eBook)
DOI 10.1007/978-3-319-17575-1

Springer Cham Heidelberg New York Dordrecht London

Printed on acid-free paper

Springer International Publishing AG Switzerland is part of Springer Science+Business Media (www.springer.com)

Preface

The purpose of this book is to provide a suitable platform for teaching and learning the theory and practice of operating systems. It covers the basic concepts and principles of operating systems, and it shows how to apply them to design and implement a complete operating system in incremental steps. Throughout the book, it uses the development of the MTX operating system to convey the real intent of this book, which is to demonstrate the design principles and implementation techniques of operating systems in general.

Due to its technical contents, this book is not intended for entry-level OS courses that teach only the basic concepts and principles of operating systems without programming practice. It is intended for technically oriented OS courses that emphasize on both theory and practice. The book's evolutional style, coupled with detailed source code and complete working sample systems, make it especially suitable for self-study. This book contains many new and original materials, especially on the design and use of parallel algorithms in SMP. It is also suitable for advanced study of operating systems.

Undertaking this book project has proved to be quite a challenge. While preparing the book for publication, I have been blessed with the encouragements and helps from many people. I would like to take this opportunity to thank all of them. I am also very grateful to Springer International Publishing AG for allowing me to disclose the source code of this book to the public for free. Hopefully, this would help further developments of the MTX system and enhancements to this book in the future.

Special thanks go to Cindy Wang for her continuing support and inspirations, which have made this book possible. Finally, I would like to thank my family for bearing with me with endless excuses of being too busy for so long.

Source code included in the book can be downloaded from the author's website at: http://www.eecs.wsu.edu/~cs460/mtxhome.

December, 2014

K. C. Wang

About the Author

 **K. C. Wang** received the BSEE degree from National Taiwan University in 1960 and the Ph.D. degree in Electrical Engineering from Northwestern University, Evanston, Ill in 1965. He is currently a Professor in the School of Electrical Engineering and Computer Science at Washington State University. His academic interests are in Operating Systems, Distributed Systems and Parallel Computing.

Contents

Chapter 1
Introduction

1.1 About This Book

This book is about the design and implementation of operating systems. An operating system (OS) is a set of programs and supporting files, which runs on a computer system to make the system convenient and easy to use. Without an operating system, a computer system is essentially useless. The study of operating systems involves a wide range of subject matters in computer science and computer engineering. These include computer architecture, computer programming and, most importantly, interface between computer software and hardware. It provides a complete set of knowledge about computer systems. Such knowledge is not only essential to computer professionals but also beneficial to all kinds of endeavors in computer related careers. This book covers the basic concepts and principles of operating systems. It shows how to apply these concepts and principles to the design and implementation of the MTX operating system in detail. MTX is a small Unix-like system intended mainly for teaching and learning the theory and practice of operating systems. It is designed for Intel x86 based PCs, and it runs on real PCs and virtual machines that emulate the PC hardware. It is written mostly in the high level language C, with less than 2% of assembly code. The MTX kernel includes process management, memory management, I/O device drivers and a Linux compatible EXT2 file system. It allows users to login from the PC's console and serial ports, and it supports executions of simple commands with I/O redirections, as well as multiple commands connected by pipes. Rather than presenting a complete system in one step and trying to dissect the system, this book shows the development of an operating system in incremental steps, starting from a simple multitasking program to a complete operating system. In each step, it shows how to apply the concepts and principles of operating systems to design and implement the various system components. Each step yields a small working system, which allows the reader to test and observe the internal operations of an operating system. In each successive step, it adds new features to the system and expands the system's capability until it evolves into a complete operating system. The design and implementation of MTX cover almost the entire spectrum of Intel x86 based system architectures, from 16-bit real mode

© Springer International Publishing Switzerland 2015
K. C. Wang, *Design and Implementation of the MTX Operating System*,
DOI 10.1007/978-3-319-17575-1_1

to 32-bit protected mode and eventually to Symmetric Multiprocessing (SMP). Despite the architectural differences, it demonstrates that the same design principle and implementation techniques can be applied to all cases.

1.2 Objective and Intended Audience

The objective of this book is to provide a suitable platform for teaching and learning the theory and practice of operating systems. It uses the development of the MTX system to demonstrate the design principles and implementation techniques of operating systems in general. Due to its technical contents, this book is not intended for entry-level OS courses that teach only the basic concepts and principles of OS without any programming practice. It is intended for computer science students and computer professionals, who wish to study the internal details of operating systems. This book covers both the theoretical and practical aspects of operating systems. It describes the design and implementation of a real operating system in detail. It is suitable as a textbook for technically oriented operating systems courses that strive for a balance between theory and practice. The book's evolutional style, coupled with detailed source code and complete working sample systems, make it especially suitable for self-study by computer enthusiasts. The book contains many new and original materials, especially on the design and use of parallel algorithms in SMP. It is also suitable for advanced study of operating systems.

1.3 Unique Features of This Book

This book has many unique features which distinguish it from other books.

1. This book is self-contained. Chapter 2 covers all the foundation and background information that are needed to study operating systems. These include CPU and I/O operations, virtual and real addresses, program development steps, linking C programs with assembly code, execution image, function call conventions and run-time stack usage. When discussing device drivers it explains the operations of each device before showing the actual driver design and implementation. When discussing file systems it describes file operations in detail before showing the implementation of a complete file system. When working with PCs in 32-bit protected mode it also explains the protected mode operations in detail.
2. Chapter 3 provides a complete coverage on operating systems booting, which is lacking in other OS books. In addition to the booting principle, it shows how to write booter programs to boot up real operating systems, such as Linux, from a variety of bootable devices. All the booters used in MTX are developed in this chapter. They are comparable to GRUB (GNU GRUB 2010) and isolinux (Syslinux 2013) in performance.

3. This book shows the design and implementation of a complete operating system in incremental steps. In Chap. 4, it uses a simple program to introduce the process concept and demonstrates the principle of context switching. It uses a process life-cycle model to illustrate the principle of multitasking. The same principle is used throughout the book to create and manage process images, independent of the memory management hardware of the system. This unique approach helps the reader better understand process management in an operating system.

4. This book begins to develop MTX in 16-bit real mode. Then it extends the real mode MTX to 32-bit protect mode and eventually to SMP. Despite the architectural differences, it demonstrates that the same design principle and implementation technique can be applied to all cases.

5. Rather than covering only the concepts and principles of threads, this book shows how to extend the process model to implement threads support and demonstrates threads applications by concurrent programs.

6. MTX uses a mixture of tools for process synchronization, which are chosen to best suit the needs, and it justifies their usage. In 16-bit real mode, it uses sleep/wakeup for process management but it uses semaphores in device drivers and file system for better efficiency. This also allows for a smooth transition from uniprocessor environment to SMP. In addition, it shows how to apply some of the classical process synchronization problems to OS design. Specifically, it uses the producer-consumer problem as a model for pipes and it applies the reader-writer problem to I/O buffer management in SMP to improve concurrency.

7. Chapter 8 covers interrupt processing and process scheduling. It covers the PC's interrupts hardware and interrupts processing in detail, and it presents a general framework for interrupt-driven device drivers design. It explains why interrupt handlers should not sleep or become blocked. It discusses the goals, polices and algorithms of process scheduling, and it demonstrates the effects of different process scheduling algorithms by sample systems.

8. Chapter 9 presents a unified treatment of interrupts and signal processing, which helps clarify the intended roles and proper usage of signals. In addition, it uses examples to illustrate the concepts and techniques of signal catchers.

9. Chapter 12 covers I/O buffer management. It discusses the buffer management algorithm of Unix (Bach, 1990) and points out it shortcomings. Then it shows how to design new algorithms to improve the buffer cache performance. Most materials presented in this chapter are new and original.

10. It explains the hierarchical relations of file operations in an OS, from user space to kernel space down to the device driver level. Then it shows the implementation of a Linux compatible EXT2 file system in detail.

11. In order to show the different capabilities of segmentation and paging, it presents three different versions of MTX in protected mode; mtx32.1 uses segmentation, mtx32.2 uses static paging and pmtx uses dynamic paging.

12. Chapter 15 on SMP is most unique. It shows how to configure SMP-compliant systems and explains the startup sequence of SMP-compliant systems. It

extends the conventional process synchronization mechanisms, such as sleep/ wakeup and semaphores, to suit the SMP environment. It presents a general methodology for SMP kernel design, and it shows how to apply the principles to adapt the UP pmtx kernel for SMP. Then it focuses on the design and use of parallel algorithms for SMP. Specifically, it uses parallel algorithms in process management, resource management, pipes and I/O buffers to improve both concurrency and efficiency. This novel approach to SMP is new and original.

13. It compares monolithic kernel and microkernel based OS design and demonstrates a hybrid system, which incorporates the strength of both approaches.

14. Throughout the book, it uses sample systems to demonstrate the design principles and implementation techniques.

1.4 Book Contents

This book is organized as follows. Chapter 2 covers the foundations and background that are needed to study operating systems. These include CPU operations, virtual and real addresses, I/O operations, program development steps, linking C programs with assembly code, program execution image, function calls and run-time stack usage. It also covers some basic information of the EXT2 file system.

Chapter 3 covers OS booting. It discusses OS booting in general and describes the booting process from real or virtual storage devices in detail. These include booting from floppy disk, hard disk partitions, CD/DVD-ROM and USB drives. Instead of writing a customized booter to boot up only MTX, it shows how to develop booter programs to boot up other operating systems, such as Linux, from a variety of bootable devices.

Chapter 4 starts to develop the MTX kernel. First, it uses a simple program to introduce the process concept and demonstrate the technique of process context switching. Then it implements a multitasking environment to support multiple processes. It extends the multitasking system to support dynamic process creation, process scheduling and process termination. It shows how to stop and continue a process, and extends stop/continue to sleep/wakeup operations for process synchronization and explain their usage in an OS kernel. Then it implements the wait operation to allow processes to wait for child process termination. In addition, it also shows how to adjust process priorities for priority-based process scheduling. These lead to a simple OS kernel for process management. In each step, it demonstrates the design principles and implementation technique by a complete sample system, which allows the reader to test and observe the internal operations of an OS kernel.

Chapter 5 covers user mode and system calls. It explains the distinction between the address spaces of kernel and user modes, the mechanism of transition between user and kernel modes and how to implement the transition. It shows how to create processes with user mode images and let them return to execute the images in user mode. Based on this, it implements simple system calls, which allow user mode processes to enter kernel, execute kernel functions and return to user mode.

Then it expands the system calls to support other process management functions. These include fork, exec and the advanced technique of vfork. With fork and exec, it shows how to start up MTX with a simple init process, which forks a rudimentary sh process to run user mode programs. These make the MTX kernel to have similar capability as Unix kernel for process management. Then it extends the process model to support threads and demonstrates threads applications by concurrent programs.

Chapter 6 covers process synchronization. It explains the concepts of concurrent processes, the basic principle of process synchronization and the hierarchical relations among the various kinds of synchronizing tools. It shows how to implement critical regions in both uniprocessor and multiprocessor environments. Then it shows how to implement the various kinds of process synchronization mechanisms. These include sleep/wakeup for uniprocessor environment, spinlock and semaphores for multiprocessor environment. It shows how to apply semaphores to both operating systems design and concurrent programming. It discusses deadlocks and how to deal with deadlocks. As an application of process synchronization, it explains the concepts of pipes and shows how to apply the producer-consumer problem to implement pipes in the MTX kernel. Then it discusses process communication by messages and shows how to design and implement message passing mechanisms, using both asynchronous and synchronous protocols. In addition, it also presents a model for server-client based process communication.

Chapter 7 covers memory management. It discusses the goals and principles of memory management, which include segmentation, paging, demand-paging, virtual memory and page replacement rules. It discusses memory management in the real mode MTX in detail. These include managing process images in kernel and dynamic memory management in user space during run-time.

Chapter 8 covers interrupt processing and process scheduling. It explains the PC's interrupts hardware and interrupts processing in detail. It incorporates the PC's timer into the MTX kernel and implements timer service functions. It discusses the principles of process scheduling in time-sharing systems. It explains the goals, policies and algorithms of process scheduling in Unix and Linux. It implements several different process scheduling algorithms in MTX and compares their effects on the system performance.

Chapter 9 covers signals and signal processing. It presents a unified treatment of interrupts and signals, which helps clarify the roles of signals and signal processing. It explains the source of signals and the proper usage of signals. It shows how to implement signals and signal handling in MTX and demonstrates signal catchers by examples.

Chapter 10 covers device drivers. These include the PC's console display, keyboard, printer, serial ports, floppy drive, IDE hard disk and ATAPI driver for CDROM. Except for the console display, which does not use interrupts, all device drivers are interrupt-driven and use semaphores for synchronization. It emphasizes on the principles of driver design and presents a general framework that is applicable to all interrupt-driven device drivers. It points out the difference between pipes and interrupt-driven drivers, and explains in detail why interrupt handlers should not sleep or become blocked. It also shows how to implement foreground and background processes. It demonstrates each device driver by a sample system, which allows the reader to test and observe device driver operations.

Chapter 11 covers file system. It explains the various levels of file operations. These include low level operations on storage devices, file system support in OS kernel, system calls for file operations, library I/O functions, user commands and sh scripts. It describes the control flow of file operations, from user space to kernel space down to the device driver level. Instead of covering only the principles, it shows the implementation of a Linux compatible EXT2 file system (Card et al. 1995) in detail.

Chapter 12 covers I/O buffer management. It discusses the I/O buffer management algorithm of Unix (Bach 1990) and points out its shortcomings. Then it shows how to design new buffer management algorithms to improve the performance of the I/O buffer cache. Most materials presented in this chapter are new and original.

Chapter 13 covers user interface. It presents a complete listing of MTX system calls and shows how to develop user mode programs. It explains the roles and algorithms of the init and login programs, which are essential to system startup. It shows how to write a simple command interpreter sh to execute user commands. The simple sh supports executions of single commands with I/O redirections as well as multiple commands connected by pipes. It also lists other user mode programs, which are used to demonstrate the capability of MTX.

Chapter 14 extends the real-mode MTX to 32-bit protected mode. It explains protected mode operations in detail and shows how to configure the PC's memory management hardware for both segmentation and paging. It shows how to set up the IDT for exception and interrupt processing. Then it extends the real-mode MTX to 32-bit protected mode. In order to illustrate the different capabilities of segmentation and paging, it presents three different versions of MTX in protected mode; mtx32.1 uses segmentation, mtx32.2 uses static paging and pmtx uses dynamic paging. It also shows how to handle page faults and discusses the principles of demand-paging and virtual memory.

Chapter 15 covers Symmetric Multiprocessing (SMP). It explains multiprocessor and SMP-compliant systems (Intel 1997), configuring IOAPIC and local APICs for SMP and the startup sequence of SMP systems. It covers the principles of SMP kernel design and presents a general methodology for adapting uniprocessor (UP) kernels for SMP. Then it extends PMTX from UP to SMP. Instead of merely using locks to protect kernel data structures, which tends to restrict concurrency, it emphasizes on the design and use of parallel algorithms to improve both concurrency and efficiency. Specifically, it uses parallel algorithms for process management, resource management, pipes and I/O buffer management. This novel approach to SMP is new and original. In addition, it also shows a SMP system in 16-bit real mode.

Chapter 16 discusses other approaches to OS design. It compares monolithic kernel based OS with microkernel (Accetta et al. 1986) based OS, and it presents a hybrid system which includes the strength of both approaches. To demonstrate the capability of such a hybrid system, it implements an iso9660 file system server in user space, which communicates with client processes by messages.

The Appendix section contains instructions on how to install and run MTX on real PCs and virtual machines. It also includes a list of all the source code for the sample systems of this book.

1.5   Use This Book as OS Textbook

This book is suitable as a textbook for technically oriented operating systems cours-es in a Computer Science/Engineering curriculum that strive for a balance between theory and practice. Prerequisites for such a course are very minimal.

- Elementary data structures and programming in C.
- An introductory OS course helps but not essential.

A one-semester OS course based on this book may include the following topics.

1. Major functions of OS, program development, execution image and run-time stack usage (Chap. 2).
2. Booting principle, develop a booter to boot up MTX from a virtual disk (Chap. 3).
3. Develop an OS kernel for process management (Chap. 4).
4. Kernel mode and user mode transitions, simple system calls, fork and exec (Chap. 5).
5. Process synchronization, semaphores, deadlocks and deadlock handling, pipes and message passing (parts of Chap. 6).
6. Memory management, principles of paging and virtual memory (Chap. 7).
7. Interrupt processing, timer, timer service and dynamic process scheduling (Chap. 8).
8. Signals and signal processing, install signal catchers to handle exceptions (Chap. 9).
9. Device drivers: console display, keyboard, serial ports and IDE drivers (Chap. 10).
10. File system: file system organization, file operations in kernel (parts of Chap. 11).
11. User interface: init, login, sh and user command programs (Chap. 13).
12. Introduction to protected mode operations, segmentation and paging (Chap. 14).
13. Introduction to SMP and real-time OS (parts of Chap. 15).

The problems section of each chapter contains questions designed to review the concepts and principles presented in the chapter. Many of the problems are suitable as programming projects to let the students experiment with alternative designs and implementations. An advanced OS course may cover Chap. 14 on protected mode in more detail. It should also include Chap. 15 on SMP, with an emphasis on the de-sign of parallel algorithms to improve concurrency. Such a course may also include and expand on Chap. 16 to study different approaches to OS design.

Most materials of this book have been used in a senior level OS course, CS460, in the School of Electrical Engineering and Computer Science at Washington State University for many years. The object of the course is to lead the students to develop a small but complete operating system that actually works. The current course syllabus, lecture notes and programming assignments, are available at http://www. eecs.wsu.edu/~cs460. Many parts of this book, e.g. process management (Chaps. 4 and 5), process synchronization (Chap. 6), interrupts processing (Chap. 8) and device drivers (Chap. 10) are also suitable for courses on embedded systems.

1.6   MTX Systems for Testing and Evaluation

Sample MTX systems are available for testing and evaluation at

http://www.eecs.wsu.edu/~cs460/mtxhome/MTXinstallCD.iso

MTXinstallCD.iso is a bootable CDROM image. It contains a virtual IDE disk image, vdisk, with 4 partitions. Each partition contains a runnable MTX system. Download the MTXinstallCD.iso file. Mount it under Linux and copy the vdisk file to a directory, as in

mount –o loop MTXinstallCD.iso /mnt ; cp /mnt/vdisk ./ ; umount /mnt

The simplest way to test MTX is to run QEMU on vdisk directly, as in

qemu –hda vdisk –m 512m –smp 8 –serial mon:stdio

Then boot up and run MTX from a partition number, where

1. RMTX in 16-bit real mode
2. PMTX in 32-bit protected mode using dynamic paging
3. SMP_MTX in 32-bit protected mode using parallel algorithms for SMP
4. MTX32.1 in 32-bit protected mode using segmentation

In all cases, login as root, password:12345. All executable commands are in the/bin directory. The reader may also run QEMU on vdisk with additional options, such as

-serial /dev/pts/2 –parallel /dev/pts/3 –fda FDimage –cdrom CDimage

In addition, MTXinstallCD.iso also contains all the source code and sample systems of this book, as well as instructions on how to install the MTX system images. The reader may consult the Appendix section of this book for details.

Finally, MTX stands for Multi-Tasking eXecutable. It began in the late 80's as a simple multitasking system used by the author to demonstrate processes, context switching and process management in an OS kernel. Over time, it has gradually evolved to its present form. MTX is a Unix-like system. Its design is heavily influenced by Unix (Ritchie and Thompson, 1978; Bach, 1990), and it borrows many implementation techniques from Unix, but it is not a simple Unix clone. For instance, the internal organization and the startup sequence of MTX are very different from that of Unix. Instead of using a single mechanism for process synchronization, MTX uses a mixture of process synchronization tools, which are chosen to best suit the needs, and it justifies their usage. In the areas of I/O buffer management and SMP, all the algorithms used in MTX are new and original. Since every Unix-like system deserves a Unix-like name, e.g. Minix, Linux, etc. it seems appropriate for me to jump on the bandwagon also to give MTX a more glamorous name, Wanix, in honor of the students at Washington State University, who took the OS course and motivated me to develop the system and write this book.

References

Accetta, M. et al., "Mach: A New Kernel Foundation for UNIX Development", Technical Conference – USENIX, 1986.

Bach, M.J., "The Design of the Unix operating system", Prentice Hall, 1990.

Card, R., Ts'o, T., Tweedie, S., "Design and Implementation of the Second Extended Filesystem", web.mit.edu/tytso/www/linux/ext2intro.html, 1995

GNU GRUB Project: http://www.gnu.org/software/grub, 2010

Intel MultiProcessor Specification, v1. 4, 1997

Ritchie, D.M.; Thompson, K., "The UNIX Time-Sharing System", Bell System Technical Journal, Vol. 57, No. 6, Part 2, July, 1978,

Syslinux project, http://www.syslinux.org, 2013

Chapter 2
Foundations and Background

2.1 Computer System

2.1.1 Computer Hardware System

Figure 2.1 shows a typical computer hardware system. It consists of one or more Processor Units (PUs), which share a common memory and a set of I/O devices. I/O devices include hard disk, CDROM, USB device, floppy drive, console, terminals and printers, etc.

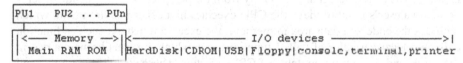

```
PU1    PU2 ... PUn
  |        |
||<—— Memory ——>||<————————————————— I/O devices ————————————————>|
|| Main RAM ROM  ||HardDisk|CDROM|USB|Floppy|console,terminal,printer
```

Fig. 2.1 Computer hardware system

The PUs may be physically separate units. With current multicore processor technology, they may reside in the same processor package. A system with only one PU is called a Uniprocessor (UP) system. Traditionally, the PU in a UP system is called the Central Processing Unit (CPU). A computer system with a multiple number of PUs is called a Multiprocessor (MP) system. In a MP system, the term CPU is also used to refer to the individual PUs. For ease of discussion, we shall assume Uniprocessor systems first.

2.1.2 CPU Operations

Every CPU has a Program Counter (PC), also known as the Instruction Pointer (IP), a flag or status register (SR), a Stack Pointer (SP) and several general registers,

© Springer International Publishing Switzerland 2015
K. C. Wang, *Design and Implementation of the MTX Operating System,*
DOI 10.1007/978-3-319-17575-1_2

where PC points to the next instruction to be executed in memory, SR contains current status of the CPU, e.g. operating mode, interrupt mask and condition code, and SP points to the top of the current stack. The stack is a memory area used by the CPU for special operations, such as push, pop call and return, etc. The operations of a CPU can be modeled by an infinite loop.

while(power-on){

> (1). fetch instruction: load *PC as instruction, increment PC to point to the next instruction;
> (2). decode instruction: interpret the instruction's operation code and generate operands;
> (3). execute instruction: perform operation on operands, write results to memory if needed; execution may use the stack, implicitly change PC, etc.
> (4). check for pending interrupts; may handle interrupts;

}

In each of the above steps, an error condition, called an exception or trap, may occur due to invalid address, illegal instruction, privilege violation, etc. When the CPU encounters an exception, it follows a pre-installed pointer in memory to execute an exception handler in software.

A CPU just keeps executing instructions. It does not know, nor care, about what it is doing. The difference, if any, is purely from the perspective of an outside observer. From a user's point of view, the CPU executes in a certain environment, which includes the code and data area in memory, the execution history, such as function calls and local variables of called functions, etc. which are usually maintained in the stack, and the current contents of CPU registers. These static (in memory) and dynamic (in CPU registers) information is called the context of an execution. If the CPU always executes in the same context of a single application, it is executing in single task mode. If the CPU can execute in the contexts of many different applications, it is executing in multitasking mode. In multitasking mode, the CPU executes different tasks by multiplexing its execution time among the tasks, i.e. it executes one task for a while, then it switches to execute another task, etc. If the switch is fast enough, it gives the illusion that all the tasks are executing simultaneously. This logical parallelism is called concurrency. In a MP system, tasks can execute on different CPUs in parallel. For the sake of simplicity, we shall consider multitasking in UP systems first. Multiprocessor systems will be covered later in Chap. 15.

2.1.3   System Mode and User Mode

CPUs designed for multitasking usually have two different execution modes, which are represented by a mode bit in the CPU's status register. If SR.mode=0, the CPU is in system mode. If SR.mode=1, it is in user mode. While in system mode, the CPU can execute any instruction and access all the memory. While in user mode, it can not execute privileged instructions, such as I/O operations or instructions that change the SR.mode, and it can only access the memory area assigned to the application. A multitasking operating system relies on the system and user modes to separate and protect the execution environments of different tasks. Instead of two modes, some CPUs may use two bits in the SR register to provide four different modes, which form a set of protection rings, in which the innermost ring 0 is the most privileged layer, and the outermost ring 3 is the least privileged layer. CPUs with protection rings are intended to implement highly secure systems. Most Unix-like systems, e.g. Linux (Bovet et al. 2005) and MTX, use only two modes. The operating system kernel runs in system mode and user applications run in user mode. It is very easy to switch the CPU from system mode to user mode, by simply changing SR.mode from 0 to 1. However, once in user mode, a program cannot change the CPU's mode arbitrarily, for obvious reasons. The only way the CPU can change from user mode to system mode is by one of the following means.

1. Exceptions or traps: when CPU encounters an exception, e.g. invalid address, illegal instruction, privilege violation, divide by 0, etc. it automatically switches to system mode to execute a trap handler routine. Trap handlers are executed in system mode because the CPU must be able to execute privileged instructions to deal with the error.
2. Interrupts: interrupts are external signals to the CPU, requesting for CPU service. When an interrupt occurs, if the CPU is in the state of accepting interrupts, i.e. interrupts are not masked out, it switches automatically to system mode to execute an interrupt handler, which again must be in system mode because I/O operations require privileged instructions (or access protected I/O memory areas). Interrupts and interrupts processing will be cover later in Chap. 8.
3. System calls: every CPU has special instructions which cause the CPU to switch from user mode to system mode. On the Intel x86 CPU it is the INT n instruction, where n is a byte value. A user mode program may issue INT n to explicitly request to enter system mode. Such requests are known as system calls, which are essential to operating systems. System calls will be covered in Chap. 5.

2.1.4 Memory and Memory Models

Memory may be composed of physically different memory chips. To reduce the access time, the memory organization may use one or more levels of cache memories, which are smaller but faster memory devices between the CPU and main memory. A CPU usually has a level-1 (L1) cache memory inside the CPU for caching both instructions and data. In addition, a system may also have L2 and L3 caches, etc. which are outside of the CPU. In a MP system the external caches may be shared by different CPUs. The memory subsystem uses a cache-coherence protocol to ensure that the contents of the various levels of caches are consistent. To most users, such hardware-level details are transparent. But they are not totally invisible to an operating system. For instance, in an OS kernel when process context switching occurs, the CPU's internal cache must be flushed to prevent it from executing stale instructions belonging to an old context.

2.1.5 Virtual Address and Physical Addresses

Ideally, memory should appear to the CPU as a sequence of linearly addressable locations which the CPU can read/write by specifying an address. In practice, this is often not the case. Usually, the CPU executes in the logical or virtual address (VA) space of a program, which may differ from the actual or physical address (PA) in memory. During execution, the CPU's memory management hardware automatically translates or maps virtual addresses to physical addresses. As an example, consider the Intel x86 CPU (Antonakos 1999). When the Intel x86 CPU starts, it is in the so called 16-bit real mode. While in real mode, the CPU can only execute 16-bit code and access the lowest 1 MB of physical memory. However, it cannot access the entire 1 MB memory all at once. Instead, the CPU regards the memory as composed of four segments. A memory segment is a block of 64 KB memory that begins from a 16-byte address boundary. Since the low 4 bits of a memory segment address are always 0, it suffices to represent a segment by the high 16 bits of the segment's 20-bit real address. The CPU has four 16-bit segment registers, denoted by CS, DS, SS, ES, which point to the segments in memory the CPU is allowed to access. Thus, the CPU can access at most 4 segments or 256 KB of real memory at any time instant. A program may consist of four distinct pieces, denoted by Code, Data, Stack and Extra sections, each up to 64 KB in size. During execution each of the sections is loaded to a memory segment, which is pointed by a corresponding CPU segment register. Within a program, every address is a 16-bit VA, which is an offset in a program's section, hence an offset in the section's segment in memory. For each VA, the CPU uses the corresponding segment register to map it to a PA by

$$(20\text{-bit})PA = (SegmentRegister \ll 4) + (16\text{-bit})VA$$

where the SegmentRegister is determined either by default or by an explicit segment prefix to the instruction. When fetching instructions the CPU uses the default CS register. When accessing stack it uses the default SS register. When reading/writing data it uses the default DS register. It uses ES if the instruction is prefixed with an ES byte.

Although the x86 CPU in real mode can support programs with four segments, a binary executable program generated by a compiler-linker may further restrict the CPU's ability to access memory. Conceptually, the run-time image of a program consists of three sections; Code, Data and Stack. Ideally, each of the sections can be loaded to a separate segment in memory and pointed by a segment register, as shown in Fig. 2.2.

In practice, some of the segments may overlap. For example, by default the binary executable generated by the compiler-linker of BCC [BCC] uses the one-seg-

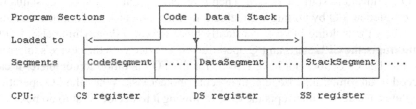

Fig. 2.2 Program sections and memory segments

ment memory model, in which the Code, Data and Stack sections are all the same. During execution, a one-segment program is loaded to a single memory segment and the CPU's CS, DS and SS registers must all point to that segment. Thus, the maximum size of a one-segment program is limited to 64 KB, but it can be loaded to, and executed from, any available segment in memory. In addition, BCC can also generate binary executables with separate I (instruction) and D (data) spaces. In the separate I&D memory model, the Code is a section, but the combined Data and Stack is a separate section. During execution, the Code section is loaded to a CS segment and the combined Data and Stack section is loaded to a combined DS and SS segment. BCC does not generate binary executables with separate data and stack segments due to potential ambiguity in dereferencing pointers in C. If the data and stack segments were separate, a pointer at run time may point to either the data area or the stack. Then *p must use the right segment to access the correct memory area, but the C compiler does not know which segment to use at compile time. For this reason, BCC's compiler and linker only generate binary executables with either one-segment or separate I&D space memory model, which limits a program's virtual address space to either 64 or 128 KB. Translation of VA to PA in general will be covered in Chap. 7 on Memory Management.

2.1.6 I/O Devices and I/O Operations

I/O devices can be classified as block and char devices. Block devices, such as disks and CDROM, transfer data in chunks or blocks. Char devices, such as console and terminals, transfer data in bytes. There are devices, e.g. USB drives, which transfer data physically in serial form but appear as a block device. I/O operations can be classified into several modes, as shown in Fig. 2.3.

In Programmed I/O (PIO), the CPU actively controls each I/O operation. In I/O by polling, the CPU first checks the device status. When the device is ready, it issues

```
                                      |- I/O by polling
                              |- PIO —|- I/O by interrupts
          I/O operations-|- DMA
                              |- I/O Processor
```

Fig. 2.3 I/O operation types

an I/O command to start the device. Then it repeatedly checks the device status for I/O completion. I/O by polling is suitable only for single task environment because while the CPU is doing I/O it is constantly busy and can't do anything else. In I/O by interrupts, the CPU starts an I/O operation on a device with the device's interrupt enabled. The CPU does not have to wait for the I/O operation to complete. It can proceed to do something else, e.g. to execute another task. When the I/O operation completes, the device interrupts the CPU, allowing it to decide what to do next. I/O by interrupts is well suited to multitasking. After starting an I/O operation, if the task has to wait for the I/O operation to complete, the CPU can be switched to run another task. In I/O by DMA (Direct Memory Access), the CPU writes the I/O operation information, such as the memory address, data transfer direction, number of bytes to transfer and the intended device, to a DMA controller and starts the DMA controller. Then the CPU can continue to execute. The DMA controller transfers data between memory and I/O device concurrently with CPU execution by sharing bus cycles with the CPU. When data transfer completes, the DMA controller interrupts the CPU. Responding to the interrupt, the CPU can check the I/O completion status and decide what to do next. I/O processors are either processors designed specially for I/O operations or general processors dedicated to I/O tasks. Unlike DMA controllers, which must be programmed by the CPU, I/O processors can execute complex I/O programs to do I/O operations without CPU supervision. In a computer system with multicore processors, some of the processors may be dedicated to I/O tasks rather than to general computing. This is because in such a system computational capacity is no longer the only factor that affects the system performance. Fast I/O and inter-processor communication to exchange data are equally important.

2.2 Operating Systems

An operating system (OS) is a set of programs and supporting files, which runs on a computer system to make the system easier and convenient to use. Without an operating system, a computer system is essentially useless. An OS may mean different things to different people. An average user may be only interested in how to use an OS. A software developer may be more interested in the tools and Application Program Interface (API) of an OS. A system designer may be more interested in the internal organization of an OS. Since this book is about the design and implementation of operating systems, we shall describe them from a functional point of view.

2.2.1 Major Functions of Operating Systems

The objective of an OS is to provide the following functions.

- Process management
- Memory management
- File system support

- Device drivers
- Networking

An OS supports the executions of processes. A process is a sequence of executions regarded by the OS kernel as a single entity for using system resources. System resources include memory space, I/O devices, and most importantly, CPU time. An operating system consists of a set of concurrent processes. Every activity in an OS can be attributed to a process running at that time. Process management includes process creation, process scheduling, changing process execution image, process synchronization and process termination. Thus, process management is the first major function of an OS.

Each process executes an image in memory. The execution image of a process is a memory area containing its code, data and stack. In an operating system, processes are dynamic; they come into existence when they are created and they disappear when their executions terminate. As processes come and go, their memory areas must be allocated and deallocated. During execution, a process may change its image to a different program. In systems with memory protection hardware, the OS kernel must ensure that each process can only access its own image to prevent processes from interfering with one another. All these require memory management, which is the second major function of an OS kernel.

In general, an OS kernel needs supporting files in order to run. During operation, it should allow users to save and retrieve information. In addition, it may also provide an environment for developing application programs. All these require file systems. Thus, the third major function of an OS is to provide file system support. File operations eventually require device I/O. An OS kernel must provide device drivers to support device I/O operations.

With the advent of networking technology, almost every computer is now connected to a network, such as the Internet. Although not essential, an OS should provide support for network access.

As an example, Linux is a general purpose OS, which has all the above functions. In comparison, MTX is a simple OS. It supports process management, memory management, a simple EXT2 file system and some device drivers, but it does not yet support networking at this moment.

2.3   Program Development

2.3.1   Program Development Steps

The steps of developing an executable program are as follows.

1. Create source files: Use a text editor, such as vi or emacs, to create one or more source files of a program. In systems programming, the most important programming languages are C and assembly. We begin with C programs first. In addition to the standard comment lines in C, we shall also use // to denote comments in

C code for convenience. Assume that t1.c and t2.c are the source files of a C program.

```
/********************** t1.c file ***********************/
int g = 100;                  // initialized global variable
int h;                        // uninitialized global variable
static int s;                 // static global variable
main(int argc, char *argv[ ]) // main function
{
    int a = 1; int b;         // automatic local variables
    static int c = 3;         // static local variable
    b = 2;
    c = mysum(a,b);           // call mysum(), passing a, b
    printf("sum=%d\n", c);    // call printf()
}
/********************** t2.c file ***********************/
extern int g;                 // extern global variable
int mysum(int x, int y)       // function heading
{
    return x + y + g;
}
```

```
                    |- non-static-|
            |- global-|           |- initialized or uninitialized
            |       |- static ----|
Variables - |
            |- local -|- register--|- in CPU register (if possible)
                      |- automatic -|- allocated on stack
                      |- static ----|- initialized or uninitialized
```

Fig. 2.4 Variables in C

Variables in C programs can be classified as global, local, static and automatic, etc. as shown in Fig. 2.4.

Global variables are defined outside of any function. Local variables are defined inside functions. Global variables are unique and have only one copy. Static globals are visible only to the file in which they are defined. Non-static globals are visible to all the files of the same program. Global variables can be initialized or uninitialized. Initialized globals are assigned values at compile time. Uninitialized globals are cleared to 0 when the program execution starts. Local variables are visible only to the function in which they are defined. By default, local variables are automatic; they come into existence when the function is entered and they logically disappear when the function exits. For register variables, the compiler tries to allocate them in CPU registers. Since automatic local variables do not have any allocated memory space until the function is entered, they cannot be initialized at compile time. Static local variables are permanent and unique, which can be initialized. In addition, C also supports volatile variables, which are used as memory-mapped I/O locations or global variables that are accessed by interrupt handlers or multiple execution threads. The volatile keyword prevents the C compiler from optimizing the code that operates on such variables.

In the above t1.c file, g is an initialized global, h is an uninitialized global and s is a static global. Both g and h are visible to the entire program but s is visible only in the t1.c file. So t2.c can reference g by declaring it as extern, but it cannot reference s because s is visible only in t1.c. In the main() function, the local variables a, b are automatic and c is static. Although the local variable a is defined as int a=1, this is not an initialization because a does not yet exist at compile time. The generated code will assign 1 to the current copy of a when main() is actually entered.

2. Use cc to convert the source files into a binary executable, as in

   cc t1.c t2.c

which generates a binary executable file named a.out. In Linux, cc is linked to gcc, so they are the same.

3. What's cc? cc is a program, which consists of three major steps, as shown in Fig. 2.5.

Step 1. Convert C source files to assembly code files: The first step of cc is to invoke the C COMPILER, which translates the .c files into .s files containing assembly code of the target machine. The C compiler itself has several phases, such as preprocessing, lexical analysis, parsing and code generations, etc, but the reader may ignore such details here.

Step 2. Convert assembly Code to OBJECT code: Every computer has its own set of machine instructions. Users may write programs in an assembly language for a specific machine. An ASSEMBLER is a program, which translates assembly code into machine code in binary form. The resulting .o files are called OBJECT code. The second step of cc is to invoke the ASSEMBLER to translate .s files to .o files. Each .o file consists of

- a header containing sizes of CODE, DATA and BSS sections
- a CODE section containing machine instructions
- a DATA section containing initialized global and static local variables
- a BSS section containing uninitialized global and static local variables
- relocation information for pointers in CODE and offsets in DATA and BSS
- a Symbol Table containing non-static globals, function names and their attributes.

Step 3: LINKING: A program may consist of several .o files, which are dependent on one another. In addition, the .o files may call C library functions, e.g. printf,

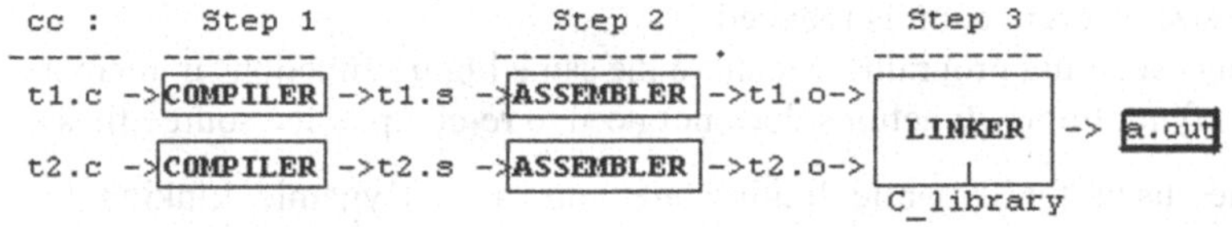

Fig. 2.5 Program development steps

which are not present in the source files. The last step of cc is to invoke the LINKER, which combines all the .o files and the needed library functions into a single binary executable file. More specifically, the LINKER does the following:

- Combine all the CODE sections of the .o files into a single Code section. For C programs, the combined Code section begins with the default C startup code crt0.o, which calls main(). This is why every C program must have a unique main() function.
- Combine all the DATA sections into a single Data section. The combined Data section contains only initialized globals and static locals.
- Combine all the BSS sections into a single bss section.
- Use the relocation information in the .o files to adjust pointers in the combined Code section and offsets in the combined Data and bss sections.
- Use the Symbol Tables to resolve cross references among the individual .o files. For instance, when the compiler sees c=mysum(a, b) in t1.c, it does not know where mysum is. So it leaves a blank (0) in t1.o as the entry address of mysum but records in the symbol table that the blank must be replaced with the entry address of mysum. When the linker puts t1.o and t2.o together, it knows where mysum is in the combined Code section. It simply replaces the blank in t1.o with the entry address of mysum. Similarly for other cross referenced symbols. Since static globals are not in the symbol table, they are unavailable to the linker. Any attempt to reference static globals from different files will generate a cross reference error. Similarly, if the .o files refer to any undefined symbols or function names, the linker will also generate cross reference errors. If all the cross references can be resolved successfully, the linker writes the resulting combined file as a.out, which is the binary executable file.

2.3.2   Static vs. Dynamic Linking

There are two ways to create a binary executable, known as static linking and dynamic linking. In static linking, which uses a static library, the linker includes all the needed library function code and data into a.out. This makes a.out complete and self-contained but usually very large. In dynamic linking, which uses a shared library, the library functions are not included in a.out but calls to such functions are recorded in a.out as directives. When execute a dynamically linked a.out file, the operating system loads both a.out and the shared library into memory and makes the loaded library code accessible to a.out during execution. The main advantages of dynamic linking are:

- The size of every a.out is reduced.
- Many executing programs can share the same library functions in memory.
- Modifying library functions does not need to re-compile the source files again.

Libraries used for dynamic linking are known as Dynamic Linking Libraries (DLLs). They are called Shared Libraries (.so files) in Linux. Dynamically loaded

(DL) libraries are shared libraries which are loaded only when they are needed. DL libraries are useful as plug-ins and dynamically loaded modules.

2.3.3   Executable File Format

Although the default binary executable is named a.out, the actual file format may vary. Most C compilers and linkers can generate executable files in several different formats, which include

1. Flat binary executable: A flat binary executable file consists only of executable code and initialized data. It is intended to be loaded into memory in its entirety for execution directly. For example, bootable operating system images are usually flat binary executables, which simplifies the boot-loader.
2. a.out executable file: A traditional a.out file consists of a header, followed by code, data and bss sections. Details of the a.out file format will be shown in the next section.
3. ELF executable file: An Executable and Linking Format (ELF) (ELF 1995) file consists of one or more program sections. Each program section can be loaded to a specific memory address. In Linux, the default binary executables are ELF files, which are better suited to dynamic linking.

2.3.4   Contents of a.out File

For the sake of simplicity, we consider the traditional a.out files first. ELF executables will be covered later in Chaps. 14 and 15 when we discuss MTX in 32-bit protected mode. An a.out file consists of the following sections:

1. header: the header contains loading information and sizes of the a.out file, where
   tsize = size of Code section;
   dsize = size of Data section containing initialized globals and static locals;
   bsize = size of bss section containing uninitialized globals and static locals;
   total_size = total size of a.out to load.
2. Code Section: also called the text section, which contains executable code of the program. It begins with the standard C startup code crt0.o, which calls main().
3. Data Section: The Data section contains initialized global and static data.
4. symbol table: optional, needed only for run-time debugging.

Note that the bss section, which contains uninitialized global and static local variables, is not in the a.out file. Only its size is recorded in the a.out file header. Also, automatic local variables are not in a.out. Figure 2.6 shows the layout of an a.out file.

where _brk is a symbolic mark indicating the end of the bss section. The total loading size of a.out is usually equal to _brk, i.e. equal to tsize + dsize + bsize. If desired, _brk can be set to a higher value for a larger loading size. The extra memory space above the bss section is the HEAP area for dynamic memory allocation during execution.

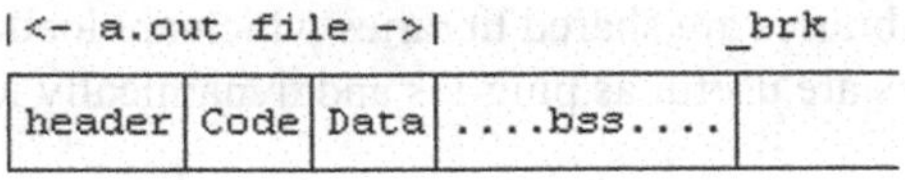

Fig. 2.6 Contents of a.out file

```
|<- a.out file ->|                    _brk

header| Code| Data| ....bss....
```

2.3.5   Program Execution

Under a Unix-like operating system, the sh command

a.out one two three

executes a.out with the token strings as command-line parameters. To execute the command, sh forks a child process and waits for the child to terminate. When the child process runs, it uses a.out to create a new execution image by the following steps.

1. Read the header of a.out to determine the total memory size needed:

TotalSize = _brk + stackSize

where stackSize is usually a default value chosen by the OS kernel for the program to start. There is no way of knowing how much stack space a program will ever need. For example, the trivial C program

main(){ main(); }

will generate a segmentation fault due to stack overflow on any computer. So the usual approach of an OS kernel is to use a default initial stack size for the program to start and tries to deal with possible stack overflow later during run-time.

2. It allocates a memory area of TotalSize for the execution image. Conceptually, we may assume that the allocated memory area is a single piece of contiguous memory. It loads the Code and Data sections of a.out into the memory area, with the stack area at the high address end. It clears the bss section to 0, so that all uninitialized globals and static locals begin with the initial value 0. During execution, the stack grows downward toward low address.

3. Then it abandons the old image and begins to execute the new image, which is shown in Fig. 2.7.

In Fig. 2.7, _brk at the end of the bss section is the program's initial "break" mark and _splimit is the stack size limit. The Heap area between bss and Stack is used by the C library functions malloc()/free() for dynamic memory allocation in the execution image. When a.out is first loaded, _brk and _splimit may coincide, so that the initial Heap size is zero. During execution, the process may use the brk(address) or sbrk(size) system call to change _brk to a higher address, thereby increasing the

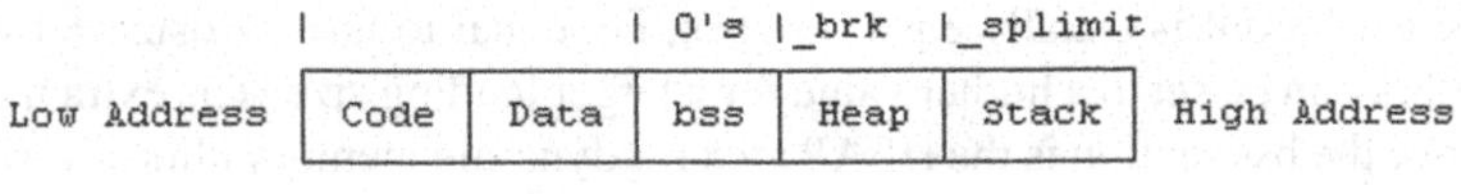

```
              |                  | 0's |_brk  |_splimit

Low Address |  Code | Data | bss | Heap | Stack |  High Address
```

Fig. 2.7 Execution image

Heap size. Alternatively, malloc() may call brk() or sbrk() implicitly to expand the Heap size. During execution, a stack overflow occurs if the program tries to extend the stack pointer below _splimit. On machines with memory protection, this will be detected by the memory management hardware as an error, which traps the process to the OS kernel. Subject to a maximal size limit, the OS kernel may grow the stack by allocating additional memory in the process address space, allowing the execution to continue. A stack overflow is fatal if the stack cannot be grown further. On machines without suitable hardware support, detecting and handling stack overflow must be implement in software.

4. Execution begins from crt0.o, which calls main(), passing as parameters argc and argv to main(int argc, char *argv[ ]), where argc = number of command line parameters and each argv entry points to a corresponding command line parameter string.

2.3.6 Program Termination

A process executing a.out may terminate in two possible ways.

1. Normal Termination: If the program executes successfully, main() eventually returns to crt0.o, which calls the library function exit(0) to terminate the process. The exit(value) function does some clean-up work first, such as flush stdout, close I/O streams, etc. Then it issues an _exit(value) system call, which causes the process to enter the OS kernel to terminate. A 0 exit value usually means normal termination. If desired, a process may call exit(value) directly without going back to crt0.o. Even more drastically, a process may issue an _exit(value) system call to terminate immediately without doing the clean-up work first. When a process terminates in kernel, it records the value in the _exit(value) system call as the exit status in the process structure, notifies its parent and becomes a ZOMBIE. The parent process can find the ZOMBIE child, get its pid and exit status by the pid = wait(int *status); system call, which also releases the ZMOBIE child process structure as FREE, allowing it to be reused for another process.

2. Abnormal Termination: While executing a.out the process may encounter an error condition, which is recognized by the CPU as an exception. When a process encounters an exception, it is forced into the OS kernel by a trap. The kernel's trap handler converts the trap error type to a magic number, called a SIGNAL, and delivers the signal to the process, causing it to terminate. In this case, the exit status of the ZOMBIE process is the signal number, and we may say that the process has terminated abnormally. In addition to trap errors, signals may also originate from hardware or from other processes. For example, pressing the Control_C key generates a hardware interrupt, which sends the signal number SIGINT(2) to all processes on that terminal, causing them to terminate. Alternatively, a user may use the command

        kill -s signal_number pid   # signal_number=1 to 31

to send a signal to a target process identified by pid. For most signal numbers, the default action of a process is to terminate. Signals and signal handling will be covered later in Chap. 9

2.4   Function Call in C

Next, we consider the run-time behavior of a.out during execution. The run-time behavior of a program stems mainly from function calls, which use the stack. The following discussions apply to running C programs on both 16-bit and 32-bit Intel x86 processors. On these machines, the C compiler generated code passes parameters on the stack in function calls. During execution, it uses a special CPU register (bp or ebp) to point at the stack frame of the current executing function. In 64-bit processors, which have more registers, the function call convention differs slightly. Some parameters are passed in specific registers. A called function may use the stack pointer itself as the stack frame pointer. Despite these minor differences, the same principle still applies.

2.4.1   Run-Time Stack Usage

Consider the following C program, which consists of a main() function shown on the left-hand side, which calls a sub() function shown on the right-hand side.

```
    main()                          |    int sub(int x, int y)
    {                               |    {
       int a, b, c;                 |       int u, v;
       a = 1; b = 2; c = 3;         |       u = 4; v = 5;
       c = sub(a, b);               |       return x+y+u+v;
       printf("c=%d\n", c);         |    }
    }                               |
```

1. When executing a.out, a process image is created in memory, which looks (logically) like the diagram shown in Fig. 2.8, where Data includes both initialized data and bss.

2. Every CPU has the following registers or equivalent, where the entries in parentheses denote registers of the x86 CPU:

   PC (IP): point to next instruction to be executed by the CPU.
   SP (SP): point to top of stack.
   FP (BP): point to the stack frame of current active function.
   Return Value Register (AX): register for function return value.

Fig. 2.8 Process execution image

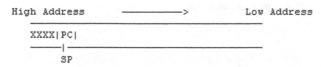

Fig. 2.9 Stack contents in function call

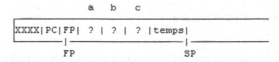

Fig. 2.10 Stack contents: Allocate local variables

3. In every C program, main() is called by the C startup code crt0.o. When crt0.o calls main(), it pushes the return address (the current PC register) onto stack and replaces PC with the entry address of main(), causing the CPU to enter main(). For convenience, we shall show the stack contents from left to right. When control enters main(), the stack contains the saved return PC on top, as shown in Fig. 2.9.

where XXXX denotes the stack contents before crt0.o calls main(), and SP points to the saved return PC from where crt0.o calls main().

4. Upon entry, the compiled code of every C function does the following:

   – push FP onto stack # this saves the CPU's FP register on stack.
   – let FP point at the saved FP # establish stack frame
   – shift SP downward to allocate space for automatic local variables on stack
   – the compiled code may shift SP farther down to allocate some scratch space.

For this example, there are 3 automatic local variables, int a, b, c, each of sizeof(int) bytes. After entering main(), the stack contents becomes as shown in Fig. 2.10, in which the spaces of a, b, c are allocated but their contents are yet undefined.

5. Then the CPU starts to execute the code a=1; b=2; c=3; which put the values 1, 2, 3 into the memory locations of a, b, c, respectively. Assume that sizeof(int) is 4 bytes. The locations of a, b, c are at −4, −8, −12 bytes from where FP points at. These are expressed as −4(FP), −8(FP), −12(FP) in assembly code, where FP is the stack frame pointer. For example, in 32-bit Linux the assembly code for b=2 in C is movl $ 2, −8(%ebp), where $ 2 means the value of 2 and %ebp is the ebp register.

6. main() calls sub() by c= sub(a, b); The compiled code of the function call consists of

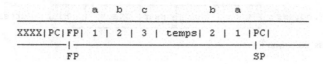

```
         a   b   c          b   a
-------------------------------------------
XXXX|PC|FP|  1 | 2 | 3 | temps| 2 | 1 |PC|
----|-------------------------------|------
    FP                              SP
```

Fig. 2.11 Stack contents: passing parameters

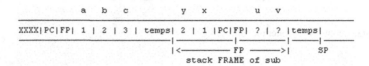

```
         a   b   c       y   x       u   v
-----------------------------------------------------
XXXX|PC|FP|  1 | 2 | 3 | temps| 2 | 1 |PC|FP|  ? | ? |temps|
----|-----------------------|-------------|----|----|------
    |                       |<------- FP ------->|  SP
                            stack FRAME of sub
```

Fig. 2.12 Stack contents of called function

- Push parameters in reverse order, i.e. push values of b=2 and a=1 into stack.
- Call sub, which pushes the current PC onto stack and replaces PC with the entry address of sub, causing the CPU to enter sub().

When control first enters sub(), the stack contains a return address at the top, preceded by the parameters, a, b, of the caller, as shown in Fig. 2.11.

7. Since sub() is written in C, it actions are exactly the same as that of main(), i.e. it

- Push FP and let FP point at the saved FP;
- Shift SP downward to allocate space for local variables u, v.
- The compiled code may shift SP farther down for some temp space on stack.

The stack contents becomes as shown in Fig. 2.12.

2.4.2 Stack Frames

While execution is inside a function, such as sub(), it can only access global variables, parameters passed in by the caller and local variables, but nothing else. Global and static local variables are in the combined Data section, which can be referenced by a fixed base register. Parameters and automatic locals have different copies on each invocation of the function. So the problem is: how to reference parameters and automatic locals? For this example, the parameters a, b, which correspond to the arguments x, y, are at 8(FP) and 12(FP). Similarly, the automatic local variables u, v are at -4(FP) and -8(FP). The stack area visible to a function, i.e. parameters and automatic locals, is called the stack FRAME of a function, like a frame of movie to a person. Thus, FP is called the Stack Frame Pointer. To a function, the stack frame looks like the following (Fig. 2.13).

From the above discussions, the reader should be able to deduce what would happen if we have a sequence of function calls, e.g.

crt0.o --> main() --> A(par_a) --> B(par_b) --> C(par_c)

```
|<───────── Stack Frame of a Function ─────────>|
| parameters | retPC | savedFP | local variables |
                         |
                  CPU.FP register
```

Fig. 2.13 Function stack frame

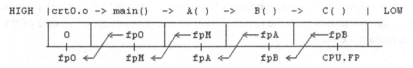

Fig. 2.14 Function call sequence

For each function call, the stack would grow (toward low address) one more frame for the called function. The frame at the stack top is the stack frame of the current executing function, which is pointed by the CPU's frame pointer. The saved FP points (backward) to the frame of its caller, whose saved FP points back at the caller's caller, etc. Thus, the function call sequence is maintained in the stack as a link list, as shown in Fig. 2.14.

By convention, the CPU's FP=0 when crt0.o is entered from the OS kernel. So the stack frame link list ends with a 0. When a function returns, its stack frame is deallocated and the stack shrinks back.

2.4.3 Return From Function Call

When sub() executes return x+y+u+v, it evaluates the expression and puts the resulting value in the return value register (AX). Then it deallocates the local variables by

.copy FP into SP;   # SP now points to the saved FP in stack.
.pop stack into FP; # this restores FP, which now points to the caller's stack frame,
                     # leaving the return PC on the stack top.
(On the x86 CPU, the above operations are equivalent to the leave instruction).
.Then, it executes the RET instruction, which pops the stack top into PC register, causing the CPU to execute from the saved return address of the caller.

8. Upon return, the caller function catches the return value in the return register (AX). Then it cleans the parameters a, b, from the stack (by adding 8 to SP). This restores the stack to the original situation before the function call. Then it continues to execute the next instruction.

It is noted that some compilers, e.g. GCC Version 4, allocate automatic local variables in increasing address order. For instance, int a, b; implies (address of a) < (address of b). With this kind of allocation scheme, the stack contents may look like the following (Fig. 2.15).

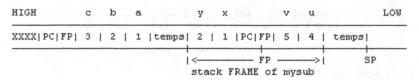

```
HIGH          c   b   a        y   x           v   u            LOW

XXXX|PC|FP|  3  |  2  |  1 |temps| 2  |  1 |PC|FP|  5  |  4  | temps|
                           +-----+          +-----+-----+-----+-----+
                      |<———————— FP ————————>|        SP
                      stack FRAME of mysub
```

Fig. 2.15 Stack contents with reversed allocation scheme

In this case, automatic local variables are also allocated in "reverse order", which makes them consistent with the parameter order, but the concept and usage of stack frames remain the same.

2.4.4 Long Jump

In a sequence of function calls, such as

$$main() \rightarrow A() \rightarrow B() \rightarrow C();$$

when a called function finishes, it normally returns to the calling function, e.g. C() returns to B(), which returns to A(), etc. It is also possible to return directly to an earlier function in the calling sequence by a long jump. The following program demonstrates long jump in Unix/Linux.

```
/***** longjump.c demonstrating long jump in Linux *****/
#include <stdio.h>
#include <setjmp.h>
jmp_buf env;              // for saving longjmp environment
main()
{
  int r, a=100;
  printf("call setjmp to save environment\n");
  if ((r=setjmp(env)) == 0){
     A();
     printf("normal return\n");
  }
  else
     printf("back to main() via long jump, r=%d a=%d\n", r, a);
}
int A()
{   printf("enter A()\n");
    B();
    printf("exit A()\n");
}
int B()
{
  printf("enter B()\n");
  printf("long jump? (y|n) ");
  if (getchar()=='y')
     longjmp(env, 1234);
  printf("exit B()\n");
}
```

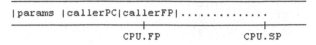

```
|params |callerPC|callerFP|..............
        +                  +
           CPU.FP                    CPU.SP
```

Fig. 2.16 Function return frame

In the above program, setjmp() saves the current execution environment in a jmp_
buf structure and returns 0. The program proceeds to call A(), which calls B(). While
in the function B(), if the user chooses not to return by long jump, the functions will
show the normal return sequence. If the user chooses to return by longjmp(env,
1234), execution will return to the last saved environment with a nonzero value. In
this case, it causes B() to return to main() directly, bypassing A(). The principle of
long jump is very simple. When a function finishes, it returns by the (callerPC, callerFP) in the current stack frame, as shown in Fig. 2.16.

If we replace (callerPC, callerFP) with (savedPC, savedFP) of an earlier function
in the calling sequence, execution would return to that function directly. In addition
to the (savedPC, savedFP), setjmp() may also save CPU's general registers and the
original SP, so that longjmp() can restore the complete environment of the returned
function. Long jump can be used to abort a function in a calling sequence, causing
execution to resume from a known environment saved earlier. Although rarely used
in user mode programs, it is a common technique in systems programming. For example, it may be used in a signal catcher to bypass a user mode function that caused
an exception or trap error. We shall demonstrate this technique later in Chap. 9 on
signals and signal processing.

2.5   Link C Program with Assembly Code

In systems programming, it is often necessary to access the hardware, such as CPU
registers and I/O port locations, etc. In these situations, assembly code becomes
necessary. It is therefore important to know how to link C programs with assembly
code. We illustrate the linking process by an example. The following program consists of a tc.c file in C and a ts.s file in assembly.

```c
/******************* tc.c file ***********************/
extern int g;          // g is extern defined in .s file
int h;                 // global h, used in .s file
main( )
{
  int a,b,c,*bp;       // locals of main()
  g = 100;             // use g in .s file
  bp = getbp();        // call getbp() in .s file
  a = 1; b = 2; h=200;
  c = mysum(a,b);      // call mysum() in .s file
  printf("a=%d b=%d c=%d\n", a,b,c);
}
```

```
!------------------- ts.s file ---------------------
        .global _h               ! IMPORT _h from C
        .global _getbp,_mysum,_g ! EXPORT global symbols to C
_getbp:                          ! int getbp() function
        mov   ax,bp
        ret
_mysum:                          ! int mysum(int x, int y)
        push bp
        mov   bp,sp              ! establish stack frame
        mov   ax,4[bp]           ! AX = x
        add   ax,6[bp]           ! add y to AX
        add   ax,_h              ! add _h to AX
        mov   sp,bp              ! return to caller
        pop   bp
        ret
_g:     .word 1234               ! global _g defined here
```

The assembly code syntax is that of BCC's as86 assembler. When generating object code BCC's compiler prefixes every identifier with an underscore, e.g. main() becomes _main and getbp() becomes _getbp, etc. BCC's assembler uses the same naming convention. An assembly program may import/export global symbols from/to C code by .global statements. Every global symbol in the assembly code must have an underscore prefix. Likewise, a C program may reference global symbols in assembly by declaring them as extern. In the C code, g is declared as an extern integer. It is the same global symbol _g in the assembly code. Similarly, the global variable h is the same _h in assembly code. In C, function names are global and the function types are int by default. If a function returns a different type, it must be either defined first or declared by a function prototype before it is used. In the C code, the statement g=100 actually changes the contents of _g in the assembly code. When it calls getbp() in assembly, the returned value is the CPU's bp register. When calling mysum(a, b) it pushes the values of b and a onto stack as parameters. Upon entry to _mysum: the assembly code first establishes the stack frame. It uses the stack frame pointer (bp) to access the parameters a, b, which are at 4[bp] and 6[bp], respectively (in BCC integers are 2 bytes). In every function call, the return value is in the AX register. Under Linux, use BCC to compile and link the C and assembly files.

```
bcc -c -ansi tc.c ts.s    # generate tc.o and ts.o
ld86 crt0.o tc.o ts.o mtxlib /usr/lib/bcc/libc.a
```

where crt0.o is the C startup code and mtxlib contains I/O and system call interface
to the MTX kernel. The resulting a.out can be executed under MTX.

2.6 Link Library

A link library contains precompiled object code. During linking, the linker searches
the link libraries for any function code and data needed by a program. Link libraries
used by the BCC linker are standard Unix archive files, which can be manipulated
by the ar utility program. The following shows how to create and maintain a link
library for use in MTX.

```
(1). Assume: getbp.s is an assebmly code file.
     !--------- getbp.s file -----------
               .globl _getbp   ! OR .global _getbp
        _getbp:  mov ax,bp
                 ret
(2). as86 -o getbp.o getbp.s   # generate getbp.o file
(3). ar r mylib getbp.o # create mylib and add the member getbp.o

(4). Assume: mysum.c is a C code file.
     /********** mysum.c file **************/
        int mysum(int x, int y){  return x+y;  }
(5). bcc -c -ansi mysum.c   # generate mysum.o file
(6). ar r mylib mysum.o     # add member mysum.o to mylib
(7)  ar t mylib             # list members of mylib
```

Similarly, we may add/delete members to/from an existing library by the ar command. Link libraries are very useful in system development. As we expand a system, we may include some of the existing parts of the system into a link library and
focus our attention on developing new features of the system.

2.7 Mailman's Algorithm

In computer systems, a problem which arises very often is as follows. A city has M
blocks, numbered 0 to $M-1$. Each block has N houses, numbered 0 to $N-1$. Each
house has a unique block address, denoted by (block, house), where $0 <= block < M$,
$0 <= house < N$. An alien from outer space may be unfamiliar with the block addressing scheme on Earth and prefers to address the houses linearly as $0,1,..N-1,N,$
$N+1.....$, etc. Given a block address BA = (block, house), how to convert it to a
linear address LA, and vice versa? If everything counts from 0, the conversion is
very simple.

$$Linear\_address\ LA = N*block + house;$$
$$Block\_address\ BA = (LA / N, LA \% N);$$

Note that the conversion is valid only if everything counts from 0. If some of the items do not count from 0, they can not be used in the conversion formula directly. The reader may try to figure out how to handle such cases in general. For ease of reference, we shall refer to the conversion method as the Mailman's algorithm.

2.7.1 Applications of Mailman's Algorithm

1. Test, Set and Clear bits in C: In standard C programs, the smallest addressable unit is a char or byte. It is often necessary to manipulate bits in a bitmap, which is a sequence of bits. Consider char buf[1024], which has 1024 bytes, denoted by buf[i], i=0, 1,...., 1023. It also has 8192 bits numbered 0,1,2,....8191. Given a bit number BIT, e.g. 1234, which byte i contains the bit, and which bit j is it in that byte? Solution:

$$i = BIT / 8; \quad j = BIT \% 8; \quad // 8 = \text{number of bits in a byte.}$$

This allows us to combine the Mailman's algorithm with bit masking to do the following bit operations in C.

```
.TST a bit for 1 or 0 :  if (buf[i] &   (1 << j))
.SET a bit to 1        :      buf[i] |=  (1 << j);
.CLR a bit to 0        :      buf[i] &= ~(1 << j);
```

It is noted that some C compilers allow specifying bits in a structure, as in

```
struct bits{
   unsigned int bit0      :  1;  // bit0 field is a single bit
   unsigned int bit123    :  3;  // bit123 field is a range of 3 bits
   unsigned int otherbits : 27;  // other bits field has 27 bits
   unsigned int bit31     :  1;  // bit31 is the highest bit
}var;
```

The structure defines var as an unsigned 32-bit integer with individual bits or ranges of bits. Then, var.bit0 =0; assigns 1 to bit 0, and var.bit123=5; assigns 101 to bits 1 to 3, etc. However, the generated code still relies on the Mailman's algorithm and bit masking to access the individual bits. The Mailman's algorithm allows us to manipulate bits in a bitmap directly without defining complex C structures.

2. Convert INODE number to inode position on disk: In an EXT2 file system, each file has a unique INODE structure. On the file system disk, inodes begin in the inode_table block. Each disk block contains

```
INODES_PER_BLOCK = BLOCK_SIZE/sizeof(INODE)
```

inodes. Each inode has a unique inode number, ino $= 1, 2, \ldots$, counted linearly from 1. Given an ino, e.g. 1234, determine which disk block contains the inode and which inode is it in that block? We need to know the disk block number because read/write a real disk is by blocks. Solution:

```
block = (ino - 1) / INODES_PER_BLOCK + inode_table;
inode = (ino - 1) % INODES_PER_BLOCK;
```

Similarly, converting double and triple indirect logical block numbers to physical block numbers in an EXT2 file system also depends on the Mailman's algorithm.

3. Convert linear disk block number to CHS = (cylinder, head, sector) format: Floppy disk and old hard disk use CHS addressing but file systems always use linear block addressing. The algorithm can be used to convert a disk block number to CHS when calling BIOS INT13.

2.8   EXT2 File System

For many years, Linux used EXT2 (Card et al.) as the default file system. EXT3 [ETX3] is an extension of EXT2. The main addition in EXT3 is a journal file, which records changes made to the file system in a journal log. The log allows for quicker recovery from errors in case of a file system crash. An EXT3 file system with no error is identical to an EXT2 file system. The newest extension of EXT3 is EXT4 (Cao et al. 2007). The major change in EXT4 is in the allocation of disk blocks. In EXT4, block numbers are 48 bits. Instead of discrete disk blocks, EXT4 allocates contiguous ranges of disk blocks, called extents. EXT4 file system will be covered in Chap. 3 when we develop booting programs for hard disks containing EXT4 file systems. MTX is a small operating system intended mainly for teaching. Large file storage capacity is not the design goal. Principles of file system design and implementation, with an emphasis on simplicity and compatibility with Linux, are the major focal points. For these reasons, MTX uses ETX2 as the file system. Support for other file systems, e.g. DOS and iso9660 (ECMA-119 1987), are not implemented in the MTX kernel. If needed, they can be implemented as user-level utility programs.

2.8.1   EXT2 File System Data Structures

Under MTX, the command, mkfs device nblocks [ninodes], creates an EXT2 file system on a specified device with nblocks blocks of 1 KB block size. The device can be either a real device or a virtual disk file. If the number of ninodes is not specified, the default number of inodes is nblocks/4. The resulting file system is totally compatible with the EXT2 file system of Linux. As a specific example, mkfs /dev/fd0

```
| 0     1     2     3     4 | 5 . .......... 49| 50 ..................|
```

```
| Boot |Super | Gd  | Bmap | Imap | Inodes blocks .... | ... data blocks .... |
```

Fig. 2.17 Simple EXT2 file system layout

1440 makes an EXT2 file system on a 1.44 MB floppy disk with 1440 blocks and 360 inodes. Instead of a real device, the target can also be a disk image file. The layout of such an EXT2 file system is shown in Fig. 2.17.

For ease of discussion, we shall assume this basic file system layout first. Whenever appropriate, we point out the variations, including those in large EXT2/3 FS on hard disks. The following briefly explains the contents of the disk blocks.

Block#0: Boot Block: B0 is the boot block, which is not used by the file system. It contains a booter program for booting up an OS from the disk.

Block#1: Superblock: (at byte offset 1024 in hard disk partitions): B1 is the superblock, which contains information about the entire file system. Some of the important fields of the superblock structure are shown below.

```
struct ext2_super_block {
    u32   s_inodes_count;        // total number of inodes
    u32   s_blocks_count;        // total number of blocks
    u32   s_r_blocks_count;
    u32   s_free_blocks_count;   // current number of free blocks
    u32   s_free_inodes_count;   // current number of free inodes
    u32   s_first_data_block;    // first data block: 1 for FD, 0 for HD
    u32   s_log_block_size;      // 0 for 1KB block, 2 for 4KB block
    u32   s_log_frag_size;       // not used
    u32   s_blocks_per_group;    // number of blocks per group
    u32   s_frags_per_group;     // not used
    u32   s_inodes_per_group;
    u32   s_mtime, s_wtime;
    u16   s_mnt_count;           // number of times mounted
    u16   s_max_mnt_count;       // mount limit
    u16   s_magic;               // 0xEF53
    // MORE non-essential fileds,
    u16 s_inode_size=256 bytes for EXT4
};
```

Block#2: Group Descriptor Block (in s_first_data_block +1 on hard disk): EXT2 divides disk blocks into groups. Each group contains 8192 (32 K on HD) blocks. Each group is described by a group descriptor structure.

```
    struct ext2_group_desc
    {
        u32   bg_block_bitmap;      // Bmap block number
        u32   bg_inode_bitmap;      // Imap block number
        u32   bg_inode_table;       // Inodes begin block number
        u16   bg_free_blocks_count; // THESE are OBVIOUS
        u16   bg_free_inodes_count;
        u16   bg_used_dirs_count;
        u16   bg_pad;               // ignore these
        u32   bg_reserved[3];
    };
```

Since a FD has only 1440 blocks, B2 contains only 1 group descriptor. The rest are 0's. On a hard disk with a large number of groups, group descriptors may span many blocks. The most important fields in a group descriptor are bg_block_bitmap, bg_inode_bitmap and bg_inode_table, which point to the group's blocks bitmap, inodes bitmap and inodes start block, respectively. Here, we assume the bitmaps are in blocks 3 and 4, and inodes start from block 5.

Block#3: Block Bitmap (Bmap): (bg_block_bitmap): A bitmap is a sequence of bits used to represent some kind of items, e.g. disk blocks or inodes. A bitmap is used to allocate and deallocate items. In a bitmap, a 0 bit means the corresponding item is FREE, and a 1 bit means the corresponding item is IN_USE. A FD has 1440 blocks but block#0 is not used by the file system. So the Bmap has only 1439 valid bits. Invalid bits are treated as IN_USE and set to 1's.

Block#4: Inode Bitmap (Imap) (bg_inode_bitmap): An inode is a data structure used to represent a file. An EXT2 file system is created with a finite number of inodes. The status of each inode is represented by a bit in the Imap in B4. In an EXT2 FS, the first 10 inodes are reserved. So the Imap of an empty EXT2 FS starts with ten 1's, followed by 0's. Invalid bits are again set to 1's.

Block#5: Inodes (begin) Block (bg_inode_table): Every file is represented by a unique inode structure of 128 (256 in EXT4) bytes. The essential inode fields are listed below.

```
struct ext2_inode {
    u16  i_mode;         // 16 bits = |tttt|ugs|rwx|rwx|rwx|
    u16  i_uid;          // owner uid
    u32  i_size;         // file size in bytes
    u32  i_atime;        // time fields in seconds
    u32  i_ctime;        // since 00:00:00,1-1-1970
    u32  i_mtime;
    u32  i_dtime;
    u16  i_gid;          // group ID
    u16  i_links_count;  // hard-link count
    u32  i_blocks;       // number of 512-byte sectors
    u32  i_flags;        // IGNORE
    u32  i_reserved1;    // IGNORE
    u32  i_block[15];    // See details below
    u32  i_pad[7];
}
```

In the inode structure, i_mode specifies the file's type, usage and permissions. For example, the leading 4 bits=1000 for REG file, 0100 for DIR, etc. The last 9 bits are the rwx permission bits for file protection. The i_block[15] array contains disk blocks of a file, which are

Direct blocks: i_block[0] to i_block[11], which point to direct disk blocks.

Indirect blocks: i_block[12] points to a disk block, which contains 256 block numbers, each of which points to a disk block.

Double Indirect blocks: i_block[13] points to a block, which points to 256 blocks, each of which points to 256 disk blocks.

Triple Indirect blocks: i_block[14] is the triple-indirect block. We may ignore this for "small" EXT2 FS.

The inode size (128 or 256) divides block size (1KB or 4KB) evenly, so that every inode block contains an integral number of inodes. In the simple EXT2 file system, the number of inode blocks is equal to ninodes/8. For example, if the number of inodes is 360, which needs 45 blocks, the inode blocks include B5 to B49. Each inode has a unique inode number, which is the inode's position in the inode blocks plus 1. Note that inode positions count from 0, but inode numbers count from 1. A 0 inode number means no inode. The root directory's inode number is 2.

Data Blocks: Immediately after the inode blocks are data blocks. Assuming 360 inodes, the first real data block is B50, which is i_block[0] of the root directory /.

EXT2 Directory Entries: A directory contains dir_entry structures, in which the name field contains 1 to 255 chars. So the dir_entry's rec_len also varies.

```
struct ext2_dir_entry_2 {
    u32 inode;                    // inode number; count from 1, NOT 0
    u16 rec_len;                  // this entry's length in bytes
    u8  name_len;                 // name length in bytes
    u8  file_type;                // not used
    char name[EXT2_NAME_LEN];     // name: 1  -255 chars, no NULL byte
};
```

2.8.2   Traverse EXT2 File System Tree

Given an EXT2 file system and the pathname of a file, e.g. /a/b/c, the problem is how to find the file. To find a file amounts to finding its inode. The algorithm is as follows.

1. Read in the superblock, which is at the byte offset 1024. Check the magic number s_magic (0xEF53) to verify it's indeed an EXT2 FS.
2. Read in the group descriptor block (1+s_first_data_block) to access the group 0 descriptor. From the group descriptor's bg_inode_table entry, find the inodes begin block number, call it the InodesBeginBlock.
3. Read in InodeBeginBlock to get the inode of /, which is INODE #2.
4. Tokenize the pathname into component strings and let the number of components be n. For example, if pathname=/a/b/c, the component strings are "a", "b", "c", with n=3. Denote the components by name[0], name[1],..,name[n-1].
5. Start from the root INODE in (3), search for name[0] in its data block(s). For simplicity, we may assume that the number of entries in a DIR is small, so that a DIR inode only has 12 direct data blocks. With this assumption, it suffices to search the 12 direct blocks for name[0]. Each data block of a DIR INODE contains dir_entry structures of the form

[ino rlen nlen NAME] [ino rlen nlen NAME] ......

where NAME is a sequence of nlen chars (without a terminating NULL char). For each data block, read the block into memory and use a dir_entry *dp to point at the loaded data block. Then use nlen to extract NAME as a string and compare it with name[0]. If they do not match, step to the next dir_entry by

$$dp = (dir\_entry *)((char *)dp + dp\text{->}rlen);$$

and continue the search. If name[0] exists, we can find its dir_entry and hence its inode number.

6. Use the inode number, ino, to locate the corresponding INODE. Recall that ino counts from 1. Use the Mailman's algorithm to compute the disk block containing the INODE and its offset in that block.

$$blk \quad = (ino - 1) \,/\, INODES\_PER\_BLOCK + InodesBeginBlock;$$
$$offset = (ino - 1) \,\% \, INODES\_PER\_BLOCK;$$

Then read in the INODE of /a, from which we can determine whether it's a DIR. If /a is not a DIR, there can't be /a/b, so the search fails. If it's a DIR and there are more components to search, continue for the next component name[1]. The problem now becomes: search for name[1] in the INODE of /a, which is exactly the same as that of Step (5).

7. Since Steps 5–6 will be repeated n times, it's better to write a search function

```
u32 search(INODE *inodePtr, char *name)
{
    // search for name in the data blocks of this INODE
    // if found, return its ino; else return 0
}
```

Then all we have to do is to call search() n times, as sketched below.

```
Assume: n, name[0], ...., name[n-1] are globals
INODE *ip points at INODE of /
for (i=0; i<n; i++){
    ino = search(ip, name[i])
    if (!ino){ // can't find name[i], exit;}
    use ino to read in INODE and let ip point to INODE
}
```

If the search loop ends successfully, ip must point at the INODE of pathname. Traversing large EXT2 FS with many groups is similar, which will be shown in Chap. 3 when we discuss booting from hard disk partitions.

2.9   The BCC Cross-Compiling Package

The initial development platform of MTX is BCC under Linux. BCC consists of an
assembler, a C compiler and a linker. It is a cross compiling package, which generates 16-bit code for execution on real-mode PC or PC emulators. The latest version
of BCC is bcc-0.16.17. Currently, BCC is included in most Linux distributions. If
not, it can be downloaded and installed easily. As usual, the bcc command accepts
both .s and .c source files and invokes the assembler, compiler and linker to generate a binary executable a.out. The resulting a.out is intended for execution on ELKS
(Embedded Linux Kernel System) [ELKS] or an ELKS simulator. To adapt BCC
to the development of MTX, we must run BCC's assembler, compiler and linker in
separate steps. Currently, MTX does not have a program development facility of
its own. Since most readers have access to Linux and are familiar with its working
environment, it is better to use Linux as the development platform of MTX. Usage
of the BCC package will be explained in Chap. 3 when we discuss booting. In addition, we also use BCC to develop MTX in 16-bit real mode in Chap. 4–13. We
shall switch to GCC's 32-bit assembler, compiler and linker when we extend MTX
to 32-bit protected mode in Chaps. 14 and 15.

2.10   Running MTX

The system image of MTX is an EXT2 file system containing the following contents.

```
           |-- bin   : binary executable programs
           |-- dev   : device special files
   /---|-- etc   : passwd file
           |-- user : user home directories
           |-- boot : mtx kernel images
```

There are two types of MTX images.

1. FDimage: These are small MTX systems, which run on (virtual) floppy disks.
   These include all the MTX systems developed in Chaps. 4 and 5. Each FDimage is a bootable floppy disk image, which can be used as the FD of a virtual
   machine. For example, to run MTX on a FDimage under QEMU, enter

   qemu -fda FDimage -no-fd-bootchk

   To run it on other virtual machines, such as DOSEMU, VMware and VirtualBox,
   etc., configure the virtual machines to boot from FDimage as the virtual FD disk.

2. HDimage: These are full-sized MTX images intended for hard disks. In order to
   run an HDimage, it must be installed to a hard disk partition, along with a MTX
   hard disk booter. The install procedure is described in the Appendix. After installation, boot up and run MTX as usual.

2.11   From Login to Command Execution

This section describes the login process of MTX. Although some of the descriptions are MTX specific, they are also applicable to all Unix-like systems. The first step of running MTX is to boot up the MTX kernel (Booting is covered in Chap. 3). When the MTX kernel starts, it initializes the system and mounts a root file system from the boot device. Then it creates a process P0, which runs only in kernel mode. P0 forks a child process P1, which executes an INIT program in user mode. P1 plays the same role as the INIT process of Unix/Linux. When P1 runs, it forks a child process on each of the login terminals. Then P1 waits for any of the login process to terminate. Each login process executes the same login program, in which it opens its own terminal (special file) to get the file descriptors in =0 for read, out =1 and err =2 for write. Then it displays login: to its own terminal and waits for users to login. When a user tries to login, the login process checks the user's login name and password in the /etc /passwd file. Each line of the passwd file is of the form

loginname:password:gid:uid:user-full-name:home-directory:program

After verifying that the user has a valid account, the login process becomes the user's process by acquiring the user's gid and uid. It changes directory to the user's home-directory and executes the listed program, which is usually the command interpreter sh. Then the user can enter commands for the sh process to execute. When the user logout, the sh process terminates, which wakes up the INIT process P1, which forks another login process on the terminal, etc.

A command is usually a binary executable file. By default, all executable programs are in the /bin directory. If an executable file is not in the /bin directory, it must be entered as a full pathname. Given a command line, such as "cat filename", sh forks a child process to execute the cat command and waits for the child process to terminate. The child process executes the command by changing its execution image to the cat program, passing as parameter filename to the program. When the child process terminates, it wakes up the parent sh process, which prompts for another command, etc. In addition to simple commands, the MTX sh also supports I/O redirections and multiple commands connected by pipes. In summary, the process of booting up MTX, login and use the MTX system is similar to, but much simpler than, that of other operating systems, such as Unix or Linux.

Problems

1. Consider the Intel x86 based PC in real-mode. Assume that the CPU's DS register contains 0×1000. What are the (20-bit) real addresses generated in the following instructions?

```
mov ax, 0x1234
add ax, 0x0002
```

A global variable char buf[1024], 20-bit real address of buf = ?

2. A binary executable a.out file consists of a header followed by TEXT and DATA sections.

```
|header| TEXT | DATA |<== BSS ===>|
```

The Unix command size a.out shows the size of TEXT, DATA, BSS of a.out. Use the following C program, t1.c, to generate t2.c to t6.c as specified below.

```
//********** t1.c file ************
   int g;
   main()
   {
       int a, b, c;
       a = 1; b = 2;
       c = a + b;
       printf("c=%d\n", c);
   }
```

t2.c: Change the global variable g to int g = 3;
t3.c Change the global variable g to int g[10000];
t4.c Change the global variable g to int g[10000] = {4};
t5.c Change the local variables of main() to int a, b,c, d[10000];
t6.c. Change the local variables of main() to static int a, b,c, d[10000];

A. In each case, use cc -m32 to generate a.out. Then use ls −l a.out to get a.out size, and use size a.out to get its section sizes. Record the observed sizes in a table:

```
Case  | a.out | TEXT | DATA | BSS |
-----------------------------------------
 (1)  |       |      |      |     |
-----------------------------------------
 etc.
-----------------------------------------
```

Then answer the following questions:

1. For the variables g, a, b, c, d, which variables are in DATA? Which variables are in BSS?
2. For the TEXT, DATA and BSS sections, which are in a.out, which is NOT in a.out? WHY?
B. In each case, use cc -static t.c to generate a.out. Record the sizes again and compare them with the sizes in (A). What are the differences and why?
3. Under Linux, use gcc -m32 to compile and run the following program.

```
int *FP; // a global pointer
main(int argc, char *argv[], char *env[])
{    int a,b,c;
     printf("enter main\n");
     a=1; b=2; c=3;
     A(a,b);
     printf("exit main\n");
}
int A(int x, int y)
{    int d,e,f;
     printf("enter A\n");
     d=4; e=5; f=6;
     B(d,e);
     printf("exit A\n");
}
int B(int x, int y)
{    int u,v,w;
     printf("enter B\n");
     u=7; v=8; w=9;
     asm("movl %ebp, FP"); // set FP=CPU's %ebp register
     // Write C code to DO (1)-(3) AS SPECIFIED BELOW
     printf("exit B\n");
}
```

1. In B(), FP points the stack frame link list in stack. Print the stack frame link list.
2. Print in HEX the address and contents of the stack from FP to the stack frame of main().
3. On a hardcopy of the output, identify and explain the stack contents in terms of function stack frames, i.e. local variables, parameters, return address, etc.
4. Run the program as a.out one two three > file. Then identify the parameters to main(), i.e. where are argc, argv, env located?

4. Under Linux, use gcc -m32 to compile and run the long jump program in Sect. 2.4.4.

1. Instead of jmp_buf env of Linux, define int *env[2]. Implement setjmp() and longjmp() as follows. In setjmp(env), save caller's [PC|FP] into env[0|1].
In longjmp(env, r), replace current [PC|FP] on stack with env[0|1], then return r.
Compile and run the program again to verify that the long jump scheme works.

2. The gcc compiler generated code may reference local variables in main() by %esp register. Show how to modify (1) to make long jump work correctly.

5. Abnormal program termination: Under Linux, try to run the following C programs. In each case, observe what happens and explain WHY?

```
5-1. int *p; main(){    *p = 1;   }
5-2. int a,b,c; main(){  c = a/b;  }
5-3. main(){ main(); }
5-4. main(){ printf("pid=%d\n", getpid()); while(1); }
```

a. From the same X-terminal, enter Control_C key. What would happen and WHY?
b. From another X-terminal, enter: kill -s 11 pid. What would happen and WHY?

6. Given an EXT2 file system, write a C program to display the contents of super-block, group descriptor 0, bitmaps as char maps, entries of the root directory.
7. Write a C program, showblock, which displays the disk block (direct, indirect and double indirect) numbers of a file in an EXT2 file system.
8. A RAM disk is a memory area used as a disk. Like a real disk, read/write a RAM disk is by 512-byte sectors. For example, in a real mode PC we may designate the 64 KB memory area from the segment 0x8000 to 0x9000 as a RAM disk. Write C functions

```
        read_sector(int sector, char buffer[512]), and
        write_sector(int sector, char buffer[512])
```

which read/write a RAM disk sector to/from a 512-byte buffer.

References

Antonakos, J.L., "An introduction to the Intel Family of Microprocessors", Prentice Hall, 1999.
BCC: Linux 8086 development environment, version 0.16.17, http://www.debath.co.uk, May, 2014
Bovet, D.P., Cesati, M., "Understanding the Linux Kernel, Third Edition", O'Reilly, 2005
Cao, M., Bhattacharya, S, Tso, T., "Ext4: The Next Generation of Ext2/3 File system", IBM Linux Technology Center, 2007.
Card, R., Theodore Ts'o, T., Stephen Tweedie, S., "Design and Implementation of the Second Extended Filesystem", web.mit.edu/tytso/www/linux/ext2intro.html, 1995
ECMA-119: Standard ECMA-119, Volume and File Structure of CDROM for Information Interchange, 2nd edition, December 1987.
ELF: Tool Interface Standard (TIS) Executable and Linking Format (ELF) Specification Version 1.2, 1995
ELKS: sourceforge.net/projects/elks, 1996
EXT2: www.nongnu.org/ext2-doc/ext2.html, 2001
EXT3: jamesthornton.com/hotlist/linux-filesystems/ext3-journal, 2015

Chapter 3
Booting Operating Systems

3.1 Booting

Booting, which is short for bootstrap, refers to the process of loading an operating system image into computer memory and starting up the operating system. As such, it is the first step to run an operating system. Despite its importance and widespread interests among computer users, the subject of booting is rarely discussed in operating system books. Information on booting are usually scattered and, in most cases, incomplete. A systematic treatment of the booting process has been lacking. The purpose of this chapter is to try to fill this void. In this chapter, we shall discuss the booting principle and show how to write booter programs to boot up real operating systems. As one might expect, the booting process is highly machine dependent. To be more specific, we shall only consider the booting process of Intel x86 based PCs. Every PC has a BIOS (Basic Input Output System) program stored in ROM (Read Only Memory). After power on or following a reset, the PC's CPU starts to execute BIOS. First, BIOS performs POST (Power-on Self Test) to check the system hardware for proper operation. Then it searches for a device to boot. Bootable devices are maintained in a programmable CMOS memory. The usual booting order is floppy disk, CDROM, hard disk, etc. The booting order can be changed through BIOS. If BIOS finds a bootable device, it tries to boot from that device. Otherwise, it displays a "no bootable device found" message and waits for user intervention.

3.1.1 Bootable Devices

A bootable device is a storage device supported by BIOS for booting. Currently, bootable devices include floppy disk, hard disk, CD/DVD disc and USB drive. As storage technology evolves, new bootable devices will undoubtedly be added to the list, but the principle of booting should remain the same. A bootable device contains a booter and a bootable system image. During booting, BIOS loads the first 512 bytes of the booter to the memory location (segment, offset)=(0x0000, 0x7C00)=0x07C00, and jumps to there to execute the booter. After that, it is

© Springer International Publishing Switzerland 2015

K. C. Wang, *Design and Implementation of the MTX Operating System,*
DOI 10.1007/978-3-319-17575-1_3

entirely up to the booter to do the rest. The reason why BIOS always loads the booter to 0x07C00 is historical. In the early days, a PC is only guaranteed to have 64 KB of RAM memory. The memory below 0x07C00 is reserved for interrupt vectors, BIOS and BASIC, etc. The first OS usable memory begins at 0x08000. So the booter is loaded to 0x07C00, which is 1 KB below 0x08000. When execution starts, the actions of a booter are typically as follows.

Load the rest of the booter into memory and execute the complete booter.
Find and load the operating system image into memory.
Send CPU to execute the startup code of the OS kernel, which starts up the OS.

Details of these steps will be explained later when we develop booter programs. In the following, we first describe the booting process of various bootable devices.

3.2 Booting from Various Devices

3.2.1 Floppy Disk Booting

As a storage device, floppy disk (FD) has almost become obsolete. Currently, most PCs, especially laptop computers, no longer support floppy drives. Despite this, it is still worth discussing FD booting for several reasons. First, booting requires writing a booter to the beginning part of a device, such as sector 0 of a hard disk, which is known as the Master Boot Record (MBR). However, writing to a hard disk is very risky. A careless mistake may render the hard disk non-bootable, or even worse, destroy the disk's partition table with disastrous consequences. In contrast, writing to a floppy disk involves almost no risk at all. It provides a simple and safe tool for learning the booting process and testing new booter programs. This is especially beneficial to beginners. Second, floppy drives are still supported in almost all PC emulators, such as QEMU, VMware and VirtualBox, etc. These PC emulators provide a virtual machine environment for developing and testing system software. Virtual machines are more convenient to use since booting a virtual machine does not need to turn off/on a real computer and the booting process is also faster. Third, for various reasons a computer may become non-bootable. Often the problem is not due to hardware failure but corrupted or missing system files. In these situations it is very useful to have an alternative way to boot up the machine to repair or rescue the system. Depending on the disk contents, FD booting can be classified into several cases, as shown in Fig. 3.1. In the following, we shall describe the setup and booting sequence of each case.

(1). FD contains a booter followed by a bootable OS image: In this case, a FD is dedicated to booting. It contains a booter in sector 0, followed by a bootable OS image in consecutive sectors, as shown in Fig. 3.2.

The size of the OS image, e.g. number of sectors, is either in the beginning part of the OS image or patched in the booter itself, so that the booter can determine how many sectors of the OS image to load. The loading address is also known, usually

```
Bootable FD
   |— 1. booter + OS image
   |— 2. booter + OS image + RAM disk image
   |— 3. booter + file system + OS image
   |— 4. booter + file system containing OS image file
   |— 5. booter for booting hard disk partitions.
```

Fig. 3.1 Bootable FDs by Contents

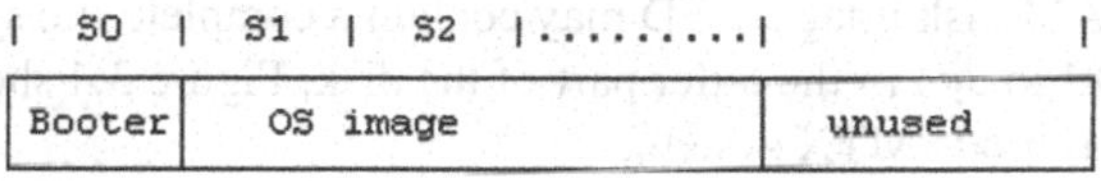

```
| S0  | S1  | S2  |.........|                 |
+--------+----------------------+-------------------+
| Booter |      OS image        |      unused       |
+--------+----------------------+-------------------+
```

Fig. 3.2 A simple bootable FD layout

by default. In this case the booter's task is very simple. All it needs to do is to load the OS image sectors to the specified address and then send the CPU to execute the loaded OS image. Such a booter can be very small and fit easily in the MBR sector. Examples of this kind of setup include MTX, MINIX and bootable FD of small Linux zImage kernel.

(2). FD with a bootable image and a RAM disk Image: Although it is very easy to boot up an OS kernel from a FD, to make the OS kernel runnable is another matter. In order to run, most OS kernels require a root file system, which is a basic file system containing enough special files, commands and shared libraries, etc. that are needed by the OS kernel. Without a root file system, an OS kernel simply cannot run. There are many ways to make a root file system available. The simplest way is to assume that a root file system already exists on a separate device. During booting the OS kernel can be instructed to mount the appropriate device as the root file system. As an example, early distributions of Linux used a pair of boot-root floppy disks. The boot disk is used to boot up the Linux kernel, which is compiled with RAM disk support. The root disk is a compressed RAM disk image of a root file system. When the Linux kernel starts up, it prompts and waits for a root disk to be inserted. When the root disk is ready, the kernel loads the root disk contents to a ram disk area in memory, un-compresses the RAM disk image and mounts the ram disk as the root file system. The same boot-root disk pair was used later as a Linux rescue system.

If the OS and RAM disk images are small, it is possible to put both images on the same floppy disk, resulting in a single-FD system. Figure 3.3 shows the layout

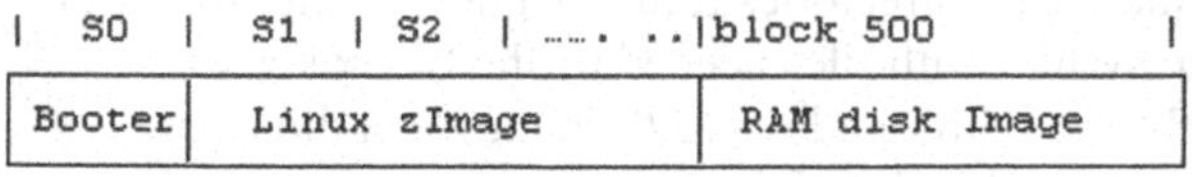

```
| S0  | S1  | S2  | ..... ..|block 500            |
+--------+-----------------+-------------------------+
| Booter |  Linux zImage   |     RAM disk Image      |
+--------+-----------------+-------------------------+
```

Fig. 3.3 Bootable FD with RAM disk image

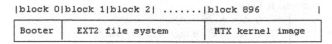

Fig. 3.4 FD with EXT2 file system and MTX kernel

of such a disk. It contains a booter and a Linux zImage followed by a compressed
RAM disk image. The Linux kernel's ramdisk parameter can be set in such a way
that when the Linux kernel starts, it does not prompt for a separate root disk but
loads the RAM disk image directly from the boot disk.

Instead of a RAM disk image, a FD may contain a complete file system in front,
followed by an OS image in the latter part of the disk. Figure 3.4 shows the layout
of a single-FD real mode MTX system.

The real mode MTX image size is at most 128 KB. We can format a FD as an
EXT2 file system with $1024 - 128 = 896$ blocks, populate it with files needed by the
MTX kernel and place the MTX kernel in the last 128 blocks of the disk. Block 0,
which is not used by the file system, contains a MTX booter. During booting, the
booter loads the MTX kernel from the last 128 disk blocks and transfers control
to the MTX kernel. When the MTX kernel starts, it mounts the FD as the root file
system. For small Linux zImage kernels, a single-FD Linux system is also possible.

(3). FD is a file system with bootable image files: In this case, the FD is a complete file system containing a bootable OS image as a regular file. To simplify booting, the OS image can be placed directly under the root directory, allowing the
booter to find it easily. It may also be placed anywhere in the file system, e.g. in
a /boot directory. In that case, the booter size would be larger since it must traverse
the file system to find the OS image. During booting, the booter first finds the OS
image file. Then it loads the image's disk blocks into memory and sends the CPU
to execute the loaded OS image. When the OS kernel starts, it mounts the FD as
the root file system and runs on the same FD. This kind of setup is very common. A
well-known example is DOS, which can boot up and run from the same FD. Here,
we describe two specific systems based on MTX and Linux.

A FD based MTX system is an EXT2 file system. It contains all the files needed
by the MTX kernel. Bootable MTX kernels are files in the /boot directory. Block0
of the disk contains a MTX booter. During booting, the booter prompts for a MTX
kernel to boot. The default is mtx but it can be any file name in the /boot directory.
With a bootable file name, the booter finds the image file and loads its disk blocks
to the segment 0x1000. When loading completes, it transfers control to the kernel
image. When the MTX kernel starts up, it mounts the FD as the root file system and
runs on the same FD. Similarly, we can create a single-FD Linux system as follows.

Format a FD as EXT2 file system (mke2fs on /dev/fd0).
Mount the FD and create directories (bin, boot,dev, etc,lib, sbin,usr).
Populate the file system with files needed by the Linux kernel.
Place a Linux zImage with rootdev=(2,0) in the /boot directory.
Install a linux booter to block0 of the FD.

After booting up, the Linux kernel can mount the FD as the root file system and run on the same FD. Although the principle is simple, the challenge is how to make a complete Linux file system small enough to fit in a single FD. This is why earlier Linux had to use a separate root disk. The situation changed when a small Linux file system, called the BusyBox (BusyBox), became available. A small BusyBox is only about 400 KB, yet it supports all the basic commands of Unix, including a sh and a text editor that emulates both vi and emacs, an incredible feat indeed. As an example, Fig. 3.13 shows the screen of booting up and running a single-FD Linux system. In addition to supporting small stand-alone Linux systems, BusyBox has become the core of almost all Linux distribution packages for installing the Linux system.

(4). FD with a booter for HD booting: This is a FD based booter for booting from hard disk partitions. During booting, the booter is loaded from a FD. Once execution starts, all the actions are for booting system images from hard disk partitions. Since the hard disk is accessed in read-only mode, this avoids any chances of corrupting the hard disk. In addition, it also provides an alternative way to boot up a PC when the normal booter becomes inoperative.

3.2.2 Hard Disk Booting

The discussion here is based on IDE hard disks but the same principle also applies to SCSI and SATA hard disks.

(1). Hard Disk Partitions: A hard disk is usually divided into several partitions. Each partition can be formatted as a unique file system and contain a different operating system. The partitions are defined by a partition table in the first (MBR) sector of the disk. In the MBR the partition table begins at the byte offset 0x1BE (446). It has four 16-byte entries for four primary partitions. If needed, one of the partitions can be EXTEND type. The disk space of an EXTEND partition can be further divided into more partitions. Each partition is assigned a unique number for identification. Details of the partition table will be shown later. For the time being, it suffices to say that from the partition table, we can find the start sector and size of each partition. Similar to the MBR, the first sector of each partition is also a (local) MBR, which may contain a booter for booting an OS image in that partition. Figure 3.5 shows the layout of a hard disk with partitions.

(2). Hard Disk Booting Sequence: When booting from a hard disk BIOS loads the MBR booter to the memory location (0x0000, 0x7C00) and executes it as usual.

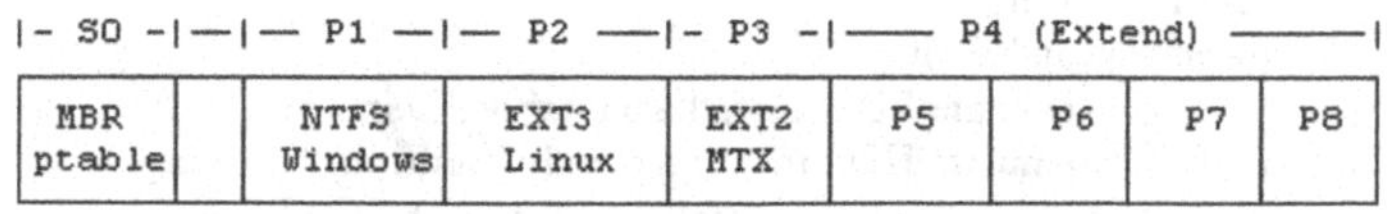

```
|- S0 -|—|— P1 —|— P2 —|- P3 -|—— P4 (Extend) ——|
```

MBR ptable		NTFS Windows	EXT3 Linux	EXT2 MTX	P5	P6	P7	P8

Fig. 3.5 Hard disk partitions

What happens next depends on the role of the MBR booter. In the simplest case, the MBR booter may ask for a partition to boot. Then it loads the local MBR of the partition to (0x0000, 0x7C00) and executes the local MBR booter. It is then up to the local MBR booter to finish the booting task. Such a MBR booter is commonly known as a chain-boot-loader. It might as well be called a pass-the-buck booter since all it does is to usher in the next booter and says "you do it". Such a chain boot-loader can be very small and fit entirely in the MBR. On the other hand, a more sophisticated HD booter should perform some of the booting tasks by itself. For example, the Linux boot loader LILO can be installed in the MBR for booting Linux as well as DOS and Windows. Similarly, GRUB (GNU GRUB Project) and the hd-booter developed in this book can also be installed in the MBR to boot up different operating systems. In general, a MBR booter cannot perform the entire booting task by itself due to its small size and limited capability. Instead, the MBR booter is only the beginning part of a multi-stage booter. In a multi-stage booter, BIOS loads stage1 and executes it first. Then stage1 loads and executes stage2, which loads and executes stage3, etc. Naturally, each succeeding stage can be much larger and more capable than the preceding stage. The number of stages is entirely up to the designer's choice. For example, GRUB version 1 and earlier had a stage1 booter in MBR, a stage1.5 and also a stage2 booter. In the latest GRUB_2, stage1.5 is eliminated, leaving only two stages. In the hd-booter of this book, the MBR booter is also part of the second stage booter. So strictly speaking it has only one stage.

3.2.3   CD/DVD_ROM Booting

Initially, CDROMs are used mainly for data storage, with proprietary booting methods provided by different computer vendors. CDROM booting standard was added in 1995. It is known as the El-Torito bootable CD specification (Stevens and Merkin 1995). Legend has it that the name was derived from a Mexican restaurant in California where the two engineers met and drafted the protocol.

(1). The El-Torito CDROM boot protocol: The El-Torito protocol supports three different ways to set up a CDROM for booting, as shown in Fig. 3.6.

(2). Emulation Booting: In emulation booting, the boot image must be either a floppy disk image or a (single-partition) hard disk image. During booting, BIOS loads the first 512 bytes of a booter from the boot image to (0x0000, 0x07C0) and execute the booter as usual. In addition, BIOS also emulates the CD/DVD drive as either a FD or HD. If the booting image size is 1.44 or 2.88 MB, it emulates the CD/

```
CD/DVD Booting
   |— emulation booting
   |       |—emulate FD  : install a bootable FD image
   |       |—emulate HD  : install a (single-partition) HD image
   |— no-emulation booting: install an arbitrary bootable image
```

Fig. 3.6 CD/DVD boot options

DVD as the first floppy drive. Otherwise, it emulates the CD/DVD as the first hard drive. Once boot up, the boot image on the CD/DVD can be accessed as the emulated drive through BIOS. The environment is identical to that of booting up from the emulated drive. For example, if the emulated boot image is a FD, after booting up the bootable FD image can be accessed as A: drive, while the original A: drive is demoted to B: drive. Similarly, if the boot image is a hard disk image, after booting up the image becomes C: drive and the original C: drive becomes D: drives, etc. Although the boot image is accessible, it is important to note that nothing else on the CD/DVD disc is visible at this moment. This implies that, even if the CD/DVD contains a file system, the files are totally invisible after booting up, which may be somewhat surprising. Naturally, they will become accessible if the booted up kernel has a CD/DVD driver to read the CD/DVD contents.

(3). No-emulation Booting: In no-emulation booting, the boot image can be any (real-mode) binary executable code. For real-mode OS images, a separate booter is not necessary because the entire OS image can be booted into memory directly. For other OS images with complex loading requirements, e.g. Linux, a separate OS booter is needed. During booting, the booter itself can be loaded directly, but there is a problem. When the booter tries to load the OS image, it needs a device number of the CD/DVD drive to make BIOS calls. The question is: which device number? The reader may think it would be the usual device number of the CD/DVD drive, e.g. 0x81 for the first IDE slave or 0x82 for the second IDE master, etc. But it may be none of the above. The El-Torito protocol only states that BIOS shall emulate the CD/DVD drive by an arbitrary device number. Different BIOS may come up with different drive numbers. Fortunately, when BIOS invokes a booter, it also passes the emulated drive number in the CPU's DL register. The booter must catch the drive number and use it to make BIOS calls. Similar to emulation booting, while it is easy to boot up an OS image from CD/DVD, to access the contents on the CD/DVD is another matter. In order to access the contents, a booted up OS must have drivers to interpret the iso9660 file system on the CD/DVD.

3.2.4 USB Drive Booting

As a storage device, USB drives are similar to hard disks. Like a hard disk, a USB drive can be divided into partitions. In order to be bootable, some BIOS even require a USB drive to have an active partition. During booting, BIOS emulates the USB drive as the usual C: drive (0x80). The environment is the same as that of booting from the first hard disk. Therefore, USB booting is identical to hard disk booting.

As an example, it is very easy to install Linux to a USB partition, e.g. partition 2 of a USB drive, and then install LILO or GRUB to the USB's MBR for booting Linux from the USB partition. The procedure is exactly the same as that of installing Linux to a hard disk partition. If the PC's BIOS supports USB booting, Linux kernel will boot up from the USB partition. However, after boot up, the Linux kernel will fail to run because it can not mount the USB partition as root device, even if all the USB drivers are compiled into the Linux kernel. This is because, when the Linux kernel starts, it only activates drivers for IDE and SCSI devices but not for USB drives. It is certainly possible to modify Linux's startup code to support USB drives, but doing so is still a per-device solution. Instead, Linux uses a general approach to deal with this problem by using an initial RAM disk image.

3.2.5   Boot Linux with Initial Ramdisk Image

Booting Linux kernel with an initial RAM disk image has become a standard way to boot up a Linux system. The advantage of using an initrd image is that it allows a single generic Linux kernel to be used on many different Linux configurations. An initrd is a RAM disk image which serves as a temporary root file system when the Linux kernel first starts up. While running on the RAM disk, the Linux kernel executes a sh script, initrc, which directs the kernel to load the driver modules of the real root device, such as a USB drive. When the real root device is activated and ready, the kernel discards the RAM disk and mounts the real root device as the root file system. Details of how to set up and load initrd image will be shown later.

3.2.6   Network Booting

Network booting has been in use for a long time. The basic requirement is to establish a network connection to a server machine in a network, such as a server running the BOOTP protocol in a TCP/IP (Comer 1995; Comer and Stevens 1998) network. Once the connection is made, booting code or the entire kernel code can be downloaded from the server to the local machine. After that, the booting sequence is basically the same as before. Networking is outside the scope of this book. Therefore, we shall not discuss network booting.

3.3   Develop Booter Programs

In this section, we shall show how to write booter programs to boot up real operating systems. Although this book is primarily about MTX, we shall also discuss Linux booting, for a number of reasons. First, Linux is a popular OS, which has a very large user base, especially among Computer Science students. A Linux distribution usually comes with a default booter, which is either LILO or GRUB. After installing Linux, it would boot up nicely. To most users the booting process remains somewhat a mystery. Many students often wish to know more about the booting process. Second, Linux is a very powerful real OS, which runs on PCs with a wide range of hardware configurations. As a result, the booting process of Linux is also fairly complex and demanding. Our purpose is to show that, if we can write a booter to boot up Linux, we should be able to write a booter to boot up any operating system. In order to show that the booters actually work, we shall demonstrate them by sample systems. All the booter programs developed in this chapter are in the MTX. src/BOOTERS directory on the MTX install CD. A detailed listing of the booter programs is at the end of this chapter.

3.3.1 Requirements of Booter Programs

Before developing booter programs, we first point out the unique requirements of booter programs.

1. A booter needs assembly code because it must manipulate CPU registers and make BIOS calls. Many booters are written entirely in assembly code, which makes them hard to understand. In contrast, we shall use assembly code only if absolutely necessary. Otherwise, we shall implement all the actual work in the high-level language C.
2. When a PC starts, it is in the 16-bit real mode, in which the CPU can only execute 16-bit code and access the lowest 1 MB memory. To create a booter, we must use a compiler-linker that generates 16-bit code. For example, we can not use GCC because the GCC compiler generates 32 or 64-bit code, which can not be used during booting. The software chosen is the BCC package under Linux, which generates 16-bit code.
3. By default, the binary executable generated by BCC uses a single-segment memory model, in which the code, data and stack segments are all the same. Such a program can be loaded to, and executed from, any available segment in memory. A segment is a memory area that begins at a 16-byte boundary. During execution, the CPU's CS, DS and SS registers must all point to the same segment of the program.
4. Booters differs from ordinary programs in many aspects. Perhaps the most notable difference is their size. A booter's size (code plus static data) is extremely limited, e.g. 512 or 1024 bytes, in order to fit in one or two disk sectors. Multistage booters can be larger but it is always desirable to keep the booter size small. The second difference is that, when running an ordinary program an operating system will load the entire program into memory and set up the program's execution environment before execution starts. An ordinary program does not have to worry about these things. In contrast, when a booter starts, it only has the first 512 bytes loaded at 0x07C00. If the booter is larger than 512 bytes, which is usually the case, it must load the missing parts in by itself. If the booter's initial memory area is needed by the OS, it must be moved to a different location in order not to be clobbered by the incoming OS image. In addition, a booter must manage its own execution environment, e.g. set up CPU segment registers and establish a stack.
5. A booter cannot use the standard library I/O functions, such as gets() and printf(), etc. These functions depend on operating system support, but there is no operat-

ing system yet during booting. The only available support is BIOS. If needed, a booter must implement its own I/O functions by calling only BIOS.

6. When developing an ordinary program we may use a variety of tools, such as gdb, for debugging. In contrast, there is almost no tool to debug a booter. If something goes wrong, the machine simply stops with little or no clue as to where and why the error occurred. This makes writing booter programs somewhat harder. Despite these, it is not difficult to write booter programs if we follow good programming practice.

3.3.2   Online and Offline Booters

There are two kinds of booters; online and offline. In an offline booter, the booter is told which OS image (file) to boot. While running under an operating system, an offline booter first finds the OS image and builds a small database for the booter to use. The simplest database may contain the disk blocks or ranges of disk blocks of the OS image. During booting, an offline booter simply uses the pre-built database to load the OS image. For example, the Linux boot-loader, LILO, is an offline booter. It uses a lilo.conf file to build a map file in the /boot directory, and then installs the LILO booter to the MBR or the local MBR of a hard disk partition. During booting, it uses the map file in the /boot directory to load the Linux image. The disadvantage of offline booters is that the user must install the booter again whenever the OS image is moved or changed. In contrast, an online booter, e.g. GRUB, can find and load an OS image file directly. Since online booters are more general and flexible, we shall only consider online booters.

3.3.3   Boot MTX from FD sectors

We begin with a simple booter for booting MTX from a FD disk. The FD disk layout is shown in Fig. 3.7.

It contains a booter in Sector 0, followed by a MTX kernel image in consecutive sectors. In the MTX kernel image, which uses the separate I&D memory model,

```
|  S0  | S1 S2 .......|   unused sectors        |

|booter|  MTX kernel  |   ..................   |
```

Fig. 3.7 MTX boot disk layout

the first three (2-byte) words are reserved. Word 0 is a jump instruction, word 1 is
the code section size in 16-byte clicks and word 2 is the data section size in bytes.
During booting, the booter may extract these values to determine the number of
sectors of the MTX kernel to load. The loading segment address is 0x1000. The
booter consists of two files, a bs.s file in BCC assembly and a bc.c file in C. Under
Linux, use BCC to generate a binary executable without header and dump it to the
beginning of a floppy disk, as in

```
as86 -o bs.o  bs.s     # assemble bs.s into bs.o
bcc  -c -ansi bc.c     # compile  bc.c into bc.o
# link bs.o and bc.o into a binary executable without header
ld86 -d -o booter bs.o bc.o /usr/lib/bcc/libc.a
# dump booter to sector 0 of a FD
dd if=booter of=/dev/fd0 bs=512 count=1 conv=notrunc
```

where the special file name, /dev/fd0, is the first floppy drive. If the target is not
a real device but an image file, simply replace /dev/fd0 with the image file name.
In that case, the parameter conv = notrunc is necessary in order to prevent dd from
truncating the image file. Instead of entering individual commands, the building
process can be automated by using a Makefile or a sh script. For simple compile-
link tasks, a sh script is adequate and actually more convenient. For example, we
may re-write the above commands as a sh script file, mk, which takes a filename
as parameter.

```
# usage: mk filename
as86 -o bs.o bs.s    # bs.s file does not change
bcc  -c -ansi $1.c
ld86 -d -o $1 bs.o $1.o /usr/lib/bcc/libc.a
dd if=$1 of=IMAGE bs=512 count=1 conv=notrunc
```

In the following, we shall assume and use such a sh script. First, we show the
booter's assembly code.

```
!======================= bs.s file ===========================
.globl _main,_prints,_NSEC                       ! IMPORT from C
.globl _getc,_putc,_readfd,_setes,_inces, _error ! EXPORT to C
        BOOTSEG  = 0x9800 ! booter segment
        OSSEG    = 0x1000 ! MTX kernel segment
        SSP      = 32*1024 ! booter stack size=32KB
        BSECTORS = 2       ! number of sectors to load initially
! Boot SECTOR loaded at (0000:7C00). reload booter to segment 0x9800
start:
        mov  ax, #BOOTSEG   ! set ES to 0x9800
        mov  es, ax
! call BIOS INT13 to load BSECTORS to (segment,offset)=(0x9800,0)
        xor  dx, dx         ! dh=head=0, dl=drive=0
        xor  cx, cx         ! ch=cyl=0,  cl=sector=0
        incb cl             ! sector=1 (BIOS counts sector from 1)
        xor  bx, bx         ! (ES,BX)= real address = (0x9800,0)
        movb ah, #2         ! ah=READ
        movb al, #BSECTORS  ! al=number of sectors to load
        int  0x13           ! call BIOS disk I/O function
! far jump to (0x9800, next) to continue execution there
        jmpi next, BOOTSEG  ! CS=BOOTSEG, IP=next
next:
        mov  ax, cs         ! Set CPU segment registers to 0x9800
        mov  ds, ax         ! we know ES=CS=0x9800. Let DS=CS
        mov  ss, ax         ! let SS = CS
        mov  sp, #SSP       ! SP = SS + 32 KB
        call _main          ! call main() in C
        jmpi 0, OSSEG       ! jump to execute OS kernel at (OSSEG,0)
!===================== I/O functions ==========================
_getc: ! char getc(): return an input char
        xorb ah, ah         ! clear ah
        int  0x16           ! call BIOS to get a char in AX
        ret
_putc: ! putc(char c): print a char
        push bp
        mov  bp, sp
        movb al, 4[bp]      ! aL = char
        movb ah, #14        ! aH = 14
        int  0x10           ! call BIOS to display the char
        pop  bp
        ret
_readfd: ! readfd(cyl,head,sector): load _NSEC sectors to (ES,0)
        push bp
        mov  bp, sp         ! bp = stack frame pointer
        movb dl, #0x00      ! drive=0 = FD0
        movb dh, 6[bp]      ! head
        movb cl, 8[bp]      ! sector
        incb cl             ! inc sector by 1 to suit BIOS
        movb ch, 4[bp]      ! cyl
        xor  bx, bx         ! BX=0
        movb ah, #0x02      ! READ
        movb al, _NSEC      ! read _NSEC sectors to (ES,BX)
        int  0x13           ! call BIOS to read disk sectors
        jb   _error         ! error if CarryBit is set
        pop  bp
        ret
_setes:                     ! setes(segment): set ES to a segment
        push bp
        mov  bp, sp
        mov  ax, 4[bp]
        mov  es, ax
        pop  bp
        ret
_inces: ! inces(): increment ES by _NSEC sectors (in 16-byte clicks)
        mov  bx, _NSEC      ! get _NSEC in BX
        shl  bx, #5         ! multiply by 2**5 = 32
        mov  ax, es         ! current ES
        add  ax, bx         ! add (_NSEC*0x20)
        mov  es, ax         ! update ES
        ret
_error:                     ! error() and reboot
        push #msg
        call _prints
        int  0x19           ! reboot
msg:    .asciz "Error"
```

In the assembly code, start: is the entry point of the booter program. During booting, BIOS loads sector 0 of the boot disk to (0x0000, 0x7C00) and jumps to there to execute the booter. We assume that the booter must be relocated to a different memory area. Instead of moving the booter, the code calls BIOS INT13 to load the first 2 sectors of the boot disk to the segment 0x9800. The FD drive hardware can load a complete track of 18 sectors at a time. The reason of loading 2 (or more) sectors will become clear shortly. After loading the booter to the new segment, it does a far jump, jmpi next, 0x9800, which sets CPU's (CS, IP)=(0x9800, next), causing the CPU to continue execution from the offset next in the segment 0x9800. The choice of 0x9800 is based on a simple principle: the booter should be relocated to a high memory area with enough space to run, leaving as much space as possible in the low memory area for loading the OS image. The segment 0x9800 is 32 KB below the ROM area, which begins at the segment 0xA000. This gives the booter a 32 KB address space, which is big enough for a fairly powerful booter. When execution continues, both ES and CS already point to 0x9800. The assembly code sets DS and SS to 0x9800 also in order to conform to the one-segment memory model of the program. Then it sets the stack pointer to 32 KB above SS. Figure 3.8 shows the run-time memory image of the booter.

It is noted that, in some PCs, the RAM area above 0x9F000 may be reserved by BIOS for special usage. On these machines the stack pointer can be set to a lower address, e.g. 16 KB from SS, as long as the booter still has enough bss and stack space to run. With a stack, the program can start to make calls. It calls main() in C, which implements the actual work of the booter. When main() returns, it sends the CPU to execute the loaded MTX image at (0x1000, 0).

The remaining assembly code contains functions for I/O and loading disk sectors. The functions getc() and putc(c) are simple; getc() returns an input char from the keyboard and putc(c) displays a char to the screen. The functions readfd(), setes() and inces() deserve more explanations. In order to load an OS image, a booter must be able to load disk sectors into memory. BIOS supports disk I/O functions via INT13, which takes parameters in CPU registers:

```
DH=head(0-1),   DL=drive(0 for FD drive 0),
CH=cyl (0-79), CL=sector (1-18)
AH=2(READ),    AL=number of sectors to read
Memory address: (segment, offset)=(ES, BX)
return status : carry bit=0 means no error, 1 means error.
```

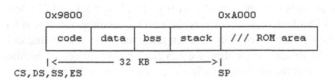

Fig. 3.8 Run-time image of booter

The function readfd(cyl, head, sector) calls BIOS INT13 to load NSEC sectors into memory, where NSEC is a global imported from C code. The zero-counted parameters, (cyl, head, sector), are computed in C code. Since BIOS counts sectors from 1, the sector value is incremented by 1 to suit BIOS. When loading disk sectors BIOS uses (ES, BX) as the real memory address. Since BX=0, the loading address is (ES,0). Thus, ES must be set, by the setes(segment) function, to a desired loading segment before calling readfd(). The function code loads the parameters into CPU registers and issues INT 0x13. After loading NSEC sectors, it uses inces() to increment ES by NSEC sectors (in 16-byte clicks) to load the next NSEC sectors, etc. The error() function is used to trap any error during booting. It prints an error message, followed by reboot. The use of NSEC as an global rather than as a parameter to readfd() serves two purposes. First, it illustrates the cross reference of globals between assembly and C code. Second, if a value does not change often, it should not be passed as a parameter because doing so would increase the code size. Since the booter size is limited to 512 bytes, saving even a few bytes could make a difference between success and failure. Next, we show the booter's C code.

```
/****************** MTX booter's bc.c file **********************
 FD contains this booter in Sector 0, MTX kernel begins in Sector 1
 In the MTX kernel: word#1=tsize in clicks, word#2=dsize in bytes
 ***************************************************************/
int tsize, dsize, ksectors, i, NSEC = 1;

int prints(char *s){  while(*s) putc(*s++); }

int getsector(u16 sector)
{  readfd(sector/36, ((sector)%36)/18, (((sector)%36)%18)); }

main()
{
  prints("booting MTX\n\r");
  tsize = *(int *)(512+2);
  dsize = *(int *)(512+4);
  ksectors = ((tsize << 4) + dsize + 511)/512;
  setes(0x1000);
  for (i=1; i<=ksectors+1; i++){
      getsector(i); inces(); putc('.');
  }
  prints("\n\rready to go?"); getc();
}
```

Explanations of C Code Disk sectors are numbered linearly as 0,1,2,..., but BIOS INT13 only accepts disk parameters in (cyl, head, sector) or CHS format. When calling BIOS INT13 we must convert the starting sector number into CHS format. Figure 3.9 shows the relationship between linear and CHS addressing of FD sectors.

Using the Mailman's algorithm, we can convert a linear sector number into CHS format as cyl=sec/36; head=(sec%36)/18; sector=(sec%36)%18;

Then write a getsector() function in C, which calls readfd() for loading disk sectors.

```
Linear:   0 ....... 17 18 .........35 36 ...... 53 54 ..... 71

sector: |S0 .... S17|S0 ..... S17|S0 ..... S17|S0 ... S17|
  head: | — head=0 — | ——head=1 —— | ——head=0 —|— head = 1-|
   cyl: |<———— cyl = 0 ————>|<——— cyl = 1 ————>| etc.
```

Fig. 3.9 Linear sector and CHS addressing

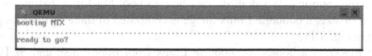

Fig. 3.10 Booting screen of MTX sector Booter

int getsector(int sec){ readfd(sec/36, (sec%36)/18, (sec%36)%18) }

In the C code, the prints() function is used to print message strings. It is based on putc() in assembly. As specified, on the boot disk the MTX kernel image begins from sector 1, in which word 1 is the tsize of the MTX kernel (in 16-byte clicks) and word 2 is the dsize in bytes. Before the booter enters main(), sectors 0 and 1 are already loaded at 0x9800. While in main(), the program's data segment is 0x9800. Thus, words 1 and 2 of sector 1 are now at the (offset) addresses 512+2 and 512+4, respectively. The C code extracts these values to compute the number of sectors of the MTX kernel to load. It sets ES to the segment 0x1000 and loads the MTX sectors in a loop. The loading scheme resembles that of a "sliding window". Each iteration calls getsector(i) to load NSEC sectors from sector i to the memory segment pointed by ES. After loading NSEC sectors to the current segment, it increments ES by NSEC sectors to load the next NSEC sectors, etc. Since NSEC = 1, this amounts to loading the OS image by individual sectors. Faster loading schemes will be discussed later is Sect. 3.3.5. Figure 3.10 shows the booting screen of the MTX.sector booter, in which each dot represents loading a disk sector.

3.3.4 Boot Linux zImage from FD Sectors

Bootable Limux images are generated as follows. Under Linux,

cd to linux source code tree directory (cd /usr/src/linux)
create a.config file, which guides make (make .config)
run make zImage to generate a small Linux image named zImage

Make zImage generates a small bootable Linux image, in which the compressed kernel size is less than 512 KB. In order to generate a small Linux zImage, we must select a minimal set of options and compile most of the device drivers as modules. Otherwise, the kernel image size may exceed 512 KB, which is too big to be loaded into real-mode memory between 0x10000 and 0x90000. In that case, we must use

```
              |BOOT|  SETUP  | (compressed) Linux kernel          |
   sector :  |   0  | 1 to n |  n+1 , (kernel size).....          |
```

Fig. 3.11 Bootable linux image

make bzImage to generate a big Linux image, which requires a different loading scheme during booting. We shall discuss how to boot big Linux bzImages later. Regardless of size, a bootable Linux image is composed of three contiguous parts, as shown in Fig. 3.11.

where BOOT is a booter for booting Linux from floppy disk and SETUP is for setting up the startup environment of the Linux kernel. For small zImages, the number of SETUP sectors, n, varies from 4 to 10. In addition, the BOOT sector also contains the following boot parameters.

```
--------   ------------------------------------------
byte 497   number of SETUP sectors
byte 498   root dev flags: nonzero=READONLY
word 500   Linux kernel size in (16-byte) clicks
word 504   ram disk information
word 506   video mode
word 508   root device=(major, minor) numbers
--------------------------------------------------
```

Most of the boot parameters can be changed by the rdev utility program. The reader may consult Linux man page of rdev for more information. A zImage is intended to be a bootable FD disk of Linux. Since kernel version 2.6, Linux no longer supports FD booting. The discussion here applies only to small Linux zImages of kernel version 2.4 or earlier. During booting, BIOS loads the boot sector, BOOT, into memory and executes it. BOOT first relocates itself to the segment 0x9000 and jumps to there to continue execution. Then it loads SETUP to the segment 0x9020, which is 512 bytes above BOOT. Then it loads the Linux kernel to the segment 0x1000. When loading completes, it jumps to 0x90200 to run SETUP, which starts up the Linux kernel. The loading requirements of a Linux zImage are:

```
         BOOT+SETUP   : 0x90000
         Linux Kernel : 0x10000
```

Our Linux zImage booter essentially duplicates exactly what the BOOT sector does. A Linux zImage boot disk can be created as follows. First, use dd to dump a Linux zImage to a FD beginning in sector 1, as in

```
dd if = zImage of = /dev/fd0 bs = 512 seek =1 conv = notrunc
```

```
|booter|<------- Linux zImage ------->|
|  S0  |  S1   S2   ....                |    unused    |

 booter BOOT SETUP kernel     .....    ............
```

Fig. 3.12 Linux boot disk layout

Then install a Linux booter to sector 0. The resulting disk layout is shown in Fig. 3.12.

The MTX booter can be adapted to booting Linux from a zImage boot disk. In the assembly code, we only need to change OSSEG to 0x9020. When main() returns, it jumps to (0x9020, 0) to execute SETUP. The C code is almost the same as that of the MTX booter. We only show the modified main() function.

```
/*********** C code for Linux zImage booter **************/
int setup, ksectors, i;
main()
{
  prints("boot linux\n\r");
  setup = *(char *)(512+497);         // number of SETUP sectors
  ksectors = *(int *)(512+500) >> 5;  // number of kernel sectors
  setes(0x9000);                      // load BOOT+SETUP to 0x9000
  for (i=1; i<=setup+ksectors+2; i++){ // 2 sectors before SETUP
    getsector(i);                      // load sector i
    i <= setup ? putc('*') : putc('.'); // show a * or .
    inces();                           // inc ES by NSEC sector
    if (i==setup+1)                    // load kernel to ES=0x1000
      setes(0x1000);
  }
  prints("\n\ready to go?"); getc();
}
```

The booting screen of the Linux zImage booter is similar to Fig. 3.10, only with many more dots. In the Linux kernel image, the root device (a word at byte offset 508) is set to 0x0200, which is for the first FD drive. When Linux boots up, it will try to mount (2,0) as the root file system. Since the boot FD is not a file system, the mount will fail and the Linux kernel will display an error message, Kernel panic: VFS: Unable to mount root fs 02:00, and stop. To make the Linux kernel runnable, we may change the root device setting to a device containing a Linux file system. For example, assume that we have Linux installed in partition 2 of a hard disk. If we change the root device of zImage to (3,2), Linux would boot up and run successfully. Another way to provide a root file system is to use a RAM disk image. As an example, in the BOOTERS directory in the MTX install CD, OneFDlinux.img is a single-FD Linux image. It contains a Linux booter and a Linux zImage in front, followed by a compressed ramdisk image beginning in block 550. The Linux kernel is compiled with ramdisk support. The ramdisk

```
RAMDISK driver initialized: 16 RAM disks of 7777K size 1024 blocksize
Uniform Multi-Platform E-IDE driver Revision: 7.00beta4-2.4
ide: Assuming 33MHz system bus speed for PIO modes; override with idebus=xx
hdc: QEMU CD-ROM, ATAPI CD/DVD-ROM drive
ide1 at 0x170-0x177,0x376 on irq 15
RAMDISK: Compressed image found at block 550
EXT2-fs warning: mounting unchecked fs, running e2fsck is recommended
VFS: Mounted root (ext2 filesystem).
Freeing unused kernel memory: 72k freed
init started: BusyBox v1.5.1 (2007-06-21 20:09:17 PDT) multi-call binary

Welcome to One FD Linux

Mounting filesystems ...

Please press Enter to activate this console.
KCW : ls
bin     dev     lib     mnt     sbin    usr
boot    etc     linuxrc proc    tmp     var
KCW : _
```

Fig. 3.13 Single-FD linux running on ramdisk

parameter is set to $16384 + 550$ (bit14 = 1 plus ramdisk begin block), which tells the Linux kernel not to prompt for a separate ramdisk but load it from block 550 of the boot disk. Figure 3.13 shows the screen of running the single-FD Linux on a ramdisk.

3.3.5   Fast FD Loading Schemes

The above FD booters load OS images one sector at a time. For small OS images, such as the MTX kernel, this works fine. For large OS images like Linux, it would be too slow to be acceptable. A faster loading scheme is more desirable. When boot a Linux zImage, logically and ideally only two loading operations are needed, as in

$$setes(0x9000); \; nsec = setup + 1; \; getsector(1);$$

$$setes(0x1000); \; nsec = ksectors; \; getsector(setup + 2);$$

Unfortunately, things are not so simple due to hardware limitations. The first problem is that FD drives cannot read across track or cylinder. All floppy drives support reading a full track of 18 sectors at a time. Some BIOS allows reading a complete FD cylinder of 2 tracks. The discussion here assumes 1.44 MB FD drives that support reading cylinders. When loading from FD the sectors must not cross any cylinder boundary. For example, from the sector number 34 (count from 0), read 1 or 2 sectors is OK but attempting to read more than 2 sectors would result in an error. This is because sectors 34 and 35 are in cylinder 0 but sector 36 is in cylinder 1; going from sector 35 to 36 crosses a cylinder boundary, which is not allowed by the drive hardware. This means that each read operation can load at most a full cylinder of 36 sectors. Then, there is the infamous cross 64 KB boundary problem, which says that when loading FD sectors the real memory address cannot cross any 64 KB boundary. For example, from the real address 0x0FE00, if we try to load 2 sectors, the second sector would be loaded to the real address 0xFE000 + 0x200 = 0x10000, which crosses the 64 KB boundary at 0x10000. The cause of the problem is due to the DMA controller, which uses 18-bit address. When the low 16 bits of an address reaches 64K, for some reason the DMA controller does not increment the high order 2 bits of the address, causing the low 16-bit address to wrap around. In this case, loading may still occur but only to the same segment again. In the above example, instead of the intended address 0x10000, the second sector would be loaded to 0x00000. This would destroy the interrupt vectors, which effectively kills BIOS. Therefore, a FD booter must avoid both problems when loading an OS image. A simple way to avoid these problems is to load sectors one by one as we have done so far. Clearly, loading one sector at a time will never cross any cylinder. If the loading segment starts from a sector boundary, i.e. a segment address divisible by 0x20, it also will not cross any 64 KB boundary. Similarly, if the OS image starts from a block boundary on disk and the loading segment also starts from a block boundary in memory, then loading 1 KB blocks would also work. In order not to cross both cylinder and 64 KB boundaries, the best we can do is loading 4 sectors at a time. The reader is encouraged to prove this. Can we do better? The answer is yes, as evidenced by many published boot-loaders, most of which try to load by tracks. Here we present a fast loading scheme, called the "cross-country" algorithm, which loads by cylinders. The algorithm resembles a cross country runner negotiating an obstacle course. When there is open space, the runner takes full strides (load cylinders) to run fast. When there is an obstacle ahead, the runner slows down by taking smaller strides (load partial cylinder) until the obstacle is cleared. Then the runner resumes fast running by taking full strides, etc. The following C code shows a Linux zImage booter that implements the cross country algorithm. In order to keep the booter size within 512 bytes, updating ES is done inside getsector() and the prints() function is also eliminated. The resulting booter size is only 484 bytes.

```
/***************** Cross Country Algorithm ************************
Load cylinders. If a cylinder is about to cross 64KB, compute NSEC =
max sectors without crossing 64KB. Load NSEC sectors, load remaining
CYL-NSEC sectors. Then load cylinders again, etc.
****************************************************************/
#define TRK 18
#define CYL 36
int setup, ksectors, ES;
int csector = 1;  // current loading sector
int NSEC = 35;  // initial number of sectors to load >= BOOT+SETUP
int getsector(u16 sector)
{
    readfd( sector/CYL,((sector)%CYL)/TRK,(((sector)%CYL)%TRK));
    csector += NSEC; inces();
}
main()
{
  setes(0x9000);
  getsector(1);              // load Linux's [boot+SETUP] to 0x9000
  // current sector = SETUP's sector count (at offset 512+497) + 2
  setup    = *(u8 *)(512+497) + 2;
  ksectors = (*(u16 *)(512+500)) >> 5;
  NSEC = CYL - setup;        // sectors remain in cylinder 0
  setes(0x1000);             // Linux kernel is loaded to segment 0x1000
  getsector(setup);          // load the remaining sectors of cylinder 0
  csector = CYL;             // we are now at begining of cyl#1
  while (csector < ksectors+setup){ // try to load cylinders
    ES = getes();            // current ES value
    if (((ES + CYL*0x20) & 0xF000) == (ES & 0xF000)){//same segment
      NSEC = CYL;            // load a full cylinder
      getsector(csector); putc('C'); // show loaded a cylinder
      continue;
    }
    // this cylinder will cross 64KB, compute MAX sectors to load
    NSEC = 1;
    while( ((ES + NSEC*0x20) & 0xF000) == (ES & 0xF000) ){
      NSEC++; putc('s'); // number of sectors can still load
    }                    // without crossing 64KB boundary
    getsector(csector);  // load partial cylinder
    NSEC = CYL - NSEC;   // load remaining sectors of cylinder
    putc('|');           // show cross 64KB
    getsector(csector);  // load remainder of cylinder
    putc('p');
  }
}
```

Figure 3.14 shows the booting screen of the linux.cylinder booter. In the figure, each C is loading a cylinder, each sequence of s is loading the sectors of a partial

Fig. 3.14 Booting linux by loading cylinders

cylinder, each | is crossing a 64 KB boundary and each p is loading the remaining sectors of a cylinder.

Instead of loading cylinders, the reader may modify the above program to load tracks. Similarly, the reader may modify the above booters to load disk blocks.

3.3.6   Boot MTX Image from File System

Our second booter is to boot MTX from a file system. A MTX system disk is an EXT2 file system containing files needed by the MTX kernel. Bootable MTX kernel images are files in the /boot directory. Block 0 of the disk contains the booter. The loading segment address is 0x1000. After booting up, the MTX kernel mounts the same boot disk as the root file system.

When booting an OS image from an EXT2 file system, the problem is essentially how to find the image file's inode. The reader may consult Sect. 2.8.2 of Chap. 2 for the algorithm. Here we only briefly review the steps. Assume that the file name is /boot/mtx. First, read in the 0th group descriptor to find the start block of the inodes table. Then read in the root inode, which is number 2 inode in the inode table. From the root inode's data blocks, search for the first component of the file name, boot. Once the entry boot is found, we know its inode number. Use Mailman's algorithm to convert the inode number to the disk block containing the inode and its offset in that block. Read in the inode of boot and repeat the search for the component mtx. If the search steps succeed, we should have the image file's inode in memory. It contains the size and disk blocks of the image file. Then we can load the image by loading its disk blocks.

When such a booter starts, it must be able to access the file system on the boot disk, which means loading disk blocks into the booter program's memory area. In order to do this, we add a parameter, buf, to the assembly function, readfd(char *buf), where buf is the address of a 1 KB memory area in the booter segment. It is passed to BIOS in BX as the offset of the loading address in the ES segment. Corresponding to this, we also modify getsector() in C to take a block number and buf as parameters. When the booter starts, ES points to the segment of the booter. In the booter's C code, if buf is global, it is relative to DS. If buf is local, it is relative to SS. Therefore, no matter how we define buf, the loading address is always in the booter segment. When loading the blocks of an OS image we can set ES to successive segments and use (ES, 0) as the loading address. The booter's assembly code is almost the same as before. We only show the booter's C code. The booter size is 1008 bytes, which can fit in the 1 KB boot block of a FD.

```
/********************************************************
*             Image file booter's bc.c code            *
********************************************************/
#include "ext2.h"  // contain EXT2 structure types
#define BLK 1024
typedef unsigned char  u8;
typedef unsigned short u16;
typedef unsigned long  u32;
typedef struct ext2_group_desc  GD;
typedef struct ext2_inode        INODE;
typedef struct ext2_dir_entry_2 DIR;
u16 NSEC = 2;
char buf1[BLK], buf2[BLK];       // 2 I/O buffers of 1KB each
int prints(char *s){ //same as before }
int gets(char *s){   // to keep code simple, no length checking
    while ((*s=getc()) != '\r')
         putc(*s++);
    *s = 0;
}
int getblk(u16 blk, char *buf)
{ readfd(blk/18, ((2*blk)%36)/18, ((2*blk)%36)%18, buf); }

u16 search(INODE *ip, char *name)
{
   int i;   char c;  DIR *dp;
   for (i=0; i<12; i++){ // assume a DIR has at most 12 direct blocks
       if ( (u16)ip->i_block[i] ){
           getblk((u16)ip->i_block[i], buf2);
           dp = (DIR *)buf2;
           while ((char *)dp < &buf2[BLK]){
               c = dp->name[dp->name_len];  // save last byte
               dp->name[dp->name_len] = 0;  // make name into a string
               prints(dp->name); putc(' '); // show dp->name string
               if ( strcmp(dp->name, name) == 0 ){
                   prints("\n\r");
                   return((u16)dp->inode);
               }
               dp->name[dp->name_len] = c;  // restore last byte
               dp = (char *)dp + dp->rec_len;
           }
       }
   }
   error();  // to error() if can't find file name
}

main()  // booter's main function, called from assembly code
{
   char  *cp, *name[2], filename[64];
   u16    i, ino, blk, iblk;
   u32   *up;
   GD    *gp;
   INODE *ip;
   DIR   *dp;
   name[0] = "boot"; name[1] = filename;
   prints("bootname: ");
   gets(filename);
   if (filename[0]==0) name[1]="mtx";
   getblk(2, buf1);     // read blk#2 to get group descriptor 0
   gp = (GD *)buf1;
   iblk = (u16)gp->bg_inode_table;  // inodes begin block
   getblk(iblk, buf1);              // read first inode block
   ip = (INODE *)buf1 + 1;          // ip->root inode #2
   for (i=0; i<2; i++){             // serach for system name
       ino = search(ip, name[i]) - 1;
       if (ino < 0) error();        // if search() returned 0
       getblk(iblk+(ino/8), buf1);  // read inode block of ino
       ip = (INODE *)buf1 + (ino % 8);
   }
   if ((u16)ip->i_block[12]) // read indirect block into buf2, if any
       getblk((u16)ip->i_block[12], buf2);
   setes(0x1000);             // set ES to loading segment
   for (i=0; i<12; i++){      // load direct blocks
       getblk((u16)ip->i_block[i], 0);
       inces(); putc('*');    // show a * for each direct block loaded
   }
   if ((u16)ip->i_block[12]){ //load indirect blocks, if any
       up = (u32 *)buf2;
       while(*up++){
          getblk((u16)*up, 0);
          inces(); putc('.'); // show a . for each ind block loaded
       }
   }
   prints("ready to go?"); getc();
}
```

The booter's C code is fairly simple and straightforward. However, it is still worth pointing out the following programming techniques, which help reduce the booter size. First, if a booter needs string data, it is better to define them as string constants, e.g. name[0] = "boot", name[1] = "mtx", etc. String constants are allocated in the program's data area at compile-time. Only their addresses are used in the generated code. Second, on a FD the number of blocks is less than 1440. However, the block numbers in an inode are u32 long values. If we pass the block number as u32 in getblk() calls, the compiled (16-bit) code would have to push the long blk value as 16-bit items twice, which increase the code size. For this reason, the parameter blk in getblk() is declared as u16 but when calling getblk(), the long blk values are typecast to u16. The typecasting not only reduces the code size but also ensures getblk() to get the right parameters off the stack. Third, in the search() function, we need to compare a name string with the entry names in an EXT2 directory. Each entry name has name_len chars without an ending null byte, so it is not a string. In this case, strncmp() would not work since !strncmp("abcde","abcd", 4) is true. In order to compare the names, we need to extract the entry name's chars to make a string first, which require extra code. Instead, we simply replace the byte at name_len with a 0, which changes the entry name into a string for comparison. If name_len is a multiple of 4, the byte at name_len is actually the inode number of the next directory entry, which must be preserved. So we first save the byte and then restore it later. Finally, before changing ES to load the OS image, we read in the image's indirect blocks first while ES still points at the program's segment. When loading indirect blocks we simply dereference the indirect block numbers in the buffer area as *(u32 *). Without these techniques, it would be very difficult to write such a booter in C in 1024 bytes. Figure 3.15 shows the screen of booting MTX from a file system. In the figure, each asterisk is loading a direct block and each dot is loading an indirect block of the image file.

3.3.7 Boot Linux zImage from File System

The MTX booter can be adapted to booting small Linux kernels from an EXT2 file system. When booting a Linux zImage there is a slight problem. The contents of an image file are stored in (1 KB) disk blocks. During booting, we prefer to load the image by blocks. As pointed out earlier, starting from segment 0x1000, loading 1 KB blocks will not cross any cylinder or 64 KB boundary. In

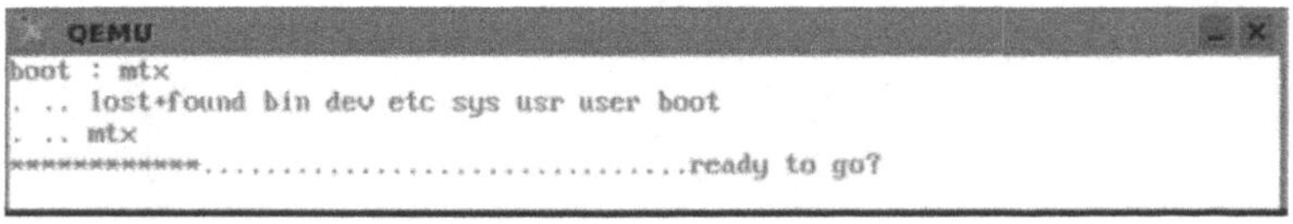

Fig. 3.15 Booting MTX from file system

a Linux zImage, the kernel image follows BOOT + SETUP immediately. If the number of BOOT + SETUP sectors is odd, the kernel image does not begin at a block boundary, which makes loading by blocks difficult. For instance, if we load the block that contains the last sector of SETUP and the first sector of kernel to 0x1000-0x20, it would cross 64 KB boundary. If we load the first kernel sector to 0x1000, followed by loading blocks, we must monitor the blocks and split up any block that crosses a 64 KB boundary. It would be very hard to write such a booter in 1 KB. There are two possible ways to deal with this problem. The simplest way is to assume that the number of SETUP sectors is odd, so that BOOT + SETUP = even. If the number of SETUP sectors is even, e.g. 10, we can always pad a dummy sector between SETUP and the kernel image to make the latter begin at a block boundary. Another way is to load the block that contains the last SETUP sector and the first kernel sector to 0x1000, followed by loading blocks. When loading completes, if the number of SETUP sectors is even, we simply move the loaded image downward (address-wise) by one sector. The Linux zImage booter uses the second technique. The booter's C code is shown below. The move(segment) function is in assembly, which is trivial and therefore not shown. The booter size is 1024 bytes, which is still within the 1 KB limit.

```
/****************** C code of Linux bzImage booter ***************/
u16 iblock, NSEC = 2;
char b1[1024],b2[1024],b3[1024]; // b2[ ] and b3[ ] are adjacent
main()
{
  char    *cp, *name[2];
  u16     i,ino, setup, blk, nblk;
  u32     *up;
  INODE   *ip;
  GD      *gp;
  name[0] = "boot"; name[1] = "linux"; // hard coded /boot/linux so far
  getblk(2, b1);
  gp=(GD *)b1; // get group0 descriptor to find inode table start block
  // read inode start block to get root inode
  iblock = (u16)gp->bg_inode_table;
  getblk(iblock, b1);
  ip = (INODE *)b1 + 1;    // ip points at root inode
  // serach for image file name
  for (i=0; i<2; i++){
      ino = search(ip, name[i]) - 1;
      if (ino < 0) error();    // if search() failed
      getblk(iblock + (ino / 8),  b1);
      ip = (INODE *)b1 + (ino % 8);
  }
  // get setup_sectors from linux BOOTsector[497]
  getblk((u16)ip->i_block[0], b2);
  setup = b2[497];
  nblk = (1 + setup)/2;  // number of [bootsector+SETUP] blocks
  // read in indirect & double indirect blocks before changing ES
  getblk((u16)ip->i_block[12], b2); // get indirect block into b2[ ]
  getblk((u16)ip->i_block[13], b3); // get db indirect block into b3[ ]
  up =(u32 *)b3;
  getblk((u16)*up, b3)         // get first double indirect into b3[ ]
  setes(0x9000);              // loading segment of BOOT+SETUP
  for (i=0; i<12; i++){       // nblk of these are bootblock+SETUP
    if (i==nblk){
      if ((setup & 1)==0) // if setp=even => need 1/2 block more
          getblk((u16)ip->i_block[i], 0);
          setes(0x1000);     // set ES for kernel image at 0x1000
      }
      getblk((u16)ip->i_block[i], 0); // setup=even:1/2 SETUP
      inces();
  }
  //load indirect and double indirect blocks in b2[]b3[]
  up = (u32 *)b2;              // access b2[ ]b3[ ] as u32's
  while(*up++){
      getblk((u16)*up, 0);        // load block to (ES,0)
      inces(); putc('.');
  }
  // finally, if setup is even, move kernel image DOWN one sector
  if ((setup & 1)==0)
    for (i=1; i<9; i++)
        move(i*0x1000); // move one 64 KB segment at a time
}
```

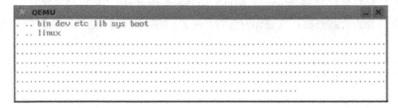

Fig. 3.16 Booting linux from file system

Figure 3.16 shows the screen of booting Linux from a file system, in which each dot represents loading a 1 KB disk block of the Linux kernel image.

When the Linux kernel boots up, it must mount a root file system in order to run. In the busyboxlinux directory, the sh script mkvfd creates a virtual FD containing a Linux root file system based on BusyBox. After booting up, the Linux kernel mounts the FD as the root file system and runs on the same FD. The screen of running such a single-FD Linux is similar to Fig. 13.13, except that it does not load any ramdisk image during booting.

3.4 Hard Disk Booter

In this section, we shall develop an online booter for booting MTX and big Linux images (bzImages) from hard disk partitions. The HD booter consists of 5 files; a bs.s in assembly, a bc.c in C, which includes io.c, bootMtx.c for booting MTX and bootLinux.c for booting Linux. During booting, it displays the hard disk partitions and prompts for a partition number to boot. If the partition type is MTX (90) or Linux (83), it allows the user to enter a filename to boot. If the user enters only the return key, it boots /boot/mtx or /boot/vmlinuz by default. When booting Linux it also supports an initial RAM disk image. For non-MTX/Linux partitions, it acts as a chain-booter to boot other operating systems, such as Windows. Since booting MTX is much simpler, we shall only discuss the Linux part of the HD booter.

The HD booter consists of five logical parts. Each part is essentially an independent programming task, which can be solved separately. For example, we may write a C program to display the partitions of a hard disk, and test it under Linux first. Similarly, we may write a program, which finds the inode of a file in an EXT2 file system and print its disk blocks. When the programs are tested to be working, we adapt them to the 16-bit environment as parts of the booter. The following describes the logical components of the HD booter.

3.4.1 I/O and Memory Access Functions

A HD booter is no longer limited to 512 or 1024 bytes. With a larger code size, we shall implement a set of I/O functions to provide better user interface during booting. Specifically, we shall implement a gets() function, which allows the user to input bootable image filename and boot parameters, and a printf() function for formatted printing. First, we show the gets() function.

```
#define MAXLEN 128
char *gets(char s[ ])  // caller must provide REAL memory s[MAXLEN]
{
    char c, *t = s; int len=0;
    while( (c=getc()) != '\r' && len < MAXLEN-1){
        *t++ = c; putc(c); len++;
    }
    *t = 0; return s;
}
```

For outputs, we first implement a printu() function, which prints unsigned short integers.

```
char *ctable = "0123456789ABCDEF";
u16 BASE = 10; // for decimal numbers
int rpu(u16 x)
{   char c;
    if (x){
        c = ctable[x % BASE];
        rpu(x / BASE);
        putc(c);
    }
}
int printu(u16 x)
{
    (x==0)? putc('0') : rpu(x);
    putc(' ');
}
```

The function rpu(x) recursively generates the digits of x % 10 in ASCII and prints them on the return path. For example, if x = 123, the digits are generated in the order of '3', '2', '1', which are printed as '1', '2', '3' as they should. With printu(), writing a printd() to print signed short integers becomes trivial. By setting BASE to 16, we can print in hex. By changing the parameter type to u32, we can print long values, e.g. LBA disk sector and inode numbers. Assume that we have prints(), printd(), printu(), printx(), printl() and printX(), where printl() and printX() print 32-bit values in decimal and hex, respectively. Then write a printf(char *fmt,...) for formatted printing, where fmt is a format string containing conversion symbols %c, %s, %u, %d, %x, %l, %X.

```
int printf(char *fmt, ...) // some C compiler requires the three dots
{
    char *cp = fmt;              // cp points to the fmt string
    u16  *ip = (u16 *)&fmt + 1; // ip points to first item
    u32  *up;                    // for accessing long parameters on stack
    while (*cp){                 // scan the format string
        if (*cp != '%'){         // spit out ordinary chars
            putc(*cp);
            if (*cp=='\n')       // for each '\n'
                putc('\r');      // print a '\r'
            cp++; continue;
        }
        cp++;                    // print item by %FORMAT symbol
        switch(*cp){
            case 'c' :   putc(*ip);   break;
            case 's' : prints(*ip);   break;
            case 'u' : printu(*ip);   break;
            case 'd' : printd(*ip);   break;
            case 'x' : printx(*ip);   break;
            case 'l' : printl(*(u32 *)ip++);   break;
            case 'X' : printX(*(u32 *)ip++);   break;
        }
        cp++; ip++;              // advance pointers
    }
}
```

The simple printf() function does not support field width or precision but it is adequate for the print task during booting. It would greatly improve the readability of the booter code. The same printf() function will also be used later in the MTX kernel. When booting a big Linux bzImage, the booter must get the number of SETUP sectors to determine how to load the various pieces of the image. After loading the image, it must set the boot parameters in the loaded BOOT and SETUP sectors for the Linux kernel to use. To do these, we implement the get_byte()/put_byte() functions in C, which are similar to the traditional peek()/poke() functions.

```
u8 get_byte(u16 segment, u16 offset)
{
    u8 byte;
    u16 ds = getds();      // getds() in assembly returns DS value
    setds(segment);        // set DS to segment
    byte = *(u8 *)offset;
    setds(ds);             // setds() in assembly restores DS
    return byte
}
void put_byte(u8 byte, u16 segment, u16 offset)
{
    u16 ds = getds();      // save DS
    setds(segment);        // set DS to segment
    *(u8 *)offset = byte;
    setds(ds);             // restore DS
}
```

Similarly, we can implement get_word()/put_word() for reading/writing 2-byte words. These functions allow the booter to access memory outside of its own segment.

3.4.2 Read Hard Disk LBA Sectors

Unlike floppy disks, which use CHS addressing, large hard disks use Linear Block Addressing (LBA), in which disk sectors are accessed linearly by 32 or 48 bits sector numbers. To read hard disk sectors in LBA, we may use the extended BIOS INT13-42 (INT 0x13, AH=0x42) function. The parameters to INT13-42 are specified in a Disk Address Packet (DAP) structure.

```
struct dap{          // DAP structure for INT13-42
    u8    len;       // dap length=0x10 (16 bytes)
    u8    zero;      // must be 0
    u16   nsector;   // actually u8; sectors to read=1 to 127
    u16   addr;      // memory address = (segment, addr)
    u16   segment;   // segment value
    u32   sectorLo;  // low  4 bytes of LBA sector#
    u32   sectorHi;  // high 4 bytes of LBA sector#
};
```

To call INT13-42, we define a global dap structure and initialize it once, as in

```
struct dap dap, *dp=&dap; // dap and dp are globals in C
dp->len = 0x10;          // dap length = 0x10
dp->zero = 0;            // this field must be 0
dp->sectorHi = 0;        // assume 32-bit LBA, high 4-byte always 0
// other fields will be set when the dap is used in actual calls
```

Within the C code, we may set dap's segment, then call getSector() to load one disk sector into the memory location (segment, offset), as in

```
int getSector(u32 sector, u16 offset)
{
    dp->nsector = 1;
    dp->addr    = offset;
    dp->sectorLo= sector;
    diskr();
}
```

where diskr() is in assembly, which uses the global dap to call BIOS int13-42.

```
!-------------------- assembly code ---------------------------
        .globl _diskr, _dap ! _dap is a global dap struct in C
_diskr:
        mov   dx, #0x0080    ! device=first hard drive
        mov   ax, #0x4200    ! aH=0x42
        mov   si, #_dap      ! (ES,SI) points to _dap
        int   0x13           ! call BIOS INT13-42 to read sectors
        jb    _error  ! to error() if CarryBit is set (read failed)
        ret
```

Similarly, the function

```
int getblk(u32 blk, u16 offset, u16 nblk)
{
    dp->nsectors = nblk*SECTORS_PER_BLOCK; // max value=127
    dp->addr     = offset;
    dp->sectorLo = blk*SECTORS_PER_BLOCK;
    diskr();
}
```

loads nblk contiguous disk blocks into memory, beginning from (segment, offset), where nblk $\leq$ 15 because dp->nsectors $\leq$ 127.

3.4.3   Boot Linux bzImage with Initial Ramdisk Image

When booting a Linux bzImage, the image's BOOT + SETUP are loaded to 0x9000 as before but the Linux kernel is loaded to the physical address 0x100000 (1 MB) in high memory. If a RAM disk image is specified, it is also loaded to high memory. Since the PC is in 16-bit real mode during booting, it cannot access memory above 1 MB directly. Although we may switch the PC to protected mode, access high memory and then switch back to real-mode afterwards, doing these requires a lot of work. A better way is to use BIOS INT15-87, which is designed to copy memory between real and protected modes. Parameters of INT15-87 are specified in a Global Descriptor Table (GDT).

```
struct GDT
{
    u32 zeros[4];       // 16 bytes 0's for BIOS to use
    // src address
    u16 src_seg_limit;  // 0xFFFF = 64KB
    u32 src_addr;       // low 3 bytes of src addr, high_byte=0x93
    u16 src_hiword;     // 0x93 and high byte of 32-bit src addr
    // dest address
    u16 dest_seg_limit; // 0xFFFF = 64KB
    u32 dest_addr;      // low 3 bytes of dest addr, high byte=0x93
    u16 dest_hiword;    // 0x93 and high byte of 32-bit dest addr
    // BIOS CS DS
    u32 bzeros[4];
};
```

The GDT specifies a src address and a dest address; both are 32-bit physical addresses. However, the bytes that form these addresses are not adjacent, which makes them hard to access. Although both src_addr and dest_addr are defined as u32, only the low 3 bytes are part of the address, the high byte is the access rights 0x93. Similarly, both src_hiword and dest_hiword are defined as u16 but only the high byte is the 4th address byte; the low byte is again the access rights 0x93. As an example, if we want to copy from the real address 0x00010000 (64 KB) to 0x01000000 (16 MB), a GDT can be initialized as follows.

```
init_gdt(struct GDT *p)
{  int i;
   for (i=0; i<4; i++)
      p->zeros[i] = p->bzeros[i] = 0;
   p->src_seg_limit = p->dest_seg_limit = 0xFFFF; // 64KB segments
   p->src_addr     = 0x93010000;         // bytes 0x00 00 01 93
   p->dest_addr    = 0x93000000;         // bytes 0x00 00 00 93
   p->src_hiword   = 0x0093;             // bytes 0x93 00
   p->dest_hiword  = 0x0193;             // bytes 0x93 01
}
```

The following code segment copies 4096 bytes from 0x00010000 (64 KB) in real mode memory to 0x01000000 (16 MB) in high memory.

```
C code:
            struct GDT gdt;      // define a gdt struct
            init_gdt(&dgt);      // initialize gdt as shown above
            cp2himem();          // assembly code that does the copying

Assembly code:
      .globl _cp2himem,_gdt   ! _gdt is a global GDT from C
_cp2himem:
            mov cx,#2048       ! CX=number of 2-byte words to copy
            mov si,#_gdt       ! (ES,SI) point to GDT struct
            mov ax,#0x8700     ! aH=0x87
            int 0x15           ! call BIOS INT15-87
            jc  _error
            ret
```

Based on these, we can load the blocks of an image file to high memory as follows.

1. load a disk block (4 KB or 8 sectors) to segment 0x1000;
2. cp2himem();
3. gdt.vm_addr+=4096;
4. repeat (1)–(3) for next block, etc.

This can be used as the basic loading scheme of a booter. For fast loading, the hd-booter tries to load up to 15 contiguous blocks at a time. It is observed that most PCs actually support loading 16 contiguous blocks at a time. On these machines, the images can be loaded in 64 KB chunks.

3.4.4   Hard Disk Partitions

The partition table of a hard disk is in the MBR sector at the byte offset 446 (0x1BE). The table has 4 entries, each defined by a 16-byte partition structure, which is

```
stuct partition {
        u8   drive;          // 0x80 - active
        u8   head;           // starting head
        u8   sector;         // starting sector
        u8   cylinder;       // starting cylinder
        u8   sys_type;       // partition type
        u8   end_head;       // end head
        u8   end_sector;     // end sector
        u8   end_cylinder;   // end cylinder
        u32  start_sector;   // starting sector counting from 0
        u32  nr_sectors;     // number of sectors in partition
    };
```

If a partition is EXTEND type (5), it can be divided into more partitions. Assume that partition P4 is EXTEND type and it is divided into extend partitions P5, P6, P7. The extend partitions form a link list, as shown in Fig. 3.17.

The first sector of each extend partition is a local MBR. Each local MBR has

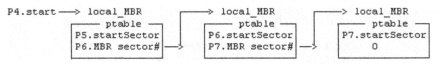

Fig. 3.17 Link list of extended partitions

a partition table, which contains only two entries. The first entry defines the start sector number and size of the extend partition. The second entry points to the next local MBR. All the local MBR's sector numbers are relative to P4's start sector. As usual, the link list ends with a 0 in the last local MBR. In a partition table, the CHS values are valid only for disks smaller than 8 GB. For disks larger than 8 GB but fewer than 4G sectors, only the last 2 entries, start_sector and nr_sectors, are meaningful. Therefore, the booter should only display the type, start sector and size of the partitions.

3.4.5   Find and Load Linux Kernel and Initrd Image Files

The steps used to find a Linux bzImage or RAM disk image are essentially the same as before. The main differences stem from the need to traverse large EXT2/EXT3 file systems on hard disks.

(1). In a hard disk partition, the superblock of an EXT2/EXT3 file system is at the byte offset 1024. A booter must read the superblock to get the values of s_first_data_block, s_log_block_size, s_inodes_per_group and s_inode_size, where s_log_block_size determines the block size, which in turn determines the values of group_desc_per_block, inodes_per_block, etc. These values are needed when traversing the file system.

(2). A large EXT2/EXT3 file system may have many groups. Group descriptors begin at the block (1+s_first_data_block), which is usually 1. Given a group number, we must find its group descriptor and use it to find the group's inodes start block.

(3). The central problem is how to convert an inode number to an inode. The following code segment illustrates the algorithm, which amounts to applying Mailman's algorithm twice.

```
/********** Algorithm: Convert inode number to inode *********/
(a). Compute group# and offset# in that group
     group   = (ino-1) / inodes_per_group;
     inumber = (ino-1) % inodes_per_group;

(b). Find the group's group descriptor
     gdblk = group / desc_per_block;   // which block this GD is in
     gdisp = group % desc_per_block;   // which GD in that block

(c). Compute inode's block# and offset in that group
     blk=inumber / inodes_per_block;   // blk# r.e.to group inode_table
     disp=inumber % inodes_per_block;  // inode offset in that block

(d). Read group descriptor to get group's inode table start block#
     getblk(1+first_data_block+gdblk, buf, 1); // GD begin block
     gp = (GD *)buf + gdisp;      // it's this group desc.
     blk += gp->bg_inode_table; // blk is r.e. to group's inode_table
     getblk(blk, buf, 1);        // read the disk block containing inode
     INODE *ip=(INODE *)buf+(disp*iratio); //iratio=2 if inode_size=256
```

When the algorithm ends, INODE *ip should point to the file's inode in memory.

(4). Load Linux Kernel and Ramdisk Image to High Memory: With getblk() and cp2himem(), loading kernel image to 1 MB in high memory is straightforward. The only complication is when the kernel image does not begin at a block boundary. For example, if the number of SETUP sectors is 12, then 5 sectors of the kernel are in block1, which must be loaded to 0x100000 first before we can load the remaining kernel by blocks. In contrast, if the number of SETUP sectors is 23, then BOOT and SETUP are in the first 3 blocks and kernel begins at block #3. In this case, we can load the entire kernel by blocks without having to deal with fractions of a block at the beginning. Although the hd-booter handles these cases properly, it is certainly a pain. It would be much better if the Linux kernel of every bzImage begins at a block boundary. This can be done quite easily by modifying a few lines in the Linux tools program when it assembles the various pieces into a bzImage file. Why Linux people don't do that is beyond me.

Next, we consider loading RAM disk images. An excellent overview on Linux initial RAM disk (initrd) is in (Jones 2006). Slackware (Slackware Linux) also has an initrd HOWTO file. An initrd is a small file system, which is used by the Linux kernel as a temporary root file system when the kernel starts up. The initrd contains a minimal set of directories and executables, such as sh, the ismod tool and the needed driver modules. While running on initrd, the Linux kernel typically executes a sh script, initrc, to install the needed driver modules and activate the real root device. When the real root device is ready, the Linux kernel abandons the initrd and mounts the real root file system to complete a 2-stage boot up process. The reason of using an initrd is as follows. During booting, Linux's startup code only activates a few standard devices, such as FD and IDE/SCSI HD, as possible root devices. Other device drivers are either installed later as modules or not activated at all. This is true even if all the device drivers are built into the Linux kernel. Although it is possible to activate the needed root device by altering the kernel's startup code, the question is, with so many different Linux system configurations, which device to activate? An obvious answer is to activate them all. Such a Linux kernel would be humongous in size and rather slow to boot up. For example, in some Linux distribution packages the kernel images are larger than 4 MB. An initrd image can be tailor-built with instructions to install only the needed driver modules. This allows a single generic Linux kernel to be used in all kinds of Linux system configurations. In theory, a generic Linux kernel only needs the RAM disk driver to start. All other drivers may be installed as modules from the initrd. There are many tools to create an initrd image. A good example is the mkinitrd command in Linux. It creates an initrd.gz file and also an initrd-tree directory containing the initrd file system. If needed, the initrd-tree can be modified to generate a new initrd image. Older initrd. gz images are compressed EXT2 file systems, which can be uncompressed and mounted as a loop file system. Newer initrd images are cpio archive files, which can be manipulated by the cpio utility program. Assume that initrd.img is a RAM disk image file. First, rename it as initrd.gz and run gunzip to uncompress it. Then run

> mkdir temp; cd temp; # use a temp DIR
> cpio -id < ../initrd   # extract initrd cc

to extract the contents. After examining and modifying files in initrd-tree, run

> find . | cpio -o -H newc | gzip > ../in

to create a new initrd.gz file.

Loading initrd image is similar to loading kernel image, only simpler. There is no specific requirement on the loading address of initrd, except for a maximum high address limit of 0xFE000000. (The reader may consult Chap. 15 on SMP for reasons). Other than this restriction, any reasonable loading address seems to work fine. The hd-booter loads the Linux kernel to 1 MB and initrd to 32 MB. After loading completes, the booter must write the loading address and size of the initrd image to SETUP at the byte offsets 24 and 28, respectively. Then it jumps to execute SETUP at 0x9020. Early SETUP code does not care about the segment register settings. In kernel 2.6, SETUP requires DS = 0x9000 in order to access BOOT as the beginning of its data segment.

3.4.6 Linux and MTX Hard Disk Booter

A complete listing of the hd-booter code is in BOOTERS/HD/MBR.ext4/. The booter can boot both MTX and Linux with initial RAM disk support. It can also boot Windows by chain-booting. For the sake of brevity, we only show the booting Linux part here.

```
!---------------- hd-booter's bs.s file -------------------------
        BOOSEG = 0x9800
        SSP    = 32*1024       ! 32KB bss + stack; may be adjusted
        .globl _main,_prints,_dap,_dp,_bsector,_vm_gdt  ! IMPORT
        .globl _diskr,_getc,_putc,_getds,_setds,        ! EXPORT
        .globl _cp2himem,_jmp_setup
! MBR loaded at 0x07C0. Load entire booter to 0x9800
start:  mov  ax, #BOOSEG
        mov  es, ax
        xor  bx, bx           ! clear BX = 0
        mov  dx, #0x0080      ! head 0, HD
        xor  cx, cx
        incb cl               ! cyl 0, sector 1
        incb cl
        mov  ax, #0x0220      ! READ 32 sectors, booter size up to 16KB
        int  0x13
! far jump to (0x9800, next) to continue execution there
        jmpi next, BOOSEG     ! CS=BOOSEG, IP=next
next:
        mov  ax, cs           ! set CPU segment registers
        mov  ds, ax           ! we know ES,CS=0x9800. Let DS=CS
        mov  ss, ax
        mov  es, ax           ! CS=DS=SS=ES=0x9800
        mov  sp, #SSP         ! 32 KB stack
        call _main            ! call main() in C
        test ax, ax           ! check return value from main()
        je   error            ! main() return 0 if error
        jmpi 0x7C00,0x0000    ! otherwise, as a chain booter
_diskr:
        mov  dx, #0x0080      ! drive=0x80 for HD
        mov  ax, #0x4200
        mov  si, #_dap
        int  0x13             ! call BIOS INT13-42 read the block
        jb   error            ! to error if CarryBit is on
        ret
error:
        mov  bx, #bad
        push bx
        call _prints
        int  0x19             ! reboot
bad:    .asciz "\n\rError!\n\r"
_jmp_setup:
        mov  ax, 0x9000       ! for SETUP in 2.6 kernel:
        mov  ds, ax           ! DS must point at 0x9000
        jmpi 0,  0x9020       ! jmpi to execute SETUP at 0x9020

_getc: ! same as before
_putc: ! same as before
_getds: ! return DS value
_setds: ! set DS to a segment
!------------------------ cp2himem() ----------------------------
! for each batch of k<=16 blocks, load to RM=0x10000 (at most 64KB)
! then call cp2himem() to copy it to     VM=0x100000 + k*4096
!----------------------------------------------------------------
_cp2himem:
        push bp
        mov  bp, sp
        mov  cx, 4[bp]        ! words to copy (32*1024 or less)
        mov  si, #_vm_gdt
        mov  ax, #0x8700
        int  0x15
        jc   error
        pop  bp
        ret
/*********** Algorithm of hd-booter's bc.c file **************/
#define BOOTSEG 0x9800
#include "bio.c"           // I/O functions such as printf()
#include "bootLinux.c"     // C code of Linux booter
int main()
{
  (1). initialize dap for INT13-42 calls;
  (2). read MBR sector;
  (3). print partition table;
  (4). prompt for a partition to boot;
  (5). if (partition type == LINUX)
            bootLinux(partition);  // no return
  (6). load partition's local MBR to 0x07C0;
       chain-boot from partition's local MBR;
}
/*********** Algorithm of bootLinux.c file ***************/
boot-Linux-bzImage Algorithm:
{
  (1). read superblock to get blockSize,inodeSize,inodes_per_group
  (2). read Group Descriptor 0 to get inode start block
  (3). read in the root INODE and let INODE *ip point at root INODE
  (4). prompt for a Linux kernel image filename to boot
  (5). tokenize image filename and search for image's INODE
  (6). handle symbolic-link filenames
  (7). load BOOT+SETUP of Linux bzImage to 0x9000;
  (8). set video mode word at 506 in BOOT to 773 (for small font).
  (9). set root dev word at 508 in BOOT to (0x03, pno) (/dev/hdapno)
  (10). set bootflags word at offset 16 in SETUP to 0x2001
  (11). compute number of kernel sectors in last block of SETUP
  (12). load kernel sectors to 0x1000, then cp2himem() to 1MB
  (13). load kernel blocks to high memory, each time load 64KB
  (14). load initrd image to 32 MB in high memory
  (15). write initrd address and size to offsets (24,28) in SETUP
  (16). jmp_setup() to execute SETUP code at 0x9020
}
```

In the above algorithm, step (8) is optional. Step (9) sets the root device, which is needed only if no initrd image is loaded. With an initrd image, the root device is determined by the initrd image. Step (10) is mandatory, which tells SETUP that the kernel image is loaded by an "up-to-date" boot loader. Otherwise, the SETUP code would consider the loaded kernel image invalid and refuse to start up the Linux kernel.

3.4.7 Boot EXT4 Partitions

At the time of this writing, many Linux distributions are switching to EXT4 (Cao et al. 2007) as the default file system. It is fairly easy to modify the booter to boot MTX and Linux from EXT4 partitions. Here, we briefly describe the EXT4 file system and the needed modifications to the HD booter.

(1). In EXT4, the i_block[15] array of an inode contains a header and 4 extents structures, each 12 bytes long, as shown below.

```
|<------ u32 i_block[15] area -------->|
|header|extent1|extent2|extent3|extent4|
struct ext3_extent_header {
        u16  eh_magic;        // 0xF30A
        u16  eh_entries;      // number of valid entries
        u16  eh_max;          // capacity of store in entries
        u16  eh_depth;        // has tree real underlaying blocks?
        u32  eh_generation;   // generation of the tree
};
struct ext3_extent {
        u32  ee_block;        // first logical block extent covers
        u16  ee_len;          // number of blocks covered by extent
        u16  ee_start_hi;     // high 16 bits of physical block
        u32  ee_start;        // low  32 bits of physical block
};
```

The root directory does not use extents, so i_block[0] is still the first data block.

(2). The GD and INODE types are the same as they are in EXT2, but the INODE size is 256 bytes. The SUPER block's magic number is also the same as in EXT2, but we may test s_feature_incompat (>0x240) to determine whether it's an EXT4 file system.

(3). Blocks in each extent are contiguous. There is no need to scan for contiguous blocks when loading an image; just load a sequence of blocks directly. For HDs, the block size is 4 KB. The maximum number of blocks per loading is still limited to 16 or less. Shown below are the search() and load() functions for EXT4 file system. Integrating them into the HD booter is left as an exercise.

```
/******* serach for name in an EXT4 DIR INODE ********/
u32 search(INODE *ip, char *name)
{
    u16  i; u32  ino;
    struct ext3_extent_header *hdp;
    struct ext3_extent *ep;
    char buf[BLK];
    hdp = (struct ext3_extent_header *)&(ip->i_block[0]);
    ep  = (struct ext3_extent *)&(ip->i_block[3]);
    for (i=0; i<4; i++){
        if (hdp->eh_entries == 0){
            getblk((u32)ip->i_block[0], buf, 1);
            i = 4; // no other extents
        }
        else{
            ep = (struct ext3_extent *)&(ip->i_block[3]);
            getblk((u32)ep->ee_start, buf, 1);
        }
        if (ino = find(buf, name))   // find name string in buf[ ]
            return ino;
    }
    return 0;
}
/******** load blocks of an INODE with EXT4 extent ********/
int loadExt4(INODE *ip, u16 startblk)
{
    int i,j,k,remain; u32 *up;
    struct ext3_extent_header *hdp;
    struct ext3_extent *ep;
    int ext;
    u32 fblk, beginblk;
    hdp = (struct ext3_extent_header *)ip->i_block;
    ep  = (struct ext3_extent *)ip->i_block + 1;
    ext = 1;
    while(1){
        if (ep->ee_len==0)
            break;
        beginblk = 0;
        if (ext==1)  // if first extent: begin from startblk
            beginblk = startblk;
        k = 16;      // load 16 contisuous blocks at a time
        fblk = ep->ee_start + beginblk;
        remain = ep->ee_len - beginblk;
        while(remain >= k){
            getblk((u32)(fblk), 0, k);
            cp_vm(k, '.');
            fblk += k;
            remain -= k;
        }
        if (remain){
            getblk((u32)(fblk), 0, remain);
            cp_vm(remain, '.');
        }
        ext++; ep++;   // next extent
    }
}
```

```
***************** HD booter : *****************
bsector=504063  inode_size=256  inode_ratio=2
Booting from EXT4 Partition
inodes_pg=7128  blocks_pg=32768  inodes_table=82  inodepbk=16  descpbk=128
Enter kernel name to boot (ENTER=vmlinuz) :
Search for /vmlinuz
serach for vmlinuz : . .. lost+found var dev sys lib mnt home usr etc boot srv b
in vmlinuz
FOUND vmlinuz
symlink -> /boot/vmlinuz-generic-smp-2.6.29.6-smp
Search for //boot/vmlinuz-generic-smp-2.6.29.6-smp
serach for boot : . .. lost+found var dev sys lib mnt home usr etc boot
FOUND boot
serach for vmlinuz-generic-smp-2.6.29.6-smp : . .. config-generic-2.6.29.6 vmlin
uz-generic-2.6.29.6 System.map-generic-2.6.29.6 vmlinuz System.map config vmlinu
z-generic-smp-2.6.29.6-smp
FOUND vmlinuz-generic-smp-2.6.29.6-smp
BIG kernel image : root=[3  7 ] setup_sectors=24 setupBlks=4 sBlks=3 sSectors=1
.............................
last loaded kernel addr=0x35EE00
load initrd (y:n) ? load initrd to 32MB
Enter initrd pathname (ENTER=/initrd.gz) :
Search for /initrd.gz
serach for initrd.gz : . .. lost+found var dev sys lib mnt home usr etc boot srv
 bin vmlinuz sbin proc media tmp root opt initrd.gz
FOUND initrd.gz
Loading image size=988301 bytes
................
ready to go?
```

Fig. 3.18 Booting linux bzImage with initrd from EXT4 partition

Figure 3.18 shows the screen of the hd-booter when booting a generic Linux kernel with initial RAM disk image, initrd.gz, from an EXT4 partition.

3.4.8 Install HD Booter

Now that we have a hard disk booter, the next problem is where to install it? Obviously, the beginning part of the booter must be installed in the HD's MBR since that's where the booting process begins. The question is where to install the remaining parts of the booter? The location chosen must not interfere with the hard disk's normal contents. At the same time it must be easy for the stage1 booter to find. The question has an interesting answer. By convention, each HD partition begins at a (logical) track boundary. Since the MBR is already in track 0, partition 1 actually begins from track 1. A track usually has 63 sectors. We can certainly put a fairly big and powerful booter in the unused space of track 0. Unfortunately, once the good news gets around, it seems that everybody tries to use that hidden space for some special usage. For example, GRUB installs its stage2 booters there, so does our hd-booter. Naturally, as a Chinese proverb says, "A single mountain cannot accommodate two tigers", only one tiger can live there at a time. The hd-booter can be installed to a HD as follows.

```
(1)  dd if=hd-booter of=/dev/hda bs=16 count=27
(2)  dd if=hd-booter of=/dev/hda bs=512 seek=1
```

Assume that the booter size is less than 31 KB (the hd-booter size is about 10 KB). Step (1) dumps the first 432 bytes of the booter to the MBR without disturbing the partition table, which begins at byte 444. Step (2) dumps the entire booter to sectors 1 and beyond. During booting, BIOS loads the MBR to 0x07C00 and executes the beginning part of the hd-booter. The hd-booter reloads the entire booter, beginning from sector 1, to 0x98000 and continues execution in the new segment. The actual number of sectors to load can be adjusted to suit the booter size, but loading a few extra sectors causes no harm.

Although installing the hd-booter is simple, a word of caution is in order. Murphy's law says anything that can go wrong will go wrong. Writing to a hard disk's MBR is very risky. A simple careless mistake may destroy the partition table and/ or corrupt the HD contents, rendering the HD either non-bootable or useless. It is therefore advised not to install the booter to a HD unless you are absolutely sure of what you are doing. Before attempting to install the booter, it's a good idea to write down the HD's partition table on a piece of paper in case you have to restore it. A vsupport loading cylinders, we only need to modify one line in the above assembly code: change mov dx, #0x0080 to mov dx, #0x0000, so that the booter will be re-loaded from a FD when it begins to run. Once the booter starts running, it actually boots from the HD. Since the HD is accessed in read-only mode, the scheme should be safe. Instead of a real HD, the reader may use a virtual HD. Similarly, the HD booter may also be installed to a USB drive. In that case, no changes are needed.

3.5 CD/DVD-ROM Booter

A bootable CD/DVD is created in two steps. First, create an iso9660 file system (Standard ECMA-119 1987) containing a CD/DVD booter. Then write the iso image to a CD/DVD by a CD/DVD burning tool. The resulting CD/DVD is bootable. If desired, the iso file can also be used directly as a virtual CD. In this section, we shall show how to develop booter programs for CD/DVD booting.

3.5.1 Emulation CDROM Booting

From a programming point of view, emulation booting is trivial. There is not much one needs to (or can) do other than preparing a bootable disk image. The following shows how to do emulation booting.

3.5.1.1 Emulation-FD Booting

Assume that fdimage is a bootable floppy disk image (size=1.44 MB). Under Linux, use the sh command

mkisofs -o /tmp/fcd.iso -v -d -R -J -N -b fdimage -c boot.catalog ./

to create a/tmp/fcd.iso file from the current directory. The reader may consult Linux man page of mkisofs for the meaning of the various flags. The iso file is a bootable CD image. It can be written to a real CD/DVD disc by using a suitable CD/DVD burning tool, such as Nero or K3b under Linux. It can also be used as a virtual CD on most virtual machines. Then boot from either a real or a virtual CD/DVD. After booting up, the environment is exactly the same as that of booting from a floppy disk.

Example 1: BOOTERS/CD/emuFD demonstrates emulation-FD booting. It contains a MTX system, MTXimage, based on MTX5.1 of Chap. 5. When creating a bootable CD image, it is used as the emulation-boot image. Upon booting up from the CD, MTX runs as if it had been booted up from a FD. As pointed out before, the MTX kernel can only access the MTXimage on the CD as if it were a FD drive, but it cannot access anything else on the CD.

3.5.1.2 Emulation-HD Booting

Similarly, assume that hdimage is a single-partition hard disk image with a HD booter installed in the MBR. Under Linux, use the sh command

mkisofs -o /tmp/hcd.iso -v -d -R -J -N-b hdimage -hard-disk-booting -c boot.catalog ./ to create a bootable CD image and burn the hcd.iso file to a CD/DVD disc. After booting up, the environment is exactly the same as that of booting from the first hard disk.

Example 2: BOOTER/CD/emuHD demonstrates emulation-HD booting. In the emuHD directory, hdimage is single-partition hard disk image. It contains a MTX system in partition 1 and a MTX booter (hd-booter of Sect. 3.4.5) in MBR. In the example, the hdimage is used as the hard-disk-boot image to create a bootable CDROM image. When booting from the CDROM, the sequence of actions is identical to that of booting MTX from a HD partition. When the MTX kernel runs, the environment is the same as that of running from the C: drive. All I/O operations to the emulated hard disk use INT13-42 calls to BIOS. Again, the MTX kernel can only access the hdimage but nothing else on the CDROM.

3.5.2 No-Emulation CDROM Booting

In no-emulation booting, if the loading requirements are simple, e.g. just load the OS image to a segment in real-mode memory, then there is no need for a separate booter because the entire OS image can be loaded by BIOS during booting.

3.5.2.1 No-Emulation Booting of MTX

Example 3: BOOTERS/CD/MTXCD demonstrates no-emulation booting of MTX. It contains a MTX system, which is again based on MTX5.1. However, the MTX kernel is modified to include an iso loader and a simple iso file system traversing program. The MTX kernel is used as the no-emulation booting image. During booting, the entire MTX kernel is loaded to the segment 0x1000 and runs from there. When the MTX starts to run, it must create a process with a user mode image from a /bin/u1 file, which means it must be able to read the CDROM contents. Loading the user mode image file is done by the isoloader. The program cd.c supports basic iso9660 file system operations, such as ls, cd, pwd and cat. These allow a process to navigate the file system tree on the CDROM. The example is intended to show that a booted up OS kernel can access the CDROM contents if it has drivers to interpret the iso file system on the CDROM.

3.5.2.2 No-Emulation Linux Booter

In no-emulation CDROM booting, a separate booter is needed only if the loading requirements of an OS image are non-trivial, such as that of Linux. In the following, we shall develop an iso-booter for booting Linux bzImage with initial RAM disk support from CDROM. To do this, we need some background information about the iso9660 file system, which are summarized below.

For data storage, CDROM uses 2048-byte sectors, which are addressed in LBA just like HD sectors. The data format in an iso9660 file system represents what may be called a masterpiece of legislative compromise. It supports both the old 8.3 filenames of DOS and, with Rock Ridge extension, it also supports Unix-style filenames and attributes. To accommodate machines using different byte orders, all multi-byte values are stored twice in both little-endian and big-endian formats. To support international encoding, chars in Joliet extension are stored in 16-bit Unicode. An iso9660 CDROM contains a sequence of Volume Descriptors (VDs), which begin at sector 16. Each VD has a type identifier, where 0=BOOT, 1=Primary, 2=Supplementary and 255=End of the VD table. Unix-style files are under the supplementary VD, which contains, among other thing, the following fields.

```
u8  type                 = VD's type
u32 type_1_path_table = start sector of Little_endian path_table
u32 path_table_size   = path_table size in bytes.
root_directory_record = root DIR iso_directory_record
```

The steps of traversing a Unix-style file system on a CDROM are as follows.

1. From sector 16, read in and step through the Volume Descriptors to search for the Supplementary VD (SVD), which has type=2.
2. SVD.root_directory_record is an iso_directory_record (DIR) of 34 bytes.

```
struct iso_directory_record {
    unsigned char length;
    unsigned char ext_attr_length;
    char extent[8];
    char size[8];
    char date[7];
    unsigned char flags;
    char file_unit_size;
    char interleave;
    char volume_sequence_number[4];
    unsigned char name_len;
    char name[0];
};
```

3. Multi-byte values are in stored in both little-endian and big-endian format. For example, DIR.extent = char extent[8] = [4-byte-little-endian, 4-byte-big-endian]. To get a DIR's extent (start sector), we may use u32 extent = *(u32 *)DIR.extent, which extracts only the first 4 little-endian bytes. Similarly for DIR.size, etc.

4. In an iso file system, FILE and DIR records are identical. Therefore, entries in a directory record are also directory records. The following algorithm shows how to search for a name string in a DIR record.

```
/** Algorithm of search for fname string in DIR **/
DIR *search(DIR, fname)
{   sector = DIR.extent (begin sector# of DIR record);
    while(DIR.size){
        read sector into a char buf[2048];
        char *cp = buf; DIR *dp = buf; // both point at buf beginning
        while(cp < buf+2048){
            each record has a length, a name_len and a name in 16-bit
            Unicode. Convert name to ascii, then compare with fname;
            if (found) we actually have fname's RECORD;
                return DIR record (pointer);
            else advance cp by record length, pull dp to next record;
        } // until buf[ ] end
        DIR.size -= 2048; sector++;
    } // until DIR.size=0
}
```

5. To search for the DIR record of a pathname, e.g. /a/b/c/d, tokenize the pathname into component name strings. Start from the root DIR, search for each component name in the current DIR. The steps are are similar to that of finding the inode of a pathname in an EXT2/EXT3 file system.

6. If we allow .. in a pathname, we must be able to get the parent of the current DIR. Similar to a Unix directory, the second entry in an iso9660 directory contains the extent of the parent directory. For each .. entry we may either return the parent DIR's extent or a DIR pointer to the second record. Alternatively, we may also search the path table to find the parent DIR's extent. This method is left as an exercise.

With this background information, we are ready to show the details of an iso-booter. First, the iso.h file contains the types of volume descriptor, directory record and path table. All entries are defined as char arrays. For ease of reference, arrays of size 1 are redefined simply as char. The primary and supplementary volume descriptors differ in only in 2 fields, flags and escape, which are unspecified in the former but specified in the latter. Since these fields are irrelevant during booting, we only use the supplementary volume descriptor. Both iso_directory_record and iso_path_table are open-ended structures, in which the name field may vary, depending on the name_len. When stepping through these records we must advance by the actual record length. Similarly, when copying a directory record we must use memcpy(p1,p2, p2-> length) to ensure that the entire record is copied.

In the iso-booter, BOOTSEG is set to 0x07C0, rather than 0x9800. This is because many older PCs, e.g. some Dell and IBM Thinkpad laptops, seem to ignore the -boot-load-seg option and always load the boot image to the segment 0x07C0. For maximum compatibility, the iso-booter is loaded to the segment 0x07C0 and runs from there without relocation. This works out fine for Linux, which does not use the memory area between 0x07C0 and 0x1000. The iso-booter's bs.s file is the same as that of the hd-booter, with only a minor difference in the beginning part. When the iso-booter starts, it is already completely loaded in and it does not need to relocate. However, it must use the boot drive number passed in by BIOS, as shown below.

```
!------------------ iso-booter's bs.s file ----------------------
! In no-emulation booting, many PCs always load booted image to 0x07C0.
! Only some PCs honor the -boot-load-seg=SEGMENT option. So use 0x07C0
!---------------------------------------------------------------------
          BOOTSEG  = 0x07C0
          SSP      = 32*1024
!         .globls : SAME as in hd-booter
          .globl   _drive     ! boot drive# in C code, passed in DL
          jmpi start,BOOTSEG   ! upon entry, set CS to BOOTSEG=0x07C0
start:
          mov     ax,cs       ! set other CPU segment registers
          mov     ds,ax       ! we know ES,CS=0x07C0. Let DS=CS
          mov     ss,ax       ! SS = CS ===> all point to 0x07C0
          mov     es,ax
          mov     sp,#SSP     ! SP = 32KB
          mov     _drive,dx   ! save drive# from BIOS to _drive in C
          call    _main       ! call main() in C
! Remaining .s code: SAME AS in hd-booter but use the boot drive#
```

The iso-booter's C code and algorithms are also similar to the hd-booter. For the sake of brevity, we only show the parts that are unique to the iso-booter. A complete listing of the iso-booter code is in BOOTERS/CD/isobooter/ directory.

```
/*******************iso-booter's bc.c file *********************/
#define BOOTSEG 0x07C0
#include "iso.h"        // iso9660 file types
#include "bio.c"        // contains I/O functions
main()
{
    (1). initialize dap and vm_gdt for BIOS calls
    (2). find supplement Volume Descriptor to get root_dir_record
    (3). get linux bzImage filename to boot or use default=/vmlinuz;
    (4). load(filename);
    (5). loadrd("initrd.gz");
    (6). jmp_setup();
}
/************* iso-booter's bootLinux.c file ********************/
u32 bsector;            // getnsector() base sector
u32 zsector, zsize;     // bzImage's begin sector# & size
struct vmgdt {          // same as in hd-booter }
init_vm_gdt(){          // same as in hd-booter }
// get nsectors from bsector+rsector to dp-segment
u16 getnsector(u16 rsector, u16 nsector);
{
    dp->nsector = nsector;
    dp->addr = (u16)0;              // load to dp->segment:0
    dp->sl = (u32)(bsector + (u32)rsector); // rsector = offset
    readcd();                       // same as diskr() but use boot drive#
}
// loadimage() : load 32 CD-sectors to high memory
int loadimage(u16 imageStart, u32 imageSize)
{
    u16 i, nsectors;
    nsectors = imageSize/2048 + 1;
    i = imageStart;
    // load 32 CD sectors at a time to 0x1000; then cp2himem();
    while(i < nsectors){
        getnsector(i, 32);
        cp2himem(32*1024);
        gdtp->vm_addr += (u32)0x10000;
        putc('.');
        i += 32;
    }
}
// dirname() : convert DIR name in Unicode-2 to ascii in temp[ ]
char temp[256];
char *dirname(struct iso_directory_record *dirp)
{ int i;
    for (i=0; i<dirp->name_len; i+=2){
        temp[i/2] = dirp->name[i+1];
    }
    temp[dirp->name_len/2] = 0;
    return temp;
}
// search DIR record for name; return pointer to name's record
struct iso_directory_record *search(struct iso_directory_record *dirp,
char *name)
{
    char *cp, dname[256];
    int  i, loop, count;
    u32  extent, size;
    struct iso_directory_record *ddp, *parent;
    printf("search for %s\n", name);
    extent = *(u32 *)dirp->extent;
    size   = *(long*)dirp->size;
    loop = 0;
    while(size){
        count = 0;
        getSector(extent, rbuf);
```

```
          cp = rbuf;
          ddp = (struct iso_directory_record *)rbuf;
          if (strcmp(name,"..")==0){   // for .., return 2nd record pointer
             cp += ddp->length;
             ddp = (struct iso_directory_record *)cp;
             return ddp;
          }
       while (cp < rbuf + SECSIZE){
          if (ddp->length==0)
             break;
          strcpy(dname, dirname(ddp)); // assume supplementary VD only
          if (loop==0){   // . and .. only in the first sector
             if (count==0) strcpy(dname, ".");
             if (count==1) strcpy(dname, "..");
          }
          printf("%s   ", dname);
          if (strcasecmp(dname, name)==0){ // ignore case
             printf(" ==> found %s : ", name);
             return ddp;
          }
          count++;
          cp += ddp->length;
          ddp = (struct iso_directory_record *)cp;
       }
       size -= SECSIZE;
       extent++;
       loop++;
    }
    return 0;
}
// getfile() : return pointer to filename's iso_record
struct iso_directory_record *getfile(char *filename)
{  int i;
    struct iso_directory_record *dirp;
    tokenize(filename);      // same as in hd-booter;
    dirp = root;
    for (i=0; i<nnames; i++){
        dirp = search(dirp, name[i]);
        if (dirp == 0){
          printf("no such name %s\n", name[i]);
          return 0;
        }
        // check DIR type
        if (i < nnames-1){    // check DIR type but ignore symlinks
           if ((dirp->flags & 0x02) == 0){
              printf("%s is not a DIR\n", name[i]);
              return 0;
           }
        }
    }
    return dirp;
}

int load_rd(char *rdname) // load_rd() : load initrd.gz image
{
    u32 rdstart,rdsize;              // initrd's start sector & size
    // (1). set vm_addr to initrd's loading address at 32MB
```

```
        dirp = getfile(rdname);
        rdstart = *(u32 *)dirp->extent;   // start sector of zImage on CD
        rdsize  = *(long  *)dirp->size;   //  size in bytes
        // (2). load initrd image
        dp->segment = 0x1000;
        bsector = rdstart;
        loadimage((u16)0,(u32)rdsize);
        // (3). write initrd loading address and size to SETUP
}

int load(char *filename)    // load() : load Linux bzImage
{
        struct iso_directory_record *dirp;
        dirp = getfile(filename);
        // dirp now points at bzImage's RECORD
        zsector = *(u32 *)dirp->extent;  // start sector of bzImage on CD
        zsize   = *(long  *)dirp->size;  // size in bytes
        /******* SAME AS in hd-booter except CD-sector size=2KB ******
        get number of 512-byte setup sectors in filename's BOOT sector
        load BOOT+SETUP to 0x9000
        set boot parameters in loaded BOOT+SETUP
        load kernel fraction sectors in SETUP to 1MB in high memory
        ****************************************************************/
        // continue to load kernel 2KB CD-sectors to high memory
        dp->segment = 0x1000;
        loadimage((u16)setupBlks, (u32)zsize);
        load_rd("/initrd.gz");      // assume initrd.gz filename
        jmp_setup();
}
```

Under Linux, run mk to generate a boot image file iso-booter as before. Next, run

```
    mkisofs -o /tmp/iso-booter.iso -v -d -R -J -N -no-emul-boot \
            -boot-load-size 20 \  # (512-byte) sectors to load
            -b iso-booter \       # boot image file
            -c boot.catalog ./    # from files in current directory
```

to generate an iso image, which can be burned to a CD disc or used as a virtual CD.

3.5.3   Comparison with isolinux CDROM Booter

isolinux (Syslinux project) is a CD/DVD Linux boot-loader. It is used in almost all CD/DVD based Linux distributions. As an example, the bootable CD/DVD of Slackware Linux 13.1 distribution contains

```
        |-- isolinux/  : isolinux.bin, isolinux.cfg, initrd.img
    /-- |-- kernels/   : huge.s/bzImage: bootable Linux bzImage file
        |-- slackware/ : Linux distribution packages
```

where isolinux.bin is the (no-emulation) booter of the CD/DVD. During booting, isolinux.bin consults isolinux.cfg to decide which Linux kernel to load. Bootable

Linux kernels are in the kernels/ directory. The user may choose a kernel that close-ly matches the target system hardware or use the default kernel. With a kernel file name, isolinux.bin loads the kernel and the initial ramdisk image, initrd.img, which is compressed root file system based on BusyBox. Then it executes SETUP. When the Linux kernel starts, it mounts initrd.img as the root device.

Example 4. Replace isolinux booter with iso-booter: The iso-booter can be used to replace the isolinux booter in a Linux distribution. As a specific example, BOOTERS/CD/slackCD/ is a copy of the Slackware 13.1 boot CD but without the installing packages of Linux. It uses the iso-booter of this book to generate a bootable iso image. During booting, enter /kernels/bzImage as the kernel and / isolinux/initrd.img as the initial ramdisk image. Slackware's install environment should start up.

Example 5. Boot generic Linux bzImage with initrd.gz: In the BOOTERS/CD/ linuxCD/ directory, vmlinuz is a generic Linux kernel, which must be booted with an initial ramdisk image. The initrd.gz file is generated by the mkinitrd command using files in the /boot/initrd-tree/ directory. The iso-booter can boot up a generic Linux kernel and load the initrd.gz for the Linux kernel to start. Figure 3.19 shows the booting screen of the iso-booter. It loads the Linux kernel to 1 MB and initrd. gz to 16 MB.

Example 6. Linux LiveCD: We can boot up a Linux kernel from a CD and let it run on the CD directly. First, create a CD containing a base Linux system. Install the iso-booter on the CD to boot up a generic Linux kernel with an initrd image. While running on the ramdisk, load the isofs driver module. Then mount the CD and switch root file system to the CD. Linux would run on the booting CD directly (albeit in read-

Fig. 3.19 CDOM iso-booter screen

only mode). This is the basis of what's commonly known as a Linux LiveCD. For more information, the reader may consult the numerous LiveCD sites on the Internet.

Example 7. MTX Install CD: The iso-booter is the booter of MTXinstallCD.iso. It boots up a generic Linux kernel (version 2.6) and loads an initial RAM disk image, initrd.gz. When Linux boots up, it runs on the RAM disk image, which is used to install MTX from the CDROM.

3.6 USB Drive Booter

USB drives are storage devices connected to the USB bus. From a user point of view, USB drives are similar to hard disks. A USB drive can be divided into partitions. Each partition can be formatted as a unique file system and installed with a different operating system. To make a USB drive bootable, we install a booter to the USB drive's MBR and configure BIOS to boot from the USB drive. On some PCs, e.g. HP and Compaq, the USB drive must have a bootable partition marked as active. During booting, BIOS emulates the booting USB drive as C: drive. The booting actions are exactly the same as that of booting from a hard disk. The booted up environment is also the same as if booted up from the first hard disk. Any booter that works for hard disk should also work for USB drives. Therefore, USB booting is identical to hard disk booting. However, depending on the booted up OS, there may be a difference. Usually, an OS that boots up from a hard disk can run directly on the hard disk. This may not be true if the OS is booted up from a USB drive. In the following, we use two specific examples to illustrate the difference.

3.6.1 MTX on USB Drive

MTX.bios is a MTX system which can be installed and run on either a floppy disk or a hard disk partition. In MTX.bios, all I/O operations are based on BIOS. When running on a FD, it uses BIOS INT13 to read-write floppy disk in CHS format. When running on a HD, it uses INT13-42 to read-write hard disk sectors in LBA. The following example shows how to install and run MTX.bios on a USB drive.

Example 8./BOOTERS/USB/usbmtx demonstrates running MTX on a USB drive, denoted by /dev/sda. If the PC's HD is a SATA drive, change the USB drive to /dev/sdb. First, run the sh script, install.usb.sh, to install MTX to a USB drive partition.

```
mke2fs /dev/sda3 -b 1024 8192   # assume USB drive partition 3
mount /dev/sda3 /mnt
mount -o loop MTX.bios /tmp     # mount MTX.bios
cp -av /tmp/* /mnt
umount /mnt; umount /tmp
```

Next, install hd-booter to the USB drive by

```
dd if=hd-booter of=/dev/sda bs=16 count=27
dd if=hd-booter of=/dev/sda bs=16 seek=1
```

Then boot from the USB drive under QEMU, as in

qemu –hda /dev/sda

When the MTX kernel starts, it can access the USB drive through BIOS INT13-42 on drive number 0x80. Since the environment is exactly the same as if running on a hard disk, MTX will run on the USB drive.

3.6.2 Linux on USB Drive

The last booting example is to create a so called "Linux Live USB". A live USB refers to a USB drive containing a complete operating system, which can boot up and run on the USB drive directly. Due to its portability and convenience, Linux live USB has received much attention and generated a great deal of interests among Linux users in recent years. The numerous "Linux live USB" sites and postings on the Internet attest to its popularity. When it first started in the late 1990's the storage capacity of USB drives was relatively small. The major effort of earlier work was to create "small" Linux systems that can fit into USB drives. As the storage capacity of USB drives increases, this is no longer a restriction. At the time of this writing, 32–64 GB USB drives are very common and affordable. It is now possible to install a full featured Linux system on a USB drive still with plenty free space for applications and data. Most Linux live USB installations seem to require a special setup environment, such as Linux running on a live CD. This example is intended to show that it is fairly easy to create a Linux live USB from a standard Linux distribution package. To be more specific, we shall again use Slackware Linux 13.1, which is based on Linux kernel version 2.6.33.4, as an example. The Slackware Linux distribution package consists of several CDs or a single DVD disc. The steps to create a Linux live USB are as follows.

1. Install Slackware 13.1 to a USB drive partition. Slackware 13.1 uses /dev/sda as the primary hard disk. The USB drive should be named /dev/sdb. Install Linux to a USB partition, e.g. /dev/sdb1, by following the installation procedures. Since our hd-booter can boot from both EXT3 and EXT4 partitions, the reader may choose either EXT3 or EXT4 file system.
2. After installing Linux, the reader may install LILO as the Linux booter. However, when the Linux kernel boots up, it will fail to run because it cannot mount the USB partition (8,17) as root device. As in CDROM booting, the missing link is again an initial RAM disk image. The Linux kernel must run on a ramdisk first in order for it to install the needed USB drivers and activate the USB drive. So the problem is how to create such an initrd.gz file.

3. While still in the installation environment, the USB partition is mounted on /mnt,
   which already has all the Linux commands and driver modules. Enter the following commands or run the commands as a sh script.

```
cd /mnt;   chroot /mnt                      # change root to /mnt
# create initrd-tree with USB drivers
mkinitrd -c -k 2.6.33.4 -f ext4 -r /dev/sdb1 -m crc16: \
         jbd2:mbcache:ext4:usb-storage:ehci-hcd:uhci-hcd:ohci-hcd
echo 10 > /boot/initrd-tree/wait-for-root  # write to wait-for-root
mkinitrd                                    # generate initrd.gz again
# if install lilo as booter
echo "initrd = /boot/initrd.gz" >> /etc/lilo.conf # append lilo.conf
lilo                                        # install lilo again
# install hd-booter to USB drive
# dd if=hd-booter of=/dev/sda bs=16 count=27
# dd if=hd-booter of=/dev/sda bs=512 seek=1
```

The above commands create a /boot/initrd.gz with USB driver modules in /boot of
the USB partition. In the directory /boot/initrd-tree/ created by mkinitrd, the default
value of wait-for-root is 1 s, which is too short for USB drives. If the value is too
small, initrc may be unable to mount the USB drive, leaving the Linux kernel stuck
on the initial ramdisk. Change it to a larger value, e.g. 10, to let the initrc process
wait for 10 s before trying to mount the USB partition. After booting up Linux, the
reader may try different delay values to suit the USB drive. Instead of LILO, the
reader may also install the hd-booter to the USB drive. Mount a CDROM or another
USB drive containing the above sh script and the hd-booter. Run the above sh script
and install the hd-booter by un-commenting the last two lines. Then boot from the
USB drive. Linux should come up and run on the USB drive.

3.7 Listing of Booter Programs

All the booters developed in this chapter have been tested on both real PCs and many
versions of virtual machines. The booter programs are in the BOOTERS directory
on the MTX install CD. Figure 3.20 shows a complete list of the booter programs.

```
FD—|—loadSector   :  linuxSector,  linux.sector.ramdisk,
    |                 OneFDlinux,   linux.cylinder, mtxSector
    |—loadBlock    :  linuxBlock,   mtxBlock
    |—FS           :  linuxFS,      mtxFS

HD—|—MBR.ext4      :  hd-booter for EXT2/3/4 file systems

CD—|——emulation   :  emuFD, emuHD
    |-no-emulation :  isobooter; linuxCD, mtxCD, slackCD

USB-|— HOWTOusblinux, usbmtx
```

Fig. 3.20 List of booter programs

Problems

1. FD booting:

   1. Assume that a one-segment program is running in the segment 0x1000. What must be the CPU's segment registers?

   2. When calling BIOS to load FD sectors into memory, how to specify the memory address?

   3. In getblk(u16 blk, char buf[ ]), the CHS parameters are computed as

      ```
      (C,H,S)=((2*blk)/36,  ((2*blk)%36)/18,  ((2*blk)%36)%18);
      ```

   The conversion formula can be simplified, e.g. C = blk/18, etc. Try to simplify the CHS expression. Write a C program to verify that your simplified expressions are correct, i.e. they generates the same (C, H,S) values as the original algorithm.

2. Assume: The loading segment of MTX is 0x1000. During booting, BIOS loads the first 512 bytes of a 1 KB MTX booter to the segment 0x07C0. The booter should run right where it is first loaded, i.e. in the segment 0x07C0 without relocation.

   1. What must the booter do first?
   2. How to set the CPU's segment registers?
   3. What's the maximum run-time image size of the booter?

3. On the MTX install CD, OneFDlinux.img is an EXT2 file system containing a bootable Linux zImage in the /boot directory.

   1. Using it as a virtual FD, verify that Linux can boot up and run on the same FD.
   2. Replace the booter in Block 0 with a suitable Linux booter developed in this chapter.

4. Prove that when loading FD sectors into memory, we can load at most 4 consecutive sectors without crossing either cylinder or 64 KB boundaries.

5. Modify the FD booter that uses the cross-country algorithm to load by tracks.

6. Ramdisk Programming: Assume: A MTX boot FD contains

   ```
   |booter|MTX kernel image|ramdiskImage|
   ```

where ramdiskImage in the last 128 blocks is a root file system for the MTX kernel. When the MTX kernel starts, it loads the ramdiskImage to the segment 0x8000. Then the MTX kernel uses the memory area between 0x8000 to 0xA000 as a ramdisk and runs on the ramdisk. Wrtie C code for the functions
      getblk(u16 blk, char buf[1024])/putblk(u16 blk, char buf[1024])
which read/write a 1 KB block from/to the ramdisk. HINT: use get_word()/put_word().

7. Under Linux, write a C program to print all the partitions of a hard disk.
8. Write a C program, showblock, which prints all the disk block numbers of a file in an EXT4 file system. The program should run as follows.

    showblock DEVICE   PATHNAME
    e.g. showblock /dev/sda2   /a/b/c/d   # /dev/sda2 for SATA hard disk partition 2

9. Assume that /boot/osimage is a bootable OS image. Write a C program, which finds the disk blocks of the OS image and store them in a /osimage.blocks file. Then write a booter, which simply loads the disk blocks in the /osimage.blocks file. Such a booter may be called an offline booter. The Linux boot-loader, LILO, uses this scheme. Discuss the advantages and disadvantages of off-line booters.
10. When booting a Linux bzImage, if the Linux kernel does not begin at a block boundary, loading the Linux kernel is rather complex. Given a Linux bzImage, devise a scheme which makes the Linux kernel always begin at a block boundary.
11. Modify the hd-booter to accept input parameters. For example, when the booter starts, the user may enter an input line

    kernel=/boot/newvmlinuz initrd=/boot/initrd.gz root=/dev/sda7

where each parameter is of the form KEYWORD=value.

12. Modify the hd-booter to allow symbolic-link filenames for initrd.gz in the hd-booter.
13. The iso-booter does not handle symbolic-link filenames. Modify the C code to allow symbolic links.
14. Use the path table of an iso9660 file system to find the parent directory record.
15. USB booting: In some USB drives, a track may have less than 20 sectors. The hd-booter size is just over 10 KB. How to install the hd-booter to such USB drives?

Use the hd-booter and a Linux distribution package, e.g. Slackware 14.0, to create a Linux Live USB.

16. The ultimate version of MTX supports SMP in 32-bit protected mode, which is developed in Chap. 15 of this book. The bootable image of a SMP_MTX is a file consisting of the following pieces:

```
Sector  0     1     2       3  | 4  ......
        ---------------------------------------------------
        |BOOT|SETUP|  APentry  | MTX kernel                |
        ---------------------------------------------------
```

where APentry is the startup code of non-boot processors in a SMP system. During booting, the booter loads BOOT+SETUP to 0x90000, APentry to 0x91000, and the MTX kernel to 0x10000. After loading completes, it sends the CPU to execute SETUP at 0x90200. Modify the MTX booter for booting SMP_MTX images.

17. Write a loader for loading a.out files into memory for execution. When loading an a.out file, it is more convenient to load the file by blocks. Assume that a one-segment a.out file (with header) is loaded at the segment address 0x2000, and it should run in that segment.

    1. How to set up the CPU's segment registers?
    2. Show how to eliminate the 32-byte header after loading a.out to a segment.

References

BusyBox: www.busybox.net, 2006

Cao, M., Bhattacharya, S, Tso, T., "Ext4: The Next Generation of Ext2/3 File system", IBM Linux Technology Center, 2007.

Comer, D.E., "Internetworking with TCP/IP: Principles, Protocols, and Architecture, 3/E", Prentice-Hall, 1995.

Comer, D.E., Stevens, D.L., "Internetworking With TCP/IP: Design, Implementation, and Internals, 3/E", Prentice-Hall, 1998.

GNU GRUB Project: www.gnu.org/software/grub/, 2010

Jones, M.T, "Linux initial RAM disk (initrd) overview", IBM developerworks, linux, Technical library, 2006

Slakware Linux: slackware.osuosl.org/slackware/README.initrd, 2013

Standard ECMA-119, Volume and File Structure of CDROM for Information Interchange,2nd edition, December 1987.

Stevens, C.E, Merkin, S. The "El Torito" Bootable CD-ROM Format Specification, Version 1.0, January, 1995

Syslinux project, www.syslinux.org, 2014

Chapter 4
A Simple Operating System Kernel

In this chapter, we start to develop a simple operating system kernel for process management. We begin in 16-bit real-mode [Antonakos 1999] for several reasons. First, the operating environment of Intel x86 based PCs in protected mode (Intel i486 1990; Intel 64 2014), is quite complex. If we begin in protected mode, it may take a long time to cover the needed background information. Most readers, especially beginners to operating systems, would be overwhelmed by the low level details and may lose interest quickly. In contrast, the 16-bit real mode environment is much simpler and easier to understand. It allows us to get a quick start without worrying about the complexity of protected mode operations. Second, before developing our own device drivers in Chap. 10, we shall use BIOS for basic I/O, which is available only in real mode. Third and more importantly, most OS design and implementation issues, such as process management, process synchronization, device drivers, file system and user interface, etc. do not depend on whether the machine is in real mode or protected mode. Their only differences are in the areas of virtual address spaces, process image size, memory protection and exception processing. These can be deferred until the reader has gained enough working experience in a simpler environment. Then the transition from real mode to protected mode would be relatively easy and smooth. This approach can be justified by the following facts. Despite its simplicity, the real-mode MTX is also the basis of all other forms of MTX in 32-bit protected mode, from uniprocessor systems to symmetric multiprocessing (SMP) (Intel 1997). Rather than presenting a complete kernel in one step, we shall develop the MTX kernel in incremental steps. In each step, we explain the concepts and principles involved and show how to apply them to design and implement the various system components. In addition, we shall demonstrate each step by a sample system, which allows the reader to test and observe the internal operations of an OS kernel. In this chapter, we first explain the principle of multitasking, the concept of processes and illustrate context switching by a simple program. Then we extend the multitasking program to support dynamic process creation, process scheduling and process termination. Based on these, we implement sleep, wakeup and wait operations for process management. This simple multitasking system serves as the starting point of the MTX kernel.

© Springer International Publishing Switzerland 2015
K. C. Wang, *Design and Implementation of the MTX Operating System,*
DOI 10.1007/978-3-319-17575-1_4

4.1 Multitasking

In general, multitasking refers to the ability of performing several independent activities at the same time. For example, we often see people talking on their cell phones while driving. In a sense, these people are doing multitasking, although a very bad kind. In computing, multitasking refers to the execution of several independent tasks at the same time. In a uniprocessor system, only one task can execute at a time. Multitasking is achieved by multiplexing the CPU's execution time among different tasks, i.e. by switching the CPU's execution from one task to another. If the switch is fast enough, it gives the illusion that all the tasks are executing simultaneously. This logical parallelism is called concurrency. In a multiprocessor system, tasks can execute on different CPUs in parallel in real time. In addition, each processor may also do multitasking by executing different tasks concurrently. Multitasking is the basis of operating systems. It is also the basis of concurrent programming in general.

4.2 The Process Concept

An operating system is a multitasking system. In an operating system, tasks are also called processes. For all practical purposes, the terms task and process can be used interchangeably. In Chap. 2, we defined an execution image as a memory area containing the execution's code, data and stack. Formally, a process is the execution of an image. It is a sequence of executions regarded by the OS kernel as a single entity for using system resources. System resources include memory space, I/O devices and, most importantly, CPU time. In an OS kernel, each process is represented by a unique data structure, called the Process Control Block (PCB) or Task Control Block (TCB), etc. In MTX, we shall simply call it the PROC structure. Like a personal record, which records all the information of a person, a PROC structure contains all the information of a process. In a single CPU system, only one process can be executing at a time. The OS kernel usually uses a global PROC pointer, running or current, to point at the PROC that is currently executing. In a real OS, the PROC structure may contain many fields and quite large. To begin with, we shall define a very simple PROC structure to represent processes.

```
typedef struct proc{
        struct proc *next;
        int         *ksp;
        int         kstack[1024];
}PROC;
```

In the PROC structure, the next field is a pointer pointing to the next PROC structure. It is used to maintain PROCs in dynamic data structures, such as link lists and queues. The ksp field is the saved stack pointer of a process when it is not executing and kstack is the execution stack of a process. As we expand the MTX kernel, we shall add more fields to the PROC structure later.

4.3 Development of the MTX Kernel

4.3.1 A Simple Multitasking Program

We begin to develop the MTX kernel by a simple program, which is used to illustrate two important points. First, how do processes in an OS begin? Second, how does an OS run different processes? The following program, denoted by MTX4.0, is similar to a booter. It can be compiled and linked by BCC to generate a binary executable, as in

```
as86 -o ts.o  ts.s    # assemble ts.s into ts.o
bcc  -c -ansi t.c      # compile t.c into t.o
as86 -d -o mtx0 ts.o t.o mtxlib /usr/lib/bcc/libc.a  #link
```

where mtxlib is a link library containing I/O functions based on BIOS. To run the mtx0 program, we need a MTX booter, which loads the mtx0 image to the segment 0x1000 and sends the CPU to execute the mtx0 code. Assume that FDimage is a bootable floppy disk image of MTX, i.e. it is an EXT2 file system with a MTX booter in block 0. At this moment, the file system contents do not matter. All we need is a boot directory containing a bootable image file. Mount the FDimage disk image and copy mtx0 to the boot directory, as in

```
mount -o loop FDimage /mnt; cp mtx0 /mnt/boot/mtx0; umount /mnt
```

We use a bootable FD image mainly for convenience because it can be used directly in a real PC or PC emulator. For example, to boot up and run mtx0 under QEMU, enter

qemu -fda FDimage -no-fd-bootchk

To run it under DOSEMU or VMware, configure the virtual machine to use FDimage as a virtual floppy disk. The following lists the assembly and C code of the MTX4.0 program. The assembly code syntax is that of BCC's as86 assembler.

```
! ---------------------- ts.s file -----------------------
        .globl _tswitch                                  !EXPORT to C
        .globl _main,_running,_scheduler,_proc0,_procSize !IMPORT
start:  mov   ax,cs          ! set DS=SS=CS = 0x1000
        mov   ds,ax
        mov   ss,ax
        mov   sp,#_proc0     ! set sp point to proc0 in C code
        add   sp,_procSize   ! sp point to high end of proc0
        call  _main          ! call main() in C
        hlt                  ! if main() returns, just halt.
_tswitch:                    ! tswitch() function
SAVE:   push  ax
        push  bx
        push  cx
        push  dx
        push  bp
        push  si
        push  di
        pushf
        mov   bx,_running    ! bx -> proc
        mov   2[bx],sp       ! save sp to proc.ksp
FIND:   call  _scheduler     ! call scheduler() in C
RESUME: mov   bx,_running    ! bx -> running proc
        mov   sp,2[bx]       ! load sp with proc.ksp
        popf
        pop   di
        pop   si
        pop   bp
        pop   dx
        pop   cx
        pop   bx
        pop   ax
        ret
/************* t.c file ******************/
#define SSIZE 1024              // 2KB stack size per PROC
typedef struct proc{           // process structure
        struct proc *next;     // next PROC pointer
        int *ksp;              // saved sp when PROC is not running
        int  kstack[SSIZE];    // process kernel mode stack
}PROC;                         // PROC is a type
int  procSize = sizeof(PROC);
PROC proc0, *running;          // proc0 structure and running pointer
int scheduler(){ running = &proc0; }
main()
{
  running = &proc0;
  printf("call tswitch()\n");
    tswitch();
  printf("back to main()\n");
}
```

During booting, the MTX booter loads mtx0 to the segment 0x1000 and jumps to there to execute the mtx0 code. When execution starts in ts.s, it sets all segment registers to 0x1000 in order to conform to the program's one-segment memory model. Then it sets the stack pointer to the high end of proc0, so that proc0.kstack is the initial stack area. Up to this point, the system has no notion of any process

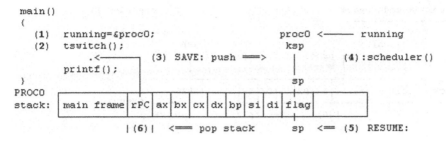

Fig. 4.1 Execution diagram of Proc0

because there is none. Then the assembly code calls main() in C. When control enters main(), we have an image in execution. By the definition of process, which is the execution of an image, we have a process in execution, although the system still does not know which process is executing. In main(), after setting running to point at proc0, the system is now running the process proc0. This is how a typical OS kernel starts to run an initial process when it begins. The initial process is handcrafted or created by brute force.

Starting from main(), the run-time behavior of the program can be traced and explained by the execution diagram of Fig. 4.1, in which the key steps are labeled (1) to (6).

At (1), it lets running point to proc0, as shown on the right-hand side of Fig. 4.1. Since we assume that running always points at the PROC of the current executing process, the system is now running the process proc0.

At (2), it calls tswitch(), which saves the return address, rPC, in stack.

At (3), it executes the SAVE part of tswitch(), which saves CPU registers into stack and saves the stack pointer sp into proc0.ksp.

At (4), it calls scheduler(), which sets running to point at proc0 again. For now, this is redundant since running already points at proc0. Then it executes the RESUME part of tswitch().

At (5), it sets sp to proc0.ksp, which is again redundant since they are already the same. Then it pops the stack, which restores the saved CPU registers.

At (6), it executes ret at the end of RESUME, which returns to the calling place of tswitch().

4.3.2   Context Switching

Besides printing a few messages, the program seems useless since it does practically nothing. However, it is the basis of all multitasking programs. To see this, assume that we have another PROC structure, proc1, which called tswitch() and executed the SAVE part of tswitch() before. Then proc1's ksp must point to its stack area, which contains saved CPU registers and a return address from where it called tswitch(), as shown in Fig. 4.2.

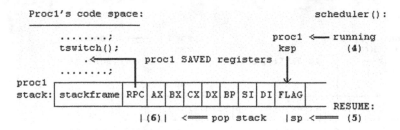

Fig. 4.2 Execution diagram of Proc1

In scheduler(), if we let running point to proc1, as shown in the right-hand side of Fig. 4.2, the RESUME part of tswitch() would change sp to proc1's ksp. Then the RESUME code would operate on the stack of proc1. This would restore the saved registers of proc1, causing proc1 to resume execution from where it called tswitch() earlier. This changes the execution environment from proc0 to proc1.

Context Switching Changing the execution environment of one process to that of another is called context switching, which is the basic mechanism of multitasking.

4.3.3 A Simple Multitasking System

With context switching, we can create a multitasking environment containing many processes. In the next program, denoted by MTX4.1, we define NPROC = 9 PROC structures. (We shall justify the assumption of 9 PROCs later in Chap. 5 when we extend the processes to have user mode images). Each PROC has a unique pid number for identification. The PROCs are initialized as follows.

```
running-> P0 -> P1 -> P1 -> P2 ->...;-> P8->|
          |                                 |
          <---------------------------------<---
```

P0 is the initial running process. All the PROCs form a circular link list for simple process scheduling. Each of the PROCs, P1 to P8, is initialized in such a way that it is ready to resume running from a body() function. Since the initialization of the PROC stack is crucial, we explain the steps in detail. Although the processes never existed before, we may pretend that they not only existed before but also ran before. The reason why a PROC is not running now is because it called tswitch() to gave up CPU earlier. If so, the PROC's ksp must point to its stack area containing saved CPU registers and a return address, as shown in Fig. 4.3, where the index -i means SSIZE-i.

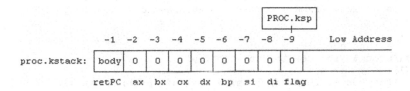

Fig. 4.3 Process stack contents

Fig. 4.4 Initial stack contents of a process

Since the PROC never really ran before, we may assume that its stack was initially empty, so that the return address, rPC, is at the very bottom of the stack. What should be the rPC? It may point to any executable code, e.g. the entry address of a body() function. What about the "saved" registers? Since the PROC never ran before, the register values do not matter, so they can all be initialized to 0. Accordingly, we initialize each of the PROCs, P1 to P8, as shown in Fig. 4.4.

With this setup, when a PROC becomes running, i.e. when running points to the PROC, it would execute the RESUME part of tswitch(), which restores the "saved" CPU registers, followed by RET, causing the process to execute the body() function.

After initialization, P0 calls tswitch() to switch process. In tswitch(), P0 saves CPU registers into its own stack, saves the stack pointer in its PROC.ksp and calls scheduler(). The scheduler() function simply changes running to running-> next. So P0 switches to P1. P1 begins by executing the RESUME part of tswitch(), causing it to resume to the body() function. While in body(), the running process prints its pid and prompts for an input char. Then it calls tswitch() to switch to the next process, etc. Since the PROCs are in a circular link list, they will take turn to run. The assembly code is the same as before, except for the initial stack pointer, which is set to proc[0]'s kstack when execution begins, as in

```
.globl _main,_running,_scheduler
.globl _proc,_procSize ! change proc0 to proc[ ]
mov    sp,#_proc        ! set sp point to proc[0]
add    sp,_procSize     ! let sp point to high end of proc[0]
```

The following lists the C code of the multitasking program.

```
/*********** t.c file of a multitasking program **************/
#define NPROC     9              // number of PROCs
#define SSIZE 1024               // proc kstack size = 2KB
typedef struct proc{
    struct proc *next;
    int    *ksp;
    int    pid;                  // add pid as proc's ID
    int    kstack[SSIZE];        // proc stack area
}PROC;
PROC proc[NPROC], *running;      // define NPROC proc structures
int procSize = sizeof(PROC);     // PROC size, needed in assembly code
int body()
{   char c;
    int pid = running->pid;
    printf("proc %d resumes to body()\n", pid);
    while(1){
        printf("proc %d running, enter a key:\n", pid); c=getc();
        tswitch();
    }
}
int init()                       // initialize PROC structures
{
    PROC *p; int i, j;
    For (i=0; i<NPROC; i++){      // initialize all PROCs
        p = &proc[i];
        p->pid = i;               // pid = 0,1,2,..NPROC-1
        p->next = &proc[i+1];     // point to next PROC
        if (i){                   // for PROCs other than P0
            p->kstack[SSIZE-1]=(int)body; // entry address of body()
            for (j=2; j<10; j++) // all saved registers = 0
                p->kstack[SSIZE-j] = 0;
            p->ksp = &(p->kstack[SSIZE-9]);// saved sp in PROC.ksp
        }
    }
    proc[NPROC-1].next = &proc[0]; // all PROCs form a circular list
    running = &proc[0];           // P0 is running;
    printf("init complete\n");
}
int scheduler()                  // scheduler() function
{ running = running->next; }
main()                           // main() function
{
    init();
    while(1){
        printf("P0 running\n");
        tswitch();
    }
}
```

The reader may compile the MTX4.1 program to generate a bootable image. Then boot up and run the program on either a real or virtual PC to observe its run-time behavior. As the system runs, each input key causes a process switch. It uses the process pid to display lines in different colors, just for fun. Figure 4.5 shows the sample outputs of running MTX4.1.

The reader may modify the C code of MTX4.1 to produce different effects. For example, add printf() statements to the scheduler() function to identify the PROCs

```
init complete
proc 0  running : enter a key :
proc 1  resumes to body()
proc 1  running : enter a key :
proc 2  resumes to body()
proc 2  running : enter a key :
proc 3  resumes to body()
proc 3  running : enter a key :
proc 4  resumes to body()
proc 4  running : enter a key :
proc 5  resumes to body()
proc 5  running : enter a key :
proc 6  resumes to body()
proc 6  running : enter a key :
proc 7  resumes to body()
proc 7  running : enter a key :
proc 8  resumes to body()
proc 8  running : enter a key :
proc 0  running : enter a key :
proc 1  running : enter a key :
```

Fig. 4.5 Sample outputs of MTX4.1

during context switch. After initialization, instead of calling tswitch(), let P0 call the body() function, etc.

Note that none of the processes, P1 to P8, actually calls body(). What we have done is to convince each process that it called tswitch() to give up CPU just before entering the body() function, and that's where it shall return to when it starts. Thus, we can set up the initial execution environment of a process to control its course of actions. The process has no choice but to obey. This is the power (and joy) of systems programming.

Note also that the processes, P1 to P8, all execute the same code, namely the same body() function. This shows the difference between programs and processes. A program is just a piece of passive code, which has no life in itself. Processes are executions of programs, which make the programs alive. Even when executing the same program each process executes in its own context. For example, in the body() function the local variable c is in the running proc's stack and pid is the running proc's pid, etc. In a multitasking environment, it is no longer appropriate to describe what a program does. We must look at a program's behavior from the viewpoint of what a process is doing while executing the program. Likewise, an OS kernel is just a (big) program, which is executed by a set of concurrent processes. For convenience, we often say what an OS kernel is doing. But we should really look at an OS kernel from the viewpoint of what the processes are doing while executing the kernel code. The main advantage of this process-based point of view is that it allows us to develop an OS kernel as a set of cooperating processes from ground zero. In fact, this is the major theme of this book, which we shall continue to demonstrate throughout the book.

The assembly function tswtich() is the key to understanding context switching and multitasking. A better way to look at tswitch() is not as a piece of code but as a relay station where processes change hands, as Fig. 4.6 shows.

Fig. 4.6 Process switch box

```
                  ---------------
proc Pi --->|  tswitch()  |---> proc Pj
                  ---------------
```

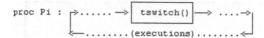

Fig. 4.7 Process execution cycle

In this view, tswitch() is a switch box where a process Pi goes in and, in general, another process Pj emerges. In tswitch(), the code of SAVE and RESUME are complementary in that whatever items are saved by SAVE, RESUME must restore exactly the same. In principle, a process may save its execution context anywhere, as long as it can be retrieved and restored when the process resumes running again. Some systems save process context in the PROC structure. Since each process already has a stack, we choose to save the process context in the process stack and only save the stack pointer in the PROC structure.

Another way of looking at process creation is as follows. Each process may be thought of as running in a perpetual cycle, in which it runs for a while, then it calls tswitch() to give up CPU to another process. Some time later, it regains CPU and emerges from tswitch() to resume running again, etc, as shown in Fig. 4.7.

To create a process to run for the first time is the same as to resume a process to run again. We can make a cut in the process execution cycle and inject a suitable condition for it to resume. The natural place to make such a cut is when the process is not running, i.e. immediately after it has executed the SAVE part in tswitch() and yielded CPU to another process. At the cut point, we can fabricate a stack frame as if it was saved by the process itself. When the process becomes running again, it will obey the stack frame and resume to wherever we want it to be.

4.4 Dynamic Process Creation and Process Scheduling

Next, we modify the multitasking program as the initial version of the MTX kernel. As we continue to develop the MTX kernel, we shall demonstrate each step by a complete sample system. For ease of identification, we shall label the sample systems MTXx.y, where x is the chapter in which the MTX kernel is developed, and y is the version number. To begin with, we shall extend MTX4.1 to support dynamic process creation and process scheduling by (static) priority. In order to do these, we need to modify the PROC structure by adding more fields to it. For convenience (mainly for ease of reference in assembly code), we assume that ksp is the second entry and the process kernel stack is always at the high end of the PROC structure. Any new PROC fields should be added between the ksp and kstack entries. The CPU in 16-bit real mode push/pop stack in 2-byte units. Any added field should also be in 2-byte units, so that we can access the stack area as an integer array in C. For the MTX4.2 kernel, the added PROC fields are

```
int status    = proc status = FREE|READY|STOP|DEAD, etc.
int priority  = proc scheduling priority
int ppid      = parent pid
```

In addition, the MTX4.2 kernel also maintains a freeList and a readyQueue, where

- freeList = a singly-linked list containing all FREE PROCs. Initially, all PROCs are in the freelist. When creating a new process we try to allocate a FREE PROC from freeList. When a process terminates, its PROC structure is eventually returned to the freeList for reuse.
- readyQueue = a priority queue containing PROCs that are READY to run. In the readyQueue, PROCs of the same priority are ordered first-in-first-out (FIFO).

When the MTX4.2 kernel starts in ts.s, the stack pointer is initialized to point to the high end of proc[0].kstack. Then it calls main(), which calls init() to initialize the data structures as follows.

- Initialize each PROC by assigning pid = PROC index, status = FREE and priority = 0.
- Enter all PROCs into freeList.
- Initialize readyQueue = 0.
- Create P0 as the first running process, i.e. allocate proc[0] and let running point to it.

When init() completes, the system is running P0. P0 calls kfork() to create a child process P1 and enters it into readyQueue. When creating a new process the caller is the parent and the newly created process is the child. But as we shall see shortly, the parent-child process relation is not permanent. The parent of a process may change if its original parent terminates first. Every newly created process has priority = 1 and begins execution from the same body() function. After creating P1, P0 enters a while(1) loop, in which it calls tswitch() whenever readyQueue is not empty. Since P1 is already in readyQueue, P0 switches to run P1. At this point, process scheduling is very simple. Among the processes, P0 has the lowest priority 0. All other processes have priority 1. This implies that P0 is always the last PROC in readyQueue. Since PROCs of the same priority are ordered FIFO, other PROCs will take turn to run. P0 will run again if and only if all other PROCs are not runnable. Process scheduling with adjustable priorities will be discussed later in Sect. 4.4. In the body() function, let the running process print its pid and prompt for a input char, where 's' is to switch process and 'f' is to create a child process. In the MTX kernel, the queue and list manipulation functions are:

```
PROC *get_proc(PROC **list) : return a FREE PROC pointer from list
int   put_proc(PROC **list, PROC *p) : enter p into list
int   enqueue(PROC **queue, PROC *p) : enter p into queue by priority
PROC *dequeue(PROC **queue) : return first element removed from queue
printList(char *name, PROC *list)    : print name=list contents
```

Since these functions will be used in all MTX kernels, we precompile them into .o
files and put them in a link library, mtxlib, for linking. As a programming exercise,
the reader is strongly encouraged to implement these functions in a queue.c file and
include it in the C code. During linking, the linker will use the reader defined functions instead of those in the mtxlib library. This is left as an exercise. The following
lists the C code of the MTX4.2 kernel.

```c
/*********** MTX4.2 kernel t.c file ********************/
#define NPROC    9
#define SSIZE 1024
/******* PROC status ********/
#define FREE     0
#define READY    1
#define STOP     2
#define DEAD     3
typedef struct proc{
    struct proc *next;
    int     *ksp;
    int     pid;              // add pid for identify the proc
    int     ppid;            // parent pid;
    int     status;          // status = FREE|READY|STOPPED|DEAD, etc
    int     priority;        // scheduling priority
    int     kstack[SSIZE];   // proc stack area
}PROC;
PROC proc[NPROC], *running, *freeList, *readyQueue;
int   procSize = sizeof(PROC);
// #include "io.c"     // include I/O functions based on getc()/putc()
// #include "queue.c" // implement your own queue functions
int body()
{
  char c;
  printf("proc %d starts from body()\n", running->pid);
  while(1){
     printList("freelist   ", freeList);// optional: show the freeList
     printList("readyQueue", readyQueue); // show the readyQueue
     printf("proc %d running: parent=%d\n",running->pid,running->ppid);
     printf("enter a char [s|f] : ");
     c = getc(); printf("%c\n", c);
     switch(c){
         case 'f' : do_kfork();    break;
         case 's' : do_tswitch();  break;
     }
  }
}
```

```c
PROC *kfork() // create a child process, begin from body()
{
    int i;
    PROC *p = get_proc(&freeList);
    if (!p){
       printf("no more PROC, kfork() failed\n");
       return 0;
    }
    p->status = READY;
    p->priority = 1;          // priority = 1 for all proc except P0
    p->ppid = running->pid;         // parent = running
    /* initialize new proc's kstack[ ] */
    for (i=1; i<10; i++)            // saved CPU registers
       p->kstack[SSIZE-i]= 0 ;     // all 0's
    p->kstack[SSIZE-1] = (int)body; // resume point=address of body()
    p->ksp = &p->kstack[SSIZE-9];   // proc saved sp
    enqueue(&readyQueue, p); // enter p into readyQueue by priority
    return p;                       // return child PROC pointer
}
int init()
{
    PROC *p; int i;
    printf("init ....\n");
    for (i=0; i<NPROC; i++){     // initialize all procs
       p = &proc[i];
       p->pid = i;
       p->status = FREE;
       p->priority = 0;
       p->next = &proc[i+1];
    }
    proc[NPROC-1].next = 0;
    freeList = &proc[0];          // all procs are in freeList
    readyQueue = 0;
    /**** create P0 as running ******/
    p = get_proc(&freeList);      // allocate a PROC from freeList
    p->ppid = 0;                  // P0's parent is itself
    p->status = READY;
    running = p;                  // P0 is now running
}
int scheduler()
{
    if (running->status == READY)      // if running is still READY
       enqueue(&readyQueue, running); // enter it into readyQueue
    running = dequeue(&readyQueue);    // new running
}
main()
{
    printf("MTX starts in main()\n");
    init();                  // initialize and create P0 as running
    kfork();                 // P0 creates child P1
    while(1){                // P0 switches if readyQueue not empty
       if (readyQueue)
          tswitch();
    }
}
```

```
/*************** kernel command functions ****************/
int do_kfork( )
{
  PROC *p = kfork();
  if (p == 0){ printf("kfork failed\n"); return -1; }
  printf("PROC %d kfork a child %d\n", running->pid, p->pid);
  return p->pid;
}
int do_tswitch(){  tswitch(); }
```

4.5   MTX4.2: Demonstration of Process Creation and Process Switch

MTX4.2 demonstrates dynamic process creation and process scheduling by static priority. Figure 4.8 shows the sample outputs of running the MTX4.2 kernel.

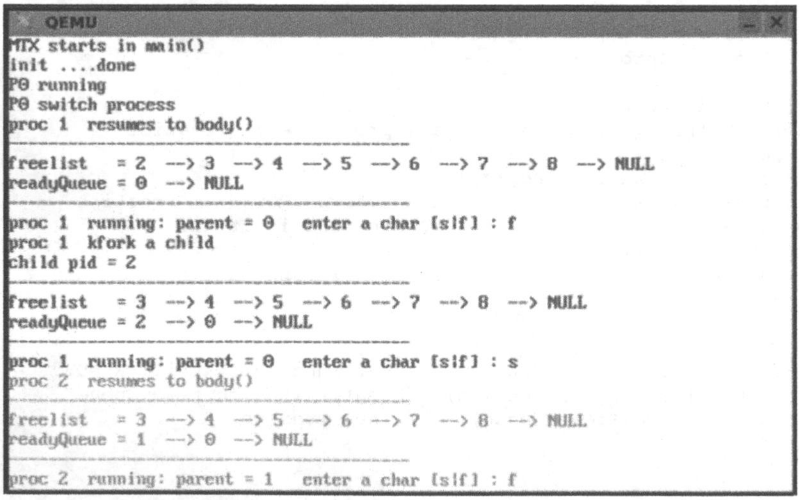

Fig. 4.8 Sample outputs of MTX4.2

4.6   Stop and Continue a Process

In the body() function, each command invokes a do_command() function, which calls a corresponding kernel function. The reader may test the kernel functions and observe their executions in action. As an exercise, the reader may modify the MTX4.2 kernel to do the following. In the body() function, add a 'q' command, which lets the running process call do_exit() to become DEAD. The algorithm of do_exit() is

```
do_exit()
{
    change running PROC's status to DEAD;
    call tswitch() to give up CPU;
}
```

Similarly, add a 't' command, which stops the current running process, and a 'c' command, which lets a stopped process continue. The algorithms of stop and continue are

```
do_stop()
{
    change running PROC.status to STOP;
    call tswitch() to give up CPU;
}
do_continue()
{
    ask for a pid to be continued; validate pid, e.g. 0 < pid < NPROC;
    find the PROC by pid; if PROC.status is STOP, change its status to
    READY and enter it into readyQueue;
}
```

4.7   MTX4.3: Demonstration of Stop/Continue Operations

Figure 4.9 shows the samples outputs of MTX4.3, which demonstrates stop/continue operations. In the figure, the running process displays its pid, asks for a command char and execute the command, where
    's' = switch process, 'f' = kfork a child process, 'q' = to become DEAD
    't' = to become STOP, 'c' = to continue a stopped process by pid
    When a process becomes STOP or DEAD, it gives up CPU by calling tswitch(). Since the process status is not READY, it will not be entered into readyQueue, which makes the process non-runnable. A stopped process becomes runnable again when another process lets it continue. As an exercise, the reader may modify stop to a stop [pid] operation, which stops a process identified by pid. If pid is not

```
 QEMU                                                                    _ X
MTX starts in main()
init ....done
P0 running
P0 switch process
proc 1  resumes to body()
─────────────────────────────────────────
freelist  = 2  --> 3  --> 4  --> 5  --> 6  --> 7  --> 8  --> NULL
readyQueue = 0 [0 ] --> NULL
─────────────────────────────────────────
proc 1 running: priority=1  parent=0  enter a char [s|f|q|t|c] : f
proc 1  kfork a child
child pid = 2
─────────────────────────────────────────
freelist  = 3  --> 4  --> 5  --> 6  --> 7  --> 8  --> NULL
readyQueue = 2 [1 ] --> 0 [0 ] --> NULL
─────────────────────────────────────────
proc 1 running: priority=1  parent=0  enter a char [s|f|q|t|c] : t
proc 1  stop running
proc 2  resumes to body()
─────────────────────────────────────────
freelist  = 3  --> 4  --> 5  --> 6  --> 7  --> 8  --> NULL
readyQueue = 0 [0 ] --> NULL
─────────────────────────────────────────
proc 2 running: priority=1  parent=1  enter a char [s|f|q|t|c] : c
enter pid to continue : 1
─────────────────────────────────────────
freelist  = 3  --> 4  --> 5  --> 6  --> 7  --> 8  --> NULL
readyQueue = 1 [1 ] --> 0 [0 ] --> NULL
─────────────────────────────────────────
proc 2 running: priority=1  parent=1  enter a char [s|f|q|t|c] :
```

Fig. 4.9 Sample outputs of MTX4.3

specified, it stops the running process itself. Similarly, the reader may modify the continue operation to let a DEAD process become runnable again. This should convince the reader that if we know the principle of process operations in an OS kernel, we may do anything to them, even perform miracles like resurrection of the dead.

4.8   Sleep and Wakeup Operations

The stop operation simply stops a process from running, and the continue operation makes a stopped process ready to run again. We can extend stop to a sleep(event) operation, which stops a running process to wait for an event, and extend continue to a wakeup(event) operation, which wakes up sleeping processes when their awaited event occurs. sleep() and wakeup() are the basic mechanism of process synchronization in the Unix kernel. Assume that every PROC has an (added) event field. The algorithms of sleep() and wakeup() are

```
sleep(int event)
{
   record event value in running PROC.event;
   change running PROC.status to SLEEP;
   switch process;
}
wakeup(int event)
{
   for every proc in the PROC array do{
        if (proc.status == SLEEP && proc.event == event){
           change proc.status to READY; // make it READY to run
           enter proc into readyQueue;
        }
   }
}
```

4.9 Sleep and Wakeup Usage

In an OS kernel, sleep and wakeup are used as follows.

1. When a process must wait for something, e.g. a resource, identified by an event value, it calls sleep(event) to go to sleep, waiting for the event to occur. In sleep(), it records the event value in the PROC structure, changes its status to SLEEP and gives up CPU. A sleeping process is not runnable since it is not in the readyQueue. It will become runnable again when the awaited event occurs, at which time another process (or an interrupt handler) calls wakeup(event) to wake it up.

2. An event is any value a process may sleep on, as long as another process will issue a wakeup call on the event value. It is up to the system designer to associate each resource with a unique event value. In Unix, event values are usually (global) variable addresses in the Unix kernel, which are unique, so that processes may sleep on distinct event values. wakeup(event) only wakes up those processes that are sleeping on the specified event value. For example, when a process waits for child process termination, it usually sleeps on its own PROC address, which is unique and also known to its children. When a process terminates, it issues wakeup(&parentPROC) to wake up its parent.

3. Many processes may sleep on the same event, which is natural because many processes may need the same resource that is currently busy or unavailable.

4. When an event occurs, someone (a process or an interrupt handler) will call wakeup(event), which wakes up ALL the processes sleeping on that event. If no process is sleeping on the event, wakeup() has no effect, i.e. it does nothing. When an awakened process runs, it must try to get the resource again since the resource may already be obtained by another process.

5. Since an event is just a value, it does not have a memory location to record the occurrence of the event. In order not to miss a wakeup call, a process must go to sleep BEFORE the awaited event occurs. In a uniprocessor system, this

is always achievable. In a multiprocessor system, the sleep_first_wakeup_later order cannot be guaranteed because processes may run in parallel in real-time. So sleep/wakeup works only for uniprocessor systems. For multiprocessor systems, we need other kinds of process synchronization tools, e.g. semaphores, which will be discussed later in Chap. 6.

6. The Unix kernel assigns a fixed priority to a process when it goes to sleep. The assigned priority is based on the importance of the resource the process is waiting for. It is the scheduling priority of the process when it wakes up. If an awakened process has a higher priority than the current running process, process switch does not take place immediately. It is deferred until the current running process is about to exit kernel mode to return to user mode. The reasons for this will also be discussed later.

7. The assigned priority classifies a sleeping process as either a SOUND sleeper or a LIGHT sleeper. A sound sleeper can only be woken up by its awaited event. A light sleeper can be woken up by other means, which may not be the event it is waiting for. For example, when a process waits for disk I/O, it sleeps with a high priority and should not be woken up by signals. If it waits for an input key from a terminal, which may not come for a long time, it sleeps with a low priority and can be woken up by signals. In the Linux kernel, a sleep process (task) is either INTERRUPTABLE or UNINTERRUPTABLE, which is the same as light or sound sleeper in Unix.

4.10   Implementation of Sleep and Wakeup

For the MTX kernel, we may implement sleep() and wakeup() as follows.

```
int sleep(int event)
{
    running->event = event;   // record event in PROC.event
    running->status = SLEEP;  // change status to SLEEP
    tswitch();                // give up CPU
}
 int wakeup(int event)
 {
    int i; PROC *p;
    for (i=1; i<NPROC; i++){    // not applicable to P0
        p = &proc[i];
        if (p->status == SLEEP && p->event == event){
            p->event = 0;       // cancel PROC's event
            p->status = READY;  // make it ready to run again
            enqueue(&readyQueue, p);
        }
    }
 }
```

Strictly speaking, the above implementation has some serious flaws but it works for the current MTX kernel because

- As of now, MTX is a uniprocessor system, in which only one process can run
  at any time instant. A process runs until it is ready to switch, e.g. when it sees a
  's' or 't' command. Process switch occurs only after a process has completed an
  operation, never in the middle of an operation. In other words, each process runs
  alone without any interference from other processes.
- So far, the MTX kernel does not have any interrupts. When a process runs, it
  cannot be interfered from any interrupt handler.

Details of how to implement sleep/wakeup and other process synchronization
mechanism properly will be covered later in Chap. 6.

4.11   MTX4.4: Demonstration of Sleep/Wakeup Operations

To demonstrate sleep and wakeup operations, we add the commands 'z' and 'a' to
the body() function, where 'z' is for a process to go to sleep on an event value and
'a' wakes up processes, if any, that are sleeping on an event value. Figure 4.10 show
the sample outputs of running MTX4.4. As an exercise, the reader may modify
MTX4.4 to do the following:

- Implement a FIFO sleepList containing all SLEEP processes. Modify the sleep()
  function to enter the sleeping process into the sleepList. Modify the wakeup()
  function to wake up sleeping processes in order.
- In the body() function, display sleeping processes and the events they are sleeping on.
- Instead of waking up all processes sleeping an event, wake up only one such
  process, and discuss its implications.

```
proc 1 running: priority=1  parent=0  enter a char [s|f|q|z|a] : f
proc 1  kfork a child
child pid = 2
----------------------------------------------------
freelist  = 3  --> 4  --> 5  --> 6  --> 7  --> 8  --> NULL
readyQueue = 2 [1 ] --> 0 [0 ] --> NULL
----------------------------------------------------
proc 1 running: priority=1  parent=0  enter a char [s|f|q|z|a] : z
input an event value to sleep: 123
proc 1  going to sleep on event=123
proc 2  resumes to body()
----------------------------------------------------
freelist  = 3  --> 4  --> 5  --> 6  --> 7  --> 8  --> NULL
readyQueue = 0 [0 ] --> NULL
----------------------------------------------------
proc 2 running: priority=1  parent=1  enter a char [s|f|q|z|a] : a
input an event value to wakeup: 123
proc 2  wakeup procs sleeping on event=123
wakeup proc 1
----------------------------------------------------
freelist  = 3  --> 4  --> 5  --> 6  --> 7  --> 8  --> NULL
readyQueue = 1 [1 ] --> 0 [0 ] --> NULL
----------------------------------------------------
proc 2 running: priority=1  parent=1  enter a char [s|f|q|z|a] :
```

Fig. 4.10 Sample outputs of MTX4.4

4.12   Process Termination

In an operating system, a process may terminate or die, which is a common term of process termination. As mentioned in Chap. 2, a process may terminate in two possible ways:

- Normal termination: The process calls exit(value), which issues _exit(value) system call to execute kexit(value) in the OS kernel, which is the case we are discussing here.
- Abnormal termination: The process terminates because of a signal. Signals and signal handling will be covered in Chap. 9.

In either case, when a process terminates, it eventually calls kexit() in the OS kernel. The general algorithm of kexit() is as follows.

4.12.1   Algorithm of kexit

```
kexit(int exitValue)
{
    1. erase process user-mode context, e.g. close file descriptors,
       release resources, deallocate usermode image memory, etc.
    2. dispose of children processes, if any.
    3. record exitValue in PROC.exitCode for parent to get.
    4. become a ZOMBIE (but do not free the PROC)
    5. wakeup parent and, if needed, also the INIT process P1.
}
```

So far, all the processes in MTX run in kernel mode, so they do not have any user mode context yet. User mode will be introduced in Chap. 5. Until then we shall ignore user mode context. So we begin by discussing Step 2 of kexit(). In some OS, the execution environment of a process may depend on that of its parent. For example, the child's memory area is within that of the parent, so that the parent process cannot die unless all of its children have died. In Unix, processes only have the very loose parent-child relation but their execution environments are all independent. Thus, in Unix a process may die any time. If a process with children dies first, all the children processes would become orphans. Then the question is: what to do with such orphans? In human society, they would be sent to grandma's house. But what if grandma already died? Following this reasoning, it immediately becomes clear that there must be a process which should not die if there are other processes still existing. Otherwise, the parent-child process relation would soon break down. In all Unix-like systems, the process P1, which is also known as the INIT process, is chosen to play this role. When a process dies, it sends all the orphaned children, dead or alive, to P1, i.e. become P1's children. Following suit, we shall also designate P1 in MTX as such a process. Thus, P1 should not die if there are other processes still existing. The remaining problem is how to implement Step 2 efficiently. In order for a dying process to dispose of orphan children, the process must be able to determine whether it has any child and, if it has children, find all the children quickly. If the number of processes is small, e.g. only a few as in MTX4.4, both questions can be answered effectively by searching all the PROC structures. For example, to determine whether a process has any child, simply search the PROCs for any one that is not FREE and its ppid matches the process pid. If the number of processes is large, e.g. in the order of hundreds or even thousands, this simple search scheme would be too slow. For this reason, most large OS kernels keep track of process relations by maintaining a process family tree.

4.12.2   Process Family Tree

Typically, the process family tree is implemented as a binary tree by a pair of child and sibling pointers in each PROC, as in

struct proc *child, *sibling, *parent;

where child points to the first child of a process and sibling points to a list of other children of the same parent. For convenience, each PROC also uses a parent pointer pointing to its parent. As an example, the process tree shown on the left-hand side of Fig. 4.11 can be implemented as the binary tree shown on the right-hand side of Fig. 4.11, in which each vertical link is a child pointer and each horizontal link is a sibling pointer. For the sake of clarity, parent and null pointers are not shown.

With a process tree, it is much easier to find the children of a process. First, follow the child pointer to the first child PROC. Then follow the sibling pointers to traverse the sibling PROCs. To send all children to P1, simply detach the children list and append it to the children list of P1 (and change their ppid and parent pointer also). Because of the small number of PROCs, MTX does not implement the process tree. This is left as a programming exercise in the Problem section. In either case, it should be fairly easy to implement Step 2 of kexit().

Each PROC has a 2-byte exitCode field, which records the process exit status. In MTX, the low byte of exitCode is the exitValue and the high byte is the signal num-

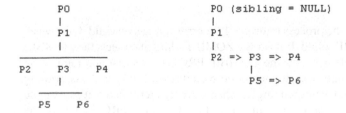

Fig. 4.11 Process tree and binary tree

ber that caused the process to terminate. Since a process can only die once, only one of the bytes has meaning. After recording exitValue in PROC.exitCode, the process changes its status to ZOMBIE but does not free the PROC. Then the process calls kwakeup(event) to wake up its parent, where event must be the same unique value used by both the parent and child processes, e.g. the address of the parent PROC structure or the parent pid. It also wakes up P1 if it has sent any orphans to P1. The final act of a dying process is to call tswitch() for the last time. After these, the process is essentially dead but still has a dead body in the form of a ZOMBIE PROC, which will be buried (set FREE) by the parent process through the wait operation.

4.13   Wait for Child Process Termination

At any time, a process may call the kernel function

pid = kwait(int *status)

to wait for a ZOMBIE child process. If successful, the returned pid is the ZOMBIE child's pid and status contains the exitCode of the ZOMBIE child. In addition, kwait() also releases the ZOMBIE PROC back to the freeList. The algorithm of kwait is

```
int kwait(int *status)
{
    if (caller has no child)
        return -1 for error;
    while(1){ // caller has children
        search for a (any) ZOMBIE child;
        if (found a ZOMBIE child){
            get ZOMBIE child pid
            copy ZOMBIE child exitCode to *status;
            bury the ZOMBIE child (put its PROC back to freeList)
            return ZOMBIE child pid;
        }
        //**** has children but none dead yet ***
        ksleep(running);  // sleep on its PROC address
    }
}
```

In the kwait algorithm, the process returns -1 for error if it has no child. Otherwise, it searches for a ZOMBIE child. If it finds a ZOMBIE child, it collects the ZOMBIE child's pid and exitCode, releases the ZOMBIE PROC to freeList and returns the ZOMBIE child's pid. Otherwise, it goes to sleep on its own PROC address, waiting for a child to terminate. Correspondingly, when a process terminates, it must issue kwakeup(parent) to wake up the parent. Instead of the parent PROC address, the reader may verify that using the parent pid should also work. In the algorithm, when the process wakes up, it will find a dead child when it executes the while loop again.

Note that each kwait() call handles only one ZOMBIE child, if any. If a process has many children, it may have to call kwait() multiple times to dispose of all the dead children. Alternatively, a process may terminate first without waiting for any dead child. When a process dies, all of its children become children of P1. As we shall see later, in a real system P1 executes in an infinite loop, in which it repeatedly waits for dead children, including adopted orphans. Therefore, in a Unix-like system, the INIT process P1 wears many hats.

- It is the ancestor of all processes except P0. In particular, it is the grand daddy of all user processes since all login processes are children of P1.
- It is the head of an orphanage since all orphans are sent to his house and call him Papa.
- It is the manager of a morgue since it keeps looking for ZOMBIEs to bury their dead bodies.

So, in a Unix-like system if the INIT process P1 dies or gets stuck, the system would stop functioning because no user can login again and the system will soon be full of rotten corpses.

4.14   Change Process Scheduling Priority

In an OS kernel, processes compete for CPU time by scheduling priority. However, process scheduling by priority is meaningful only if process priority can be changed dynamically. Factors that affect process priority typically involve some measure of time. For example, when a process is scheduled to run, it is given a certain amount of time to run. If a process uses up its allotted time whenever it runs, its priority should decrease. If a process gives up CPU before its allotted time expires, the remaining time may be credited to the process, allowing its priority to increase. If a ready process has not run for a long time, its priority should also increase, etc. Since the MTX kernel does not yet have a timer (timer will be introduced in Chap. 8), it is not possible to adjust process priorities dynamically. However, we can simulate dynamic process priority and observe its effect by the following means.

1. Add a time field to the PROC structure to simulate process time quantum. When a process is scheduled to run, set its time quantum to a limit value, e.g. 5. While a process runs, decrement its time by 1 for each command it executes. When the simulated time reaches 0, switch process. If a process switches before its time expires, use the remaining time to adjust its scheduling priority. This would simulate process scheduling by time slice and dynamic priority. Implementation of such a scheme is left as an exercise in the Problem section.
2. Alternatively, we may implement a change priority operation, which changes the priority of a process. Changing process priority may reorder the readyQueue, which in turn may trigger a process switch.

4.15   MTX4.5: Demonstration of Process Management

In the above sections, we have discussed the concepts and principles of process management in an OS kernel. These include context switching, process creation, process termination, process goes to sleep, wake up processes, wait for child process termination and change process priority. In the sample system MTX4.5, we integrate these concepts and principles and implement the algorithms to demonstrate process management in an OS kernel. The following lists the C code of the MTX4.5 kernel. In order to make the code modular, related functions are implemented in separate files for easier update and maintenance. For example, type.h contains system constants and data structure types, wait.c contains sleep/wakeup, exit and wait functions, kernel.c contains kernel command functions, etc.

```
/*************** type.h file ****************/
#define NPROC    9
#define SSIZE 1024
#define FREE     0
#define READY    1
#define RUNNING  2      // for clarity only, not needed or used
#define STOPPED  3
#define SLEEP    4
#define ZOMBIE   5
typedef struct proc{
    struct proc *next;
    int   *ksp;
    int   pid;          // process ID number
    int   status;       // status = FREE|READY|RUNNING|SLEEP|ZOMBIE
    int   ppid;         // parent pid
    struct proc *parent; // pointer to parent PROC
    int   priority;
    int   event;        // sleep event
    int   exitCode;     // exit code
    int   kstack[SSIZE];
}PROC;

/****************** wait.c file ***************************/
int ksleep(int event) { // shown above }
int kwakeup(int event){ // shown above }
int ready(PROC *p) { p->status=READY; enqueue(&readyQueue, p); }
int kexit(int exitValue)
{
   int i, wakeupP1 = 0;
   if (running->pid==1 && nproc>2){ // nproc = number of active PROCs
      printf("other procs still exist, P1 can't die yet\n");
      return -1;
   }
   /* send children (dead or alive) to P1's orphanage */
   for (i = 1; i < NPROC; i++){
      p = &proc[i];
      if (p->status != FREE && p->ppid == running->pid){
         p->ppid = 1;
         p->parent = &proc[1];
         wakeupP1++;
      }
```

```
    }
    /* record exitValue and become a ZOMBIE */
    running->exitCode = exitValue;
    running->status = ZOMBIE;
    /* wakeup parent and also P1 if necessary */
    kwakeup(running->parent); // parent sleeps on its PROC address
    if (wakeupP1)
        kwakeup(&proc[1]);
    tswitch();                     // give up CPU
}
int kwait(int *status)  // wait for ZOMBIE child
{
    PROC *p; int i, hasChild = 0;
    while(1){                              // search PROCs for a child
        for (i=1; i<NPROC; i++){           // exclude P0
            p = &proc[i];
            if (p->status != FREE && p->ppid == running->pid){
                hasChild = 1;              // has child flag
                if (p->status == ZOMBIE){  // lay the dead child to rest
                    *status = p->exitCode; // collect its exitCode
                    p->status = FREE;      // free its PROC
                    put_proc(&freeList, p); // to freeList
                    nproc--;               // once less processes
                    return(p->pid);        // return its pid
                }
            }
        }
        if (!hasChild) return -1;          // no child, return ERROR
        ksleep(running); // still has kids alive: sleep on PROC address
    }
}
/******************** kernel.c file **********************/
int do_tswitch() { // same as in MTX4.4 }
int do_kfork()   { // same as in MTX4.4 }
int do_exit()    { kexit(0);             }
int do_stop()    { // same as in MTX4.4 }
int do_continue(){ // same as in MTX4.4 }
int do_sleep()   { // same as in MTX4.4 }
int do_wakeup()  { // same as in MTX4.4 }
// added scheduling functions in MTX4.5
int reschedule()
{
    PROC *p, *tempQ = 0;
    while ( (p=dequeue(&readyQueue)) ){ // reorder readyQueue
        enqueue(&tempQ, p);
    }
    readyQueue = tempQ;
    rflag = 0;                          // global reschedule flag
    if (running->priority < readyQueue->priority)
        rflag = 1;
}
int chpriority(int pid, int pri)
{
    PROC *p; int i, ok=0, reQ=0;
    if (pid == running->pid){
        running->priority = pri;
        if (pri < readyQueue->priority)
```

```
            rflag = 1;
      return 1;
   }
   // if not for running, for both READY and SLEEP procs
   for (i=1; i<NPROC; i++){
      p = &proc[i];
      if (p->pid == pid && p->status != FREE){
         p->priority = pri;
         ok = 1;
         if (p->status == READY)   // in readyQueue==> redo readyQueue
            reQ = 1;
      }
   }
   if (!ok){
      printf("chpriority failed\n");
      return -1;
   }
   if (reQ)
      reschedule(p);
}
int do_chpriority()
{
   int pid, pri;
   printf("input pid " );
   pid = geti();
   printf("input new priority " );
   pri = geti();
   if (pri<1) pri = 1;
   chpriority(pid, pri);
}
int body()
{
   char c;
   while(1){
      if (rflag){
         printf("proc %d: reschedule\n", running->pid);
         rflag = 0;
         tswitch();
      }
      printList("freelist  ", freeList);    // show freelist
      printQ("readyQueue", readyQueue);      // show readQueue
      printf("proc%d running: priority=%d parent=%d enter a char
             [s|f|t|c|z|a|p|w|q]: ",
             running->pid, running->priority, running->parent->pid );
      c = getc(); printf("%c\n", c);
      switch(c){
         case 's' : do_tswitch();      break;
         case 'f' : do_kfork();        break;
         case 'q' : do_exit();         break;
         case 't' : do_stop();         break;
         case 'c' : do_continue();     break;
         case 'z' : do_sleep();        break;
         case 'a' : do_wakeup();       break;
         case 'p' : do_chpriority();   break;
         case 'w' : do_wait();         break;
         default: printf("invalid command\n'); break;
      }
```

```c
    }
}
/********************* main.c file of MTX4.5 kernel ******************/
#include "type.h"
PROC proc[NPROC], *running, *freeList, *readyQueue, *sleepList;
int procSize = sizeof(PROC);
int nproc, rflag;           // number of procs, re-schedule flag
#include "io.c"             // may include io.c and queue.c here
#include "queue.c"
#include "wait.c"           // ksleep(), kwakeup(), kexit(), wait()
#include "kernel.c"         // other kernel functions
int init()
{
    PROC *p; int i;
    for (i=0; i<NPROC; i++){  // initialize all procs
        p = &proc[i];
        p->pid = i;
        p->status = FREE;
        p->priority = 0;
        p->next = &proc[i+1];
    }
    freeList = &proc[0]; proc[NPROC-1].next = 0; // freeList
    readyQueue = sleepList = 0;
    /**** create P0 as running ******/
    p = get_proc(&freeList); // get PROC from freeList
    p->status = READY;
    running = p;
    nproc = 1;
}
int scheduler()
{
    if (running->status == READY)
        enqueue(&readyQueue, running);
    running = dequeue(&readyQueue);
    rflag = 0;
}
main()
{
    printf("MTX starts in main()\n");
    init();                     // initialize and create P0 as running
    kfork();                    // P0 kfork() P1 to run body()
    while(1){
        while(!readyQueue);     // P0 idle loop while readyQueue empty
        tswitch();              // P0 switch to run P1
    }
}
```

Figure 4.12 shows the sample outputs of MTX4.5, in which the commands are:

s = switch process, f = fork a child process, q = terminate with an exit value

t = stop running process, c = continue a stopped process

z = running process sleep on an event value, a = wake up processes by event value

p = change process priority, w = wait for a ZOMBIE child

```
proc 1 [1 ] running: parent=0
enter a char [slfltlclzlalplwlq] : f
proc 1  kfork a child
child pid = 2

freelist  = 3 [0 ] -> 4 [0 ] -> 5 [0 ] -> 6 [0 ] -> 7 [0 ] -> 8 [0 ] -> NULL
readyQueue = 2 [1 ] -> 0 [0 ] -> NULL
sleepList  = NULL

proc 1 [1 ] running: parent=0
enter a char [slfltlclzlalplwlq] : w
proc 2  resumes to body()

freelist  = 3 [0 ] -> 4 [0 ] -> 5 [0 ] -> 6 [0 ] -> 7 [0 ] -> 8 [0 ] -> NULL
readyQueue = 0 [0 ] -> NULL
sleepList  = 1 [1 ] -> NULL

proc 2 [1 ] running: parent=1
enter a char [slfltlclzlalplwlq] :
```

Fig. 4.12 Sample outputs of MTX4.5

4.16   MTX Development Environment

The initial development platform of MTX is BCC under Linux. Figure 4.13 shows
the development and running environment of MTX. The right-hand side of the
figure shows two X-window terminals. X-window#1 is for developing the MTX
kernel. X-window#2 is for running the MTX kernel on a virtual machine. The software tools used include Linux editors, such as vi or emacs, the BCC compiler-
linker package and the archive utility ar for creating and maintaining link library.
After creating the source files, the user may use either a Makefile or a mk script to
compile-link the source files into a MTX kernel image. There are two ways to test
the MTX kernel. The left-hand side of the figure shows a real x86 PC with bootable
devices, e.g. a FD containing a MTX disk image. To test the MTX kernel on a real
PC, simply copy the MTX kernel to the disk image as /boot/mtx and then boot up
MTX on the PC. Until we add a file system to MTX, the MTX system operates in
read-only mode. So a FD-emulation CDROM may also be used as the boot device.

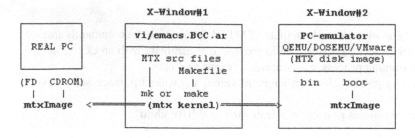

Fig. 4.13 Development environment of MTX

MTX is intended to be a real operating system. It should work on real PCs, not just in an emulated environment. However, booting from a real PC requires turning off/on a real machine and the booting process is also slow. A faster and more convenient way to run MTX is to use a PC emulator, such as QEMU, DOSEMU or VMware, as shown in the right-hand side box X-Winodw#2. When running MTX on virtual machines the simplest way is to use the mtximage file as a bootable virtual floppy disk.

```
.QEMU    : qemu -fda mtximage -no-fd-bootchk
.DOSEMU  : configure DOSEMU to use mtximage as virtual FD
.VMware  : configure VM to boot from mtximage as virtual FD
```

In all the cases, MTX will boot up and run in a separate window. Thus, we can develop and run MTX without ever leaving the working environment of Linux. Due to its fast turn around time and convenience, most students prefer this method. Alternatively, MTX can also be installed to, and run from, hard disk partitions of virtual machines. The install procedures are described in the Appendix of this book.

Problems

1. The Intel x86 CPU has a pusha instruction, which pushes (in order) all the general registers ax,cx,dx,bx,oldsp,bp,si,di into stack, where oldsp is the sp value before the pusha instruction. Correspondingly, the popa instruction pops the saved registers in reverse order. Assume that tswitch() is modified as

```
_tswitch:
SAVE:    pusha
         pushf
         mov    bx,_running
         mov    2[bx], sp
FIND:    call _scheduler
RESUME:
```

(1). Write assembly code for the RESUME part.
(2). Corresponding to this tswitch(), show how to initialize the kernel stack of a new process to let it resume to the body() function. Test MTX with the modified tswitch().

2. In addition to general registers, the x86 CPU's segment registers should also be part of the context of a process. As such, they should also be saved and then restored during context switching. Assume that tswitch() is modified as

```
  _tswitch:
SAVE:    push   ax,bx,cx,dx,bp,si,di   ! in pseudo-code
         pushf
! ADD THESE LINES, WHICH SAVE THE CPU'S SEGMENT REGISTERS
         push   ds
         push   ss
! END OF ADDED LINES
         mov    bx,_running
         mov    2[bx], sp
FIND:    call   _scheduler
RESUME:
```

(1). Write assembly code for the RESUME part of the modified tswitch().
(2). Corresponding to the modified tswitch(), show how to initialize the kernel stack of a new process. Pay special attention to the contents of ds and ss, which cannot be arbitrary but must be initialized with some specific values. Test MTX with the modified tswitch().
(3). The ADDED LINES are not in MTX's tswitch() because they are redundant. WHY are they redundant?

3. In the MTX kernel, a process gives up CPU by calling tswitch(). Since this is a function call, it is unnecessary to save all the CPU registers. For instance, it is clearly unnecessary to save and restore the AX register. Assume: tswitch() is modified as follows.

```
  _tswitch:
SAVE:    push   bp                      ! save bp only
         mov    bx,_running
         mov    2[bx], sp
FIND:    call   _scheduler
RESUME:
```

(1). Write assembly code for the RESUME part of the modified tswitch().
(2). Corresponding to this tswitch(), show how to initialize the kernel stack of a new process to let it resume to the body() function. Test MTX with the modified tswitch().
(3). Delete the "push bp" instruction. Repeat (2) and (3). Does MTX still work?
(4). Why is it necessary to save the bp register of a process? (HINT:stack frames)

4. In MTX, context switching begins when the current running process calls tswitch(), which changes the execution to a new process. Some people refer to this as a co-routine call, not a complete context switching. To soothe such critics, we may implement tswitch() as

```
_tswitch:   INT 100
            ret
```

When the x86 CPU executes the INT 100 instruction, it first saves the CPU's [FLAG, CS, PC] registers onto the (current) stack. Then, it loads the contents of the memory locations [400, 402] into CPU's [PC, CS], causing it to execute from the newly loaded [PC, CS]. Corresponding to INT 100, the instruction IRET pops 3 items into the CPU's [PC, CS, FLAG] registers. Assume that the memory contents of [400, 402]=[SAVE, 0x1000]. Then, after INT 100, the CPU would execute SAVE in our MTX kernel. Assume: the code of SAVE is:

```
SAVE:   push DS,ES,SS,ax,bx,cx,dx,bp,si,di;
save sp into running PROC's ksp;
FIND:   call scheduler() to find next running PROC;
-------------------------------------------------
RESUME:
```

(1). Complete the RESUME part, using pseudo-assembly code.
(2). With this tswitch(), show how to initialize the kstack of a new process for it to begin execution in body().
(3). Justify whether it is really necessary to implement context switching this way?

5. In MTX, tswitch() calls scheduler(), which essentially picks a runnable process from readyQueue as the next running process. Rewrite tswich() as tswitch(PROC *current, PROC *next), which switches from the current running process to the next running process.

6. In MTX, there is only one readyQueue, which contains all the processes that are READY to run. A multi-level priority queue (MPQ) consists of, e.g. n+1 priority queues, each at a specific priority level, as shown in the following figure.

```
MPQ --|-- level_0_queue : lowest priority 0
      |-- level_1_queue : 2nd lowest priority 1
      |-- ...........................
      |-- level_n_queue : highest priority n
```

In each priority queue, processes have the same priority and are ordered FIFO. Redesign the ready queue in MTX to implement a multi-level priority queue.

7.   Implement process family tree for the MTX kernel.
8.   Modify the kexit() function to implement the following.

(1). A dying process must dispose of its ZOMBIE children first.
(2). A process can not die until all the children processes have died.

Discuss the advantages, if any, and disadvantages of these schemes.

9.   Linux has a waitpid(int pid, int *status) kernel function, which is equivalent to wait4(int pid, int *status) in Unix. Both allow a process to wait for a specific ZOMBIE child specified by pid. Implement the waitpid()/wait4() function for the MTX kernel.
10.   Assume: A bootable MTX kernel image begins with

```
jmp go              ! a jmp instruction of 2 bytes
.word kernel_size
go:                 ! assembly code of ts.s
```

where kernel_size is the MTX kernel size in bytes, which is the total size of the kernel's code, data and bss sections. When the MTX kernel starts, it can read the kernel_size to determine the starting address and size of the initial FREE memory area, which is all the memory area from the end of the MTX kernel to the segment 0x2000. Assume that in the MTX kernel the PROC structure is defined as

```
typedef struc proc{
    struct proc *next;
    int *ksp, pid, status;
    int *kstack; // pointer to per process kernel stack area
}PROC;
PROC *running, *readyQueue;
```

Note that the PROC structure only has a stack pointer but without a stack area, and the MTX kernel does not have an array of PROC structures.

(1). Implement a PROC *allocate_proc(sizeof(PROC)) function, which allocates a piece of memory from the FREE memory area as a new proc structure.
(2). Implement an int *allocate_stack(SSIZE) function, which allocates a stack area of SSIZE bytes for an allocated PROC structure.

(3). When a process dies, it must release the stack area back to the FREE memory. Implement the free_stack(PROC *p) function.
(4). When a process finds a ZOMBIE child, it should release the ZOMBIE PROC back to the FREE memory. Implement the free_proc(PROC *p) function.

(5). Re-write the MTX kernel code using these allocation/deallocation functions for PROCs and process stacks.

11. In the MTX kernel, when a process Pi switches to another process Pj, the kernel stack changes from Pi's kstack to Pj's kstack directly. In many Unix-like systems, the PROC structure of a process and its kernel mode stack are allocated dynamically as in Problem 7. When a process Pi switches to another process Pj, the kernel stack first changes from Pi's kstack to a temporary stack, such as that of an idle process P0, and then to Pj's kstack. Why the difference?

12. In the MTX kernel, each process has a unique pid, which is the index of its PROC structure. In most Unix-like systems, the pid of a process is assigned a unique number in the range [2, 32768]. When the pid number exceeds the maximum limit, it wraps around.

(1). Why are pid's assigned this way?

(2). Implement this kind of pid assignment scheme for the MTX kernel.

13. In the MTX kernel, kfork() creates a child process which starts execution from the body() function. Assume: the body() function is modified as follows.

                    int body(int pid){....... print pid.........}

where pid is the process pid. Furthermore, when a process finishes executing the body() function, it returns to kexit(0) with a 0 exit value. Modify kfork() to accomplish these.

14. In the MTX kernel, kfork() creates a child process which starts execution from the body() function.

(1). Assume that a process Pi has executed the following function calls.

```
----------------------------------------------------------------------------------
body()            |   int A(int x)   |   int B(int y)   |   int C(int z)
{ int m = 1;      |   { int a = 2;   |   { int b = 3;   |   { int c = 4;
   A(m);          |      B(a);       |      C(b);        |      HERE:
}                 |   }              |   }               |   }
----------------------------------------------------------------------------------
```

Draw a diagram to show the stack contents of Pi when execution is at the label HERE in the function C().

(2). Assume that while in the function C(), Pi calls kfork() to create a child process Pj, as shown below.

```
int C(int z){
    int pid = kfork();        // creates a child process Pj
    < -------------------      // RESUME POINT of Pj
    if (pid==0) {printf("this is the child Pj")
}
```

When the child process Pj runs, it should resume to the same place where it is created, i.e. to the statement pid = kfork() but with a 0 return value. Modify kfork() to accomplish these. Ensure that your kfork() algorithm works for any number of function calls.

HINTS:
(1). Copy parent's stack to child's stack, add a stack frame for the child to resume.
(2). Fix up copied stack frame pointers to point to child's stack area.

15. Modify the MTX4.4 kernel to simulate process scheduling by dynamic priority:

(1). Add a time field to the PROC structure to simulate the CPU use time.
(2). When a process (other than P0) is scheduled to run, give it a time quantum of 5. In the body() function, decrement the running process time by 1 for each command it executes. When the time field reaches 0, switch process. If a process switches before its time expires, add the remaining time to its new priority.
(3). In the scheduler() function, if the process is not P0 and still ready, set its new priority to remaining time + 1, which determines its position in the readyQueue.

Boot up and run the system to observe process scheduling by dynamic priority.

16. User-level multitasking under Linux:

(a). Given: the following ts.s in 32-bit GCC assembly code:

```
#------------ ts.s file --------------------
    .global tswitch, running, scheduler # no underscore prefix
tswitch:
SAVE:      pushal
           pushfl
           movl    running,%ebx
           movl    %esp, 4(%ebx)    # integers in GCC are 4 bytes
FIND:      call    scheduler
RESUME:    movl    running, %ebx
           movl    4(%ebx), %esp
           popfl
           popal
           ret
```

(b). The following t.c file
```
/*********** t.c file for multitasking under Linux ***********/
#include <stdio.h>
#include <stdlib.h> // Linux header files
#include "type.h"   // PROC struct type, same as in MTX4.1
#include "queue.c"  // getproc(),enqueue(),dequeue(); same as in MTX4.1
#define NPROC 9

PROC proc[NPROC], *running, *freeList, *readyQueue;

int body()
{ int c;
  while(1){
    printf("\n****************************************\n");
    printf("I am task %d My parent=%d\n", running->pid, running->ppid);
    printf("input a char [f|s] : ");
    c = getchar();
    switch(c){

        case 'f': kfork();       break;
        case 's': tswitch();     break;
    }
  }
}

PROC *kfork()
{ PROC *p = get_proc(&freeList);
  if (!p)
     return 0;
  /* initialize the new proc and kstack */
  p->status = READY;
  p->ppid = running->pid;
  p->priority = 1;                     // priority = 1
  p->kstack[SSIZE-1] = (int)body;      // start to run body()
  p->ksp = &(p->kstack[SSIZE - ?]);    // SEE REQUIREMENTS BELOW
  enqueue(&readyQueue, p);
  return p;
}

int init()
{ int i;   PROC *p;
  // initialize all PROCs in a freeList, readyQueue=0
}
```

```
main()
{
  init();
  kfork();    // create P1
  printf("P0 switch to P1\n");
  tswitch();
}

int scheduler()
{
  if (running->status == READY)
      enqueue(&readyQueue, running);
  running = dequeue(&readyQueue);
}
```

(1). In the kfork() function, there is a line

$$p->ksp = \&(p->kstack[SSIZE - ?]);$$

Fix up the ? entry to make the kfork() code work.

(2). Under Linux, use gcc to compile-link t.c and ts.s into a.out, as in

gcc -m32 t.c ts.s

Then run a.out.; enter 'f' or 's' and observe the outputs.

(3). Modify t.c to implement exit(), sleep(), wakeup() and wait() functions as in MTX4.5.

(4). The multitasking environment of (3) is the basis of so called user-level threads. Discuss the similarity and difference between a multitasking kernel, e.g. MTX4.5, and user-level threads.

References

Antonakos, J.L., "An introduction to the Intel Family of Microprocessors", Prentice Hall, 1999.
Intel 64 and IA-32 Architectures Software Developer's Manual, Volume 3, 2014
Intel i486 Processor Programmer's Reference Manual, 1990
Intel MP: Intel MultiProcessor Specification, v1. 4, 1997

Chapter 5
User Mode and System Calls

In Chap. 4, we developed a simple OS kernel for process management. The simple kernel supports dynamic process creation, process termination, process synchronization by sleep/wakeup operations, wait for child process termination and priority-based process scheduling. In MTX4.5, all processes run in kernel mode since they execute in the same address space of the MTX kernel. In a real operating system, processes may execute in two different modes; kernel mode and user mode. In this chapter, we shall extend the simple MTX kernel to support process executions in user mode. First, we explain the difference between the address spaces of kernel and user modes, the mechanism of transition between user and kernel modes, and how to implement the transition. Then we show how to create processes with user mode images and let them return to execute images in user mode. Based on these, we implement simple system calls, which allow user mode processes to enter kernel mode, execute kernel functions and return to user mode. Then we implement other system call functions for process management. These include fork, exec and the advanced technique of vfork (Goldt et al. 1995). This would make the MTX kernel to have similar capability as the Unix kernel for process management. In addition to the fork-exec paradigm of Unix, we also point out other alternative schemes, such as the create and attach operations in MVS [IBM MVS]. Then we discuss the concepts and advantages of threads (POSIX 1995) and extend the process model to implement threads support in the MTX kernel. In addition, we also demonstrate threads applications by concurrent programs and show how to synchronize threads executions to prevent race conditions. In the Problem section, we point out variations to the kernel design and encourage the reader to explore alternative ways to implement the kernel functions.

5.1 Process Execution Image

The execution image of a process consists of three logical segments; Code, Data and Stack, as shown in Fig. 5.1.

© Springer International Publishing Switzerland 2015   133
K. C. Wang, *Design and Implementation of the MTX Operating System*,
DOI 10.1007/978-3-319-17575-1_5

Fig. 5.1 Process execution image

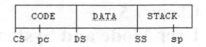

In theory, all the segments can be independent, each in a different memory area, as long as they are pointed by the CPU's segment registers. In practice, some of the segments may coincide. For example, in the single-segment memory model, all segments are the same. During execution, the CPU's CS, DS and SS all point to the same segment of the execution image. In the separate I&D space memory model, CS points to the Code segment, but DS and SS point to the combined Data and Stack segment. For the sake of simplicity, we shall assume the single-segment memory model first. Each process image has only one segment and the segment size is 64 KB. Process images with separate I&D spaces and variable sizes will be considered later in Chap. 7 when we discuss memory management.

5.2   Kernel and User Modes

From now on we shall assume that a process may execute in two different modes; kernel mode and user mode, denoted by Kmode and Umode for short. While in Kmode, all processes share the same Code and Data of the OS kernel, but each process has its own kernel mode stack (in the PROC structure), which contains the execution context of the process while in Kmode. When a process gives up CPU, it saves its dynamic context (CPU registers) in kstack. When a process becomes running again, it restores the saved context form kstack. In Umode, process images are in general all different. Each process has a separate Umode memory area containing the user mode code, data and stack, denoted by Ucode, Udata and Ustack, of the process. For ease of discussion, we begin with the following assumptions.

1. The MTX kernel runs in the segment 0x1000.
2. The system has 9 PROC structures, P0 to P8. P0 always runs in Kmode.
3. Only P1 to P8 may run in Umode, each has a distinct 64 KB Umode image in the segment (pid+1)* 0x1000, e.g. P1 in 0x2000, P2 in 0x3000, P8 in 0x9000, etc.

The fixed segment memory assignment of process images is just for ease of discussion. It will be removed later when we implement memory management.

Fig. 5.2 Processes with Umode images

Next, assume that the process P5 is running in Umode now, P2 is READY but not running. Figure 5.2 shows the current memory map of the MTX system.

Since P5 is running in Umode, the CPU's CS, DS, SS registers must all point to P5's Umode image at 0x6000. P5's ustack is in the upper region of Uimage5. When P5 enters Kmode, it will execute the Kernel image in the segment 0x1000. The CPU's CS, DS, SS registers must be changed to point to 0x1000, as shown by the kCS, kDS, kSS in the figure. In order for P5 to run in kernel, the stack pointer must also be changed to point to P5's kstack. Naturally, P5 must save its Umode segment registers, uCS, uDS, uSS, and usp if it intends to return to Uimage5 later.

Assume that, while in Kmode, P5 switches to P2, which may return to its Umode image at 0x3000. If so, P2 must change CPU's segment registers to its own uCS, uDS, uSS, all of which must point to 0x3000. When P2 runs in Umode, its ustack is in the upper region of Uimage2. Similarly, the reader may deduce what would happen if P2 enters Kmode to switch to another process, etc.

5.3 Transition Between User and Kernel Modes

In an OS, a process migrates between Umode and Kmode many times during its lifetime. Although every process begins in Kmode, we shall assume that a process is already executing in Umode. This sounds like another chicken-egg problem, but we can handle it easily. A process in Umode will enter Kmode if one of the following events occurs:

- Exceptions : also called traps, such as illegal instruction, invalid address, etc.
- Interrupts : timer interrupts, device I/O completion, etc.
- System calls : INT n (or equivalent instructions on other CPUs).

Exceptions and interrupts will be covered in later chapters. Here, we only consider system calls. System call, or syscall for short, is a mechanism which allows a process in Umode to enter Kmode to execute kernel functions. Syscalls are not ordinary function calls because they involve CPU operating in different modes (if so equipped) and executing in different address spaces. However, once the linkage is set up, syscalls can be used as if they were ordinary function calls. Assume that there are N kernel functions, each corresponds to a call number $n = 0$, $1, ., N - 1$, e.g.

```
Call#   Kernel Function
-----   ----------------
  0       kgetpid()    // get process pid
  1       kfork()      // fork a child process
  2       kexec()      // change Umode image
  3       kwait()      // wait for ZOMBIE child process
  ...............
  6       kexit()      // terminate
```

where the prefix k of the function names emphasizes that they are functions in the OS kernel. A Umode process may use

```
int r = syscall(call#, parm1, parm2, .... );
```

to enter Kmode to execute the corresponding kernel function, passing parameters to the kernel function as needed. When the kernel function finishes, the process returns to Umode with the desired results and a return value. For most syscalls, a 0 return value mean success and − 1 means failure.

5.3.1   System Calls

Assuming 4 parameters, the implementation of syscall() is shown below.

```
!===========================================================
!  int syscall(int a,b,c,d); issue INT 80 to enter Kernel
!===========================================================
_syscall:
            INT n     <==== This is the magic wand!
returnHERE:   ret
```

On the Intel x86 CPU, syscall is implemented by the INT n instruction, where n is a byte value (0–255). Although we may use different INT n to implement different syscalls, it suffices to use only one number: INT 80, since the parameter a represents the syscall number. The choice of INT 80 is quite arbitrary. We may choose any other number, e.g. 0x80, as long as it is not used as IRQ of the interrupt hardware or by BIOS. When the CPU executes INT 80, it does the following.

PUSH: push flag register, clear flag register's T-bit and I-bit; push uCS and uPC.
LOAD: load (PC, CS) with contents of (4*80, 4*80+2)=(_int80h, KCS).
HANDLER: continue execution from the loaded (PC, CS)=(_int80h, KCS).

Since these operations are crucial to understanding both system call and interrupts processing in later chapters, we shall explain them in more detail.

   PUSH: INT n causes the CPU to push the current uFlag, uCS, uPC into stack. On most other machines, a special instruction like INT n causes the CPU to enter a separate Kmode and switches stack to Kmode stack automatically. The Intel x86 CPU in 16-bit real mode does not have a separate Kmode or a separate Kmode stack pointer. After executing INT 80, it only switches the execution point from (uPC, uCS) to (kPC, kCS), which changes the code segment from UCode to KCode. All other segments (DS, SS, ES) and CPU registers are still those in Umode. Thus, when CPU first enters the int80h() handler function, the stack is still the process

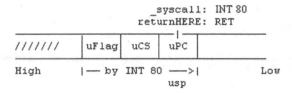

Fig. 5.3 Stack contents by INT 80

ustack in the uSS segment. It contains the saved uFlag, uCS, uPC at the top, where uPC points at the address of returnHERE in _syscall, as shown in Fig. 5.3.

Corresponding to INT n, the instruction IRET pops three items off the current stack into CPU's PC, CS, Flag registers, in that order. It is used by interrupt handlers to return to the original point of interruption.

LOAD: For the x86 CPU in 16-bit real mode, the lowest 1 KB area of physical memory is dedicated to 256 interrupt vectors. Each interrupt vector area contains a pair of (PC, CS), which points to the entry point of an interrupt handler. After saving uFlag, uCS and uPC of the interrupted point, the CPU turns off the T (trace) and I (Interrupt Mask) bits in the flag register to disable trace trap and mask out interrupts. Then it loads (PC, CS) with the contents of interrupt vector 80 as the new execution point. The interrupt vector 80 area must be initialized before executing INT 80, as shown below.

```
set_vector(80, (int)int80h);  // int80h() is _int80h: in ts.s file
int set_vector(int vector, int handler)
{
  put_word(handler, 0x0000, vector*4);    // KPC points to handler
  put_word(0x1000,  0x0000, vector*4+2);  // KCS segment=0x1000
}
```

5.3.2   System Call Interrupt Handler

After loading the vector 80 contents into (PC, CS) registers, the CPU executes int80h() in the code segment of the MTX kernel. int80h() is the entry point of INT 80 interrupt handler in assembly code, which is shown below.

```
HANDLER: INT80 interrupt handler
|=================================================================
|  int80h() is the entry point of INT 80 interrupts
|=================================================================
_int80h:
! (1). SAVE Umode registers into ustack, save uSS,uSP into running PROC
! Accordingly, we modify the PROC structure as follows.
!     typedef struct proc{
!        struct proc *next;
!        int    *ksp;
!        int     uss, usp;  // ADD uss, usp at byte offsets 4, 6
!        Other PROC fields are the same as before
!     } PROC;
!     int procSzie = sizeof(PROC): // a global used in assembly code
!     When a process enters Kmode, saves (uSS,uSP) to PROC.(uss,usp)
! (2). Set stack pointer sp to running PROC's kstack HIGH END
!      Then call handler function in C
! (3). RETURN to Umode
! Details of the steps (1) to (3) are shown below.
! ************** SAVE U mode registers ***************************
KSAVE:
        push ax  ! save all Umode registers into ustack
        push bx
        push cx
        push dx
        push bp
        push si
        push di
        push es
        push ds
! ustack contains: |uflag,uCS,uPC|ax,bx,cx,dx,bp,si,di,ues,uds|
!                                                          usp
! change DS to KDS in order to access data in Kernel space
        mov ax,cs      ! assume one-segment kernel, change DS to kDS
        mov ds,ax      ! let DS=CS = 0x1000 = kernel DS
USS = 4                ! offsets of uss, usp in PROC
USP = 6
! All variables are now offsets relative to DS=0x1000 of Kernel space
! Save running proc's Umode (uSS, uSP) into its PROC.(uss, usp)
        mov bx,_running ! bx points to running PROC in K space
        mov USS(bx),ss ! save uSS in proc.uss
        mov USP(bx),sp ! save uSP in proc.usp
! change ES,SS to Kernel segment 0x1000
        mov ax,ds      ! CPU must mov segments this way!
        mov es,ax
        mov ss,ax      ! SS is now KSS = 0x1000
! switch running proc's stack from U space to K space.
        mov sp,bx      ! sp points at running PROC
        add sp,procSize ! sp -> HIGH END of running's kstack
! We are now completely in K space, stack=running proc's EMPTY kstack
! **********   CALL handler function in C  *******************
        call_kcinth    ! call kcinth() in C;
! *************   RETURN TO Umode *************************
_goUmode:
        cli            ! mask out interrupts
        mov bx,_running ! bx -> running PROC
        mov ax,USS(bx)
        mov ss,ax      ! restore uSS
        mov sp,USP(bx) ! restore uSP
        pop ds
        pop es
        pop di
        pop si
        pop bp
        pop dx
        pop cx
        pop bx
        pop ax  ! NOTE: return value must be in AX in ustack
        iret
```

The C handler function, kcinth(), actually handles the syscall. When the C handler function finishes, the process returns to execute the assembly code _goUmode. It first restores the Umode stack from running PROC.(uss, usp). Then it restores the saved Umode registers, followed by IRET, causing the process to return to the interrupted point in Umode. Since _goUmode is a global symbol, a process in Kmode may call goUmode() directly to return to Umode.

5.3.3   Enter and Exit Kernel Mode

The assembly code _int80h and _goUmode are the keys to understanding transitions between Umode and Kmode. Logically, int80h() and goUmode() are similar to the SAVE and RESUME operations of tswitch() in Kmode. The following compares their similarity and differences.

```
tswitch() in Kmode:
{
   SAVE   : save CPU registers in kstack; save kSP in PROC;
   FIND   : // call scheduler() to find next running PROC;
   RESUME : restore kSP from running PROC and CPU regs from kstack;
   RET    : return to where it called tswitch() earlier;
}
int80h()
{
   1. save CPU registers in ustack;
   2. switch CPU from Umode to Kmode, save uSS and uSP in PROC;
      change stack to running PROC's EMPTY kstack;
   3. call handler function kcinth() in C;
}
// kernel may switch running to a different PROC before goUmode()
goUmode()
{
   1. restore Umode uSS and uSP from running PROC;
   2. restore saved CPU registers from ustack;
   3. iret back to Umode;
}
```

The major difference is 2 in int80h(), which changes the CPU's execution environment from Umode to Kmode and saves Umode's uSS and uSP in the running PROC. In most CPUs designed for Kmode and Umode operations, the switch is automatic. When such a CPU executes the syscall instruction (or accepts an interrupt), it automatically switches to Kmode and saves the interrupt context in Kmode stack. Since the x86 CPU in real mode does not have this capability, we have to coerce it to do the switch manually, which is both a curse and blessing. It's a curse because we have to do the extra work. It's a blessing because it allows the reader to better understand how CPU switches mode and execution environment. _int80h and _goUmode() are the entry and exit code of the syscall handler. Since syscall is just a special kind of interrupt, the same entry and exit code can also be used to handle other kinds of interrupts and exceptions. We shall show this later in Chaps. 8 and 9 when we discuss interrupt and exception processing.

5.3.4 System Call Handler Function in C

kcinth() is the syscall handler function in C. The parameters used in syscall(a,b,c,d) are in the process ustack, which contains the entries as shown in Fig. 5.4.

The Umode segment is saved in PROC.uss, and usp is saved in PROC.usp. Using the inter-segment copying functions, get_word()/put_word(), we can access the process ustack. For example, we can get the syscall number a (at index 13) by

int ka = get_word(running->uss, running->usp+2*13);

Similarly, we can get other syscall parameters from the ustack. Based on the call number a, we can route the syscall to a corresponding kernel function, passing parameters b, c, d to it as needed. The kernel function actually handles the syscall. As an example, assume that the syscall number 0 is to get the process pid. The call is routed to

int r = kgetpid(){ return running->pid;}

which simply returns the running process pid. Likewise, we can write to the ustack of a process to change its contents. In particular, we can change the saved uax (at index 8) as the return value to Umode by put_word(r, running->uss, running->usp+2*8);

5.3.5 Return to User Mode

Each kernel function returns a value back to Umode, except kexit(), which never returns, and kexec(), which returns to a different image if the operation succeeds. The return value is carried in the CPU's AX register. Since goUmode() pops the saved uax from ustack, we must fix up the saved uax with the desired return value before executing goUmode(). This can be done in the C handler function kcinth() before it returns to execute goUmode().

The above describes the control flow of syscalls. It shows the execution locus of a process when it issues a syscall to enter kernel, executes kernel functions and returns to Umode with a return value. Syscalls are the main mechanism in support

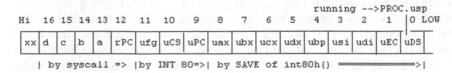

Fig. 5.4 Process system call stack contents

of kernel mode and user mode operations. Implementation of the syscall mechanism is a major step in the development of an OS kernel. In the following, we shall show how to implement syscalls in MTX. This should allow the reader to better understand the internal operations of an operating system kernel.

5.4   User Mode Programs

In order to issue syscalls, we need a Umode image file, which is a binary executable to be executed by a process in Umode.

5.4.1   Develop User Program Programs

The following shows a simple Umode program. As usual, it consists of a u.s file in BCC assembly and a ul.c file in C.

```
!================= u.s file of Umode image ====================
             .globl _main,_syscall,_exit,_getcs
start:       call _main
! if main() returns, syscall exit(0) to terminate in MTX kernel
             push #0              ! push exitValue 0
             call _exit           ! call exit(value) function in Umode
! int syscall(a,b,c,d) from C code
_syscall:    int 80
             ret
_getcs:      mov ax,cs            ! getcs() return CS segment register
             ret

/*********** ul.c file of Umode image ************************/

main()
{
    int pid = getpid();
    printf("I am proc %d in Umode: running segment=%x\n",pid,getcs());
    printf("Enter a key : "); getc();
    printf("proc %d syscall to kernel to die\n", pid);
    exit(0);
}
int getpid()                      // assume : getpid() call# = 0
{ return syscall(0, 0, 0, 0); }

int exit(int exitValue)           // assume : exit() call# = 6
{ syscall(6, exitValue, 0, 0); }
```

The u.s file is necessary because we can only issue syscalls by INT 80 in assembly. It also serves as the entry point of Umode programs. As will be seen shortly, when a Umode program begins execution, the CPU's segment registers are already set up by the kernel code and it already has a ustack. So upon entry, u.s simply calls main() in C.

A Umode program can only do general computations. Any operation not available in Umode must be done by syscalls to the OS kernel. For example, both get-pid() and exit() are syscalls. This is because a process can only get its pid from kernel space and it must terminate in kernel. Each syscall has an interface function, which issues an actual syscall to the kernel. For convenience, syscall interface functions are implemented in a single file, ucode.c, which is shared by all Umode programs. Usually, they are precompiled as part of the system linking library. Umode programs may call syscall interface functions, such as getpid(), exit(), etc. as ordinary function calls.

As of now, the MTX kernel does not yet have its own device drivers. All I/O operations in MTX are based on BIOS. I/O functions, such as getc(), putc(), gets(), printf(), are precompiled object code in a mtxlib library, which is used by both the MTX kernel and Umode programs. Therefore, getc() and putc() in Umode are also BIOS calls. Strictly speaking, Umode programs should not be able to do I/O directly. Basic Umode I/O, e.g. getc() and putc(), should also be syscalls. This is left as an exercise. As before, use BCC to generate a binary executable (with header, which is needed by the loader), as in

```
as86 -o u.o u.s
bcc  -c -ansi u1.c
ld86 -o u1 u.o u1.o mtxlib/usr/lib/bcc/libc.a
mount-o loop mtximage /mnt; cp u1 /mnt/bin; umount /mnt
```

The last command line copies u1 to /bin/u1 in a bootable MTX system image.

5.4.2 Program Loader

Executable a.out files generated by BCC have a 32-bit header containing 8 long values.

```
struct header{
  u32 ID_space: // 0x4100301:combined I&D|0x4200301:separate I&D
  u32 magic_number; // 0x00000020
  u32 tsize;        // code section size in bytes
  u32 dsize;        // initialized data section size in bytes
  u32 bsize;        // bss section size in bytes
  u32 zero;         // 0
  u32 total_size;   // total memory size, including heap
  u32 symbolTable_size; // only if symbol table is present
}
```

A loader is a program which loads a binary executable file into memory for execution. In a real OS kernel with file system support, the loader typically uses the kernel's internal open() function to open the image file for read. Then it uses the kernel's internal read() function to load the image file into memory. We shall show this later when we add file system support to the MTX kernel. In the meantime, we shall modify the MTX booter as a loader. In this case, the loader is almost the same as a booter, except that it is not a standalone program but a callable function in kernel. The loader's algorithm is

```
/********  Algorithm of MTX Loader *********/
int load(char *filename, u16 segment)
{
   1. find the inode of filename; return 0 if fails;
   2. read file header to get tsize, dsize and bsize;
   3. load [code|data] sections of filename to memory segment;
   4. clear bss section of loaded image to 0;
   5. return 1 for success;
}
```

5.5   Create Process with User Mode Image

In the MTX kernel, we modify kfork() to kfork(char *filename), which creates a new process and loads filename as its Umode image. The following show the modified kfork algorithm.

```
PROC *kfork(char *filename)
{
  (1). creat a child PROC ready to run from body()in Kmode
  (2). segment=(child pid + 1)*0x1000; //child Umode segment
       if (filename){
  (3).     load filename to child segment as its Umode image;
  (4).     set up child's ustack for it to return to Umode to execute
           the loaded image;
       }
  (5). return child PROC pointer;
}
```

In the modified kfork(), Step (1) is the same as before. The MTX kernel has 9 PROCs but only P1 to P8 may run in Umode. The Umode segment of each process is statically assigned in Step (2) as (pid + 1)*0x1000, so that each process runs in a unique Umode segment. In Step (3), it calls load("/bin/u1", segment), which loads /bin/u1 into the Umode segment of the new process and clears the bss section in the Umode image to 0. Step (4) is most crucial, so we shall explain it in detail.

5.6   Initialize Process User Mode Stack

Our objective here is to set up the ustack of a new process for it to return to Umode to execute the loaded image. To do this, we again think of each process as running in a perpetual cycle, as shown in Fig. 5.5.

```
Kmode : ┌─>  tswitch()  =>  X  => goUmode()
        │                (cut)            ║
    ────┴──────────────────────────────  ║─────────
Umode :syscall()  <= run in Umode  <═════╝
```

Fig. 5.5 Process execution cycle

In Fig. 5.5, a process in Umode does a syscall to enter Kmode, executes in Kmode until it calls tswitch() to give up CPU and stays in the readyQueue until it runs again. Then it executes goUmode() to return to Umode and repeats the cycle. We can make a cut in the process execution cycle and inject a condition for it to resume to Umode. The cut point is labeled X, just before the process executes goUmode(). In order to create a suitable condition for a process to goUmode(), we may ask the question: how did a process come to the cut point? The sequence of events must be as follows:

4. It did an INT 80 in Umode by

```
                    INT 80 ---------> _int80h: in Kmode
        returnHERE: ret
```

When the process first enters Kmode, its ustack contains

where the saved uPC points to returnHERE: in the Umode code section. Then it executes _int80h: to save CPU registers to its ustack, which becomes

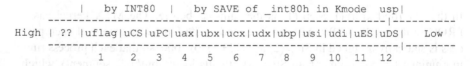

Then it saves the Umode segment in its PROC.uss and the stack pointer in PROC. usp. Our task here is to create a ustack for the newly created process to goUmode(). We shall fill in the ustack contents as if it was done by the process itself when it entered Kmode. After loading the Umode image to a segment, the ustack is at the high end of the segment. Although the process never existed before, we pretend that

The process executed INT 80 from the virtual address 0 in Umode, and that is where it shall return to when it goUmode(). Furthermore, before executing INT 80 its ustack was empty, the CPU segment registers CS, DS, ES, SS all pointed at its Umode segment and all other registers were 0's, except uflag, which should allow interrupts while in Umode. Therefore, the saved process context should be as shown in Fig. 5.6.

In Fig. 5.6, uflag = 0x0200 (I-bit = 1 to allow interrupts), uCS = uDs = uES = Umode segment, uPC = 0 (for virtual address 0) and all other "saved" registers are 0. In the process PROC, we set PROC.(uss, usp) = (Umode segment, −24). The reader may wonder why −24? In the ustack, the saved uDS is the 12th entry from the left. Its offset is −2 * 12 = −24 from the high end of ustack. In 16-bit binary, −24 is 1111111111101000 (in 2's-complement form) or 0xFFE8 in hex, which is exactly the offset address of the saved uDS in ustack. In other words, a virtual address in a segment can be expressed either as a positive offset from the low end or as a negative offset from the high end (64 KB = 0) of the segment.

5.7 Execution of User Mode Image

With the ustack contents as shown in Fig. 5.6, when the PROC becomes running and executes _goUmode, it would do the steps (R1) to (R3) shown in Fig. 5.6.

(R1): Restore CPU's (SS, SP) registers from (PROC.uss, PROC.usp). The stack is now the process ustack as shown in the figure.

(R2). Pop "saved" registers into CPU, which sets DS and ES to Umode segment.

(R3). Execute IRET, which pops the remaining 3 items off ustack into CPU's flag, CS, PC registers, causing the CPU to execute from (CS, PC) = (seg, 0), which is the beginning of the Umode image program.

When execution of the Umode image begins, the ustack is logically empty. As soon as execution starts, the ustack contents will change. As the process continues to execute, the ustack frames will grow and shrink as described in Chap. 2. Note that when control first enters the Umode image, the CPU's bp register is initially 0. Recall that bp is the stack frame pointer in function calls. This is why the Umode stack frame link list ends with a 0.

In the body() function, add a 'u' command, which calls goUmode() to let the running process return to Umode. Alternatively, we may modify kfork() by setting the resume point of every newly created process to goUmode(). In that case, a process would return to Umode immediately when it begins to run. The following lists the changes to the MTX5.0 system code.

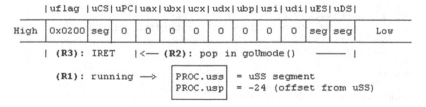

Fig. 5.6 Process context before goUmode()

5.8   MTX5.0: Demonstration of Simple System Calls

```
! ------------------- u.s file -----------------------------
          .globl _main,_syscall,_exit,_getcs
          call  _main
! if main() returns, call exit(0)
          push  #0
          call  _exit
_syscall: int   80
          ret
_getcs:   mov   ax,cs
          ret

/********* ucode.c file: syscall interface fucntions *******/
int getpid()              { return syscall(0,0,0,0);  }
int ps()                  { return syscall(1,0,0,0);  }
int chname(char *s)       { return syscall(2,s,0,0);  }
int kfork()               { return syscall(3,0,0,0);  }
int kswitch()             { return syscall(4,0,0,0);  }
int wait(int *status)     { return syscall(5,status,0,0); }
int exit(int exitValue)   {        syscall(6,exitValue,0,0); }
/************* common code of Umode programs **************/
char *cmd[]={"getpid","ps","chname","kfork","switch","wait","exit",0};
int show_menu()
{
    printf("***************** Menu ******************\n");
    printf("* ps  chname  kfork  switch  wait  exit *\n");
    printf("****************************************\n");
}
int find_cmd(char *name) // convert cmd to an index
{
    int i=0; char *p=cmd[0];
    while (p){
        if (!strcmp(p, name))
            return i;
        i++;
        p = cmd[i];
    }
    return -1;
}
/****************** Umode command functions *******************/
int ukfork() { kfork(); }
int uswitch(){ kswitch(); }
int uchname()
{ char s[32];
    printf("input new name : ");
    chname(gets(s)); // assume gets() return pointer to string
}
int uwait()
{   int child, status;
    child = wait(&status);
    printf("proc %d, dead child=%d\n", getpid(), child);
    if (child >= 0)  // only if has child
        printf("status=%d\n", status);
}
int uexit()
{ char s[16]; int exitValue
    printf("enter exitValue : ");
    exitValue = atoi(gets(s));
```

```
        exit(extiValue);
}
/*********************** u1.c file **************************/
#include "ucode.c"
main()
{
  char command[64];
  int pid, cmd, segment;
  while(1){
     pid = getpid();                // sycall to get process pid
     segment = getcs();             // getcs() return CS register
     printf("---------------------------------------------\n");
     printf("I am proc %d in U mode: segment=%x\n", pid, segment);
     show_menu();
     printf("Command ? "); gets(command);
     if (command[0]==0) continue;
     cmd = find_cmd(command);
     switch(cmd){
        case 0 : getpid();         break;
        case 1 : ps();             break;
        case 2 : uchname();        break;
        case 3 : ukfork();         break;
        case 4 : uswitch();        break;
        case 5 : uwait();          break;
        case 6 : uexit();          break;
        default: printf("Invalid command %s\n", command); break;
     }
  }
}
```

When a process executes u1 in Umode, it runs in a while(1) loop. After printing its
pid and segment, it displays a menu

```
******************* Menu *********************
*  ps   chname   kfork   switch   wait   exit *
**********************************************
```

Then it prompts for an input command. Each command invokes a user command
function, which calls a syscall interface function to issue a syscall to the MTX5.0
kernel. Each syscall is routed to a corresponding kernel function by the syscall
handler kcinth() in kernel, which is shown below.

```
/****** MTX5.0 syscall handler: ustack layout in syscall ************
 usp  1   2   3   4   5   6   7   8   9  10   11   12  13  14  15  16
--|-----------------------------------------------------------------
|uds|ues|udi|usi|ubp|udx|ucx|ubx|uax|upc|ucs|uflag|rPC| a | b | c | d |
------------------------------------------------------------------*/
#define AX  8
#define PA 13
int kcinth()
{
    u16 segment, offset; int a, b, c, d, r;
    segment = running->uss; offset = running->usp;
    /* get syscall parameters from ustack */
    a = get_word(segment, offset + 2*PA);
    b = get_word(segment, offset + 2*(PA+1);
    c = get_word(segment, offset + 2*(PA+2);
    d = get_word(segment, offset + 2*(PA+3));
    /* route syscall call to kernel functions by call# a */
    switch(a){
        case 0 : r = getpid();     break;
        case 1 : r = kps();        break;
        case 2 : r = kchname(b);   break;
        case 3 : r = kkfork();     break;
        case 4 : r = kswitch();    break;
        case 5 : r = kwait(b);     break;
        case 6 :     kexit(b);     break;
        default: printf("invalid syscall %d\n", a);
    }
    put_word(r, segment, offset + 2*AX); // return value in uax
}
```

If the number of syscalls is small, it suffices to use a switch table to route the syscalls. When the number of syscalls is large, it is better to use a branch table containing kernel function pointers. The following illustrates the function pointer table technique.

1. Define kernel function prototypes.

```
int kgetpid(),kps(),kchname(),kkfork(),kswitch(),kwait(),kexit();
```

2. Set up a table of function pointers, each index corresponds to a syscall number.

```
                    0      1       2        3        4       5       6
int (*f[ ])()={kgetpid, kps, kchname, kkfork, kswitch, kwait, kexit};
```

3. Call the kernel function by the call# a, passing parameters to the function as needed.

```
              int r = (*f[a])(b,c,d);
```

At this point, our purpose is to show the control flow of syscalls. Exactly what each syscall does is unimportant. The user commands are designed in such a way that the corresponding kernel functions either already exist or are very easy to implement. For example, kgetpid() returns the running process pid, kps() prints the status information of the PROCs, kkfork() calls kfork() to create a child process and returns its pid, kswitch() calls tswitch() to switch process, kwait() and kexit() already exist in the MTX kernel. The chname syscall is intended to show the different address spaces of Umode and Kmode. Each PROC has a char name[32] name field, which is initialized with the name of a heavenly body in the Solar system. The chname syscall changes the running PROC's name to a new string. Before fully understand the distinction between user and kernel mode address spaces, many students try to implement the change name function in kernel as

```
int kchname(char *newname)
{
  strcpy(running->name, newname);return 0 for SUCCESS;
}
```

To their dismay, it only changes the PROC's name to some unrecognizable garbage or, even worse, causes their kernel to crash. The reader is encouraged to figure out the reason and try to implement it correctly.

5.8.1   Validation of System Call Parameters

Besides illustrating the difference between user and kernel mode address spaces, the chname syscall is also intended to bring out another important point, namely the kernel must validate system call parameters. In the chname(char *newname) syscall, the parameter newname is a virtual address in user space. What if it is an invalid address? In the real mode MTX, this can not happen since an offset in a segment is always a valid virtual address. In systems with memory protection hardware, the kernel may generate an exception if it tries to access an invalid address. In addition, the chname syscall also has an implicit value parameter, the length of the newname string. In the MTX5.0 kernel, the name field of each PROC only has room for 32 chars. What if the user tries to pass in a newname string longer than 32 chars? If the kernel simply accepts the entire string, it may overflow the PROC's name field and write to some other areas in kernel space, causing the kernel to crash. Similarly, in some syscalls the kernel may write information to uses space. If the syscall address parameter is invalid, the kernel may generate a protection error or write to the wrong process image. For these reasons, the kernel must validate all syscall parameters before processing the syscall.

MTX5.0 demonstrates Umode to Kmode transitions and simple syscalls. Figure 5.7 shows the sample outputs of running MTX5.0 under QEMU. The reader may run the system to test other syscall commands.

```
proc 1  running: parent = 0   enter a char [s|f|w|q|u] : u

I am proc 1  in U mode: running segment=0x2000
******************* Menu *********************
* ps  chname  kfork  switch  wait  exit *
*********************************************
Command ? ps
=============================================
  name          status        pid       ppid

Sun             READY         0          0
Mercury         running       1          0
Venus           FREE
Earth           FREE
Mars            FREE
Jupiter         FREE
Saturn          FREE
Uranus          FREE
Neptune         FREE
---------------------------------------------

I am proc 1  in U mode: running segment=0x2000
******************* Menu *********************
* ps  chname  kfork  switch  wait  exit *
*********************************************
Command ?
```

Fig. 5.7 Sample outputs of MTX5.0

5.9   fork-exec in Unix/Linux

In Unix/Linux, the system call
$$int\ pid = fork();$$

creates a child process with a Umode image identical to that of the parent. If successful, fork() returns the child process pid. Otherwise, it returns −1. When the child process runs, it returns to its own Umode image and the returned pid is 0. This is the basis of the C code in user mode programs

```
int pid = fork(); // fork a child process
    if (pid){  // parent executes this part; }
    else    {  // child  executes this part; }
```

The code uses the returned pid to differentiate between the parent and child processes. Upon return from fork(), the child process usually uses the system call

$$int\ r = exec(char\ *filename);$$

to change image to that of a different program and return to Umode to execute the new image. If successful, exec() merely replaces the original Umode image with a new image. It is still the same process but with a different Umode image. This allows a process to execute different programs. In general, exec takes more parameters than a single filename. The extra parameters, known as command line parameters, are passed to the new image when execution starts. To begin with, we shall consider exec with only a filename first, and consider command line parameters later.

Fork and exec may be called the bread and butter of Unix because almost every operation in Unix depends on fork-exec. For example, when a user enters a command, the sh process forks a child process and waits for the child to terminate. The child process uses exec to change its image to the command file and executes the command. When the child process terminates, it wakes up the parent sh, which prompts for another command, etc. While Unix uses the fork-exec paradigm, which creates a process to execute a different program in two steps, there are alternative schemes. In the MVS [IBM MVS] operating system, the system call create(filename) creates a child process to execute filename in one step, and attach(filename) allows a process to execute a new file without destroying the original execution image. Variations to the fork-exec paradigm are listed in the Problem section as programming exercises. In the following, we shall implement fork and exec exactly the same as they are in Unix.

5.9.1 Implementation of fork in MTX

First, we outline the algorithm of fork. Then we explain the steps by a specific example.

```
/******************** Algorithm of fork ************************/
1. create a child proc ready to run in Kmode, retrun -1 if fails;
2. copy parent Umode image to child Umode segment;
3. oct child PROC.(uss, usp)=(child segment, parent PROC.usp);
4. fix up child's ustack to let it return to Umode image with 0;
5. return child pid
```

Assume that process P1 calls pid=fork() from Umode, as shown in Fig. 5.8.

In Fig. 5.8, the left-hand shows P1's Code and Data sections and the right-hand side shows changes to its ustack. When P1 executes fork(), it calls syscall(7,0,0,0) in assembly. The saved fPC on its ustack points to the return point in fork(). In _syscall, it executes INT 80 to enter the MTX kernel. In int80h(), it saves CPU registers in ustack and saves uSS=0x2000 and uSP into PROC[1].(uss, usp). Then, it calls kfork(0) to create a child process P2 in the segment 0x3000 but does not load any Umode image file. Instead, it copies the entire Umode image of P1 to the child segment. This makes the child's Umode image identical to that of the parent. Figure 5.9 shows the copied image of the child process.

Since PROC[2]'s Umode image is in the segment 0x3000, its saved uss must be set to 0x3000. Since usp is an offset relative to the PROC's segment, PROC[2]'s saved usp should be the same as that of the parent. However, if we let the child return to Umode as is, it would goUmode with the ustack contents as shown in Fig. 5.9, causing it to return to the segment 0x2000 since the copied **DS, ES, CS** in

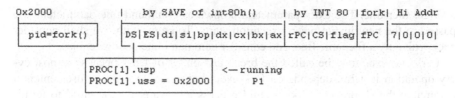

Fig. 5.8 fork() diagram of parent process

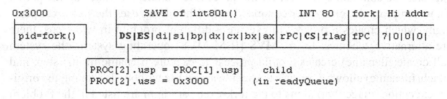

Fig. 5.9 Copied user mode image of child process

its ustack are all 0x2000. This would send P2 to execute in P1's segment also, like sending two fellows to the same bed. Interesting perhaps but not very good since the processes will interfere with each other. What we need is to send P2 back to its own bed (segment). So we must fix up P2's ustack before letting it goUmode. In order to let the child process return to its own segment, we must change the copied **DS**, **ES** and **CS** to child's segment 0x3000. All other entries in the copied image, such as rPC and fPC, do not need any change since they are offset values relative to a segment. To let the child return pid=0, simply change its saved uax to 0. With these modifications, the child will return to a Umode image identical to that of the parent but in its own segment 0x3000. Because of the copied rPC and fPC values, the child will return to the same place as does the parent, i.e. to the statement pid=fork(); as if it had called fork() before, except that the returned pid is 0. The C code of fork() in the MTX5.1 kernel is shown below.

```
/**************** fork()in MTX5.1 kernel ******************/
int copyImage(u16 pseg, u16 cseg, u16 size)
{  u16 i;
   for (i=0; i<size; i++)
       put_word(get_word(pseg, 2*i), cseg, 2*i);
}
int fork()
{ int pid; u16 segment;
  PROC *p = kfork(0);        // kfork() a child, do not load image file
  if (p==0) return -1;       // kfork failed
  segment = (p->pid+1)*0x1000; // child segment
  copyImage(running->uss, segment, 32*1024); // copy 32K words
  p->uss = segment;          // child's own segment
  p->usp = running->usp;     // same as parent's usp
  //*** change uDS, uES, uCS, AX in child's ustack ****
  put_word(segment, segment, p->usp);        // uDS=segment
  put_word(segment, segment, p->usp+2);      // uES=segment
  put_word(0,       segment, p->usp+2*8);    // uax=0
  put_word(segment, segment, p->usp+2*10);   // uCS=segment
  return p->pid;
}
```

5.9.2   Implementation of exec in MTX

The implementation of exec is also very simple. The algorithm of exec is

```
/***************** Algorithm of exec(filename) **************/
1. get filename from Umode space;
2. load filename to running proc's segment; return -1 if fails;
3. initialize proc's ustack for it to execute from VA=0 in Umode.
```

Note that exec() return − 1 if the operation fails. It does not return any value on success. In fact, it never returns. The reader is encouraged to figure out why? The C code of kexec() is shown below.

```
/******** kexec(filename) in MTX5.1 kernel ****************/
int kexec(char *y)    // y points at filenmae in Umode space
{
    int i, length = 0;
    char filename[64], *cp = filename;
    u16 segment = running->uss;    // same segment
    /* get filename from U space with a length limit of 64 */
    while( (*cp++ = get_byte(running->uss, y++)) && length++ < 64 );
    if (!load(filename, segment)); // load filename to segment
        return -1;        // if load failed, return -1 to Umode
    /* re-initialize process ustack for it return to VA=0 */
    for (i=1; i<=12; i++)
        put_word(0, segment, -2*i);
    running->usp = -24;                    // new usp = -24
    /* -1   -2 -3  -4 -5 -6 -7 -8 -9 -10 -11 -12  ustack layout */
    /* flag uCS uPC ax bx cx dx bp si  di uES uDS              */
    put_word(segment, segment, -2*12);    // saved uDS=segment
    put_word(segment, segment, -2*11);    // saved uES=segment
    put_word(segment, segment, -2*2);     // uCS=segment; uPC=0
    put_word(0x0200, segment, -2*1);      // Umode flag=0x0200
}
```

5.9.3   MTX5.1: Demonstration of fork-exec in MTX

To test fork and exec, we add the user commands fork, exec and the corresponding syscall interface functions to MTX5.1.

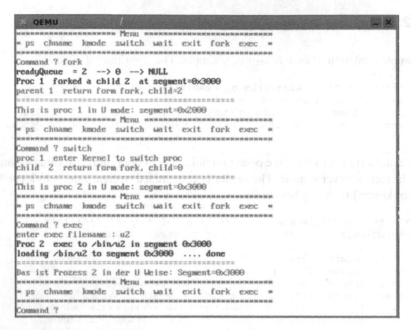

Fig. 5.10 Sample outputs of MTX5.1

```
int fork()        { return syscall(7,0,0,0); }
int exec(char *s){ return syscall(8,s,0,0); }
int ufork()       // user fork command
{   int child = fork();
    (child)? printf("parent ") : printf("child  ")
    printf("%d return form fork, child_pid=%d\n", getpid(), child);
}
int uexec()       // user exec command
{   int r; char filename[64];
    printf("enter exec filename : ");
    gets(filename);
    r = exec(filename);
    printf("exec failed\n");
}
```

In order to demonstrate exec, we need a different Umode image. The image file u2
is the same as u1 except that it displays in German. The reader may create other
Umode image files to speak different languages, just for fun. Figure 5.10 shows the
sample outputs of running MTX5.1.

5.10   Command Line Parameters

In Unix/Linux, when a user enter a command line="cmd a1 a2... an", sh forks a
child process to execute the cmd program, which can be written as

> main(int argc, char *argv[], char *env[ ])
> {
>   // argc, argv are passed to main() by exec()
> }

Upon entry to main(), argc=n+1, argv points to a null terminated array of string
pointers, each points to a parameter string, as shown in Fig. 5.11
    The env parameter points to a null terminated array containing environment string
pointers similar to argv. By convention, argv[0] is the program name and argv[1]
to argv[argc-1] are command line parameters to the program. In Unix/Linux, the
command line parameters are assembled in Umode before calling kexec() in kernel
via the syscall

> execve(char *cmd, char *argv[ ], char *env[ ]);

The Unix kernel passes argv and env to the new image. Because of the limited space
in the MTX kernel, we shall implement command line parameters in a different
way, but with the same end results. In MTX, the exec syscall takes the entire command line as parameter, i.e.

> int r = exec("cmd a1 a2 ... an");

We modify kexec() in kernel by using the first token, cmd, as the filename. After
loading the filename, we set up the ustack of the new Umode image as shown in
Fig. 5.12.

Fig. 5.11 Command-line
parameters

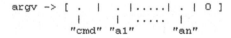

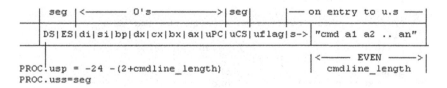

Fig. 5.12 Command line parameter in user mode stack

First, we pad the command line with an extra byte to make the total length even, if necessary. Next, we put the entire string into the high end of ustack and let s point at the string in ustack. Then we create a syscall interrupt stack frame for the process to goUmode, as shown in the left-hand side of Fig. 5.12. When execution begins in Umode, the ustack top contains s, which points to the command string in ustack. Accordingly, we modify u.s to call main0(), which parses the command line into string tokens and then calls main(int argc, char *argv[]). The algorithm of main0() is shown below.

```
main0(char *s) // *s is the original command line "cmd a1 a2 … an"
{
    tokenize *s into char *argv[ ] with argc = number of token strings;
    main(argc, argv);
}
```

5.11   Simple sh for Command Execution

With fork and exec, we can standardize the execution of user commands by a simple sh. First, we precompile main0.c as crt0.o and put it into the link library mtxlib as the C startup code of all MTX Umode programs. Then we write Umode programs in C as

```
/********** filename.c file ***************/
#include "ucode.c"  // user commands and syscall interface
main(int argc, char *argv[ ])
{   // C code of Umode program }
```

Then we implement a rudimentary sh for command execution as follows.

```
/******************** sh.c file **********************/
#include "ucode.c"  // user commands and syscall interface
main(int argc, char *argv[ ])
{
    int pid, status;
    while(1){
        display executable commands in /bin directory
        prompt for a command line cmdline = "cmd a1 a2 .... an"
        if (!strcmp(cmd,"exit"))
            exit(0);
        // fork a child process to execute the cmd line
        pid = fork();
        if (pid)                    // parent sh waits for child to die
            pid = wait(&status);
        else                        // child exec cmdline
            exec(cmdline);          // exec("cmd a1 a2 ... an");
    }
}
```

Then compile all Umode programs as binary executables in the /bin directory and run sh when the MTX starts. This can be improved further by changing P1's Umode image to an init.c file.

```
/******* init.c file : initial Umode image of P1 ********/
main( )
{
  int sh, pid, status;
  sh = fork();
  if (sh){                    // P1 runs in a while(1) loop
     while(1){
        pid = wait(&status); // wait for ANY child to die
        if (pid==sh){         // if sh died, fork another one
           sh = fork();
           continue;
        }
        printf("P1: I just buried an orphan %d\n", pid);
     }
  }
  else
     exec("sh");              // child of P1 runs sh
}
```

MTX5.2 demonstrates a simple sh for command execution. In MTX5.2, P1 is the INIT process, which executes the /bin/init file. It forks a child process P2 and waits for any ZOMBIE children. P2 exec to /bin/sh to become the sh process. The sh process runs in a while(1) loop, in which it displays a menu and asks for a command line to execute. All commands in the menu are user mode programs. When the user enters a command line of the form cmd parameter-list sh forks a child process to execute the command line and waits for the child process to terminate. The child process uses exec to execute the cmd file, passing parameter-list to the program. When the child process terminates, it wake up the sh process, which prompts for another command line. When the sh process itself terminates, the INIT process P1 forks another sh process, etc.

Eventually, we shall expand init.c to let P1 fork several login processes on different terminals for users to login. When a user login, the login process becomes the user process and executes sh. This would make the running environment of MTX identical to that of Unix/Linux. Figure 5.13 shows the sample outputs of MTX5.2

5.12   vfork

In a Unix-like system the usual behaviors of parent and child processes are as follows.

```
if (fork())              // parent fork() a child process
   wait(&status);        // parent waits for child to terminate
else
   exec(filename);       // child executes a new image file
```

```
 X  QEMU                                                              _ X
Proc 1  forked a child 2  at segment=0x3000
init waits
Proc 2  exec to /bin/sh in segment 0x3000
loading /bin/sh to segment 0x3000  .... done
sh 2  running
========= commands in /bin =========
newname ps fork exec u1 u2
===================================
enter command (cmd in /bin OR exit) : exec u1 test command line parameters
Parent sh 2  fork a child
readyQueue  = 3  --> 0  --> NULL
Proc 2  forked a child 3  at segment=0x4000
parent sh 2  waits
child  sh 3  running
Proc 3  exec to /bin/exec in segment 0x4000
loading /bin/exec to segment 0x4000  .... done
Proc 3  exec to /bin/u1 in segment 0x4000
loading /bin/u1 to segment 0x4000  .... done
enter main() : argc = 5
argv[0 ] = u1
argv[1 ] = test
argv[2 ] = command
argv[3 ] = line
argv[4 ] = parameters
=============================================
I am proc 3 in U mode: segment=0x4000
******************* Menu ***************************
* ps  chname  kmode  switch  wait  exit  fork  exec  *
***************************************************
Command ?
```

Fig. 5.13 Sample outputs of MTX5.2

After creating a child, the parent waits for the child to terminate. When the child
runs, it changes Umode image to a new file. In this case, copying image in fork()
would be a waste since the child process abandons the copied image immediately.
For this reason, most Unix systems support a vfork, which is similar to fork but
does not copy the parent image. Instead, the child process is created to share the
same image with the parent. When the child does exec, it only detaches itself from
the shared image without destroying it. If every child process behaves this way, the
scheme would work fine. But what if users do not obey this rule and allow the child
to modify the shared image? It would alter the shared image, causing problems to
both processes. To prevent this, the system must rely on memory protection. In systems with memory protection hardware, the shared image can be marked as read-
only so that a process can only execute the image but not modify it. If either process
tries to modify the shared image, the image must be split into separate images. So
far, MTX runs on Intel x86 machines in real mode, which does not have memory
protection mechanism. Despite this, we can implement vfork also, provided that the
child process only does exec without modifying the shared image.

5.12.1   Implementation of vfork in MTX

The algorithm of vfork is as follows.

```
/*************************** Algorithm of vfork ***********************************/
1. kfork(0) a child process ready to run in Kmode, return -1 if fails;
2. copy a section of parent's ustack from parent.usp all the way back
   to where it called pid = vfork(), as shown in Figure 5.14.
3. Let child PROC.uss = parent PROC.uss, so that they share the same
   segment, set child PROC.usp = parent PROC.usp-1024, change ax in
   child's goUmode frame to 0 for it to return 0 to pid=vfork();
4. return child pid;
```

Figure 5.14 illustrates Step 2 of the vfork algorithm.

In Fig. 5.14, the right-hand side shows the Umode stack frame of the parent process in a vfork() system call. The stack frame is copied to a low area in the parent's ustack as the Umode stack frame of the vforked child process, as shown on the left-hand side of the figure. When the parent returns, it executes goUmode() by the stack frame from parent.usp, and the returned value is child pid. When the child runs, it executes goUmode() by the stack frame from child.usp. The stack frames are identical, except for the return values. Therefore, the child also returns to pid=vfork() with a 0. When the child returns to Umode, it runs in the same image as the parent. Then it issues an exec syscall to change image. When it enters kexec(), the Umode segment is still that of the parent. The child can fetch the command line and then exec to its own segment. To support vfork, kexec() only needs a slight modification. If the caller is a vforked process, instead of the caller's current segment, it loads the new image to the caller's default segment (by pid), thereby detaching it from the parent image. The following shows the vfork code in the MTX5.3 kernel.

```
/**************** vfork() in MTX5.3 kernel ********************/
int vfork()
{
  int pid, i, w;   u16 segment;
  PROC *p = kfork(0);     // kfork() child, do not load image file
  if (p==0)
      return -1;          // kfork() failed
  p->vforked = 1;         // set vforked flag, used in kexec()
  /* copy a section of parent ustack for child to return to Umode */
  for (i=0; i<24; i++){   // 24 words is enough; > 24 should also work
      w = get_word(running->uss, running->usp+i*2);
      put_word(w, running->uss, running->usp-1024+i*2);
  }
  p->uss = running->uss;
  p->usp = running->usp - 1024;
  put_word(0,running->uss,p->usp+8*2);// set child's return value to 0
  p->kstack[SSIZE-1] = goUmode;       // child goUmode directly
  return p->pid;
}
```

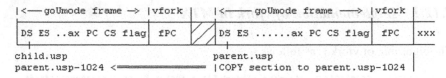

Fig. 5.14 goUmode stack frames in vfork()

5.12.2   MTX5.3: Demonstration of vfork in MTX

MTX5.3 demonstrates vfork in MTX. To do this, we add a uvfork syscall interface
and a user mode vfork command program.

```
/*************** User mode Program of vfork() *****************/
int uvfork(){return syscall(9,0,0,0);} // vfork() system call
int vfork(int argc, char *argv[ ])
{
  int pid, status;
  pid = uvfork();  // call uvfork() to vfork a child
  if (pid){
     printf("vfork parent %d waits\n", getpid());
     pid = wait(&status);
     printf("parent %d waited, dead child=%d\n", getpid(), pid);
  }
  else{ // vforked child process
     printf("vforked child %d in segment %x\n", getpid(), getcs());
     printf("This is Goldilocks playing in Papa bear's bed\n");
     printf("EXEC NOW! before he wakes up\n");
     exec("u2 Bye Bye! Papa Bear");
     printf("exec failed! Goldilocks in deep trouble\n");
     exit(1); // better die with dignity than mauled by a big bear
  }
}
```

When running the vfork command it will show that every vforked child process
begins execution in the same segment of the parent, like Goldilocks playing in Papa
bear's bed. If the child process exec to its own segment before the parent runs or
while the parent is sleeping in wait(), the Papa bear would never know Goldilocks
played in his bed before. Figure 5.15 shows the sample outputs of running the vfork
command in MTX5.3.

5.13   Threads

5.13.1   Principle of Threads

Threads are independent execution units in the same address space of a process.
In the process model, each process is an independent execution unit but each process has only one execution path. In the thread model, a process contains multiple

```
This is proc 1 in U mode: segment=0x2000
************************* Menu ****************************
* ps chname kmode switch wait exit fork exec vfork *
*********************************************************
Command ? vfork
vfork() in kernel Proc 1 forked a child 2  at segment=0x3000
fix ustack for child to return to Umode
vfork parent 1  waits
proc 1  enter Kernel to wait for a child to die
vforked child 2  in segment=0x2000
This is Goldilocks playing in Papa bear's bed
EXEC NOW! before he wakes up
Proc 2  exec to /bin/u2 in segment 0x3000
loading /bin/u2 to segment 0x3000  .... done
main0: s=u2 Bye Bye! Papa Bear
enter main : argc = 5
argv[0 ] = u2
argv[1 ] = Bye
argv[2 ] = Bye!
argv[3 ] = Papa
argv[4 ] = Bear
=============================================
Das ist Prozess 2 in der U Weise: Segment=0x3000
```

Fig. 5.15 Sample outputs of MTX5.3

threads, each of which is an independent execution unit. When creating a process it is created in a unique address space with a main thread. When a process begins to run, it runs the main thread of the process. With only a main thread, there is virtually no difference between a process and a thread. However, the main thread may create other threads. Each thread may create yet more threads, etc. All threads in a process execute in the same address space of the process but each thread is an independent execution unit. In addition to sharing a common address space, threads also share many other resources of a process, such as user id, opened file descriptors and signals, etc. A simple analogy is that a process is a house with a house master (the main thread). Threads are people living in the same house of a process. Each person in a house can carry on his/her daily activities independently, but they share some common facilities, such as the same mailbox, kitchen and bathroom, etc. Historically, most OS used to support their own proprietary threads. Currently, almost all OS support Pthreads, which is the threads standard of IEEE POSIX 1003.1c (POSIX 1995). For more information, the reader may consult numerous books (Buttlar et al. 1996) and on-line articles on Pthreads programming [Pthreads]. Threads have many advantages over processes.

5.13.2   Advantages of Threads

1. Thread creation and switching are faster
   In general, creating a thread is faster than creating a process since it does not need to allocate memory space for the thread image. Also, thread switching is faster than process switching. The context of a process is complex and large. The complexity stems mainly from the process image. For example, in a system

with virtual memory, a process image may be composed of many pages. During execution some of the pages are in memory while others are not. The OS kernel must use several page tables and many levels of hardware assistances to keep track of the pages of each process. Process switching involves replacing the complex paging environment of one process with that of another, which requires a lot of operations and time. In contrast, threads of a process share the same address space. Switching among threads in the same process is much simpler and faster because the OS kernel only needs to switch the execution points without changing the process image.

2. Threads are more responsive

A process has only a single execution path. When a process becomes blocked, the entire process execution stops. In contrast, when a thread is suspended, other threads in the same process can continue to execute. This allows a program with threads to be more responsive. For example, in a process with threads, while one thread is blocked for I/O, other threads can still do computations in the background. In a server with threads, the server can serve multiple clients concurrently.

3. Threads are better suited to parallel computing

The goal of parallel computing is to use multiple execution paths to solve problems faster. Algorithms based on the principle of divide and conquer, e.g. binary search and quicksort, etc. often exhibit a high degree of parallelism, which can be exploited by using parallel or concurrent executions to speed up the computation. Such algorithms often require the executions to share common data. In the process model, processes cannot share data efficiently because their address spaces are all distinct. To remedy this, processes must use Inter-Process Communication (IPC) or other means to include a common data area in their address spaces. In contrast, threads in the same process share all the (global) data in the same address space. Thus, writing programs for parallel executions using threads is simpler and more natural than using processes.

5.13.3   Threads Operations

The execution locus of a thread is similar to that a process, i.e. it can execute in either Umode or Kmode. In Umode, threads run in the same address space of a process but each has its own execution stack. As an independent execution unit, a thread can make syscalls to the OS kernel, subject to the kernel's scheduling policy, becomes suspended, and resumes to continue execution, etc. From the execution locus point of view, threads are just like processes. To take advantage of the share address space of threads, the kernel's scheduling policy may favor threads of the same process over those in different processes. As of now, almost all OS provide Pthreads compatible threads support, which includes

- thread creation and termination: thread_create(), thread_exit(), etc.
- threads synchronization: thread_join(), mutex, condition_variables, etc.

In the following, we shall discuss the implementation of threads in MTX.

5.14   Implementation of Threads in MTX

Ideally, a PROC structure should contain a process part and a thread part. The process part contains process information that is common to all threads in the process. The thread part contains information that is unique to each thread. Rather than drastically altering the PROC structure, we shall add a few new fields to the current PROC structure and use it for both processes and threads.

5.14.1   Thread PROC Structure

```
typedef struct proc{
      /* same as current PROC sturct but add new entries */
      int type;            // PROCESS|THREAD
      int tcount           // total number of threads in PROC
      struct proc *tlist;  // a list of all threads in PROC
      struct resouce *resourcePtr; // pointer to process "resource"
      int kstack[SSIZE]    // kstack[] must be the last entry
} PROC;
```

Add NTHREAD PROCs to the MTX kernel, as in

```
#define NPROC   9        // same as before
#define NTHREAD 16       // added PROCs for threads
PROC proc[NPROC+NTHREAD];
```

The first NPROC PROCs are for processes and the remaining ones are for threads. Free process PROCs are maintained in a freeList as before. Free thread PROCs are maintained in a separate tfreeList. When creating a process by fork/vfork we allocate a process PROC from freeList and the PROC type is PROCESS. When creating a thread we allocate a thread PROC from tfreeList and the PROC type is THREAD. When a process is created by fork/vfork, the process PROC is also the main thread of the new process. When creating a thread the new PROC is a thread in the same process of the caller. When a thread creates another thread, the usual parent-child relation applies. In MTX, P0 runs only in Kmode. All processes with Umode images, begin from P1. Thus, user processes form a process family-tree with P1 as the root. Similarly, threads in a process form a thread family-tree with the main thread as the root, as shown in Fig. 5.16.

In order to maintain the parent-child relation of processes, we require that P1 cannot die if there are other processes still existing. Similarly, the main thread of a process cannot die if there are other threads still existing in the process. From a thread PROC, we can always find the main thread PROC by following the parent PROC pointers. Therefore, there is no need to actually implement the thread family-tree in a process. In the main thread PROC, tcount records the total number of threads in the process. For thread PROCs, tcount is not used. In every PROC,

```
              ┌─P2=(main thread)                      ┌─thread_11
  P0──P1─┤                              ┌─thread_9─┤
              ├─P3=(main thread)─┤              └─thread_12
              │                                 └─thread_10
              └─P4=(main thread)
```

Fig. 5.16 Process and thread family tree

the resourcePtr points to a resource structure containing the per-process resources, such as uid, opened file descriptors and signals, etc. The per-process resource is allocated once only in the main thread. All other threads in a process point to the same resource. At this point, MTX processes do not have any resource yet, so the resource pointer field is not used until later. The added thread PROCs allow for an easy extension of MTX to support threads. For instance, the system falls back to the pure process model if NTHREAD = 0.

5.14.2   Threads Management Functions

Threads management in MTX includes the following functions

```
thread creation        : thread(int *fn, *stack, flag, *ptr);
thread termination     : texit(int exitValue);
thread join            : tjoin(int n);
thread synchronization : mutex_create(), mutex_destroy(),
                         mutex_lock(), mutex_unlock();
```

5.14.3   Thread Creation

Thread creation in MTX is similar to Linux's clone(). The thread creation function is

```
int kthread(int fn, int *stack, int flag, int *ptr)
{   // create a thread, where
    fn    = function entry address to be executed by the thread,
    stack = high end address of a ustack area,
    flag  = thread options; 0 or 1 to determine thread's ustack
    ptr   = pointer to a list of parameters for fn(ptr);
}
```

The function kthread() creates a thread to execute the function fn(ptr) with a ustack at the high end of the stack area. In Linux's clone() syscall, the flag parameter allows the thread to have many options, e.g. keep newly opened file descriptors private, etc. For simplicity reasons, we shall not support such options. Besides, our MTX processes do not have any resource yet anyway. So the flag parameter is

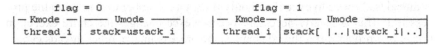

Fig. 5.17 Umode thread stack assignment

only used to determine the thread's ustack. When flag=0, the parameter stack is the high end of the thread's ustack. When flag=1, stack is the high end of a total ustack area. The ustack of each thread is a section of the total ustack area determined by its pid. This simplifies the ustack area management when threads are created and terminated dynamically. The ustack usage is shown in Fig. 5.17.

Due to the limited number of thread PROCs and the Umode address space size of each process (64 KB), we set TMAX <=NTHREAD=16 as the maximal number of threads in a process. The algorithm of thread creation is as follows.

```
              Algorithm of thread creation in MTX
------------------------------------------------------------------------
1. if process tcount > TMAX return -1 for error
2. allocate a free THREAD PROC and initialize it ready to run as before,
   i.e. initialize its kstack[ ] to resume to goUmode() directly.
3. determine its ustack high end, initialize the ustack for it return
   to execute fn(ptr) in the Umode image of the caller.
4. enter thread PROC into readyQueue, increment process t_count by 1;
5. return thread pid;
------------------------------------------------------------------------
```

Most of the steps are self-explanatory. We only explain step 3 in more detail. In order for a thread to return to Umode to execute fn(ptr), we pretend again that it had done an INT 80 from the virtual address fn. Therefore, its ustack must contain an INT80 stack frame for it to return to Umode. Furthermore, when execution begins from fn, it appears as if the thread had called fn with the parameter ptr. Accordingly, we set up its ustack to contain the contents as shown in Fig. 5.18.

In Fig. 5.18, DS=ES=CS=caller's segment, all "saved registers" are 0's, saved-PC=fn and flag=0x0200. When the thread executes goUmode(), it will return to (CS, fn) with the ustack top containing |3|ptr|, as if it had called fn(ptr) from the virtual address 3. At the virtual address 3 (in u.s) is a call to exit(0). When fn() finishes, it returns to the virtual address 3, causing the thread to terminate by exit(0). In addition, we also impose the following restrictions on threads.

4. When a process with threads does fork or vfork, it creates a new process with only the main thread, regardless of how many threads are in the caller's process.

Fig. 5.18 Thread Umode stack contents

5. A thread is allowed to exec if and only if the total number of threads in the process is 1. This is clearly necessary because exec changes the entire execution image of a process. If a thread changes the process image, other threads cannot survive. So we modify kexec() in the MTX kernel to enforce this rule, which effectively says that only the main thread with no child threads may change image.

5.14.4   Thread Termination

In the process model, when a process terminates, it sends all orphaned children to P1, which can not die if there are other processes still existing. Similarly, in the thread model, the main thread of a process can not die if there are other threads still existing in the process, for the following reasons. First, if the main thread dies first, the entire process address space would be freed. This would make the "house" of the remaining threads disappear, which is clearly unacceptable. Second, if the main thread dies first, the children threads would have no parent. If the dying main thread sends the orphaned children to P1, P1 cannot maintain the thread count of all the orphaned threads. If any of the surviving thread continues to create threads, P1 would not know what to do with this. So a dying thread should not send its orphans to P1 but to the main thread. This implies that the main thread cannot die if there are other threads in the process. In order for process with threads to terminate properly, we modify kexit() in the MTX kernel as follows, which can be used by both processes and threads to terminate.

```
kexit(int exitValue)
{
    if (caller is a THREAD){
        dec process t_count by 1;
        send all children, if any, to main thread of process;
    }
    else { // caller is a PROCESS)
        while (process t_count > 1)
            wait(&status);  // wait for all other threads to die
            /* caller is a process with only the main thread */
            send all children to P1;
    }
    record exitValue in PROC;
    become a ZOMBIE;
    wakeup parent;
    if (has sent children to P1) wakeup P1;
    tswitch();
}
```

5.14.5   Thread Join Operation

The thread join(thread_id) operation suspends a thread until the designated thread terminates. In general, a thread may join with any other thread. In practice, a thread usually joins with either a specific child or all of its children. To support the former, we may implement a wait4(chid_pid) function, which waits for a specific child process to die. This is left as an exercise. To support join with all children, the current kwait() function is sufficient, as in

```
join(int n)   // wait for n children threads to terminate
{
    int pid, status;
    while(n--)
        pid = wait(&status);
}
```

5.14.6   Threads Synchronization

Since threads execute in the same address space of a process, they share all the global variables in a process. When several threads try to modify the same shared variable or data structure, if the outcome depends on the execution order of the threads, it is called a race condition. In concurrent programming, race conditions must not exist. Otherwise, the results may be inconsistent. In order to prevent race conditions among threads, we implement mutex and mutex operations in MTX. A mutex is a data structure

```
struct mutex{
    int status;    // FREE|inUSE|LOCKED|UNLOCKED|etc.
    int owner;     // owner pid, only owner can unlock
    PROC *queue;   // waiting proc queue
}mutex[NMUTEX];   // all initialized as FREE
```

Define the following mutex operations

```
struct mutex *m = mutex_create(); // create a mutex, return pointer
mutex_lock(m)    : lock mutex m;
mutex_unlock(m) : unlock mutex
mutex_destroy(m): destroy mutex.
```

Threads use mutex as locks to protect shared data objects. A typical usage of mutex is as follows. A thread first calls m=mutex_create() to create a mutex, which is visible to all threads in the same process. A newly created mutex is in the unlocked state and without an owner. Each thread tries to access a shared data object by

mutex_lock(m);
    access shared data object;
mutex_unlokc(m);

When a thread executes mutex_lock(m), if the mutex is unlocked, it locks the mutex, becomes the owner and continues. Otherwise, it blocks and waits in the mutex (FIFO) queue. Only the thread which has acquired the mutex lock can access the shared data object. When the thread finishes with the shared data object, it calls mutex_unlock(m) to unlock the mutex. A locked mutex can only be unlocked by the current owner. When unlocking a mutex, if there are no waiting threads in the mutex queue, it unlocks the mutex and the mutex has no owner. Otherwise, it unblocks a waiting thread, which becomes the new owner and the mutex remains locked. When all the threads are finished, the mutex may be destroyed for possible reuse. Although the MTX kernel supports mutex operations, we shall discuss their implementations in Chap. 6 in the context of process synchronization.

5.14.7   Threads Scheduling

Since thread switching is simpler and faster than process switching, the kernel's scheduling policy may favor threads in the same process over threads in different processes. To illustrate this, we implement a user command, chpri, which changes the scheduling priority of a process and all the threads in the same process. Correspondingly, we implement kchpri() and reschedule() functions in the MTX kernel. Whenever a process changes priority, it also calls resehedule(), which reorders the readyQueue by the new priority. If a process has a higher priority than other processes, the kernel will always run a thread from that process until either there are no runnable threads in the process or its priority is changed to a lower value.

5.15   Concurrent Program Examples Using Threads

We demonstrate the threads capability of MTX by the following concurrent programs.

Example 1. Quicksort by threads: The qsort.c file implements quicksort of an array of 10 integers by threads. When the program starts, it runs as the main thread of a MTX process. The main thread calls qsort(&arg), with arg's lowerbound=0 and upperbound=arraySize-1. In qsort(), the thread picks a pivot element to divide the array range into two parts such that all elements in the left part are less than the pivot and all elements in the right part are greater than the pivot. Then it creates 2 children threads to sort each of the two parts, and waits for the children to die. Each child thread sorts its range by the same algorithm recursively. When all the children threads finish, the main thread resumes. It prints the sorted array and terminates. As is well known, the number of sorting steps of quicksort depends on the order of the unsorted data, which affects the number of threads needed in the qsort program. To test qsort on larger data arrays, the number of threads, NTHREAD, in type.h may have to be increased, but keep in mind that each thread PROC requires a kstack of SSIZE bytes and the MTX kernel space in real mode is only 64 KB.

Example 2. Compute sum of matrix elements by threads: The matrix.c program computes the sum of the elements in a matrix, int A[8][8], by threads. When the program starts, it runs as the main thread of a MTX process. The main thread creates $n<=8$ children threads, denoted by thread[n]. In the thread() call, we set the parameter flag=0 to show that the user program must manage the thread stacks. After creating the children threads, the main threads waits for all the children to terminate by tjoin(n). Each child thread[i] computes the sum of the i_th row of the matrix and deposits the partial sum into sum[i]. When the main thread resumes, it computes the total sum by adding all the partial sums.

Example 3. Race condition and threads synchronization: The race.c file is identical to matrix.c except that, instead of depositing each row sum into a distinct sum[i], all threads try to update the same total, as in

```
                 int total = 0;
 each thread :   compute row_sum;
                 read current total;
                 update total by total += row_sum;
 =======> utswitch()          // simulate interrupt
                 write total back;
```

Before writing the updated total back, we intentionally insert a utswitch() syscall to switch process. This creates race conditions among the threads. Each thread writes to the same total with its old value. The final total value depends on the execution order of the threads and the result is most likely incorrect. However, if we protect the updating code by a mutex lock, as in

```
 main thread : MUTEX *mutex = mutext_create();
 each thread : compute row sum;
               mutex_lock(mutex);
                 read current total;
                 current total += row sum;
 =======> utswitch()
                 write total back
               mutex_unlock(mutex);
```

Then there will be no race condition. This is because mutex_lock() allows only one thread to continue. Once a thread begins to update total, any other thread trying to do the same will be blocked by the mutex lock. When the thread that holds the mutex lock finishes, it releases the mutex lock, allowing another thread to do the updating. Since the threads update total one at a time, the final total value will be correct regardless of the execution order of the threads.

5.16   MTX5.4: Demonstration of Threads in MTX

MTX5.4 demonstrates threads in MTX. The concurrent programs using threads are qsort, matrix, race and norace.

Figure 5.19 shows the sample outputs of the concurrent matrix computation program using four threads. As the figure shows, all the threads execute in the same segment address of a process. The reader may also test other threads programs, especially race and norace, and compare their outputs.

Problems

1. Rewrite int80h() and goUmode() by using pusha and popa instructions to save and restore the CPU general registers. Then, show how to initialize the Umode stack when creating a process to run in Umode.
2. Rewrite int80h() in the assembly file to do the following:

   (1). Instead of saving Umode registers in ustack, save them in the process PROC structure.

```
 QEMU                                                          _ x
enter ? for help menu
kcsh # : matrix 4
Parent sh 2 fork a child  parent sh 2  waits
child   sh 6  running
proc 6  exec matrix
Number of threads = 4
proc 6  creates a thread using stack 0x1D24
readyQueue  = 17  --> 0  --> NULL
proc 6  created a thread 17  in segment=0x46A8  tcount=2
proc 6  creates a thread using stack 0x2124
readyQueue  = 17  --> 18  --> 0  --> NULL
proc 6  created a thread 18  in segment=0x46A8  tcount=3
proc 6  creates a thread using stack 0x2524
readyQueue  = 17  --> 18  --> 19  --> 0  --> NULL
proc 6  created a thread 19  in segment=0x46A8  tcount=4
proc 6  creates a thread using stack 0x2924
readyQueue  = 17  --> 18  --> 19  --> 20  --> 0  --> NULL
proc 6  created a thread 20  in segment=0x46A8  tcount=5
main thread 6  waits in thread_join()
thread 17  : row[0 ] sum = 28
thread 18  : row[1 ] sum = 36
thread 19  : row[2 ] sum = 44
thread 20  : row[3 ] sum = 52
main thread compute total = 160
kcsh # : █                                          04:29:09
```

Fig. 5.19 Sample outputs of MTX5.4

(2). Show the corresponding code for goUmode().

(3). Discuss the advantages and disadvantages of this scheme.

3. Redesign the syscall interface to pass syscall parameters in CPU registers

(1). Implement syscall (a,b,c,d) as_syscall:
! put syscall parameters a,b,c,d in CPU registers ax,bx,cx,dx, respectively,
then issue

$$INT\ 80$$
$$ret$$

(2). Re-write the syscall handler in C as int kcinth(int ka, int kb, int kc, int kd)
{...............}which receives a,b,c,d as parameters.

4. Assume: the syscall int get_name(char *myname) gets the running PROC's
name string and returns the length of the name string. Implement the get_
name() syscall and test it under MTX5.0.

5. On some CPUs designed for kernel-user mode operations, the CPU has two
separate stack pointers; a ksp in kernel mode and a usp in user mode. When an
interrupt occurs, the CPU enters kernel mode and pushes [SR,PC] of the interrupted point into kernel stack. Assume such a CPU. Show how to initialize the
kernel stack of a newly created process for it to begin execution from VA=0 in
user mode.

6. Assume: In MTX, P1 is a Casanova process, which hops, not from bed to bed,
but from segment to segment. Initially, P1 runs in the segment 0×2000. By a
hop(u16 segment) syscall, it enter kernel to change segment. When it returns to
Umode, it returns to an IDENTICAL Umode image but in a different segment,
e.g. 0×4000. Devise an algorithm for the hop() syscall, and implement it in
MTX to satisfy the lusts of Casanova processes.

7. When a Casanova process tries to change its Umode segment, the target segment may already be occupied by another process. If so, the original process
must be evicted to make room for the Casanova process. Devise a technique
that would allow the Casanova process to move into a segment without destroying the original process in that segment.

8. In a swapping OS, a process Umode image may be swapped out to a disk to
make room for another process. When a swapped out process is ready to run,
its image is swapped in by a swapping process again. In the MTX kernel, P0
can be designated as the swapping process. Design an algorithm to make MTX
a swapping OS.

9. What would happen if a process executing a.out issues another exec("a.out")?

$$main()\ \{exec("a.out");\ \}$$

10. Both Unix and MTX support the system calls fork(), exec() and wait(), each
returns -1 if the syscall fails. Assume that a.out is the binary executable of the
following program.

```
main(int argc, char *argv[ ])
{
    if (fork()==0)
A:    exec("a.out again");
    else
B:    wait(&argc);
}
```

(1). Start from a process, e.g. P2. After fork(), which process executes the state-
    ment A and what does it do? Which process executes the statement B and
    what does it do?
(2). Analyze the run-time behavior of this program. If you think it would cause
    MTX to crash, think carefully again.
(3). Run a.out under MTX and compare the results with your analysis

11. (1). Modify exec() as execv(char *filename, char *argv[]) as in Unix/Linux.
    (2). Assume: char *env="PATH=bin HOME=/" is an "environment string" in
        Umode. Modify exec() so that every Umode main() function can be written
        as

                    main(int argc, char *argv[ ], char *env[ ])

12. In IBM MVS, pid=create(filename, arg_list); creates a child process, which
    executes filename with arg_list as parameters in a single operation.
    (1). Design an algorithm for the create() operation.
    (2). Compare create() with fork()/exec() of Unix; discuss their advantages and
        disadvantages.

13. The MTX kernel developed in this chapter can only run 8 processes in user
    mode. This is because each process is assigned a unique 64 KB segment.
    Assume that each user mode image needs only 32 KB space to run. Modify the
    MTX kernel to support 16 user mode processes, each runs in a unique 32 KB
    memory area.

14. In MTX, the Umode images of all processes are different. Assume that Umode
    image files have separate I&D spaces. The code of an image file can be loaded
    to a code segment, and the data+stack can be in a separate segment. Different
    Umode processes may execute the same file by sharing the same Code seg-
    ment. Each process still has its own data+stack segment. Redesign the MTX
    kernel to allow processes to share "common code".

15. Pthreads programming: Implement the matrix operations and qsort using
    Pthreads of Linux.

16. Pthreads support a barrier-wait operation, which allows a set of threads to wait
    until a specified number of threads have called the wait() function of a barrier.
    Implement the barrier–wait operation in MTX.

References

Buttlar, D, Farrell, J, Nichols, B., "PThreads Programming, A POSIX Standard for Better Multi-processing", O'Reilly Media, 1996

Goldt, S, van der Meer, S., Burkett, S., Welsh, M. The Linux Programmer's Guide, Version 0.4. March 1995.

IBM MVS Programming Assembler Services Guide, Oz/OS V1R11.0, IBM, 2010

POSIX. 1 C, Threads extensions, IEEE Std 1003.1c, 1995

Pthreads: https://computing.llnl.gov/tutorials/pthreads, 2015

The Linux Man page Project: https://www.kernel.org/doc/man-pages, 2004

References

Chapter 6
Process Synchronization

An operating system consists of many concurrent processes and threads. Each process or thread may execute in two different modes. While in kernel mode, all processes and threads share the same address space of the OS kernel. While in user mode, each process executes in a unique address space but threads in a process share the same address space of the process. When concurrent processes or threads execute in the same address space, they may access and modify common data objects in the shared address space. Process synchronization refers to the mechanisms and rules used to ensure the integrity of shared data objects in a concurrent execution environment. The principle and technique are applicable to both processes and threads in an OS, as well as processes in concurrent programming systems, since their synchronization problem is essentially the same. In this chapter, we shall discuss process synchronization. First, we illustrate the need for process synchronization. Then we show how to implement synchronizing tools and use them for process synchronization. Then we discuss possible problems, such as deadlock and starvation, due to misuse of these tools and how to deal with such problems. Lastly, we show how to apply the principle of process synchronization to design and implement pipes and message passing in an OS kernel.

6.1 Concurrent Processes

Although this book is primarily about operating systems, we shall discuss process synchronization in the general model of concurrent processes. Figure 6.1 shows a system of concurrent processes. The system consists of n processes, denoted by P1 to Pn, which share some data objects in their address space, e.g. in the kernel space of an OS or in the same address space of threads. Each process runs on a virtual processor, denoted by VP1 to VPn. Several virtual processors may be mapped to a real CPU, denoted by CPU1 to CPUm, by multitasking on the CPUs. The CPUs access data objects in physical memory, denoted by x and $Y=(y, \dots ,z)$, which are in the shared address space of the processes. From a logical point of view, processes run concurrently, independent of the number of real CPUs. Similar to virtual processors,

© Springer International Publishing Switzerland 2015
K. C. Wang, *Design and Implementation of the MTX Operating System*,
DOI 10.1007/978-3-319-17575-1_6

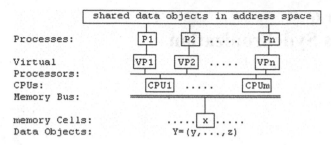

Fig. 6.1 Concurrent processes

which ultimately run on real CPUs, shared data objects ultimately reside in physical memory. When accessing shared data objects processes must be synchronized to ensure the integrity of the shared data objects.

6.2   Process Synchronization Problem

First, we illustrate the need for process synchronization by the following examples.

Example 1. Concurrent updates: Assume that int $x=0$ is in the address space of many processes, all of which try to update x by $x=x+1$. The update operation actually consists of three steps:

S1: read x from memory into CPU;

S2: increment x by 1 inside CPU;

S3: write x back to memory;

Assume that a process P1 has executed S1 but not yet S2 and S3. Meantime, another process P2 executes S1 also. P2 would read the old value of x, which is still 0. Then P1 executes S2 and S3, which change x to 1. Then P2 executes S2 and S3, which write 1 to x again. The value of x is still 1. Since both P1 and P2 have incremented x by 1, the value of x should be 2, not 1. So the result is incorrect. On the other hand, if either process completes the sequence of steps S1 to S3 before another process is allowed to do the same, the result will be correct regardless of the execution order of the processes. This is exactly the same kind of race condition in the concurrent program example in Chap. 5, in which threads update a shared variable in the same address space. To prevent race conditions, processes must execute the sequence of operations S1 to S3 one at a time. While a process executes S1 to S3, it must exclude all other processes from doing the same. This is known as the principle of Mutual Exclusion (ME), which is the foundation of all solutions to the process synchronization problem.

Example 2. Resource management: Assume that a resource is something which can be used by only one process at a time, e.g. a memory area for updating or a printer. In order to ensure the exclusive use of a resource, we may try to protect the resource as follows. Define a global status variable

```
int s = FREE if resource is available, BUSY otherwise;
```

Any process which needs the resource must check the status variable s, as in

```
check:
if (s == FREE){
    s = BUSY;                 // acquire the resource
        use the resource;
    s = FREE;                 // release the resource
}
else{                  // resource not available, what to do?
    option 1 : goto check; // keep trying
    option 2 : sleep(&s); goto check; // workable but must retry
    option 3 : block the process; when the process runs again,
               it is guaranteed to have the resource;
}
```

The above code segment may look good but it would not work in a concurrent
system. This is because several processes may arrive at the label check at the same
time. If so, all such processes would see s as FREE before any of them has changed
it to BUSY. Then all the processes would think they have got the resource. The
example shows that when we try to use a status variable to protect a resource, the
status variable itself needs protection. Thus, the mutual exclusion problem is recursive in the sense that the problem repeats itself. The recursion must stop some-
where. Otherwise, the problem would have no solution. As we shall see shortly, the
buck stops at the memory access hardware level. Next, assume that we can protect
the status variable s to make the above code work. What should a process do if it
finds s BUSY? The example lists three options. In option 1, the process repeatedly
checks the status variable until it succeeds. This is known as a spinlock, which is
viable in multiprocessor systems but not a good option in uniprocessor systems. In
option 2, the process goes to sleep to wait for the resource. When the process wakes
up, it must execute the check code again since the resource status may be changed
when it runs. So the process must retry, which means inefficiency. In the third option, the process blocks itself to wait for the resource. When a blocked process runs
again, it is guaranteed to have the resource so that it does not need to retry again.
Under normal conditions, option 3 would be the best. This shows that process synchronization can be achieved by using different kinds of tools. Such tools form a
hierarchy, ranging from simple spinlocks to very sophisticated mechanisms, all of
which depend on the principle of mutual exclusion. Figure 6.2 shows the hierarchy
of process synchronization tools.

   In the bottom part of Fig. 6.2, x and Y=(y, ... ,z) denote shared data objects in
memory. Above the memory box are mechanisms for process synchronization. The
mechanisms form a hierarchy. Each level includes more mechanisms with improved
functionality, all of which depend on the mechanisms at lower levels. At the lowest
level, disable CPU interrupts ensures only one process is running on a CPU. The
machine instructions TS and XCHG are for modifying memory locations as atomic
or indivisible operations. Above the level of atomic instructions are synchroniz-

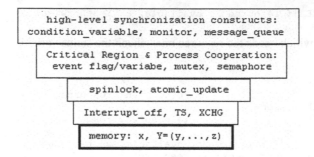

Fig. 6.2 Hierarchy of process synchronization tools

ing tools implemented in software. These include spinlocks and atomic updates for multiprocessor systems. At the next higher level are synchronization primitives, such as event flags, event variables, mutex and semaphores, etc. which are used for both process mutual exclusion and cooperation. At the highest level are synchronizing constructs, such as condition variables, monitors and message queues, etc. When accessing shared data objects concurrent processes rely on the various levels of mechanisms for synchronization.

6.3 Critical Region

A Critical Region (CR) or Critical Section (Silberschatz et al. 2009; Stallings 2011) is a sequence of operations on shared data objects by only one process at a time. Critical regions are intended to protect shared data objects, not code. Regardless of how we write the code, either as one piece or as separate pieces, they are parts of the same critical region if they access the same shared data objects. As a specific example, consider the following code segment:

```
            SHARED int s;
------------------------------
inc_s(int *s)|     dec_s(int *s)
{            |     {
  (*s)++;    |        (*s)
}            |     }
------------------------------
Processes: inc_s(&s); dec_s(&s);
```

Both inc_s() and dec_s() modify the shared variable s. The CR here is associated with the shared variable s, not the individual pieces of code that operate on s. If a process is already executing inc_s(), no other process is allowed to execute inc_s(), dec_s() or any other code that operate on s at the same time. This is very different from saying that each of the individual functions is a CR. Instead, it means that any code which operates on the shared variable s is part of the same CR associated with s. Critical regions realize the principle of process mutual exclusion, which is the basis of process synchronization. So the fundamental problem is how to implement critical regions.

6.4 Implementation of Critical Region

Assume that x is an addressable memory location, e.g. a byte or a word. In every computer system, read(x) and write(x) are atomic operations. No matter how many CPUs try to read or write the same x, even at the same time, the memory controller allows only one CPU to access x at a time. Once a CPU starts to read or write x, it completes the operation before any other CPU is allowed to access the same x. However, the individual atomicity of read and write does not guarantee that x can be updated correctly. This is because updating x requires read(x) and then write(x) in two steps. Between the two steps other CPUs may cut in, which either read the yet to be updated old value of x or write values to x that will be over-written. These are exactly the reasons of the race condition in Example 1. To remedy this, CPUs designed for multiprocessing usually support a Test-and-Set (TS) or equivalent instruction, which works as follows. Assume again that x is an addressable memory location and x=0 initially. The TS(x) instruction performs the following sequence of actions on x as a single indivisible (atomic) operation.

$$TS(x) = \{\text{read x from memory; test x for 0 or 1; write 1 to x}\}$$

No matter how many CPUs try to do TS(x), even at the same time, only one CPU can read x as 0, all others will read x as 1. On the Intel x86 CPU, the equivalent instruction is XCHG, which exchanges a CPU register with a memory location in a single indivisible operation. With the TS or equivalent instruction, we can implement a CR associated with x as follows Fig. 6.3.

On every CPU, process switching is usually triggered by interrupts. Step (1) disables CPU interrupts to prevent process switching. This ensures that each process keeps running on a CPU. At (2), the process loops until TS(x) gets a 0 value. Among the CPUs trying to execute TS(x), only one can get 0 to enter the CR. All

```
         byte x = 0        // x represents a CR
(1).   int_off;          // disable CPU interrupts
(2).   while (TS(x));    // busy wait until x==0, as a spinlock

(3).   |          CR          |

(4).   x = 0;            // write 0 to x; release the spinlock
(5).   int_on;           // enable CPU interrupts
```

Fig. 6.3 Implementation of basic CR

other CPUs will get the value 1 and continue to execute the while loop. Therefore, only one process can be inside the CR at any time. When the process finishes the CR, it sets x to 0, allowing another process to pass through (2) to enter the CR. At (5), the process enables CPU interrupts to allow process switching, but the process has already exited the CR.

The busy waiting loop at (2) is called a spinlock because the processes which get the value 1 keep on spinning while the gate is "locked". With only the TS or equivalent instruction, spinlocks are necessary to implement CRs. If process switching time is longer than the CR execution time, it would be better to wait for the CR rather than to block and switch process. Therefore, spinlocks are convenient to use in multiprocessor systems when the CR duration is short. For uniprocessor systems, spinlock is not necessary and can be omitted. The Intel x86 CPU uses a single I-bit in the flag register to disable/enable interrupts. Some CPUs use an interrupts priority in the status register to disable/enable interrupts selectively. In order to adapt the basic CR to different CPUs, int_off and int_on can be defined as

```
#define int_off   { int SR = lock(); }
#define int_on    { unlock(SR);      }
```

where lock() disables CPU interrupts and returns the original CPU status register, and unlock(SR) restores CPU's status register to its original value. On the Intel x86 CPU, lock() and unlock() can be implemented in assembly, which use CLI/ STI instructions to clear/set the I-bit in the CPU's flag register. To enable interrupts unconditionally, unlock() can be called with a 0 value. In addition to TS or XCHG, many CPUs also support updating memory locations as atomic instructions. In the Intel x86 CPU, XADD and several other instructions can be executed as atomic operations by a LOCK prefix, e.g. LOCK ADD x, ax, which atomically adds ax to x. However, these instructions can only protect memory contents of limited size, e.g. bytes, words, etc. To protect multiple data objects of arbitrary sizes, general CRs are needed.

6.5   Implementation of Process Synchronization Mechanisms

With the basic CR of Fig. 6.3, we can implement other mechanisms for process synchronization.

6.5.1   Sleep/Wakeup

As pointed out in Chap. 4, sleep/wakeup works only for UP kernels. In a UP kernel, only one process runs at a time. Process switch takes place only when the running process

.terminates,

.goes to sleep or becomes STOPPED or BLOCKed,

.has finished kernel mode execution and is about to return to user mode.

Otherwise, the current process just keeps on running. When a process executes sleep or wakeup in kernel, it cannot be interfered by other processes since no other process can run at the same time. However, interference may come from interrupt handlers. While a process executes, if an interrupt occurs and the CPU is ready to accept interrupts, the process is diverted to execute the interrupt handler, which may interfere with the process. To prevent this, it suffices to disable interrupts upon entry to sleep or wakeup, and enable interrupts when the execution finishes. Since sleep and wakeup may be called with interrupts disabled, they should restore CPU's original interrupt mask rather than always enable interrupts at the end. The proper implementation of sleep and wakeup is outlined below.

```
-------------------------------------------------------------------
sleep(int event)                    |   wakeup(int event)
{                                   |   {
 int_off;                           |    int_off;
 // same C code as in Chapter 4     |    // same C code as in Chapter 4
 int_on;                            |    int_on;
}                                   |   }
-------------------------------------------------------------------
```

Modifications of sleep/wakeup for multiprocessing systems will be shown later in Chap. 15 when we discuss SMP. It is also worth noting that an interrupt handler should never sleep or become blocked. We shall justify this in Chap. 8 on interrupts. Therefore, interrupt handlers may only call wakeup or other unblocking operations but should never call sleep or operations that may block the interrupted process.

6.5.2   Semaphore

A (counting) semaphore is a data structure

```
struct semaphore{
        byte lock;       // represents a CR; initial value = 0;
        int  value;      // initial value of semaphore
        PROC *queue;     // a FIFO queue of BLOCKed processes
}s;
```

In the semaphore structure, lock=0 represents the CR, value is the initial value of the semaphore and queue is a FIFO queue of processes blocked on the semaphore. All operations on a semaphore must be performed in the same CR of the semaphore's lock. In order to shorten the notations in the following discussions, we define

```
---------------------------------------------------------
enterCR(byte *lock)         |    exitCR(byte *lock)
{                           |    {
    int_off;                |        *lock = 0;
    while(TS(*lock));       |        int_on;
}                           |    }
---------------------------------------------------------
```

The most well-known operations on semaphores are P and V, which are defined as follows.

```
---------------------------------------------------------
P(struct sempahore *s)      |    V(struct semaphore *s)
{                           |    {
    enterCR(&s->lock);      |        enterCR(&s->lock);
    s->value--;             |        s->value++;
    if (s->value < 0)       |        if (s->value <= 0)
        BLOCK(s);           |            SIGNAL(s);
    else exitCR(&s->lock);  |        exitCR(&s->lock);
}                           |    }
---------------------------------------------------------
```

where BLOCK(s) blocks the process in the semaphore's FIFO queue, and SIGNAL(s) unblocks the first process from the semaphore's FIFO queue.

```
---------------------------------------------------------
BLOCK(struct semaphore *s)       |   SINGAL(struct semaphore *s)
{                                |   {
    running->status = BLOCK;     |       PROC *p;
    enqueue(&s->queue,running);  |       p = dequeue(&s->queue);
    s->lock = 0; // only for MP  |       p->status = READY;
    switch process;  int_on;     |       enqueue(&readyQueue, p);
}                                |   }
---------------------------------------------------------
```

For uniprocessor systems, s.lock is not needed and can be omitted, reducing enterCR() and exitCR() to int_off and int_on, respectively. The above shows the implementation of P and V operations in detail. The syntax assumes a programming language which passes parameters by value, such as C. For ease of discussion, we shall hide the implementation details and use the following short notations for P and V.

```
SEMAPHORE s = value; // s.value=value and s.queue=0
---------------------------------------------------------
P(s)                        |    V(s)
{                           |    {
    s--;                    |        s++;
    if (s<0) BLOCK(s);      |        if (s<=0) SIGNAL(s);
}                           |    }
---------------------------------------------------------
```

It is noted again that any operation on a semaphore must be implemented as a CR. Let us examine what would happen if this requirement is not met. Assume that s=0 and a process P1 has executed s-- in P(s) and is about to block itself in the semaphore queue. If another process P2 is allowed to do V(s) at this moment, P2 would execute s++, which would make P1's decision based on s<0 incorrect. Similarly, when P2 executes s++ and finds s=0, P2 would expect to SIGNAL a blocked process but the semaphore queue is empty. Thus, both P1 and P2 would end up in error due to race conditions to access the semaphore queue. On machines with atomic update instructions, e.g. XADD, we may even assume that both --s and ++s are atomic, but this still does not prevent the race condition.

6.5.3   Semaphore Operations for Multiprocessor Systems

Semaphore operations are not limited to P and V. We may define additional semaphore operations to suit the needs, provided that they operate in the CR of the semaphore. For multiprocessor systems, we define the following additional semaphore operations.

(1). Conditioanl_P (CP) and Conditonal_V (CV) operations:

```
----------------------------------------------------------
int CP(SEMAPHORE s)       |       int CV(SEMAPHORE s)
{                         |       {
   if (s>0){              |           if (s < 0 ){
      s--;                |              s++;   SIGNAL(s);
      return 1;           |           return 1;
   }                      |           }
   return 0;              |           return  0;
}                         |       }
----------------------------------------------------------
```

CP(s) operates exactly as P(s) and returns 1 if s>0. Otherwise, it returns 0 without changing the semaphore value. Likewise, CV(s) operates exactly as V(s) and returns 1 if s<0. Otherwise, it returns 0 without changing the semaphore value. CP can be used to avoid deadlocks in concurrent programs. CV can be used to simulate wakeup in a concurrent process environment.

(2). PV() operation: In a multiprocessor system, it is often necessary for a process to release one lock and wait for another lock. Using conventional P/V on semaphores may cause race conditions in the time gap after the process has done V on one semaphore but before it has completed P on another semaphore. In order to prevent race conditions, we define a PV(s1, s2) operation as follows.

```
PV(SEMAPHORE s1, SEMAPHORE s2){ atomically P(s1), V(s2) }
```

PV(s1,s2) allows a process to complete the blocking operation on semaphore s1 before releasing the semaphore s2 in a single indivisible operation. It eliminates the time gap between V(s2) and P(s1), thereby preventing any race condition. PV(s1,s2) requires a process to acquire the spinlock of s1 while holding the spinlock of s2.

We shall ensure that it is used in such a way that the locking order is always unidirectional, so that cross-locking can never occur. Usage of these semaphore operations will be shown later in Chap. 15 on SMP. Although we may define any new semaphore operations, we must ensure that the operations are meaningful and their usage is correct. For instance, we may define a VALUE(s) operation, which returns the current value of a semaphore. Many students often try to use such a function in concurrent programs, as in

```
(1)   int r = VALUE(SEMAPHORE s);
(2)   if (r>0){ // decision based on semaphore value > 0 }
      else    { // decision based on semaphore value <=0 }
```

Unfortunately, such a concurrent program is incorrect. This is because when we test the semaphore value at (2), the semaphore may already be changed by other processes. It can only be used in a system environment in which only one process runs at a time, e.g. in a uniprocessor kernel.

6.6   Applications of Semaphores

6.6.1   Semaphore Lock

A semaphore with an initial value=1 can be used as a lock for critical regions of long durations. Processes access the CR by using P/V on the semaphore as lock/unlock, as in

```
              SEMAPHORE s = 1;
   Processes:   P(s);
                // CR protected by lock semaphore s
              V(s);
```

With the semaphore lock, the reader may verify that only one process can be inside the CR at any time.

6.6.2   Mutex Lock

A mutex is a lock semaphore (initial value=1) with an additional owner field, which identifies the current process that holds the mutex lock. When a mutex is in the unlocked state, its ownership is 0 (no owner). When a process performs mutex_lock(s) on an unlocked mutex, it locks the mutex and becomes the owner. If the mutex is already locked, it waits in the mutex queue. A locked mutex can only be unlocked by its owner. Unlocking a mutex wakes up a waiting process, if any, which becomes the new owner and the mutex remains locked. If no process is waiting, the mutex becomes unlocked with no owner. Modifications to P and V for mutex operations are trivial. A major difference between mutex and semaphore is that processes must use mutex_lock() followed by mutex_unlock() in matched pairs, a process may do V on a semaphore without having done P on the semaphore. Thus, mutexes are strictly for locking, semaphores can be used for both locking and process cooperation.

6.6.3 Resource Management

A semaphore with initial value n>0 can be used to manage n identical resources. Each process tries to get a unique resource for exclusive use. This can be achieved as follows.

```
                    SEMAPHORE s = n;
        Processes:  P(s);
                        use a resource exclusively;
                    V(s);
```

As long as s>0 a process can succeed in P(s) and get a resource. When all the resources are in use, requesting processes will be blocked at P(s). When a resource is released by V(s), a blocked process, if any, will be allowed to continue to use a resource. At any time the following invariants hold.

```
    s >= 0 :  s   = the number of resources still available;
    s <  0 :  |s| = number of processes waiting in s queue
```

6.6.4 Wait for Interrupts and Messages

A semaphore with initial value 0 is often used to convert an external event, such as hardware interrupt, arrival of messages, etc. to unblock a process that is waiting for the event. As an example, assume that a process issues a disk I/O operation to start the disk hardware. It then waits for I/O completion by P(s=0). When the I/O operation completes, the interrupt handler issues V(s) to unblock the waiting process. Similarly, a process may use P(s=0) to wait for messages, etc.

6.6.5 Process Cooperation

6.6.5.1 Producer-Consumer Problem

A set of producer and consumer processes share a finite number of buffers. Each buffer contains a unique item at a time. Initially, all the buffers are empty. When a producer puts an item into an empty buffer, the buffer becomes full. When a con-

```
        DATA buf[N];                  /* N buffer cells  */
        int  head=tail=0;            /* index to buffer cells */
        SEMAPHORE empty = N; full = 0; pmutex = 1; cmutex = 1;
        ----------Producer: ----------|---------- Consumer: ----------
    while(1){                         |    while(1){
        produce an item;             |
        P(empty);                    |        P(full);
          P(pmutex);                 |          P(cmutex);
            buf[head++]  = item;     |            item = buf[tail++];
            head %= N;               |            tail %= N;
          V(pmutex);                 |          V(cmutex);
        V(full);                     |        V(empty);
    }                                |    {
```

Fig. 6.4 Producer-Consumer problem solution

sumer gets an item from a full buffer, that buffer becomes empty, etc. A producer must wait if there are no empty buffers. Similarly, a consumer must wait if there are no full buffers. Furthermore, waiting processes must be allowed to continue when their awaited events occur. Figure 6.4 shows a solution of the Producer-Consumer problem using semaphores.

In Fig. 6.4, processes use mutex semaphores to access the circular buffer as CRs. Producer and consumer processes cooperate with one another by the semaphores full and empty.

6.6.5.2   Reader-Writer Problem

A set of reader and writer processes share a common data object, e.g. a file. The requirements are: an active writer must exclude all others. However, readers should be able to read the data object concurrently if there is no active writer. Furthermore, both readers and writers should not wait indefinitely (starve). Figure 6.5 shows a solution of the Reader-Writer Problem using semaphores.

In Fig. 6.5, the semaphore rwsem enforces FIFO order of all incoming readers and writers, which prevents starvation. rsem is for readers to update the nreader variable in a CR. The first reader in a batch of readers locks the wsem to prevent any writer from writing while there are active readers. On the writer side, at most one writer can be either actively writing or waiting in wsem queue. In either case, new writers will be blocked in the rwsem queue. Assume that there is no writer blocked at rwsem. All new readers can pass through both P(rwsem) and P(rsem), allowing them to read the data concurrently. When the last reader finishes, it issues V(wsem) to allow any writer blocked at wsem to continue. When the writer finishes, it unlocks both wsem and rwsem. As soon as a writer waits at rwsem, all new comers will be blocked at rwsem also. This prevents readers from starving writers.

There are many other classical process synchronization problems which can be solved effectively by using semaphores. Most of these problems are of academic interests only, which are rarely, if ever, used in real operating systems. Interested readers may consult other OS books or online articles on the subject matter.

```
            SEMAPHORE  rwsem = 1,  wsem = 1,   rsem = 1;
            int nreader = 0  /* number of active Readers */
```

ReaderProcess	WriterProcess

`{`
`  while(1){`
`    P(rwsem);`
`    P(rsem);`
`      nreader++;`
`      if (nreader==1)`
`        P(wsem);`
`    V(rsem);`
`    V(rwsem);`
`      /* read data */`
`    P(rsem);`
`      nreader--;`
`      if (nreader==0)`
`        V(wsem);`
`    V(rsem);`
`  }`
`}`
	`{`
	`  while(1){`
	`    P(rwsem);`
	`    P(wsem);`
	`      /** write data **/`
	`    V(wsem);`
	`    V(rwsem);`
	`  }`
	`}`

Fig. 6.5 Reader-Writer problem solution

6.7   Other Synchronization Mechanisms

Many OS kernels use other mechanisms for process synchronization. These include

(1). Event Flags in OpenVMS (formerly VAX/VMS) [OpenVMS 2014]: In its simplest form, an event flag is a single bit, which is in the address spaces of many processes. Either by default or by explicit syscall, each event flag is associated with a specific set of processes. OpenVMS provides service functions for processes to manipulate their associated event flags by

```
set_event(b)   : set b to 1 and wakeup waiter(b) if any;
clear_event(b): clear b to 0;
test_event(b)  : test b for 0 or 1;
wait_event(b)  : wait until b is set;
```

Naturally, access to an event flag must be mutually exclusive. The differences between event flags and Unix events are:

A Unix event is just a value, which does not have a memory location to record the occurrence of the event. A process must sleep on an event first before another process tries to wake it up later. In contrast, each event flag is a dedicated bit, which can record the occurrence of an event. This implies that when using event flags the order of set_event and wait_event does not matter. Another difference is that Unix events are only available to processes in kernel mode, event flags in OpenVMS can also be used by processes in user mode.

Event flags in OpenVMS are in clusters of 32 bits each. A process may wait for a specific bit, any or all of the events in an event cluster. In Unix, a process can only sleep for a single event.

As in Unix, wakeup(e) in OpenVMS also wakes up all waiters on an event.

(2). Event variables in MVS: IBM's MVS [IBM MVS 2010] uses event variables for process synchronization. An event variable is a structure

```
struct event_variable{
        bit w;              // wait flag initial = 0
        bit p;              // post flag initial = 0
        struct proc *ptr;  // pointer to waiting PROC
} e1, e2,..., en;          // event variables
```

Each event variable e can be awaited by at most one process at a time. However, a process may wait for any number of event variables. When a process calls wait(e) to wait for an event, it does not wait if the event already occurred (post bit=1). Otherwise, it turns on the w bit and waits for the event. When an event occurs, another process uses post(e) to post the event by turning on the p bit. If the event's w bit is on, it unblocks the waiting process if all its awaited events have been posted.

(3). ENQ/DEQ in IBM MVS: In their simplest form, ENQ(resource) allows a process to acquire the exclusive control of a resource. The resource can be specified in a variety of ways, such as a memory area, the contents of a memory area, etc. The process blocks if the resource is unavailable. Otherwise, it gains the exclusive control of the resource until it is released by a DEQ(resource) operation. Like event variables, a process may call ENQ(r1,r2, ... rn) to wait for all or a subset of multiple resources.

6.8   High-level Synchronization Constructs

Although P/V on semaphores are powerful synchronization tools, their usage in concurrent programs is scattered. Any misuse of P/V may lead to problems, such as deadlocks. To remedy this, many high-level process synchronization mechanisms have been proposed.

6.8.1   Condition Variables in Pthreads

In Pthreads [Pthreads 2015], threads may use condition variables for synchronization. To use a condition variable, first create a mutex, m, for locking a CR containing shared variables, e.g. a counter. Then create a condition variable, con, associated with the mutex. When a thread wants to access the shared variable, it locks the mutex first. Then it checks the variable. If the counter value is not as expected, the thread may have to wait, as in

```
int count                        // shared variable of threads
pthread_mutex_lock(m);           // lock mutex first
 if (count is not as expected)
   pthread_cond_wait(con, m);  // wait in con and unlock mutex
pthread_mutex_unlock(m);         // unlock mutex
```

where pthread_cond_wait(con, m) blocks the calling thread on the condition variable, which automatically and atomically unlocks the mutex m. While a thread is blocked on the condition variable, another thread may use pthread_cond_ signal (con) to unblock a waiting thread, as in

```
pthread_lock(m);
   change the shared variable count;
   if (count reaches a certain value)
      pthread_cond_signal(con);
pthread_unlock(m);
```

When an unblocked thread runs, the mutex m is automatically and atomically locked, allowing the unblocked thread to resume in the CR of the mutex m. In addition, a thread may use pthread_cond_broadcast(con) to unblock all threads that are waiting for the same condition variable, which is similar to wakeup in Unix. Thus, mutex is strictly for locking, condition variables may be used for threads cooperation.

6.8.2   Monitors

A monitor (Hoare 1974) is an Abstract Data Type (ADT), which includes shared data objects and all the procedures that operate on the shared data objects. Like an ADT in object-oriented programming (OOP) languages, instead of scattered codes in different processes, all codes which operate on the shared data objects are encapsulated inside a monitor. Unlike an ADT in OOP, a monitor is a CR which allows only one process inside the monitor at a time. Processes can only access shared data objects of a monitor by MONITOR m.procedure(parameters) calls. The concurrent programming language compiler translates monitor procedure calls as entering the monitor CR, and provides run-time protection automatically. When a process finishes executing a monitor procedure, it exits the monitor, which automatically unlocks the monitor, allowing another process to enter the monitor. While executing inside a monitor, if a process becomes blocked, it automatically exits the monitor first. As usual, a blocked process will be eligible to enter the monitor again when it is SINGALed up by another process. Monitors are similar to condition variables but without an explicit mutex lock, which makes them somewhat more "abstract" than condition variables. The goal of monitor and other high-level synchronization constructs is to help users write "synchronization correct" concurrent programs. The idea is similar to that of using strong type-checking languages to help users write "syntactically correct programs". These high-level synchronizing tools are used mostly in concurrent programming but rarely used in real operating systems.

6.9   Deadlock

Semaphores are convenient and powerful tools for process synchronization. They are used in both OS kernels and user mode concurrent programming. For example, almost all multiprocessor OS kernels use semaphores. In System V Unix (Bach 1990), semaphores are the basic mechanism for Inter-process Communication (IPC). Although not native to Pthreads, most Pthreads implementations also support semaphore. As any other tools, improper usage of semaphores may lead to problems. The most well known problem is deadlock.

6.9.1   Deadlock Definition

First, consider the following concurrent program.

```
              SEMAPHORE s1=1,  s2=1;
    Process P1:                    Process P2:
    ------------------------------------------
       P(s1);              |          P(s2);
       P(s2);              |          P(s1);
    ------------------------------------------
```

In the program, P1 holds semaphore s1 and requests semaphore s2, which is already held by P2. While holding s2, P2 requests s1, which is already held by P1. In this case, P1 and P2 are in a deadlock because they mutually wait for each other, and neither one can proceed. Formally, deadlock is a condition in which a set of processes mutually wait for one another and none of the processes can continue.

6.9.2   Necessary Conditions for Deadlock (Coffman et al. 1971)

In order for deadlock to occur, the following conditions must be true.
  C1: mutual exclusion: only one process at a time.
  C2: no preemption: hang on to what you already got, never give them away.
  C3: partial allocation: greedy; already got something but want more.
  C4: circular waiting: processes wait for one another in circles.
  The most famous method to deal with deadlocks is the ostrich algorithm of Professor Tanenbaum (Tanenbaum and Woodhul 2006): "stick your head in the sand and pretend there is no problem at all". Of course, Professor Tanenbaum was only joking.

6.9.3 Deadlock Prevention

Similar to dealing with diseases, the best way to deal with deadlock is prevention. We may prevent deadlock by eliminating any of the above necessary conditions. However, not every such condition can be eliminated from a real system. For example, it is impossible to eliminate C1 and it may be too costly to eliminate C2. So the only viable options are C3 and C4. The opposite of C3 is Total Allocation, in which every process must obtain all the needed resources before it starts to run. With Total Allocation, it is obvious there can't be any deadlock. To defeat C4, we may rank the resources as R1, R2, ... , Rn, and enforce the following rule, which can be checked at run-time: Processes can only request resources in a unidirectional order. If a process has requested Ri, it can only request Rj for $j > i$, but not for $j <= i$. Using this scheme, it is easy to prove (by induction) that there cannot be any loop in the requests, hence no chance of deadlock.

6.9.4 Deadlock Avoidance

The basic principle of deadlock avoidance is as follows. For each resource request, pretend to grant the request and evaluate the resulting system state. If the state is SAFE, which means the system has at least one way to let all the processes run to completion, actually grant the request. Otherwise, deny the request. This is known as the Banker's algorithm (Dijkstra 1965). We illustrate the algorithm by an example. Assume that a system has 10 units of the same type of resources. Three processes, [P1, P2, P3], each declares a maximum number of resources needed as [m1, m2, m3] = [6, 5, 8], where each $mi <= 10$. The following table shows the initial state of the system.

```
       State:            S0
                 Max.    Has    Need
       =============================
       P1         6        0      6
       P2         5        0      5
       P3         8        0      8
       =============================
       Available: 10
```

The initial state S0 in clearly SAFE because we may choose any process and let it run to completion. Then choose another process and let it run to completion, etc. Assume that the system is in the state S1, as shown in the right-hand side of the following table.

```
State:           S0                    S1
        Max.  Has   Need          has   need
    ====================|------------
    P1    6    0     6   |    1      5
    P2    5    0     5   |    2      3
    P3    8    0     8   |    3      5
    ====================|------------
    Available: 10                   4
```

S1 is SAFE because we my let P2 run to completion first, and then let either P1 or P3 run to completion. While in the state S1, assume that P1 requests 3 additional resources. Should we grant the request? First, pretend to grant it. The resulting state is S2:

```
State:         S0              S1             S2
        Max.  Has   Need  |  has   need  |  Has   Need
    ====================|------------|-------------
    P1    6    0     6   |   1     5    |   4     2
    P2    5    0     5   |   2     3    |   2     3
    P3    8    0     8   |   3     5    |   3     5
    ====================------------------------------
    Available: 10                  4              1
```

The state S2 is UNSAFE because, with only 1 available resource, there is no way to let any of the processes run to completion. In this case, the request should be denied. Thus, the algorithm starts from a SAFE (initial) state and moves forward only if the next state is SAFE. The algorithm can be generalized to handle $n > 1$ resource types. In that case, each entry in the state table becomes a row vector of size n.

Despite its theoretical elegance, Banker's algorithm is impractical for the following reasons: First, in a real system, especially in an interactive system, it is impossible to know how many resources a process will ever need. Without this information, the algorithm can't even start. Second, for m processes and n resource types, the computational complexity of the algorithm is $m.n**2$. Since the algorithm must be invoked once for each resource request, it would incur too much system overhead, turning a rabbit into a snail (slower than a turtle!). Third, even in a safe state the system cannot run processes arbitrarily; it may have to run the processes in some specific order in order to maintain the safety of the system state, which complicates process scheduling. Finally, the algorithm is overly conservative. An UNSAFE state only has the potential of deadlock but may not lead to a deadlock. In the above example, even in the UNSAFE state S2, if either P2 or P3 releases one of its resources the system would become SAFE. Since we cannot predicate the process behavior, the algorithm simply assumes the worst case.

6.9.5 *Deadlock Detection and Recovery*

In this scheme, allow the system to run, with the possibility of deadlocks. Try to detect deadlocks when they occur. Then take remedial actions to break up the deadlock. Recall that a deadlock is a condition in which a set of processes is engaged in a circular waiting loop, which can only be broken up by the processes themselves in the set. In other words, every process involved in the circular waiting has no other way out. The "no other way out" condition is both necessary and sufficient for deadlock to occur. For example, A waits only for B, which waits only for A, is a deadlock. However, A waits only for B, which waits for A or C, may not be a deadlock because B may proceed via C. So circular waiting is only a necessary, but not sufficient, condition for deadlock to occur. A set of deadlocked processes may contain many circular waiting loops. Deadlock detection amounts to checking for such a condition among some of the processes. The problem can be formulated in terms of a resource allocation graph. Assume that the resources r1,r2,.rn are all distinct, and process can only wait for one resource at a time. Construct a directed graph G as follows:

1. Nodes = {r1,r2, ... ,rm, P1,P2, ... ,Pn};
2. Add an arc (ri, Pj) iff ri is allocated to (and held by) Pj.
3. Add an arc (Pj, rk) iff Pj is waiting for rk.

Then every closed loop in the graph G represents a deadlock. As an example, assume that
    P1 holds r1 and waits for r2; P2 holds r2 and waits for r3; P3 holds r3 and waits for r2. The corresponding graph G is

```
        r1 --> P1 --> r2 --> P2 --> r3 --> P3
                       |                     |
                       |<--------------------|
```

which shows that P2 and P3 are in a deadlock. The above technique can be extended to handle resources with multiple copies. In that case, a loop in the allocation graph only represents a possible deadlock. Once a deadlock is detected, the processes involved in the deadlock, as well as the resources that cause the deadlock, are also known. Recovery from deadlock can be done by aborting some of the processes involved in a deadlock, allowing others to proceed. Again, the technique is rarely used in real OS. In practice, a much simpler scheme is often used for deadlock detection. If there is no progress among a set of processes for an extended period of time, chances are that these processes are deadlocked.

6.10   Deadlock Prevention in Concurrent Programs

(1). Assume semaphores. Identify the critical regions as R1, R2, ... Rm, each protected by a semaphore lock. Try to design the algorithm in such a way that every
process requests the CRs in a unidirectional chain of P operations. The algorithm
will be free of deadlock since there is no waiting loop.

(2). If cross requests cannot be avoided, e.g. some process must do P(Ri); P(Rj); but
others must do P(Rj); P(Ri); in reverse order, then there are two options: combine Ri and Rj into a single CR, which reduces concurrency. If this is not permissible, use the following strategy. Whenever we detect a potential deadlock, try
to release some of the acquired semaphores in order to prevent deadlock, which
amounts to defeating the necessary condition C2. For example, we may use the
Conditional_P operation to prevent deadlock as follows.

```
Process P1: P(Ri); ....; P(Rj);
Process P2: P(Rj); ....; if (!CP(Ri)){V(Rj); retry the algorithm }
```

In the example, both P1 and P2 try to lock Ri and Rj, but in reverse order. Instead of
using P(s), which blocks a process if s is already locked, P2 uses CP on the second
semaphore Ri. If CP(Ri) fails, P2 unlocks Rj and retries the algorithm. As long as
one of the processes backs off, deadlock cannot occur.

6.11   Livelock

A set of processes mutually cause others to proceed but they all run in circles doing
nothing logically useful. From the process point of view, they are all running. From
the user point of view, they are all running but accomplish nothing. For instance, in
the above example of using CP, if both P1 and P2 back off when they fail to lock
a semaphore, it is possible that both processes may retry the algorithm forever. A
simple way to prevent livelock is to ensure only one of the processes backs off.

6.12   Starvation

Starvation is a condition in which a process waiting for resources may be blocked
indefinitely. For example, if the semaphore queue is a priority queue, then some
processes may wait in the queue forever or starve. A fundamental cause of starvation is unfair competition; some big bully always steps in front of you while you
wait in line. As in human society, there are many ways to ensure fairness. The simplest way is to enforce FIFO. With FIFO, there will be no big bullies and therefore
no starvation.

6.13 Process Synchronization in MTX

In MTX, we intentionally use a mixture of process synchronization tools, which are chosen to best suit the problem at hand. For process management, we use sleep/ wakeup because they are easy to understand and compatible with Unix. For resource management, we use semaphores because each V operation unblocks only one waiting process, which eliminates unnecessary process switching. In file system and device drivers, we also use semaphores because they simplify the transition from uniprocessor environment to SMP on multiprocessor systems.

6.14 Pipes

Pipes are unidirectional inter-process communication channels for processes to exchange data. A pipe has a read end and a write end. Data written to the write end of a pipe can be read from the read end of the pipe. Since their debut in the original Unix, pipes have been incorporated into almost all OS, with many variations. Some systems allow pipes to be bidirectional, in which data can be transmitted in both directions. Ordinary pipes are for related processes. Named pipes are FIFO communication channels between unrelated processes. Reading and writing pipes are usually synchronous and blocking. Some systems support non-blocking and asynchronous read/write operations on pipes. For the sake of simplicity, we shall consider a pipe as a finite-sized FIFO communication channel between a set of related processes. Reader and writer processes of a pipe are synchronized in the following manner. When a reader reads from a pipe, if the pipe has data, the reader reads as much as it needs (up to the pipe size) and returns the number of bytes read. If the pipe has no data but still has writers, the reader waits for data. When a writer writes data to a pipe, it wakes up the waiting readers, allowing them to continue. If the pipe has no data and also no writer, the reader returns 0. Since readers wait for data if the pipe still has writers, the 0 return value means only one thing, namely the pipe has no data and also no writer. In that case, the reader can stop reading from the pipe. When a writer writes to a pipe, if the pipe has room, it writes as much as it needs to or until the pipe is full, i.e. no more room. If the pipe has no room but still has readers, the writer waits for room. When a reader reads data from the pipe to create more rooms, it wakes up the waiting writers, allowing them to continue. However, if a pipe has no more readers, the writer must detect this as a broken pipe error and aborts.

6.14.1 Pipe Programming in Unix/Linux

In Unix/Linux, pipes are supported by a set of pipe related syscalls. The syscall pipe(int pd[2]) creates a pipe in kernel and returns two file descriptors in pd[2], where pd[0] is for reading from the pipe and pd[1] is for writing to the pipe. However, a pipe is not intended for a single process. For example, after creating a pipe, if the process tries to read even 1 byte from the pipe, it would never return from the read syscall. This is because when the process tries to read from the pipe, there is no data but the pipe has a writer, so it waits for data. But who is the writer? It's the process itself. So the process waits for itself, thereby locking itself out so to speak. Conversely, if the process tries to write more than the pipe size (4 KB in most cases), the process would again wait for itself when the pipe becomes full. Therefore, a process can only be either a reader or a writer on a pipe, but not both. The correct usage of pipe is as follows. After creating a pipe, the process forks a child process to share the pipe. During fork, the child inherits all the opened file descriptors of the parent. The user must designate one of the processes as a writer and the other one as a reader of the pipe. The order does not matter as long as each process is designated to play only a single role. Assume that the parent is chosen as the writer and the child as the reader. Each process must close its unwanted pipe descriptor, i.e. writer must close its pd[0] and reader must close its pd[1]. Then the parent can write to the pipe and the child can read from the pipe. The following diagram shows the system model of pipe operations.

```
-------------------------------------- Unix Kernel ----------------------------------------
 WriterProc                                                      ReaderProc
 fd[pd[1]] ---> writeOFT --> PIPE --> readOFT --> fd[pd[0]]
 ---- | --------------------------------------------------------| ---------
int n=write(pd[1],wbuf,nbytes) | int n=read(pd[0],rbuf,nbytes)
------- Writer process image --|----- Reader process image ------
```

On the left-hand side of the diagram, a writer process issues a write(pd[1], wbuf, nbytes) syscall to enter the OS kernel. It uses the file descriptor pd[1] to access the PIPE through the writeOFT. It executes write_pipe() to write data into the PIPE's buffer, waiting for room if necessary. On the right-hand side of the diagram, a reader process issues a read(pd[0],rbuf, nbytes) to enter the OS kernel. It uses the file descriptor pd[0] to access the PIPE through the readOFT. Then it executes read_pipe() to read data from the PIPE's buffer, waiting for data if necessary. The writer process may terminate first when it has no more data to write, in which case the reader may continue to read as long as the PIPE still has data. However, if the reader terminates first, the writer should see a broken pipe error and also terminate. Note that the broken pipe condition is not symmetrical. It is a condition of a communication channel in which there are writers but no reader. The converse is not a broken pipe since readers can still read as long as the pipe has data. The following program demonstrates pipes in Unix/Linux.

```
/********************** Unix Pipe Example ************************/
#include <stdio.h>
#include <stdlib.h>
#include <string.h>
int  pd[2], n, i;
char line[256], *s="data from pipe ";
main()
{
    pipe(pd);               // create a pipe
    if (fork()){            // fork a child as READER, parent as WRITER
        printf("parent %d close pd[0]\n", getpid());
        close(pd[0]);
        while(i++ < 10){ // parent writes to pipe t0 times
            printf("parent %d writing pipe : %s\n", getpid(), s);
            write(pd[1], s, strlen(s));
        }
        printf("parent %d exit\n", getpid());
        exit(0);
    }
    else{                   // child as pipe READER
        printf("child  %d close pd[1]\n", getpid());
        close(pd[1]);
        while(1){           // child read from pipe
            printf("child  %d reading from pipe\n", getpid());
            if ((n = read(pd[0], line, 256)) == 0)
                exit(0);
            line[n]=0; printf("%s  n=%d\n",line,  n);
        }
    }
}
```

The reader may run the program under Linux and observe its behavior. In the program, both the parent and child will terminate normally. The reader may modify the program to do the following experiments and observe the results.

(1). Let the parent be the reader and child be the writer.

(2). Let the writer write continuously and the reader only read a few times.

In the second case, the writer should terminate by a BROKEN_PIPE error.

6.14.2   Pipe and the Producer-Consumer Problem

In principle, pipes are similar to the producer-consumer problem, but there are differences. In the producer-consumer problem, processes run forever. They are synchronized beautifully as long as both producers and consumers exist. However, processes do not behave that way in the real world. For instance, what if all the consumers have died? Should the producers still deposit items to the shared buffer? If they do, it would be a waste of effort since there is no one to consume the items anymore. Worse yet, if the producers continue to deposit items, eventually all of them will be blocked when all the buffers are full, resulting in a degenerated form of deadlock. On the consumer side, what if all the producers have died? Should they still wait for items that will never come? If they do, they also will be blocked forever. In the idealistic producer-consumer problem, such real issues are completely ignored. The solution may be very elegant but has little practical value. However, if we amend the producer-consumer problem to handle the exceptional conditions, it could be a suitable model of pipes. Despite the strong similarity between pipes and the producer-consumer problem, in practice pipes usually do not use semaphores for synchronization, for the following reasons. First, semaphores are suitable for read/write data objects of the same size, e.g. a byte at a time, but not for a variable number of bytes. In contrast, writers and readers of a pipe do not have to write/read data of the same size. For example, writers may write lines but readers read chars, and vice versa. Second, the V operation on a semaphore unblocks at most one waiting process. Although rare, a pipe may have multiple writers and readers at both ends. When either side of a pipe changes the pipe status, it should unblock all waiting processes on the other side. In this case, sleep/wakeup are more suitable than P/V operations on semaphores.

6.14.3   Implementation of Pipes in MTX

This section describes the implementation of pipes in the MTX kernel. It also introduces the concepts of opened file descriptors and opened file instances.

(1). A process creates a pipe by the syscall pipe(pd[2]). The pipe() syscall allocates a PIPE object.

```
typedef struct pipe{
    char  buf[PSIZE];      // circular data buffer
    int   head, tail;      // circular buf index
    int   data, room;      // number of data & room in pipe
    int   nreader, nwriter; // number of readers, writers on pipe
}PIPE;
```

A PIPE object has a read end and a write end. Each end is represented by an Open File Table (OFT) object.

```
typedef struct oft{
    int mode;              // READ_PIPE|WRITE_PIPE
    int refCount;          // number of PROCs using this pipe end
    struct pipe *pipe_ptr; // pointer to the PIPE object
}OFT;
```

In an OFT, mode=READ_PIPE or WRITE_PIPE, which identifies the pipe end, refCount records the number processes at the pipe end, and pipe_ptr points to the PIPE object. From a process point of view, it can access a PIPE object if it has pointers to the PIPE's OFTs. Thus, we add a field OFT *fd[NFD] to every PROC structure. The fd[] array contains pointers to OFTs, which are opened file instances. Each index of the fd [] array is called a file descriptor. When a process opens a file, it uses a free entry in the fd[] array to point at the OFT of the opened file. When a process creates a pipe, it uses two fd entries, each points to an OFT of the PIPE object. Based on these, the pipe creation algorithm is as follows.

```
/*------ Algorithm of pipe creation: pipe(int pd[2]) ----------*/
1. Add a file descriptor array, fd[NFD], to every PROC structure:
   typedef struct proc{
       // same as before
       OFT  *fd[NFD];  // opened file descriptors; copy on fork()
       int kstack[SSIZE];
   }PROC;
2. Allocate a PIPE object. Initialize the PIPE object with
   head=tail=0; data=0; room=PSIZE; nreaders=nwriters=1;
3. Allocate 2 OFTs. Initialize the OFTs as
   readOFT.mode = READ_PIPE; writeOFT.mode = WRITE_PIPE;
   both OFT's refCount=1 and pipe_ptr points to the same PIPE object.
4. Allocate 2 free entries in the PROC.fd[] array,e.g.fd[i] and fd[j].
   Let fd[i] point to readOFT and fd[j] point to writeOFT.
5. write index i to pd[0] and index j to pd[1]; both are in Uspace.
6. return 0 for OK;
```

(2). After creating a pipe, the process must fork a child to share the pipe. Modify fork() to let the child process inherit all the opened file descriptors of the parent.

```
int fork()                       // same modifications to vfork():
{
    // same as before but Add copy opened file descriptors
    // assume PROC *p points at the child PROC
    for (int i=0; i<NFD; i++){
        if (running->fd[i]){       // copy only non-zero entries
            p->fd[i] = running->fd[i];
            p->fd[i]->refCount++; // inc OFT.refCount by 1
            if (p->fd[i]->mode == READ_PIPE)
                p->fd[i]->pipe_ptr->nreader++; // pipe.nreader++
            if (p->fd[i]->mode == WRITE_PIPE)
                p->fd[i]->pipe_ptr->nwriter++; // pipe.nwriter++
        }
    }
}
```

(3). After fork, both processes have 2 file descriptors; pd[0] for reading from the pipe and pd[1] for writing to the pipe. Since a process can only be either a reader or a writer but not both, each process must close an unwanted pipe end. The following shows the close_pipe algorithm.

```
/*---------------------- Algorithm of close_pipe : close(int fd) ----------------------*/
1.   Validate fd to make sure it's a valid opened file descriptor
2.   Follow PROC.fd[fd] to its OFT. Decrement OFT.refCount by 1;
3.   if (WRITE_PIPE){
         decrement nwriter by 1;
         if (nwriter==0){          // last writer on pipe
            if (nreader==0)
               deallocate PIPE;
            deallocate writeOFT;
         }
         wakeup(data);             // wakeup ALL blocked readers
     }
4.   else{ // READ_PIPE
         decrement nreader by 1;
         if (nreader==0){          // last reader on pipe
            if (nwriter==0)
               deallocate PIPE;
            deallocate readOFT;
         }
         wakeup(room);             // wakeup ALL blocked writers
     }
5.   Clear caller's fd[fd] to 0; return OK;
```

(4). Next, we show the read and write pipe algorithms.

```
/*---------- Algorithm of read_pipe  -------------*/
int read_pipe(int fd, char *buf, int n)
{   int r = 0;
    if (n<=0)
        return 0;
    validate fd; from fd, get OFT and pipe pointer p;
    while(n){
        while(data){
            read a byte form pipe to buf;
            n--; r++; data--; room++;
            if (n==0)
                break;
        }
        if (r){                     // has read some data
            wakeup(room);
            return r;
        }
        // pipe has no data
        if (nwriter){               // if pipe still has writer
            wakeup(room);           // wakeup ALL writers, if any.
            sleep(data);            // sleep for data
            continue;
        }
        // pipe has no writer and no data
        return 0;
    }
}


/*---------- Algorithm of write_pipe -------------*/
int write_pipe(int fd, char *buf, int n)
{   int r = 0;
    if (n<=0)
        return 0;
    validate fd; from fd, get OFT and pipe pointer p;
    while (n){
        if (!nreader)               // no more readers
            kexit(BROKEN_PIPE);     // BROKEN_PIPE error
        while(room){
            write a byte from buf to pipe;
            r++; data++; room--; n--;
            if (n==0)
                break;
        }
        wakeup(data);               // wakeup ALL readers, if any.
        if (n==0)
            return r;               // finished writing n bytes
        // still has data to write but pipe has no room
        sleep(room);                // sleep for room
    }
}
```

Note that when a process tries to read n bytes from a pipe, it may return less than n bytes. If the pipe has data, it reads either n or the number of available bytes in the pipe, whichever is smaller. It waits for data only if the pipe has no data but still has writers. If the pipe has no data and no writer, it returns 0. In that case, the process must stop reading from the pipe. Variations to the read algorithm will be discussed in the Problem section.

(5). When a process exits, it closes all opened file descriptors. So we modify kexit() in the MTX kernel to close opened pipe file descriptors.

To support pipe operations, we add pipe related syscalls to the MTX kernel.

```
case 30 : r = kpipe(b);            break;
case 31 : r = read_pipe(b,c,d);    break;
case 32 : r = write_pipe(b,c,d);   break;
case 33 : r = close_pipe(b);       break;
case 34 : r = pfd();               break;
```

where pfd() displays the opened pipe descriptors of the running process. Similarly, we also add pipe related syscall interface to the ucode.c file.

6.14.4   MTX6.pipe: Demonstration of Pipes in MTX

MTX6.pipe1 and MTX6.pipe2 demonstrate pipes in MTX. MTX6.pipe1 is for testing pipes manually. The reader may consult the README file for the testing commands. MTX6.pipe2 has a unixpipe command, which is the same Unix pipe program in Section 6.14.1. In the unixpipe program, the pipe writer terminates first, so all the processes terminate normally. The reader may modify the program to let the pipe reader process terminate first and observe its effect. In a pipe program, the parent process, which creates the pipe, normally does not wait for the child process to terminate. If the parent terminates first, the child would become an orphan. The reader may also observe what happens to such orphans. Figure 6.6 show the screen of running the unixpipe command of MTX6.pipe2.

6.15   Message Passing

Message passing allows processes to communicate with one another by exchanging messages. Message passing has a wide range of applications. In operating systems, it is a general form of Inter-Process Communication (IPC) (Accetta et al. 1986). In computer networks, it is the basis of server-client oriented programming. In distributed computing, it is used for parallel processes to exchange data and synchronization. In operating system design, it is the basis of so called microkernel, etc. In this

Fig. 6.6 Demonstration of pipe in MTX

section, we shall show the design and implementation of several message passing schemes using semaphores.

The goal of message passing is to allow processes to communicate by exchanging messages. Since processes have distinct (Umode) address spaces, they cannot access each other's memory area directly. Therefore, message passing must go through the kernel. The contents of a message can be designed to suit the needs of the communicating processes. For simplicity, we shall assume that message contents are text strings of finite length, e.g. 128 bytes. To accommodate the transfer of messages, we assume that the kernel has a finite set of message buffers, which are defined as

```
typedef struct mbuf{
      struct mbuf *next;      // pointer to next mbuf
      int pid;                // sender pid
      int priority;           // message priority
      char contents[128];     // message contents
}MBUF;   MBUF mbuf[NMBUF]; // NMBUF = number of mbufs
```

Initially, all message buffers are in a free mbufList. To send a message, a process must get a free mbuf first. After receiving a message, it releases the mbuf as free. Since the mbufList is accessed by many processes, it is a CR and must be protected. So we define a semaphore mlock=1 for processes to access the mbufList exclusively. The algorithm of get_mbuf() and put_mbuf() is

```
MBUF *get_mbuf()
{
    P(mlock);
      MBUF *mp = dequeue(mbuflList);
    V(mlock);
    return mp;
}
int put_mbuf(MBUF *mp)
{
    P(mlock);
      enqueue(mbufList)
    V(mlock);
}
```

Instead of a centralized message queue, we assume that each PROC has a private message queue, which contains mbufs delivered to, but not yet received by, the process. Initially, every PROC's mqueue is empty. The mqueue of each process is also CR because it is accessed by all the sender processes as well as the process itself. So we define a semaphore PROC.mlock=1 for protecting the process message queue.

6.15.1   Asynchronous Message Passing

In the asynchronous message passing scheme, both send and receive operations are non-blocking. If a process can not send or receive a message, it returns a failed status, in which case the process may retry the operation again later. Asynchronous communication is intended mainly for loosely-coupled systems, in which interprocess communication is infrequent, i.e. processes do not exchange messages on a planned or regular basis. For such systems, asynchronous message passing is more suitable due to its greater flexibility. The algorithms of asynchronous send-receive operations are as follows.

```
int a_send(char *msg, int pid) // send msg to target pid
{
  MBUF *mp;
  // validate target pid, e.g. proc[pid] must be a valid processs
  if (!(mp = get_mbuf()))      // try to get a free mbuf
      return -1;               // return -1 if no mbuf
  mp->pid = running->pid;      // running proc is the sender
  mp->priority = 1;        // assume SAME priority for all messages
  cpfu(msg, mp->contents);     // copy msg from Umode space to mbuf
  // deliver mbuf to target proc's message queue
  P(proc[pid].mlock);          // enter CR
    enter mp into PROC[pid].mqueue  by priority

  V(proc[pid].lock);           // exit CR
  V(proc[pid].message);    // V the target proc's messeage semaphore
  return 1;                    // return 1 for SUCCESS
}
int a_recv(char *msg)      // receive a msg from proc's own mqueue
{
  MBUF *mp;
  P(running->mlock);           // enter CR
  if (running->mqueue==0){     // check proc's mqueue
     V(running->mlock);        // release CR lock
     return -1;
  }
  mp = dequeue(running->mqueue); // remove first mbuf from mqueue
  V(running->mlock);           // release mlock
  cp2u(mp->contents, msg);     // copy contents to msg in Umode
  put_mbuf(mp);                // release mbuf as free
  return 1;
}
```

The above algorithms work under normal conditions. However, if all processes only send but never receive, or a malicious process repeatedly sends messages, the system may run out of free message buffers. When that happens, the message facility would come to a halt since no process can send anymore. One good thing about the asynchronous protocol is that there cannot be any deadlocks because it is non-blocking.

6.15.2 Synchronous Message Passing

In the synchronous message passing scheme, both send and receive operations are blocking. A sending process must "wait" if there is no free mbuf. Similarly, a receiving process must "wait" if there is no message in its message queue. In general, synchronous communication is more efficient than asynchronous communication. It is well suited to tightly-coupled systems in which processes exchange messages on a planned or regular basis. In such a system, processes can expect messages to come when they are needed, and the usage of message buffers is carefully planned. Therefore, processes can wait for messages or free message buffers rather than relying on retries. To support synchronous message passing, we define additional semaphores for process synchronization and redesign the send-receive algorithm as follows.

```
SEMAPHORE nmbuf = NMBUF; // number of free mbufs
SEMAPHORE PROC.nmsg = 0; // for proc to wait for messages

MBUF *get_mbuf()           // return a free mbuf pointer
{
    P(nmbuf);              // wait for free mbuf
    P(mlock);
      MBUF *mp = dequeue(mbufList)
    V(mlock);
    return mp;
}
int put_mbuf(MBUF *mp)    // free a used mbuf to freembuflist
{
    P(mlock);
      enqueue(mbufList, mp);
    V(mlock);
    V(nmbuf);
}

int s_send(char *msg, int pid)// synchronous send msg to target pid
{
    // validate target pid, e.g. proc[pid] must be a valid processs
    MBUF *mp = get_mbuf();     // BLOCKing: return mp must be valid
    mp->pid = running->pid;   // running proc is the sender
    cpfu(msg, mp->contents);  // copy msg from Umode space to mbuf
    // deliver msg to target proc's mqueue
    P(proc[pid].mlock);       // enter CR
      enqueue(proc[pid].mqueue, mp);
    V(proc[pid].lock);        // exit CR
    V(proc[pid].nmsg);        // V the target proc's nmsg semaphore
}

int s_recv(char *msg) // synchronous receive from proc's own mqueue
{
    P(running->nmsg);         // wait for message
    P(running->mlock);        // lock PROC.mqueue
      MBUF *mp = dequeue(running->mqueue); // get a message
    V(running->mlock);        // release mlock
    cp2u(mp->contents, msg);  // copy contents to Umode
    put_mbuf(mp);             // free mbuf
}
```

6.15.3   MTX6.message1: Demonstration of Synchronous Message Passing

The sample system MTX6.message1 demonstrates synchronous message passing. When the system starts, the menu includes the send and recv commands. The reader may test the message passing functions as follows. First, fork a few processes. Then run the send and recv commands. If a process has no pending message, attempting to recv would block the process and switch process automatically. Otherwise, use the switch command to switch process.

The above s_send/s_recv algorithm is correct in terms of process synchronization, but there are other problems. Whenever a blocking protocol is used, there are chances of deadlock. Indeed, the s_send/s_recv algorithm may lead to the following deadlock conditions.

(1). If processes only send but do not receive, all processes would eventually be blocked at P(nmbuf) when there are no more free mbufs.

(2). If no process sends but all try to receive, every process would be blocked at its own nmsg semaphore.

(3). A process Pi sends a message to another process Pj and waits for a reply from Pj. Pj does exactly the opposite. Then Pi and Pj would mutually wait for each other, which is the familiar cross-locked deadlock.

How to deal with these problems? For (1), we may use a quota to limit the number of messages each process is allowed to send, e.g. QUOTA=NMBUF/NPROC. In get_mbuf(), if a process' quota is 0, return −1 for failure. Otherwise, we decrement its quota by 1. In put_mbuf(), we increment the process' quota by 1, etc. But this would change the s_send operation from synchronous to asynchronous. For (2), we may try to apply the principles of deadlock handling. The first approach is deadlock prevention, which does not seem possible since we do not know the (future) behavior of processes. The second approach is deadlock avoidance, which can be implemented as follows. Define nwait as the number of processes waiting for messages. In s_recv(), if nwait=NPROC-1, the state is unsafe and the process must not wait. Like (1), this would change s_recv to asynchronous also. Lastly, it is easy to implement deadlock detection and recovery by simply checking whether nwait=NPROC. If so, send a dummy message to every blocked process to let it continue. The reader may wonder if all processes are blocked, who will do the deadlock detection and recovery? The answer is based on the old story of how "the cat taught the tiger"; the cat taught the tiger all the skills except one, which saved the cat's life. In most OS kernels, there is usually a process which is always ready to run but has the lowest priority. In MTX, it is the process P0. When all other processes become blocked and non-runnable, the lowest priority process resumes. So there is always a cat alive. For (3), there is no direct solution. In fact, s_send/s_recv can be used to replace V/P on semaphores. When a process waits for an event, it uses s_recv to wait for a message. When the awaited event occurs, another process uses s_send to send a message to unblock it. Like semaphores, misuse of s_send/s_recv may also lead to deadlocks.

It is worth noting that the s_send/s_recv algorithm is similar to the Producer-Consumer algorithm. Whereas there is no deadlock in the Producer-Consumer algorithm, deadlock is possible in the s_send/s_recv algorithm. The underline reason is that in the Producer-Consumer algorithm, each process plays only one role; either as a producer or as a consumer, but not both. In the s_send_s_recv algorithm, a process can be both a sender and receiver, thus the complication. If we restrict the roles of the processes, deadlock may not occur. This leads us to the Server-Client communication model.

6.15.4   Server-Client Message Passing

In a simple server-client communication system, there are two kinds of processes; servers and clients. Clients can only communicate with servers and servers can only communicate with clients. Each client has either a guaranteed or dedicated message buffer. After sending a request to a server, a client immediately waits for a reply since there is nothing else the client can do. Upon receiving a client request, a server handles the request, which may require some time delay, but it eventually sends a reply to the client. With these restrictions, there is no deadlock. To prove this, it suffices to show the following.

(1). Waiting loops among clients or servers cannot exist.
(2). Since each client has a message buffer, send() is non-blocking. A server blocked in recv() will be unblocked by a client request. Similarly, a client blocked in recv() will be unblocked by a server reply.

6.15.5   Multi-level Server-Client Message Passing

The simple server-client model can be extended to handle multiple levels of clients and servers. In a multi-level server-client system, processes are divided into levels, from 1 to N, where 1 is the lowest and N is the highest level. Every process at level-1 is a client, which can only send a request and immediately waits for a reply. Every process at level-N is a server, which can only receive a request, handle it and send a reply to the client. A process at level i, ($1 < i < N$), can be both a server and a client, which obeys the following rules.

(1). As a server, it may receive requests from clients at lower levels. For every received request, it should complete the requested service and send a reply to the client as soon as possible. If it has to defer the processing of a request, it must be due to a lack of resource, which can only be obtained from a higher level server. For each deferred request, it must send a request to a higher level server and is expecting a reply in order to receive again. Otherwise, a server may keep receiving client requests but never process them, which logically do not make sense. For any deferred request, it must eventually complete the requested service and send a reply to the client.
(2). As a client, it may send requests to higher level servers. However, it sends such requests only if it has un-replied requests of its own. Thus, the number of requests sent can never be greater than the number of un-replied requests.

Let L be the number of levels and N1 be the number of processes in level-1. In a multi-level server-client message passing system, if the number of message buffers is NMBUF>=(L-1)*N1, then there is no deadlock. To prove this, it suffices to show the following:

(1). All requests originate from processes in level-1. When replying to a request a server does not need a new buffer because it can use the same buffer of the

States	send(): reply request		recv(): reply request	
(0, 0)	NO	— —	request: —	(0,1)
(0, 1)	YES:	(0,0) (1,1)	NO:	— —
(1, 0)		— NOT ALLOWED —		
(S>0, R>0)				
S>R		— NOT ALLOWED —		
S=R	NO:	— —	YES: (S-1,R)	(S,R+1)
S<R	YES: (S,R-1)	(S+1,R)	YES: (S-1,R)	(S,R+1)

Fig. 6.7 States of multi-level Server_Client

request. In the worst case, every server, except those in the highest level, may have to defer the processing of a received request and send a request of its own. The number of message buffers needed by the system is at most $(L-1)*N1 <= NMBUF$. Therefore, send() is non-blocking.

(2). Consider a process in recv(). If a server has not received any request, it may call recv() without being blocked forever because some clients will call send() to unblock it. If it has sent a request but has not yet received a reply, it may also call recv() because a reply will eventually come. The only possible deadlock is the following situation. A server has received requests from all its clients, which are all waiting for replies but the server has not replied to any of them yet, and the server itself did not send any requests with expected replies. If such a server calls recv(), it would result in a deadlock because all clients are already waiting for the server's replies and the server is now waiting for requests from the clients. But such a server is not allowed to receive. Hence, deadlock cannot occur.

To implement a multi-level server-client message system, we define

```
PROC.S = number of expected replies of a process =
         number of requests sent - number of replies received
PROC.R = number of un-replied requests of a process =
         number of requests received - number of replies sent
```

PROC.(S, R) may be regarded as the state of a process. Initially, all PROC.(S, R)=(0,0), except for each level-1 process, which has the initial values (0,1), as if it had received a "dummy" request from a "phantom client" (the user). Figure 6.7 shows the process states in a multi-level server-client system.

The following code segments implement a multi-level server-client message passing system. It is assumed that each PROC has a level field, which is assigned a value 1 to L in init(). Each process at level-1 can only be a client, which may use send followed by recv or a separate sendrecv to send a request to a higher level server and waits for a reply. A process at level between 1 and L can be both a server and a client. It may use recv to receive either requests from clients or replies from higher level servers. It uses send to reply to a client from which it has received a request earlier or to send requests to higher level servers. Each PROC also has the S and R fields and a replylist. The replylist of a process contains received but not yet replied requests. The send/recv algorithms follow the process state transitions in Fig. 6.7. Any attempts to use send/recv which violates the server-client protocol will result in errors with appropriate error messages.

```
/* C code of a multi-level server-client message passing system */
#define NMBUF NPROC
MBUF mbuf[NPROC], *freeMbuflist;
SEMAPHORE mlock;
/******************** utility functions ************************/
int enmqueue(MBUF **queue, MBUF *p){ // enqueue p by priority }
PROC *demqueue(MBUF **queue){         // return first MBUF in queue}
int cpfu(char *src, char *dest){      // copy from U space }
int cp2u(char *src, char *dest){      // copy  to U space }
int printmlist(MBUF *p){              // print message list }
MBUF *get_mbuf(){                     // return a free mbuf }
int put_mbuf(MBUF *mp){               // release a mbuf }
MBUF *findClient(int pid){// find a client mbuf in server replylist }
int mbuf_init(){          // initialize freeMbuflist and semaphores }

/***************** send()-recv() functions *******************/
int send(char *msg, int pid)  // send msg to target pid
{
    MBUF *mp; PROC *p = &proc[pid];
    /*********** check not allowed to send cases *************/
    if (p->status == FREE || p->status == ZOMBIE){
        printf("target %d invlaid\n", pid); return -1;
    }
    if (running->level == p->level){
        printf("can't send to the same level\n"); return -1;
    }
    if (running->S==0 && running->R==0){
        printf("%d:(s,r)=(0,0), can't send\n", running->pid); return -1;
    }
    if (running->S==1 && running->R==0){
        printf("%d:(s,r)=(1,0) should never happen\n",
                running->pid);return -1;
    }
    if ((running->S == running->R) && running->S > 0){
        printf("(s,r)=(%d, %d): can't send\n", running->S, running->R);
        return -1;
    }
    /******************** OK to send ************************/
    if (running->S < running->R){  // PROC.S < PROC.R
        if (running->level > proc[pid].level){
            printf("%d send reply\n", running->pid);
            if ( (mp = findClient(pid)) == 0){ // find client's request
                printf("has not received a request from client %d\n",pid);
                return -1;
            }
            running->R--;
            mp->pid = running->pid;
            cpfu(msg, mp->contents); //copy server's msg from U space
            printf("%d[%d] sending reply %s to %d[%d]\n", running->pid,
                    running->level, mp->contents, p->pid, p->level);
        }
        else{
            printf("send request to server\n");
            if( !(mp=get_mbuf()) ){
                printf("PANIC: null mbuf pointer; should not happen\n");
                return -1;
            }
            mp->pid = running->pid;
            cpfu(msg, mp->contents); // copy server's msg from U space
            running->S++;
```

```
        }
        // deliver mp to pid's mqueue
        P(&proc[pid].mlock);
          enmqueue(&proc[pid].mqueue, mp);
        V(&proc[pid].mlock);
        V(&proc[pid].nmsg);
        return 1;
    }
    printf("S >= R: can't send\n");
    return 0;
}

int recv(char *msg)   // receive a mbuf from proc's own mqueue
{
  MBUF *mp;
  if (running->S==0 && running->R>0){
      printf("(s r)=(%d %d): can't recv()\n", running->S,running->R);
      return -1;
  }
  if (running->S > running->R){ // this case should never happen
      printf("PANIC:(%d>%d)\n",running->S, running->R);
      return -1;
  }
  // OK to receive: running->S <= running->R
  P(&running->nmsg);
  P(&running->mlock);
    mp = demqueue(&running->mqueue);
  V(&running->mlock);
  printf("%d[%d] recv: from %d[%d] contents=%s\n", running->pid,
         running->level, mp->pid, proc[mp->pid].level, mp->contents);
  cp2u(mp->contents, msg);
  if (running->level < proc[mp->pid].level){// reply from a server
      printf("recved a reply\n");
      running->S--;
      put_mbuf(mp);   // release mbuf
  }
  else{ // recevied a client request
      printf("recved a client request\n");
      // enter client request into replylist; do not free mbuf yet
      enmqueue(&running->replylist, mp);
      running->R++;
  }
  return 1;
}

int sendrecv(char *msg, int pid) // sendrecv: for level-1 clinets only
{   send(msg, pid); recv(msg); }
```

6.15.6 MTX6.message2: Demonstration of Server-Client Message Passing

MTX6.message2 demonstrates multi-level message passing. When the system starts, P1 begins to run u1 in Umode. While in P1, fork several processes, e.g. P2 to

P6, at different levels. The process levels are assigned in init() as (P1, P2) at level-1, (P3, P4) at level-2, (P5, P6) at level-3, etc. In this case, (P1, P2) can only be clients. (P3, P4) can be both server and client, (P5, P6) can only be servers if there is no process above level-3. While in Umode, each process displays its pid and level value. User mode commands are s(send), r(recv) or sr(sendrecv). The reader may test the message passing facility as follows.

1. While in P1: enter sr with a message to P3. P1 should block in recv() and switches to P2.
2. In P2, enter sr to send a message to P4. P2 should block and switch to P3.
3. In P3, enter r to receive a request, which should get P1's request and enter it into P3's replylist. Then enter s with a reply message to P1, which should unblock P1.
4. Enter switch until P1 becomes running again. P1 should be back to Umode with P3's reply.
5. Switch back to P4. Enter recv and then send reply to P2. Switch to P2 to see its reply from P4.
6. Try to enter s/r commands that violate the client-server protocol. The operation should fail with appropriate error messages.
7. Experiment with (P3, P4) as clients and (P5, P6) as servers, etc.

Multi-level server-client message passing is not intended as a general mechanism for IPC. It is suitable for systems with a hierarchical communication organization, such as microkernel based operating systems. A microkernel is a kernel with only the essential functions of an operating system, such as process scheduling and message passing. All other functions, such as process management, memory management, device drivers and file system, etc. can be implemented as server processes. In a microkernel based system, user processes do not execute kernel functions directly. They send request messages to various servers and wait for answers and results. In this sense, the reader may regard MTX6.message2 as a microkernel, but it is far from being a complete operating system. In contrast, a monolithic kernel includes all the functions of an operating system. It is essentially a complete operating system. In a monolithic kernel based system, user processes enter kernel mode to execute kernel functions directly. Both kinds of systems have advantages and disadvantages. Most traditional operating systems, e.g. Unix and Linux, are monolithic kernel based systems. Likewise, MTX is also a monolithic kernel based system. We shall explain and justify this later in Chap. 16.

Problems

1. ASSUME: A (counting) SEMAPHORE s=2;/* initial s.value=2, s.queue=0 */

Processes perform the following sequence of P/V operations on s.

```
Process   : P1  P2  P3  P4  P5  P1  P2
Operation : P   P   P   P   P   V   V
```

Show the value and queue of the semaphore AFTER each P/V operation.

2. In IBM's MVS, the general form of WAIT() is

   WAIT(EVENT e1,EVENT e2, ..., EVENT en, int k);   /* k <= n */

which allows a process to wait for any k out of n events. The general form of
POST() is POST(e1,e2,..,em), which posts the specified m events.

   (1). Design an algorithm (in pseudo-C) for the general WAIT()/POST()
        operations.
   (2). Can WAIT()/POST() lead to deadlock? If so, how to prevent deadlock?

3. A resource is an item which can be used by only one process at a time. Assume
   N resources. In IBM MVS, a process may issue the system call

                         ENQ(r1,r2,...,rn);

to request for n<=N resources. The process does not resume until it has acquired
ALL n resources. A process may issue DEQ(r) to release a resource it has acquired
earlier.

   (1). Design an algorithm (in pseudo-C) for the ENQ()/DEQ() operations.
   (2). Can ENQ()/DEQ() lead to deadlock? If so, how to prevent deadlock?

4. Implement pipes in MTX using semaphores. Pay attention to how to handle
   abnormal process termination, e.g. when the last reader terminates, it must
   unblock all the waiting writers, if any. Similarly, when the last writer terminates,
   it must unblock all the waiting readers, if any.
5. Assume that a pipe has k bytes of data. When a process tries to read n>k bytes
   from a pipe, instead of waiting for n bytes of data, it only reads k<n bytes and
   returns. Re-write the read_pipe algorithm in such a way that the reader process
   does not return unless it has read n bytes. Discuss the advantages and disadvantages of such an algorithm.
6. In the read_pipe and write_pipe algorithms, the pipe variables data and room are
   decremented and incremented on each byte read/written. Re-write the algorithms
   to minimize the number of operations on these variables.
7. If a pipe has no more readers, a writer considers this as a BROKEN_PIPE error
   and aborts. On the other hand, if a pipe has no more writers, it is not a BRO-
   KEN_PIPE to a reader. Why?
8. bi-directional pipe: A bi-directional pipe is a pipe that supports R/W in both
   directions.

   (1). A process creates a pipe but does not close the R/W ends of the pipe. Can
        such a pipe be bi-directional?
   (2). Write a user interface function pipe2(pipe1, pipe2]), which creates 2 pipes.
        Then show how to support bi-directional pipes.

9. Implement pipe as files:

(1). As an ordinary file, which is read/written as a pipe.

(2). As a RAM disk in memory.

10. Named pipes: A named pipe is a FIFO device which can be accessed by unrelated processes for R/W. Named pipes are usually implemented as files of the PIPE type. R/W of named pipes are synchronized in the same way as pipes. Design an algorithm for named pipes.

11. Message buffers and message queues can be eliminated if processes exchange messages by rendezvous. In this scheme, a sender tries to find whether an intended receiver is waiting for its message. If so, it copies the message to the receiver's address space and unblocks the receiver. If not, it waits. When a receiver runs, it tires to find a waiting sender which has message for it. If so, it copies the message and unblocks the sender. Otherwise, it waits.

(1). Prove that, in a uniprocessor kernel, both sender and receiver wait for each other cannot occur.

(2). In a multiprocessor kernel, processes may run on separate processors in parallel. Can process rendezvous still work?

12. In a multi-level server-client model, an intermediate server may need to send more than one request for a received client request. For example, when a user process requests a file system server to read a file block, the FS server may ask the disk driver server to read the requested block and also the next (contiguous) disk block to pre-read in the next block. How to modify the server-client model to support this?

References

Accetta, M. et al., "Mach: A New Kernel Foundation for UNIX Development", Technical Conference—USENIX, 1986

Bach, M.J., "The Design of the Unix operating system", Prentice Hall, 1990

Coffman, E.G, Merwin-Dagget, M., Shoshani, A, "System Deadlocks", Computing Surveys, vol. 3, 1971

Dijkstra, E.W., "Co-operating Sequential Processes", in Programming Languages, Academic Press, 1965

Hoare, C.A.R, "Monitors: An Operating System Structuring Concept", CACM, Vol. 17, 1974

IBM MVS Programming Assembler Services Guide, Oz/OS V1R11.0, IBM, 2010

OpenVMS: HP OpenVMS systems Documentation, http://www.hp.com/go/openvms/doc, 2014

Pthreads: https://computing.llnl.gov/tutorials/pthreads/, 2015

Silberschatz, A., P.A. Galvin, Gagne, G, "Operating system concepts, 8th Edition", John Wiley & Sons, Inc. 2009

Stallings, W. "Operating Systems: Internals and Design Principles (7th Edition)", Prentice Hall, 2011

Tanenbaum, A.S., Woodhul, A.S., "Operating Systems, Design and Implementation, third Edition", Prentice Hall, 2006

Chapter 7
Memory Management

7.1 Goals of Memory Management

In an operating system, many processes are running concurrently. In order to run, each process needs a memory area for its user mode image. A computer system has only a finite amount of physical memory. The first goal of memory management is to ensure that processes run in their own address spaces without interference from one another. The second goal is to run as many processes as possible in the finite amount of physical memory. The third goal is to run processes with virtual address spaces larger than the amount of physical memory allocated to them. Memory management varies from simple schemes, which do not need much hardware support, to very sophisticated schemes, which combine both hardware support and good management policies implemented in software. In this chapter, we shall discuss the general principles of memory management. Details of advanced memory management schemes, such as segmentation, paging and virtual memory, will be covered later in Chap. 14 when we discuss the Intel x86 CPU in 32-bit protected mode. In this chapter, we shall focus on the real-mode MTX and describe the memory management schemes in detail. These include managing process images in kernel and dynamic memory management in user space.

7.2 Virtual Address and Physical Address

A Virtual Address (VA) is an address used in a program. A Physical Address (PA) is an address used by the CPU to access physical memory. A program image generated by a compiler and linker typically uses VA. During execution of a program image, the CPU's memory management unit (MMU) automatically translates or maps each VA to a PA. Most memory management schemes depend on VA to PA mapping.

© Springer International Publishing Switzerland 2015
K. C. Wang, *Design and Implementation of the MTX Operating System,*
DOI 10.1007/978-3-319-17575-1_7

7.3   Variable Sized Partitions

When running multiple processes in a system, the most commonly used memory management scheme is to treat process images as variable-sized partitions. In this scheme, each process image is loaded to a contiguous piece of memory, which is allocated by the image size. When a process terminates, its memory is released as free for reuse. This is the memory management scheme used in the real mode MTX, which will be discussed in detail in Sect. 7.12.

7.4   Overlay

Overlay is a memory management scheme which allows a program to use the same memory area at different stages of execution. In this scheme, a program is organized to consist of several disjoint pieces, which are not needed at the same time during execution. To run a program, load in only the parts that are needed by the program to start. During execution, load in the needed pieces on demand, overlying the program memory areas that are not needed by the current execution. Program overlays were popular in the early days when computer memories were expensive and small. It is rarely used nowadays. However, dynamic loading, which loads in the needed modules of a running system to overlay those which are no longer needed, is based on the principle of overlay.

7.5   Swapping

Swapping is a technique used to increase the number of runnable processes in a system. It swaps process images between memory and a storage area, which can be either a swap disk or a swap file. The candidates for swap-out are typically non-runnable processes, i.e. processes that are sleeping or blocked. When a swapped out process becomes ready to run, its image is loaded into memory, allowing it to continue again. A swapper process tries to swap-in as many ready processes as possible. If there is no room and also no stopped processes in memory, it may swap-out some ready processes to make room for processes that need to be swapped in. The swapping policy is similar to process scheduling by dynamic priority.

7.6 Segmentation

In segmentation (Intel 2011), a program image is divided into many independent parts, called segments. Each segment may be loaded to a separate memory area. During execution, the CPU is told which segment to use and where the segment is in memory. Each VA is an offset relative to the beginning of a segment. The segment's physical address is kept in either a segment register or a segment table. The CPU automatically maps each VA to a PA in physical memory.

Example: The Intel x86 CPU in real mode uses segmentation. Since this is already discussed in Chap. 2.1.5, we only add the following comments. When executing a program image in real mode the CPU only knows the beginning PA of each segment but it does not know how big the segment is. So it simply treats each segment as 64KB in size. Assume that a process image size is only 20KB, which is loaded in a segment. During execution, the process may read/write any PA in the segment, although it should only access the 20KB area in that segment. The CPU has no way to prevent the process from accessing PAs outside of its image area. This implies that if we implement a multitasking system based on the x86 CPU in real mode, there is no protection against invalid memory access by processes.

To remedy the lack of memory protection problem, some CPUs designed for segmentation allow a program to have a large number, e.g. 256, of segments and define each segment by a pair of segment descriptors.

Segment Address Descriptor = Segment begin address

Segment Usage Descriptor = Segment size, Access, R/W

Corresponding to these, a loaded program image has a Segment Table containing up to 256 pairs of segment descriptors. Assuming 4 bytes per entry, the Segment Table has a size of 2KB, which may be too large to be kept in the CPU all at once. So the CPU uses a Segment Base Register to point to the Segment Table of the running process. Assume that the segments are numbered 0 to 255. Each VA is of the form VA = [Segment#, Offset]. During execution, the CPU uses the corresponding Segment Table entry to map the VA to a PA. At the same time, it uses the Segment Usage Descriptor to validate the intended memory access. If the VA exceeds the segment size, it would be an invalid memory reference. Similarly, the CPU can check the access field for READ_ONLY or READ/WRITE of the Segment Usage Descriptor to ensure that the intended access is valid. Segments are best suited to logical units of a program image, such as Code, Data, Stack, Procedures, common data, etc. An excellent usage of segmentation is to allow processes share segments, such as Dynamic Linking Library (DLL) modules.

7.7   Paging

7.7.1   One-Level Paging

Segments are of variable sizes. Each segment must be loaded to a contiguous memory area. The disadvantage of segmentation is that it may cause memory fragmentation, in which the memory contains many unused spaces or holes but none big enough for the current needs. Paging is designed to reduce memory fragmentation. Instead of variable sized segments, all pages are the same size, e.g. 4KB each. Physical memory is divided into 4KB page frames. Then loading pages into memory becomes trivial:

1. Find enough page frames to load the pages. Allocation/deallocation of page frames can be done by either a bit-map or a link list.
2. It does not matter which page is loaded to which page frame, as long as we record them in a Page Table, which looks like the following:

```
        VA Page#      PAgeFrameAddr      Usage
        ------------------------------------------
           0           0x30000           RO
           1           0x20000           R/W
           .............................
          255          0x00000           R/W
        ------------------------------------------
```

The CPU has a Page Table register, which points to the Page Table of an executing image. Given a VA=[Page#, Offset], the CPU uses the corresponding Page Table entry to map it to a PA and validate the intended memory access.

7.7.2   Multi-Level Paging

The one-level paging scheme is impractical because, with 256 4KB-pages, each process image is limited to only 1024 KB. With 32-bit memory addressing, the maximal VA space of a process should be 4 GB. Assuming 4KB page size and 4 GB VA space, each process needs 1M pages or 4 MB memory just for its Page Table alone. The solution to this problem is to use multiple levels of paging. In a 2-level paging scheme, each VA is divided into 3 parts: VA=[Page#1, Page#2, Offset]. Given a VA, the CPU first uses Page#1 in a Level-1 page table to find the physical address of the Level-2 page table. It then uses Page#2 in the Level-2 page table to determine the page frame address. The final PA is the page frame address + Offset. In each step, the CPU uses the page table entry to validate the intended memory access. With 2-level paging, each page table size is only 4KB, which can be loaded into memory. When the CPU translates a VA to PA, it has to access the page tables in memory twice. To speed up address translation, the CPU typically keeps the most recently used page table entries in a translation-lookaside buffer (TLB), which is a small cache memory within the CPU.

7.7.3 Other Paging Schemes

SUN's SPARC RICS machines use 3-level paging. Motorola 6803X's can be programmed for up to 4 paging levels. At the other extreme, MIPS R2000 uses 0-level, i.e. all VA to PA translations are done through a cache buffer inside the CPU.

7.8 Demand-Paging and Virtual Memory

In general, virtual memory refers to the memory management scheme in which VA differs from PA. However, most people tend to think of Virtual Memory (Corman 2004) as the scheme in which the VA space of a program is much larger than the real memory allocated to the program. The goal of VM is to run large program images with less real memory. VM is based on the following principles.

1. Multiplexing: Try to satisfy the needs for many items with only a few at different times.
2. Program locality: During execution, a program tends to access instructions and data in a small area in memory, but not everything within its VA space all at once.
3. Trade time with space: If we try to run a large process image with less real memory, the process must stop from time to time, waiting for the needed pages to be loaded into memory.

7.8.1 Demand-Paging

In demand-paging, the OS loads only a few pages of a program image for execution to start. It loads additional pages only when they are needed by the program execution. This allows a system to run programs with VA much larger than the actual amount of physical memory. Details of paging and demand-paging will be covered later in Chap. 14.

7.8.2   Page Replacement Rules

In demand-paging, when a process attempts to reference a page that is not present in memory, it generates a page fault, which traps to the OS kernel. The kernel's page fault handler can load in the needed page to a page frame, update the page table entry and let the process continue. Loading in a new page is straightforward, except when all the page frames are in use. If that case, a loaded page must be evicted to make room for the new page. This is known as the Page Replacement Problem, which has been studied extensively in the literature and discussed in most OS books. Some of the page replacement rules are:

1. Optimal Replacement Rule: Replace those pages which will cause the least number of page faults in the future. This is unrealizable because it depends on the future behavior of processes.
2. FIFO algorithm: This is the simplest page replacement algorithm to implement but it has been shown to have poor performance.
3. Second Chance Algorithm: Same as FIFO but give each referenced page a second chance. If the oldest page's Reference bit R is 0, choose it to replace. Otherwise, clear its R bit to 0 and continue to look for page with a 0 R bit. If all pages' R bits are 1, this reduces to FIFO but with one round of searching overhead.
4. LRU algorithm: Replace the Least Recently Used page. LRU is realizable but expensive to implement.
5. Use R and M bits: Each page has a Referenced bit and a Modified bit. Page replacement is based on the (R, M) bits. Details will be shown in Chap. 14 when we discuss memory management in protected mode
6. Use a fixed sized pool of free page frames: The OS kernel maintains a certain number of free page frames in a free pool. During page replacement, a victim is selected as before. Instead of waiting for a free page fame to become available, the needed page is loaded into a frame allocated from the free pool. This allows the page faulted process to continue as soon as possible. When the victim's page frame is freed, it is added to the free pool for future allocation.
7. Use a dynamic free page frame pool: The free page frame pool is maintained dynamically. When a page is released, it goes to the free pool. Whenever the free pool reaches a low-water mark, a special process, called the page stealer, is scheduled to run, which collects the pages of idle (sleeping or blocked) processes into the free pool. Page frames in the free pool are maintained in an ordered list to honor LRU.

7.9   Virtual Memory Based File Mapping

Virtual memory maps process images from disks into memory. File I/O maps file contents from disks into memory. File-mapping unifies the two schemes. The following program illustrates file mapping in Linux.

```
/*************** filemap.c file *******************/
#include <stdio.h>
#include <fcntl.h>
#include <sys/mman.h>
int fd, i, BLK=4096;
main(int argc, char *argv[ ]) // usage: a.out filename
{ if ((fd = open(argv[1], O_RDONLY)) < 0)
   { printf("open %s failed\n", argv[1]); exit(1) }
   /* mmap(startAddr, nbytes, usage flags, fileDes, offset) */
   char *p = mmap(0, BLK, PROT_READ, MAP_SHARED, fd, 0);
   printf("-------- file contents --------\n");
   for (i=0; i<BLK; i++) putchar(*p++);
}
```

The example program maps the first 4096 bytes of an opened file (descriptor) to memory at the starting address p. This allows the process to access the file contents as if they were memory locations. When running the program as a.out filename, it displays the first 4096 bytes of the opened file. File mapping is a natural and powerful extension of the VA concept. In addition to its execution image in memory, a process may include all opened files in its VA space.

7.10   Distributed Shared Memory System

Another extension of the process VA space is the distributed shared memory system (DSM) (Li and Hudak 1989). A DSM system consists of many computers in a computer network. Each individual computer is called a node, which has its own CPU and local memory. The address space of a process running on a node includes the local memories of all the nodes in the DSM system. As in a paging system, the total address space is divided into pages. At each node, pages are either local or remote. When a process executes at a particular node, it may reference any of the pages in its VA space, which includes all the memories in the entire network. If a referenced remote page is not available at the local machine, a page fault occurs and the needed page is fetched from the remote node. DSM is a novel idea but it also has many problems, both technical and non-technical. In addition to network traffic, an immediate problem with DSM is page consistency. A page that is local to a node may be in use by many processes running on different nodes. Therefore, a page may have many separate copies residing in different machines. If one of the local copies gets modified, all other copies of the same page must be updated as well. This is the same as the cache coherence problem in a multi-CPU system. Over a network, it is certainly a nontrivial problem. Non-technical problems with DSM may involve security and privacy, which are even more difficult to resolve.

7.11   General Demand-Paging Model

In a multitasking system, demand-paging involves much more than page replacement alone. Processes may share pages. To load a page, a process must check first whether the needed page already exists. If the needed page already exists, the process may simply attach itself to the page frame as a user. When a page frame is freed, it is released into the free pool. A released page frame should be kept in the free pool for as long as possible. If a process needs a page that is still in the free pool, it may reuse the page if its contents are still valid. The VAX's VMS (OpenVMS) uses this scheme, along with the FIFO page replacement algorithm. The scheme is not limited to demand-paging. It is really a multi-user cache memory management problem, which may be defined as follows. A set of processes share a finite pool of free objects (page frames, I/O buffers, cache memory slots, etc.) Each process may behave as a reader or writer. As usual, readers may use the same object concurrently. Writers must exclude all others. In addition, usage of the objects must meet the following requirements:

1. Consistency: the objects must be used in a consistent manner, e.g. every free page frame is represented by a unique free object, every disk block is represented by a unique I/O buffer, etc.
2. Cache effect: the objects must retain their contents for reuse until they are reassigned, e.g. the cache effect may be improved by a LRU replacement algorithm.

In Chap. 15, we shall show a parallel algorithm for managing the I/O buffer cache in a multiprocessor system, which is based on the general demand-paging model.

7.12   Memory Management in Real-Mode MTX

In this section, we shall discuss memory management in the real mode MTX. Up to this point, the real mode MTX can only run 8 processes, P1 to P8, in user mode. Each process is assigned a fixed 64KB segment at the segment address (pid+1)*0×1000. Most user mode programs do not need a full 64KB segment to run. Allocating a full 64KB segment for every process does not use the memory space efficiently. With memory management, we can remove the fixed segment limitation, allowing the system to run more than 8 processes at the same time.

As will be shown later, when we add device drivers and a file system, the real mode MTX kernel size will eventually exceed 64 KB. In that case, the MTX kernel is a binary executable with separate I&D spaces for a maximum kernel space

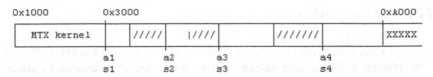

Fig. 7.1 Memory map of MTX

of 128 KB. For ease of discussion, we shall assume that the MTX kernel size is
128 KB, which begins at the segment 0×1000. When the real-mode MTX kernel
starts, the memory area from the segment 0×3000 to 0×A000 is free. When creating
the process P1 we allocate a piece of memory from the free area to load the init program. To keep track of the memory usage, we record the segment address and size
of the loaded image of each process in the PROC structure. When a process forks a
child, we allocate a memory area for the child of the same size as the parent. When
a process exec to a file, if the new image size is larger than the old image size, we
allocate a memory area to load the new image and release the old image area. Otherwise, we load the new image in the old segment and release the extra memory space
as free. When a process terminates, we release its Umode image memory as free for
reuse. During system operation, as process images come and go the memory area
eventually becomes fragmented and looks like a checkerboard, in which some areas
are occupied by process images while other areas are free, as shown in Fig. 7.1.

In Fig. 7.1, each white area represents a free area or a hole and each shaded area
represents an area in use.

7.12.1   Free Memory List

When allocating memory for a process we assume that the entire process image is
loaded to a contiguous memory area. This is clearly needed if the image has only
one segment. Even for programs with separate I&D spaces, we still prefer to load
the entire image to a contiguous memory area, which simplifies the memory management functions. To keep track of the available memory areas, we build a free
memory list containing the holes in memory, as shown in Fig. 7.2. Each list element
contains the beginning address and size of a hole in memory.

Fig. 7.2 Free memory list

7.12.2   Memory Allocation

When a process forks a new process or exec to a new image, it calls kmalloc(size), which allocates a piece of free memory of the needed size. If successful, kmalloc() returns a pointer to the allocated memory segment. It returns 0 if no free memory can be allocated. The algorithm of kmalloc() is

```
segment *kmalloc(u16 request_size)
{
    search free memory list for a HOLE with size >= request_ize:
    if find such a HOLE at, say [ai, si]:
        if (si == request_size){ // exactly fit
            delete the hole from free memory list
            return ai;
        }
        // hole size > request_size
        allocate request_size from HIGH end of the hole by
        changing [ai,si] to [ai, si-request_size];
        return   ai + si - request_size;
    }
    return 0;   // no hole big enough
}
```

kmalloc() tries to allocate memory from the first hole that is big enough to satisfy the requested size. It is therefore known as the First-Fit Algorithm. There are variations to this scheme, such as Best-Fit and Worst-Fit algorithms, which are rarely used in practice.

7.12.3   Memory Deallocation

When a process terminates or changes image size, it calls kmfree(beginAddress, size), which releases the area back to the free memory list. In the free memory list, every hole is of maximal size, so there are no adjacent holes. When releasing a piece of memory three possible cases may arise, as shown in Fig. 7.3. For case 1, we create a new hole to represent the released area. For case 2, we absorb the released area into an adjacent hole. For case 3, we consolidate the three adjacent holes into a single hole, which actually deletes a hole from the free memory list. The algorithm of kmfree() is

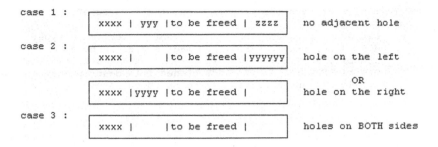

Fig. 7.3 Memory maps during release

```
kmfree(address, size) //chunk=[address,size]=released area
{
    if (chunk has no adjacent holes)
        insert chunk as a new node into free memory list;
    else if (chunk is adjacent to a hole on both left and right)
        combine [left_hole,chunk,right_hole] into a single node;
    else if (chunk has a left adjacent hole)
        absorb chunk into left hole;
    else
        absorb chunk into right hole;
}
```

The free memory list can be implemented in two different ways. The first way is to maintain the link list inside the holes. Each hole contains a triple=(address, size, next) at the beginning, in which next is the beginning address of the next hole. The second way is to implement it as a link list containing memory node structures of the form

```
typedef struct mnode{
        struct mnode *next;
        u16     addr;
        u16     size;
}MNODE; MNODE mnode[NPROC+1];
```

To support memory management, the MTX kernel is modified as follows.

```
PROC.res: pointer to a per-process "resource structure".
typedef struct res{
        u16 segment, size, SEP;   // segment, size, image type.
        u16 tsize, dsize, bsize;  // image's size in bytes
        u16 brk, splimit;         // brk mark and stack low limit
        OFT *fd[NFD];             // opened file descriptors
        // signals and handlers   // to be added later
}RES;
```

fork(): Allocate a memory area of the same size as the parent. Record the segment and size in child PROC.res structure. Copy parent image to child segment. Set child Code segment and Data+Stack segment by parent's image type, e.g. SEP=0 for single segment image or SEP=1 for image with separate I&D spaces.

exec(): If the new image is larger than old image, allocate memory by new image size and release old image. Otherwise, use the same old image and release any extra memory space.

kexit(): When a process terminates, release Umode image by kmfree(segment, size).

7.13   Memory Compaction

Memory management using variable-sized partitions may cause memory fragmentation. When memory becomes severely fragmented, the memory may contain many unused holes but none big enough for the requested size. Memory compaction is a scheme, which consolidates all the holes into a single hole of maximal size. In this scheme, whenever the memory manager can not find enough memory and there are multiple holes, it moves all the process images to one end of the memory and adjusts their saved segment registers to suit the new segments. Then it tries to allocate memory again. However, the scheme is rarely used in practice due to its excessive run-time overhead. The principle of memory compaction has other applications as well. For instance, when applied to files on storage devices, it is known as file system defragmentation.

7.14   Swapping

Even with memory compaction, the number of runnable processes in a system may still be limited due to a lack of available memory. Swapping is a technique to make more memory available by swapping out process images that are not runnable. For example, when the sh process executes a command, it forks a child to execute the command and waits for the child to terminate. While the child is executing, the sh process is not runnable but it still occupies a memory area. In a swapping system, the sh process image could be swapped out to create space for processes that need memory to run. When a swapped out process becomes ready to run, its image is loaded into memory by a swapper process, allowing it to resume running again. A simple algorithm for the swapper process is as follows.

```
while(1){
    sleep(need_to_swap_in);
    while (there are processes need to swap in){
        swap in a process image; continue;
        if (no memory){
            swap out a non-runnable process; continue;
            swap out a ready process; continue;
            break; // if can't swap out any, to while(1)loop
        }
    }
}
```

A process may swap itself out voluntarily. For example, when a process tries to expand its image size but there is not enough memory, it may write its own image out, including the expanded size, to a swap disk, and wakes up the swapper process. When a swapped out process becomes ready, the swapper process is woken up to run, which tries to swap in as many ready process images as possible. If there is no memory, it tries to swap out non-runnable processes. If there are no non-runnable processes, it may swap out some processes that are still runnable. The choice of which process to swap out usually involves some time information. Since MTX dose not yet have a timer, we can only swap out non-runnables processes. Implementations of memory compaction and swapping in MTX are left as an exercise in the Problem section.

7.15   MTX7.1. Demonstration of Memory Management in MTX

The sample system MTX7.1 demonstrates memory management in the MTX kernel. It is based on MTX5.1. In MTX7.1, when a process forks a child, it allocates a child image of the same size. When a process does exec, the user may enter a size of 16 to 64 KB for the new image. In kexec(), the process creates a new image of the specified size and releases the old image. In each case, it displays the free memory list before and after each allocation and deallocation of memory. The move operation allows a process to migrate to different memory areas, which demonstrates the principle and techniques needed for memory compaction and swapping. Figure 7.4 shows the screen of running MTX7.1.

```
===========================================
This is proc 1 in U mode: segment=0x9000
****************** Menu ******************
* ps chname kmode switch wait exit fork exec move *
***********************************************************
Command ? exec
enter exec filename : u2
enter size in KB[16!24!32!48!64] : 64
filename=u2 size=64
KEXEC: size=0x1000
kmalloc req_size=0x1000
mem_list = [0x2000  0x7000 ] =>
mem_list = [0x2000  0x6000 ] =>
segment=0x8000  size=0x1000
Proc 1  exec to /bin/u2 in segment 0x8000
loading /bin/u2 to segment 0x8000  .... done
1  kmfree: [0x9000  0x1000 ]
mem_list = [0x2000  0x6000 ] =>
mem_list = [0x2000  0x6000 ] =>[0x9000  0x1000 ] =>
enter main : argc = 1
argv[0 ] = u2
===========================================
Das ist Prozess 1 in der U Weise: Segment=0x8000
****************** Menu ******************
* ps chname kmode switch wait exit fork exec move *
***********************************************************
Command ?
```

Fig. 7.4 Demonstration system of MTX7.1

7.16   Memory Management in User Space.

In addition to fork, exec and exit, which require memory management in kernel, dynamic memory management in user space may also invoke the kernel memory manager. During execution, a user mode program may use the run-time library functions malloc()/free() to allocate/free memory in the image's heap area dynamically. When a Umode image is first loaded, the image's brk mark is usually set to the end of the image's bss section, so that the initial heap size is 0. Whenever there is not enough space in the heap area, malloc() issues a brk() or sbrk() syscall to increase the heap size. The former sets the brk mark to a specified address and the latter increases the heap size in increments. After obtaining a block of memory for the heap, malloc() tries to allocate a piece of memory of the requested size form the heap. When a dynamically allocated memory area is no longer needed, the program may use free(ptr) to release it back to the heap's free area. In principle, malloc()/free() can be implemented by the same first-fit algorithm, which manages the heap area as variable-sized partitions. Here, we only focus on the effects of brk() and sbrk() system calls. Since brk() and sbrk() change the Umode image size, they may invoke the memory manager in kernel to adjust the Umode image size and relocate, if necessary, the Umode image. For clarity, the MTX kernel implements two separate syscalls, sbrk(), which increases the heap size, and rbrk(), which reduces the heap size, both in 16-byte clicks. When a process calls sbrk() to increase the heap size, it allocates a larger memory area for the new image, copies the old image to the new memory area and releases the old image. During image expansion, the maximal size of the combined data and stack is limited to a full segment of 64KB. When a process calls rbrk() to reduce the heap size, it shrinks the image size and releases the extra memory space. The following describes the algorithms of sbrk() and rbrk() in the MTX kernel.

7.16.1   Expand Heap Size by sbrk()

```
/********* Algorithm of sbrk in MTX *********/
int sbrk(u16 v)   // request v is in 16-byte clicks
{
    if (v==0) return current brk mark;
    newsize = PROC.size + v;
    if (image has separate I&D space)
        newsize = newsize - image's tsize
    if (newsize > 4096) // max. 64KB limit
        newsize = 4096; v=newsize-size;
    new_segment = kmalloc(newsize);   // allocate newsize
    copy |code|data|bss|heap| to new_segment;
    copy old stack to high end of new_segment;
    mfree(PROC.segment, PROC.size);
    change PROC.CS  to new_segment;
    change PROC.USS to new_segment if not separate I&D space
    change PROC.USS to new_segment+PROC.tsize if separate I&D sapce
    adjust saved stack frame pointers in new image;
    set image's new segment, size and brk mark; return brk;
}
```

The actions of sbrk() can be best illustrated by the following diagrams.

1. Image before expansion

```
-------------------------------------------
|Code|Data|Bss|heap|             old stack |
------------------- |----------------------
old segment        old_brk
```

2. One-segment Image after expansion

```
------------------------------------------------------
|Code|Data|Bss|heap| NEW HEAP  |       new stack     |
------------------- |-----------|----------------------
UCS,UDS,USS                      brk
```

3. Separate I&D Image after expabsion

```
 ---------------------    ------------------------------
 |Code|Data|Bss|heap|  NEW HEAP  |        new stack       |
 |----|-------------|-----------|---------------------
 UCS   UDS,USS                     brk
```

When expand an image, sbrk() first computes the new image size (in 16-byte clicks) and allocates a memory area of new image size. Then it copies the old image's [code | data | bss | heap] to the beginning of the new segment and the old stack to the high end of the new segment. The gap between the old heap and the copied stack is the added new heap area. Then it releases the old image memory area and sets the PROC's saved UCS and USS to point to the code and data areas in the new segment. All these operations are simple and straightforward except for the following complication. In the new image, the copied data, bss and (old) heap are still relative to the new segment and hence remain valid. However, the stack is now preceded by a new heap area but all the saved stack frame pointers are still offsets relative to the old stack segment. In the execution image generated by C compiler and linker, data and stack must be in the same segment. Moving the stack area alone would cause references to local variables to be incorrect due to the changed stack position in the new image. Although the stack has been moved, all the saved stack frame pointers still point to locations in the old stack. We must adjust the saved stack frame pointers to suit the new image. As pointed out in Chap. 2, the stack frame pointers form a link list which ends with a 0. It is fairly easy to traverse the link list to adjust all the saved stack frame pointers by a linear shift. For the same reason, pointers which already point at local variables must also be adjusted. Since it is impossible to know whether there are such pointers, the only solutions are: (1). do not use pointers to point at local variables, and (2). after each sbrk() call, such variables must be reassigned again.

7.16.2   Reduce Heap Size by rbrk()

```
/******* Algorithm of rbrk in MTX *******/
int rbrk(u16 v)         // request v in 16-byte clicks
{
    newsize = PROC.size - v;
    if (newsize < 1024){//assume: minimal size=16KB=1024 clicks
        newsize = 1024;
        v = PROC.size - newsize;
    }
    copy old stack forward by v;
    mfree(PROC.segment+newsize, v);
    adjust PROC.usp;
    adjust saved stack frame pointers in new image;
    set image's new size and brk mark; return brk;
}
```

The actions of rbrk() is the reverse of sbrk() but within the same image. It moves the stack area downward by v clicks and releases the extra memory at the high end. As in image expansion, the saved stack frame pointers must also be adjusted to suit the changed stack position. Alternative scheme to implement sbrk() and rbrk(), which do not need adjustment of stack frames, is listed as a programming exercise in the Problem section.

Implementation of malloc() and free() operations for dynamic memory management in the user mode heap space is also listed as an exercise in the Problem section.

7.17 Memory Protection in MTX

The Intel x86 CPU in real-mode does not have any memory protection mechanism in hardware. Therefore, MTX in real-mode also has no memory protection. A user mode program may crash if it misuses its virtual address. The most common type of user program error is illegal address, due to incorrect pointers or array out of bounds. The real mode MTX kernel has no protection against such errors. Another common error is stack overflow, which is handled in software as follows. MTX provides a check_stack() syscall, which checks the current stack pointer against the image's splimt. If the stack pointer is below the image's splimit, it prints a stack overflow warning and returns 0. A user program may include a check_stack() syscall upon entry to every function. When check_stack() returns 0, the program may abort the function execution. In that case, the user must redesign the program to avoid stack overflow.

```
This program demo sbrk [size] syscall: EXPAND image by 256
sbrk v=256  0x100
Kernel sbrk:  v=0x100
oldImage_size=0x790    newImage_size=0x890
kmalloc: size=0x100
mem_list=[0x2000  0x6460 ]->[0x8BF0  0x140 ]->[0x9600  0x500 ]->NULL
mem_list=[0x2000  0x6360 ]->[0x8BF0  0x140 ]->[0x9600  0x500 ]->NULL
expand to left by v
newsegment=0x8360    newusp=0x88B0
back from sbrk() syscall brk = 0x390
local variables a=1  b=2  c=3
enter a key for rbrk syscall: Kernel rbrk v=0x40
oldImage_size=0x890    newImage_size=0x850
mfree:[0x8BB0  0x40 ]
mem_list=[0x2000  0x6360 ]->[0x8BF0  0x140 ]->[0x9600  0x500 ]->NULL
mem_list=[0x2000  0x6360 ]->[0x8BB0  0x100 ]->[0x9600  0x500 ]->NULL
back from rbrk() syscall brk = 0x23
local variables a=1  b=2  c=3
3  in kexit keixt:3  mfree 0x8360  0x850
mfree:[0x8360  0x850 ]
mem_list=[0x2000  0x6360 ]->[0x8BB0  0x100 ]->[0x9600  0x500 ]->NULL
mem_list=[0x2000  0x6D30 ]->[0x9600  0x500 ]->NULL
wakeup proc 2
================= commands in /bin =================
ps matrix race norace qsort pipe sbrk rbrk srbrk chstack
===================================================
enter command in /bin OR exit):
```

Fig. 7.5 Demonstration of sbrk/rbrk in MTX7.2

7.18 MTX7.2. Demonstration of Memory Management in User Space

The sample system MTX7.2 demonstrates memory management in user space. Figure 7.4 shows the screen of running the srbrk program of MTX7.2. The program first issues a sbrk() syscall to expand the heap size by 0×100 clicks. Then it issues a rbrk syscall to reduce the heap size by 0×40 clicks. In both cases, changing the heap size also changes the stack position in the new images. Despite these, it shows that the local variable values remain the same after the sbrk and rbrk syscalls. In addition, it also shows the free memory lists before and after each allocation and deallocation of memory (Fig. 7.5).

Problems

1. Implement sbrk(v), which expands a process image by v clicks, by the following algorithm.

    (1). Allocate an area of size v to the left of the old image. Then, move Code + Data + bss + old_heap "left" by v.
    (2). Allocate an area of size v to the right of the old image. Then, move the old stack right.
    (3). Allocate a new image and release the old image only if (1) and (2) are not possible.

2. Conceptually, the heap area of an execution image is in between the Data and Stack areas. This is because we would like to keep the stack at the high end of the virtual address space. In practice, the heap area can be located after the stack area, as shown below.

```
-------------------------------------------
|Code|Data|Bss| old stack | heap|
-------------------------------|------
segment                         old_brk
```

In this case, brk()/sbrk() would extend the heap area toward the right. Assume that the maximal heap size is 16KB.

(1). Show how to set the initial stack pointer of an image.
(2). When the heap is expanded by brk()/sbrk(), is it necessary to adjust the stack frame pointers in the new image? Justify.
(3). Design an algorithm for this kind of brk()/sbrk() and implement it in MTX.

3. In MTX, the default stack size of a one-segment execution image is 20KB. Implement a expand stack system call, which increases the stack size of a process image by 4KB. Discuss any possible problem and how to deal with the problem.

4. In all Unix-like systems the C library functions malloc()/free() are used for dynamic allocation/deallocation of memory from/to the heap area in user space, where

$$\text{void } *ptr = malloc(int \ size);$$

allocates size bytes from the heap area and returns a pointer to the allocated memory, and

$$\text{void free(void } *ptr);$$

frees the memory space pointed by ptr, which must have been returned by a previous call to malloc(size).

Assume: each MTX process has a heap size of HSIZE bytes. Implement malloc()/free() for dynamic memory management in user mode heap space.

5. Implement memory compaction for the real mode MTX kernel. In kmalloc(), if there is not enough memory and there are multiple holes, move all the process images to the high end of memory and try to allocate memory again. Note that, if a process image is moved, its saved segment registers in both the PROC and user mode stack must be adjusted to suit the new segments.

6. Implement process swapping in MTX by using P0 as the swapping process.

References

Corman, M., "Understanding the Linux Virtual Memory Manager", Prentice Hall PTR, 2004

"Intel® 64 and IA-32 Architectures Software Developer's Manuals Vol.1". Intel Corporation, 2011.

Li, K., Hudak, P. "Memory Coherence in Shared Virtual Memory Systems", ACM Trans. On Computer Systems, Vol. 7, 1989

OpenVMS: HP OpenVMS systems Documentation, http://www.hp.com/go/openvms/doc, 2014

Chapter 8
Interrupt Processing and Process Scheduling

8.1 Interrupts

Interrupts are external signals from devices to CPU, requesting for CPU service. The Intel x86 CPU has 2 binary interrupt request lines: NMI, which stands for Non-Maskable Interrupt, and INTR, which stands for Interrupt Request. An interrupt is present if any of the lines is asserted. The CPU always accepts any NMI request, hence the name NMI. For an INTR request, the CPU may mask out the request if the CPU flag register's I bit is 0. A masked out interrupt is kept pending until the CPU flag.I_bit is changed to 1. The instruction CLI clears the flag.I_bit and STI sets the flag.I_bit.

8.2 Interrupts Hardware

In Intel x86 based PCs, interrupts are configured as shown in Fig. 8.1.

The interrupts hardware consists of two interconnected 8259 Programmable Interrupt Controllers (PICs) (Intel 8259A 2014). The first PIC is the master and the second PIC is the slave. Each PIC has 8 inputs, denoted by IRQ0 to IRQ7. Among the IRQ's, IRQ0 has the highest priority. The 8259 PIC is a priority encoder, which behaves as a dog-fight box, where the top-dog (highest priority IRQ) emerges as the winner. The PIC sends the IRQ with the highest priority to the CPU's INTR input. The slave PIC's INT request line is fed to IRQ2 of the master PIC. The IRQs of the slave PIC are also known as

```
IRQ8=real-time clock, IRQ9=redirected IRQ2, IRQ10-12=general use,
IRQ13=FPU, IRQ14=IDE channel 1 (HD), IRQ15=IDE channel 2 (CDROM)
```

© Springer International Publishing Switzerland 2015

K. C. Wang, *Design and Implementation of the MTX Operating System,*
DOI 10.1007/978-3-319-17575-1_8

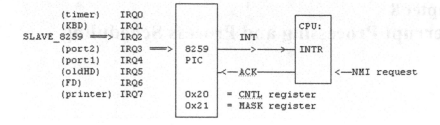

Fig. 8.1 Interrupts configuration of PC

Each 8259 PIC has an interrupt control (INT_CNTL) register and an interrupt mask (INT_MASK) register.

```
INT_CNTL   control  register at 0x20  (Slave : 0xA0)
INT_MASK   mask     register at 0x21  (Slave : 0xA1)
```

The INT_MASK register is used to enables/disable individual IRQ lines. An IRQn line is enabled if bit n of INT_MASK register = 0; bit $n=1$ disables IRQn. The INT_CNTL register is used to signal End-Of-Interrupt (EOI) processing. After sending an IRQn interrupt to the CPU, the 8259 PIC automatically blocks all IRQs of the same or lower priority. The software interrupt handler must explicitly write EOI to the INT_CNTL register at the end of interrupt processing. Otherwise, no further interrupts of the same or lower priority can occur again. The above information is summarized below.

1. The 8259 PIC orders the interrupt requests from IRQ0 (highest) to IRQ7 (lowest).
2. Each IRQn can be enabled/disabled by writing to the INT_MASK register at 0×21 or 0xA1, in which bitn = 0 enables IRQn, bitn = 1 disables IRQn.
3. When interrupt requests occur, the 8259 PIC routes the highest priority IRQn to INTR of the CPU. Meanwhile, it blocks any interrupt requests of the same or lower priority, but it will route any higher priority requests to the CPU.
4. When INTR is asserted, the CPU does not accept the request until its flag.I bit is 1. While the flag.I bit is 0, INTR will remain asserted, which keeps the interrupt request pending.

8.3   Interrupt Processing

When an interrupt occurs, if the CPU's flag.I_bit is 1, the CPU accepts the interrupt and starts interrupt processing at the end of current instruction or at an interruptible point in a long instruction. The sequence of events during interrupt processing is as follows.

1. CPU issues an INT_ACK signal to the 8259 PIC, asking for an interrupt vector.
2. The 8259 PIC spits out a byte value, known as the interrupt vector, to the data bus, allowing the CPU to read the vector. When the PC starts, the interrupt vectors of the PICs are initialized by BIOS to the default values

```
Master PIC : IRQ0-7 :  0x08 -0x0F
Slave  PIC : IRQ8-15:  0x70 -0x77
```

The interrupt vectors can be changed by programming the 8259 interrupt controllers. Since it is unnecessary to remap IRQ vectors in 16-bit real mode, we shall use the default vector values.

3. For PCs in real mode, the lowest 1KB memory contains 256 interrupt vectors. Each vector area contains a pair of [PC, CS], which point to the entry point of an interrupt handler. In order to handle an interrupt at IRQn, an interrupt handler must be installed for the interrupt vector before the interrupt occurs.
4. After acquiring the vector n, the CPU's actions are identical to that of executing an INT n instruction. It first saves [flag, CS, PC] into the CURRENT stack, changes flag register's T and I bits to 0, load [PC, CS] from the vector location [4*n, 4*n+2] and continues execution from the new [PC, CS], which is the entry point of the IRQn interrupt handler.

8.4 TIMER and Timer Service

The PC's timer (Intel 8253 2010) has three independent channels. The channel-0 timer is connected to the master PIC at IRQ0. It can be programmed to generate square waves, which are used to trigger periodic timer interrupts. In this section, we shall incorporate PC's timer into the MTX kernel to provide timer based service functions.

8.4.1 PC's Timer Operation

(1). The PC's channel-0 timer has a base frequency of 1193182 Hz. It can be programmed to generate 60 interrupts per second. The time interval between timer interrupts is called a tick, like the tick of a clock. It interrupts at IRQ0 (vector 8).
(2). Timer Initialization: The code segment shown below initializes the timer.

```
#define TIMER_COUNT   0x00    // cc00xxxx, cc=channel=00, x=any
#define SQUARE_WAVE   0x36    // ccaammmb, aa=access,mmm=mode,b=BCD
#define TIMER_FREQ 1193182L   // timer frequency
#define TIMER_COUNT TIMER_FREQ/60      //initial value of counter
#define TIMER_PORT    0x40    // channel 0 timer port address
#define TIMER_MODE    0x43
#define TIMER_IRQ        0    // IRQ0
#define INT_CNTL      0x20    // master PIC control register
#define INT_MASK      0x21    // master PIC mask reg:bit i=0=enable
int tick = 0;                 // tick count
int timer_init()// Initialize channel 0 of the 8253A timer to 60 Hz
{
    out_byte(TIMER_MODE, SQUARE_WAVE); // set timer continuous MODE
    out_byte(TIMER_PORT, TIMER_COUNT)      // write timer low byte
    out_byte(TIMER_PORT, TIMER_COUNT >> 8);// write timer high byte
}
```

(3). Install a timer handler to vector 8 and enable timer interrupt: Assume that _tinth is the entry point of the timer interrupt handler in assembly code. First, install the timer interrupt handler by

```
int tinth();            // declare tinth() as a function
set_vector(8, tinth);   // install address of tinth() to vector 8
```

which writes [_tinth, 0×1000] to [4*8, 4*8+2], similar to installing int80h() for syscalls.

Then enable timer interrupts by

```
    // Assume IRQ 0-7 ONLY. clear bit 0 in PIC mask register
    int enable_irq(u16 irq)
    {  out_byte(INT_MASK, in_byte(INT_MASK) & ~(1 << irq)); }
    enable_irq(TIMER_IRQ);
```

Once initialized and enabled, the timer will interrupt at IRQ0 once every 1/60 s. If the system is not yet ready to handle interrupts, we can mask out CPU interrupts until it is ready to accept interrupts.

(4). Interrupt Processing Stack: Unlike system calls, which can only occur in Umode, interrupts may occur in either Umode or Kmode. Interrupt processing must be done in Kmode. When a timer interrupt occurs, the CPU saves [flag, CS, PC] of the interrupted point in the current stack, which may be either the user mode stack or the kernel mode stack. Then it follows the vector 8 contents to continue execution from [_tinth, 0×1000] in the MTX kernel. At this moment, only CS=0×1000. All other CPU registers are still those of the interrupted point. Similar to _int80h, we may let _tinth save all CPU registers into the current stack. Then a decision must be made in order to set up the correct execution environment.

(4).1. If the CPU was in Umode before the interrupt, we must change DS, SS, ES to the kernel segment 0×1000, save the interrupted Umode (SS, SP) and switch to the running process' kstack. Then call a handler function to continue processing the interrupt. In this case, the situation is exactly the same as that of syscall when the process enters Kmode via INT 80. So we may save CPU registers into the running proc's ustack, save (SS, SP) into its PROC. (uss, usp), and use the proc's empty kstack, i.e. let sp point to the high end of running proc's kstack.

(4).2. If the CPU was in Kmode before the interrupt, then there is no need to change DS, SS, ES, since they already point to the kernel segment 0×1000. In this case, we must continue to use the running proc's kstack since it not only contains the saved context of the interrupted point but also the execution history of the interrupted process in Kmode. It would be a disaster if we try to use the proc's kstack from scratch again.

How do we know in which mode the CPU was executing before an interrupt? The reader is encouraged to think about this problem first. Some CPU's status register has a current/previous mode field, which allows an interrupt handler to determine in which mode the interrupt occurred. In other CPUs, e.g. the x86 in protected mode, the CPU switches to the kernel mode stack automatically following an interrupt, so there is no need to decide which stack to use. Since the x86 CPU in real mode does not have this capability, we have to use some other means to determine whether an interrupt occurred in Umode or Kmode. In either case, we must ensure that interrupt processing is performed in Kmode, so that CS = Kernel code segment, DS = SS = Kernel data + stack segment and stack is the running proc's kstack.

(5). After establishing an appropriate kernel mode stack, we may call thandler() in C, which implements the actual timer interrupt processing. In thandler(), we may update the current time, display a wall clock, update running proc's CPU usage time, adjust process priorities and start time dependent work, etc. Then issue EOI to signal end of interrupt processing.

(6). When thandler() finishes, it returns to the calling place in _tinth, which returns to the interrupted point by

```
_ireturn: ! same as _goUmode
     cli   ! mask out interrupts
     if (process was in Umode){
          restore (SS,SP) from running PROC.(uss,usp);
     }
     pop saved registers in reverse order
     iret
```

(7). When control enters an interrupt handler, the CPU's interrupts are masked out. After saving the interrupted context, the interrupt handler typically unmasks interrupts to allow the CPU to accept other interrupts of higher priority. If so, the CPU may handle another interrupt before the current interrupt handler finishes. Thus, interrupt processing may be nested. For nested interrupts, the first interrupt may occur in Umode. Any subsequent interrupts must occur in Kmode, i.e. in the middle of processing an interrupt. In the latter case, we continue to use the proc's kstack to save and return to the last interrupted point. Therefore, our scheme can handle nested interrupts. The maximal depth of nested interrupts is limited by the number of different IRQs, which is 15 in the case of Intel x86 based PCs (Intel 64, 2011; Intel 64, 2011). This also implies that every proc's kstack must be big enough to contain up to 15 layers of saved interrupted contexts and their stack frames. Instead of requiring every process to have such a big kernel stack, some CPUs use a single hardware interrupt stack for interrupt processing. In that case, each proc's kstack only needs enough space to maintain its execution context in Kmode.

8.5   Implementation of Timer in MTX

In the MTX kernel, the implementation of timer interrupts processing is as follows.

1. Mask out all interrupts by lock(), which issues CLI.
2. Initialize MTX kernel as before. Create P0 and let P0 kfork P1 with a Umode image. In kfork(), set the saved flag register to 0×0200 (I_bit=1) so that P1 will run with interrupts enabled when it starts.
3. Set syscall and timer interrupt vectors by set_vector(80, int80h); set_vector(8, tinth);
4. Initialize and enable timer by timer_init(). Timer interrupts will occur immediately but they are masked out for now.
5. tswitch() to P1, which loads CPU's flag register with I_bit=1, allowing CPU to accept interrupts.

The following code segments show the timer implementation in MTX8.timer1, which is based on MTX5.1. The major changes in MTX8.timer1 are in the assembly code. First, with interrupts, the entire tswitch() code must be executed with interrupts masked out. Second, it uses a macro, INTH, to generate appropriate entry and exit code for both syscall and timer interrupts. Since the same INTH macro will also be used later for other interrupts, we shall show the entire INTH macro code and explain it in more detail.

First, we add an inkmode field to every PROC structure at the byte offset 8. When a process is created in kernel, we initialize its inkmode to 1. When a process goes to Umode, we decrement its inkmode by 1. When a process enters or re-enters Kmode, we increment its inkmode by 1, etc. Thus, we may use the running proc's inkmode value to determine in which mode an interrupt occurred. If inkmode = 1, it occurred in Umode. If inkmode > 1, it occurred in Kmode. Alternatively, we may also use the saved segment register to determine the CPU mode. For example, if the saved CS is not the kernel segment (0×1000), the interrupt must have occurred in Umode. The following shows the modified PROC structure and the INTH macro.

```
    struct proc{
        struct proc *next;
        int  *ksp;
        int  uss, usp;
        int  inkmode;  // ADD: process in Kmode flag; initial = 1
        // remaining fields same as before
    }
!********** For timer interrupt : ADD THESE to ts.s file*************
        .globl _tinth,_thandler
USS = 4; USP = 6; INK = 8  ! byte offset of inkmode in PROC
    MACRO INTH  ! as86 macro: parameters are ?1 ?2, etc
        push ax
        push bx
        push cx
        push dx
        push bp
        push si
        push di
        push es
        push ds
        mov  ax,cs
        mov  ds,ax     ! Assume one-segment kernel: set DS to kDS=0x1000
        mov  bx, _running    ! bx points to running PROC
        inc INK[bx]          ! enter Kmode : inc proc.inkmode by 1
        cmp INK[bx],#1       ! if proc.inkmode=1,interrupt was in Umode
        jg  ?1               ! inkmode > 1 : interrupt was in Kmode
!---- interrupt in Umode: save interrupted (SS,SP) into PROC -------
        mov bx,_running      ! ready to access running PROC
        mov USS[bx],ss       ! save SS in PROC.uss
        mov USP[bx],sp       ! save SP in PROC.usp
! change ES,SS to Kernel segment
        mov  ax,ds
        mov  es,ax           ! CS=DS=SS=ES in Kmode
        mov  ss,ax
        mov  sp, _running    ! sp -> running PROC
        add  sp, _procSize   ! sp -> running proc's kstack high end
?1:     call _?1             ! call handler in C
        br   _ireturn        ! return to interrupted point
     MEND
!********  INSTALL INTERRUPT HANDLERS **********
_int80h: INTH  kcinth        ! install syscall INT 80 handler
_tinth:  INTH  thandler      ! install timer   INT 8 handler
```

Interrupt handlers are installed by INTH macro calls of the form

_entryPoint:INTH chandler

Each INTH macro call generates a block of assembly code, in which the symbol ?1 is replaced with the parameter chandler. In the generated assembly code, it saves all the CPU registers in the current stack. Then it switches DS to kernel's data segment to access the PROC structure of the interrupted process. It uses the proc's inkmode to determine whether the interrupt occurred in Umode or Kmode. If the interrupt occurred in Umode, the actions are the same as that of INT 80. In this case, it uses the running proc's empty kstack to call chandler(). If the interrupt occurred in Kmode, it continues to use the running proc's kstack to call chandler() directly. When the chandler() function finishes, it returns to _ireturn, which is the same as _goUmode. Depending on the proc's inkmode value, it uses the saved interrupt stack frame in either the proc's ustack or kstack to return to the interrupted point.

```
_ireturn:_goUmode:
        cli
        mov bx,_running        ! bx points at running PROC
        dec INK[bx]            ! dec proc.inkmode by 1
        cmp _inkmode,#0        ! inkmode==0 means proc was in Umode
        jg  xkmode            ! by pass return to Umode code
! return to Umode: restore uSS, uSP from running PROC.(uss,usp)
        mov ax,USS[bx]
        mov ss,ax             ! restore SS
        mov sp,USP[bx]        ! restore SP
xkmode: pop ds
        pop es
        pop di
        pop si
        pop bp
        pop dx
        pop cx
        pop bx
        pop ax
        iret

/********* main.c file of MTX8.timer1 with timer *******/
main()
{
  printf("MTX starts in main()\n");
  lock();                  // CLI to mask out interrupts
  init();                  // initialize and create P0 as running
  set_vector(80,int80h);   // set syscall vector
  set_vector(8, tinth);    // install timer interrupt handler
  kfork("/bin/init");      // P0 kfork() P1 to execute /bin/init
  timer_init();            // initialize and start timer
  while(1){
     while(!readyQueue);
     tswitch();            // P0 switch to run P1 with flag.I bit=1
  }
}
/*=========== timer interrupt handler ============*/
int tick = 0;            // global tick count
int thandler()
{
  tick++; tick %= 60;
  if (tick == 0){          // at each second
     printf("1 second timer interrupt in ");
     running->inkmode > 1 ? putc('K') : putc('U'); printf("mode\n");
  }
  out_byte(0x20, 0x20);    // issue EOI to 8259 PIC
}
```

MTX8.timer1 is a sample system which demonstrates the simple timer interrupt handler. At each second, it displays a line to show whether the timer interrupt occurred in Kmode or Umode. Despite frequent timer interrupts, the reader may enter commands to run the system as usual. The reader may also modify the timer interrupt handler to perform other time dependent tasks, such as

1. Display a "wall clock" to show the system time in hr: min: sec format.
2. Let a running process sleep for a few seconds and wakeup the process when its sleeping time expires, etc.

8.6 Process Switch by Time Slice

With a timer, we can extend MTX8.timer1 to implement timer based process switching.

In MTX.timer2, when a process is scheduled to run, it is given a time slice of, say 5 s. While a process runs, we decrement its time by 1 at each second if it is running in Umode. When the process' time slice expires, switch process to run another process. Figure 8.2 shows the screen of running MTX8.timer2.

Figure 8.2 shows two user mode processes, P1 and P2, each runs for 5 s. When a process time slice expires, it switches process automatically. Note that process

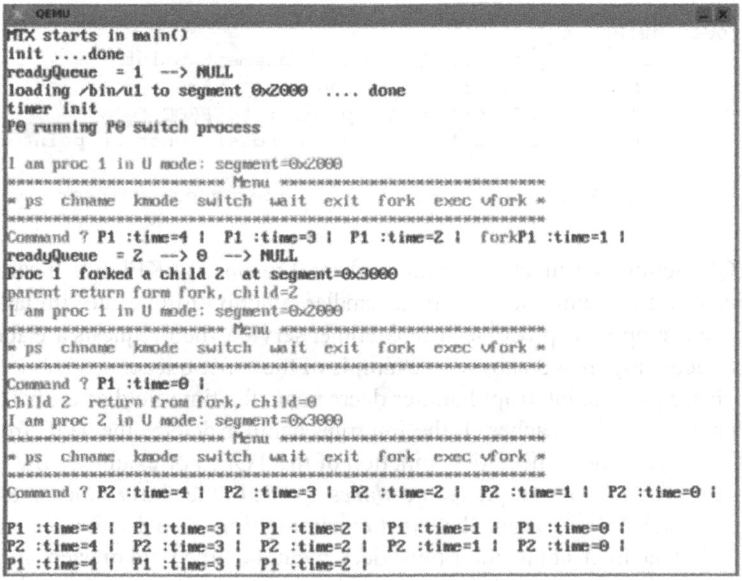

Fig. 8.2 Timer based process switch

switch occurs only when the process is running in Umode. This is because the uni-processor MTX kernel can only support one process running in Kmode at a time. Time slice based process switch is a simple form of process scheduling. We shall discuss general process scheduling in Section 8.9.

8.7 Implementation of Timer Service in MTX

An operating system kernel usually provides the following timer services to processes.

. pause(t) : suspend the process for t seconds.
. itimer(t) : set an interval timer of t seconds. When the interval time expires, notify
         the process. If t=0, cancel an earlier interval timer request.

To simplify the discussion, we shall assume that each process has only one outstanding timer request and the time unit is in seconds in real time, i.e. the process' virtual timer continues to run whether the process is executing or not.

(1). Timer Request Queue: Timer service provides each process with a virtual or logical timer by a single physical timer. This is achieved by maintaining a timer queue to keep track of process timer requests. A timer queue element (TQE) is a structure

```
typedef struct tq{
        struct tq *next;    // next element pointer
        int       time;     // requested time
        struct PROC *proc;  // pointer to PROC
        int     (*action)(); // 0|1|handler function pointer
}TQE;
TQE *tq, tqe[NPROC];        // tq = timer queue pointer
```

In the TQE, action is a function pointer, where 0 means WAKEUP, 1 means NO-TIFY, other value = entry address of a handler function to execute. Initially, the timer queue is empty. As processes invoke timer service, their requests are added to the timer queue. Figure 8.3 shows an example of the timer queue.

At each second, the interrupt handler decrements the time field of each TQE by 1. When a TQE's time reaches 0, the interrupt handler deletes the TQE from the timer queue and invokes the action function of the TQE. For example, after 5 s, it deletes tqe[2] from the timer queue and wakes up P2. In the above timer queue, the time field of each TQE contains the exact remaining time. The disadvantage of this scheme is that the interrupt handler must decrement the time field of each and every TQE. In general, an interrupt handler should complete the interrupt processing as quickly as possible. This is especially important for the timer interrupt handler. Otherwise, it may loss ticks or even never finish. We can speed up the timer interrupt handler by modifying the timer queue as shown in Fig. 8.4.

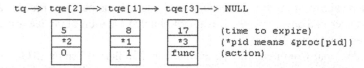

Fig. 8.3 Timer request queue

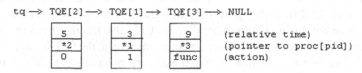

Fig. 8.4 New timer request queue

In the modified timer queue, the time field of each TQE is relative to the cumulative time of all the preceding TQEs. At each second, the timer interrupt handler only needs to decrement the time of the first TQE and process any TQE whose time has expired. With this setup, insertion and deletion of a TQE must be done carefully. For example, if a process P4 makes an itimer(10) request, its TQE should be inserted after TQ[1] with a time $= 2$, which changes the time of TQ[3] to 7. Similarly, when P1 calls itimcr(0) to cancel its timer request, its TQE[1] will be deleted from the timer queue, which changes the time of TQE[3] to 12, etc. The reader is encouraged to figure out the general algorithms for insertion and deletion of TQEs.

(2). Timer Queue as a Critical Region: The timer queue data structure is shared by processes and the timer interrupt handler. Access to the timer queue must be synchronized to ensure its integrity. MTX in real mode is a uniprocessor OS, which allows only one process to execute in kernel at a time. In the MTX kernel a process cannot be interfered by another process, so there is no need for process locks. However, while a process executes, interrupts may occur. If a timer interrupt occurs while a process is in the middle of modifying the timer queue, the process would be diverted to execute the interrupt handler, which also tries to modify the timer queue. To prevent interference from interrupt handler, the process must mask out interrupts when accessing the timer queue. The following shows the algorithm of itimer().

```
/*************** Algorithm of itimer() *********************/
int itimer(t)
{
    (1). Fill in TQE[pid] information, e.g. proc pointer, action.
    (2). lock();        // mask out interrupts
    (3).  traverse timer queue to compute the position to insert TQE;
    (4).  insert the TQE and update the time of next TQE;
    (5). unlock();      // unmask interrupts
}
```

The itimer() algorithm is the first example of interactions between process and interrupt handler in a device driver. Design and implementation of device drivers will be covered in Chapter 10.

(3). Additional Comments on Timer interrupt handler: When an IRQn interrupt occurs, the PIC interrupt controller automatically masks out all interrupts of IRQn of the same or lower priority. Since timer interrupts at IRQ0, which has the highest priority among the IRQs, all interrupts are disabled when the CPU enters the timer interrupt handler. To allow further interrupts to occur again, an interrupt handler must explicitly write EOI (0×20) to port 0×20 to signal End-Of-Interrupt processing. In addition, upon entry to an interrupt handler, the CPU also has interrupts masked out because its flag.I bit $=0$. In order to accept other interrupts, the CPU's flag.I bit must be set to 1. The internal organization of a timer interrupt handler falls into two cases.

a. At each tick, it must update the tick count and process CPU usage time, etc. Execution of this part must complete within one tick time. Otherwise, the handler would incur an infinite recursion, resulting in stack overflow on any machine. Since this part cannot last longer than one tick time, whether to re-enable and unmask interrupts is unimportant.

b. At some regularly scheduled time, e.g. at each second, the handler may need to re-compute all process priorities for process scheduling. If the computation can be completed in one tick time, there is no need to enable timer interrupts. Otherwise, timer interrupts must be re-enabled and unmasked in order not to lose ticks. However, this would create the following problem. If the current processing can not be completed within one second time, re-entering the timer interrupt handler would cause an infinite recursion again. The reader is encouraged to think about how to handle such cases.

8.8   Timer Service in MTX

The MTX kernel supports the following timer service to processes.

1. pause(t): the process goes to sleep for t seconds.
2. itimer(t): sets an interval timer of t seconds. Send a SIGALRM (14) signal to the process when the interval timer expires.

Signals and signal handling will be covered in Chapter 9. Before then, we shall assume that a process goes to sleep after requesting an interval timer.

3. A process executing the floppy disk driver waits for 0.5 s after turning on the drive motor. It also issues a timer request to turn off the drive motor after 2 s. Although these can be integrated into the itimer() service function framework, it is implemented separately in the timer interrupt handler.

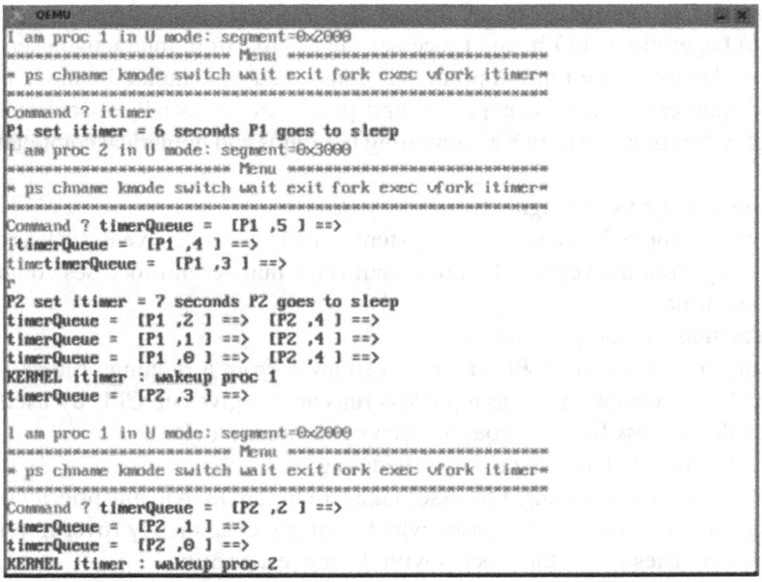

```
QEMU                                                                    _ x
I am proc 1 in U mode: segment=0x2000
********************** Menu ******************************
* ps chname kmode switch wait exit fork exec vfork itimer*
****************************************************
Command ? itimer
P1 set itimer = 6 seconds P1 goes to sleep
I am proc 2 in U mode: segment=0x3000
********************** Menu ******************************
* ps chname kmode switch wait exit fork exec vfork itimer*
****************************************************
Command ? timerQueue =  [P1 ,5 ] ==>
itimerQueue =  [P1 ,4 ] ==>
timetimerQueue = [P1 ,3 ] ==>
r
P2 set itimer = 7 seconds P2 goes to sleep
timerQueue =  [P1 ,2 ] ==>  [P2 ,4 ] ==>
timerQueue =  [P1 ,1 ] ==>  [P2 ,4 ] ==>
timerQueue =  [P1 ,0 ] ==>  [P2 ,4 ] ==>
KERNEL itimer : wakeup proc 1
timerQueue =  [P2 ,3 ] ==>

I am proc 1 in U mode: segment=0x2000
********************** Menu ******************************
* ps chname kmode switch wait exit fork exec vfork itimer*
****************************************************
Command ? timerQueue =  [P2 ,2 ] ==>
timerQueue =  [P2 ,1 ] ==>
timerQueue =  [P2 ,0 ] ==>
KERNEL itimer : wakeup proc 2
```

Fig. 8.5 Demonstration of interval timer in MTX

MTX8.timer3 demonstrates the interval timer service of MTX. When a process requests an interval timer of t seconds, it goes to sleep. At each second, the timer interrupt handler displays the timer queue and wakes up the process when its interval timer expires. Figure 8.5 show the screen of running MTX8.timer3.

8.9 Process Scheduling

8.9.1 Process Scheduling Terminology

In a multitasking operating system, there are usually many processes ready to run. The number of runnable processes is in general greater than the number of CPUs. Process scheduling is to decide when and on which CPU to run the processes in order to achieve an overall good system performance. Before discussing process scheduling, we first clarify the following terms, which are usually associated with process scheduling.

1. I/O-bound vs. compute-bound processes:

A process is considered as I/O-bound if it suspends itself frequently to wait for I/O operations. I/O-bound processes are usually from interactive users who expect fast response time. A process is considered as compute-bound if it uses CPU time extensively. Compute-bound processes are usually associated with lengthy computations, such as compiling programs and numerical computations, etc.

2. Response time vs. throughput:
   Response time refers to how fast a system can respond to an event, such as entering a key from the keyboard. Throughput is the number of processes completed per unit time.

3. Preemption vs. non-preemption:
   Preemption means the CPU can be taken away from a running process at any time. Non-preemption means a process runs until it gives up CPU by itself, e.g. when the process finishes, goes to sleep or becomes blocked.

4. Round-robin vs. dynamic priority scheduling:
   In round-robin scheduling, processes take turn to run. In dynamic priority scheduling, each process has a priority, which changes dynamically (over time), and the system tries to run the process with the highest priority.

5. Real-time vs. time-sharing:
   A real-time system must respond to external events, such as interrupts, within a minimum response time, e.g. within a few msec. In addition, the system may also need to complete the processing of such events within a guaranteed time interval. In a time-sharing system, each process runs with a guaranteed time slice so that all processes receive their fair share of CPU time. Immediate response is desired but not guaranteed. Because of their critical timing requirements, process scheduling in real-time systems differ from that of time-sharing systems. Most general purpose OS, such as Unix and Linux, are time-sharing systems. In the following, we shall only consider process scheduling in time-sharing systems.

8.9.2 Goals, Policy and Algorithms of Process Scheduling

Process scheduling is intended to achieve the following goals.

> .high utilization of system resources, especially CPU time,
> .fast response to interactive processes,
> .fairness to all processes for good throughput, etc.

It is easy to see that some of goals are conflicting to one another. For example, fast response time and good throughput usually cannot be achieved at the same time. A scheduling policy is a set of rules, by which a system tries to achieve good system performance by striving for a balance among the conflicting goals. A scheduling algorithm is a set of methods that implements a scheduling policy. In an OS kernel, the various components (data structures and code) that implement the scheduling algorithm are collectively known as the process scheduler. It is worth noting that in most OS there is not a single piece of code or module that can be identified as the scheduler. The functions of a scheduler are implemented in many places, e.g. in wakeup(), exit() and, most notably, the timer interrupt handler, of an OS kernel.

8.9.3 Process Scheduling in Time-Sharing Operating Systems

The primary goal of a time-sharing system is to ensure fast response time to interactive processes. Other goals, such as resource utilization, fairness to all processes and throughput, are also important but only secondary to response time. In order to achieve a balanced system performance, the scheduling policy usually favors I/O-bound processes over compute-bound processes. Since the OS kernel cannot know whether a process is I/O-bound or compute-bound ahead of time, the only way to judge is by the process behavior, typically by its CPU usage time. Thus, timer becomes an indispensable part of process scheduling. The scheduling algorithm of most time-sharing systems is based on a multi-level priority queue (MPQ). The MPQ may only be conceptual, a system may not actually maintain such a queue, but it helps explain the principle of priority-based scheduling. Figure 8.6 shows the organization of a MPQ.

In a MPQ, each process has a priority. Process priorities are divided into levels, each level includes a range of priority values. Within the same priority level, processes are ordered by priority or FIFO if they have the same priority. With the MPQ, selecting the next process to run is simple; the scheduler simply selects the process with the highest priority in the highest queue level. When a process' priority changes, it may be reordered in the same level, or even moved to a different level, in the MPQ. The scheduler periodically computes the priorities of all the processes. It rewards processes whose behavior helps achieving the scheduling goals and penalizes those which do not. For example, if a process waits for I/O frequently (I/O-bound), its priority should rise because it did not use much CPU time but most likely expects fast (terminal) response. On the other hand, if a process uses CPU time extensively (compute-bound), its priority should drop because it degrades the response time of other processes. Likewise, if a process has not run for some time, its priority should also rise in order to ensure fairness. Thus, the central problem is how to adjust the process priorities dynamically. Instead of discussing process

Fig. 8.6 Multi-level scheduling queue

```
MPQ = level_1 : highest priority
      level_2 : 2nd highest priority
      ..........................
      level_n : lowest priority
```

scheduling in abstract terms, we shall examine the scheduling algorithms of some real OS, e.g. Unix, Linux and MTX.

8.9.3.1   Process Scheduling in Unix

Unix (Bach 1990) is a general purpose time-sharing system, which is intended to support many users. As such, it must provide fast response time to interactive users and at the same time tries to complete as many background processes as possible. To Unix, response time, throughput and resource utilization are equally important. Therefore, the scheduling policy of Unix tries to strive for a balance among these goals. In Unix, processes have two kinds of priorities, Kmode priority and Umode priority. In each mode, process priorities are divided further into different levels. Kmode priorities are fixed, which never change. Umode priorities are adjusted dynamically over time. The scheduling policy favors processes in Kmode in order to speed up kernel operations. At the same time, it tries to improve the response time of Umode processes and also to ensure fairness. When a process is created, it is assigned a base value of Umode priority, say 60. While a process runs in Umode, its priority is adjusted as follows. On each timer tick, the CPU usage time of the running process is incremented by 1. At each second, the priority values of all Umode processes are recomputed by the formula

$$priority\ value = decay(CPU\_time) + base(60) + nice;$$

where decay() is a non-linear decreasing function on the CPU time used by the process and nice is an optional value requested by the process. In Unix, a smaller priority value means higher priority. The decay function is non-linear, e.g. $decay(t) = t/2$, which has a faster decay rate when t is large. Thus, the priority of a process decreases rapidly if it has used a lot of CPU time recently. While this favors I/O-bound processes, it does not totally discriminate against compute-bound processes. If a process has not used any CPU time recently, its priority will rise. To ensure fairness, when a process is selected to run, it is given a time quantum, which is the maximum time a process is allowed to run. When a process runs in Umode, its time quantum is decremented by 1 on each timer tick. When a process has exhausted its time quantum, it is pre-emptied, giving CPU to another runnable process. When a process first enters Kmode, it runs with the same Umode priority but its CPU usage time is no longer incremented, meaning that a process runs in Kmode with no time limit. While in Kmode, if a process goes to sleep, it is assigned a fixed Kmode priority by the sleep reason, which reflects the importance of the resource the process is waiting for. For example, if a process waits for disk I/O completion, it goes to sleep with the highest priority. If a process waits for an I/O buffer, it sleeps with the next highest priority. This is because a process must already have an I/O buffer before issuing a disk I/O. If a process waits for an inode, its priority is even lower, etc. All Kmode priority values are less than the Umode base value, i.e. Kmode priorities are always higher than Umode priorities. When a process runs in Kmode, it may wake up a sleeping process with a higher priority. If so, it sets a switch process flag but does not switch process immediately. When the running process exits Kmode to return to Umode, it drops back to Umode priority and switches process if the switch process flag is set. From a process viewpoint, the running process is preempted, but only in Umode. A process in Kmode is never preempted. In addition, Unix also has a fair share scheduler, which divides CPU time among different user groups proportionally, regardless of how many processes are in the groups.

In summary, the scheduling algorithm of Unix uses dynamic priority to improve response time. It uses time quanta to ensure fairness. However, dynamic priority and time quanta only apply to processes in Umode. Processes running in Kmode have no time limit. When a blocked process wakes up in Kmode, it resumes running with a fixed high priority until it exits Kmode. This speeds up the execution of the Unix kernel, which improves system resource utilization and throughput.

8.9.3.2 Process Scheduling in Linux

Linux is intended primarily for the personal use of a single user. Most people run Linux on a personal computer. Many Linux users often run audio/video applications, which demand extreme fast response. To a Linux user, resource utilization is not an issue. Fast response time is the primary goal. Because of these unique requirements, process scheduling in Linux (Bovet and Cesati 2005) is very different from that of Unix. The first major difference is that Linux does not differentiate between kernel mode and user mode processes. Instead, it divides processes into two types; real-time or conventional. Real-time processes are those which demand very quick response time. They are given static priorities, which range from 1 to 99, and which never change. Real-time processes may run either by FIFO with no time limit or by round-robin with a time quantum. The scheduling policy is to run real-time processes first until there are no such runnable processes. All other processes are conventional, which are scheduled by dynamic priority.

The second difference is that Linux's scheduler does not re-compute process priorities at fixed time instants, e.g. at each second as does in Unix. Instead, it divides CPU time into intervals, called epochs. An epoch is a time interval in which there are still runnable processes with remaining time quanta. When an epoch begins, each runnable process is given a time quantum duration, which is computed by the scheduling parameters of the process. If a process has used up its time quantum in the previous epoch, it is assigned a base quantum, which is also the base priority of the process. If it has some quantum remaining, the remaining quantum is converted to a bonus added to its base quantum. This increases the priority of I/O-bound processes. When forking a child process, the parent's remaining quantum is divided in half between the parent and the child. Without this feature, a user process could fork a child just before its time quantum expires and let the child continue the parent's work. If the child were given a full base time quantum, the user would be able to run a process which never exhausts its time quantum. When selecting the next process to run, the scheduler chooses a runnable process with the highest priority in the current epoch. An epoch ends when all runnable processes have exhausted their quanta, at which time a new epoch begins.

The third difference is in the way of computing process priority. In Linux, the dynamic priority of a process is the sum of its base time quantum (also the base priority) and its remaining time in the current epoch. The scheduler itself is invoked on one of three occasions:

1. when a process goes to sleep to become blocked for a resource, it invokes the scheduler directly to select a next runnable process.
2. When the current process has exhausted its time quantum or when it wakes up a sleeping process with a higher priority. In the latter case, it evaluates the goodness of the awakened process and sets a need_switch flag only if the awakened process is more worthy to run. The goodness test function on an awakened process returns a large value for real-time process which ensures that the real-time process will run next. It returns 0 if the process has no time quantum left. Otherwise, it returns the current priority of the process. If the candidate and the current process have the same address space, it returns the candidate's current priority + 1. This helps reschedule threads in the same process.
3. when a process explicitly yields CPU to another runnable process.

In the cases (2) and (3), process switching does not take place immediately. It occurs only when the running process exits Kmode to return to Umode. In SMP Linux, the scheduling algorithm is similar but modified in order to boost system performance in a multiprocessor environment.

In summary, the scheduling algorithm of Linux divides processes into two types; real-time and conventional. Real-time processes have fixed priorities which are always higher than that of conventional processes. Linux does not distinguish between processes in Kmode or Umode. All conventional processes are scheduled by dynamic priority. Instead of re-computing process priorities at fixed time instants, Linux uses epochs. Although Linux tries to support real-time processes, it is not a real-time system in the true sense.

8.10   Process Scheduling in MTX

As in Linux, the process scheduling goals of MTX are ordered as

fast response time to interactive processes,
fairness to non-interactive processes,
resource utilization is only a minor objective.

Instead of a single process scheduling policy, MTX supports three different kinds of process schedulers. We demonstrate process scheduling in MTX by the sample systems MTX8.sch1 to MTX8.sch3. These are the initial versions of MTX for hard disk partitions. The reader may consult the README files on how to install and test the systems on virtual machines of QEMU or VMware.

8.10.1 MTX8.sch1: Time Slice

The scheduling policy is to treat all the processes equally. To ensure both fast response and fairness, each process runs with a fixed time slice of 6–10 timer ticks. When the time slice of a process expires, it switches process when it exits Kmode.

8.10.2 MTX8.sch2: Fixed Process Priority and Time Slice

The scheduling policy is to speed up kernel operation as well as to ensure fast response to interactive processes. All processes run in Umode with the same priority 128. When a blocked process is woken up in Kmode, it is assigned a fixed priority 256. When a process exits Kmode, it drops back to the Umode priority (128), which may trigger a process switch if there is a runnable process with higher priority (256). As in MTX8.sch1, each process runs with a time slice of 6–10 timer ticks. When a running process has exhausted its time quantum, it is preempted to run another process.

8.10.3 MTX3.sch3: Dynamic Process Priority and Time Slice

The scheduling policy is the same as in MTX8.sch2 but with the following refinements to the scheduling algorithm. Each process has a CPU_time usage field. When a process is selected to run, it is assigned a base priority of 128 and its CPU_time used is set to 0. While a process runs, its CPU_time is incremented by 1 at each timer tick, with a maximum limit of 127. At each 20 ticks, or any value $<=$ time quantum, the priorities of all processes are recomputed as
  priority $= 128-$ CPU_time
When a process is unblocked in Kmode, it is assigned a base priority $=256-$ CPU_time. When a process exits Kmode, either by system call or at the end of interrupt processing, it drops back to Umode priority, which is 128-CPU_time. It switches process if there is a higher priority process in the ready queue.

8.10.4 Comparison of MTX Scheduling Algorithms

The difference between the three scheduling algorithms can be best illustrated by an example. In MTX, there are no compute-bound processes. Instead, we simulate compute-bound processes by running while(1) looping programs in the background.

1. Assume that the time quantum of each process is 120 ticks (2 s).
2. Under the MTX sh, enter loop & to run a looping process in the background.
3. Then try to run another command, e.g. cat file.

While the looping process is running, the sh process is waiting for a command line. In MTX8.sch1, as a command is entered, the first input char causes a keyboard interrupt, which unblocks the sh process in Kmode. But the sh process cannot run because its priority is also 128. It will run only when the looping process has exhausted its time quantum of 2 s. When the sh process eventually runs it reads whatever keys are available in the keyboard input buffer. If the user has not entered a complete command line, the sh will go back to wait again. In this case, the user would experience a delay of up to 2 s between each key input. Most interactive users would consider this unacceptable. When the sh has read a complete command line, it will run until its time quantum expires. The only way to prevent the excessive delays is to use a very short time quantum, e.g. 6 ticks.

In MTX8.sch2, the situation is different. The looping process runs in Umode with a priority 128. When sh waits for a command line, the first input key interrupt wakes up the sh process with a higher priority (256). When the looping process exits Kmode, it immediately switches to the sh process. If the sh process needs more keys, it goes back to Kmode to wait for another key, which switches back to the looping process. However, the user would see each input key immediately after it is typed. When sh eventually gets a complete command line, it will keep running for a time quantum of 2 s before switching to the looping process.

In MTX8.sch3, the situation is similar to that of MTX8.sch2, except that the sh process will respond even faster. The looping process simulates a pure compute-bound process, which issues no I/O operations at all. Whenever it runs, it tries to use up its full time quantum of 2 s. Since the process priorities are recomputed dynamically based on their CPU time used, a running process may be preempted before its time quantum expires. This is even more obvious if we run several looping processes in the background. In that case, the response time to interactive processes is still quite good.

In summary, MTX allows the reader to experiment with different scheduling algorithms and observe their effects on the system performance. The MTX kernel is simple but table enough to support this kind of experiments, which is hard to do on other operating systems.

Problems

1. Assume that when the MTX kernel starts, it remaps the vectors of IRQ0-IRQ15 to 0×20-0×2F. Show how to set the timer interrupt vector in MTX to make the timer work.
2. Assume that in a Timer Request Queue the timer request elements (TQEs) are maintained in such a way that the time of each TQE is relative to the cumulative time of all the preceding TQEs. Devise algorithms for insertion and deletion of a TQE.
3.(1). Rewrite the INTH macro as

```
MACRO INTH
    call save
    call _?1
    br   _ireturn
MEND
```

where save() is a function which saves CPU registers of the interrupted point, changes the execution environment to Kmode and uses the running proc's kstack. Then install interrupt handlers as

_int80h: INTH _kcinth
_tinth: INTH _thandler

(2). Assume 10 interrupt handlers are to be installed with this new INTH macro. Determine the number of bytes saved in the kernel code space.

4. In order to support nested interrupts, each process' kstack must have enough space for saving up to 15 levels of interrupt contexts in the worst case. To save kernel space, try to use a single stack area, denoted by Istack, for interrupt processing. Implement an Istack for interrupt processing in MTX.

5. The MTX kernel has only a single priority process scheduling queue. Assume that processes have $N=4$ distinct priorities. Implement a N-level priority scheduling queue for MTX.

6. Assume: each semaphore has a priority field, which is used as follow.

(1). During initialization, assign a fixed priority value to each semaphore.

(2). Modify V(s) such that, when unblocking a process from a semaphore queue the unblocked process shall run with the semaphore priority. Answer the following questions.

(1). How to assign semaphore priority values in an OS kernel?

(2). How would the semaphore priorities affect process scheduling?

References

Intel 8253 Programmable Interval Timer, http://en.wikipedia.org/wiki/Intel_8253, 2010

Intel 8259A PIC: http://pdos.csail.mit.edu/6.828/2014/readings/hardware/8259A.pdf, 2014

Bach, M.J., "The Design of the Unix operating system", Prentice Hall, 1990

Bovet, D.P., Cesati, M., "Understanding the Linux Kernel, Third Edition", O'Reilly, 2005

"Intel 64 and IA-32 Architectures Software Developer's Manuals Vol. 1". Intel Corporation, 2011.

"Intel 64 and IA-32 Architectures Software Developer's Manuals Vol. 3A". Intel Corporation, 2011

Chapter 9
Signals and Signal Processing

9.1 Signals and Interrupts

In Chap. 8, we have seen that interrupts are requests sent to a CPU, which divert the CPU from its normal executions to do interrupt processing. Like interrupts to a CPU, signals are requests sent to a process, which divert the process from its normal executions to do signal processing. Before discussing signals and signal processing, we shall review the concepts and mechanism of interrupts, which help put signals in an OS into a proper perspective.

(1). First, we generalize the notion of process to mean: a "process" (in quotes) is a sequence of activities. Examples of generalized "processes" include

.a person, who carries on his/her daily routine chores.
.a Unix (or MTX) process, which runs in its address space(s).
.a CPU, which executes machine instructions.

(2). An "interrupt" is an event delivered to a "process", which diverts the "process" from its normal activities to do something else, called "interrupt processing". The "process" may resume its normal activities when it finishes processing the "interrupt".

(3). The term "interrupt" can be applied to any "process", not just to a CPU in a computer. For example, we may speak of the following kinds of "interrupts".

(3). 1. PERSON interrupts:

While I am reading, grading, day-dreaming, etc. in my office, some real events may occur, such as

© Springer International Publishing Switzerland 2015
K. C. Wang, *Design and Implementation of the MTX Operating System,*
DOI 10.1007/978-3-319-17575-1_9

Real Events	ID	Action Function
Building on fire	1	Get out immediately!
Telephone rings	2	Pick up phone to chat with the caller.
Telephone rings	3	Yell come in (or pretend not there).
Cut own finger	4	Apply band-aid.

All these may be called PERSON interrupts since they divert a person from his/her normal activities to "process or handle the interrupt". After processing an interrupt, a person may resume whatever he/she was doing before (if the person survives and still remembers what he/she was doing before). Each interrupt is assigned a unique ID number for identification, and has a pre-installed action function, which a person can "execute" upon receiving an interrupt. Depending on their origin, interrupts may be classified into 3 categories:

From hardware: building on fire, alarm clock goes off, etc.
From other person: phone call, knocking on door, etc.
Self-inflicted: cut own finger, eat too much, etc.

Depending on their urgency, interrupts can be classified as

Non-maskable (NMI): Building on fire!
Maskable: Knocking on door, etc.

Each of the action functions of a PERSON is installed either by instincts or by experience. It is impossible to complete the above table since there are too many different kinds of PERSON interrupts, but the idea should be clear.

(3). 2. PROCESS interrupts:
These are interrupts sent to a process. While a process is executing, it may receive interrupts from 3 different sources:
From hardware: Control_C key from terminal, interval timer, etc.
From other process: kill(pid, SIG#), death_of_child, etc.
Self-inflicted: divide by zero, invalid address, etc.

Each process interrupt is converted to a unique ID number, which is delivered to the process. Unlike PERSON interrupts, which has too many kinds, we can always limit the number of interrupts to a process. In Unix, process interrupts are called SIGNALS, which are numbered 1 to 31. For each signal, a process has an action function in its PROC structure, which the process can execute upon receiving a signal. Similar to a person, a process may mask out certain kinds of signals to defer their processing. If needed, a process may also change its signal action functions.

(3). 3. HARDWARE Interrupts:
These are signals sent to a processor or CPU. They also originate from 3 possible sources:

From hardware: Timer, I/O devices, etc.
From other processors: FFP, DMA, other CPUs in a multiprocessor system.
Self-inflicted: divide by 0, protection error, INT instruction.

Each interrupt has a unique interrupt vector number. The action function is an interrupt handler in the interrupt vector table. Recall that a CPU is always executing a process. The CPU does not cause any self-inflicted interrupts (unless faulty). Such interrupts are due to the process that is using or, in most cases, misusing the CPU. The former includes the INT n or equivalent instructions, which cause the CPU to switch from Umode to Kmode. The latter includes all trap errors recognized by the CPU as exceptions. Therefore, we may rule out the self-inflicted interrupts from a CPU, leaving only those external to the CPU.

(3). 4. Trap Errors of Process:

A process may cause self-inflicted interrupts to itself. Such interrupts are due to errors, e.g. divide by 0, invalid address, illegal instruction, privilege violation, etc. which are recognized by the CPU as exceptions. When a process encounters an exception, it traps to the OS kernel, converts the trap reason to a signal number and delivers the signal to itself. If the exception occurs in user mode, the default action of a process is to terminate, with an optional memory dump for debugging. As we shall see later, a process may replace the default action function with a signal catcher, allowing it to handle signal in user mode. If the trap occurs in kernel mode, which must be due to hardware error or, most likely, bugs in the kernel code, there is nothing the kernel can do. In Unix/Linux, the kernel simply prints a PANIC error message and stops. Hopefully the problem can be traced and fixed in the next kernel release. MTX adopts the same humble attitude. Despite my best effort, I have no doubt there are still bugs in the MTX kernel.

9.2 Examples of Unix/Linux Signals

(1). Pressing the Control_C key usually causes a running process to terminate. Here is why. The Control_C key generates a keyboard hardware interrupt. The keyboard interrupt handler converts the Control_C key to a SIGINT(2) signal delivered to all processes on the terminal and wake up such processes if they are waiting for keyboard inputs. While in Kmode, every process is required to check and handle outstanding signals. For most signals, the default action of a process is to call the kernel's kexit(exitValue) function to terminate. In Linux, the low byte of exitValue is the signal number that caused the process to terminate.

(2). The user may use the nohup a.out & command to run a process in the background. The process will continue to run even after the user logout. The nohup command causes the sh to fork a child to execute the program as usual, but the child ignores the SIGHUP(1) signal. When the user logout, the sh sends a SIGHUP signal to all processes associated with the terminal. Upon receiving such a signal, the background process simply ignores it and continues to run.

To prevent the background process from using the terminal for I/O, the background process usually disconnects itself from the terminal (by redirecting its file descriptors 0,1,2 to /dev/null), making it totally immune to any terminal oriented signals.

(3). Perhaps a few days later the user login again and finds (by ps -u UID) that the background process is still running. The user may use the sh command

$$\text{kill pid   (or kill -s 9 pid)}$$

to kill it. Here is how. The process executing kill sends a SIGTERM(15) signal to the target process identified by pid, requesting it to die. The targeted process will comply with the request and terminate. If the process has chosen to ignore the SIGTERM signal, it may refuse to die. In that case, we may use kill -s 9 pid, which will kill it for sure. This is because processes cannot change their actions for the number 9 signal. The reader may wonder, why number 9? In the original Unix, there were only 9 signals. The number 9 signal was reserved as the last resort to kill a process. Although later Unix systems expand the signal numbers to 31, the meaning of signal number 9 is still retained.

9.3   Signal Processing in Unix (Bovet and Cesati 2005)

(1). Signal types in Unix: Unix supports 31 different signals, which are defined in the signal.h file. Each signal has a symbolic name, such as SIGHUP(1), SIGINT(2), SIGKILL(9), SIGSEVG(11), etc.

(2). Origins of signals: Signals to a process originate from 3 sources:

Hardware Interrupts: While a process executes, some hardware interrupts are converted to signals delivered to the process. Examples of hardware signals are

Interrupt key (Control-C), which results in a SIGINT(2) signal.
Interval timer, which delivers an SIGALRM(14) signal when time expires.
Other hardware errors, such as bus-error, IO trap, etc.

Self-inflicted: When a process in Umode encounters a trap (error), it goes to Kmode to deliver a signal to itself. Examples of familiar trap signals are SIGFPE(8) for floating point exception (divide by 0) and the most common and dreadful SIGSEGV(11) for segmentation fault, etc.
.From other process by the kill(pid, sig#) syscall, which delivers a sign# signal to a target process identified by pid. The reader may try the following experiment. Under Linux, run the trivial C program

$$\text{main()\{ while(1); \}}$$

which causes the process to loop forever. From another (X-window) terminal, use ps -u to find the looping process pid. Then enter the sh command

kill -s 11 pid

The looping process will die with segmentation fault. The reader may say: that's incredible! All the process does is executing in a while(1) loop, how can it commit a segmentation fault? The answer is: it does not matter. Whenever a process dies by a signal, its exitValue contains the signal number. The parent sh simply converts the signal number of the dead child process to an error string, whatever that is.

(3). Signals in process PROC: Each PROC has a 32-bit vector, which records signals sent to the process. In the bit vector, each bit (except bit 0) represents a signal number. In addition, it also has a MASK bit-vector for masking out the corresponding signals. A set of syscalls, such as sigmask, sigsetmask, siggetmask, sigblock, etc. can be used to set, clear and examine the MASK bit-vector. A pending signal becomes effective only if it is not masked out. This allows a process to defer processing masked out signals, similar to CPU masking out certain interrupts.

(4). Singal Handlers: Each process PROC has a signal handler array, int sig[32]. Each entry of the sig[32] array specifies how to handle a corresponding signal, where 0 means DEFault, 1 means IGNore, other nonzero value means by a preinstalled signal catcher (handler) function in Umode.

(5). Change Signal Handlers: A process may use the syscall

int r = signal(int signal_number, void *handler);

to change the handler function of a selected signal number except 9 and 19(SIGSTOP). The installed handler, if not 0 or 1, must be the entry address of a function in user space of the form

void catcher(int signal_number){.............}

(6). A process may use the syscall

int r = kill(pid, signal_number);

to send a signal to another process identified by pid. The sh command

kill -s signal_number pid

uses the kill syscall. In general, only related processes, e.g. those with the same uid, may send signals to each other. However, a superuser process (uid=0) may send signals to any process. The kill syscall uses an invalid pid, to mean different ways of delivering the signal. For example, pid=0 sends the signal to all processes in the same process group, pid=−1 for all processes with pid>1, etc. The reader may consult Linux man pages on signal/kill for more details.

(7). A process checks signals and handles outstanding signals when it is in Kmode. If a signal has a user installed catcher function, the process first clears the signal, fetches the catcher's address, and resets the installed catcher to DEFault. Then it manipulates the return path in such a way that it returns to execute the catcher function in Umode. When the catcher function finishes, it returns to the original point of interruption, i.e. from where it lastly entered Kmode. Thus, the process takes a detour to execute the catcher function first. Then it resumes normal execution.

(8). Reset user installed signal catchers: User installed catcher functions are intended to deal with trap errors in user code. Since the catcher function is also executed in Umode, it may commit the same kind of traps again. If so, the process would end up in an infinite loop, jumping between Umode and Kmode forever. To prevent this, the Unix kernel typically resets the handler to DEFault before letting the process execute the catcher function. This implies that a user installed catcher function is good for only one occurrence of the signal. To catch another occurrence of the same signal, the catcher must be installed again. For simplicity reasons, we shall adopt this rule in MTX also. However, the treatment of user installed signal catchers is not uniform as it varies across different versions of Unix. For instance, in BSD the signal handler is not reset but the same signal is blocked while executing the signal catcher. Interested readers may consult the man pages of signal and sigaction of Linux for more details.

(9). Signal and Wakeup: There are two kinds of SLEEP processes in the Unix kernel; sound sleepers and light sleepers. The former are non-interruptible, but the latter are interruptible by signals. If a process is in the non-interruptible SLEEP state, arriving signals (which must originate from hardware interrupts or another process) do not wakeup the process. If it is in the interruptible SLEEP state, arriving signals will wake it up. For example, when a process waits for terminal inputs, it sleeps with a low priority, which is interruptible, a signal such as SIGINT will wake it up. In MTX, a signal always wakes up a process if it is sleeping or blocked for terminal inputs. It does not wake up those processes if they are waiting for file operations or I/O for block devices.

(10). Proper use of signals: Unix signals are originally designed for these purposes.

As a unified treatment of process traps: When a process encounters an exception, it traps to kernel mode, converts the trap reason to a signal number and delivers the signal to itself. If the exception occurred in Kmode, the kernel prints a PANIC message and stops. If the exception occurred in Umode, the process typically terminates with a memory dump for debugging.

To allow processes to handle program errors in Umode by preinstalled signal catchers. This is similar to the ESPIE macro in MVS [IBM MVS 2010].

Under unusual conditions, it allows a process to kill another process by a signal. Note that kill does not kill a process outright; it is only a "please die" plea to the target process. Why can't we kill a process outright? The reader is encouraged to think of the reasons. (Hint: the large number of unclaimed bank accounts in Swiss banks).

(11). Misuse of Signals: In many OS books, signals are classified as a mechanism for inter-process communication. The rationale is that a process may send a signal to another process, causing it to execute a preinstalled handler function. The classification is highly debatable, if not inappropriate, for the following reasons.

The mechanism is unreliable due to possible missing signals. Each signal is represented by a single bit in a bit-vector, which can only record one occurrence of a signal. If a process sends two or more identical signals to another process, they may show up only once in the recipient PROC.

Race condition: Before processing a signal, a process usually resets the signal handler to DEFault. In order to catch another occurrence of the same signal, the process must reinstall the catcher function BEFORE the next signal arrives. Otherwise, the next signal may cause the process to terminate. Although the race condition could be prevented by blocking the same signal while executing the signal catcher, there is no way to prevent missing signals.

Most signals have predefined meaning. Indiscriminate use of signals may not achieve communication but confusion. For example, sending a SIGSEGV(11) segmentation fault signal to a looping process is like yelling to a swimmer in the water: "Your pants are on fire!".

Therefore, trying to use signals for inter-process communication is over stretching the intended purpose of signals. If needed, the message passing mechanism presented in Chap. 6 is a much better way for IPC.

9.4   Implementation of Signals in MTX

9.4.1   Signal Types in MTX

The real-mode MTX uses a 16-bit vector for signals. Therefore, it supports only 15 types of signals, which are the first 15 signals in Unix.

```
#define NSIG     16
#define SIGHUP    1
#define SIGINT    2
#define SIGQUIT   3
#define SIGILL    4
#define SIGTRAP   5
#define SIGABRT   6
#define SIGBUS    7
#define SIGFPE    8
#define SIGKILL   9
#define SIGUSR1  10
#define SIGSEGV  11
#define SIGUSR2  12
#define SIGPIPE  13
#define SIGALRM  14
#define SIGTERM  15
```

In fact, the actual number of signals in the real mode MTX is much less. This is because the Intel x86 CPU in real mode recognizes only a few traps. For instance, it recognizes divide-by-0 and single-step traps by the vector number 0 and 1, respectively, but it does not recognize most other types of traps. For demonstration purpose, other traps are simulated by INT n instructions, where $n=2$ to 7. The full set of signals will be used later in protected mode MTX in Chaps. 14 and 15.

9.4.2   Signals in PROC Resource

Each MTX PROC has a pointer to a resource structure, which contains the following fields for signals and signal handling.

   u16 signal;   // 15 signals; bit 0 is not used.
   int sig[16]; // signal handlers: 0=default,1=ignore, else a catcher in Umode.

For the sake of simplicity, MTX dose not support signal masking. If desired, the reader may add signal masking to the MTX kernel.

9.4.3   Signal Origins in MTX

(1). Hardware: MTX supports only the Control-C key from terminal, which is converted to SIGINT(2), and the interval timer of a process, which is converted to INTALRM(14).
(2). Traps: MTX in real mode only supports the divide-by-0 trap. Other traps are simulated by a simu_trap(int n) function, which issues an INT n.

(3). From Other Process: MTX supports the kill(pid, signal) syscall, but it does
not enforce permission checking. Therefore, a process can kill any process. If
the target process is in the SLEEP/BLOCKED state, kill() normally wakeup/
unblock the process.

9.5   Deliver Signal to Process

The algorithm of the kill syscall is

```
/************* Algorithm of kill syscall  ****************/
int kkill(int pid, int sig_number)
{
   (1). validate signal number and pid;
   (2). check permission to kill; // not enforced, may kill any pid
   (3). set proc.signal.[bit_sig_number] to 1;
   (4). if proc is SLEEP, wakeup pid;
   (5). if proc is BLOCKed for terminal inputs, unblock proc;
   (6). return 0 for success;
}
```

9.5.1   Change Signal Handler in Kernel

MTX supports the siganl syscall, which changes the handler function of a specified
signal. The algorithm of the signal syscall is

```
/*********** Algorithm of signal syscall ***************/
int ksignal(u16 sig_number, u16 catcher)
{
   (1). validate sig number, e.g. cannot change signal number 9;
   (2). int oldsig = running->sig[sig_number];
   (3). running->sig[sig_number] = catcher;
   (4). return oldsig;
}
```

9.5.2   Signal Processing in MTX

A CPU usually checks for pending interrupts at the end of executing an instruction. Likewise, it suffices to let a process check for pending signals at the end of
Kmode execution, i.e. when it is about to return to Umode. However, if a process
enters Kmode via a syscall, it should check and handle signals first. This is because
if a process already has a pending signal, which may cause it to die, executing the
syscall would be a waste of time. On the other hand, if a process enters Kmode

due to an interrupt, it must handle the interrupt first. The algorithm of checking for pending signals is

```
/************ Algorithm of Check Signals ***********/
int check_sig()
{
   int i;
   for (i=1; i<NSIG; i++){
        if (running->signal & (1 << i)){
             running->signal &= ~(1 << i);
             return i;
        }
   }
   return 0;
}
```

A process handles outstanding signals by the code segment

```
            if (running->signal)
                 psig();
```

The algorithm of psig() is

```
/************* Algorithm psig() *****************/
int psig(int sig)
{
   while(int n=check_sig()){              // for each pending signal do
(1).   clear running PROC.signal[bit_n]; // clear the signal bit
(2).   if (running->sig[n] == 1)         // IGNore the signal
          continue;
(3).   if (running->sig[n] == 0)         // DEFault : die with sign#
          kexit(n<<8);       // high byte of exitStatus=signal number
(4).   // execute signal handler in Umode
       fix up running PROC's "interrupt stack frame" for it to return
       to execute catcher(n) in Umode;
   }
}
```

9.5.3   Dispatch Signal Catcher for Execution in User Mode

In the algorithm of psig(), only step (4) is interesting and challenging. Therefore, we shall explain it in more detail. The goal of (4) is to let the process return to Umode to execute a catcher(int sig) function. When the catcher() function finishes, it should return to the point where the process lastly entered Kmode. The following diagrams show how to accomplish these. When a process enters Kmode from Umode, its

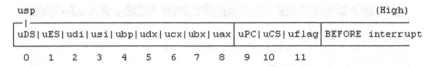

```
usp                                                                 (High)
 ┌─│──────────────────────────────────────────────────────────────────────
 │uDS|uES|udi|usi|ubp|udx|ucx|ubx|uax│uPC|uCS|uflag│ BEFORE interrupt
   0   1   2   3   4   5   6   7   8    9  10   11
```

Fig. 9.1 Process interrupt stack frame

```
usp                                      |replace|          | insert |
 ┌─│─────────────────────────────────────────────────────────────────────
 │uDS|uES|udi|usi|ubp|udx|ucx|ubx|uax│catcher│uCS|uflag│uPC|sig#│ intr
   0   1   2   3   4   5   6   7   8     9      10   11    12  13
```

Fig. 9.2 Modified process interrupt stack frame

ustack top contains an "interrupt stack frame" consisting of the 12 entries, as shown in Fig. 9.1.

In order for the process to return to catcher() with the signal number as a parameter, we modify the interrupt stack frame as follows.

(1). replace the uPC (at index 9) with the entry address of catcher();
(2). insert the original return address, uPC, and the signal number after the interrupt stack frame, as shown in Fig. 9.2.

This can be done by shifting the interrupt stack frame downward 2 slots, then inserting the entries (uPC, sig#) immediately after the interrupt stack frame. This changes the saved usp to usp-4. In a system with stack size limit, the ustack itself may have to be expanded first. Here, we assume that the ustack always has space for the added entries. With the modified ustack, when the process exits kernel, it will return to catcher() as if it had called catcher(sig#) from the place pointed by the original uPC. When the catcher() function finishes, it returns by uPC, causing it return to the original point of interruption.

It is observed that in some PC emulators the interrupt stack frame may contain extra entries. For instance, the interrupt stack frame of DOSEMU contains |SP| F800 |uPC |uCS |uflag| rather than |uPC|uCS|uflag| as in a real PC. For such emulators, the interrupt stack frame is meant to contain all the (extra) entries pushed on the stack by the emulator. Otherwise, the above scheme may not work. The virtual machines of QEMU and VMware do not have such problems.

9.6 MTX9.Signal: Demonstration of Signal Processing in MTX

MTX9.signal demonstrates signals and signal processing. In MTX9.signal, when running the sh command, P1 creates a child P2 to run sh and waits for the child to terminate. P2 shows the commands in the /bin directory. The commands include divide, itimer, trap and kill, which demonstrate signals and signal handling. Figure 9.3 shows the screen of running the divide and itimer commands, which are explained below.

```
loading /bin/divide to segment 0x4000  .... done
try to divide by zero
install catcher ? (y|n) : y
ksignal: sig=8  catcher=0x423   installed sig 8  0x423
here it goes : c = a/0 !
proc 3  divide error => SIGFPE=8
in catcher : signal# = 8
AMAZING GRACE! I survived divide by zero
proc 2  found a ZOMBIE child 3  exitValue=0
=============== commands in /bin ===============
u1 u2 sh divide itimer trap kill
==============================================
enter command in /bin OR exit): itimer 2
proc 2  forked a child 3  in segment=0x4000
proc 3  exec to /bin/itimer in segment 0x4000
loading /bin/itimer to segment 0x4000  .... done
$$$$$$$$$$$$$$$$$$$$$$$$$$$$$$$$$$$$$$$$$$$$$$$$$$
          This is MTX's itimer in action
$$$$$$$$$$$$$$$$$$$$$$$$$$$$$$$$$$$$$$$$$$$$$$$$$$
install catcher? [y|n]proc3  : set itimer 2
timerQ =  [3 , 2 ] ==>
proc3  : looping until SIGALRM ....
timerQ =  [3 , 1 ] ==>
timerQ =  [3 , 0 ] ==>
proc 3  dying by signal# 14
proc 2  found a ZOMBIE child 3  exitValue=3584
=============== commands in /bin ===============
u1 u2 sh divide itimer trap kill
==============================================
enter command in /bin OR exit):
```

Fig. 9.3 Demonstration of signal processing in MTX

9.6.1 Divide Trap Catcher

The PC in real mode recognizes divide-by-zero, which traps to the vector number 0. To catch divide-by-zero errors, we can install a trap handler for vector 0 by the INTH macro

_divide INTH kdivide

In the C handler function kdivide(), it sends a SIGFPE(8) signal to the running process. If the process has not installed a catcher, it will die by the signal number 8. Before the divide error, the user may choose to install a catcher for the divide trap. In that case, the process will execute the catcher in Umode. The catcher uses a long jump to bypass the function containing the divide instruction that caused the exception, allowing the process to continue and terminate normally.

9.6.2 Other Traps

The trap.c program issues an INT n ($n=2$ to 7) to simulate a hardware exception, which sends a signal number n to the process. Similar to the divide trap, the user may install a catcher for the simulated trap n error. In that case, the process will execute the catcher, which uses a long jump to let the process terminate normally.

9.6.3 Interval Timer and Alarm Signal Catcher

In the USER directory, the itimer.c program demonstrates interval timer, alarm signal and signal catcher.

```
/******************* itimer.c file *********************/
void catcher(int sig)
{
  printf("proc %d in catcher: sig-%d\n", getpid(), sig);
  itimer(1); // set a 1 second itimer again
}
main(int argc, char *argv[])
{
  int t = 1;
  if (argc>1) t = atoi(argv[1]);      // timer interval
  printf("install catcher? [y|n]");
  if (getc()=='y')
     signal(14, catcher);  // install catcher() for SIGALRM(14)
   itimer(t);                // set interval timer in kernel
  printf("proc %d looping until SIGALRM\n", getpid());
  while(1);                 // looping until killed by a signal
}
```

In the itimer.c program, the process sets an interval timer of t seconds. Then, it executes a while(1) loop. When the interval timer expires, the timer interrupt handler sends a SIGALRM(14) signal to the process. If the user has not installed a signal catcher, the process will die by the signal. Otherwise, it will execute the catcher once and continues to loop. In the latter case, the process can be killed by other means, such as the Control_C key, which will be shown later when we develop the keyboard driver. In the meantime, we let the catcher() function set another itimer request. When the second itimer expires, the process will die by SIGALRM(14). The reader may modify the catcher() function to install the catcher again. Recompile and run the system to observe the effect.

9.6.4 The Kill Command

The kill command demonstrates the kill system call. To test the kill command, let P1 fork a child (P2) first. Then run the sh process and enter

kill pid signal_number

which sends a signal to the targeted process, causing it to die. Based on this, the reader may try to develop a program to do inter-process communication using the signal and kill system calls, but watch what would happen if a process repeatedly send the same signal to the target process.

Problems

1. Review Questions:

(1). Define "interrupts" in your own words.
(2). What are Hardware interrupts, Process interrupts?
(3). INT n instructions are usually called software interrupts. What's the difference between INT n and PROCESS interrupt?
(4). How does a process get PROCESS interrupts?
(5). How does a process handle PROCESS interrupts?

2. What is the role of signal 9? Why is it needed?
3. A CPU usually checks for pending interrupts at the end of current instruction. What are the time and places for a process to check for pending signals?
4. Before handling a signal, the kernel usually resets the signal's handler to DEFault. Why is this necessary?
5. In C programming, a callback function (pointer) is passed as a parameter to a called function, which may execute the callback function. What's the difference between callback functions and signal catchers?
6. Assume that a process has installed a signal catcher for SIGALRM(14). What if the process exec to a different image? How to deal with this kind of problem?
7. A super user process may kill any other process. An non-super user process may only kill processes of the same user. Implement permission checking in the kill system call.
8. Implement signal masking in MTX.
9. Use SIGUSR1(10) signal to implement Inter-Process Communication (IPC) in MTX. Compare it with message passing by send/recv in Chap. 6.

10. Implement a death-of-child (SIGCHLD) signal. When a process terminates, it sends a SIGCHILD signal to the parent, causing the parent to execute the wait() function.
11. A process gets user inputs to update a counter. Every t seconds it sends the counter value to another process in a message. Design an algorithm for such a process and implement it under MTX. (HINT: use the interval timer and enforce critical regions).
12. Assume that processes communicate by send/recv messages, which are unreliable, e.g. messages may be lost during send/recv. After sending a message, a process expects a reply. If it does not receive a reply within t seconds,

it re-sends the same message again. If it receives a reply within t seconds, it must not send the same message again. Design an algorithm for the sending process and implement it in MTX.

References

Bovet, D.P., Cesati, M., "Understanding the Linux Kernel, Third Edition", O'Reilly, 2005
IBM MVS Programming Assembler Services Guide, Oz/OS V1R11.0, IBM, 2010
Linux: http://www.linux.org, 2015

Chapter 10
Device Drivers

10.1 Device Drivers

A device driver is a piece code which controls a device for I/O operations. It is an interface between a physical device and processes doing I/O on the device. So far, MTX uses BIOS for I/O. In this chapter, we shall develop our own device drivers to replace BIOS for I/O operations. These include drivers for the console display, keyboard, parallel printer, serial ports, floppy drives, IDE hard disk and CD/DVD ROM. In a multitasking system, I/O operations should be done by interrupts, not by polling. Therefore, all the device drivers, except the console display, are interrupt-driven. When developing the device drivers we shall focus on the principles of driver design, rather than trying to implement complete drivers. For example, in the console display driver, we only show how to display ordinary chars, but not all the special chars. In the keyboard driver, we only show how to handle ordinary keys and some of the function and control keys, but not all the escape key sequences. In the disk and CDROM drivers, we only show how to recognize exceptions but do not attempt to handle all the error conditions, etc. Despite these simplifications, all the device drivers presented in this chapter are functional, but they are by no means complete. Interested readers may try to improve on the drivers to make them complete. As usual, after presenting the design and implementation of each device driver, we shall demonstrate the driver operations by a sample system. Since the main objective is to demonstrate the device drivers, most of the sample systems are based on MTX5.1. For ease of reference, we shall label the sample systems MTX10.xy, where the suffix letters indicate the included drivers. Among the I/O devices, the console display is the simplest because it is a memory mapped device, which does not use interrupts. So we begin with the console display driver.

K. C. Wang, *Design and Implementation of the MTX Operating System*,
DOI 10.1007/978-3-319-17575-1_10

10.2   Console Display Driver

The console display of IBM compatible PCs has many modes, ranging from the original VGA to what's broadly referred to as SVGA. MTX does not support graphic display. It only uses the basic VGA mode to display text in 16 colors with 640×400 resolutions. From a programming point of view, the PC's display works as follows. It is a memory mapped device. The display screen is organized as 25 rows by 80 columns, for a total of $25 \times 80 = 2000$ characters. The display memory, known as the video RAM, is a memory area containing characters to be displayed. Each character in the video RAM is represented by 2 bytes = [attribute, character], where the attribute byte determines how to display the character, e.g. color, intensity, reverse video, blinking, etc. The second byte is the ASCII code of the character to be displayed. The video RAM begins at the segment address 0xB800. The size of the video RAM varies from 16 to 32 KB, which is much larger than the 4000 bytes needed to display a screen. The interface between the video RAM and the display screen is a Video Display Controller (VDC), which has a cursor position register and a display start address register. The VDC simply displays the 4000 2-byte words, beginning from the start address, in the video RAM to the screen as 2000 characters in a 25×80 layout. The cursor shape and size can be programmed through the cursor height register. The cursor location is determined by the cursor position register. For proper visual effect, the cursor is positioned at where the next character is to be displayed. The relationship between the video RAM contents and the display screen is shown in Fig. 10.1.

Assume that each box of the video RAM in Fig. 10.1 contains 2000 words. The VDC simply displays the words in the box pointed by the start address. If we move the start address up one line (toward low address), the displayed screen would show wxyz at the top. The visual effect is that the entire screen is scrolled downward one line. If we move the start address down one line, the screen would be scrolled up one line. When moving the start address downward (toward higher address) we must monitor its position in the video RAM area. If the remaining RAM area is less than a screen size, we must copy the next screen to the beginning of the RAM area and reset the start address to the video RAM beginning address. This is because the

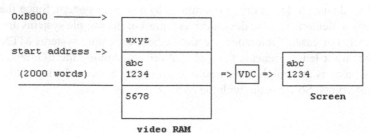

Fig. 10.1 Video RAM and display

video RAM address does not wrap around by itself. The VDC registers can be accessed through the display adaptor's index register at the I/O port address 0x3D4. To change a VDC register, first select the intended register. Then write a (2-byte) value to the data register at 0x3D5 to change the selected register. When programming the VDC the most important VDC register pairs are start_address=0x0C-0x0D and cursor_position=0x0E-0x0F. The display driver algorithm is as follows.

(1). call vid_init() to initialize the cursor size, cursor position and, VID_ORG of the VDC hardware. Initialize the driver variables row and column to 0. Clear the screen and position the cursor at the top left corner.

(2). A screen=25 rows by 80 columns=2000 words=[attribute byte, char byte] in the video RAM, beginning at start_address=0xB8000.

(3). To display a screen: write 4000 bytes (2000 words) to the video RAM at the current VID_ORG location. The VDC will display the 2000 chars from start_address=VID_ORG in the video RAM to the screen.

(4). The driver must keep track of the Cursor position (row, col). After displaying a char, the driver must advance the Cursor by one word, which may change (row, col). When col >=80, reset col to 0 and increment row by 1. When row >=25, scroll up one row. Handle special chars such as \n and \b to produce the right visual effect.

(5). Scroll up or down:

(5).1. To scroll up one row: increment VID_ORG by one row. Write a row of blanks to the last row on screen. If the last row exceeds video RAM size, copy current screen to the video RAM beginning and reset VID_ORG to 0.

(5).2. To scroll down one row: decrement VID_ORG by one row.

The following lists the display driver code.

```
/*********** Display Driver vid.c file of MTX kernel ************/
#define VDC_INDEX      0x3D4
#define VDC_DATA       0x3D5
#define CUR_SIZE        10  // cursor size register
#define VID_ORG         12  // start address register
#define CURSOR          14  // cursor position register
#define LINE_WIDTH      80  // # characters on a line
#define SCR_LINES       25  // # lines on the screen
#define SCR_BYTES     4000  // bytes of one screen=25*80
#define CURSOR_SHAPE    15  // block cursor for EGA/VGA
// attribute byte: 0x0HRGB, H=highLight; RGB determine color
u16 base = 0xB800;          // VRAM base address
u16 vid_mask = 0x3FFF;      // mask=Video RAM size - 1
u16 offset;                 // offset from VRAM segment base
int color;                  // attribute byte
int org;                    // current display origin, r.e. VRAM base
int row, column;            // logical row, col position

int vid_init() // initializes org=0 (row,column)=(0,0)
{ int i, w;
  org = row = column = 0; // initialize globals
  color = 0x0A;                     // high YELLOW;
  set_VDC(CUR_SIZE, CURSOR_SHAPE);  // set cursor size
  set_VDC(VID_ORG, 0);              // display origin to 0
  set_VDC(CURSOR, 0);               // set cursor position to 0
  w = 0x0700;                       // White, blank char
  for (i=0; i<25*80; i++)           // clear screen
      put_word(w, base, 0+2*i);     // write 25*80 blanks to VRAM
}
int scroll() //scroll UP one line
{ u16 i, w, bytes;
  // test offset = org + ONE screen + ONE more line
  offset = org + SCR_BYTES + 2*LINE_WIDTH;
  if (offset <= vid_mask)   // offset still within VRAM area
      org += 2*LINE_WIDTH;  // just advance org by ONE line
  else{   // offset exceeds VRAM area ==> reset to VRAM beginning by
          // copy current rows 1-24 to BASE, then reset org to 0
      for (i=0; i<24*80; i++){
          w = get_word(base, org+160+2*i);
          put_word(w, base, 0+2*i);
      }
      org = 0;
  }
  // org has been set up properly
  offset = org + 2*24*80;   // offset = beginning of row 24
  // copy a line of BLANKs to row 24
  w = 0x0C00;   // HRGB=1100 ==> HighLight RED, Null char
  for (i=0; i<80; i++)
      put_word(w, base, offset + 2*i);
  set_VDC(VID_ORG, org >> 1);   // set VID_ORG to org
}
int move_cursor()  // move cursor to current position
{   int pos = 2*(row*80 + column);
    offset = (org + pos) & vid_mask;
    set_VDC(CURSOR, offset >> 1);
}
```

```
// display a char, handle special chars '\n','\r','\b'
int putc(char c)
{ u16 w, pos;
  if (c=='\n'){
     row++;
     if (row>=25){
        row = 24;
        scroll();
     }
     move_cursor();
     return;
  }
  if (c=='\r'){
     column=0;
     move_cursor();
     return;
  }
  if (c=='\b'){
     if (column > 0){
        column--;
        move_cursor();
        put_word(0x0700, base, offset);
     }
     return;
  }
  // c is an ordinary char
  pos = 2*(row*80 + column);
  offset = (org + pos) & vid_mask;
  w = (color << 8) + c;
  put_word(w, base, offset);
  column++;
  if (column >= 80){
     column = 0;
     row++;
     if (row>=25){
        row = 24;
        scroll();
     }
  }
  move_cursor();
}
int set_VDC(u16 reg, u16 val) //set VDC register reg to val
{
  lock();
  out_byte(VDC_INDEX, reg);          // set index register
  out_byte(VDC_DATA,  (val>>8)&0xFF); // output high byte
  out_byte(VDC_INDEX, reg + 1);       // next index register
  out_byte(VDC_DATA,  val&0xFF);       // output low byte
  unlock();
}
```

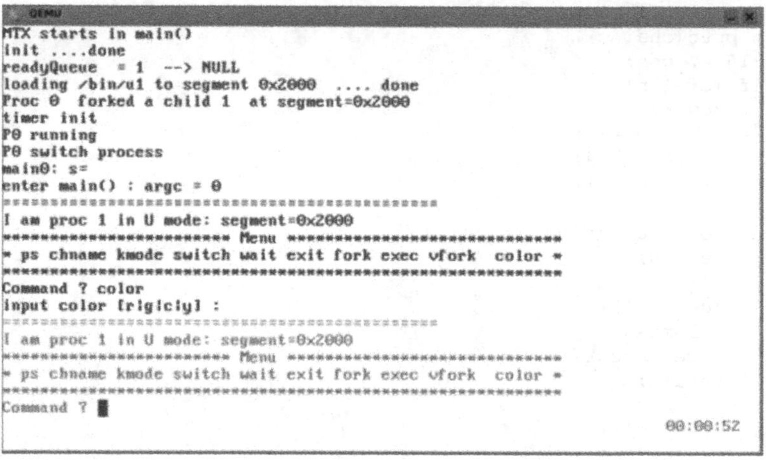

Fig. 10.2 Demonstration of timer and display drivers

10.3   MTX10.tv: Demonstration of Timer and Display Driver

MTX10.vt includes both the timer and display drivers. The following describes the changes in MTX10.vt for testing the console display driver.

1. When MTX10.vt starts, the video driver must be initialized first. It is observed that, in order for the video driver to work in color mode, the PC must start in mono display mode. This is done by a BIOS 0x10 call in assembly before calling main() in C. Upon entry to main(), the first action is to call vid_init(), which initializes the display driver.
2. Change putc() in Umode to a syscall, which calls putc() in the display driver.
3. Add a Umode command, color, which issues a syscall (9, color) to change the display color by changing the color bits in the attribute byte.
4. Modify the timer interrupt handler to display a wall clock on the lower right corner of the display screen. Figure 10.2 shows the display screen of running MTX10.tv.

10.4   Keyboard Driver

In this section, we shall develop a simple keyboard driver for the MTX kernel. Instead of showing a complete driver all at once, we shall develop the keyboard driver in several steps. First, we focus on the design principles of interrupt-driven device drivers and present a general framework that is applicable to all interrupt-driven

```
#define NSCAN 58
/* Scan codes to ASCII for unshifted keys */
char unshift[NSCAN] = { // NSCAN=58
   0, 033,'1','2','3','4','5','6','7','8','9','0','-','=','\b','\t',
  'q','w','e','r','t','y','u','i','o','p','[',']', '\r', 0,'a','s',
  'd','f','g','h','j','k','l',';', 0,  0,  0,  0, 'z', 'x','c','v',
  'b','n','m',',','.','/', 0, '*', 0, ' ' };
/* Scan codes to ASCII for shifted keys */
char shift[NSCAN] = {
   0, 033,'!','@','#','$','%','^','&','*','(',')','_','+','\b','\t',
  'Q','W','E','R','T','Y','U','I','O','P','{','}', '\r', 0,'A','S',
  'D','F','G','H','J','K','L',':', 0, '~', 0,  '|','Z','X','C','V',
  'B','N','M','<','>','?', 0, '*', 0, ' ' };
```

Fig. 10.3 Key mapping tables

drivers. For the keyboard driver, we begin by considering only lower case ASCII keys first, in order not to be distracted by the details of handling special keys. After showing the basic driver design, we extend it to handle upper case and special keys. The last step is to link the keyboard driver with user mode processes, allowing them to get chars in RAW mode (get keys as they are) or COOKED mode (after processing special keys).

10.4.1 The Keyboard Hardware

Instead of ACSII code, the keyboard of IBM compatible PCs generates scan codes. A complete listing of scan codes is included in the keyboard driver. Translation of scan code to ASCII is by mapping tables in software. This allows the same keyboard to be used for different languages. For each key typed, the keyboard generates two interrupts; one when the key is pressed and another one when the key is released. The scan code of key release is 0x80+the scan code of key press, i.e. bit-7 is 0 for key press and 1 for key release. When the keyboard interrupts, the scan code is in the data port (0x60) of the keyboard interface. The interrupt handler reads the data port to get the scan code and acknowledges the input by strobe PORT_B at 0x61. Some special keys generate escape key sequences, e.g. the UP arrow key generates 0xE048, where 0xE0 is the escape key itself. The following shows the mapping tables for translating scan codes into ASCII. The keyboard has 105 keys. Scan codes above 0x39 (57) are special keys, which cannot be mapped directly, so they are not shown in the key maps. Such special keys are recognized by the driver and handled accordingly. Figure 10.3 shows the key mapping tables.

10.4.2 Interrupt-Driven Driver Design

Every interrupt-driven device driver consists of three parts; a lower-half part, which is the interrupt handler, an upper-half part, which is called by processes and a com-

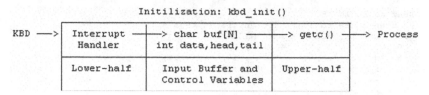

Fig. 10.4 KBD driver organization

mon data area, which are shared by the lower and upper parts. Figure 10.4 shows the organization of the keyboard driver. The top of the figure shows kbd_init(), which initialize the KBD driver when the system starts. The middle part shows the control and data flow path from the KBD device to a process. The bottom part shows the lower-half, input buffer, and the upper-half organization of the KBD driver.

When MTX boots up, the keyboard hardware is already initialized by BIOS and is ready for use. kbd_init() only initializes the driver's control variables. When a key is typed, the KBD generates an interrupt, causing the interrupt handler to be executed. The interrupt handler fetches the scan code from KBD's data port. For normal key presses, it translates the scan code into ASCII, enters the ASCII char into an input buffer, buf[N], and notifies the upper-half of the input char. When a process needs an input char, it calls getc() of the upper-half driver, trying to get a char from buf. The process waits if there is no char in buf. The control variable, data, is used to synchronize the interrupt handler and process. The choice of the control variable depends on the synchronization tool used. To begin with, we shall use sleep/wakeup for synchronization. The following shows the C code of a simple KBD driver. The driver handles only lower case keys. Upper case and special keys will be considered later.

10.4.3   A Simple Keyboard Driver Using Sleep/Wakeup

```c
/******************* A simple KBD Driver ************************/
#define KEYBD    0x60    // I/O port for keyboard data
#define PORT_B   0x61    // port_B of 8255
#define KBIT     0x80    // bit used to ack chars to keyboard
#define KBLEN      64    // size of input buffer in bytes
#define NSCAN      58    // number of scan codes to map
#define SPACE    0x39    // space char, above which are special keys
#include "keymap.c"      // keymap tables shown above
struct kbd{
  char buf[KBLEN];       // CIRCULAR buffer for input chars
  int  head, tail;
  int  data;             // number of chars in buf[ ]
} kbd;                   // keyboard driver structure
int kbd_init()
{
  kbd.head = kbd.tail = kbd.data = 0;
  enable_irq(1);         // enable IRQ1
  out_byte(0x20, 0x20);
}

int kbhandler()
{ int scode, value, c;
  // get scan code from keyboard's data port and ack it.
  scode = in_byte(KEYBD);            // get scan code
  value = in_byte(PORT_B);           // strobe PORT_B to ack the key
  out_byte(PORT_B, value | KBIT);    // first, set the bit high
  out_byte(PORT_B, value);           // then set it low
  //printf("kbd interrupt %x\n", scode);
  if (scode & 0x80 || scode > SPACE) // ignore release OR special keys
     goto out;
  c = unshift[scode];                // map scan code to ASCII char
  if (kbd.data == KBLEN){            // sound warning if buf is full
     printf("%c kbd buf FULL!\n", 007);
     goto out;
  }
  kbd.buf[kbd.head++] = c;           // enter ASCII char into buf[ ]
  kbd.head %= KBLEN;                 // buf[ ] is circular
  kbd.data++;
  wakeup(&kbd.data);                 // wakeup process in upper half
out:
  out_byte(0x20, 0x20);              // send EOI to 8259 PIC controller
}

/***************** upper-half driver routine ****************/
int getc()
{   u8 c;
    lock();                  // kbd.buf[ ] and kbd.data form a CR
    while (kbd.data==0){     // between process and interrupt handler
       unlock();
       sleep(&kbd.data);     // wait for data
       lock();
    }
    c = kbd.buf[kbd.tail++];
    kbd.tail %= KBLEN;
    kbd.data--;
    unlock();
    return c;
}
```

The simple KBD driver is intended mainly to illustrate the design principle of an interrupt-driver input device driver. The driver's buffer and control variables form a critical region since they are accessed by both process and interrupt handler. When the interrupt handler executes, the process is logically not executing. So process can not interfere with interrupt handler. However, while a process executes, interrupts may occur, which diverts the process to execute the interrupt handler, which may interfere with the process. For this reason, when a process calls getc(), it must mask out interrupts to prevent keyboard interrupts from occurring. Then it checks whether there are any keys in the input buffer. If there is no key, it sleeps with interrupt enabled. Upon waking up, it disables interrupts before checking for input keys again. If there are input keys, it gets a key, modifies the input buffer and the number of input keys while still inside the critical region. Finally, it enables interrupts before return a key. On the x86 CPU it is not possible to mask out only keyboard interrupts. The lock() operation masks out all interrupts, which is a little overkill but it gets the job done. Alternatively, we may write to the PIC mask register to disable/enable the keyboard interrupt.

10.4.4   A Simple Keyboard Driver Using Semaphore

Instead of sleep/wakeup, we may also use semaphore to synchronize the process and interrupt handler. In that case, we only need to define data as a semaphore with a 0 initial value and replace sleep/wakeup with P/V on the semaphore, as shown below.

```
struct kbd{
    char buf[KBLEN];
    int  head, tail;
    SEMAPHORE data;            // use semaphore for synchronization
}kbd;

int kbd_init()
{
  kbd.head = kbd.tail = 0;
  kbd.data.value = kbd.data.queue = 0; // initialize semaphore to 0
}
int kbhandler()
{
    /**** same as before ****/
    V(&kbd.data);
out:
    out_byte(0x20, 0x20);
}
int getc()
{   u8 c;
    P(&kbd.data); // wait for input key if necessary
    lock();
      c = kbd.buf[kbd.tail++];
      kbd.tail %= KBLEN;
    unlock();
    return c;
}
```

The advantages of using a semaphore is that it combines a counter, testing the counter and deciding whether to proceed or not all in an indivisible operation. In getc(), when a process passes through the P() statement, it is guaranteed to have a key in the input buffer. The process does not have to retry as in the case of using sleep/wakeup. However, when implementing input device drivers there is a practical problem, which must be handled properly. While a process waits for terminal inputs, it is usually interruptible. The process may be woken up or unblocked by a signal even if no key is entered. When the process resumes, it still tries to get a key. We must adjust the input buffer, e.g. by inserting a dummy key for the process to get. Otherwise, the buffer's head and tail pointers would be inconsistent, causing the next process to get wrong keys.

10.4.5 Interrupt Handlers Should Never Sleep or Block

In the KBD driver, the interrupt handler puts chars into the input buffer and process gets chars from the input buffer. It looks like a pipe but there is a major difference. In the pipe case, both ends are processes. In the KBD driver case, the write-end is not a process but an interrupt handler. Unlike a process, an interrupt handler should never sleep or become blocked, for the following reasons.

1. Sleeping or blocking applies only to a process, not to a piece of code. When an interrupt occurs, the current running process is diverted to handle the interrupt, but we do not know which process that is. If an interrupt handler sleeps or blocks, it would cause the interrupted process to sleep or block. The interrupted process may have nothing to do with the interrupt reason. It happens to be the running process when the interrupt occurs, and it is performing the interrupt processing service. Blocking such a good samaritan process logically does not make sense.

2. Blocking a process implies process switch. In all uniprocessor Unix-like systems, switch process in kernel mode is not allowed because the entire kernel is a critical region form process point of view.

3. If the interrupted process was executing in user mode, switch process is possible, but this would leave the interrupt handler in an unfinished state, rendering the interrupting device unusable for an unknown period of time. If the switched process terminates, the interrupt handler would never finish. This amounts to a lost interrupt, which confuses the device driver.

4. In a multiprocessor system, if the interrupted process has set a lock and the interrupt handler tries to acquire the same lock again, the process would lock itself out.

Therefore, an interrupt handler should only do wakeup or unblocking operations but should never sleep or become blocked. For instance, in the KBD driver the interrupt handler never waits. If the input buffer is full, it simply sounds a warning beep, discards the input char and returns.

10.4.6   Raw Mode and Cooked Mode

In the KBD driver, the interrupt handler deposits keys into the input buffer without echoing them. This has two effects. The first one is that, if no process is getting input keys and echoing them, the user would not see the keys as they are typed. The second effect is that the input buffer contains raw keys. For example, when a user types 'a', followed by backspace '\b' and then 'c', the normal interpretation is that the user intends to erase the last 'a' and replace it with 'c'. In raw mode, all three keys are entered into the input buffer. The interpretation of these keys and their visual effects on the display screen are left for the process to decide. Raw inputs are often necessary. For example, when executing a full screen text editor a process may need raw keys to move the cursor and process the edited text. If a process only needs input lines, as most processes executing in command-line mode do, the raw inputs must be processed or cooked into lines. Again, this is left for the process to decide outside of the KBD driver.

10.4.7   Foreground and Background Processes

The KBD driver works fine if only one process tries to get inputs from the keyboard. If several processes try to get inputs from the keyboard, the results may differ depending on the synchronization tools used. In Unix, wakeup() wakes up all processes sleeping on the same event without any specific order. If several processes are sleeping for inputs, each input key will wake up all such processes but only one process will get the key, so that each process may get a different key. The result is that no process can get a complete line, which is clearly unacceptable. Using semaphores makes the situation even worse. If several processes try to get input keys, they are all blocked in the semaphore queue of the KBD driver. As input chars are entered, the processes are unblocked one at a time, each gets a different key. The result is the same as before; namely no process can get a complete line. In the simple KBD driver using sleep/wakeup for synchronization, sleeping processes are maintained in a FIFO sleepList. If we run several processes under MTX, only one process will get all the input keys. The reader may verify this and try to figure out why? It turns out that the problem can not be solved by the driver alone. Some protocol at a higher level is needed. In practice, when several processes share the same input device, e.g. a keyboard, only one of the processes is designated as the foreground process. All others, if any, are in the background. Only the foreground process is allowed to get inputs. A special fg command can be used to promote a background process to the foreground, which automatically demotes the original foreground process to background. In MTX, this is implemented by a lock semaphore in the KBD driver. Alternative ways to implement foreground and background processes are listed as programming exercises in the Problem section.

10.4.8   Improved KBD Driver

The following shows an improved keyboard driver, which handles upper case keys and some special keys. It uses semaphores for synchronization.

```
/*********************************************************************
                  An improved KBD driver: kbd.c file
**********************************************************************/
#define KEYBD      0x60      // I/O port for keyboard data
#define PORT_B     0x61      // port_B of 8255
#define KBIT       0x80      // ack bit
#define NSCAN        58      // number of scan codes
#define KBLEN        64
#define BELL       0x07
#define F1         0x3B      // scan code of function keys
#define F2         0x3C
#define CAPSLOCK 0x3A        // scan code of special keys
#define LSHIFT     0x2A
#define RSHIFT     0x36
#define CONTROL    0x1D
#define ALT        0x38
#define DEL        0x53

#include "keymap.c"
struct kbd{
    char buf[KBLEN];
    int  head, tail;
    SEMAPHORE data;              // semaphore between inth and process
    SEMAPHORE lock;              // ONE active process at a time
    struct proc *blist;          // (background) PROCS on the KBD
    int intr,kill,xon,xoff;      // examples of KBD control keys
}kbd;
int alt, capslock, esc, shifted, control, arrowKey; // state variables

int kbd_init()
{
  esc=alt=control=shifted=capslock = 0; // clear state variables
  kbd.head = kbd.tail = 0;
  // define default control keys
  kbd.intr = 0x03;        // Control-C
  kbd.kill = 0x0B;        // Control-K
  kbd.xon  = 0x11;        // Control-Q
  kbd.xoff = 0x13;        // Control-S
  // initialize semaphores
  kbd.data.value = 0; kbd.data.queue = 0;
  kbd.lock.value = 1; kbd.lock.queue = 0;
  kbd.blist = 0;         // no background PROCs initially
  enable_irq(1);
  out_byte(0x20, 0x20);
}
/*************** lower-half driver ***********************/
int kbhandler()
{
  int scode, value, c;
  // Fetch scab code from the keyboard hardware and acknowledge it.
  scode = in_byte(KEYBD);     // get scan code
  value = in_byte(PORT_B);    // strobe PORT_B to ack the char
  out_byte(PORT_B, value | KBIT);
  out_byte(PORT_B, value);

  if (scode == 0xE0)     // ESC key
    esc++;               // inc esc count by 1
  if (esc && esc < 2)    // only the first ESC key, wait for next code
    goto out;
```

```
    if (esc == 2){          // two 0xE0 means escape sequence key release
       if (scode == 0xE0) // this is the 2nd ESC, real code comes next
          goto out;
       // with esc==2, this must be the actual scan code, so handle it
       scode &= 0x7F;             // leading bit off
       if (scode == 0x38){        // Right Alt
          alt = 0;
          goto out;
       }
       if (scode == 0x1D){        // Right Control release
          control = 0;
          goto out;
       }
       if (scode == 0x48)         // up arrow
          arrowKey = 0x0B;
       esc = 0;
       goto out;
    }
    if (scode & 0x80){// key release: ONLY catch shift,control,alt
       scode &= 0x7F;             // mask out bit 7
       if (scode == LSHIFT || scode == RSHIFT)
          shifted = 0;            // released the shift key
       if (scode == CONTROL)
          control = 0;            // released the Control key
       if (scode == ALT)
          alt = 0;                // released the ALT key
       goto out;
    }

    // from here on, must be key press
    if (scode == 1)               // Esc key on keyboard
       goto out;
    if (scode == LSHIFT || scode == RSHIFT){
       shifted = 1;               // set shifted flag
       goto out;
    }
    if (scode == ALT){
       alt = 1;
       goto out;
    }
    if (scode == CONTROL){
       control = 1;
       goto out;
    }
    if (scode == 0x3A){
       capslock = 1 - capslock;   // capslock key acts like a toggle
       goto out;
    }
    if (control && alt && scode == DEL){
       printf("3-finger salute\n");
       goto out;
    }
    /************* Catch and handle F keys for debugging *************/
    if (scode == F1){ do_F1(); goto out;}
    if (scode == F2){ do_F2(); goto out;}   // etc
    // translate scan code to ASCII, using shift[ ] table if shifted;
    c = (shifted ? shift[scode] : unshift[scode]);
```

```
    // Convert all to upper case if capslock is on
    if (capslock){
      if (c >= 'A' && c <= 'Z')
        c += 'a' - 'A';
      else if (c >= 'a' && c <= 'z')
        c -= 'a' - 'A';
    }
    if (control && (c=='c'||c=='C')){// Control-C on PC are 2 keys
      //Control-C Key; send SIGINT(2) signal to processes on console;
      c = '\n'; // force a line, let procs handle SIG#2 when exit Kmode
    }
    if (control && (c=='d'|| c=='D')){  // Control-D, these are 2 keys
      printf("Control-D: set code=4 to let process handle EOF\n");
      c = 4;                            // Control-D
    }
    /* enter the char in kbd.buf[ ] for process to get */
    if (kbd.data.value == KBLEN){
      printf("%c\n", BELL);
      goto out;                         // kb.buf[] already FULL
    }
    kbd.buf[kbd.head++] = c;
    kbd.head %= KBLEN;
    V(&kbd.data);
out:
    out_byte(0x20, 0x20);               // send EOI

}
/********************** upper-half driver **********************/
int getc()
{
    u8 c;
    if (running->fground==0)
      P(&kbd.lock);     // only foreground proc can getc() from KBD
    P(&kbd.data);
    lock();
    c = kbd.buf[kbd.tail++]; kbd.tail %= KBLEN;
    unlock();
    return c;
}
```

In the KBD structure of the improved keyboard driver, data is a semaphore with initial value 0. The semaphore lock (initial value = 1) ensures that only one process can get inputs from the keyboard. In addition, the KBD structure also has a few other control variables. For example, intr defines the interrupt key, which generates a SIGINT(2) signal to all processes on the keyboard. It is set to Control-C by default. The kill key (Control-K) is for erasing an entire input line, etc. The control variables are usually managed by stty() and ioctl() syscalls. The improved KBD driver is intended to show how to detect and handle some of the special keys, which are explained below.

1. The KBD driver uses the state variables, esc, control, shifted, alt to keep track of the states of the driver. For example, esc = 1 when it sees the first ESC (0xE0). With esc = 2, the next scan code determines the actual special key, which also clears esc to 0.

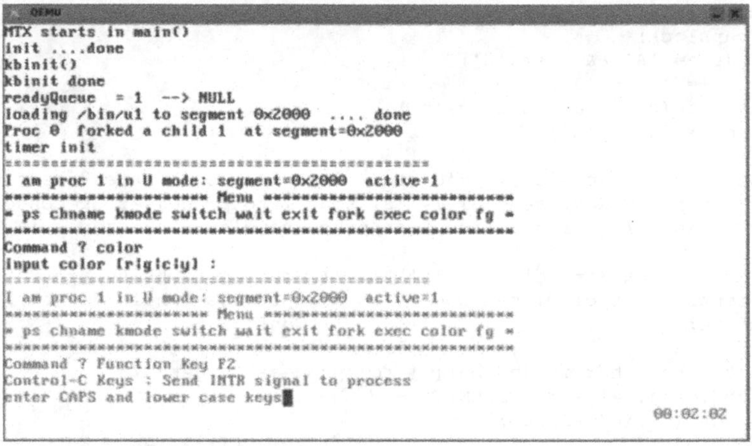

```
 QEMU                                                                          - x
MTX starts in main()
init ....done
kbinit()
kbinit done
readyQueue  = 1  --> NULL
loading /bin/u1 to segment 0x2000  .... done
Proc 0 forked a child 1 at segment=0x2000
timer init
===========================================================
I am proc 1 in U mode: segment=0x2000 active=1
***************** Menu ***************************
* ps chname kmode switch wait exit fork exec color fg *
*************************************************
Command ? color
input color [r|g|c|y] :
===========================================================
I am proc 1 in U mode: segment=0x2000 active=1
***************** Menu ***************************
* ps chname kmode switch wait exit fork exec color fg *
*************************************************
Command ? Function Key F2
Control-C Keys : Send INTR signal to process
enter CAPS and lower case keys█
                                                                   00:02:02
```

Fig. 10.5 Display screen of MTX10.vtk

2. Key press or release: Key release is of interest only to shift, control and Alt keys because releasing such keys resets the state variables shifted, control and alt.
3. Special key processing examples:

   .Function Keys: These are the simplest to recognize. Some of the function keys may be used as hot keys to perform specific functions. For example, pressing the F1 key may invoke ps() to print the process status in kernel.
   .Shift key: (LeftShift=0x2A, RightShift=0x36): When either shift key is pressed but not yet released, set shifted to 1 and use the shifted keymap to translate the input chars. Releasing either LSHIFT or RSHIFT key resets shifted to 0.
   .Control key sequence: Control-C: Left CONTROL key (0x1D) down but not released, set control=1. Releasing the CONTORL key resets control to 0. With control=1 and a key press, determine the Control-key value.
   .Esc Key sequence: Many special keys, e.g. arrow keys, Delete, etc. generate scan code E0xx, where E0 is the ESC key. After seeing 2 ESC keys, set esc=2. With esc=2, get the next key press, e.g. UP arrow=E048, to determine the special key value.

10.4.9 MTX10.vtk: Demonstration of Keyboard Driver

MTX10.vtk is a sample system which includes the display, timer and keyboard drivers. The keyboard driver handles upper and lower cases keys and some special keys. It also supports foreground and background processes. When MTX10.vtk boots up, it runs P1 as the foreground process in Umode. The reader may fork several background processes and use the fg command to change the active process on the keyboard. Figure 10.5 shows the screen of running MTX10.vtk.

```
      Parallel ports:       LPT1        LPT2
              DATA          0x378       0x3BC
              STATUS        0x379       0x3BD
              COMMAND       0x37A       0x3BE
                7       6     5       4       3       2     1     0
     Status : NOTBUSY  - NOPAPER SELECT NOERROR   -      -     -
     Command:    -       -     -   EnableIRQ INIT  SELECT - STROBE
```

Fig. 10.6 Parallel port address and registers

10.5 Parallel Printer Driver

10.5.1 Parallel Port Interface

A PC usually has two parallel ports, denoted by LPT1 and LPT2, which support parallel printers. Each parallel port has a data register, a status register and a command register. Figure 10.6 shows the parallel port addresses and the register contents.

Before printing, the printer must be initialized once by:

INIT: write 0x08 to COMMAND register first, then
select: write 0x0C to COMMAND register.

To print, write a char to DATA register. Then strobe the printer once by writing a 1, followed by a 0, to bit 0 of the command register, which simulates a strobe pulse of width >0.5 usec. For example, writing $0x1D=00011101$ followed by $0x1C=00011100$ strobes the printer with interrupts enabled. When the printer is ready to accept the next char, it interrupts at IRQ7, which uses vector 15. In the interrupt handler, read the status register and check for error. If no error, send the next char to the printer and strobe it once again, etc.

10.5.2 A Simple Printer Driver

Like any interrupt-driven device driver, a printer driver consists of an upper-half part and a lower-half part, which share a common buffer area with control variables. The following shows a simple printer driver. We assume that each process prints one line at a time, which is controlled by a mutex semaphore. Process and interrupt handler share a circular buffer, pbuf[PLEN], with head and tail pointers. To print a line, a process calls prline(), which calls prchar() to deposit chars into pbuf, waiting for room if necessary. It prints the first char if the printer is not printing. After writing the entire line to pbuf, the process waits for completion by P(done). The interrupt handler will print the remaining chars from pbuf. When a line is completely printed, it V(done) to unblock the process, which V(mutex) to allow another process to print.

```
/********** C Cdoe of a Simple Printer Driver ****************/
#define NPR       1
#define PORT      0x378    // #define PORT 0x3BC for LPT2
#define STATUS PORT+1
#define COMD      PORT+2
#define PLEN      128
#include "semaphore.c" // SEMAPHORE type and P/V operations
struct para{            // printer data structure
   int port;            // I/O port address
   int printing;        // 1 if printer is printing
   char pbuf[PLEN];     // circular buffer
   int head, tail;
   SEMAPHORE mutex, room, done; // control semaphores
}printer[NPR];
pr_init()               // initialize or reset printer
{  struct para *p;
   p = &printer[0];     // assume only one printer
   printf("pr_init %x\n", PORT);
   p->port = PORT;
   p->head = p->tail = 0;
   p->mutex.value = 1;  p->mutex.queue = 0;
   p->room.value = PLEN; p->room.queue = 0;
   p->done.value = 0;    p->done.queue = 0;
   /* initialize printer at PORT */
   out_byte(p->port+2, 0x08);   // init
   out_byte(p->port+2, 0x0C);   // int, init, select on
   enable_irq(7);
   p->printing = 0;             // is NOT printing now
}
int strobe(struct para *p)
{  out_byte(p->port+2, 0x1D);   // may need delay time here
   out_byte(p->port+2, 0x1C);
}
/*************** Lower-half printer driver ******************/
int phandler()                  // interrupt handler
{ u8 status, c;
   struct para *p = &printer[0];
   status = in_byte(p->port+1);
   //printf("printer interrupt status = %x\n", status);
   if (status & 0x08){          // check for noError status only
      if (p->room.value == PLEN){  // pbuf[] empty, nothing to print
         out_byte(p->port+2, 0x0C); // turn off printer interrupts
         V(&p->done);              // tell process print is DONE
         p->printing = 0;         // is no longer printing
         goto out;
      }
      c = p->pbuf[p->tail++];     // print next char
      p->tail %= PLEN;
      out_byte(p->port, c);
      strobe(p);
      V(&p->room);
      goto out;
   }
   // abnormal status: should handle it but ignored here
out:  out_byte(0x20, 0x20);        // issue EOI
}
/************** Upper-half printer driver ****************/
int prchar(char c)
{  struct para *p = &printer[0];
   P(&p->room);                   // wait for room in pbuf[]
```

```
      lock();
        if (p->printing==0){          // print the char
            out_byte(p->port, c);
            strobe(p);
            p->printing = 1;
            unlock();
            return;
        }
        // already printing, enter char into pbuf[]
        p->pbuf[p->head++] = c;
        p->head %= PLEN;
    unlock();
}
int prline(char *line)
{   struct para *p = &printer;
    P(&p->mutex);                     // one process prints LINE at a time
        while (*line)
            prchar(*line++);          // print chars
        P(&p->done);                  // wait until pbuf[ ] is DONE
    V(&p->mutex);                     // allow another process to print
}
```

10.5.3   MTX10.pr: Demonstration of Printer Driver

MTX10.pr demonstrates the printer driver. To test the printer driver on a virtual machine, configure the VM's parallel port to use a pseudo-terminal. Boot up MTX and run the pr command from user mode. Figure 10.7 shows the screen of running MTX10.pr on QEMU using /dev/pts3 as the parallel port. For each interrupt, the printer driver displays a "printer interrupt" message. Eventually, the printer will be represented by a special file, /dev/lp0, in the MTX file system. In that case, writing to the special file invokes the printer driver.

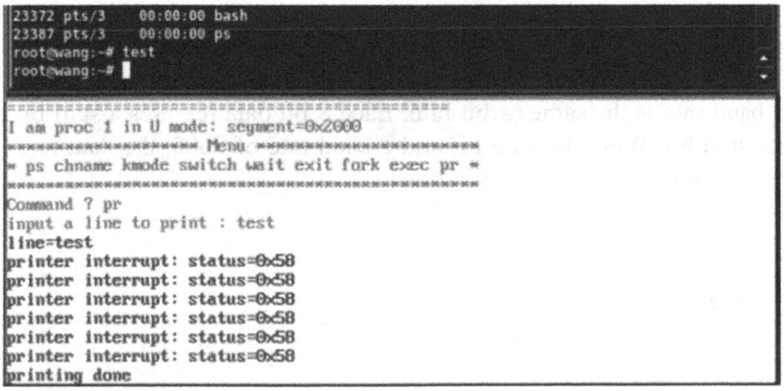

Fig. 10.7 Demonstration of printer driver

```
        DTE                                      DCE
        ────                                     ────
Pin  2    <────────      Rx    <────────  2
     3    ════════>      Tx    ════>       3
     4    ════════>      RTS   ════>       4
     5    <────────      CTS   <────────  5
     6    <────────      DSR   <────────  6
     7    ──────────     Ground ──────────  7
     8    <────────      DCD   <────────  8
    20    ════════>      DTR   ════>      20
```

Fig. 10.8 RS232C signal lines

10.6   Serial Port Driver

10.6.1   RS232C Serial Protocol

RS232C is the standard protocol for serial communication. The RS232C protocol defines 25 signal lines between a Data Terminal Equipment (DTE) and a Data Communication Equipment (DCE). Usually, a computer is a DTE, a modem or serial printer is a DCE. Figure 10.8 shows the most commonly used signal lines and data flow directions of the serial interface.

To establish a serial connection between a DTE and a DCE, a sequence of events goes like this. First, the DTE asserts the DTR (Data Terminal Ready), which informs the DCE that the DTE is ready. The DCE responds by asserting DSR (Data Set Ready) and DCD (Data Carrier Detect), which informs the DTE that the DCE is also ready. When the DTE has data to send, it asserts RTS (Request To Send), which asks the DCE for permission to send. If the DCE is ready to receive data, it asserts CTS (Clear To Send). Then the DTE can send data through Tx while CTS is on. The DCE can send data through Rx to DTE anytime without asking for permission first.

10.6.2   Serial Data Format

Figure 10.9 shows the serial data format.

Bits timing is controlled by a (local) clock, which determines the baud rate. Technically, baud rate refers to the number of signal changes per second. For binary signals, baud rate is the same as bit rate. Each 8-bit data requires a start bit and at least one stop bit. With one stop bit and a baud rate of 9600, the data rate is 960 chars per second.

```
     Space                                             Space
 ───────────|    7   6   5   4   3   2   1   0   |───────────
            |───|───|───|───|───|───|───|───|───|───|
         start|<──────────  8 data bits ──────────>|Stop
          bit                                        bit
```

Fig. 10.9 Serial data format

```
Index Name       Function        COM1    COM2

   0   DATA    Rx or Tx data      3F8    2F8
   1   IER     Interrupt Enable   3F9    2F9
   2   IIR     Interrupt ID       3FA    2FA
   3   LCR     Line Control       3FB    2FB
   4   MCR     Modem Control      3FC    2FC
   5   LSR     Line Status        3FD    2FD
   6   MSR     Modem Status       3FE    2FE

IER:   bit0=RX enable, bit1=Tx enable
IIR:   bits2-1=error(00),Tx(01) Rx(10),Modem(11)
LCR:   number of data bits, stop bits, parity, etc.
MCR:   bit0=DTR, bit1=RTS, bit2=enable hardware interrupt
LSR:   bit0=Rx data ready, bit5=Tx register empty
```

Fig. 10.10 Serial ports registers

Fig. 10.11 DTE-to-DTE
connection

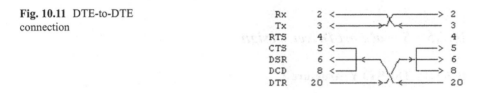

```
Rx    2  <───────────X───────>  2
Tx    3  <───────>─/\─<───────   3
RTS   4                          4
CTS   5  <─┐              ┌───>  5
DSR   6  <─┤─<──┐  ┌─>┤──>  6
DCD   8  <─┘    \/      └───>  8
DTR  20  ───────>─/\─<───────  20
```

10.6.3   PC Serial Ports

Most PCs have two serial ports, denoted by COM1 and COM2. Figure 10.10 shows
the serial port registers and their contents.

10.6.4   Serial Terminals

PC's serial ports are DTE's by default. They are intended to connect to DCE's, such
as modems, serial terminals and serial printers, etc. We cannot connect the serial
ports of PCs directly because both are DTEs. In order for the connection to work,
one must be a DCE, or at least each serial port thinks the other side is a DCE. There
are two possible ways to do this.

1. Configure one of the PC's serial port as a DCE. Then connect the two serial ports
   by an ordinary DTE to DCE cable, which is wired straight-through.
2. Make both DTEs think the other side is a DCE by crossing some wires in the
   cable, as shown in Fig. 10.11.

Unlike the PC's console keyboard, which generates scan codes, a serial terminal generates ASCII code directly. The most widely used serial terminal standard is the VT100 protocol. In addition to ordinary ASCII keys, VT100 also supports special keys as escape sequence codes. For example, Cursor UP is ESC [A, Cursor Down is ESC [B, etc. A virtual serial terminal is a device which emulates a real serial terminal. There are many ways to connect a PC to a virtual serial terminal.

. Connect to a PC running a program which emulates a serial terminal.
. Enable serial port support of a PC emulator. For example,
  QEMU: run QEMU with –serial option, e.g. -serial mon:stdio -serial /dev/pts/2
  VMware/VirtualBox: configure VM to use virtual serial terminals.

It is noted that VMware's virtual serial ports may be sockets, which require a socket interface program, such as socat, for both input and output.

10.6.5   Serial Port Driver Design

10.6.5.1   The STTY Structure

Each serial port is represented by a stty structure.

```
struct stty {
    // input section
    char inbuf[BUFLEN]; int inhead,intail;
    SEMAPHORE inchars;
    // output section
    char outbuf[BUFLEN];int outhead,outtail;
    SEMAPHORE outspace;
    // Control section
    char erase,kill,intr,x_on,x_off,tx_on;
    // I/O port base address
    int port;
} stty[NSTTY];   // NSTTY = mumber of serial ports
```

The stty structure consists of three sections. The input section contains a circular buffer, inbuf, for storing input chars and a semaphore, inchars=0, for synchronization. The output section contains a circular buffer, outbuf, for storing outgoing chars, a semaphore, outspace=BUFLEN, for synchronization and a tx_on flag for output interrupt enabled. The control section defines control chars, such as intr, echo, kill, etc. The I/O port field stores the serial port base address.

10.6.5.2   Serial Port Initialization

To initialize the serial ports, write values to their control registers in the following order.

```
0x80 to DATA : bit#7=1              // Use DATA, IER registers
0x00 to IER  : 0 value             // for divisor
0x0C to DATA : divisor=12          // divisor=12 for 9600 bauds
0x03 to LCR : Line Control = 00000011 // no parity, 8_bit data
0x0B to MSR : Modem Control= 00001011 // turn on IRQ, RTS, DTR
0x01 to IER : Int Enablee  = 00000001 // Tx off, Rx on.
tx_on = 0;                         // Tx interrupt disabled
```

10.6.5.3   Lower-Half Serial Port Driver

The lower-half of the serial port drivers is the interrupt handler, which is set up as follows.

1. Set interrupt vectors for COM1 (IRQ4) and COM2 (IRQ3) by

```
set_vector(12, s0inth);    // vector 12 for COM1
set_vector(11, s1inth);    // vector 11 for COM2
```

Install interrupt handler entry points by the INTH macro in assembly:

```
_s0inth: INTH s0handler    // entry points of
_s1inth: INTH s1handler    // serial interrupt handlers
```

2. Write s0handler() and s1handler() functions, which call shandler(int port):

```
int s0handler(){ shandler(0);}
int s1handler(){ shandler(1);}
```

3. Serial Port Interrupt Handler Function in C:

```
int shandler(int port) // port=0 for COM1; 1 for COM2
{
    struct stty *tty = &stty[port];
    int IntID, LineStatus, ModemStatus, intType;
    IntID       = in_byte(tty->port+IIR);  // read InterruptID
    LineStatus  = in_byte(tty->port+LSR);  // read LineStatus
    ModemStatus = in_byte(tty->port+MSR);  // read ModemStatus
    intType = IntID & 0x07;      // mask in lowest 3 bits of IntID
    switch(intType){
        case 0 : do_modem(tty);   break;
        case 2 : do_tx(tty);      break;
        case 4 : do_rx(tty);      break;
        case 6 : do_errors(tty);  break;
    }
    out_byte(0x20, 0x20);        // issue EOI to PIC Controller
}
```

Upon entry to shandler(), the port parameter identifies the serial port. The actions of
the interrupt handler are as follows.
. Read interrupt ID register to determine the interrupt cause.
. Read line and modem status registers to check for errors.
. Handle the interrupt.
. Issue EOI to signal end of interrupt processing.

In order to keep the driver simple, we shall ignore errors and modem status changes
and consider only rx and tx interrupts for data transfer.

4. Input Interrupt Handler:

```
int do_rx(struct stty *tty)
{
  (1). char c = in_byte(tty ->port); // get char from data register
  (2). if (tty->inchars.value >= BUFLEN){ // if inbuf is full
          out_byte(tty, BEEP);            // sound BEEP=0x7
            return;
       }
  (3). if (c==0x3){                        // Control_C key
          send SIGINT(2)   signal to processes;
          c = '\n';                        // force a line
       }
       tty ->inbuf[tty->inhead++] = c; // put char into inbuf
       tty ->inhead %= BUFLEN;         // advance inhead
  (4). V(&tty->inchars);    // inc inchars and unblock sgetc()
}
```

In do_rx(), it only catches Control_C as the interrupt key, which sends a SIGINT(2)
signal to the process on the terminal and forces a line for the unblocked process to
get. It considers other inputs as ordinary keys. The circular input buffer is used in
the same way as in the keyboard driver. Similar to the keyboard driver case, we assume that there is a process running on the serial terminal. So do_rx() only enters
raw inputs into the input buffer. The process will cook the raw inputs into lines and
echo the chars.

5. Output Interrupt Handler:

```
int do_tx(struct stty *tty)
{
  (1). if (no more chars in outbuf[]){        // no more outputs
          turn_off Tx interrupt;
          return;
       }
  (2). char c = tty->outbuf[tty->outtail++]; // output next char
       tty->outtail %= BUFLEN;
       out_byte(tty->port, c);
  (3). V(&tty->outspace);
}
```

In do_tx(), if there are no more chars to output, it turns off Tx interrupt and returns.
Otherwise, it outputs the next char from outbuf and V the outspace semaphore to
unblock any process that may be waiting for room in outbuf.

10.6.5.4 Upper-Half Serial Port Driver

The upper-half driver functions are sgetc() and sputc(), which are called by processes to input/output chars from/to the serial port.

```
char sgetc(struct stty *tty)    // return a char from serial port
{
    char c;
    P(&tty->inchars);           // wait if no input char yet
    lock();                     // disable interrupts
      c = tty->inbuf[tty->intail++];
      tty->intail %= BUFLEN;
    unlock();                   // enable interrupts
    return c;
}
int sputc(struct stty *tty, char c)
{
    P(&tty->outspace);          // wait for space in outbuf[]
    lock();                     // disalble interrupts
      tty->outbuf[tty->outhead++] = c;
      tty->outhead %= BUFLEN;
      if (!tty->tx_on)
        enable_tx(tty);         // trun on tty's tx interrupt;
    unlock();                   // enable interrupts
}
```

When a process calls sputc(), it first waits for room in the output buffer. Then it deposits the char into outbuf and turns on Tx interrupt, if necessary. The interrupt handler, do_tx(), will write out the chars from outbuf on successive Tx interrupts. When the interrupt for the last char occurs, the interrupt handler turns off Tx interrupt.

10.6.6 MTX10.serial: Demonstration of Serial Port Driver

MTX10.serial demonstrates the serial port driver. Figure 10.12 shows the screen of running MTX10.serial under QEMU. To test the serial port driver, configure QEMU to use a pseudo-terminal, e.g./dev/pts/3, as serial port. In the pseudo-terminal, enter sleep 10,000 to suspend the Linux sh process. After booting up MTX, serial port I/O can be done in either Kmode or Umode. In Kmode the commands are

```
i : get a line from serial port;
o : send a line to serial port
```

In Umode, the commands are sin for input a line and sout for output a line. On inputs, it prints a rx interrupt for each char. On outputs, it prints a tx interrupt for each line. In the demonstration system, we assume that no process is running on the serial terminal to echo the inputs. In order to let the user see the input chars, do_rx() uses a small echo buffer to echo the inputs and it also handles the backspace key. The reader may consult the driver code for details. In the final versions of MTX, we shall use the serial port driver to support multiple user logins from serial terminals.

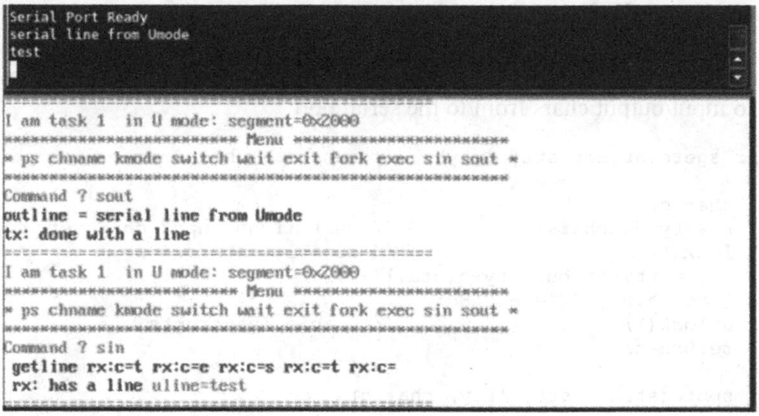

```
Serial Port Ready
serial line from Umode
test
I
===========================================================
I am task 1  in U mode: segment=0x2000
*************************** Menu *************************
* ps chname kmode switch wait exit fork exec sin sout *
***********************************************************
Command ? sout
outline = serial line from Umode
tx: done with a line
===========================================================
I am task 1  in U mode: segment=0x2000
*************************** Menu *************************
* ps chname kmode switch wait exit fork exec sin sout *
***********************************************************
Command ? sin
 getline rx:c=t rx:c=e rx:c=s rx:c=t rx:c=
 rx: has a line uline=test
===========================================================
```

Fig. 10.12 Demonstration of serial port driver

10.7 Floppy Disk Driver

10.7.1 FDC Controller

The PC's floppy disk controller (FDC) uses the NEC µPD765 or Intel 82072A floppy disk controller chip. For basic FD operations, they use the same programming interface. The FDC has several registers at the I/O port addresses shown in Fig. 10.13.

The status bits in ST0-ST2 are listed in the driver code. The reader may also consult FDC documentations [FDC 2012] for more information. The FDC uses channel 2 DMA of the ISA bus for data transfer. When executing a R/W command the sequence of operations is as follows.

Register	Primary	7	6	5	4	3	2	1	0
DOR	0x3F2	motor-on: B		A		IRQ-DMA	~RESET	DRIVE	
STATUS	0x3F4	RDY DIR DMA BSY				drive is seeking			
DATA	0x3F5	Data reg : write commands, read results							
ST0-ST2	0x3F5	Result status; read from DATA register							

Fig. 10.13 FDC registers

10.7.2 FDC R/W Operation Sequence

1. Turn on the drive motor with the IRQ_DMA bit set, wait until drive motor is up to running speed, which can be done by either a delay or a timer request. Also, set a timer request to turn off the drive motor with an appropriate delay time, e.g. 2 s, after the command is finished.
2. If needed, reset, recalibrate the drive and seek to the right cylinder.
3. Set up the DMA controller for data transfer.
4. Poll the main status register until drive is ready to accept command.
5. Write a sequence of command bytes to the DATA register. For example, in a read/write sector operation, the 9 command bytes are:
   opcode, head+drive, cyl, head, sector, // drive=00,01,10,11
   bytes_per_sector, sector_per_track, gap_length, data_length.

For a specific drive type, the last 4 command bytes are always the same and can be regarded as constants.

6. After executing the command, the FDC will interrupt at IRQ6. When a FD interrupt occurs, if the command has a result phase, the driver can read the result status ST0-ST2 from DATA register. Some commands do not have a result phase e.g. recalibrate and seek, which require an additional sense command to be sent in order to read the status bytes ST0-ST2.
7. Wait for FDC interrupt; send a sense command if needed. Read results from DATA register to get status ST0-ST2 and check for error. If error, retry steps (2)-(7).
8. If no error, the command is finished. Start next command. If no more commands in 2 s, turn off the drive motor by timer.

10.7.3 FD Driver Design

1. Floppy drive data structure: Each drive is represented by a floppy structure.

```
struct floppy {      // drive struct, one per drive
    u16 opcode;       // FDC_READ or FDC_WRITE
    u16 cylinder;     // cylinder number
    u16 sector;       // sector : counts from 1 NOT 0
    u16 head;         // head number
    u16 count;        // byte count (BLOCK_SIZE)
    u16 address;      // virtual address of data area
    u16 curcyl;       // current cylinder number
    u8  results[7];   // each cmd may generate up to 7 result bytes
    u8  calibration;  // drive is CALIBRATED or UNCALIBRATED flag
} floppy[NFDC];       // NFDC = 1
```

In order to keep the driver simple, we assume that the FD driver supports only one 1.44 MB drive for READ/WRITE operations. It should be quite easy to extend the driver to support more drives and other operations, such as format, etc.

2. FD semaphores: the FD driver uses two semaphores for synchronization:

```
SEMAPHORE fdio=1;    // process execute FD driver one at a time,
SEMAPHORE fdsem=0;   // for process to wait for FD interrupts.
```

3. fd_init(): initialize the FD structure, including semaphores and status flags. Write 0x0C to DOR register, which turns A: drives's motor off and sets the drive with interrupts enabled and using DMA.

```
int fd_init()
{
   struct floppy *fp = floppy[0];
   fdio.value = 1; fdsem.queue = 0;
   fdsem.value = fdsem.queue = 0;
   fp->curcyl = 0; fp->calibration = 0;
   need_reset = 0;
   motor_status = 0x0C;   // 0x0C;          (0x0D for B drive)
   out_byte(DOR,  0x0C);  // DOR=00001100 (0x0D for B drive)
}
```

4. Upper-half FD driver: the upper-half of the FD driver includes almost the entire driver's C code. In the FD driver, the process runs in several stages, which are interleaved by FD interrupts. After issuing a command, it waits for interrupt by P(fdsem). When the interrupt occurs, the FD interrupt handler does V(fdsem) to unblock the process, which reads and checks the result status and continues to the next stage, etc.

5. Lower-half FD driver: The FD interrupt handler is very simple. All it does is to issue V(fdsem) to unblock the process. Then it issues EOI and returns.

6. FD motor on/off control: The motor status is maintained in a motor_status variable. After turning on the drive motor, the process sets a timer request of 20 ticks and waits on the fdsem semaphore for the drive motor to get up to speed. After 20 ticks, the timer interrupt handler unblocks the process. For each read/write operation, it also sets 120 timer ticks to turn off the motor, which is done by the timer interrupt handler.

7. Main FD driver function: read/write a disk block to an address in kernel space:

```
int fdrw(u16 rw, u16 blk, char *addr)
{
   struct floppy *fp = floppy[0];
   int r, i;
   P(&fdio);     // one process executes fd_rw() at a time
   motor_on();  // turn on motor if needed, set 2 sec. turn off time
   fp->opcode = rw;                   // opcode
   r = (2*blk) % CYL_SIZE;            // compute CHS
   fp->cylinder = (2*blk) / CYL_SIZE;
   fp->head = r / TRK_SIZE;
   fp->sector = (r % TRK_SIZE) + 1;   // sector counts from 1, NOT 0
   fp->count = BLOCK_SIZE;            // block size
   fp->address = addr;                // address
   for (i=0; i<MAX_RETRY; i++){       // try MAX_RETRY times
        // First check to see if FDC needs reset
        if  (need_reset) // printf("fd reset\n");
           fd_reset();
        // May also need to recalibrate, especially after a reset
        if (fp->calibration == UNCALIBRATED)
           calibrate(fp);
        // Seek to the correct cynlinder if needed
        if (fp->curcyl != fp->cylinder)
           seek(fp);
        // Set up DMA controller
        setup_dma(fp);
        // write commands to FDC to start RW
        r = commands(fp);
        if (r==OK) break;
   }
   if (i>=MAX_FD_RETRY)
       printf("FDC error\n");// error, most likey hardware failure
   V(&fdio);                 // unlock fdio semaphore
}
```

fdrw() is the main FD driver function. It reads/writes a 1 K block (2 sectors) at the linear block number, blk, into the virtual address addr (in Kmode). The reason of reading only 2 sectors is because the FD driver is intended to work with the MTX file system, which uses 1 KB I/O buffers for both FD and HD. When a process enters fdrw(), it first locks the fdio semaphore to prevent other process from executing the same FD driver. The fdio lock is released only after the current process has finished the read/write operation. Then it calls motor_on(), which turns on the drive motor and sets the motor-off time to 2 s. Then it computes the CHS values of the blk. Then it executes the retry loop up to MAX_FD_RETRY (5) times. In the retry loop, it first ensures that the drive does not need reset, has been calibrated and seek to the right cylinder so that the drive is ready to accept commands. Then it calls setup_dma(), which programs the DMA controller for the intended data transfer. It writes the command bytes to the DATA register. Then it waits for interrupt by P(fdsem). When the expected interrupt occurs, the FD interrupt handler issues V(fdsem) to unblock the process, which continues to read the result status and checks for error. For a recalibrate or seek command, it issues a sense command before reading the status ST0-ST2. Error conditions in the recalibration and seek stages are checked but ignored. Such errors would most likely lead to a R/W error eventually. So we only focus on checking the result status after a R/W command. Any error at this stage causes the

```
 OEMU
password:12345
++++++++++++++++++++++++++++
KCLOGIN : Welcome! root
KCLOGIN : cd to HOME=/  change uid to 0 exec to /bin/sh .....
enter ? for help menu
kcsh # : mount /dev/fd0 /mnt
Parent sh 2 fork a child  child  sh 4  running
proc 4  exec mount
parent sh 2  waits
bmap=3    imap=4    iblock=5
mount : mounted /dev/fd0 on /mnt
kcsh # : mount
Parent sh 2 fork a child  child  sh 5  running
proc 5  exec mount
/dev/hda3 mounted on /
/dev/fd0 mounted on /mnt
parent sh 2  waits
kcsh # : cat /mnt/f1
Parent sh 2 fork a child  child  sh 6  running
proc 6  exec cat
            KC's cool cat MEOW!
This is a small file on a virtual FD

parent sh 2  waits                                          09:35:09
kcsh # :
```

Fig. 10.14 Demonstration of FD driver and mount

driver to re-execute the retry loop. When the R/W operation finishes, either successfully or due to error, the process unlocks the fdio semaphore.

10.7.4 Implications on I/O Buffers in MTX

MTX uses I/O buffers for block devices, which include both FD and HD. For HD,
all writes to disk blocks use the delay-write policy. When a process writes a disk
block, it writes data to a buffer assigned to the disk block, which is marked as dirty
for delay-write. A dirty buffer is written out to disk asynchronously only when it is
to be reassigned to a different disk block. For removable devices, such as FD disks,
delay-write is undesirable. For this reason, the FD driver uses synchronous write to
ensure that data are written to the FD disk directly.

10.7.5 Demonstration of FD Driver

MTX10.fd demonstrates the FD driver. Since the FD driver takes over FD interrupts, it is not possible to run MTX on a FD image and operate on a FD at the same
time. For this reason, MTX10.fd runs only on HD. The reader may test it on virtual
machines by the following steps.

1. Run the sh script mk PARTITION qemu|vmware, e.g. mk 3 qemu, which installs
   a complete rmtx system to partition 3 of a virtual HD named vdisk.
2. Run qemu –had vdisk –fda fd # fd is a FD image containing an EXT2 FS
3. Boot up MTX from partition 3. Mount the virtual FD by mount /dev/fd0 /mnt
4. Then copy files to/from the mounted FS. When finished, umount /dev/fd0.

Figure 10.14 shows the screen of running MTX10.fd. It first mounts the virtual FD.
Then it cat the contents of a file from the mounted FD. The reader may also run the
cp command to copy files to/from the FD.

```
Control Register:
  0x3F6 = 0x80 (0000 1REO): R=reset, E=0=enable interrupt
Command Block Registers:
  0x1F0 = Data Port
  0x1F1 = Error
  0x1F2 = Sector Count
  0x1F3 = LBA low byte
  0x1F4 = LBA mid byte
  0x1F5 = LBA hi  byte
  0x1F6 = 1B1D TOP4LBA: B=LBA,D=driv
  0x1F7 = Command/status
                            7      6     5     4    3   2    1     0
Status Register(0x1F7)= BUSY READY FAULT SEEK DRQ CORR IDDEX ERROR
Error Register (0x1F1)=  BBK    UNC    MC  IDNF MCR ABRT TONF AMNF
The error bits are: BBK=Bad Block,UNC=Uncorrectable data error,
MC=Media Changed,IDNF=ID mark Not Found,MCR=Media Change Requested,
ABRT=Aborted,TONF=Track 0 Not Found,AMNF=Address Mark Not Found
```

Fig. 10.15 IDE ports and registers

10.8   IDE Hard Disk Driver

There are two kinds of hard disk interface; Parallel ATA (PATA) [PATA 2015] and Serial ATA (SATA) [SATA 2012]. PATA is also known as IDE. SATA stands for serial ATA interface, which uses SCSI like packets and is different from IDE interface. In some PCs, SATA can be configured to be backward compatible with PATA but not vice versa. Older PATA uses PIO (Programmed I/O). Newer PATA, e.g. ATA-3, may use either PIO or DMA. In order to use DMA the PC must be in protected mode to access the PCI bus. In general, DMA is faster and more suited to transferring large amounts of data. For small amount of data, e.g. in usual file system operations, it is actually better to use PIO due to its simplicity. This section presents IDE hard disk drivers using PIO. In order to illustrate different driver designs, we shall show three different versions of the HD driver. The first driver relies entirely on the process, which actively controls each r/w operation. In the second driver, process and interrupt handler cooperate, each performs part of the r/w operation. In the third version, the HD driver is an integral part of the block device I/O buffer management subsystem of the MTX kernel. It works with a disk I/O queue and supports both synchronous (blocking) read and asynchronous (non-blocking) write operations.

10.8.1   IDE Interface

A PC usually has two IDE channels, denoted as IDE0 and IDE1. Each IDE channel can support two devices, known as the master and slave. A hard disk drive is usually the master device of IDE0. Each IDE channel has a set of fixed I/O port addresses. Figure 10.15 lists the port addresses of IDE0 and their contents.

10.8.2   IDE R/W Operation Sequence

(1). Initialize HD:Write 0x08 to Control Register (0x3F6): (E bit=0 to enable interrupt).

(2). Read Status Register (0x1F7) until drive is not Busy and READY;

(3). Write sector count, LBA sector number, drive (master=0x00, slave=0x10) to command registers (0x1F2-0x1F6).

(4). Write READ|WRITE command to Command Register (0x1F7).

(5). For a write operation, wait until drive is READY and DRQ (drive request for data).

Then, write data to data port.

(6). Each (512-byte) sector R|W generates an interrupt. I/O can be done in two ways:

(7a). Process waits for each interrupt. When a sector R/W completes, interrupt handler unblocks process, which continues to read/write the next sector of data from/to data port.

(7b). Process starts R/W. For write (multi-sectors) operation, process writes the first sector of data, then waits for the FINAL status interrupt. Interrupt handler transfers remaining sectors of data on each interrupt. When R/W of all sectors finishes, it unblocks the process. This scheme is better because it does not unblock or wakeup processes unnecessarily.

(8). Error Handling: After each R/W operation or interrupt, read status register. If status.ERROR bit is on, detailed error information is in the error register (0x1F1). Recovery from error may need HD reset.

10.8.3   A Simple HD Driver

Shown below is a simple HD driver based on 10.7.2.(7a). For each hd_rw() call, the process starts the r/w of one sector and blocks itself on the hd_sem semaphore, waiting for interrupts. When an interrupt occurs, the interrupt handler simply unblocks the process, which continues to r/w the next sector. The hd_mutex semaphore is used to ensure that processes execute hd_rw() one at a time.

```
/********** A Simple IDE hard disk driver using PIO *********/
#define HD_DATA        0x1F0  // data port for R/W
#define HD_ERROR       0x1F1  // error register
#define HD_SEC_COUNT   0x1F2  // R/W sector count
#define HD_LBA_LOW     0x1F3  // LBA low  byte
#define HD_LBA_MID     0x1F4  // LBA mid  byte
#define HD_LBA_HI      0x1F5  // LBA high byte
#define HD_LBA_DRIVE   0x1F6  // 1B1D0000=>B=LBA,D=drive=>0xE0 or 0xF0
#define HD_CMD         0x1F7  // command : R=0x20 W=0x30
#define HD_STATUS      0x1F7  // status register
#define HD_CONTROL     0x3f6  // 0x08(0000 1RE0):Reset,E=1:NO interrupt
/* HD disk controller command bytes. */
#define HD_READ        0x20   // read
#define HD_WRITE       0x30   // write
#define BAD            -1     // return BAD on error
struct semaphore hd_mutex;    // for procs hd_rw() ONE at a time
struct semaphore hd_sem;      // for proc to wait for IDE interrupts
// read_port() reads count words from port to (segment, offset)
int read_port(u16 port, u16 segment, u16 *offset, u16 count)
{ int i;
  for (i=0; i<count; i++)
     put_word(in_word(port), segment, offset++);
}
// write_port() writes count words from (segment, offset) to port
int write_port(u16 port, u16 segment, u16 *offset, u16 count)
{ int i;
  for (i=0; i<count; i++)
     out_word(port, get_word(segment, offset++));}
}
int delay(){ }
int hd_busy() {return in_byte(HD_STATUS) & 0x80;} // test BUSY
int hd_ready(){return in_byte(HD_STATUS) & 0x40;} // test READY
int hd_drq()  {return in_byte(HD_STATUS) & 0x08;} // test DRQ
int hd_reset()
{  /***************** HD software reset sequence *******************
   ControlRegister(0x3F6)=(0000 1RE0); R=reset, E=0:enable interrupt
   Strobe R bit from HI to LO; with delay time in between:
         Write 0000 1100 to ControlReg; delay();
         Write 0000 1000 to ControlReg; wait for notBUSY & no error
   ****************************************************************/
   out_byte(0x3F6, 0x0C);      delay();
   out_byte(0x3F6, 0x08);      delay();
   if (hd_busy() || cd_error()) {
       printf("HD reset error\n"); return(BAD);
   }
   return 0;      // return 0 means OK
}
int hd_error()  // test for error
{ int r;
   if (in_byte(0x1F7)& 0x01){  // status.ERROR bit on
      r = in_byte(0x1F1);       // read error register
      printf("HD error=%x\n", r); return r;
   }
   return 0;                    // return 0 if no error
}
int hd_init()
{
  printf("hd_init\n");
  hd_mutex.value = 1;
```

```
  hd_mutex.queue = 0;
  hd_sem.value = hd_sem.queue = 0;
}
int hdhandler()
{
  printf("hd interrupt! ");
  V(&hd_sem);                    // unblock process
  out_byte(0xA0, 0x20);    // send EOI
  out_byte(0x20, 0x20);
}
int set_ide_regs(int rw, int sector, int nsectors)
{
  while(hd_busy() && !hd_ready());    // wait until notBUSY & READY
  printf("write to IDE registers\n");
  out_byte(0x3F6, 0x08);             // control = 0x08; interrupt
  out_byte(0x1F2, nsectors);         // sector count
  out_byte(0x1F3, sector);           // LBA low  byte
  out_byte(0x1F4, sector>>8);        // LBA mid  byte
  out_byte(0x1F5, sector>>16);       // LBA high byte
  out_byte(0x1F6, ((sector>>24)&0x0F) | 0xE0); // use LBA for drive 0
  out_byte(0x1F7, rw);               // READ | WRITE command
}
int hd_rw(u16 rw, u32 sector, char *buf, u16 nsectors)
{
  int i;
  P(&hd_mutex);            // procs execute hd_rw() ONE at a time
  hd_sem.value = hd_sem.queue = 0;
  set_ide_regs(rw, sector, nsector);     // set up IDE registers
  // ONE interrupt per sector read|write; transfer data via DATA port
  for (i=0; i<nsectors; i++){          // loop for each sector
      if (rw==HD_READ){
          P(&hd_sem);                  // wait for interrupt
          if (err = hd_error())
              break;
          read_port(0x1F0, getds(), buf, 256); // 256 2-byte words
          buf += 512;
      }
      else{   // for HD_WRITE, must wait until notBUSY and DRQ=1
          while (hd_busy() && !hd_drq());
          write_port(0x1F0, getds(), buf, 256);
          buf += 512;
          P(&hd_sem);                  // wait for interrupt
          if (hd_error())
          break;
      }
  }                                    // end loop
  V(&hd_mutex);                        // release hd_mutex lock
  if (hd_error()) return BAD;
  return 0;
}
```

10.8.4   Improved HD Driver

The second HD driver is based on 10.7.2.(7b). In this case, the process sets up a data
area containing disk I/O parameters, such as R|W operation, starting sector, number
of sectors, etc. Then it starts R|W of the first sector and blocks until all the sectors are
read or written. On each interrupt, the interrupt handler performs R|W of the remaining
sectors. When all sectors R|W are finished, it unblocks the process on the last interrupt.

```
/*********** HD driver for synchronous disk I/O ***************/
/** HD I/O parameters common to hd_rw() and interrupt handler */
u16  opcode;        // HD_READ | HD_WRITE
char *bufPtr;       // pointer to data buffer
int  ICOUNT;        // sector count
u16  hderror        // error flag
int hdhandler()     // HD interrupt handler
{
  printf("HD interrupt ICOUNT=%d\n", ICOUNT);
  if (hderror = hd_error())   // check for error
     goto out;
  // ONE interrupt per sector read|write; transfer data via DATA port
  if (opcode==HD_READ){
     read_port(0x1F0, getds(), bufPtr, 512);
     bufPtr += 512;
  }
  else{  // HD_WRITE
     if (ICOUNT > 1){
        unlock();    // allow interrupts
        write_port(0x1F0, getds(), bufPtr, 512);
        bufPtr += 512;
     }
  }
  if (--ICOUNT == 0){
     printf("HD inth: V(hd_sem)\n");
     V(&hd_sem);
  }
out:
  if (hderror && ICOUNT)
     V(&hd_sem);            // must unblock process even if ICOUNT > 0
  out_byte(0xA0, 0x20);   // send EOI
}
int hd_rw(u16 rw, u32 sector, char *buf, u16 nsectors)
{
    P(&hd_mutex);          // one proc at a time executes hd_rw()
    hd_sem.value = hd_sem.queue = 0;
    printf("hd_rw: setup I/O paremeters for interrupt handler\n");
    opcode = rw;           // set opcode
    bufPtr = buf;          // pointer to data buffer
    ICOUNT = nsectors;     // nsectors to R/W
    hderror = 0;           // initialize hderror to 0
    set_ide_regs(rw, sector, sectors);  // set up IDE registers
    if (rw==HD_WRITE){  // must wait until notBUSY and DRQ=1
       while (hd_busy() && !hd_drq());
       write_port(0x1F0, getds(), buf, 512);
       bufPtr += 512;
    }
    P(&hd_sem);        // block until r/w of ALL nsectors are done
    V(&hd_mutex);      // unlock hd_mutex lock
    return hderror;
}
```

10.8.5   HD Driver with I/O Queue

In an operating system, read operations are usually synchronous, meaning that a process must wait for the read operation to complete. However, write operations are usually asynchronous. In the MTX kernel, all HD write operations are delay

writes. After issuing a write request, the process continues without waiting for the
write operation to complete. Actual writing to the HD may take place much later by
the I/O buffer subsystem. Since the interrupt handler also issues R/W operations,
hd_rw() cannot contain any sleep or P operations which would block the caller. The
algorithm of the MTX HD driver is shown below.

```
------------ MTX HD driver: Shared Data Structure ------------
    struct request{
        struct request *next; // next request pointer
        int    opcode;         // READ|WRITE
        u32    sector;         // start sector (or block#)
        u16    nsectors;       // number of sectors to R/W
        char   buf[BLKSIZE];   // data area
        SEMAPHORE io_done;     // initial value = 0
    };  I/O_queue = a (FIFO) queue of I/O requests;

------------ MTX HD Driver Upper-half Process) ---------------
hd_read()
{
    1. construct an "I/O request" with SEMAPHORE request.io_done=0;
    2. hd_rw(request);
    3. P(request.io_done);          // "wait" for READ completion
    4. read data from request.buf;
}

hd_write()
{
    1. construct an "I/O request";
    2. write data to request.buf;
    3. hd_rw(request);              // do not "wait" for completion
}

hd_rw(I/O_request)
{
    1. enter request into (FIFO) I/O_queue;
    2. if (fisrt in I/O_queue)
         start_io(request);         // issue actual I/O to HD
}
-------------- MTX HD Driver Lower-half --------------------
InterruptHandler()
{
    request = first request in I/O_queue;
    1. while (request.nsectors){
         transfer data;
         request.nsectors--;
         return;
       }
    2. request = dequeue(I/O_queue); // 1st request from I/O queue
       if (request.opcode==READ)      // READ is synchronous:
           V(request.io_done);        // unblock waiting process
       else
           release the request buffer;// dealy write; release buffer
    3. if (!empty(I/O_queue))         // if I/O_queue not-empty
           start_io(first request in I/O_queue); // start next I/O
}
```

Details of the MTX HD driver will be shown later when we discuss I/O buffer management for block devices in Chap. 12.

10.8.6 MTX10.hd: Demonstration of IDE Driver

MTX10.hd demonstrates the IDE driver. It implements the second HD driver described in Sect. 10.7.4. After booting up MTX10.hd, enter the hd command from Umode. It issues a syscall(10) to execute the hd() function in kernel. In hd(), it first calls hd_rw() to read the HD's MBR sector to find out the start sectors of the partitions. It writes 10 lines of text to block 0 of partition 1. Then it reads the same block back to verify that the write operations are completed successfully. For each read/write operation, the driver displays messages to show the interactions between the process and the interrupt handler. The reader may modify the hd() code to choose an appropriate free partition to read/write.

10.9 ATAPI Driver

CDROM drives use the ATAPI (AT Attachment Packet Interface) protocol (ATA 1996), which is an extension of PATA. At the hardware level, ATAPI allows ATAPI devices, e.g. CD/DVD drives, to be connected directly to the IDE bus. All the I/O port addresses are the same as in PATA. However, some of the command registers are redefined in ATAPI. The major difference between PATA and ATAPI is that ATAPI uses SCSI-like packets to communicate with ATAPI devices. A packet consists of 12 bytes, which are written to the data port when the drive is ready to accept the packet. Once a packet is issued, interactions between the host and the device are governed by the ATAPI protocol.

10.9.1 ATAPI Protocol [ATAPI 2006; AT Attachment 1998]

Figure 10.16 shows the I/O ports of the ATAPI interface.

The status (0x177) and error (0x171) registers are the same as in PATA, except that some of the bits, especially those in the error register, are redefined for ATAPI devices (Fig. 10.17).

The interrupt reason register (0x172) is new in ATAPI. When an ATAPI interrupt occurs, IO indicates the data direction (0=toDevice, 1=toHost) and CoD indicates whether the request is for Command packet (0) or data (1). The meaning of the (IO, CoD,DRQ) bits are shown in Fig. 10.18.

```
// ATAPI I/O ports: registers 0x172,0x174,0x175 are REDEFINED in ATAPI
#define CD_DATA      0x170    // data port for R/W
#define CD_ERROR     0x171    // error register/write=features register
#define CD_INTREA    0x172    // Interrupt reason (see below)
#define CD_NO_USE    0x173    // not used by ATAPI
#define CD_LBA_MID   0x174    // byte_count LOW byte
#define CD_LBA_HI    0x175    // byte_count HI byte
#define CD_DRIVE     0x176    // drive select   (0x00=master,0x10=slave)
#define CD_CMD       0x177    // command: 0xA0 (packet command)
#define CD_STATUS    0x177    // status register   (see below)
```

Fig. 10.16 ATAPI I/O Ports

```
                        7     6     5     4     3     2     1   0
status reg : 0x177 = BUSY REDY FAULT SEEK DRQ   CO  - ERR
error  reg : 0x171 = | sense key error | MCR ABRT EOM ILI
sense key error=notReady,hardware,illegal request,unit attention
MCR=media change,ABRT=abort,EOM=end of media,TLT=illegal length
```

Fig. 10.17 ATAPI status and error registers

```
Interrupt reason register = 0x172; with DRQ in status register 0x177
    7 6 5 4 3   2  1   0 status
| reserved   |Rel| IO CoD DRQ(IO:0=toDev,1=toHost;CoD:0=data,1=command)
                  ── ── ──
              0  0   1  ready for data from host(PIO write data)
              0  1   1  ready to accept command packet
              1  0   1  data to host ready      (PIO read  data)
              1  1   0  final status interrupt
```

Fig. 10.18 ATAPI interrupt reason register

The byte count registers (0x174-175) are used in 2 ways. When issuing a command packet to a device, byte count is the number of bytes needed by the host. After a DRQ interrupt, byte count is the actual number of bytes transferred by the device. A device may use several data transfer operations, each identified by a separate DRQ interrupt, to satisfy the needed byte count. On each DRQ interrupt, the host must examine the interrupt reason. If the interrupt reason is (10), the host must continue to read data until it sees the final status interrupt (11) with DRQ=0.

10.10   ATAPI Operation Sequence

The following shows the operation sequence of the ATAPI protocol.

(1). host : poll for BSY=0 and DRQ=0; then write to feature, byteCount, drive registers (0x171,0x174,0x176); then, write packet command 0xA0 to command register (0x177).

(2). drive: set BSY, prepares for command packet transfer. Then set (IO,coD) to (01) and assert DRQ, cancel BSY.

(3). host : when DRQ=1, write 12 command bytes to Data Register 0x170; then wait for drive interrupt;

(4). drive: clear DRQ, set BSY, read feature & byteCount Regs. For PIO mode, put byte count into byteCount regs, set (IO,coD)=(10), DRQ=1, BSY=0, then generate interrupt INTRQ.

(5). host : interrupt handler: read status register (to clear INTRQ) to get DRQ. DRQ=1 means data ready for PIO. Read data port by actual byte count.

(6). drive: After data read by host, clears DRQ=0. If more data, set BSY=1, repeat (4) to (6) until all needed bytes are transferred.

(7). drive: When all needed data are transferred, issue final status interrupt by BSY=0, (IO,Cod,DRQ)=(110) and INTRQ.

(8). host : final status interrupt: read status register and error register.

10.10.1   ATAPI Driver Code

```
// ATAPI registers 0x172,0x174,0x175 are REDEFINED in ATAPI
#define CD_DATA      0x170  // data port for R/W
#define CD_ERROR     0x171  // error register/write=features register
#define CD_INTREA    0x172  // Read:interrupt reason register with DRQ
#define CD_NO_USE    0x173  // not used by ATAPI
#define CD_LBA_MID   0x174  // byte count LOW byte bits0-7
#define CD_LBA_HI    0x175  // byte count HI byte  bits 8-15
#define CD_DRIVE     0x176  // drive select
#define CD_CMD       0x177  // command : R=0x20 W=0x30
#define CD_STATUS    0x177  // status register
/*********** (1) utility functions ********************/
int cd_busy() { return (in_byte(0x177) & 0x80);}
// BUSY and READY are complementary; only need cd_busy()
int cd_ready(){ return (in_byte(0x177) & 0x40); }
int cd_DRQ()  { return (in_byte(0x177) & 0x08);}
int cd_error()
{   int r = in_byte(0x177);   // read status REG
    if (r & 0x01){            // if status.ERROR bit on
        r = in_byte(0x171);   // read error REG
        printf("CD RD ERROR = %x\n", r);
        return r;
    }
    return 0;
}
/********* (2). Common database of ATAPI driver ********/
int   cderror;
char *bufPtr;
u16   byteCount;
u16   procSegment;   // calling process Umode segment
/********* (3) ATAPI Driver Upper-half (Process) *************/
int getSector(u32 sector, char *buf, u16 nsector)
{
    int i;   u16 *usp;   u8  *cp;
    printf("CD/DVD getSector : sector=%l\n", sector);
    cderror = 0;                    // clear error flag
    bufPtr = buf;                   // pointer to data area
    procSegment = running->uss;     // if buf is in Umode
    cd_sem.value = cd_sem.queue = 0; // initialize cd_sem to 0
    /************** READ 10 packet layout *******************
                    0   1  | 2 3 4 5| 6 |7 8 9 | 10 11|
            .byte   0x28 0  |  LBA   | 0 | len  |  0  0|
    *******************************************************/
    // create packet: packet.lba[4];low-byte=MSB hi-byte=LSB
    zeropkt();
    pkt[0] = 0x28;                // READ 10 opcode in pkt[0]
    cp = (u8 *)&sector;           // sector LBA in pkt[2-5]
    pkt[2] = *(cp+3);             // low byte = MSB
    pkt[3] = *(cp+2);             // LBA byte 1
    pkt[4] = *(cp+1);             // LBA byte 2
    pkt[5] = *cp;                 // high byte= LSB
    pkt[7] = 0                    // pkt[7-8]=number of sectors to READ
    pkt[8] = nsector;             // nsector's LSB
    out_byte(0x376, 0x08);        // nInt=0 => enable drive interrupt
    out_byte(0x176, 0x00);        // device : 0x00=master;
    //(1). poll for notBUSY and then ready:
    while (cd_busy() || cd_DRQ()); // wait until notBUSY and DRQ=0
    // 2. write to festures regs 0x171, byteCount, drive registers
    out_byte(0x171, 0);  // feature REG = PIO (not DMA)
    // write host NEEDED byte_count into byteCount regs 0x174-0x175
    out_byte(0x174, (nsector*2048) & 0xFF); // Low byte
```

```
      out_byte(0x175, (nsector*2048) >> 8);    // high byte
      // 3.write 0xA0 to command register 0x177
      //printf("write 0xA0 to cmd register\n");
      out_byte(0x177, 0xA0);        // drive starts to process packet
      // wait until notBUSY && READY && DRQ is on
      while (cd_busy() || !cd_DRQ()); // wait until notBUSY and DRQ=1
      //printf("write 6 words of packet to 0x170\n");
      usp = &pkt;
      for (i=0; i<6; i++)
         out_word(0x170, *usp++);
      P(&cd_sem);        // process "wait" for FINAL status interrupt
      return cderror;
}
/****** (4). ATAPI Driver Lower-half: Interrupt Handler ********/
int cdhandler()
{
   u8 reason, status, err;  u16 byteCount;
   //read status, interrupt reason and error registers; get status.DRQ:
   status = in_byte(0x177);
   reason = in_byte(0x172) & 0x03;
   err = in_byte(0x171);
   if (status & 0x01){ // status.ERROR bit on ==> set cderror flag
      cderror = 1;
      V(&cd_sem);        // unblock proc
      if (err & 0x08)    // err=xxxxMyyy : M=need media change => ignore
         printf("media change error\n");
      //printf("CD error : status=%x  err=%x\n", status, err);
      goto out;
   }
   if ((reason==0x01) && (status & 0x08)){ // 011=ready for command
      //printf("CD ready for commands\n");
      goto out;
   }
   if ((reason==0x02) && (status & 0x08) && !(status & 0x80)){
      //printf("CD data ready for PIO ");
      byteCount=(in_byte(0x175) << 8 ) | (in_byte(0x174));
      //printf("byteCount=%d\n", byteCount);
      /********* PIO data to Kmode or Umode *********************/
      read_port(0x170, getds(), bufPtr, byteCount);    // PIO to KMODE
      //read_port(0x170, procSegment, bufPtr, byteCount); // to Umode
      goto out;
   }
   if (reason==0x03 && !(status & 0x08)){ // 110: FINAL status interrupt
      //printf("final status interrupt:status=%x:V(cd_sem)\n", status);
      V(&cd_sem);
   }
out:
   out_byte(0xA0, 0x20);    // EOI to slave 8259 PIC
   out_byte(0x20, 0x20);    // EOI to master PIC
}
```

10.10.2   MTX10.hd.cd: Demonstration of ATAPI Driver

MTX10.hd.cd is a sample MTX system with both IDE and ATAPI drivers. First, run
mk to install MTX to a FD image. Then run QEMU or VMware on the FD image.
Configure QEMU or VMware with either a real or virtual CDROM containing an
iso9660 file system. When MTX boots up, enter the cd command to test the ATAPI
driver. The driver testing program, cd.c, supports such operations as ls, cd, pwd and

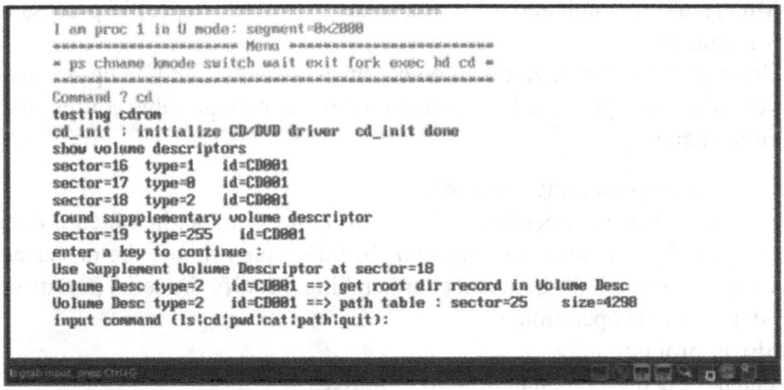

```
############################################
I am proc 1 in U mode: segment=0x2000
********************** Menu ************************
* ps chname kmode switch wait exit fork exec hd cd *
***************************************************
Command ? cd
testing cdrom
cd_init : initialize CD/DVD driver  cd_init done
show volume descriptors
sector=16  type=1   id=CD001
sector=17  type=0   id=CD001
sector=18  type=2   id=CD001
found suppplementary volume descriptor
sector=19  type=255   id=CD001
enter a key to continue :
Use Supplement Uolume Descriptor at sector=18
Uolume Desc type=2   id=CD001 ==> get root dir record in Uolume Desc
Uolume Desc type=2   id=CD001 ==> path table : sector=25   size=4298
input command (ls!cd!pwd!cat!path!quit):
```

Fig. 10.19 Demonstration of HD and CD drivers

cat, which allow the user to navigate the iso9660 file system tree on the CDROM. Figure 10.19 shows the screen of running MTX10.hd.cd

Problems

1. The console display driver only handles the special chars \n, \r and \b. Modify it to handle the tab char, \t. Each \t should be expanded to, e.g. 8 spaces. Alternatively, each \t should advance the Cursor to the beginning of the next display boundary.
2. Modify the console display driver to support scroll-down. Use either a function key or the up-arrow key to initiate the scroll-down action.
3. Virtual Console: virtual consoles, which are often called the poor man's X-windows, provide logical display screens for different processes. In this scheme, each PROC has a 2000 words area for saving the current display screen in the video RAM. During process switch (e.g. by a function key), save current PROC's screen and restore the saved screen of the new process. The visual effect is as if the display is switched from one PROC to another. Implement virtual consoles for processes in MTX.
4. Keyboard driver Programming problems

   1. Use Control-C key to send a SIGNINT(2) signal to all processes associated with the keyboard. Install handler function to ignore the signal or as a software interrupt.
   2. Use Control-K as the kill key, which erases the current input line.
   3. Catch F2, F3 as hot keys to display sleeping PROCs, semaphore values and queues.
   4. Implement uV(semaphore *s, PROC *p), which unblocks a process p from a semaphore queue.
   5. Use process status, e.g. STOPPED, to implement background processes.

6. Modify the fg command to fg pid, which promotes a specific process to the foreground.
7. Command history: Save executed commands in a buffer. Use up-down arrow keys to recall a previously executed command, with possible editing, for execution again.

5. Serial Ports Programming Problems
The serial port driver operates in the "half-duplex" mode, in which it does not echo input chars as they are received. In full-duplex mode, the driver echoes each input char, including special char handling. Modify the serial port driver for full-duplex mode operation.
6. FD driver programming:
Extend the FD driver to support two FD drives.
7. The HD driver works for the master drive of IDE0. Modify the HD driver to support two IDE0 drives.
8. The ATAPI driver works for the second IDE master drive. Extend it to support two IDE1 drives.

References

ATA: "ATA Interface for CD-ROMs", rev 2.6, SFF Committee, Jan., 1996.
ATAPI: "ATA/ATAPI Command Set (ATA8-ACS)", 2006, http://www.t13.org/documents/up-loadeddocuments/docs2006/d1699r3f-ata8-acs.pdf
FDC: "Floppy Disk Controller", http://wiki.osdev.org/Floppy_Disk_Controller, 2012
PATA: Parallel ATA: http://en.wikipedia.org/wiki/Parallel_ATA, 2015
SATA: "Serial ATA: A Comparison with Ultra ATA Technology". Seagate Technology, 2012
SVGA: http://en.wikipedia.org/wiki/Super_video_graphics_array, 2009
T13 AT Attachment (1998). AT Attachment Interface for Disk Drives (ATA-1)
VDC: Motorola 6845 VDC: http://www.tinyvga.com/6845, 2008

Chapter 11
File System

This chapter describes the implementation of a simple EXT2 file system [Card et al. 1995; Cao et al. 2007; EXT2 2001; EXT3 2015]. We choose the EXT2 file system for MTX mainly for two reasons. First, EXT2 is a simple file system, which is easy to understand but powerful enough for practical use. Second and more importantly, it is Linux compatible. Since we use Linux as the development platform of MTX, compatibility with Linux avoids unnecessary file conversions, which greatly simplifies the development of the MTX system. In this chapter, we first present an overview of file operations in an operating system. Next, we show how to format a disk image as an EXT2 file system. Then we describe the implementation of a simple EXT2 file system in detail.

11.1 File Operation Levels

File operations consist of five levels, from low to high, as shown in the following hierarchy.
(1) **Hardware Level:** File operations at hardware level include

fdisk: divide a hard disk or usb drive into partitions for file systems.
mkfs: format a disk partition to make it ready for file system.
fsck: check and repair file system.
defragmentation: compact files in a file system.

Most of these are system-oriented utility programs. An average user may never need them, but they are indispensable tools for creating and maintaining file systems.

(2) **File System Functions in OS Kernel:** Every operating system kernel provides support for basic file operations. The following lists some of these functions in a Unix-like system kernel, where the prefix k denotes kernel functions.

© Springer International Publishing Switzerland 2015
K. C. Wang, *Design and Implementation of the MTX Operating System,*
DOI 10.1007/978-3-319-17575-1_11

```
kmount(), kumount()              (mount/umount file systems)
kmkdir(), krmdir()               (make/remove directory)
kchdir(), kgetcwd()              (change directory, get CWD pathname)
klink(), kunlink()               (hard link/unlink files)
kchmod(), kchown(), ktouch()     (change r|w|x permissions,owner,time)
kcreat(), kopen()                (create/open file for R,W,RW,APPEND)
kread(), kwrite()                (read/write opened files)
klseek(); kclose()               (lseek/close file descriptors)
ksymlink(), kreadlink()          (create/read symbolic link files)
kstat(), kfstat(), klstat()      (get file status/information)
kopendir(), kreaddir()           (open/read directories)
```

(3) **System Calls:** User mode programs use system calls to access kernel functions. As an example, the following program reads the second 1024 bytes of a file.

```c
#include <fcntl.h>
main(int argc, char *argv[ ])    // run as a.out filename
{
    int fd, n;
    char buf[1024];
    if ((fd = open(argv[1], O_RDONLY)) < 0) // if open() fails
        exit(1);
    lseek(fd, 1024, SEEK_SET);    // lseek to byte 1024
    n = read(fd, buf, 1024);      // try to read 1024 bytes
    close(fd);
}
```

The functions open(), read(), lseek() and close() are C library functions. Each library function issues a system call, which causes the process to enter kernel mode to execute a corresponding kernel function, e.g. open goes to kopen(), read goes to kread(), etc. When the process finishes executing the kernel function, it returns to user mode with the desired results. Switch between user mode and kernel mode requires a lot of actions (and time). Data transfer between kernel and user spaces is therefore quite expensive. Although it is permissible to issue a read(fd, buf, 1) system call to read only one byte of data, it is not very wise to do so since that one byte would come with a terrific cost. Every time we have to enter kernel, we should do as much as we can to make the journey worthwhile. In the case of read/write files, the best way is to match what the kernel does. The kernel reads/writes files by block size, which ranges from 1KB to 8KB. For instance, in Linux, the default block size is 4KB for hard disks and 1KB for floppy disks. So each read/write system call should also try to transfer one block of data at a time.

(4) **Library I/O Functions:** System calls allow the user to read/write chunks of data, which are just a sequence of bytes. They do not know, nor care, about the meaning of the data. A user often needs to read/write individual chars, lines or data structure records, etc. With only system calls, a user mode program must do these operations from/to a buffer area by itself. Most users would consider this too inconvenient. The C library provides a set of standard I/O functions for convenience, as well as for run-time efficiency. Library I/O functions include:

```
FILE mode I/O: fopen(),fread();  fwrite(),fseek(),fclose(),fflush()
char mode I/O: getc(), getchar() ugetc(); putc(),putchar()
line mode I/O: gets(), fgets(); puts(), fputs()
formatted I/O: scanf(),fscanf(),sscanf(); printf(),fprintf(),sprintf()
```

With the exceptions of sscanf()/sprintf(), which read/write memory locations, all other library I/O functions are built on top of system calls, i.e. they ultimately issue system calls for actual data transfer through the system kernel.

(5) **User Commands:** Instead of writing programs, users may use Unix/Linux commands to do file operations. Examples of user commands are

mkdir, rmdir, cd, pwd, ls, link, unlink, rm, cat, cp, mv, chmod, etc.

Each user command is in fact an executable program (except cd), which typically calls library I/O functions, which in turn issue system calls to invoke the corresponding kernel functions. The processing sequence of a user command is either

```
   Command => Library I/O function => System call => Kernel Function
OR Command ======================== > System call => Kernel Function
```

(6) **Sh Scripts**: Although much more convenient than system calls, commands must be entered manually, which is tedious and time-consuming. Sh scripts are programs written in the sh programming language, which can be executed by the command interpreter sh. The sh language include all valid Unix commands. It also supports variables and control statements, such as if, do, for, while, case, etc. In practice, sh scripts are used extensively in Unix systems programming. In addition to sh, many other script languages, such as Perl and Tcl, are also in wide use.

11.2 File I/O Operations

Figure 11.1 shows the diagram of file I/O operations.

In Fig. 11.1, the upper part above the double line represents kernel space and the lower part represents user space of a process. The diagram shows the sequence of actions when a process read/write a file stream. Control flows are identified by the labels (1–10), which are explained below.

User Mode Operations

--------------------------------- User Mode Operations --
(1). A process in User mode executes
```
    FILE *fp = fopen("file", "r"); or FILE *fp = fopen("file", "w");
```
which opens a file stream for READ or WRITE.

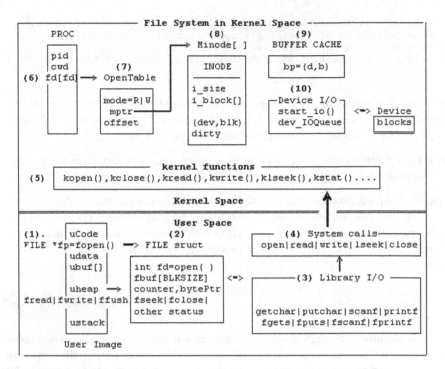

Fig. 11.1 File operation diagram

(2). fopen() creates a FILE structure in user (heap) space containing a file descriptor, fd, and a fbuf[BLKSIZE]. It issues a fd = open("file", flags = READ or WRITE) syscall to kopen() in kernel, which constructs an OpenTable to represent an instance of the opened file. The OpenTable's mptr points to the file's INODE in memory. For non-special files, the INODE's i_block array points to data blocks on the storage device. On success, fp points to the FILE structure, in which fd is the file descriptor returned by the open() syscall.

(3). fread(ubuf, size, nitem, fp): READ nitem of size each to ubuf by

. copy data from FILE structure's fbuf to ubuf, if enough, return;
. if fbuf has no more data, then execute (4a).

(4a). issue read(fd, fbuf, BLKSIZE) syscall to read a file block from kernel to fbuf, then copy data to ubuf until enough or file has no more data.

(4b). fwrite(ubuf, size, nitem, fp): copy data from ubuf to fbuf;

. if (fbuf has room): copy data to fbuf, return;
. if (fbuf is full) : issue write(fd, fbuf, BLKSIZE) syscall to write a block to kernel,
                       then write to fbuf again.

Thus, fread()/fwrite() issue read()/write() syscalls to kernel, but they do so only if necessary and they transfer data in chunks of block size for better efficiency. Similarly, other Library I/O Functions, such as fgetc/fputc, fgets/fputs, fscanf/fprintf, etc. also operate on fbuf in the FILE structure, which is in user space.

=================== **Kernel Mode Operations** ===================

(5).File system functions in kernel:
Assume read(fd, fbuf[ ], BLKSIZE) syscall of non-special file.

(6). In a read() syscall, fd is an opened file descriptor, which is an index in the running PROC's fd array, which points to an OpenTable representing the opened file.

(7). The OpenTable contains the files's open mode, a pointer to the file's INODE in memory and the current byte offset into the file for read/write. From the OpenTable's offset,

. Compute logical block number, lbk;
. Convert logical block number to physical block number, blk, via INODE.i_
   block array.

(8). Minode contains the in-memory INODE of the file. The INODE.i_block array contains pointers to physical disk blocks. A file system may use the physical block numbers to read/write data from/to the disk blocks directly, but these would incur too much physical disk I/O.

(9). In order to improve disk I/O efficiency, the OS kernel usually uses a set of I/O buffers as a cache memory to reduce the number of physical I/O. Details of I/O buffer management will be covered in Chap. 12.

(9a). For a read(fd, buf, BLKSIZE) syscall, determine the needed (dev, blk) number, then consult the I/O buffer cache to

```
.get a buffer = (dev, blk);
.if (buffer's data are invalid){
    start_io on buffer;
    wait for I/O completion;
}
.copy data from buffer to fbuf;
.release the buffer to buffer cache;
```

(9b). For a write(fd, fbuf, BLKSIZE) syscall, determine the needed (dev, blk) number, then consult the I/O buffer cache to

```
.get a buffer = (dev, blk);
.write data to the I/O buffer;
.mark buffer as dataValid and DIRTY (for delay-write to disk);
.release the buffer to buffer cache;
```

(10): Device I/O: Physical I/O on the I/O buffers ultimately go through the device driver, which consists of start_io() in the upper-half and disk interrupt handler in the lower-half of the driver.

```
--------------- Upper-half of disk driver ----------------------
start_io(bp): //bp=a locked buffer in dev_list, opcode=R|W(ASYNC)
{
   1. enter bp into dev's I/O_queue;
   2. if (bp is FIRST in I/O_queue)
         issue I/O command to device;
}
--------------- Lower-half of disk driver --------------------
Device_Interrupt_Handler:
{
   bp = dequeue(first buffer from dev.I/O_queue);
   if (bp was READ){
      mark bp data VALID;
      wakeup/unblock waiting process on bp;
   }
   else       // bp was for delay write
      release bp into buffer cache;
   if (dev.I/O_queue NOT empty)
      issue I/O command for first buffer in dev.I/O_queue;
}
```

11.3   EXT2 File System Specification

Chapter 2 contains a brief description of the EXT2 file system, which is sufficient for the following discussions. For more information, the reader may consult EXT2 file system documentations [Card et al. EXT2] for details.

11.4   A Simple mkfs Program

On the MTX Install CD, MTX.programs/mkfs.c is a C program, which formats a disk image as an EXT2 file system. For the sake of simplicity, we assume that the file system has only one disk block group. The maximal number of disk blocks is 8192. The program is intended to be compiled and run under Linux, but it can be adapted to any system environment which supports the write disk block operation. Under Linux, the program runs as follows.

mkfs device nblocks [ninodes]

where nblocks is the number of (1KB) blocks and niondes is the number of inodes. If ninodes is not specified, the program computes a default number of ninodes based on nblocks. The algorithm of mkfs is outlined below.

```
/*********** Algorithm of mkfs devive, nblocks, [ninode]*********/
1. open device for RW mode, write to last disk block;
2. if ninodes is not specified, compute ninodes=8*((nblocks/4)/8);
3. based on ninodes, compute number of inode blocks and used blocks.
4. create super block, write to block#1
5. create group descriptor 0, write to block#2
6. create blocks bitmap; write to blcok#3
7. create inodes bitmap; write to block#4
8. clear inodes blocks on disk; allocate a data block, create a root
   inode in memory with i_blokc[0]=allocated data block, write the
   root inode to #2 inode on disk.
9. initialize root inode's data block to contain . and .. entries;
   write data block to disk;
```

The basic technique used is to create the needed data structure in a 1KB buffer area in memory and then write it to a corresponding block of the disk image. The resulting disk image file can be used as a virtual disk.

11.5 Implementation of EXT2 File System

11.5.1 File System Organization

Figure 11.2 shows the internal organization of an EXT2 file system. The organization diagram is explained by the labels (1–5).

(1). is the PROC structure of the running process. Each PROC has a cwd, which points to the in-memory INODE of the PROC's Current Working Directory. It also has an array of file descriptors, fd[], which point to opened file instances.

(2). is the root pointer of the file system. It points to the in-memory root INODE. When the system starts, one of the devices is chosen as the root device, which must be a valid EXT2 file system. The root INODE (inode #2) of the root device is loaded into memory as the root (/) of the file system. This operation is known as "mount root file system".

(3). is an openTable entry. When a process opens a file, an entry of the PROC's fd array points to an openTable, which points to the in-memory INODE of the opened file.

(4). is an in-memory INODE. Whenever a file is needed, its INODE is loaded into a minode slot for reference. Since INODEs are unique, only one copy of each INODE can be in memory at any time. In the minode, (dev, ino) identify where the INODE came from, for writing the INODE back to disk if modified. The refCount field records the number of processes that are using the minode. The dirty field indicates whether the INODE has been modified. The mounted flag indicates whether the INODE has been mounted on and, if so, the mntabPtr points to the mount table entry of the mounted file system. The lock field is to ensure that an in-memory INODE can only be accessed by one process at a time, e.g. when modifying the INODE or during a read/write operation.

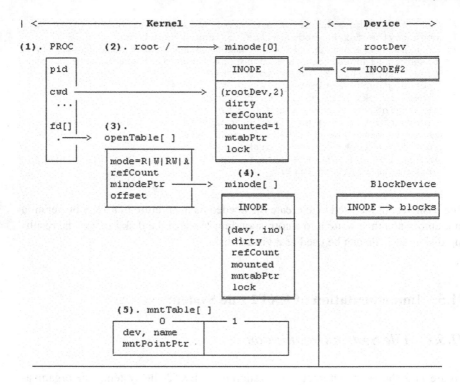

Fig. 11.2 EXT2 File system data structures

(5). is a table of mounted file systems. For each mounted file system, an entry in the mount table is used to record the mounted file system information. In the in-memory INODE of the mount point, the mounted flag is turned on and the mntabPtr points to the mount table entry. In the mount table entry, mntPointPtr points back to the in-memory INODE of the mount point. As will be shown later, these doubly-linked pointers allow us to cross mount points when traversing the file system tree. In addition, a mount table entry may also contain other information of the mounted file system, such as the device name, superblock, group descriptor and bitmaps, etc. for quick reference.

11.5.2 Files in the MTX/FS directory

In the MTX kernel source tree, the FS directory contains files which implement the EXT2 file system. The files are organized as follows.

```
------------------ Common files of FS -----------------------------
type.h  : EXT2 data structure types
global.c: global variables of FS
util.c  : common utility functions: getino(), iget(), iput(), search(), etc.
allocate_deallocate.c : inodes/blocks management functions
```

Implementation of the file system is divided into three levels. Each level deals with a distinct part of the file system. This makes the implementation process modular and easier to understand. Level-1 implements the basic file system tree. It contains the following files, which implement the indicated functions.

```
-------------------- Level-1 of FS ----------------------------
mkdir_creat.c      : make directory, create regular and special file
cd_pwd.c           : change directory, get CWD path
rmdir.c            : remove directory
link_unlink.c      : hard link and unlink files
symlink_readlink.c : symbolic link files
stat.c             : return file information
misc1.c            : access, chmod, chown, touch, etc.
-----------------------------------------------------------------
```

User level programs which use the level-1 FS functions include

mkdir, creat, mknod, rmdir, link, unlink, symlink, rm, ls, cd and pwd, etc.

Level-2 implements functions for reading/writing file contents.
```
---------------------- Level-2 of FS -----------------------------
open_close_lseek.c  : open file for READ|WRITE|APPEND, close file and lseek
read.c              : read from an opened file descriptor
write.c             : write to an opened file descriptor
opendir_readdir.c   : open and read directory
dev_switch_table    : read/write special files
block device I/O buffer management : I/O buffer management
```

Level-3 implements mount, umount and file protection.

```
---------------------- Level-3 of FS ----------------------------
mount_umount.c      : mount/umount file systems
file protection     : access permission checking
file-locking        : lock/unlock files
-----------------------------------------------------------------
```

11.5.3   Implementation of Level-1 FS

(1) type.h file: This file contains the data structure types of the EXT2 file system, such as superblock, group descriptor, inode and directory entry structures. In addition, it also contains the open file table, mount table, pipes and PROC structures and constants of the MTX kernel.

(2) global.c file: This file contains global variables of the MTX kernel. Examples
of global variables are

```
MINODE  minode[NMINODES];    // in memory INODEs
MOUNT   mounttab[NMOUNT];     // mount table
OFT     oft[NOFT];            // Opened file instance
```

(3) util.c file: This file contains utility functions of the file system. The most
important utility functions are getino(), iget() and iput(), which are explained in
more detail.

(3).1. u32 getino(int *dev, char *pathname): getino() returns the inode number of
a pathname. While traversing a pathname the device number may change if the
pathname crosses mounting point(s). The parameter dev is used to record the final
device number. Thus, getino() essentially returns the (dev, ino) of a pathname. The
function uses token() to break up pathname into component strings. Then it calls
search() to search for the component strings in successive directory minodes.

(3).2. MINODE *iget(in dev, u32 ino): This function returns a pointer to the in-
memory INODE of (dev, ino). The returned minode is unique, i.e. only one copy of
the INODE exists in memory. In addition, the minode is locked for exclusive use
until it is either released or unlocked.

(3).3. iput(MINODE *mip): This function releases and unlocks a minode pointed by mip. If the process is the last one to use the minode (refCount = 0), the INODE
is written back to disk if it is dirty (modified).

(3).4. Use of getino()/iget()/iput(): In a file system, almost every operation begins with a pathname, e.g. mkdir pathname, cat pathname, etc. Whenever a pathname is needed, its inode must be loaded into memory for reference. The general
pattern of using an inode is

> . ino = getino(&dev, pathname);
> . mip = iget(dev, ino);
> .   use the mip->INODE, which may modify the INODE;
> . iput(mip);

There are only a few exceptions to this usage pattern. For instance,
    chdir: iget the new DIR minode but iput the old DIR minode.
    open: iget the minode of a file, which is released when the file is closed.
    mount: iget the minode of mountPoint, which is released later by umount.

In general, iget and iput should appear in pairs, like a pair of matching parentheses. We may rely on this usage pattern in the implementation code to ensure that
every INODE is loaded and then released properly.

(3).5. Minodes Locking: Every minode has a lock field, which ensures that a minode can only be accessed by one process at a time, especially when modifying the
INODE. Unix uses a busy flag and sleep/wakeup to synchronize processes accessing the same minode. In MTX, each minode has a lock semaphore with an initial

value 1. A process is allowed to access a minode only if it holds the semaphore lock. The reason for minodes locking is as follows.

Assume that a process Pi needs the inode of (dev, ino), which is not in memory. Pi must load the inode into a minode entry. The minode must be marked as (dev, ino) to prevent other processes from loading the same inode again. While loading the inode from disk Pi may wait for I/O completion, which switches to another process Pj. If Pj needs exactly the same inode, it would find the needed minode already exists. Without the lock, Pj would proceed to use the minode before it is even loaded in yet. With the lock, Pj must wait until the minode is loaded, used and then released by Pi. In addition, when a process read/write an opened file, it must lock the file's minode to ensure that each read/write operation is atomic.

(4). allocate_deallocate.c file: This file contains utility functions for allocating and deallocating minodes, inodes, disk blocks and open file table entries. It is noted that both inode and disk block numbers count from 1. Therefore, in the bitmaps bit i represents inode/block number $i+1$.

(5). mount_root.c file

This file contains the mount_root() function, which is called during system initialization to mount the root file system. It reads the superblock of the root device to verify the device is a valid EXT2 file system. It loads the root INODE (ino $=2$) into a minode and sets the root pointer to the root minode. Then it unlocks the root minode to allow all processes to access the root minode. A mount table entry is allocated to record the mounted root file system. Some key parameters on the root device, such as the starting blocks of the bitmaps and inodes table, are also recorded in the mount table for quick reference.

(6). mkdir_creat.c file

This file contains mkdir and creat functions for making directories and creating files, respectively. mkdir and creat are very similar, so they share some common code. Before discussing the algorithms of mkdir and creat, we first show how to insert/delete a DIR entry into/from a parent directory. Each data block of a directory contains DIR entries of the form

```
|ino rlen nlen name|ino rlen nlen name|  ...
```

where name is a sequence of nlen chars without a terminating NULL byte. Since each DIR entry begins with a u32 inode number, the rec_len of each DIR entry is always a multiple of 4 (for memory alignment). The last entry in a data block spans the remaining block, i.e. its rec_len is from where the entry begins to the end of block. In mkdir and creat, we assume the following.

(a). A DIR file has at most 12 direct blocks. This assumption is reasonable since, with 1KB block size and an average file name of 16 chars, a DIR can contain more than 500 file names. We may assume that no user would put that many entries in a directory.

(b). Once allocated, a DIR's data block is kept for reuse even if it becomes empty. With these assumptions, the insertion and deletion algorithms are as follows.

```
/************* Algorithm of Insert_dir_entry *****************/
(1). need_len = 4*((8+name_len+3)/4); // new entry need length
(2). for each existing data block do {
         if (block has only one entry with inode number==0)
             enter new entry as first entry in block;
         else{
(3).         go to last entry in block;
             ideal_len = 4*((8+last_entry's name_len+3)/4);
             remain = last entry's rec_len - ideal_len;
             if (remain >= need_len){
                 trim last entry's rec_len to ideal_len;
                 enter new entry as last entry with rec_len = remain;
             }
(4).         else{
                 allocate a new data block;
                 enter new entry as first entry in the data block;
                 increase DIR's size by BLKSSIZE;
             }
         }
         write block to disk;
     }
(5). mark DIR's minode modified for write back;

/************* Algorithm of Delete_dir_entry (name) *************/
(1). search DIR's data block(s) for entry by name;
(2). if (entry is the only entry in block)
         clear entry's inode number to 0;
     else{
(3).     if (entry is last entry in block)
             add entry's rec_len to predecessor entry's rec_len;
(4).     else{ // entry in middle of block
             add entry's rec_len to last entry's rec_len;
             move all trailing entries left to overlay deleted entry;
         }
     }
(5). write block back to disk;
```

Note that in the Delete_dir_entry algorithm, an empty block is not deallocated but kept for reuse. This implies that a DIR's size will never decrease. Alternative schemes are listed in the Problem section as programming exercises.

11.5.3.1 Mkdir-creat-mknod

mkdir creates an empty directory with a data block containing the default. and.. entries. The algorithm of mkdir is

```
/********* Algorithm of mkdir *********/
int mkdir(char *pathname)
{
  1. if (pathname is absolute) dev = root    ->dev;
         else                          dev = PROC's cwd->dev
  2. divide pathname into dirname and basename;
  3. // dirname must exist and is a DIR:
     pino = getino(&dev, dirname);
     pmip = iget(dev, pino);
     check pmip      ->INODE is a DIR
  4. // basename must not exist in parent DIR:
         search(pmip, basename) must return 0;
  5. call kmkdir(pmip, basename) to create a DIR;
         kmkdir() consists of 4 major steps:
         5-1. allocate an INODE and a disk block:
              ino = ialloc(dev); blk = balloc(dev);
                mip = iget(dev,ino);   // load INODE into an minode
         5-2. initialize mip->INODE as a DIR INODE;
                mip->INODE.i_block[0] = blk; other i_block[ ] are 0;
                mark minode modified (dirty);
                iput(mip);   // write INODE back to disk
         5-3. make data block 0 of INODE to contain . and .. entries;
                write to disk block blk.
         5-4. enter_child(pmip, ino, basename); which enters
                (ino, basename) as a DIR entry to the parent INODE;
  6. increment parent INODE's links_count by 1 and mark pmip dirty;
     iput(pmip);
}
```

Creat creates an empty regular file. The algorithm of creat is

```
/**************** Algorithm of creat ()************************/
creat(char * pathname)
{
    This is similar to mkdir() except
    (1). the INODE.i_mode field is set to REG file type, permission
              bits set to 0644 for rw-r--r--, and
    (2). no data block is allocated for it, so the file size is 0.
    (3). Do not increment parent INODE's links_count
}
```

It is noted that the above creat algorithm differs from that in Unix/Linux. The new file's permissions are set to 0644 by default and it does not open the file for WRITE mode and return a file descriptor. In practice, creat is rarely used as a stand-alone syscall. It is used internally by the open() function, which may create a file, open it for WRITE and return a file descriptor. The open operation will be described later.

mknod creates a special file which represents either a char or block device with a device number=(major, minor). The algorithm of mknod is

```
/***************** Algorithm of mknod () **********************/
mknod(char *name, int type, int device_number)
{
    This is similar to creat() except
    (1). the default parent directory is /dev;
    (2). INODE.i_mode is set to CHAR or BLK file type;
    (3). INODE.I_block[0] contains device_number=(major, minor);
}
```

11.5.3.2 Chdir-getcwd-stat

Each process has a Current Working Directory (CWD), which points to the CWD minode of the process in memory. chdir(pathname) changes the CWD of a process to pathname. getcwd() returns the absolute pathname of CWD. stat() returns the status information of a file in a STAT structure. The algorithm of chdir() is

```
/********** Algorithm of chdir ************/
int chdir(char *pathname)
{
    (1). get INODE of pathname into a minode;
    (2). verify it is a DIR;
    (3). change running process CWD to minode of pathname;
    (4). iput(old CWD); return 0 for OK;
}
```

getcwd() is implemented by recursion. Starting from CWD, get the parent INODE into memory. Search the parent INODE's data block for the name of the current directory and save the name string. Repeat the operation for the parent INODE until the root directory is reached. Construct an absolute pathname of CWD on return. Then copy the absolute pathname to user space. stat(pathname, STAT *st) returns the information of a file in a STAT structure. The algorithm of stat is

```
/********* Algorithm of stat *********/
int stat(char *pathname, STAT *st)
{
    (1). get INODE of pathname into a minode;
    (2). copy (dev, ino) of minode to (st_dev, st_ino) of the STAT
         structure in user space;
    (3). copy other fields of INODE to STAT structure in user space;
    (4). iput(minode); retrun 0 for OK;
}
```

11.5.3.3 Rmdir

As in Unix/Linux, in order to rm a DIR, the directory must be empty, for the following reasons. First, removing a non-empty directory implies removing all the files

and subdirectories in the directory. Although it is possible to implement a rmdir()
operation, which recursively removes an entire directory tree, the basic operation
is still to remove one directory at a time. Second, a non-empty directory may contain files that are actively in use, e.g. opened for read/write, etc. Removing such a
directory is clearly unacceptable. Although it is possible to check whether there are
any active files in a directory, it would incur too much overhead in the kernel. The
simplest way out is to require that a directory must be empty in order to be removed.
The algorithm of rmdir() is

```
/*********** Algorithm of rmdir *************/
  rmdir(char *pathname)
  {
    1. get in-memory INODE of pathname:
       ino = getino(&de, pathanme);
       mip = iget(dev,ino);
    2. verify INODE is a DIR (by INODE.i_mode field);
       minode is not BUSY (refCount = 1);
       DIR is empty (traverse data blocks for number of entries = 2);
    3. /* get parent's ino and inode */
       pino = findino(); //get pino from .. entry in INODE.i_block[0]
       pmip = iget(mip->dev, pino);
    4. /* remove name from parent directory */
       findname(pmip, ino, name); //find name from parent DIR
       rm_child(pmip, name);
    5. /* deallocate its data blocks and inode */
       truncat(mip);   // deallocate INODE's data blocks
    6. deallocate INODE
       idalloc(mip->dev, mip->ino); iput(mip);
    7. dec parent links_count by 1;
       mark parent dirty; iput(pmip);
    8. return 0 for SUCCESS.
  }
```

11.5.3.4   Link-unlink

The link_unlikc.c file implements link and unlink. link(old_file, new_file) creates
a hard link from new_file to old_file. Hard links can only be to regular files, not
DIRs, because linking to DIRs may create loops in the file system name space. Hard
link files share the same inode. Therefore, they must be on the same device. The
algorithm of link is ·

```
         /********* Algorithm of link ********/
         link(old_file, new_file)
         {
         1. // verify old_file exists and is not DIR;
            oino = getino(&odev, old_file);
            omip = iget(odev, oino);
            check file type (cannot be DIR).
         2. // new_file must not exist yet:
            nion = get(&ndev, new_file) must return 0;
            ndev of dirname(newfile) must be same as odev
         3. // creat entry in new_parent DIR with same ino
            pmip -> minode of dirname(new_file);
            enter_name(pmip, omip->ino, basename(new_file));
         4. omip->INODE.i_links_count++;
            omip->dirty = 1;.
            iput(omip);
            iput(pmip);
         }
```

unlink decrements the file's links_count by 1 and deletes the file name from its
parent DIR. When a file's links_count reaches 0, the file is truly removed by deallocating its data blocks and inode. The agorithm of unlink() is

```
/***********  Algorithm of unlink *************/
unlink(char *filename)
{
  1. get filenmae's minode:
     ino = getino(&dev, filename);
     mip = iget(dev, ino);
     check it's a REG or SLINK file
  2. // remove basename from parent DIR
     rm_child(pmip, mip->ino, basename);
     pmip->dirty = 1;
     iput(pmip);
  3. // decrement INODE's link_count
     mip->INODE.i_links_count--;
     if (mip->INODE.i_links_count > 0){
     mip->dirty = 1; iput(mip);
           }
  4. if (!SLINK file)          // assume:SLINK file has no data block
     truncate(mip); // deallocate all data blocks
     deallocate INODE;
     iput(mip);
}
```

11.5.3.5 Symlink-readlink

symlink(old_file, new_file) creates a symbolic link from new_file to old_file. Unlike hard links, symlink can link to anything, including DIRs or files not on the same
device. The algorithm of symlink is

```
Algorithm of symlink(old_file, new_file)
{
    1. check: old_file must exist and new_file not yet exist;
    2. create new_file; change new_file to SLINK type;
    3. // assume length of old_file name <= 60 chars
       store old_file name in newfile's INODE.i_block[ ] area.
       mark new_file's minode dirty;
       iput(new_file's minode);
    4. mark new_file parent minode dirty;
       put(new_file's parent minode);
}
```

readlink(file, buffer) reads the target file name of a SLINK file and returns the length of the target file name. The algorithm of readlink() is

```
Algorithm of readlink (file, buffer)
{
    1. get file's INODE into memory; verify it's a SLINK file
    2. copy target filename in INODE.i_block into a buffer;
    3. return strlen((char *)mip->INODE.i_block);
}
```

11.5.3.6   Other Level-1 Functions

Other level-1 functions include access, chmod, chown, touch, etc. The operations of all such functions are of the same pattern:

```
    (1). get the in-memory INODE of a file by
            ino = getinod(&dev, pathname);
            mip = iget(dev,ino);
    (2). get information from the INODE or modify the INODE;
    (3). if INODE is modified, mark it DIRTY for write back;
    (4). iput(mip);
```

11.5.4   Implementation of Level-2 FS

Level-2 of FS implements read/write operations of file contents. It consists of the following functions: open, close, lseek, read, write, opendir and readdir.

11.5.4.1   Open-close-lseek

The file open_close_lseek.c implements open(), close() and lseek(). The system call
    int open(char *filename, int flags);
opens a file for read or write, where flags = 0|1|2|3|4 for R|W|RW|APPEND, respectively. Alternatively, flags can also be specified as one of the symbolic con-

stants O_RDONLY, O_WRONLY, O_RDWR, which may be bitwise or-ed with file
creation flags O_CREAT, O_APPEND, O_TRUNC. These symbolic constants are
defined in type.h. On success, open() returns a file descriptor for subsequent read()/
write() system calls. The algorithm of open() is

```
/**************  Algorithm of open()  **********/
int open(file, flags)
{
 1. get file's minode:
    ino = getino(&dev, file);
    if (ino==0 && O_CREAT){
    creat(file); ino = getino(&dev, file);
    }
    mip = iget(dev, ino);
 2. check file INODE's access permission;
    for non-special file, check for incompatible open modes;
 3. allocate an openTable entry;
    initialize openTable entries;
    set byteOffset = 0 for R|W|RW; set to file size for APPEND mode;
 4. Search for a FREE fd[ ] entry with the lowest index fd in PROC;
    let fd[fd]point to the openTable entry;
 5. unlock minode;
    return fd as the file descriptor;
}
```

Figure 11.3 show the data structure created by open(). In the figure, (1) is the PROC
structure of the process that calls open(). The returned file descriptor, fd, is the index of the fd[ ] array in the PROC structure. The contents of fd[fd] points to a OFT,
which points to the minode of the file. The OFT's refCount represents the number
of processes which share the same instance of an opened file. When a process opens
a file, the refCount in the OFT is set to 1. When a process forks, the child process

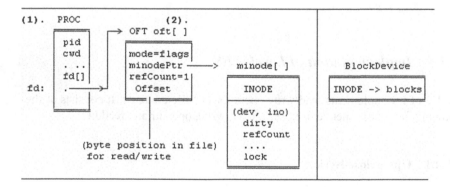

Fig. 11.3 Data Structures of open()

inherits all the opened file descriptors of the parent, which increments the refCount of every shared OFT by 1. When a process closes a file descriptor, it decrements the OFT's refCount by 1, etc. The OFT's offset is a conceptual pointer to the current byte position in the file for read/write. It is initially set to 0 for R|R|RW or to file size for APPEND.

In MTX, lseek(fd, position) sets the offset in the OFT of an opened file descriptor to the byte position relative to the beginning of the file. Once set, the next read/write begins from the current offset position. The algorithm of lseek () is trivial. For files opened for READ, it only checks the position value to ensure it's within the bounds of [0, file_size]. If fd is a regular file opened for WRITE, it allows the byte offset to go beyond the current file size but does not allocate any disk block. Disk blocks will be allocated when data are actually written to the file. The algorithm of closing a file descriptor is

```
/************* Algorithm of close()  ****************/
int close(int fd)
{
  (1). check fd is a valid opened file descriptor;
  (2). if (PROC's fd[fd] != 0){
  (3).     if (openTable's mode == READ/WRITE PIPE)
               return close_pipe(fd); // close pipe descriptor;
  (4).     if (--refCount == 0){ // if last process using this OFT
               lock(minodeptr);
               iput(minode);      // release minode
               }
         }
  (5). clear fd[fd] = 0;         // clear fd[fd] to 0
  (6). return SUCCESS;
}
```

11.5.4.2   Read Regular Files

The system call int read(int fd, char buf[ ], int nbytes); reads nbytes from an opened file descriptor into a buffer area in user space. read() invokes kread() in kernel, which implements the read system call. The algorithm of kread() is

```
/**************** Algorithm of kread() in kernel ****************/
int kread(int fd, char buf[ ], int nbytes, int space) //space=K|U
{
  (1). validate fd; ensure oft is opened for READ or RW;
  (2). if (oft.mode = READ_PIPE)
          return read_pipe(fd, buf, nbytes);
  (3). if (minode.INODE is a special file)
          return read_special(device,buf,nbytes);
  (4). (regular file):
          return read_file(fd, buf, nbytes, space);
}


/*************** Algorithm of read regular files ****************/
int read_file(int fd, char *buf, int nbytes, int space)
{
(1). lock minode;
(2). count = 0;              // number of bytes read
     compute bytes available in file: avil = fileSize - offset;
(3). while (nbytes){
        compute logical block: lbk  = offset / BLKSIZE;
        start byte in block:   start = offset % BLKSIZE;
(4).    convert logical block number, lbk, to physical block number,
        blk, through INODE.i_block[ ] array;
(5).    read_block(dev, blk, kbuf); // read blk into kbuf[BLKSIZE];
        char *cp = kbuf + start;
        remain = BLKSIZE - start;
(6)     while (remain){// copy bytes from kbuf[ ] to buf[ ]
           (space)? put_ubyte(*cp++, *buf++) : *buf++ = *cp++;
           offset++; count++;          // inc offset, count;
           remain--; avil--; nbytes--; // dec remain, avil, nbytes;
           if (nbytes==0 || avail==0)
              break;
        }
     }
(7). unlock minode;
(8). return count;
}
```

The algorithm of read_file() can be best explained in terms of Fig. 11.4. Assume that fd is opened for READ. The offset in the OFT points to the current byte position in the file from where we wish to read nbytes. To the kernel, a file is just a sequence of contiguous bytes, numbered from 0 to fileSize-1. As Fig. 11.4 shows, the current byte position, offset, falls in a logical block, lbk = offset/ BLKSIZE, the byte to start read is start = offset % BLKSIZE and the number of bytes remaining in the logical block is remain = BLKSIZE—start. At this moment, the file has avail = file-Size—offset bytes still available for read. These numbers are used in the read_file algorithm. In MTX, block size is 1 KB and files have at most double indirect blocks.

The algorithm of converting logical block number to physical block number for read is

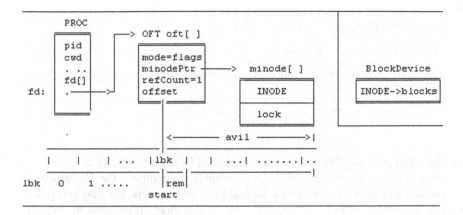

Fig. 11.4 Data Structures for read_file()

```
/* Algorithm of Converting Logical Block to Physical Block */
u32 map(INODE, lbk){               // convert lbk to blk
    if (lbk < 12)                  // direct blocks
        blk = INODE.i_block[lbk];
    else if (12 <= lbk < 12+256){ // indirect blocks
        read INODE.i_block[12] into u32 ibuf[256];
        blk = ibuf[lbk-12];
    }
    else{                          // doube indirect blocks
        read INODE.i_block[13] into u32 dbuf[256];
        lbk-=(12+256);
        dblk=dbuf[lbk / 256];
        read dblk into dbuf[ ];
        blk =dbuf[lbk % 256];
    }
    return blk;
}
```

11.5.4.3 Write Regular Files

The system call int write(int fd, char ubuf[ ], int nbytes) writes nbytes from ubuf in user space to an opened file descriptor and returns the actual number of bytes written. write() invokes kwrite() in kernel, which implements the write system call. The algorithm of kwrite() is

```
/************** Algorithm of kwrite () in kernel ***********/
int kwrite(int fd, char *ubuf, int nbytes)
{
  (1). validate fd; ensure OFT is opened for write;
  (2). if (oft.mode = WRITE_PIPE)
          return write_pipe(fd, buf, nbytes);
  (3). if (minode.INODE is a special file)
          return write_special(device,buf.nbytes);
  (4). return write_file(fd, ubuf, nbytes);
}
```

The algorithm of write_file() can be best explained in terms of Fig. 11.5.

In Fig. 11.5, the offset in the OFT is the current byte position in the file for write. As in read_file(), it first computes the logical block number, lbk, the start byte position and the number of bytes remaining in the logical block. It converts the logical block to physical block through the file's INODE.i_block array. Then it reads the physical block into a buffer, writes data to it and writes the buffer back to disk. The following shows the write_file() algorithm.

```
/************** Algorithm of write regular file ***************/
int write_file(int fd, char *ubuf, int nbytes)
{
(1). lock minode;
(2). count = 0;           // number of bytes written
(3). while (nbytes){
        compute logical block: lbk = oftp->offset / BLOCK_SIZE;
        compute start byte:    start = oftp->offset % BLOCK_SIZE;
(4).    convert lbk to physical block number, blk;
(5).    read_block(dev, blk, kbuf); //read blk into kbuf[BLKSIZE];
        char *cp = kbuf + start; remain = BLKSIZE - start;
(6)     while (remain){   // copy bytes from kbuf[ ] to ubuf[ ]
            put_ubyte(*cp++, *ubuf++);
            offset++;  count++;     // inc offset, count;
            remain --; nbytes--;    // dec remain, nbytes;
            if (offset > fileSize) fileSize++; // inc file size
            if (nbytes <= 0) break;
        }
(7).    wrtie_block(dev, blk, kbuf);
        }
(8). set minode dirty = 1; // mark minode dirty for iput()
     unlock(minode);
     return count;
}
```

The algorithm of converting logical block to physical block for write is similar to that of read, except for the following difference. During write, the intended data block may not exist. If a direct block does not exist, it must be allocated and recorded in the INODE. If the indirect block does not exist, it must be allocated and initialized to 0. If an indirect data block does not exist, it must be allocated

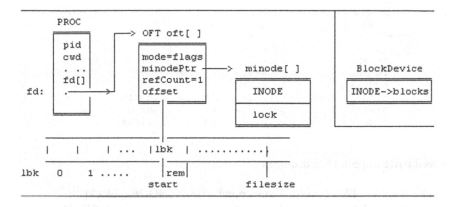

Fig. 11.5 Data structures for write_file()

and recorded in the indirect block, etc. The reader may consult the write.c file for details.

11.5.4.4 Read-Write Special Files

In kread() and kwrite(), read/write pipes and special files are treated differently. Read/write pipes are implemented in the pipe mechanism in the MTX kernel. Here we only consider read/write special files. Each special file has a file name in the /dev directory. The file type in a special file's inode is marked as special, e.g. 0060000= block device, 0020000=char device, etc. Since a special file does not have any disk block, i_block[0] of its INODE stores the device's (major, minor) number, where major = device type and minor = unit of that device type. For example,/dev/fd0=(2,0),/dev/tty0=(4,0) and /dev/ttyS1=(5,1), etc. The major device number is an index in a device switch table, dev_sw[ ], which contains pointers to device driver functions, as in

```
struct dev_sw {
    int (*dev_read)();
    int (*dev_write)();
} dev_sw[];
```

Assume that int nocall(){ } is an empty function, and are device driver functions. The device switch table is set up to contain the driver function pointers.

```
struct dev_sw dev_sw[ ] =
{ //   read               write
  //--------            --------
      nocall,           nocall,        // 0 /dev/null
      nocall,           nocall,        // 1 kernel memory
      fd_read,          fd_write,      // 2 FD
      hd_read,          hd_write,      // 3 HD
      console_read,     console_write, // 4 console
      serial_read,      serial_write,  // 5 serial ports
      nocall,           printer_write  // 6 printer
};
```

Then read/write a special file becomes

(1). get special file's (major, minor) number from INODE.i_block[0];

(2). return (*dev_sw[major].dev_read) (minor, parameters);   // READ

OR return (*dev_sw[major].dev_write)(minor, parameters);   // WRITE

(2). invokes the corresponding device driver function, passing as parameters the minor device number and other parameters as needed. The device switch table is a standard technique used in all Unix-like systems. It not only makes the I/O subsystem structure clear but also greatly reduces the read/write code size. Hopefully, this also helps answer the question from many curious students, namely why the device number of floppy drives is 2 and that of hard drives is 3, etc. It's because the original Unix designers set up their device switch table this way, and everyone else has been a copycat ever since.

11.5.4.5   Opendir-readdir

Unix considers everything as a file. Therefore, we should be able to open a DIR for read just like a regular file. From a technical point of view, there is no need for a separate set of opendir() and readdir() functions. However, different Unix systems may have different file systems. It may be difficult for users to interpret the contents of a DIR file. For this reason, POSIX specifies opendir and readdir operations, which are independent of file systems. Support for opendir is trivial; it's the same open system call, but readdir() has the form

struct dirent *ep = readdir(DIR *dp);

which returns a pointer to a dirent structure on each call. This can be implemented in user space as a library I/O function. Since MTX does not have user-level library stream I/O, we shall implement opendir() and readir() as system calls.

```
int opendir(pathaname)
{    return open(pathname, O_RDONLY|O_DIR); }
```

where O_DIR is a bit pattern for opening the file as a DIR. In the open file table, the mode field contains the O_DIR bit.

```
int readdir(int fd, struct udir *dp) // struct udir{DIR; name[256]};
{
    // same as read() in kernel except:
    use the current byte offset in OFT to read the next DIR record;
    copy the DIR record into *udir in Umode;
    advance offset by DIR entry's rec_len;
}
```

User mode programs must use the readdir(fd, struct udir *dir) system call instead of the readdir(DP) call.

11.5.5 Implementation of Level-3 FS

Level-3 of FS implements mount and umount of file systems and file protection.

11.5.5.1 Mount-umount

The mount command, mount filesys mount_point, mounts a file system to a mount_ point directory. It allows the file system to include other file systems as parts of an existing file system. The data structures used in mount are the MOUNT table and the in-memory minode of the mount_point directory. The algorithm of mount is

```
/********* Algorithm of mount **********/
mount()  // Usage: mount [filesys mount_point]
{
1. If no parameter, display current mounted file systems;
2. Check whether filesys is already mounted:
     The MOUNT table entries contain mounted file system (device) names
     and their mounting points. Reject if the device is already mounted.
     If not, allocate a free MOUNT table entry.
3. filesys is a special file with a device number dev=(major,minor).
     Read filesys' superblock to verify it is an EXT2 FS.
4. find the ino, and then the minode of mount_point:
          call ino = get_ino(&dev, pathname);  to get ino:
          call mip = iget(dev, ino); to load its inode into memory;
5. Check mount_point is a DIR and not busy, e.g. not someone's CWD.
6. Record dev and filesys name in the MOUNT table entry;
     also, store its ninodes, nblocks, etc. for quick reference.
7. Mark mount_point's minode as mounted on (mounted flag = 1) and let
     it point at the MOUNT table entry, which points back to the
     mount_point minode.
}
```

The operation Umount filesys detaches a mounted file system from its mounting point, where filesys may be either a special file name or a mounting point directory name. The algorithm of umount is

```
/****************** Algorithm of umount ***********************/
umount(char *filesys)
{
1. Search the MOUNT table to check filesys is indeed mounted.
2. Check (by checking all active minode[].dev) whether any file is
   active in the mounted filesys; If so, reject;
3. Find the mount_point's in-memory inode, which should be in memory
   while it's mounted on. Reset the minode's mounted flag to 0; then
   iput() the minode.
4. return SUCCESS;
}
```

11.5.5.2   Implications of mount

While it is easy to implement mount and umount, there are implications. With mount, we must modify the get_ino(&dev, pathname) function to support crossing mount points. Assume that a file system, newfs, has been mounted on the directory /a/b/c. When traversing a pathname, mount point crossing may occur in both directions.

(1)   Downward traversal: When traversing the pathname /a/b/c/x, once we reach the minode of /a/b/c, we should see that the minode has been mounted on (mounted flag = 1). Instead of searching for x in the INODE of /a/b/c, we must

  − . Follow the minode's mountTable pointer to locate the mount table entry.
  − . From the newfs's dev number, get its root (ino = 2) INODE into memory.
  − . Then continue search for x under the root INODE of newfs.

(2)   Upward traversal: Assume that we are at the directory /a/b/c/x and traversing upward, e.g. cd ../../, which will cross the mount point /a/b/c. When we reach the root INODE of the mounted file system, we should see that it is a root directory (ino = 2) but its dev number differs from that of the real root, so it is not the real root yet. Using its dev number, we can locate its mount table entry, which points to the mounted minode of /a/b/c/. Then, we switch to the minode of /a/b/c/ and continue the upward traversal. Thus, crossing mount point is like a monkey or squirrel hoping from one tree to another and then back.

11.5.5.3   File Protection

In Unix, file protection is by permission checking. Each file's INODE has an i_mode field, in which the low 9 bits are for file permissions. The 9 permission bits are

```
owner   group   other
-----   -----   -----
r w x   r w x   r w x
------  ------  -----
```

where the first 3 bits apply to the owner of the file, the second 3 bits apply to users in the same group as the owner and the last 3 bits apply to all others. For directories, the x bit indicates whether a process is allowed to go into the directory. Each process has a uid and a gid. When a process tries to access a file, the file system checks the process uid and gid against the file's permission bits to determine whether it is allowed to access the file with the intended mode of operation. If the process does not have the right permission, it is not allowed to access the file. For the sake of simplicity, MTX ignores gid. It uses only the process uid to check for file access permission.

11.5.5.4 Real and Effective uid

In Unix, a process has a real uid and an effective uid. The file system checks the access rights of a process by its effective uid. Under normal conditions, the effective uid and real uid of a process are identical. When a process executes a setuid program, which has the setuid bit (bit 11) in the file's i_mode field turned on, the process' effective uid becomes the uid of the program. While executing a setuid program, the process effectively becomes the owner of the program. For example, when a process executes the mail program, which is a setuid program owned by the superuser, it can write to a mail file of another user. When a process finishes executing a setuid program, it reverts back to the real uid. For simplicity reasons, MTX does not yet support effective uid. Permission checking is based on real uid.

11.5.5.5 File Locking

File locking is a mechanism which allows a process to set locks on a file, or parts of a file to prevent race conditions when updating files. File locks can be either shared, which allows concurrent reads, or exclusive, which enforces exclusive write. File locks can also be mandatory or advisory. For example, Linux supports both shared and exclusive files locks but file locking is only advisory. In Linux, file locks can be set by the fcntl() system call and manipulated by the flock() system call. In MTX, file locking is enforced only in the open() syscall of non-special files. When a process tries to open a non-special file, the intended mode of operation is checked for compatibility. The only compatible modes are READs. If a file is already opened for updating mode, i.e. W|RW|APPEND, it cannot be opened again. This does not apply to special files, e.g. terminals. A process may open its terminal multiple times even if the modes are incompatible. This is because access to special files is ultimately controlled by device drivers.

11.6   Extensions of MTX File System

The simple EXT2 FS in MTX uses 1KB block size and has only 1 disk block group.
It can be extended easily as follows.

(1)   Multiple groups: The size of group descriptor is 32 bytes. With 1KB block size,
a block may contain 1024/32=32 group descriptors. With 32 groups, the FS
size can be extended to 32*8=256 MB.
(2)   4KB block size: With 4KB block size and only one group, the FS size would be
4*8=32 MB. With one group descriptor block, the FS may have 128 groups,
which extend the FS size to 128*32=4 GB. With 2 group descriptor blocks, the
FS size would be 8 GB, etc. Most of the extensions are straightforward, which
are suitable topics for programming projects.
(3)Pipe files: It's possible to implement pipes as regular files, which obey the read/
write protocol of pipes. The advantages of this scheme are: it unifies pipes and
file inodes and it allows named pipes, which can be used by unrelated processes.
In order to support fast read/write operations, pipe contents should be in memory, such as a RAMdisk. If desired, the reader may implement named pipes as
FIFO files.

Problems

1. In the read_file algorithm of Sect. 11.5.2, data can be read from either user space
or kernel space.

(1). Justify why it is necessary to read data to kernel space.

(2). In the inner loop of the read_file algorithm, data are transferred one byte at
a time for clarity. Optimize the inner loop by transferring chunks of data at a time
(HINT: minimum of data remaining in the block and available data in the file).

2. Modify the write-file algorithm in Sect. 11.5.3 to allow

(1). Write data from kernel space, and
(2). Optimize data transfer by copying chunks of data.

3. Consider the cp f1 f2 operation, which copies file f1 to file f2.

(1). Design an algorithm for the cp program.
(2). What if f1 and f2 are the same file?
(3). With hard links, two filenames may refer to the same file. How to determine
whether two filenames are the same file?

4. Assume: dir1 and dir2 are directories. cpd2d dir1 dir2 recursively copies dir1
into dir2.

(1). Write C code for the cpd2d program.
(2). What if dir1 contains dir2, e.g. cpd2d /a/b /a/b/c/d?
(3). How to determine whether dir1 contains dir2?

5. Modify the Delete_dir_entry algorithm as follows. If the deleted entry is the only entry in a data block, deallocate the data block and compact the DIR INODE's data block array. Modify the Insert_dir_entry algorithm accordingly and implement the new algorithms in the MTX file system.

5. In EXT2, the algorithms of inserting/deleting DIR entries amount to applying memory compaction to disk blocks, so that each data block of a directory has only one hole of maximal size at the end of the block. Consider the following Delete_dir_entry algorithm.

```
Delete_dir_entry // delete an entry from a DIR's data block
{
  (1). search DIR's data block(s) for the entry;
  (2). clear entry's inode number to 0;
  (3). if (not first entry in block)
         add entry's rec_len to predecessor entry's rec_len;
}
```

In the algorithm, if the entry to be deleted is the first entry in a data block, clearing its inode number to 0 makes the entry invalid. If it is not the first entry in the block, absorbing its rec_len into its predecessor effectively hides the deleted entry, making it invisible. In both cases, the deleted space is not wasted since it may be reused later when inserting a new entry.

(1). Corresponding to this Deletion algorithm, design an Insertion algorithm which enters a new entry name into a DIR.

(2). Discuss the advantages and disadvantages of the new Insertion/Deletion algorithms.

(3). Implement the new Insertion/Deletion algorithms and compare their performance with that of EXT2.

6. MTX does not yet support file streams. Implement library I/O functions to support file streams in user space.
7. Implement real and effective user IDs in MTX file system.
8. In MTX, mount can only mount block special files, e.g./dev/fd0 and hard disk partitions. Modify mount.c in FS to mount EXT2 disk image files as loop devices.

References

Cao, M., Bhattacharya, S, Tso, T., "Ext4: The Next Generation of Ext2/3 File system", IBM Linux Technology Center, 2007.
Card, R., Theodore Ts'o, T., Stephen Tweedie, S., "Design and Implementation of the Second Extended Filesystem", web.mit.edu/tytso/www/linux/ext2intro.html, 1995
EXT2: http://www.nongnu.org/ext2-doc/ext2.html, 2001
EXT3: http://jamesthornton.com/hotlist/linux-filesystems/ext3-journal, 2015

Chapter 12
Block Device I/O and Buffer Management

12.1 Block Device I/O Buffers

In Chap. 11, we showed the algorithms of read/write regular files. The algorithms rely on two key operations, read_block and write_block, which read/write a disk block to/from a buffer in kernel memory. Since disk I/O are slow in comparison with read/write memory, it is undesirable to read/write disk blocks on every read/ write file operation. For this reason, most OS kernels use I/O buffering to reduce the number of physical I/O. I/O buffering is especially important for block devices containing file systems. A well designed I/O buffering scheme can significantly improve I/O efficiency and increase system throughput.

The basic principle of I/O buffering is very simple. The kernel uses a set of I/O buffers as a cache memory for block devices. When a process tries to read a disk block identified by (dev, blk), it first searches the buffer cache for a buffer already assigned to the disk block. If such a buffer exists and contains valid data, it simply reads from the buffer without reading in the disk block again. If such a buffer does not exist, it allocates a buffer for the disk block, reads data from disk into the buffer, then reads data from the buffer. Once a block is read in, the buffer will remain in the buffer cache for the next read/write requests of the same block by any process. Similarly, when a process writes to a disk block, it first gets a buffer assigned to the block. Then it writes data to the buffer, marks the buffer as dirty and releases it to the buffer cache. Since a dirty buffer contains valid data, it can be used to satisfy subsequent read/write requests for the same block without incurring real disk I/O. Dirty buffers will be written to disk only when they are to be reassigned to different blocks.

Before discussing buffer management algorithms, we first introduce the following terms. In read_file/write_file, we have assumed that they read/write from/to a dedicated buffer in kernel memory. With I/O buffering, the buffer will be allocated dynamically from a buffer cache. Assume that BUFFER is the structure type of buffers (defined below) and getblk(dev, blk) allocates a buffer assigned to (dev, blk)

© Springer International Publishing Switzerland 2015   345
K. C. Wang, *Design and Implementation of the MTX Operating System*,
DOI 10.1007/978-3-319-17575-1_12

from the buffer cache. Define a bread(dev, blk) function, which returns a buffer (pointer) containing valid data.

```
BUFFER *bread(dev,blk) // return a buffer containing valid data
{
   BUFFER *bp = getblk(dev,blk); // get a buffer for (dev,blk)
   if (bp data valid)
   return bp;
   bp->opcode = READ;              // issue READ operation
   start_io(bp);                   // start I/O on device
   wait for I/O completion;
   return bp;
}
```

After reading data from a buffer, the process releases the buffer back to the buffer cache by brelse(bp). Similarly, define a write_block(dev, blk, data) function as

```
write_block(dev, blk, data)        // write data from U space
{
   BUFFER *bp = bread(dev,blk); // read in the disk block first
   write data to bp;
   (synchronous write)? bwrite(bp) : dwrite(bp);
}
```

where bwrite(bp) is for synchronous write and dwrite(bp) is for delay-write, as shown below.

```
------------------------------------------------------------------
bwrite(BUFFER *bp){             |  dwrite(BUFFER *bp){
   bp->opcode = WRITE;          |     mark bp dirty for delay_write;
   start_io(bp);                |     brelse(bp); // release bp
   wait for I/O completion;     |  }
   brelse(bp); // release bp    |
}                               |
------------------------------------------------------------------
```

Synchronous write waits for the write operation to complete. It is used for sequential or removable block devices, e.g. tape drives or floppy disks. For random access devices, e.g. hard disks, all writes can be delay writes. In delay write, dwrite(bp) marks the buffer as dirty and releases it to the buffer cache. Since dirty buffers contain valid data, they can be used to satisfy subsequent read/write requests of the same block. This not only reduces the number of physical disk I/O but also improves the buffer cache effect. A dirty buffer will be written to disk only when it is to be reassigned to a different disk block, at which time the buffer is written out by

```
awrite(BUFFER *bp)
{
   bp->opcode = ASYNC;        // for ASYNC write;
   start_io(bp);
}
```

which calls start_io() on the buffer but does not wait for I/O completion.

Physical Block Device I/O   Each device has an I/O queue which contains buffers of pending I/O. The start_io() operation on a buffer is

```
start_io(BUFFER *bp)
{
    enter bp into device I/O queue;
    if (bp is first buffer in I/O queue)
        issue I/O command for bp to device;
}
```

When an I/O operation completes, the device interrupt handler finishes the I/O operation on the current buffer and starts I/O for the next buffer in the I/O queue if it is non-empty. The algorithm of the disk I/O interrupt handler is

```
InterruptHandler()
{
    bp = dequeue(device I/O queue); // bp = remove head of I/O queue
    (bp->opcode == ASYNC)? brelse(bp) : unblock process on bp;
    if (!empty(device I/O queue))
        issue I/O command for first bp in I/O queue;
}
```

12.2   Unix I/O Buffer Management Algorithm

Unix I/O buffer management algorithm first appeared in (Ritchie and Thompson 1978; Lion 1996). It is discussed in detail in Chap. 3 of Bach (Bach 1990). The Unix buffer management subsystem consists of the following components.

(1). I/O buffers: A set of NBUF buffers in kernel is used as a buffer cache. Each buffer is represented by a structure.

```
typdef struct buf{
    struct buf *next_free;      // freelist pointer
    struct buf *next_dev;       // dev_list pointer
    u16 dev,blk;                // assigned disk block;
    u16 opcode;                 // READ|WRITE
    u16 dirty;                  // buffer data modified
    u16 async;                  // ASYNC write flag
    u16 valid;                  // buffer data valid
    u16 busy;                   // buffer is in use
    u16 wanted;                 // some process needs this buffer
    struct semaphore lock=1;    // buffer locking semaphore; value=1
    struct semaphore iodone=0;  // for process to wait for I/O completion;
    char buf[BLKSIZE];          // block data area
} BUFFER;
BUFFER buf[NBUF], *freelist; // NBUF buffers and free buffer list
```

The buffer structure consists of two parts; a header part for buffer management and a data part for a block of data. To conserve kernel memory, the status fields may be defined as a bit vector, in which each bit represents a unique status condition. They are defined as u16 here for clarity and ease of discussion.

(2). Device Table: Each block device is represented by a device table structure.

```
struct devtab{
   u16   dev;                    // major device number
   u32   start_sector;          // for hard disk partitions
   u32   size;                   // size of device in blocks
   BUFFER *dev_list;            // device buffer list
   BUFFER *io_queue;            // device I/O queue
} devtab[NDEV];
```

Each devtab has a dev_list, which contains I/O buffers currently assigned to the device, and an io_queue, which contains buffers of pending I/O operations on the device. The I/O queue may be organized for optimal I/O operations. For instance, it may implement the various disk scheduling algorithms, such as the elevator algorithm or the linear-sweep algorithm, etc. For the sake of simplicity, we shall assume FIFO I/O queues.

(3). Buffer Initialization: When the system starts, all I/O buffers are in the freelist and all device lists and I/O queues are empty.

(4). Buffer Lists: When a buffer is assigned to a (dev, blk), it is inserted into the devtab's dev_list. If the buffer is currently in use, it is marked as BUSY and removed from the freelist. A BUSY buffer may also be in the I/O queue of a devtab. Since a buffer cannot be free and busy at the same time, the device I/O queue is maintained by using the same next_free pointer. When a buffer is no longer BUSY, it is released back to the freelist but remains in the dev_list for possible reuse. A buffer may change from one dev_list to another only when it is reassigned. As shown before, read/write disk blocks can be expressed in terms of bread, bwrite and dwrite, all of which depend on getblk and brelse. Therefore, getblk and brelse form the core of the Unix buffer management scheme. The algorithm of getblk and brelse is as follows.

(5). Unix getblk/brelse algorithm: (Lion 1996, Chap. 3 of (Bach 1990)).

```
/* getblk: return a buffer=(dev,blk) for exclusive use */
BUFFER *getblk(dev,blk){
while(1){
  (1). search dev_list for a bp=(dev,blk);
  (2). if (bp in dev_lst){
            if (bp BUSY){
                set bp WANTED flag;
                sleep(bp);
                continue;
            }
            /* bp not BUSY */
            take bp out of freelist;
            mark bp BUSY;
            return bp;
       }
  (3). /* bp not in cache; try to get a free buf from freelist */
       if (freelist empty){
            set freelist WANTED flag;
            sleep(freelist);
            continue;
       }
  (4). /* freelist not empty */
       bp = first bp taken out of freelist;
       mark bp BUSY;
       if (bp DIRTY){           // bp is for delayed write
            awrite(bp);         // write bp out ASYNC;
            continue;
       }
  (5). reassign bp to (dev,blk); // set bp data invalid, etc.
       return bp;
}

/** brelse: releases a buffer as FREE to freelist **/
brelse(BUFFER *bp){
  if (bp WANTED)
      wakeup(bp);          // wakeup ALL proc's sleeping on bp;
  if (freelist WANTED)
      wakeup(freelist); // wakeup ALL proc's sleeping on freelist;
  clear bp and freelist WANTED flags;
  insert bp to (tail of) freelist;
}
```

It is noted that in (Bach 1990), buffers are maintained in hash queues. When the number of buffers is large, hashing may reduce the search time. If the number of buffers is small, hashing may actually increases the execution time due to additional overhead. Furthermore, studies (Wang 2002) have shown that hashing has almost no effect on the buffer cache performance. In fact, we may consider the device lists as hash queues by the simple hashing function hash(dev, blk)=dev. So there is no loss of generality by using the device lists. The Unix algorithm is very simple and easy to understand. Perhaps because of its extreme simplicity, most people are not very impressed by it at first sight. Some may even consider it naive because of the repeated retry loops. However, the more you look at it, the more it makes sense. This amazingly simple but effective algorithm attests to the ingenuity of the original Unix designers. Some specific comments about the Unix algorithm follow.

(1). Data Consistency: In order to ensure data consistency, getblk must never assign more than one buffer to the same (dev, blk). This is achieved by having the process re-execute the "retry loops" after waking up from sleep. The reader may verify that every assigned buffer is unique. Second, dirty buffers are written out before they are reassigned, which guarantees data consistency.

(2). Cache effect: Cache effect is achieved by the following means. A released buffer remains in the device list for possible reuse. Buffers marked for delay-write do not incur immediate I/O and are available for reuse. Buffers are released to the tail of freelist but allocated from the front of freelist. This is based on the LRU ((Least-Recent-Used) principle, which helps prolong the lifetime of assigned buffers, thereby increasing their cache effect.

(3). Critical Regions: Device interrupt handlers may manipulate the buffer lists, e.g. remove a bp from a devtab's I/O queue, change its status and call brelse(bp). So in getblk and brelse, device interrupts are masked out in these critical regions. These are implied but not shown in the algorithm.

(4). Shortcomings of the algorithm:

(4)-1. Inefficiency: the algorithm relies on retry loops, which would cause excessive process switches. For example, releasing a buffer may wake up two sets of processes; those who want the released buffer, as well as those who just need a free buffer. Since only one process can get the buffer, all other awakened processes would have to sleep again.

(4)-2. Unpredictable cache effect: In the Unix algorithm, every released buffer is up for grabs. If the buffer is obtained by a process which needs a free buffer, the buffer would be reassigned, even though there may be processes which still need the buffer.

(4)-3. Possible starvation: The algorithm is based on the principle of "free economy", in which every process is given chances to try but with no guarantee of success. Therefore, process starvation may occur.

(4)-4. The algorithm uses sleep/wakeup, which is only suitable for uniprocessor kernels.

12.3   New I/O Buffer Management Algorithms

In this section, we shall develop new algorithms for I/O buffer management. Instead of sleep/wakeup, we shall use P/V on semaphores for process synchronization. The main advantages of semaphores over sleep/wakeup are

Counting semaphores can be used to represent the number of available resources, e.g. the number of free buffers. When processes wait for a resource, the V operation unblocks only one waiting process, which is guaranteed to have the resource.

These semaphore properties can be used to design more efficient algorithms for buffer management. Formally, we specify the problem as follows.

Assume a uniprocessor kernel (one process runs at a time). Use P/V on counting semaphores to design new buffer management algorithms which meet the following requirements:

1. Guarantee data consistency.
2. Good cache effect.
3. High efficiency: No retry loops and no unnecessary process "wakeups".
4. Free of deadlocks and starvation.

It is noted that merely replacing sleep/wakeup in the Unix algorithm by P/V on semaphores is not an acceptable solution because doing so would retain all the retry loops. We must redesign the algorithm to meet all the above requirements and justify that the new algorithm is indeed better than the Unix algorithm. First, we define the following semaphores.

```
BUFFER buf[NBUF];          // NBUF I/O buffers
SEMAPHORE free = NBUF;      // counting semaphore for FREE buffers
SEMAPHORE buf[i].sem = 1;   // each buffer has a lock sem=1;
```

To simplify the notations, we shall refer to the semaphore of each buffer by the buffer itself. As in the Unix algorithm, initially all buffers are in the freelist and all device lists and I/O queues are empty. Before presenting solutions to the problem, we first illustrate the subtlety of the problem by an example. Most students tend to mimic the getblk/brelse algorithm of Unix and propose the following algorithm.

```
BUFFER *getblk(dev, blk) // return a locked buffer pointer
{
     while(1){
(1). if (bp in dev_list){
          P(bp);
          remove bp from freelist;
          return bp;
     }
     // bp not in cache, try to create a bp=(dev,blk)
(2). P(free);   // wait for a free buffer
     bp = remove a buffer from freelist;
     P(bp);       // lock buffer
     if (buffer is delay-write){
          awrite(bp);
          goto (2);
     }
     assign buffer to (dev,blk);
     return bp;
     }
}
brelse(BUFFER *bp)
{
(3). enter bp into freelist;
(4). V(bp); V(free);
}
```

Unfortunately, such an algorithm is incorrect. To see this, assume that several processes need the same buffer, which does not exist and there are no more free buffers.
Then all of such processes would be blocked at (2) in getblk(). When buffers are
released as free at (4), these processes would be unblocked one at a time to create
the same buffer multiple times. To prevent multiple buffers, such processes would
have to execute from (1) again, which is the same as retry. However, by rearranging
the execution path of the algorithm slightly, we come up with a simple workable
algorithm, which is shown below.

12.4   Simple PV-Algorithm

```
BUFFER *getblk(dev, blk)
{   while(1){
  (1).     P(free);              // get a free buffer first
  (2).     if (bp in dev_list){
  (3).          if (bp not BUSY){
                    remove bp from freelist;
                    P(bp);        // lock bp but does not wait
                    return bp;
                }
                // bp in cache but BUSY
                V(free);          // give up the free buffer
  (4).          P(bp);           // wait in bp queue
                return bp;
           }
           // bp not in cache, try to create a bp=(dev,blk)
  (5).     bp = frist buffer taken out of freelist;
           P(bp);                // lock bp, no wait
  (6).     if (bp dirty){
                awrite(bp);       // write bp out ASYNC, no wait
                continue;         // continue from (1)
           }
  (7).     reassign bp to (dev,blk); // mark bp data invalid, not dirty
           return bp;
       }                          // end of while(1)
}

brelse(BUFFER *bp)
{
  (8). if (bp queue has waiter){ V(bp); return; }
  (9). if (bp dirty && free queue has waiter){ awrite(bp); return; }
  (10). enter bp into (tail of) freelist; V(bp); V(free);
}
```

Next, we show that the simple PV-algorithm is correct and meets the requirements.
   (1). Buffer uniqueness: In getblk, if there are free buffers, the process does not
wait at (1). Then it searches the dev_list. If the needed buffer already exits, the
process does not create the same buffer again. If the needed buffer does not exist,
the process creates the needed buffer by using a free buffer, which is guaranteed to
have. If there are no free buffers, it is possible that several processes, all of which

need the same buffer, are blocked at (1). When a free buffer is released at (10), it unblocks only one process to create a needed buffer. Once a buffer is created, it will be in the dev_list, which prevents other processes from creating the same buffer again. Therefore, every assigned buffer is unique.

(2). No retry loops: The only place a process re-executes the while(1) loop is at (6), but that is not a retry because the process is continually executing.

(3). No unnecessary wakeups: In getblk, a process may wait for a free buffer at (1) or a needed buffer at (4). In either case, the process is not woken up to run again until it has a buffer. Furthermore, at (9), when a dirty buffer is to be released as free and there are waiters for free buffers at (1), the buffer is not released but written out directly. This avoids an unnecessary process wakeup. The reader is encouraged to figure out why?

(4). Cache effect: In the Unix algorithm, every released buffer is up for grabs. In the new algorithm, a buffer with waiters is always kept for reuse. A buffer is released as free only if it has no waiters. This should improve the buffer's cache effect.

(5). No deadlocks and starvation: In getblk(), the semaphore locking order is always unidirectional, i.e. P(free), then P(bp), but never the other way around, so deadlock cannot occur. If there are no free buffers, all requesting processes will be blocked at (1). This implies that while there are processes waiting for free buffer, all buffers in use cannot admit any new users. This guarantees that a BUSY buffer will eventually be released as free. Therefore, starvation for free buffers cannot occur.

The simple PV-algorithm is very simple and easy to implement, but it does have the following two weaknesses. First, its cache effect may not be optimal. This is because as soon as there is no free buffer, all requesting processes will be blocked at (1), even if their needed buffer may already exist in the buffer cache. Second, when a process wakes up from the freelist queue, it may find the needed buffer already exists but BUSY, in which case it will be blocked again at (4). Strictly speaking, the process has been woken up unnecessarily since it gets blocked twice. The following algorithm, which is optimal in terms of the number of process switches, does not have such weaknesses.

12.5 Optimal PV-Algorithm

In the Optimal PV-algorithm, we assume that every PROC structure has the added fields (dev, blk) and a buffer pointer, BUFFER *bp. In addition, we also assume that the V operation on a semaphore with waiters returns a pointer to the un-blocked process PROC, which is a trivial extension of the standard V operation. In order to simplify the discussion, we ignore starvation for free buffers first. Starvation prevention will be considered later. The following shows the optimal PV-algorithm.

```
BUFFER *getblk(dev,blk)
{
(1). set running PROC.(dev,blk)=(dev,blk) and PROC.bp=0;
(2). search dev_list for bp=(dev,blk);
(3). if (found bp){
         if (bp is FREE){
             P(free);          // dec free.value by 1; no wait
             take bp out out freelist;
             P(bp);            // lock bp; no wait
             return bp;
         }
         // bp BUSY
         P(bp);               // wait in bp.queue
(4).     return PROC.bp;      // return buffer pointer in PROC
      }
      // buffer not in cache, try to create the needed buffer
      while(1){
(5).     P(free);             // try to get a free buffer
(6).     if (PROC.bp)         // if waited in free.queue
             return PROC.bp;  // return buffer pointer in PROC
(7).     bp = first buffer removed from from freelist;
(8).     P(bp);               // lock bp
         if (bp dirty){
             awrite(bp);      // asynchronous write, no wait
             continue;        // continue from (5)
         }
(9).     reassign bp to (dev,blk);
         return bp;
      }
}
brelse(BUFFER *bp)
{
 (10). if (bp queue has waiter){
          PROC *p=V(bp); p->bp=bp; // give bp to first waiter
          return;
       }
       /* bp queue has no waiter */
 (11). if (free queue has waiter){

 (12).     if (bp is dirty){ // never release dirty buffer as free
               awrite(bp); return;
           }
           /* free queue has waiter && bp not dirty */
 (13).     swapQueue(free, bp);  // bp.queue=0 but swap anyway
           goto (10)
       }
       // no waiter in both bp and free queues
 (14). enter bp into tail of freelist; V(bp); V(free);
   }
```

In general, the swapQueue() operation at (13) consists of the following steps.

```
(1). Let P1 = first waiter in free queue;
      m = number of PROCs in free.queue;
      n = number of PROCs in free.queue waiting for the same bp as P1;
      k = number of PROCs in bp.queue
(2). Reassign bp to P1.(dev,blk);
(3). Swap bp.queue with PROCs waiting for the same bp in free.queue;
(4). Adjust semaphore values: free.value = -(m+k-n); bp.value = -n;
```

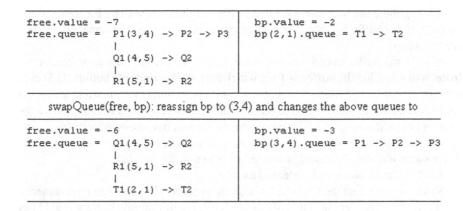

Fig. 12.1 General swapQueue operation

Conceptually, the free.queue may be regarded as a 2-dimensional queue, in which the horizontal queue contains PROCs all of which need the same bp = (dev, blk), and the vertical queue contains PROCs in their requesting order. swapQueue(free, bp) swaps the first horizontal queue of free.queue with bp.queue, adjusts the semaphore values and reassigns bp to the (dev, blk) of the first horizontal queue. Figure 12.1 shows an example of the general swapQueue() operation.

After swapQueue(), bp is reassigned to a new block and its queue contains all the PROCs which were waiting for the newly assigned buffer. The situation becomes identical to that of releasing a buffer with waiters. In comparison with the Unix algorithm, brelse here is slightly more complex, which also makes the algorithm more balanced. The following is a quick walk-through of the Optimal PV-algorithm.

At (1), the process records its (dev, blk) in PROC.(dev, blk) and sets PROC. bp = 0. The recorded PROC.(dev, blk) allows brelse to see what a blocked process is waiting for, and PROC.bp is for a blocked process to return the needed buffer upon wakeup.

(2) and (3) are obvious. At (4), the process returns PROC.bp, which may not be the bp it found earlier. In the optimal PV-algorithm, if a process ever becomes blocked, it simply returns PROC.bp when it runs again.

At (5), the process tries to get a free buffer. If there are free buffers, the process does not wait and its PROC.bp is still 0, in which case it proceeds to (7). Otherwise, it must have waited in free.queue, in which case it simply returns the buffer in its PROC.bp.

(7) to (9) are self-explanatory. (9) is the only place where a process creates a new buffer for itself.

At (10), if the buffer has waiters, the buffer should be kept for reuse. So it is given to the next waiter, which corresponds to Step (4) in getblk. Thus, a buffer with waiters is never released as free, which should improve the cache effect.

At (11), there are no waiters for this buffer but there are waiters for free buffers. At (12), if the buffer is dirty, it is written out directly to avoid an unnecessary process wakeup.

At (13), the buffer has no waiters, is not dirty and there are waiters in free.queue. Instead of releasing the buffer as free, which may lead to multiple buffers, (13) uses a "planned economy" strategy by creating the needed buffer for the waiting process (or processes which need the same buffer). In this case, bp.queue is empty, so swapQueue() only fills bp.queue with those processes from free.queue which are waiting for the same buffer. This ensures that only one buffer is created for such processes. After swapQueue(), the buffer is handed over to a waiter as usual.

At (14), the buffer is truly released as free.

Next, we show that the Optimal PV-algorithm meets all the design requirements.

(1). Buffer Uniqueness: The only possible source of multiple buffers is at (5) of getblk. If several PROCs wanting for the same bp are blocked at P(free), the needed buffer is created at either (10) or (12) by swapQueue() in brelse, which creates only one buffer for all such processes. Therefore, every assigned buffer is unique.

(2). No retry loops: This is obvious. As before, the while(1) is not a retry loop because the process is continually executing.

(3). No race conditions: Race conditions may only occur in the following way. When a buffer bp is released as free, it unblocks a process from free.queue. Before the unblocked process runs, another process may find the bp via its dev_list as exactly what it needs and removes bp from freelist. When the unblocked process runs, the intended free buffer may no longer exist. This is not possible in the Optimal PV-algorithm because such a time gap does not exist. If there are processes waiting for free buffer, their needed buffer is handcrafted and handed over to them directly. Therefore, race conditions cannot occur.

(4). No unnecessary process wakeups: The behavior of every process in getblk is

(a). if it finds the needed buffer in cache and the buffer is free, it returns the buffer.

(b). if it can create the needed buffer by using a free buffer, it creates the buffer and returns the buffer. In these two cases, the process does not wait.

(c). if a process has waited in a semaphore queue, it just returns PROC.bp. When and how did it get such a buffer is of no concern to the process. So there is absolutely no unnecessary process wakeups. The algorithm is therefore optimal in terms of the number of process switches.

(5). Good cache effect: In the new algorithm, buffers that are still in demand are never released as free. Such buffers are always kept for reuse. In the Unix algorithm every released buffer is open to competition, even if there are processes still need that buffer. Therefore, the cache effect of the PV algorithm should be better than that of the Unix algorithm. This is confirmed by simulation study results.

(6). No deadlocks: This is because the semaphore locking order is unidirectional.

(7). Starvation prevention: The only possible cause of starvation is when buffers are always in use, so that some process may wait for free buffer forever. Whereas there is no starvation in the simple PV-algorithm, it is possible in the Optimal PV-algorithm. We can modify the algorithm to prevent starvation as follows.

(7)-1. Assume that every buffer has a use_count and MAX_COUNT is a constant, which can be set to an arbitrarily large value.

(7)-2. In brelse, when a buffer is kept for reuse at (10) and if there are waiters for free buffers, we increment the buffer's use_count by 1. If free.queue is empty, we reset the buffer's use_count to 0. Thus, a buffer's use_count increases only if there are processes waiting for free buffers.

(7)-3. When a buffer's use_count reaches MAX_COUNT, the buffer will be reassigned to prevent starvation. Then the problem is: what to do with those processes still in the buffer's waiting queue? The swapQueue() operation simply swaps the buffer's waiting queue with a horizontal queue of free.queue, reassigns the buffer and adjust the semaphore values accordingly. This would move the processes in the buffer's original waiting queue to the free.queue as if they did not find the buffer before. Thus, while waiting for a needed buffer a process may be moved to different waiting queues, possibly many times. But this should be of no concern to the process. When a blocked process runs again, it simply returns the buffer (pointer) in its PROC.

After swapQueue(), the buffer is reassigned to a new block and its queue contains all the PROCs which were waiting for the newly assigned buffer. The situation becomes identical to that of releasing a buffer with waiters. Implementation of the Optimal PV-algorithm with starvation prevention is left as an exercise.

12.6 Comparisons of I/O Buffer Management Algorithms.

In the above sections, we presented two new I/O buffer management algorithms using semaphores. Simulation studies (Wang 2002) have shown that, under certain conditions, the PV-algorithms perform better than the Unix algorithm. The results are summarized briefly below.

1. When NBUF/NPROC >4, the Unix algorithm is about 10% faster than the PV-algorithms and the buffer cache hit ratio is virtually the same. If we replace the function calls to P/V with in-line code, their running times are also nearly identical. Thus, when there is less process competition for buffers, the retry strategy of the Unix algorithm is very effective.
2. When NBUF/NPROC <=4, the PV-algorithm starts to run faster and the hit ratio is also higher. As the NBUF/NPROC ratio decreases, the PV-algorithms perform much better than the Unix algorithm in both execution time and hit ratio.
3. The test results suggest a hybrid algorithm, which combines the strengths of both algorithms. In the hybrid algorithm, use the Unix algorithm when the ratio of NBUF to NPROC is large. Switch to the PV-algorithm when the ration becomes <=4.

The real mode MTX implements the simple PV-algorithm. With only 4 buffers, the hit ratio is normally around 50% but it can reach over 90% if several processes try to access the same file.

Problems

1. The MTX kernel uses the simple PV algorithm for buffer management. Implement the Optimun-PV algorithm with starvation prevention for buffer management.
2. In the real mode MTX, the number of block device I/O buffers are fixed as NBUF=4 due to kernel memory size limit. Implement the following schemes:

   a. Define NBUF=64 buffer heads in kernel with each buffer's 1KB data area in the segment 0×9000–0×A000. This allows the MTX kernel to have 64 I/O buffers at the expense of reducing available free memory by 64KB.
   b. Dynamic buffers: whenever a new buffer is needed, use kmalloc (sizeof(BUFFER)) to allocate a piece of memory for the buffer. When loading a user mode image, if there is not enough memory, evict some of the free buffers to make room for the new image. The advantage of this scheme is that the number of I/O buffers can be very large since all available memory can be used as I/O buffers. The disadvantage is that loading a large user image may trigger a cascade of delay writes of dirty buffers. This is another example of trading space with time.

3. In the optimum-PV algorithm, write operations are assumed to be asynchronous, i.e. process does not wait for the write operation to complete. This depends on the block device driver design. Assume: write operations are asynchronous for IDE hard disks but synchronous for floppy disk. Modify the optimum-PV algorithm for it to work for both kinds of disks.

References

Bach, M.J., "The Design of the Unix operating system", Prentice Hall, 1990
Lion, J., "Commentary on UNIX 6th Edition, with Source Code", Peer-To-Peer Communications, ISBN 1-57398-013-7, 1996.
Ritchie, D.M., Thompson, K., "The UNIX Time-Sharing System", Bell System Technical Journal, Vol. 57, No. 6, Part 2, July, 1978,
Wang, X., "Improved I/O Buffer Management Algorithms for Unix Operating System", M.S. thesis, EECS, WSU, 2002

Chapter 13
User Interface

User interface is a mechanism which allows users to interact with an operating system. As such, it is an indispensable part of every operating system. There are two kinds of user interfaces; Command Line Interface (CLI) and Graphic User Interface (GUI). Since MTX does not yet support graphic display, we shall only discuss command-line user interface. User interface consists of a set of user mode programs, which rely on system calls to the operating system kernel. In this chapter, we first list all the system calls to the RMTX kernel and explain their functions. Then we show how to develop user mode programs that are essential to system operations. Specifically, we shall develop an init program for system startup, a login program for users to login and a simple sh for users to execute commands. In addition, we also list other user mode programs which help demonstrate the capabilities of the RMTX system. Then we present a comprehensive description of the design and implementation of the RMTX kernel. Lastly, we explain the startup sequence of RMTX and how to recompile the RMTX system.

13.1   User Interface in MTX

As an educational system, MTX has several different versions. In addition to RMTX, which is MTX in 16-bit real mode, it also has several versions in 32-bit protected mode, which will be developed in Chaps. 14 and 15. The following discussion applies to all versions of MTX since their user interfaces are identical. Table 13.1 lists the system calls in RMTX.

The system calls are divided into four groups. Group 1 (number 0–19) is for process management. Group 2 (number 20–49) is for file system operations. Group 3 (number 50–53) is for signals and signal processing and Group 4 is for miscellaneous system calls. All the system call functions in Groups 1–3 are compatible with those of Unix/Linux. The only exception is exec. In MTX, when a user enters a command line

   a.out arg1 arg2... argn

© Springer International Publishing Switzerland 2015
K. C. Wang, *Design and Implementation of the MTX Operating System,*
DOI 10.1007/978-3-319-17575-1_13

Table 13.1 System calls in RMTX Kernel

```
================== RMTX System Call Functions ======================
Number  Name           Usage                        Function
------  -------        --------------------         ----------------------
   0    getpid         getpid()                     get process pid
   1    getppid        getppid()                    get parent pid
   2    getpri         getpri()                     get priority
   3    setpri         setpri(pri)                  set priority
   4    getuid         getuid()                     get uid
   5    chuid          chuid(uid,gid)               set uid,gid
   6    yield          yield()                      switch process
   9    exit           exit(value)                  terminate process
  10    fork           fork()                       fork child process
 *11    exec           exec(cmd_line)               change image
  12    wait           wait(&status)                wait child to die
  13    vfork          vfork()                      fork child process
  14    thread         thread(fd,stack,flag,prt)    create thread
  15    mutex_creat    mutex_creat()                mutex functions
  16    mutex_lock     mutex_lock(&mutex)
  17    mutex_unlock   mutex_unlock(&mutex)
  18    mutex_destroy  mutex_destroy(&mutex)
-----------------------------------------------------------------
  20    mkdir          mkdir(pathname)              make directory
  21    rmdir          rmdir(pathname)              rm   directory
  22    creat          creat(pathname)              creat file
  23    link           link(oldname, newname)       hard link to file
  24    unlink         unlink(pathname)             unlink
  25    symlink        symlink(oldname,newname)     create sym link
  26    readlink       readlink(name, buf[ ])       read symlink
  27    chdir          chdir(pathname)              change dir
  28    getcwd         getcwd(buf[ ])               get cwd pathname
  29    stat           stat(filename, &stat_buf)    stat file
  30    fstat          fstat(fd, &stat_buf)         stat fd
  31    open           open(filename, flag)         open for R|W|APP
  32    close          close(fd)                    close fd
 *33    lseek          lseek(fd, position)          lseek
  34    read           read(fd, buf[ ], nbytes)     read file
  35    write          write(fd,buf[ ], nbytes)     write to file
  36    pipe           pipe(pd[2])                  carete pipe
  37    chmod          chmod(filename, mode)        change permission
  38    chown          chown(filname, uid)          change file owner
  39    touch          touch(filename)              change file time
  40    settty         settty(tty_name)             set proc.tty name
  41    gettty         gettty(buf[ ])               get proc.tty name
  42    dup            dup(fd)                      dup file descriptor
  43    dup2           dup2(fd1, fd2)               dup fd1 to fd2
  44    ps             ps()                         ps in kernel
  45    mount          mount(FS, mountPoint)        mount file system
  46    umount         umount(mountPoint)           umount file system
  47    getSector      getSector(sector, buf[ ])    read CDROM sector
  48    cd_cmd         cd_cmd(cmd)                  cmd to CD driver
-----------------------------------------------------------------
  50    kill           kill(pid, sig#)              send signal to pid
  51    signal         signal(sig#, catcher)        siganl handler
  52    pause          pause(t)                     pause for t seconds
  53    itimer         itimer(sec, action)          set timer request
  54    send           send(msg, pid)               send msg to pid
  55    recv           sender=recv(msg)             receive msg
  56    tjoin          tjoin(n)                     threads join
  57    texit          texit(value)                 thread exit
  58    hits           hits()                       I/O buffer hit ratio
  59    color          color(v)                     display color
  60    sync           sync()                       sync file system
==================================================================
```

the entire command line is used in the exec system call but it passes the entire command line to the new image when execution starts. Parsing the command line into argc and argv is done by the startup code, crt0, in the new image.

13.2 User Mode Programs

In RMTX, every user mode program consists of the following parts.

(1). Entry point in u.s file:

```
        .globl  _main0, _exit
        call    _main0          ! call main0()
        push    #0              ! exit(0)
        call    _exit
  ! other assembly code, e.g. syscall which issues INT 80
```

The function main0() is in crt0.c, which is precompiled and installed in a mtxlib for linking.

(2).   /********** crt0.c file ******************/
```
        main0(char *cmdLine)
        {
          // parse cmdLine as argv[0], argv[1],...., argv[n]
          //      int argc = |<--------- argc -----------|
          main(argc, argv);  // call main(), passing argc and argv
        }
```

(3). The main.c file: As usual, every user mode program can be written as

```
        #include "ucode.c"  // system call interface functions
        main(int argc, char *argv[])
        {
          // main function of C program
        }
```

Then use BCC to generate a binary executable (with header), as in

```
        as86 -o u.o  u.s
        bcc -c -ansi $1.c
        ld86 u.o $1.o mtxlib /usr/lib/bcc/libc.a
```

Alternatively, the reader may also use a Makefile to do the compile and linking.

13.3   User Mode Programs for MTX Startup

From the MTX system point of view, the most important user mode programs are init, login and sh, which are necessary to start up the MTX system. In the following, we shall explain the roles and algorithms of these programs.

13.3.1   The INIT Program

When MTX starts, init is loaded as the Umode image of the INIT process P1. It is the first user mode program executed by MTX. A simple init program, which forks only one login process on the PC's console, is shown below. The reader may modify it to fork several login processes, each on a different terminal.

```
/*********************** init.c file ****************************/
#include "ucode.c"
int console;
main()
{  int in, out;       // file descriptors for terminal I/O
   in  = open("/dev/tty0", O_RDONLY);
   out = open("/dev/tty0", O_WRONLY); // for display to console
   printf("INIT : fork a login proc on console\n");
   console = fork();
   if (console)
      parent();
   else               // child exec to login on tty0
      exec("login /dev/tty0");
}
int parent()
{ int pid, status;
  while(1){
      printf("INIT : wait for ZOMBIE child\n");
      pid = wait(&status);
      if (pid==console){
          printf("INIT: forks a new console login\n");
          console = fork();
          if (console)
             continue;
          else
             exec("login /dev/tty0");
      }
      printf("INIT: I just buried an orphan child proc %d\n", pid);
  }
}
```

13.3.2   The login Program

All login processes executes the same login program, each on a different terminal, for users to login. The algorithm of the login program is

```
/****************** Algorithm of login ******************/
// login.c : Upon entry, argv[0]=login, argv[1]=/dev/ttyX
#include "ucode.c"
int in, out, err;
main(int argc, char *argv[])
{
    (1). close file descriptors 0,1 inherited from INIT.
    (2). open argv[1] 3 times as in(0), out(1), err(2).
    (3). settty(argv[1]); // set tty name string in PROC.tty
    (4). open /etc/passwd file for READ;

         while(1){
    (5).     printf("login:");     get user name;
             printf("password:"); get user password;
             for each line in passwd file do{
                 tokenize account line;
    (6).         if (user has a valid account){
    (7).             change uid, gid to user's uid, gid; // chuid()
                     change cwd to user's home DIR      // chdir()
                     close opened /etc/passwd file       // close()
    (8).             exec to program in user account     // exec()
                 }
             }
             printf("login failed, try again \n");
         }
}
```

13.3.3   The sh Program

After login, the user process typically executes the command interpreter sh, which gets commands from the user and executes the commands. Before showing the algorithm of sh, we need to review I/O redirection and pipe operation first.

(1). I/O Redirection: I/O redirection is based on manipulations of file descriptors. Consider the command a.out < infile, which redirects inputs from a file. Without input redirection, a.out gets all inputs from stdin, whose file descriptor is 0. To redirect inputs from a file, the process can close the file descriptor 0 and then open infile for READ. The file descriptor of the newly opened file would be 0. This is because the kernel's open() function always uses the lowest numbered file descriptor for a newly opened file. After these, a.out would receive inputs from infile rather than from the keyboard. Similarly, for the command a.out > outfile, the process can

close its file descriptor 1 and then open outfile for WRITE, with CREAT if necessary. In addition to the close-open paradigm, file descriptors can also be manipulated directly by dup and dup2 system calls. The syscall newfd = dup(fd) creates a
copy of fd and returns the lowest numbered file descriptor as newfd. The sysccall
dup2(oldfd, newfd) copies oldfd to newfd, closing newfd first if necessary. After
either dup or dup2, the two file descriptors can be used interchangeably since they
point to the same open file instance (OFT).

   (2). Pipe Operation: Consider the command cmd1 | cmd2, which connects 2
commands by a pipe. The algorithm of a process executing the pipe command is as
follows.

```
int pid, pd[2];
pipe(pd);           // creates a pipe
pid = fork();       // fork a child to share the pipe
if (pid){           // parent as pipe READER
   close(pd[1]); dup2(pd[0],0); close(pd[0]);
   exec(cmd1);
}
else{               // child as pipe WRITER
   close(pd[0]); dup2(pd[1],1); close(pd[1]);
   exec(cmd2);
}
```

Multiple pipes in a command line can be handled recursively. Based on these, we
formulate an algorithm for the sh program as follows.

```
/******************** Algorithm of sh *************************/
while (1){
    get a command line; e.g. cmdLine = cmd | cam2 | .... | cmdn &
    get cmd token from command line;
    if (cmd == cd || logout || su){  // built-in commands
       do the cmd directly;
       continue;
    }
    // for binary executable command
    pid = fork();                  // fork a child sh process
    if (pid){                      // parent sh
       if (no & symbol)            // assume at most one & for main sh
          pid = wait(&status);
       continue;                   // main sh does not wait if &
    }
    else                           // child sh
       do_pipe(cmd_line, 0);
}
int do_pipe(char *cmdLine, int *pd)
{
    if (pd){ // if has a pipe passed in, as WRITER on pipe pd:
       close(pd[0]); dup2(pd[1],1); close(pd[1]);
    }
    // divide cmdLine into head, tail by rightmost pipe symbol
    hasPipe = scan(cmdLine, head, tail);
    if (hasPipe){
       create a pipe lpd;
       pid = fork();
       if (pid){ // parent
             as READER on lpd:
                close(lpd[1]); dup2(lpd[0],0); close(lpd[0]);
             do_command(tail);
       }
       else
             do_pipe(head, lpd);
    }
    else
       do_command(cmdLine);
}
int do_command(char *cmdLine)
{
    scan cmdLine for I/O redirection symbols;
    do I/O redirections;
    head = cmdLine BEFORE redirections
    exec(head);
}
int sacn(char *cmdLine, char *head, char *tail)
{
  // divide cmdLine into head and tail by rightmost | symbol
  // cmdLine = cmd1 | cmd2 |...|cmdn-1 |  cmdn
  //           |<------- head --------->| tail |; return 1;
  // cmdLine = cmd1 ==> head=cmd1, tail=null;    return 0;
}
```

We illustrate the sh algorithm by an example. Consider the command line

```
cmdLine = "cat < infile | lower2upper | grep print > outfile"
```

where lower2upper converts lower-case letters to upper-case. Assume that the main sh process is P2, the processing sequence of the command line is as follows.

1. The main sh forks a child P3, and waits for the child to terminate.
2. The child sh, P3, calls do_pipe(cmdLine, 0). Since the pipe parameter is 0, P3 skips the "as writer on pipe" part and calls sacn() to look for any pipe symbol. scan() divides the cmdLine, by the rightmost | symbol, into head = "cat < infile | lower2upper"; tail = "grep print > outfile".
3. P3 creates a pipe, lpd[2]. Then it forks a child, P4, which receives the same file descriptors lpd[2]. Then P3 sets itself up as a reader on this pipe and calls do_command(tail). P3 first redirects its outputs to outfile, then it exec("grep print").
4. P4 calls do_pipe("cat < infile | lower2upper", lpd). Since lpd is not null, P4 sets itself up as a writer on the parameter pipe, lpd. Thus, P4 is a writer on lpd and P3 is a reader on lpd. Then P4 calls scan(), which divides the cmdLine parameter into head = "cat < infile", tail = "lower2upper". Then P4 creates a pipe, which is a new instance of lpd[2], and fork a child, P5, which shares the current pipe with P4. P4 sets itself up as the reader on this pipe and exec("lower2upper"). P4 and P3 are thus connected by the pipe created by P3.
5. P5 calls do_pipe("cat < infile", lpd). P5 sets it self up as a writer to the parameter pipe, which connects P5 to P4 through the pipe created by P4. Since there is no more pipe symbol in "cat < infile", P5 calls do_command(), in which it first sets up the input redirection and then exec("cat").

The following pipe-line diagram depicts the processes that execute the above pipe command, in which ==> stands for pipe and –> stands for I/O redirection.

infile --> P5 (cat) ==> P4 (lower2upper) ==> P3 (grep --> outfile):

Note that in the recursive calls to do_pipe(), the command line is processed from right to left, so that the main sh's child is the reader process on the rightmost pipe. In a sequence of commands connected by pipes, the rightmost pipe reader is normally the last one to terminate. In this scheme, the main sh will not prompt again until all the pipe operations have ended. As far as the pipes are concerned, the processing order does not matter. It is also possible to reverse the direction of command line processing, i.e. from left to right. The disadvantage of this scheme is that the main sh will prompt again as soon as the writer on the leftmost pipe finishes, which may confuse the user since the sh's prompt may become lost among the pipe outputs. In either case, all other processes on the pipes will become orphans, which are released by the INIT process P1.

Sometimes a running program may need to know whether its stdin/stdout has been redirected or not. For example, when the cat program is run without a filename, it should get inputs from stdin (file descriprot 0) but it should also echo the inputs to let the user see the input chars. However, if it is used behind a pipe, as in cat f | cat, it should not echo the inputs. Similarly, when displaying the contents of a file, it must print a\r for each\n in order to produce the right visual effects. This is because in Unix each line of a file ends with a\n without a\r char. If the stdout has been redirected, as in "cat filename > outfile", it must not add a\r to each line. There are many ways to write the cat program to meet these requirements. For example, we may display the\r chars to fd = 2. Alternatively, we may determine whether stdin/ stdout has been redirected or not by the following means.

(1). stat(gettty(), &st_tty); fstat(0, &st0); fstat(1, &st1);
(2). 0 has been redirected if st_tty.(dev,ino) != st0.(dev,ino)
(3). 1 has been redirected if st_tty.(dev,ino) != st1.(dev,ino)

13.4 Other User Mode Programs

All the commands in the/bin directory are user-mode programs, which are developed in the same way as described above. If needed, the reader may develop other user-mode programs. Table 13.2 lists all the user-mode programs in RMTX.

Table 13.2 User Programs in RMTX

```
Commands        Usage Example                        Function
---------      ------------------      ------------------------------------
cat      :  cat file             :  display file contents to screen
chmod    :  chmod file 0644      :  change permission bits of file
chown    :  chown uid file       :  change file's uid
cp       :  cp src dest          :  copy files or directories
creat    :  creat filename       :  creat a new file
grep     :  grep pattern file :  grep lines matching the pattern
init     :                       :  program of INIT process
kill     :  kill sig# pid        :  send sign# to procees pid
link     :  link oldf newf       :  hard link newfile to oldfile
login    :                       :  program of login processes
lpr      :  lpr file             :  print file
man      :  man                  :  a short on-line man page of MTX
mkdir    :  mkdir name           :  make a new directory
more     :  more file            :  display file one page/line at a time
mount    :  mount FS mountDir :  mount (EXT2) FS on mountDir
mv       :  mv file1 file2       :  rename files
ps       :  ps                   :  display PROC status
reboot   :  reboot               :  flush kernel buffers and reboot
rm       :  rm file              :  remove file (unlink)
rmdir    :  rmdir DIR            :  remove directory
sh       :  sh                   :  command interpreter
symlink  :  symlink old new      :  create a symlink from new to old
sync     :  sync                 :  flush kernel I/O buffers
touch    :  touch file           :  update time fields of file
umount   :  umount mountDir      :  umount a mounted FS
unlink   :  unlink file          :  decrement link count; rm if count=0
whoami   :  whoami               :  dispaly login uid
---------------- Demonstration Programs -------------------------
Signal catchers:
divide   :  divide               :  install handler for divide-by-0 trap
signal   :  signal               :  demonstrate signal and kill syscalls
trap     :  trap 2-7             :  simulate trap errors with trap handler
Control-C  key                   :  send SIGINT(2) to proc on terminal
timer Service:
pause    :  pause t              :  sleep for t seconds
itimer   :  itimer t             :  set timer t seconds; end by SIGALRM(14)
catcher  :  catcher              :  re-install signal catcher for SIGALRM
Process Management:
vfork:   :  vfork                :  demonstrate vfork()/exec() in MTX
loop     :  loop                 :  simulate compute-bound process
Threads and synchronization:
matrix, race, norace             :  matrix operations by threads
qsort                            :  demonstrate quicksort by threads
Message passing:
sendrecv                         :  send/recv messages
cdserver                         :  CDROM file server: receive message
cdclient                         :  CDROM file system client: send request
Misc.
sbrk/rbrk:                       :  inc/dec user program heap size
hits                             :  Block device I/O buffer hit ratio
mp                               :  display MP table of SMP-compliant PC
================================================================
```

13.5   Summary of RMTX

This section presents a comprehensive description of the RMTX operating system.

13.5.1   RMTX Source File Tree

The source file tree of RMTX contains the following files and directories.

```
RMTX:
|-- SETUP  : boot.s, setup.s, apentry.s
|-- type.h, Makefile, mk script
|-- kernel  : kernel source directory
|-- fs        : file system directory
|-- driver   : device driver directory
|-- USER   : use commands directory
```

A detailed listing of the RMTX kernel source files follow.

SETUP : RMTX only uses boot.s in which bytes 510-511 contain the boot signature 'RR' for real mode kernel.

type.h   : type.h defines RMTX kernel data structure types, such as PROC, PIPE, EXT2 and other data structure types.

Makefile: top-level Makefile for recompiling RMTX by the make utility.

mk   : a sh script for recompiling and installing RMTX.

/********** Kernel: Process Management Part **********/

ts.s   : startup code, tswitch, interrupt handler entry points and port I/O functions

io.c   : kernel I/O functions; printf(), get_byte()/put_byte(), etc.

queue.c : enqueue, dequue, printQueue functions

wait.c   : ksleep, kwakeup, kwait, kexit functions

loader.c : executable image loader

mem.c   : memory manager

fork.c   : kfork, fork, vfork functions

exec.c   : kexec function

threads.c : threads and mutex functions

pipe.c   : pipe and pipe read/write functions

mes.c   : message passing: send/recv functions

syscall.c : implementation of other syscall functions

int.c   : syscall routing table

t.c   : main entry, initialization, parts of process scheduler

/********** Device Drivers ***********************/

vid.c   : console display driver

timer.c   : timer and timer service functions

pv.c   : semaphore operations

kbd.c   : console keyboard driver

pr.c   : parallel printer driver

serial.c   : serial ports driver

fd.c   : floppy disk driver

hd.c   : IDE hard disk driver

atapi.c   : ATAPI CDROM driver

/********** File system ***********************/

fs   : implementation of a simple EXT2 file system

The RMTX kernel contains approximately 11000 lines of C code, with 300 lines of assembly code. The USER directory contains approximately 5000 lines of C code.

13.5.2   Process Management in RMTX

(1). PROC structure

In RMTX, each process or thread is represented by a PROC structure, which consists of three parts:

fields for process management,
a resource pointer to a per-process resource structure,
process kernel mode stack.

Since the PROC structure encompasses most of the design decisions of an OS, which in turn affects the implementation of the system, we shall explain it in more detail. In RMTX, the PROC structure is

```
typedef struct proc{
        struct  proc *next;
        int     *ksp;       // saved kstack pointer
        int     uss,usp;    // saved Umode uSS and uSP
        int     inkmode;    // in Kmode counter
        int     pid;        // proc ID
        int     ppid;       // parent pid
        int     status;     // process status
        int     priority;   // scheduling priority
        int     event;      // event to sleep on
        int     exitValue;  // exit status
        int     time;       // time quantum
        int     cpu;        // CPU time ticks used in ONE second
        int     pause;      // pause time
        int     type;       // PROCESS|THREAD type
    struct proc *parent;    // pointer to parent PROC
    struct proc *proc;      // process pointer for threads
    struct semaphore *sem;  // semaphore ptr if proc is BLOCKed
    struct pres *res;       // resource structure pointer
    int kstack[SSIZE];      // per process kernel mode stack
    }PROC;
```

In the PROC structure, the next field is used to link the PROCs in various lists or queues. For example, free PROCs are in a freeList, PROCs that are ready to run are in a readyQueue, sleeping PROCs are in a sleepList and a PROC that is blocked on a semaphore is in the semaphore's waiting queue, etc. In RMTX, all link lists and queues are singly-linked. Since the number of PROCs is small, hashing is not used. For the same reason, there are also no child and sibling process point- ers in the PROC structure. The ksp field is the saved kernel mode stack pointer of the process. When a process gives up CPU, it saves CPU registers in kstack and saves the stack pointer in ksp. When a process regains CPU, it resumes running from the stack frame pointed by ksp. The fields uss and usp are for saving the process Umode stack segment and stack pointer. When a process enters Kmode from Umode, by either a syscall or an interrupt, it saves CPU registers in its Umode stack and saves the stack segment and stack pointer in PROC.[uss, usp]. At the end of a syscall or interrupt processing, it restores the Umode stack segment and stack pointer from PROC.[uss, usp] and returns to Umode by the saved interrupt stack frame. The inkmode field is a counter used to keep track of the number of times a process enters Kmode. Since every process begins in Kmode, inkmode = 1 when a process is created. It is decremented by 1 when a process exits Kmode and incremented by 1 when it enters Kmode. For example, if an interrupt occurred in Umode, upon entry to the interrupt handler, inkmode must be 1. On the other hand, if the interrupt occurred in Kmode, the process re-enters Kmode and inkmode must be greater than 1. This allows the interrupt handler to decide whether to return via saved context in Kmode stack or Umode stack. The fields pid, ppid, priority and status are obvious. In most large OS, each process is assigned a unique pid from a range of pid numbers. In MTX, we simply use the PROC index as the process pid, which simplifies the kernel code and also makes it easier for discussion. When a process terminates or exits, it must wakeup the parent, which may be waiting at its PROC address. For convenience, the parent pointer points to the parent PROC. This allows a dying process to find its parent quickly. The event field is the event value when a process goes to sleep. The exitValue field is the exit status of a process. If a process terminates normally by an exit(value) syscall, the exit value is recorded in the low byte of exitValue. If it terminates by a signal, the high byte of exitValue is the signal number. This allows the parent process to extract the exit status of a ZOMBIE child to determine whether it terminated normally or abnormally. The time field is the maximum run time quantum of a process and cpu is its CPU usage time. They are used to compute the dynamic process scheduling priority. The pause field is for a process to sleep for a number of seconds. In MTX, process and thread PROCs are identical. The type field identifies whether a PROC is a PROCESS or THREAD. RMTX uses sleep/wakeup for process management and pipes but it uses semaphores in device drivers and file system for process synchronization. When a process becomes blocked in a semaphore queue, the PROC's sem points to the semaphore. This allows the kernel to unblock a process from a semaphore queue, if necessary. For example, when a process waits for keyboard inputs, it is blocked in the keyboard driver's input semaphore queue. A kill signal delivered to the process should let the process continue. Unlike wakeup(), which simply changes a SLEEP process status to READY and enters it into readyQueue, unblocking a process from a semaphore queue must modify the semaphore's value and waiting queue. Each PROC has a res pointer pointing to a resource structure, PRES, which is

```
typedef struct pres{
   int    uid;                    // user id
   int    gid;                    // group id
   u16    segment,size,tsize,dsize,SEP; // Umode image memory and size
   MINODE *cwd;                    // Current Working Directory pointer
   char   tty[16];                 // terminal special file name
   char   name[32];                // program name string
   int    tcount;                  // number of threads in process
   u16    signal;                  // 15 signals = bits 1 to 14
   u16    sig[NSIG];               // 15 signal handlers
   struct semaphore mlock;         // messageQ lock
   struct semaphore message;       // # of messages
   struct mbuf      *mqueue;       // message queue
   OFT    *fd[NFD];                // open file descriptors
} PRES;
```

The PRES structure contains per-process information. It includes the process uid, gid, Umode image segment and size, current working directory, terminal special file name, program name, signal and signal handlers, message queue and file descriptors, etc. In RMTX the first NPROC PROCs are for processes and the remaining NTHREAD PROCs are for threads. To the RMTX kernel, processes and threads are independent execution units. Each process executes in a unique address space but threads in a process execute in the same address space of a process. During system initialization, each PROCESS PROC is assigned a unique PRES structure pointed by the res pointer. A process is also the main thread of the process. When creating a new thread in a process, its res pointer points to the same PRES structure of the process and its proc pointer points to the process PROC. In MTX all threads in a process share the same resources of the process. For example, they share the same file descriptors, so that opened files are available to all threads in a process. Some OS kernels allow individual threads to open files, which are private to the threads. In that case, each PROC must have its own file descriptor array. Similarly for signals and messages. In the PROC structure, kstack is the process kernel mode stack. It is defined as the last field of PROC for a simple reason. When a process enters kernel from user mode, we must change the execution environment from Umode to Kmode. In particular, we must set the stack pointer to the process kstack in kernel space. All these can only be done in assembly code at the interrupt handler entry point. By placing the kstack at the end of the PROC structure makes these operations easier. The following global variables are defined in the t.c file, which also contains the main() function and the initialization function init().

```
PROC[NPROC+NTHREAD]: first NPROC PROCs for processes, remaining
                     NTHREAD PROCs for threads.
freeList  = a list of free PROCs
tfreeList = a list of free THREAD PROCs
readyQueue= a priority queue of ready processes and threads.
PROC *running = pointer to the current running process.
sleepList = a FIFO list of sleeping processes;
```

(2). io.c: This file implements printf() and a few other I/O functions. In kernel mode, printf() is based on putc() in the display driver. In user mode, it is based on uputc(), which writes to file descriptor 1 of the process.

(3). queue.c:

This file implements get_proc()/put_proc() and enqueue()/dequeue() functions. get_proc() allocates a free PROC for a new process or thread. put_proc() returns a ZOMBIE PROC to a free PROC list. Processes and threads that are ready to run are maintained in a readyQueue by priority. enqueue() enters a PROC into the ready-Queue by priority, and dequeue() returns a pointer to the highest priority PROC removed from the readyQueue. In addition, there are also other list/queue manipulation functions, e.g. enter/remove a sleeping process to/from the sleepList, etc. They are implemented in the relevant files for clarity.

(4). wait.c:

This file implements ksleep(), kwakeup(), kwait() and kexit() for process management.

ksleep()/kwakeup():

A process calls ksleep(event) to go to sleep on an event. An event is just a value which represents the sleep reason. When the awaited event occurs, another process or an interrupt handler calls kwakeup(event), which wakes up all the processes sleeping on the event. To ensure that processes are woken up in order, sleeping processes are maintained in a FIFO sleepList.

kwait():

kwait() allows a process to wait for a ZOMBIE child. If a process has children but no ZOMBIE child yet, it sleeps on its own PROC address. When a process terminates, it calls kexit() to becomes a ZOMBIE and wakes up the parent by kwakeup(running->parent). As in Unix, orphan processes become children of the INIT process P1, which repeatedly waits for any ZOMBIE children.

kexit(): every process calls kexit(exitValue) to terminate. The actions of kexit() are:

.give away children, if any, to P1;

.release resources, e.g. free Umode image memory, dispose of cwd, close opened file descriptors and release message buffers in message queue.

.record exitValue in PROC, become a ZOMBIE, wakeup parent and also P1 if it has sent any children to P1.

.call tswitch() to give up CPU for the last time.

ZOMBIE PROCs are freed by their parents through kwait(). Orphaned ZOMBIEs are freed by the INIT process P1.

(5). fork.c: This file contains kfork(), fork() and vfork(), which are implemented as follows.

kfork():

When RMTX starts, it first initializes the kernel data structures. Then it creates a process P0 as the initial running process. P0 runs only in Kmode and has the lowest priority 0. P0 continues to initialize the rest of the RMTX system. When initialization completes, P0 calls kfork("/bin/init") to create a child process P1. kfork()

calls fork1(), which is the common code of creating new processes. fork1() creates a child process ready to run in kernel but without a Umode image. When fork1() returns, kfork() allocates a Umode memory area for P1, loads the /bin/init file as the Umode image and sets up the Umode stack of P1 for it to resume. Then P0 switches process to run P1. P1 returns to Umode to execute /bin/init. P1 is the only process created by kfork(). After P1 runs, all other processes are created by fork() or vfork() as usual. The startup sequence of RMTX is unique. In most other Unix-like systems, the initial image of P1 is a piece of pre-compiled binary executable code containing an exec("/etc/init") system call. After system initialization, P1 is sent to execute the exec() syscall code in Umode, which changes P1's image to /etc/init. In RMTX, when P1 starts to run, it returns to Umode to execute the INIT image directly.

fork():

As in Unix/Linux, fork() creates a child process with an Umode image identical to that of the parent. If fork() succeeds, the parent returns the child's pid and the child returns 0. In RMTX, fork() is implemented as follows.

First, fork() calls fork1() to create a child process ready to run in Kmode. The child PROC inherits all the open file descriptors of the parent but without an Umode image. The child PROC is assigned the base priority of 127 and its resume point is set to _goUmode, so that when the child is scheduled to run, it returns to Umode immediately. Next, fork() allocates a Umode image area for the child of the same size as the parent and copies the parent's Umode image to the child. It then changes the copied DS, ES and CS in the child's Umode stack to child's segments, and sets the child's saved uss to its own data + stack segment. The child's saved usp is identical to that of the parent since it's the same offset relative to the saved uss segment. Then it changes the saved AX register in the child's Umode stack frame to 0. Finally, it returns the child's pid. When the child runs, it returns to its own Umode image with a 0. Because of the image copying, the child's Umode image is identical to that of the parent. The implementation of fork() in MTX is also unique. It only guarantees that the two Umode images are identical. The return paths of the parent and the child processes are very different.

vfork():

After forking a child, the parent usually waits for the child to terminate and the child immediately does exec() to change its Umode image. In such cases, copying image in fork() would be a waste. For this reason, many OS kernels support vfork(), which forks a child process without copying the parent image. RMTX also supports vfork(), which is implemented as follows.

a. Create a child process which shares the same image of the parent. vfork() first calls fork1() to create a child process ready to run in Kmode. When fork1() returns, vfork() does not allocate a Umode image for the child but lets it share the same Umode image with the parent, i.e. let the child PROC.uss be the same as that of the parent.

b. In the ustack area of the parent, create an interrupt stack frame for the child to return to pid=vfork() in Umode with a 0. This is done by copying the parent's interrupt stack frame to a low address area, e.g. at parent's saved usp—1KB and set the child's saved usp point to that area, as if the child had done a vfork() syscall by itself.

c. When either process returns to Umode, it would run in the same image of the parent. In an OS with memory protection hardware, the shared image can be marked as read-only. If either process tries to write to the shared image, the image is split into individual images. Since RMTX in real mode does not have any mechanism for memory protection, we must assume that, after vfork(), both the parent and child execute in read-only mode; either the parent executes wait() or the child executes exec() immediately.

d. In kexec(), a vforked child process creates a new Umode image but does not destroy the shared parent image.

e. In order to ensure that the child runs first, vfork() sets the child's priority to the maximum value 256. When the parent exits Kmode, it will switch process, allowing the child to return to Umode first.

Under normal conditions, vfork() can be used interchangeably with fork(). All the fork() syscalls in RMTX can be replaced with vfork(). However, as noted above, the vfork() in RMTX cannot support processes that modify the (shared) image. In such cases, fork() must be used instead.

(6). loader.c: This file implements the Umode image loader, which loads an executable file to a segment. The load() function uses the internal open() of the file system to open the file for read. It first calls the header() function, which reads the file header to determine the file's tsize, dsize and bss size. Then it loads the file's code+data sections to the specified segment and clears the bss section to 0. The header() function is also used in kexec() to calculate the total memory size needed by a new image.

(7). exec.c: This file implements the kexec() syscall. Unlike exec() in other OS, the parameter to kexec() is the entire command line of the form "cmd argv1 argv2... argvn". kexec() uses the first token, cmd, to create the new image, but it passes the entire command line to the new image. Parsing the command line to argc and argv is done in the new image in user mode. As of now, MTX does not support the PATH environment variable. All executable commands are assumed to be in the /bin directory. If the cmd file name does not begin with a /, it is assumed in the /bin directory by default. kexec() supports binary executable images with either a single segment or separate I&D spaces. It reads the file header to determine the total memory size needed to load the image. For single-segment images, the total memory size is the image's tsize+dsize+bssize plus a defualt ustack size of 20KB. If an image has separate I&D spaces, the image's combined data+stack size is set to the maximum value of 64KB. If the total needed size is not greater than the current image size, it simply loads the new image into the old image area. Otherwise, it calls kmalloc() of the memory manager to allocate the needed space, loads in the new image and releases the old image. Then it re-initializes the ustack to let the process execute from the beginning of the new image when it returns to Umode. When a vforked process calls kexec(), it only creates a new image without releasing the (shared) old image. In addition, kexec() also checks the process thread count. A process may exec() only if its tcount=1, i.e. when there are no other active threads in the process. kexec() clears the process signals and resets the signal handlers to default. MTX does not support close on exec() file descriptors. All opened files remain open after exec(). If needed, the reader may add this and other features to the kexec() function.

(8). mem.c file: This file implements the RMTX kernel memory manager. The RMTX kernel image is a binary executable with separate I&D spaces. The maximum size of the kernel image is 128KB bytes. When RMTX boots up, the kernel image is loaded at the segment 0×1000. Ideally, the entire memory area from the end of the RMTX kernel to the segment 0xA000 should be the initial free memory area. In order to keep the system initialization code simple, the free memory area begins from the segment 0×3000.The memory manager consists of the following components.

freeMem = a list of current free memory areas; initial free memory is from the segment
        0x3000 to 0xA000.
kmalloc(size): allocate space for process Umode image size.
kmfree(segment, size): deallocate memory at (segment, size)
sbrk()/rbrk(): increase/decrease heap size of process Umode image.

Free memory areas are managed as variable-sized partitions by the first-fit algorithm. When a process forks, it calls kmalloc() to allocate a Umode image of the same size for the child. When a process terminates, it calls kmfree() to release the Umode image space back to the freeMem list. Similarly, when a process does exec(), it may call kmalloc() and kmfree() if the new image size is larger than the current image size. sbrk() and rbrk() adjust the heap size of the Umode image. They may call kmalloc() and kmfree() as needed. The function kmalloc() is non-blocking. Instead of waiting for free memory to become available, it prints an "out of memory" message and returns 0 if there is not enough free memory for the requested size. Currently, RMTX does not implement memory compaction and user mode image swapping. Both are suitable programming projects for possible improvements to the RMTX system.

(9). threads.c: MTX supports threads. In the RMTX kernel, there are NTHREAD PROCs dedicated to threads. A process PROC is also the main thread of the process. Each process has a tcount, which is the number of threads currently in the process. When a thread is created inside a process, it is allocated a THREAD PROC, which is linked to the process PROC. Threads in a process share the same resources of the process. MTX uses mutex for threads synchronization. Threads implementation and synchronization are discussed in Chap. 5. Several user mode programs, such as matrix, race, norace and qsort, are used to demonstrate the thread capability of RMTX. Due to the small number of thread PROCs (16), the reader should observe this limit when experimenting with threads programming in RMTX.

(10). pipe.c:
This file implements pipes in RMTX. Each pipe is a PIPE structure.

```
typedef struct pipe{
        char   buf[PSIZE];          // PSIZE = 64 chars
        int    head, tail, data, room;
        int    nreader, nwriter;    // number of readers/writers
        int    busy;                // FREE or in use
}PIPE;   PIPE pipe[NPIPE];          // NPIPE = 10
```

A PIPE contains a circular char buffer, buf[PSIZE], with head and tail pointers. The control variables are data, room, nreader and nwriter, where data=number of chars in the buffer, room=number of spaces in the buffer, nreader=number of reader processes on the pipe and nwriter=number of writer processes on the pipe. These variables are used for process synchronization during pipe read/write. When RMTX starts, pipe_init() is called to initialize all the PIPE structures as free. When a process creates a pipe by the pipe(int pd[2]) syscall, it executes kpipe() in kernel. kpipe() allocates a PIPE structure, initializes the pipe variables and allocates two file descriptors, pd[0] and pd[1], which point to the READ_PIPE and WRITE_PIPE OFT instances, respectively. After creating a pipe, a process normally forks a child process to share the pipe. During fork(), the child inherits all the open file descriptors of the parent. If the file descriptor is a pipe, fork() increments the reference count of the OFT by 1 and updates the number of readers or writers in the PIPE structure as needed. Then, each process calls close_pipe() to close its unwanted pipe descriptor. close_pipe() deallocates the PIPE structure if there are no more reader and writer. Otherwise, it does the normal closing of the file descriptor and wakes up any waiting reader/writer processes on the pipe. read_pipe() is for reading from a pipe, and write_pipe() is for writing to a pipe. Processes reading/writing pipes are synchronized by ksleep() and kwakeup(). A reader process returns 0 if the pipe has no data and no writer. Otherwise, it reads as much as it needs, up to the pipe size, and returns the number of bytes read. It waits for data only if the pipe has no data but still has writers. A writer process detects a BORKEN_PIPE error and aborts if there are no readers on the pipe. Otherwise, it writes as much as it can to the pipe. It may wait if there is no room and the pipe still has readers. After each read, the reader wakes up any waiting writers. After each write, the writer wakes up any waiting readers.

The pipe implementation has the following implications. In RMTX, when a process is woken up in kernel, it is assigned a high priority. If user mode processes read/writes pipes one byte at time, it would incur a process switch after each read/write syscall, which may be undesirable. There are two possible ways to remedy this. The first one is to let processes read/write pipes in chucks of data, e.g. by user level I/O buffering as in the standard I/O library functions. The second one is to modify the RMTX process scheduling algorithm. When waking up a process from a pipe, do not assign it a high priority. The reader may try either of these approaches to reduce the number of process switches.

(11). syscall.c:

This file implements the miscellaneous syscalls, such as getpid(), kps(), etc. Any additional syscall functions can also be added here.

(12). signal.c:

This file implements signals and signal handling in RMTX. It contains the following functions.

kkill(sig, pid) implements the kill(sig, pid) syscall. It delivers a signal, sig, to the target process. To keep things simple, MTX does not enforce kill permissions, so a process may kill any other process. If desired, the reader may modify kkill() to enforce permission checking. RMTX supports only 15 signals, each corresponds to a bit (1–15) in PROC.res.signal. Delivering a signal i sets the i-th bit in the target PROC. res.signal to 1. In Unix/Linux, if a process is in the "uninterruptible sleep" state, it cannot be woken up by signals. In RMTX, processes only sleep for ZOMBIE children and reading/writing pipes, so they are interruptible. Therefore, a signal always wakes up a target process if it is sleeping. If the target process is waiting for block device I/O, it is blocked on a semaphore in the device driver. Unblocking such a process may confuse the device driver. However, if the process is waiting for terminal inputs, it will be unblocked by signals. Since the unblocked process resumes running inside a device driver, the driver's I/O buffer must also be adjusted to ensure consistency.

ksignal() implements the signal(sig, catcher) syscall. It installs a catcher function as the signal handler for the signal sig, except for signal number 9, which cannot be changed. When a process enters Kmode via a syscall and when it is about to return to Umode, it checks and handles outstanding signals by calling kpsig().

kpsig() calls cksig(), which resets the signal bit of an outstanding signal and returns the signal number. For each outstanding signal number n, if the process signal handler function, sig[n], is 0, the process calls kexit(n<<8) to die with an exit status=n<<8. If sig[n] is 1, the process ignores the signal. Otherwise, kpsig() sets up the process interrupt ustack frame in such a way that, when the process returns to Umode, it first returns to the signal catcher function. When the catcher function finishes, it returns to the place where it lastly entered kernel.

kdivide()/ktrap(): kdivide is the divide-by-zero trap handler. When the CPU in real mode encounters a divide-by-zero error, it traps to vector 0, which points to the divide-by-zero trap handler entry point, _divide, in ts.s. The trap handler calls kdivide(), in which the process delivers a number 1 signal to itself followed by kpsig(). If the process has not changed its default sig[1] handler, it would die by the signal. If the process has installed a handler to catch the signal, it will execute the handler function in Umode. A user mode program, divide.c, demonstrates the handling of divide-by-zero trap. When running the divide program, if the user chooses not to install a catcher, the program will die when it tries to divide by 0. If the user has installed a catcher, the program will execute the catcher when it tries to divide by 0. The catcher function uses a long jump to bypass the code containing the divide-by-zero instruction, allowing the program to continue. Handling other kinds of trap errors is similar. Since the PC in real mode does not recognize other kind of traps, trap errors are simulated by INT n instructions, where $1 < n < 8$. The trap.c program demonstrates trap handling by installed trap handlers. Another program that demonstrates signal handling is the itimer.c program, which catches signals from an interval timer.

```
/****** itimer.c: handle SIGALRM (14) signals *********/
int t = 1;                    // default timer interval
void catcher(int sig)
{
   signal(14, catcher);       // install signal# 14 catcher again
   printf("catcher() in Umode, sig=%d\n", sig);
   itimer(t);                 // set a t sec. interval timer
}

main(int argc, char *argv[])
{
   signal(14, catcher);       // install catcher() for SIGALRM (14)
   if (argc > 1)
       t = atoi(argv[1]);
   printf("request interval timer = %d\n", t);
   itimer(t);                 // call itimer() in kernel
   while(1);                  // looping
}
```

The program first installs a signal 14 catcher and sets an interval timer of t seconds. Then it loops forever. After the timer interval expires, the kernel's timer interrupt handler sends it a SIGALRM(14) signal. Without the catcher function, the process would die by default. If the catcher is not installed again, the process will die when it gets the next SIGALRM signal. Since the catcher is installed again, the process will be directed to execute the catcher function once every t seconds.

(13). int.c

This file implements the syscall routing table. First, a function pointer table is set up to contain all the syscall function entry addresses.

   int (*f[ ])()={getpid, getppid, getpri, ksetpri, getuid,.......};

When a process issues a syscall, e.g. syscall(a, b,c, d,e), it enters kernel by INT 80, which sends it to _int80h: in ts.s, which calls kcinth().

```
int kcinth()
{
   int a,b,c,d,e,r;
   unlock();                  // handle syscall with interrupts on
   if (running->res->signal)  // check and handle outstanding signals
      kpsig();
   // get syscall parameters a,b,c,d,e from ustack, a=syscall number
   r = (*f[a])(b,c,d,e);      // invokde the syscall function
   if (running->res->signal)  // check and handle signal again
      kpsig();
   put_uword(r, running->usp + 2*8); // return r into saved AX in ustack
   running->pri = 128-running->cpu;  // drop back to Umode priority
}
```

In kcinth(), the process checks and handles signals first. This is because, if the process already has a pending signal, which may cause it to terminate, processing the syscall would be a waste of time. If the process survives the signal processing, it fetches the syscall parameters from the Umode stack, where a is the syscall number. Then it calls the corresponding syscall function by r=(*f[a])(b, c,d, e) to process the syscall. When the syscall function returns, it checks and handles signals again. Each syscall function returns a value r, except kexit(), which never returns, and exec(), which does not return if the operation succeeds. Before returning to _goUmode in assembly, it writes r to the saved AX register in the interrupt stack frame as the return value to Umode.

(14). t.c

This is the main file of RMTX. When RMTX starts, it executes the startup code in ts.s, which calls main(). main() first calls init() to initialize the RMTX kernel and creates P0 as the initial running process. P0 kforks P1 with a Umode image,/bin/init, and switches to P1. When P1 runs, it forks one or more login processes, each on a separate terminal, and waits for any of the login processes to terminate. When the login processes run, the RMTX system is ready for use. In the t.c file, the functions nextrun(), schedule() and reschedule() are parts of the process scheduler. Process scheduling in RMTX is by both time slice and dynamic process priority, which is discussed in detail in Chap. 8. To observe process switches due to dynamic priorities, the reader may uncomment the print statement in reschedule() and recompile the RMTX kernel. Similarly, the reader may also enable the print statements in the timer interrupt handler (in timer.c) to observe timer based process switching.

(15). ts.s

This is the only assembly code file of RMTX. It consists of four parts:

a. RMTX startup code: The lines from start to call _main are the startup code of the RMTX kernel. During booting, the booter calls the time-of-day function of BIOS and saves it at 0×90000. When the MTX kernel starts, it retrieves the saved BIOS TOD as the system time base. In all versions of MTX, the time is maintained as follows. In the EXT2 file system, the INODE size is 128 bytes but the last 28 bytes are not used. So we define the last two INODE fields as u32 i_date; u32 i_time which contain the date and time in BCD format. The date and time of each INODE are based on the time-of-day (TOD), which is the initial TOD of BIOS plus the current time in seconds. While RMTX runs, it displays the TOD at the lower right corner of the screen.

b. _tswitch: This is the context switching function. When a process relinquishes CPU, it calls tswitch(), in which it saves CPU registers into its kstack and saves the stack pointer into PROC.ksp. Then, it calls nextrun() to pick a ready PROC with the highest priority as the next running process. Since P0 has the lowest priority, it runs only when all other PROCs are non-runnable. During system initialization, P0 itself may be blocked when it reads the hard disk partition table to initializes the HD driver. In that case, P0 puts the CPU in idle state with interrupts enabled. When the HD interrupt occurs, the HD interrupt handler unblocks P0 and enters it into readyQueue. In nextrun(), it picks a ready PROC with highest priority as the next running PROC, sets the PROC's run time to QUANTUM (6–10 ticks), resets the PROC's CPU usage time to 0 and clears the switch process flag, sw_flag, to 0. Then execution returns to the RESUME part of tswitch(), which resumes the new running process from the saved stack frame in kstack. Since tswitch() is always called in Kmode, there is no need to save/restore CPU segment registers because they are always the same.

c. Interrupt handler entry and exit code: These are calls to the INTH macro. Each
   macro call is of the form _xinth: INTH chandler, which defines the entry point of
   an interrupt or trap handler. Interrupt and trap handlers are implemented in C in
   various parts of the RMTX kernel. When an interrupt handler finishes, execution
   returns to the interrupted point by _ireturn. If the interrupt occurred in Kmode,
   it returns via the process kstack. Otherwise, it returns via the process ustack.
   Before a process returns to Umode, it calls kpsig() to handle any outstanding
   signal first. If it survives the signal processing, it then calls reschedule(), which
   may switch to a process with higher priority.
d. The remaining assembly code contains port I/O and CPU interrupts masking
   functions for implementing critical regions.

13.5.3   Device Drivers

(1). Timer and Timer Service (timer.c):
    The PC's channel 0 timer is programmed to generate interrupts every 1/60th of
a second. During booting, the booter reads the BIOS time-of-day (TOD) and saves
the information at 0×90000. When a MTX kernel starts, it retrieves the saved TOD
and uses it as the real time base. At each second, it displays a wall clock. RMTX
uses the timer interrupts for process scheduling, as described in Chap. 8 on process
scheduling. Timer service is implemented by a TimerQueue, which is a list of interval timer requests (TQEs). Each TQE has a time field and an action function. When
a TQE's time expires, the timer interrupt handler invokes the action function, which
typically unblocks the process or sends an SIGALRM signal to the process.
    (2). Other Device Drivers: MTX supports the following devices:

> console video driver (vid.c)
> keyboard driver (kbd.c)
> printer driver (pr.c)
> serial port driver (serial.c)
> floppy disk driver (fd.c)
> IDE hard disk driver (hd.c)
> ATAPI CDROM driver (atapi.c)

All device drivers, except the console video driver, are interrupt-driven. Their interrupt handler entry points are installed in the assembly code file, ts.s, as INTH macro
calls of the form _xinth: INTH xhandler, where xhandler is the interrupt handler in
C. All device drivers use semaphores for synchronization. Details of device driver
design and implementation are discussed in Chap. 10. Therefore, we shall not repeat
them here.

13.5.4   File System

MTX implements a simple EXT2 file system, which is described in Chap. 11. The file system is completely Linux compatible.

13.6   Install RMTX

RMTX can be installed to either a real or a virtual PC. The install procedure is described in the Appendix.

13.7   RMTX Startup Sequence

(1). The RMTX kernel image is a binary executable with separate I&D spaces. The first 5 (2-byte) words of the image contains

```
         jmp start
kds:     .word   0      ! RMTX kernel DS=0x1000+tsize/16
dsize:   .word   0      ! RMTX kernel dsize in bytes
bsize:   .word   0      ! RMTX kernel bss size in bytes
rootdev: .word   0x0303 ! default root device (major,minor) number
start:                  ! RMTX startup assembly code begins here
```

When compiling the RMTX kernel, the kernel image is first generated as an a.out file with separate I&D spaces. A utility program, h.c, is used to read the file header and patch in the values of kds, dsize and bsize at the word locations 1, 2, 3. Then, it deletes the file header, making the mtx kernel image suitable for booting. In order to be compatible with MTX in protected mode, a bootable RMTX image consists of the following pieces.

```
Sector:|  S0    S1    S3    S4  |  S5 ...................|
       |------|-----|-----|-----|-----------------------|
       | BOOT |SETUP|  APentry  |<------ mtx kernel ----->|
```

where BOOT is for booting the image from a FD, SETUP and APentry are for booting MTX in protected mode. The last 2 bytes in the BOOT sector contain the boot signature, which is PP (0×5050) for protected mode MTX kernel, or RR (0×5252) for real-mode MTX kernel.

(2). Booting RMTX:

Typically, RMTX is installed on a hard disk partition. During booting, the hd-booter loads BOOT+SETUP to 0×90000, APentry to 0×91000 and the RMTX kernel to 0×10000. Then the booter checks the boot signature in the BOOT sector. If the word in 'RR', it jumps to 0×10000 to start the RMTX kernel in real mode. The booter also writes the boot partition number into word 4 of the RMTX kernel image as the rootdev. When the RMTX kernel starts, it gets the kds segment value at word 1 and uses dsize and bsize to clear the bss section to 0. It sets the segment registers to CS=0×1000, DS=SS=ES=kds and the stack pointer to the high end of proc[0]. kstack. Then it calls main(), passing rootdev, dsize, bsize as parameters.

(3). RMTX main() function: The actions of main() are as follows:

(3)-1. Call vid_init() to initialize the console display driver to make printf() work. Extract

rootdev minor number as the root device HD.

(3)-2. Call init(HD) to initialize the RMTX kernel. The actions of init() are

Initialize kernel data structures;

Create P0 as the running process.

Initialize interrupt vectors and device drivers. During system initialization, the kernel must read the HD's MBR to find out the start_sector and size of the RMTX partition. Reading HD requires a process to wait on a semaphore for the read operation to complete. Hence P0 must be running first.

Initialize other kernel data structures, e.g. pipes and message buffers.

Initialize memory manager; free memory is from 0×30000 to 0xA0000.

Initialize file system and mount the root file system from rootdev.

(4). After init(), P0 calls kfork("/bin/init") to create P1 and load/bin/init as its Umode image. Then P0 switches to run P1. If all procs are blocked, P0 resumes to a while(1) loop in which it puts the CPU in HLT, waiting for any interrupt. It switches process when the readyQueue is not empty.

(5). Process P1: P1 executes/bin/init in Umode. It forks a login process on the console (/dev/tty0). If desired, it can also fork login processes on serial ports (/dev/ttyS0 and /dev/ttyS1). Then, it waits for any child process to terminate. Another option of P1 is to fork a cdserver process, which runs in Umode and communicates with CDROM client processes by messages. A cdclient process can request the cd-server to display or copy iso9600 files on the CD/DVD-ROM.

(6). Each login process uses exec("login /dev/ttyX") to run the login program on a terminal. It opens the terminal special file 3 times to get the file descriptors 0,1,2 as in, out, err, respectively. Then it displays a login: prompt, waiting for a user to login. Figure 13.1 shows the startup screen of the RMTX operating system.

(7). RMTX is now up and running. When a user tries to login, the login process reads the user name and password. Then it checks the password file,/etc/passwd, to verify the user account. The passwd file has the same format as that of Linux, except that it does not use encryption. If the user has a valid account, the login process becomes the user process by acquiring the user's uid. Then it changes directory to the user's home directory and exec() to run the program listed in the user account, which is usually the command interpreter sh.

(8). The user process in now running sh. The user may enter commands for sh to execute. As of now, the RMTX sh can only execute binary executable files, not sh scripts. However, it supports I/O redirections, background process and multiple commands connected by pipes.

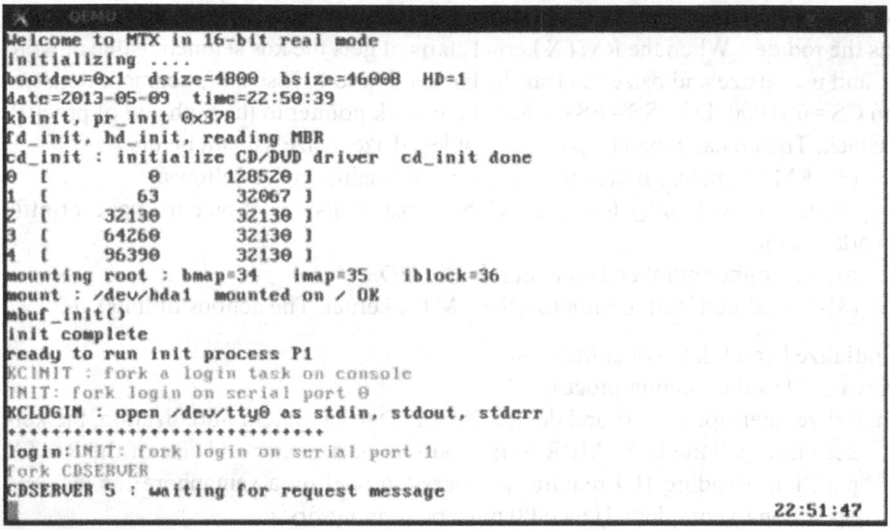

```
X      QEMU
Welcome to MTX in 16-bit real mode
initializing ....
bootdev=0x1  dsize=4800  bsize=46008  HD=1
date=2013-05-09  time=22:50:39
kbinit, pr_init 0x378
fd_init, hd_init, reading MBR
cd_init : initialize CD/DVD driver  cd_init done
0 [            0     128520 ]
1 [           63      32067 ]
2 [        32130      32130 ]
3 [        64260      32130 ]
4 [        96390      32130 ]
mounting root : bmap=34   imap=35   iblock=36
mount : /dev/hda1  mounted on / OK
mbuf_init()
init complete
ready to run init process P1
KCINIT : fork a login task on console
INIT: fork login on serial port 0
KCLOGIN : open /dev/tty0 as stdin, stdout, stderr
++++++++++++++++++++++++++++++
login:INIT: fork login on serial port 1
fork CDSERVER
CDSERVER 5 : waiting for request message
                                                     22:51:47
```

Fig. 13.1 Startup screen of RMTX

(9). When the user logout by entering logout or the Control_D key, the login sh terminates, which wakes up the INIT process P1, which forks another login process on the terminal, etc. In addition, P1 also frees any orphaned ZOMBIE processes.

(10). Shutdown and Reboot RMTX:

RMTX uses I/O buffers to keep recently used disk blocks in a buffer cache. The proper way to shutdown RMTX is by the reboot command or the usual 3-finger salute (Control_Alt_Del). These allow the RMTX kernel to flush the buffer cache and umount any mounted file system before shutdown. At any time, the user may also run the sync command to flush dirty I/O buffers to disk.

13.8   Recompile the RMTX Kernel

To recompile and install the RMTX kernel, from the RMTX source directory, run make followed by make install. Alternatively, mk partition# qemu|vmware, e.g. mk 2 qemu or mk 3 vmware, may also be used to recompile and install the RMTX system. The reader may consult the install procedures in the Appendix for more details.

13.9   Future Development

Although RMTX is a fully functional operating system, it does have some limitations. The most obvious limitation is that it only runs on PCs or virtual machines in 16-bit real mode, so it may not be suitable for practical use. As stated before, the object of this book is to provide a suitable platform for teaching and learning the theory and practice of operating systems. In order to do these in a meaningful way, it uses the development of RMTX to convey the real intent of this book, which is to show the design principles and implementation techniques of real operating systems in general. On the other hand, small systems like RMTX also have advantages and a wide range of potential applications. The main advantage of RMTX lies in its small size and its ability to run on hardware systems with limited capabilities and resources. The RMTX kernel requires less than 128 KB memory to run, but it supports multitasking, interrupts processing, I/O devices and a complete file system. With the current trend in computing technology, more and more portable devices, such as smart phones, hand-held devices, head-wearing gadgets and embedded systems, etc. will be developed. As such devices and systems become more common, it is only natural for users to expect and demand more functionalities from them, which point to the need for small operating systems designed for simple processors and limited memory space. It is hoped that the design and implementation of RMTX may help shed some light on the development of such systems in the future. In the remaining chapters of this book, we shall extend RMTX to 32-bit protected mode operations.

Problems

1. Create a /sbin directory containing system programs, e.g. login. Set up a /etc/inittab file containing

```
ID    ACTION       PROCESS (terminal and protocol)
----: --------- :  --------------------------------
c1 :  respawn   :  /sbin/login -L tty0   console
s1 :  respawn   :  /sbin/login -L ttyS0 9600 vt100
s2 :  respawn   :  /sbin/login -L ttyS1 9600 vt100
```

Rewrite init.c as follows. When init starts up, it forks a login process for each line in the inittab file. The respawn field tells init to fork a new login process on the terminal when the original login process terminates.

2. In RMTX, all commands are in the /bin directory by default. Extend sh to support environment variables, such as PATH=/bin:/sbin:/local/bin, which defines directories containing commands.

3. Extend the sh program to execute simple script files containing command lines.

4. Implement a command history file containing previous input commands. Use the arrow keys to recall previous commands for sh to execute.

5. Currently, RMTX only supports mount/umount of floppy drives containing an EXT2 FS. Modify the RMTX kernel to support mount/umount of hard disk partitions.

6. RMTX uses BCC under Linux for developing both the RMTX kernel and user mode programs. This author has successfully ported BCC's assembler (as86) and linker (ld86) to RMTX, but porting the bcc compiler remains unfinished. Interested readers are invited to port the bcc compiler over to RMTX, which would make RMTX a standalone system.

Chapter 14
MTX in 32-bit Protected Mode

14.1 Introduction to 32-bit Protected Mode

After power on or reset, the x86 CPU (Antonakos 1999) starts execution in 16-bit real mode. The CPU can be switched to 32-bit protected mode (Intel 1990) by setting bit 0 of control register CR0 to 1. Once in protected mode, the CPU's operating environment changes completely. First, the memory management scheme is totally different from that of real mode. Each segment register becomes a segment selector, which is used to select a segment descriptor in a global or local descriptor table. Each segment descriptor specifies the base address, type and size limit of a segment. A logical address comprises a segment selector and a 32-bit offset. The linear address is the segment base address plus the offset. With only segmentation, a linear address is also the physical address. If paging is enabled, the CPU translates the linear address to physical address through two levels of page tables. Second, exception and interrupt vectors are no longer in the low 1 KB of real mode memory. Instead, they are represented by trap and interrupt gates in an interrupt descriptor table. The CPU uses the interrupt descriptor table for exceptions and interrupts processing. The descriptor tables must be set up properly before switching the CPU to protected mode. If using paging, the page tables must also be set up before enabling the paging hardware. The following sections describe protected mode operations in more detail.

14.2 Memory Management in Protected Mode

Memory management consists of address translation and memory protection. In protected mode, the memory management hardware of the x86 CPU supports both segmentation and paging.

© Springer International Publishing Switzerland 2015   387
K. C. Wang, *Design and Implementation of the MTX Operating System*,
DOI 10.1007/978-3-319-17575-1_14

Fig. 14.1 Segment register

```
  15                     3  2  1  0
 ┌─────────────────────────┬──┬────┐
 │   (13 bits)  index      │ T│ RPL│
 └─────────────────────────┴──┴────┘
```

14.2.1   Segmentation

A x86 CPU in protected mode has 6 segment registers, denoted by cs, ds, ss, es, fs
and gs. Each segment register is 16 bits but its content is no longer a base address
as in real mode. Instead, it specifies the index of a segment descriptor in a descriptor table. Each segment descriptor contains the base address and size limit of the
intended segment. The linear address, which is also the physical address, is the
segment base address plus the offset. The format of a segment register is shown in
Fig. 14.1.

where index = 13-bit offset into a descriptor table, T = 0 means the Global Descriptor Table (GDT), T = 1 means the Local Descriptor Table (LDT), RPL is the
segment's privilege level for protection. The 2-bit privilege level varies from 00,
which is the highest, to 11, which is the lowest. The four privilege levels form a
set of protection rings, which can be used to implement secure operating systems
with multiple layers of protections. All Unix-like systems use only two privilege
levels; kernel level and user level. For MTX in protected mode, we shall also use
two privilege levels; RPL = 0 for kernel mode and 3 for user mode. When a process
executes at privilege level 0, it can execute any code segment and access any data
segment. When a process executes at privilege level 3, it cannot access any segment
of RPL 0 directly. This prevents user mode programs from executing kernel code
or accessing kernel data. As usual, a user mode process can enter kernel mode only
through interrupts, exceptions or by explicit system calls.

In protected mode, a logical address comprises two parts: a 16-bit segment se-
lector and a 32-bit offset, which specifies the relative address within the segment.
Given a logical address LA = [segment: offset], the CPU uses the segment selector's
T bit to access either the GDT or LDT. If T = 0, it uses the GDT, which is pointed by
the CPU's GDTR register. If T = 1, it uses the LDT, which is pointed by the CPU's
LDTR register. A system has only one GDT, which specifies the kernel code and
data segments that are common to all processes. Each process may have its own
LDT, which specifies the user mode address space of that process.

14.2.1.1   Segment Descriptors

Figure 14.2 shows the format of a Code or Data segment descriptor, each 8 bytes
long.

Segment Descriptors are in either the GDT or LDT. The CPU's GDTR register
points to a GDT descriptor containing the address and size of the GDT. Similarly,
the CPU's LDTR register points to a LDT selector in the GDT, which points to the
LDT.

```
63          |      48| 47      40 |39          |            16 15        |
|-----------|----|----|----|----|-------|--------|--------|--------|----|
|   base    |GDOA| Lm |PpLS|type|          base           |      limit     |
|  (31-24)  |(4) |    |    |    |         (23-0)          |     (15-0)     |

base  = 32-bit base address in bytes
limit = 20-bit segment size limit (Lm = high 4 bits of limit)
G=Granularity: 0 in bytes, 1 in 4KB blocks
D=1 for 32-bit operands, A=1 for available, P=1 for segment present
pL (2 bits) = Privilege level (00=kernel, 11=user), S=1 (application)
type (4 bits): code or data segment and R/W access
```

Fig. 14.2 Format of code/data descriptor

When setting up the GDT and LDT it is convenient to define a few segment descriptor prototypes. For example, the following define 4 GB (limit=0xFFFFF) GDT code and data segments.

```
u64 gdt_code = 0x00CF9A000000FFFF; // pL=00,type=0xA=non-conform code
u64 gdt_data = 0x00CF92000000FFFF; // pL=00,type=0x2=read/write data
```

Similarly, the following define 2 MB (limit=0x1FF for 512*4KB) LDT code and data segments.

```
u64 ldt_code = 0x00C0FA000000001FF; // pL=11 type=0xA=non-conform code
u64 ldt_data = 0x00C0F2000000001FF; // pL=11 type=0x2=read/write data
```

For different base address, simply change the address field (byte 7 and bytes 4-2) in the prototype. Similarly, change the limit fields for different segment size. In addition to code and data segment descriptors, the GDT may also contain Task State Segment Descriptors (TSSD). A TSSD refers to a Task State Segment (TSS), which is a data structure used by the CPU to save CPU registers during hardware task switching. It also specifies the logical address of the stacks for privilege levels 0, 1 and 2.

14.2.1.2   Segmentation Models

Memory management by segmentation may use several different memory models:

Flat model: In the flat model, all segments have base=0, G=1 (4KB) and limit=0xFFFFF (1M). In this case, virtual address to physical address mapping is one-to-one. A 32-bit virtual address is an offset from 0, so it's also a physical address. A special usage of the flat model is for paging. Before enabling the paging hardware, all segments are set to the maximum size so that the linear address range is 4 GB.

Protected flat model: In the protected flat model, segments are mapped to existing memory by setting the size limit to available physical memory. Any attempt to access memory outside the segment limit will generate a protection error.

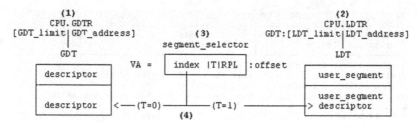

Fig. 14.3 Address translation in segmentation

Multi-segment model: In the multi-segment model, a program may use all the segment registers to access up to 6 protected segments.

Figure 14.3 shows the CPU's address translation and memory protection scheme in segmentation, which is explained by the labels (1) to (4).

(1). The CPU's GDTR register contains a GDT descriptor=[GDT_limit |GDT_address]. The GDT contains 8-byte global segment descriptors. Each segment descriptor has a 32-bit base address, a size limit and a 2-bit privilege level.

(2). Like the GDT, the LDT also contains 8-byte local segment descriptors. Unlike the GDT, which can be located anywhere in memory, the LDT descriptor must be placed in the GDT and load LDTR with its selector in the GDT.

(3). A virtual address VA=[16-bit segment_selector: 32-bit offset].

(4). The 13-bit index is used to access a segment descriptor in either the GDT (T=0) or LDT (T=1). A program executes at the privilege level (CPL) of its code segment selector. When a program uses a selector (RPL) to access a data segment descriptor (DPL), the CPU checks privilege by max(CPL, RPL)<=DPL. If the intended access passes the privilege checking, the physical address PA=segment_base+offset, which must be within the segment limit. A stack segment is a R|W data segment in which the segment type's E bit is set for expand-down and a PA in a stack segment must be greater than the segment limit. As in 16-bit real mode, we shall not use stack segments due to constraints of pointer variables in C.

In general, a program executes in code segments of the same privilege level. It may call procedures in a conforming code segment of higher privilege level but executes at the privilege level of the original program. This feature allows user mode programs to call shared procedures in kernel's conforming code segments. A program can only transfer control to a non-conforming code segment of higher privilege level through gates in the Interrupt Descriptor Table (IDT). For MTX in protected mode, we shall assume two privilege levels and use only non-conforming code segments, which prevent user mode programs from executing kernel code directly.

Fig. 14.4 Linear address
under paging

```
31            22 21           12 11              0
|----10----|----10----|------12-----|
|  pageDir | pageTable |    offset    |
```

14.2.2   Paging

In protected mode, memory can also be managed by paging. In the x86 CPU, paging is implemented on top of segmentation. A logical address is first mapped by segmentation to a linear address. If paging is not enabled, the linear address is also the physical address. If paging is enabled, the linear address is further mapped by the CPU's paging hardware to a physical address. In most paging systems, the term paging refers to pure paging, which does not have any notion of segments. Most Unix-like systems use pure paging. In the x86 CPU, there is no way to disable segmentation but there is a way to get around it. When using paging, we first set up a flat segment model in which all the segments are 4 GB in size. This makes the linear address range from 0 to 4 GB, which effectively hides the segmentation layer, making it transparent. Then we set up page tables and turn on paging. With paging enabled, a 32-bit linear address is treated by the CPU's memory Management Unit (MMU) as a triple = [pageDir, pageTable, offset], as shown in Fig. 14.4.

14.2.2.1   Page Directory and Page Tables

In a linear address, pageDir refers to an entry in a level-1 page table, pageTable refers to an entry in a level-2 page table and offset is the relative address in the page. Normal page size is 4KB. With Page Size Extension (PSE), some x86 CPUs also support super page size of 4 MB. When using paging the MMU first uses the control register CR3 to locate the page directory, which is the level-1 page table. Each page table entry has the format shown in Fig. 14.5.

```
31---------------------------12|11-----------------------0
 page frame address (31-12)  |AVAIL|0 0 D A P P U R P
                                         C W / /
                                         D T S W
```

P=1 if page present; 0 if not; R/W=read(0) or write(1);
U/S=user(1)/system(0); PWT=page write transparent;
PCD=page cache disable; A(1)=accessed, D(1)=dirty or modified
AVIAL=available for systems programmer use

Fig. 14.5 Page table entry format

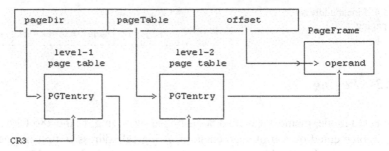

Fig. 14.6 Address translation in paging

14.2.2.2 Address Translation in Paging

Figure 14.6 depicts the address translation procedure of paging. The CPU's CR3 points to the level-1 page table. Given a linear address, the MMU first uses the 10-bit pageDir to locate an entry in the level-1 page table. Assume that the directory page table entry is present and the access checking is OK. It uses the 20-bit page frame address of the page table entry to locate the level-2 page table. Then it uses the 10-bit pageTable to locate the entry in the level-2 page table. Assume that the page entry is present and access checking is OK also. The level-2 page table entry contains the page frame address in memory. The final physical address is PA = (page frame address ≪ 12) + offset. Since paging usually relies on the flat segment model, protection by checking segment limits no longer makes sense. With paging, protection is enforced by the individual page table entries. A page is either present or not present. Attempt to access a non-present page generates a page fault. In addition, a page table entry can be marked as either read-only or writeable. Attempt to write to a read-only page also generates a page fault. The access (A) and dirty (D) bits can be used to implement page replacement in demand-paging.

14.2.2.3 Translation Lookaside Buffer (TLB)

In order to speed up the paging translation process, the CPU stores the most recently used page table entries in an internal cache, called the TLB. Most paging is performed by using the contents of the TLB. Bus cycles are performed only when a new page is used. Whenever the page tables are changed, the OS kernel must flush the TLB to prevent it from using old page entries in the TLB. Flushing the TLB can be done by reloading the CR3 control register. Individual entries in the TLB can also be flushed by the INVPLG instruction.

14.2.2.4 Full Paging

The simplest paging scheme is full paging. In this scheme, all the pages of a process image are allocated physical page frames at once. After loading a process image into page frames, the pages are always present. The full paging scheme can be either static or dynamic, depending on how page frames are allocated. In static paging, each image is allocated a single piece of contiguous physical memory aligned to a page boundary. The memory area is divided into a sequence of page frames, which are used as page table entries. The main advantage of static paging is that it is extremely easy to implement. First, process images can be managed as variable-sized partitions by the simple first-fit algorithm. Second, it is very easy to construct the page tables since all the page frames are contiguous. Third, there is no need to maintain a separate data structure to manage free page frames. In dynamic paging, the pages of an image are allocated dynamically. The main advantage of this scheme is that an image can be loaded to any available page frames, which do not have to be contiguous.

14.2.2.5   Demand-Paging

In demand-paging, the page tables of a process image are built by the image size, but not all the pages are allocated page frames. The pages which do not have page frames are marked as not present. The frame address in an absent page table entry may point to its location in a physical device, e.g. a block number in a swap disk containing the page image. During execution, when a process attempts to reference a page that is not present, it generates a page fault, which traps to the OS kernel. The OS kernel's page fault handler can allocate a page frame for the page, load the missing page into the page frame and change the page table entry to present. Then it lets the process continue with the valid page table entry. Demand-paging is the basis of virtual memory, in which the virtual address space of a process can be much larger than the physical memory allocated to it.

14.3   Interrupt and Exception Processing

14.3.1   Exceptions in Protected Mode

Interrupt and exception processing in protect mode differ from that of real mode in two areas. First, the first 32 interrupt vectors are reserved for exceptions, which are listed in Fig. 14.7. The exception vectors overlap with the traditional interrupt vectors of IRQ0 to IRQ7 (0x08 to 0x0F). The IRQ vectors must be remapped to different locations. Second, the exception vectors are no longer in the low 1KB memory area as in real mode. Instead, they are defined as interrupt descriptors in an Interrupt Descriptor Table (IDT).

Exception	Description
0x00	Divide error:
0x01	Single-step/debug exception:
0x02	Non-maskable interrupt:
0x03	Breakpoint by INT 3 instruction
0x04	Overflow
0x05	Bounds check
0x06	Invalid opcode
0x07	Coprocessor not available
0x08	Double fault
0x09	Coprocessor segment overrun
0x0A	Invalid TSS
0x0B	Segment not present
0x0C	Stack exception
0x0D	General protection violation
0x0E	Page fault
0x0F	(Reserved)
0x10	Coprocessor error
0x11-0x1F	(Reserved)

Fig. 14.7 Exception Vectors in Protected Mode

14.3.2 Interrupt Descriptor Table (IDT)

The IDT is a data structure containing interrupt and trap gates. It is pointed by the CPU's IDTR register. The IDT contents are essentially descriptors but Intel chooses to call them interrupt or trap gates. Figure 14.8 shows the format of an interrupt or trap gate.

where P is the present bit, pL is the privilege level, TYPE=1110 for interrupt gates and 1111 for trap gates. The difference between them is that invoking an interrupt gate automatically disables interrupts but invoking a trap gate does not. Since interrupts and exceptions are processed in kernel mode, the privilege level should be set to 00. It can be set to 11 to allow user mode programs to handle software generated interrupts. For convenience, we define the following prototypes of interrupt and trap gates.

```
u64 int_gate = 0x00008E0000080000; // int  gate(E), seg(08)=Kcode
u64 exe_gate = 0x00008F0000080000; // trap gate(F), seg(08)=Kcode
```

The address fields of the IDT gates can be set to point to the entry points of different exception and interrupt handler functions in the kernel code segment. In addition to interrupt and trap gates, the IDT may also contain call gates and task gates. Calling

63	48	47		32	31	16	15	0
offset (31-16)		PpL-	TYPE	000-	----	seg selector	offset(15-0)	

Fig. 14.8 Format of interrupt/trap gate

```
/************* Contents of TSS **************/
u32 *TSS                       // pointer to next TSS
u32 esp0,ss0;                  // privilege 0 esp, ss
u32 esp1,ss1,esp2,ss2;         // privilege 1,2 esp, ss
u32 CR3
u32 eip,eglags,eax,ecx,edx,ebx,esp,ebp,esi,edi
u32 es,cs,ss,ds,fs,gs          // all in low 2 bytes
u32 ldt, iomap
```

Fig. 14.9 Task state segment

a task or interrupt gate may trigger a task switch by hardware. For MTX in protected mode, we shall not use hardware task switch for the following reasons. First, task switch involves much more than just switching the hardware context of tasks. Second, software task switch is more flexible since it is under the direct control of the OS designer. Last but not least, hardware task switch is only supported in 32-bit CPUs. It is no longer supported in 64-bit x86 CPUs. For MTX in protected mode, we only use TSS to define the process kernel mode stack. To do this, we define a TSS in the PROC structure, place the TSS descriptor in the GDT and let CPU's Task Register (TR) point to the TSS descriptor in the GDT. Figure 14.9 shows the TSS data structure.

14.3.3   Task State Segment (TSS)

In the TSS structure, the fields from eip to gs are saved CPU registers during hardware task switch. Since we assume only two privilege levels without hardware task switching, the most important fields are esp0 and ss0, which define the CPU's interrupt stack. When an interrupt or exception occurs, the CPU automatically uses [ss0:esp0] as the interrupt stack. Therefore, [ss0:esp0] must point to the kernel mode stack of the current running process. The following discussions help clarify this important point.

14.3.4   TSS and Process Interrupt Stack

Assume that the CPU is executing a process in user mode. At this moment, the process kernel mode stack is empty. The CPU's TR register points to a TSS selector in the GDT, which points to the process TSS, in which [ss0:esp0] points to the (high end of) the process kernel stack, as shown in the following diagram.

```
TR->GDT.TSS->PROC.TSS   hi           PROC.kstack[ ]                low
---------   -------------------------------------
            [ss0:ssp0]->| (emtpy kernel mode stack)
            -------------------------------------
```

When an interrupt occurs, the CPU saves uSS, uSP, uflags, uCS, ueip into the interrupt stack, which becomes

```
TR->GDT.TSS->PROC.TSS    hi                         esp          low
---------   ----------------------  |---------------
            [ss0:ssp0]->|uSS|uesp|uflag|uCS|ueip|
            --------------------------------------
```

where the prefix u denotes user mode registers and the saved uSS, uesp are user mode stack at the point of interruption. If an exception occurs in user mode, the situation is exactly the same, except that for some exceptions the CPU also pushes an error number, err#, onto the interrupt stack, which becomes

```
TR->GDT.TSS->PROC.TSS    hi                          esp         low
---------   -------------------------  |------------
            [ss0:ssp0]->|uSS|uesp|uflag|uCS|ueip|err#|
                        ---------------------------------------
```

While in kernel mode, if another interrupt or exception occurs, the CPU continues to use the same interrupt stack to push one more layer of interrupted context. If the CPU is already in kernel mode, re-enter kernel mode does not involve privilege change. In this case, the saved context only has the kernel mode |kflags|kCS|keip|, as shown in the next diagram.

```
TR->GDT.TSS->PROC.TSS    hi                                    | INT:---> esp|
---------   ---------------------------------------------|--
            [ss0:ssp0]->|uSS|uesp|uflag|uCS|ueip|err#|....|kflag|kCS|keip
                        ---------------------------------------------------
```

When return from an interrupt/exception handler, the iret operation supports several different types of actions in general. We only consider the relevant case of two privilege levels without hardware task switch. In this case, iret checks the CPLs of the current and the next code segments. If the CPLs are the same, i.e. from kernel back to kernel, it only pops the saved kernel mode registers [keip, kCS,kflags]. If the CPL of the next code segment is greater, i.e. from kernel back to user mode, it pops the saved user mode registers, which includes the saved uesp and uSS.

14.3.5   Process Kernel Stack in Protected Mode

(1). Context switching: As in real mode, context switching in protected mode MTX is also by tswitch(), which is shown below in 32-bit pseudo assembly code.

```
tswitch:
            cli
ENTRY:      pushl   %eax,%ebx,%ecx,%edx,%ebp,%esi,%edi # may use pushal
            pushfl
            movl    running, %ebx     # save Kmode esp in PROC.ksp
            movl    %esp, 4(%ebx)
FIND:       call    scheduler         # find next running PROC
RESMUE:     movl    running, %ebx
            movl    4(%ebx),%esp      # restore running's Kmode esp
            popfl
            popl    %edi,%esi,%ebp,%edx,%ecx,%ebx,%eax # may use popal
            sti
            ret
```

As in real mode, there is no need to save kernel mode segment registers in tswitch() since they are always the same. Corresponding to the ENTRY and RESUME code of tswitch(), the kernel stack frame for a process to resume running is of the form

```
                                         |<-saved PROC.ksp
            |kPC|kax|kbx|kcx|kdx|kbp|ksi|kdi|kflag|
            |<------ for RESUME in tswitch()------|
```

(2). Entry and exit code of interrupt handlers: As in real mode, the entry points of interrupt handlers, including system call, are also defined by an INTH macro, which is shown below in pseudo code.

```
.MACRO INTH handler
    pushl   %eax,%ebx,%ecx,%edx,%ebp,%esi,%edi,%ds,%es,%fs,%gs
    set     %ds,%es,%fs,%gs to KERNEL DS_SELECTOR
    movl    running, %ebx    # ebx -> running PROC
    incl    8(%ebx)          # PROC.inkmode++;
    call    handler          # call handler() in C
    jmp     ireturn
.ENDM
```

Entry points of interrupt handlers are installed as calls to the INTH macro, e.g

```
    int80h: INTH   kcinth      # system call handler
    tinth:  INTH   thandler    # timer interrupt handler, etc.
```

Each interrupt handler calls a handler function in C, which actually handles the interrupt. When the C handler function finishes, it issues EOI and returns to execute the ireturn/goUmode code. If the interrupt occurred in kernel mode, the process restores saved CPU registers and IRET back to the point of interruption directly. Otherwise, it handles signal first and may switch process before returning to user mode. The following shows the pseudo code of ireturn/goUmode.

```
ireturn/goUmode:
      cli
      movl    running, %ebx
      decl    8(%ebx)                    # PROC.inkmode--;
      jg      xkmode
      call    kpsig                      # handle signal before return to Umode
      call    reschedule                 # call reschedule(); may switch process
xkmode:
      popl    %gs,%fs,%es,%ds,%edi,%esi,%ebp,%edx,%ecx,%ebx,%eax
      iret
```

As in real mode, we use a PROC.inkmode counter to keep track of the number of times a process enters kernel mode. In real mode, when a process issues a system call, the CPU saves [uflag, uCS, uPC] in the process user mode stack. The entry code of the interrupt handler, int80h(), continues to save other CPU registers, also in user mode stack. When the system call handler finishes, the process returns to user mode by the interrupt stack frame in the user mode stack. The situation changes only slightly in protected mode. Instead of the user mode stack, all the stack frames are in the process kernel mode stack. In protected mode, we shall implement syscall by INT 0x80, same as in Linux and xv6. When a process issues a syscall, the CPU saves [uSS, usp, uflag, uCS, uPC] into the process kernel stack, which becomes

```
TR->GDT.TSS->PROC.TSS      high                 esp              low
  ----------        --------------------|-----------------
     [ss0:ssp0] -> |uSS|usp|uflag|uCS|uPC|
                    -------------------------------------
```

The syscall handler entry code, int80h(), continues to save other CPU registers in the process kernel stack, which becomes

```
high                                                                    esp
-----------------------------------------------------------------|----
|uSS|usp|uflag|uCS|uPC|uax|ubx|ucx|udx|ubp|usi|udi|uDS|uES|uFS|uGS|
-----------------------------------------------------------------------
|--- by INT 0x80----->|-------------- by int80h()---------------->|..
```

While in kernel mode, if the process gives up CPU by calling tswitch(), it adds a resume stack frame to the top of the process kernel stack. Therefore, to let a process return to user mode immediately when it resumes running, we can set up its kernel stack to contain two frames; an interrupt stack frame as shown above, followed by a resume stack frame, as shown below.

```
              |goUmode|kax|kbx|kcx|kdx|kbp|ksi|kdi|kflag|
              |<-------- for RESUME in tswitch()  --|-->|
                                              PROC.ksp
```

This technique will be used in all versions of MTX in protected mode.

14.4   GCC in 32-bit Mode

For MTX in 32-bit protected mode, we shall use GCC's assembler, compiler and linker to generate 32-bit code. In 32-bit Linux, GCC generates 32-bit code by default. In 64-bit Linux, use gcc –m32 to generate 32-bit code.

14.4.1   Inline Assembly

The C compiler of GCC supports inline assembly, which is often used in OS kernel code for convenience. The basic format of inline assembly is

> __asm__("assembly code"); or simply asm("assembly code");

If the assembly code has more than one line, the statements can be separated by \n\t ; as in

> asm("movl %eax, %ebx\n\t; addl $10,%eax\n\t");

Inline assembly code can also specify operands. The template of such inline assembly code is

> asm (assembler template
>   : output operands
>   : input operands
>   : list of clobbered registers
>   );

The assembly statements may specify output and input operands, which are referenced as %0, %1. For example, in the following code segment,

```
int a, b=10;
asm("movl %1,%%eax; movl %%eax,%0;"   // use %%REG for registers
    :"=r"(a)                          // output MUST have =
    :"r"(b)                           // input
    :"%eax"                           // clobbered registers
   );
```

%0 refers to a, %1 refers to b, %%eax refers to the eax register. The constraint operator "r" means to use a register for the operand. The above code is equivalent to
    "movl b, %eax\n\t; movl %eax, a";
    It also tells the GCC compiler that the eax register will be clobbered by the inline code. Although we may insert fairly complex inline assembly code in a C program, overdoing it may compromise the readability of the program. In practice, inline assembly should be used only if the code is very short, e.g. a single assembly

instruction or the intended operation involves a CPU control register. In such cases, inline assembly code is not only clear but also more efficient than calling an assembly function.

14.4.2   Constant, Volatile and Packed Attributes

In a C program, variables or function parameters that are intended for read-only can be declared with a const qualifier to prevent them from being modified accidentally. If the program code tries to modify a const item, it will be detected as an error at compile-time. For static constants, such as the strings in char *p="abcd"; printf("%d %s\n", ...); etc. the C compiler usually puts them in a read-only data section. During execution, trying to write to read-only memory will generate a segmentation fault. The GCC is an optimizing compiler. When writing device drivers, interrupt handlers or multi-thread C code, it is often necessary to declare variables as volatile, which prevents the GCC compiler from optimizing the code involving such variables. Likewise, the packed attribute of a C structure tells the GCC compiler not to pad the structure with extra bytes for memory alignment.

14.4.3   GCC Linker and Executable File Format

GCC's linker can generate executable files in several different formats. In Linux, the default executable file format is ELF (Tool 1995; Youngdale 1995), which is better suited to dynamic linking. Since MTX does not yet support dynamic linking, we shall use ELF format for statically linked files only.

(1). Linker Script: A linker script is a text file which specifies linking options to the linker. Its usage is

ld -T ld.script [other linker flags]

As an example, the following shows a simple linker script, which may be used to generate either flat binary or ELF executable files.

```
/************** ld.script **************/
OUTPUT_FORMAT("binary")
/* OUTP UT_FORMAT("elf32  -linux") */
OUTPUT_ARCH(i386)
ENTRY(u_entry)
SECTIONS
{ . = 0x0;   /* change this if begin VA is not 0 */
    .text : { *(.text) }
    .data : { *(.data) }
    .bss  : { *(.bss)  }
}
```

A flat binary executable file is a single piece of binary code, which does not have separate code and data sections. By changing the output file format to "elf32-linux", the linker will generate an ELF executable file. For this example, the resulting ELF file has only one (loadable) program section. If desired, the linker script can be modified to generate an ELF executable with separate code, data and bss sections, as in

```
SECTIONS
{ . = 0x0;
  .text : { *(.text) }
  . = 0x8000;
  .data : { *(.  data) }
  . = 0xC000;
  .bss  : { *(.bss)  }
}
```

The resulting ELF file will have separate code, data and bss sections, each with a different starting virtual address.

(2). ELF executable file format: An ELF executable file begins with an elf-header, followed by one or more program section headers, which are defined as

```
struct elfhdr {    // ELF File header
    u32 magic;       // ELF_MAGIC 0x464C457F
    u8  elf[12];
    u16 type;
    u16 machine;
    u32 version;
    u32 entry ;
    u32 phoffset;    // byte offset of program header
    u32 shoffset;    // byte offset of sections
    u32 flags;
    u16 ehsize;      // elf header size
    u16 phentsize;   // program header size
    u16 phnum;       // number of program section headers
    u16  shentsize;
    u16 shnum;
    u16 shstrndx;
};
// ELF Program section header
struct proghdr {
    u32 type;        // 1 = loadable image
    u32 offset;      // byte offset of program section
    u32 vaddr;       // virtual address
    u32 paddr;       // physical ad     dress
    u32 filesize;    // number of bytes of program section
    u32 memsize;     // load memory size
    u32 flags;       // R|W|Ex flags
    u32 align;       // alignment
};
```

(3). ELF executable file loader: When loading an ELF file the loader must load the various sections of an ELF file to their specified virtual addresses. In addition, each loaded section should be marked with appropriate R|W|Ex attributes for protection.

For example, the code section pages should be marked as REx, data section pages should be marked as RW, etc.

(4). Program Loader in Protected Mode: The program loader of MTX in protected mode can load either flat binary or ELF image files. The loader's algorithm is as follows.

```
/***************   Loader Algor ithm  ********************/
   Open the image file for read (Use MTX's internal open)
   Read the elf -header to check whether it's an ELF file;
   if (!ELF){ // assume flat BINARY file
       determine file size; (by MTX's internal kfdsize())
       load file contents to process image area;
       return;
   }
   /********** ELF file *************/
   locate program header(s);
   for each program header do{
       get section's offset, loading address and memory size;
       load section to virtual address until memory size;
       set section's R|W|Ex attributes in loaded pages;
   }
```

In summary, for protected mode operations we must set up the GDT, remap IRQ vectors, install interrupt and exception handlers in the IDT and define CPU's interrupt stack by a TSS in the GDT. As in real mode, knowing the kernel mode stack contents is essential to understanding how to set up process for execution in protected mode. In the following sections, we shall describe the design and implementation of MTX in 32-bit protected mode. In order to illustrate the different capabilities of the PC's memory management hardware, we shall present three different versions of MTX in 32-bit protect mode, each uses a distinct memory management scheme. The three versions of MTX in 32-bit protected mode are

> MTX32.1, which uses protected segments.
>
> MTX32.2, which uses static paging.
>
> PMTX, which uses dynamic paging.

Among these, MTX32.1 and MTX32.2 are intended for demonstration only. PMTX is the final version of MTX in 32-bit protected mode for uniprocessor systems.

14.5   MTX Kernel in 32-bit Protected Mode

The kernel source tree of MTX in 32-bit protected mode is organized as

```
                      |-- SETUP  : boot.s, setup.s, apentry.s
      MTX_kernel--|--kernel    : kernel files
                  |--fs        : file system
                  |--driver    : device drivers
```

Each directory has a Makefile for GCC's compiler and linker. The top level Makefile invokes the Makefile of kernel, which in turn invokes those of fs and driver to generate the various objects code files. The object code files are linked by GCC's ld linker to generate a flat binary executable, which is the 32-bit MTX kernel. Then a sh script is used to assemble the binary files of BOOT, SETUP, APentry and MTX kernel into a bootable MTX image consisting of the following pieces.

```
    Sector | 0  |  1  |  2    3   | 4 ......................|
           ------------------------------------------------------
           |BOOT|SETUP|  APentry  | 32-bit MTX kernel ......|
           ------------------------------------------------------
```

In the bootable image, BOOT is for booting the MTX kernel image from a floppy disk. In protected mode, it is used as a communication area between the booter and kernel. SETUP is for transition from 16-bit real mode to protect mode and APentry is the startup code of non-boot processors in SMP mode (SMP MTX is covered in Chap. 15). When installed to a hard disk partition, the entire bootable image is a file,/boot/mtx, in an EXT2/3 file system. A suitable hard disk booter, e.g. the hd-booter developed in Chap. 3 of this book, is needed to boot up the MTX kernel. The booting sequence is similar to booting Linux as described in Chap. 3.

14.5.1   Protected Mode MTX Kernel Startup Sequence

(1). Hd-booter: During booting, the hd-booter loads BOOT+SETUP to 0x90000, APentry to 0x91000 and the MTX kernel to 0x10000. It also writes some boot parameters, such as Time-of-Day (TOD) of BIOS, the boot device number and the start sector of the boot partition, etc. to the BOOT sector for the kernel to use. Then it checks the boot signature at the end of the BOOT sector. If the word is 'RR', it jumps to 0x10000 to run MTX in 16-bit real mode. If the word is 'PP', it jumps to 0x90200 to run SETUP, which brings up MTX in 32-bit protected mode.

(2). SETUP: SETUP is a piece of 16-bit and 32-bit mode code in GCC assembly. It sets up an initial GDT containing 4 GB code and data segments and enters protected mode. Then it moves the MTX kernel to 1 MB (0x100000) and jumps to the entry address of the MTX kernel. The actions of SETUP are identical for all 32-bit MTX. Their only difference is in the number of segments in the initial GDT. During booting, SETUP serves as a transition stage from 16-bit real mode to 32-bit protected mode. Since the transition is crucial, we show the entire SETUP code of MTX32.1 and explain the steps in detail.

```
#--------------- setup.s file for MTX32.1 --------------------------
            .text
            .set KCODE,    0x08      # kernel code segment selector
            .set KDATA,    0x10      # kernel data segment selector
            .set K_ORG,    0x10000   # MTX kernel loaded here by booter
            .set K_HIM,    0x100000  # MTX kernel running address (1MB)
            .set GDT_ADDR,0x9F000    # hard coded GDT address
            .set GDT_SZIE 40         # GDT size in bytes
            .org 0
.code16  # 16-bit code
# set segments registers cs,ds,ss=0x9020, stack size=8KB
            ljmp  $0x9020, $go
go:         movw  %cs, %ax
            movw  %ax, %ds           # ds = 0x9020
            movw  %ax, %ss           # stack segment = 0x9020
            movw  $8192,%sp          # 8KB stack size
# mov setup_gdt to GDT_ADDR=0x9F000
            movw  $GDT_ADDR>>4,%ax
            movw  %ax, %es
            movw  $gdt,%si
            xorw  %di, %di
            movw  $GDT_SIZE>>2,%cx
            rep
            movsl
# load GDTR with gdt_desc = [GDT_limit|GDT_ADDR]
            lgdt  gdt_desc
# enter protected mode by writing 1 to CR0
            cli
            movl  %cr0,%eax
            orl   $0x1,%eax
            movl  %eax,%cr0
# do a "ljmp" to flush instruction pipeline and set CS to KCODE
            .byte 0x66, 0xea         # prefix + ljmp-opcode
            .long 0x90200+next       # SETUP is at 0x90200
            .word KCODE              # CS selector
# the handcrafted ljmp is equivalent to ljmpl of GCC's 32-bit assembly
#           ljmpl $KCODE,$(0x90200+next)

.code32  # 32-bit code
next: # load other selectors with 0x10 for kernel data entry in GDT
            movl  $KDATA,%eax
            movw  %ax,    %ds
            movw  %ax,    %es
            movw  %ax,    %fs
            movw  %ax,    %gs
            movw  %ax,    %ss
# move MTX kernel from 0x10000 to 0x100000, then jump to 0x100000
            cld
            movl  $K_ORG,%esi
            movl  $K_HIM,%edi
            movl  $1024*64,%ecx      # assume MTX kernel < 256KB
            rep
            movsl
            ljmp  $KCODE,$K_HIM      # ljmp to 0x08:0x100000
gdt:        .quad 0x0000000000000000 # null descriptor
            .quad 0x00CF9A000000FFFF # kernel cs
            .quad 0x00CF92000000FFFF # kernel ds
            .quad 0x0000000000000000 # task tss
            .quad 0x0000000000000000 # task ldt
gdt_desc: .word .-gdt-1
            .long GDT_ADDR # hard coded at 0x9F000; can be changed
            .org 512
#------------- end of setup.s file ----------------------------------
```

Upon entry, SETUP begins execution in 16-bit real mode. First, it initializes the CPU's execution environment by setting the segment registers CS, DS, SS to 0x9020 and SP to 8 KB. For MTX32.1, which uses protected segments, SETUP defines an initial GDT containing 5 entries, in which only the kernel code and data segments are initialized as 4 GB segments. It moves the initial GDT to a known physical address, GDT_ADDR=0x9F000, and loads the GTDR with the 6-byte GDT descriptor at gdt_desc. Then it enters protected mode by setting bit 0 of control register CR0 to 1. Then it executes a handcrafted ljmp to flush the instruction pipeline, preventing the CPU from executing any stale 16-bit code. The ljmp also loads the CS register with KCODE=0x08, which refers to the kernel code segment descriptor in the GDT. The handcrafted ljmp instruction is equivalent to

```
ljmpl $KCODE, $(0x90200+next)
```

which is supported by GCC's assembler. Then it loads other segment registers, ds to gs, with KDATA=0x10, which refer to the data segment descriptor in the GDT. The CPU is now executing 32-bit code in protected mode, and it can access the entire physical memory via segmentation. It moves the MTX kernel from 0x10000 to 0x100000 (1 MB). Finally it ljmp to [0x08: 0x100000], which sends the CPU to pmode_entry in the MTX kernel. In both MTX32.1 and MTX32.2, the kernel's starting address is 0x100000 (1 MB), which is directly accessible via segmentation. Therefore, their entry.s file is very simple.

(2). entry.s file:
```
            .global pmode_entry
            .extern p0stack    # high end address of proc[0].kstack
            .org 0             # virtual address=0x100000 (1MB)
pmode_entry:    .code32
            cli
            movl p0stack,%esp # set stack pointer to P0's kstack
            call init
```

pmode_entry is the entry point of the MTX kernel and p0stack is the high end address of proc[0].kstack. It sets the stack pointer to p0stack and calls init() in init.c. (3). init.c: The following shows the init() function of mtx32.1.

```
/********************* init.c file *********************/
#include "include.h"                    // extern symbols in MTX kernel
int init()
{   vid_init();                         // initialize display driver
    printf("Welcome to MTX in 32-bit Protected Mode\n");
    kernel_init(); // initialize kernel data structs, create and run P0
    // ---------- initialize IRQ and IDT -------------------
    printf("remap IRQs; install IDT vectors\n");
    remap_IRQ();                        // remap IRQ0-15 to 0x20-0x2F
    trap_install();                     // install trap handlers
    printf("install interrupt vectors and handlers\n");
    int_install(0x20, (int)tinth);      // timer IRQ was   0
    int_install(0x21, (int)kbinth);     // KBD   IRQ was   1
    int_install(0x23, (int)slinth);     // serial port 1   3
    int_install(0x24, (int)s0inth);     // serial port 0   4
    int_install(0x26, (int)fdinth);     // FD IRQ was      6
    int_install(0x27, (int)printh);     // printer IRQ was 7
    int_install(0x2E, (int)hdinth);     // IDE0 was IRQ   14
    int_install(0x2F, (int)cdinth);     // IDE1 was IRQ   15
    int_install(0x80, (int)int80h);     // syscall  =    0x80

    //----------------------------------------------------------
    printf("initialize I/O buffers and device drivers\n");
    binit();                  // I/O buffers
    fd_init(); hd_init(); kb_init(); serial_init(); etc.
    timer_init();             // timer; 8-byte BIOS TOD at 0x90000
    fs_init();                // initialize FS and mount root FS
    running->res->cwd = root; // set P0's CWD to root
    main();                   // call main() in t.c
}
```

Init() first initializes the display driver to make printf work. It calls kernel_init() to initialize the kernel data structures, create and run the initial process P0. Then it remaps IRQs, sets up the IDT and installs exception and interrupt vectors and handlers. Besides memory management, this is the second major difference between protected mode and real mode. Since these steps are needed for all protected mode operations, regardless of the memory management scheme used, we shall explain the steps once in detail.

14.5.2   Interrupt and Exception Processing

14.5.2.1   Remap IRQ Vectors

The interrupt vectors of IRQ 0-15 are remapped to 0x20-0x2F by programming the 8259 PICs.

```
#define PIC1 0x20          // master PIC controller register
#define PIC2 0xA0          // slave  PIC controller register
#define ICW1 0x11          // command word 1
#define ICW4 0x01          // command word 4
void remap_IRQ(int irq0, int irq8)
{
   out_byte(PIC1, ICW1);    // write ICW1 to both PICs command regs
   out_byte(PIC2, ICW1);
   out_byte(PIC1+1, irq0); // write ICW2 to both PICs data register
   out_byte(PIC2+1, irq8);
   out_byte(PIC1+1, 4) ;    // write ICW3 for cascaded PICs
   out_byte(PIC2+1, 2);
   out_byte(PIC1+1, ICW4); // write ICW4 for 8086 architecture
   out_byte(PIC2+1, ICW4);
}
remap_IRQ(0x20, 0x28);      // remap IRQ0-15 to 0x20-0x2F
```

14.5.2.2   IDT and Exception Handlers

The Interrupt Descriptor Table (IDT) has 256 entries, which requires 256*8 = 2KB space. The IDT can be located anywhere in memory. In MTX32.1 and MTX32.2, it is placed directly after the GDT but aligned to a 16-byte boundary for better CPU data cache efficiency. The CPU's IDTR is loaded with the 6-byte IDT descriptor

```
          -----------------------------------------------------
CPU.IDTR = |u16 size=256*8 -1| u32 address=IDT _ADDR (0x9F040) |
          -----------------------------------------------------
```

The IDT must be set up properly before the CPU can accept interrupts or handle exceptions. The steps to set up the IDT entries are as follows.

(1). IDT and Exception Handlers: The first 32 IDT entries are filled with trap gates, each points to the entry address of an exception or trap handler function.

(a). Exception Handler Entry Points: Among the 32 exceptions, some exceptions generate an error number on the interrupt stack while others do not. In order to generate appropriate entry code for different exception handlers, we define the macros, ECODE and NOECODE, which take a vector number n = 0x00 to 0x1F as parameter.

```
        .MACRO   ECODE n        # for exceptions with error number
          .global trap\n
  trap\n:  pushl   $\n            # push vector number
           jmp     trap_all
        .ENDM

        .MACRO NOECODE n         # for exceptions without error number
          .global trap\n
  trap\n:  pushl   $0             # push a 0 as error number
           pushl   $\n            # push vector number
           jmp     trap_all
        .ENDM
```

In both macros, trap_all is a piece of assembly code common to all exception handlers. For each exception vector number, 0x00 to 0x1F, call the macro ECODE or NOECODE, depending on whether the exception generates an error number or not. For example, for the vector 0x00, which corresponds to divide error, call NOECODE 0x00 because it does not generate an error number. For the vector 0x0E, which corresponds to page fault, call ECODE 0x0E because it generates an error number, etc. These macro calls generate the entry points labeled trap0x00 to trap0x1F, which are the contents of the trapEntry[ ] table.

```
int (*trapEntry[ ])() =
{ /****************** 32 trap/fault entryPoints ********************/
trap0x00,trap0x01,trap0x02,trap0x03,trap0x04,trap0x05,trap0x06,trap0x07,
trap0x08,trap0x09,trap0x0A,trap0x0B,trap0x0C,trap0x0D,trap0x0E,trap0x0F,
trap0x10,trap0x11,trap0x12,trap0x13,trap0x14,trap0x15,trap0x16,trap0x17,
trap0x18,trap0x19,trap0x1A,trap0x1B,trap0x1C,trap0x1D,trap0x1E,trap0x1F
};
```

In the IDT, the first 32 trap gates point to the entry points of trap handlers. The remaining 224 entries are filled with a default trap gate. This is done by trap_install(), which calls trap_entry() to install trap handlers in the IDT. It also loads the IDTR pointing to the IDT.

```
/************** set interrupt/trap gates in IDT *****************/
struct idt_descr{        // to be loaded into CPU's IDTR
        u16 length;
        u32 address;
} __attribute__((packed)) idt_descr = {256*8-1, IDT_ADDR};

void trap_entry(int index, u32 entryPoint)
{
    u64 idt_gate = 0x00008F0000080000ULL; // 8F:DPL=0,TRAP gate, 8=KCODE
    u64 addr = (u64)entryPoint;
    idt_gate |= (addr<<32) & 0xffff000000000000ULL;
    idt_gate |= addr & 0xffff;
    idt[index] = idt_gate;
}
void trap_install()
{  int i;
    for (i=0; i<32; i++)                        // 32 exception vectors
        trap_entry(i, (int)(trapEntry[i]));
    for (i=32; i<256; i++)                      // fill rest with default
        trap_entry(i, (int)default_trap);
    asm("lidt %0\n\t"::"m"(idt_descr));         // load CPU's IDTR
}
```

(b). All exception handlers jump to the same assembly code, trap_all, which is

```
trap_all:
                pushal        # save all CPU registers in stack
                pushl  %ds  # save seg registers, may be of Umode
                pushl  %es
                pushl  %fs
                pushl  %gs
                pushl  %ss
                # change to kernel data segments
                movw   $KDATA,%ax
                movw   %ax, %ds
                movw   %ax, %es
                movw   %ax, %fs
                movw   %ax, %gs

HIGH --------- exception stack contents at this moment ------------esp
|oss|osp|oflg|cs|eip|0/err#|nr|ax|cx|dx|bx|esp|bp|si|di|ds|es|fs|gs|ss|
|<----- by exception ----->|  |<----- by pushal ------>| push ds-ss ->|
|                           13 12 11 10  9  8  7  6  5  4  3  2  1  0 |
----------------------------------------------------------------------
                movl   running, %ebx  # ruuning->inkmode++
                incl   8(%ebx)         # inkmode at byte offset 8 in PROC
                movl   52(%esp),%ecx   # get nr at byte offset 4*13=52
# Use nr to call the corresponding handler (*trapHandler[nr])()
                call   *trapHandler(, %ecx, 4) # use 0 + %ecx*4 as index
    ereturn:
                movl   running, %ebx  # running->inkmode--
                decl   8(%ebx) # test whether was in Umode or Kmode
                jg     kreturn # to kreturn if was in Kmode
                call   kpsig   # return to Umode: handle signal first
    kreturn: # return to point of exception; kmode traps never return
                addl $4, %esp       # for %ss
                popl %gs
                popl %fs
                popl %es
                popl %ds
                popal
                addl $8, %esp       # pop vector_nr and err_code
                iret
```

trap_all saves all CPU registers on the interrupt stack and changes data segments to
that of kernel. Then, depending on the vector number nr, which was pushed on the
interrupt stack by entryPoint (at byte offset 4*13=52), it calls the corresponding
handler function in the trapHandler[ ] table.

(c). trapHandler[ ] is a table of function pointers to the entry addresses of 32
exception handler functions, which are defined as divide_error(), general_protec-
tion(), page_fault(), reserved(), etc.

```
int (*trapHandler[ ]) ()= /* exception handler function pointers */
{
  divide_error, debug_exception,  nmi,             breakpoint,
  overflow,       bounds_check,   invalid_opcode, cop_not_avail,
  double_fault, overrun,          invalid_tss,     seg_not_present,
  stack_exception, general_protection, page_fault, reserved,
  floating_point, reserved,       reserved,        reserved,
  reserved,       reserved,       reserved,        reserved,
  reserved,       reserved,       reserved,        reserved,
  reserved,       reserved,       reserved,        reserved
};
```

(d). Signal number: In all Unix-like systems, an exception is converted to a signal
number delivered to the running process. Many exception handler functions share
the same entry code because they are assigned the same signal number. In MTX,
exceptions (traps in Unix term) are converted to signal numbers as follows.

```
                # all these traps in Umode get the SIGFPE (8) signal
          divide_error: floating_point: cop_not_avail:

                        pushl $0x08  #SIGFPE 8
                        call  ehandler
                        addl  $4,%esp
                        ret
```

all these traps in Umode get the SIGTRAP (5) signal
  debug_exception: nmi:breakpoint: overflow: bounds_check: invalid_opcode:
overrun:

```
        invalid_tss:reserved:
                        pushl $0x05          #SIGTRAP 5
                        call  ehandler
                        addl  $4,%esp
                        ret
```

Treat double_fault as ABORT(6)

```
double_fault:   pushl  $0x06          #SIGABRT 6
                call   ehandler
                addl   $4,%esp
                ret
```

\# consider these as SIGMENTATION FAULTS (11):
   general_protection:seg_not_present:stack_exception: page_fault:

```
                pushl  $0x0B          #SIGSEGV 11
                call   ehandler
                addl   $4,%esp
                ret
```

Each handler function pushes a signal number corresponding to the exception on the interrupt stack and calls ehandler(), which actually handles the exception.

14.5.2.3   The Ultimate Exception Handler in C

The C function, ehandler(), is the ultimate handler of all exceptions. Upon entry, the process interrupt stack contains

```
|SS|SP|FLAG|CS|PC|err/0|nr|ax|cx|dx|bx|sp|bp|si|di|ds|es|fs|gs|ss| retPC  |sig|
|-- by exception -->|entry|---------- by trap_all   ----------->|trap0xYY|
```

Thus, ehnadler() can be written with all the interrupt stack contents as parameters.

```
void ehandler(sig,retPC,ss,gs,fs,es,ds,edi,esi,ebp,esp,ebx,edx,ecx,eax,
     nr,err,eip,cs,eflags,old_esp,old_ss)   //all parameters are u32
{
  if (exception occurred in Umode){
      send signal sig to current running process;
      printf("proc%d trap%d in Umode:sig=%d\n",running->pid,nr,sig);
      setsig(sig);   // send signal sig to running process
  }
  else{              // exception occurred in Kmode
      printf("proc%d kernel PANIC trap=%x\n", nr);
      display CPU registers (parameters) for kernel debugging
      halt();
  }
}
```

In ehandler(), if the exception occurred in user mode, it sends the signal number, sig, to the running process. When the process returns to ereturn: (in trap_all), it checks for signals and handles any pending signal, as described in Chap. 9 on signal processing. The process may return to Umode to continue if it survives the signal processing. If the exception occurred in kernel mode, which must be due to either

```
exception_nr:->IDT[nr]->trapnr:->trap_all:->trapHandler[nr]:sig# ->
   ehandler(sig#, CPU registers, nr, error#, interrupt_point){
           if (trap in Umode)
               send sig# to running process;
           else
               PANIC and halt;
   }
```

Fig. 14.10 Exception processing sequence

a hardware error or most likely a kernel bug, there is nothing the kernel can do. So
it prints a PANIC message, displays the CPU registers for debugging and stops.
The exception processing sequence is rather long and complex, which may be quite
confusing for most beginners. It may help by looking at Fig. 14.10, which depicts
the control flow of the exception processing sequence.

In Fig. 14.10, when an exception of vector nr=0xXY occurs, the CPU uses the
vector number nr to access the trap gate in the IDT, which routes the CPU to the entry
point trap0xXY. In trap0xXY, it pushes a 0 and nr on the stack, if no error number, or
just nr, if the exception generates an error number. Then it jumps to the common code
trap_all, which saves all CPU registers in the interrupt stack. It uses the vector number
nr to call the corresponding handler function in trapHandler[]. trapHandler[nr] pushes
a signal number on the stack and calls the ultimate ehandler() in C. By then the interrupt stack contains all the information about the exception, which can be accessed as
function parameters. In ehandler(), if the exception occurred in Umode, the process
gets a signal number and handles the signal before return to Umode. If the exception
occurred in Kmode, the kernel displays a PANIC message and stops. The logic is quite
simple. The seemingly complexity is because we are trying to set up the exception
handlers in a systematic way, rather than trying to do it one at a time and repeat it 32
times.

14.5.2.4   Interrupt Vectors and Handlers

Interrupt vectors and handlers of I/O devices are installed by int_install(), which is

```
int int_install(int vector, int entryPoint)
{
  u64 int_gate = 0x00008E0000080000ULL; // 8E:DPL=0,INT gates;8=KCODE
  if (vector==0x80)                      // syscall vector
     int_gate = 0x0000EE0000080000ULL;  // EE:DPL=3,INT gate; 8=KCODE
  int_gate |= ((u64)entryPoint <<32) & 0xffff000000000000ULL;
  int_gate |= ((u64)entryPoint) & 0xffff;
  idt[vector] = int_gate;
}
```

For the interrupt vectors 0x20 to 0x2F, the IDT gates are interrupt gates with RPL=0.
For the system call vector 0x80, it is an interrupt gate with RPL=3. It may also be
a trap gate with RPL=3. In that case, interrupts will be enabled during syscall. The
kernel must explicitly disable interrupts in critical regions. As in real mode, interrupt handler entry points, tinth, kbinth, etc. are installed by an INTH macro.

```
.MACRO INTH handler
    pushl %eax    # save CPU registers in    KSTACK; may use pushal
    pushl %ebx
    pushl %ecx
    pushl %edx
    pushl %ebp
    pushl %esi
    pushl %edi
    pushl %ds               # save CPU selectors
    pushl %es
    pushl %fs
    pushl %gs
    movw  $DATA_SEL,%ax   # change to kernel data segments
    movw  %ax,%ds
    movw  %ax,%es
    movw  %ax,%fs
    movw  %ax,%gs
    movl  running,%ebx    # %ebx points to running PROC
    incl  INK(%ebx)       # INK=8: running    ->inkmode++
    call  \handler        #  \handler is a parameter
    jmp   ireturn
.ENDM


# interrupt handler entry points
tinth:  INTH  thandler        # PIC timer
kbinth: INTH  kbhandler       # KBD
# Similarly for other interrupt handlers

ireturn/goUmode:              # return to point of interruption
    cli
    movl  running, %ebx   # %ebx points at running PROC
    decl  INK(%ebx)       # running->inkmode--
    jg    xkmode          # if interrupt occurred in Kmode
    call  kpsig           # before return to Umode, handle signal
    call  reschedule      # switch task if sw_flag is set
xkmode:
    popl  %gs
    popl  %fs
    popl  %es
    popl  %ds
    popl  %edi            # may use popal
    popl  %esi
    popl  %ebp
    popl  %edx
    popl  %ecx
    popl  %ebx
    popl  %eax            # NOTE: eax = syscall return value
    iret
```

Summarizing, we note that remap IRQ, set up the IDT and install exception/interrupt vectors are necessary for all protected mode operations, regardless of the memory management scheme used. The good news is that we only need to set up the IDT once for all protected mode operations.

14.6   MTX32.1: 32-bit Protected Mode MTX Using Segmentation

The first version of 32-bit MTX is MTX32.1, which uses protected segments. In MTX32.1, the PROC structure is modified to contain a TSS and 2 LDT descriptors.

```
typedef struct proc{
    // same as bef ore but ADD these for segmentation:
    TSS tss;              // TSS type in type.h
    u64 ldt[2];          // Umode code and data segments
    u32 kstack[SSIZE];   // PROC kstack must be the last field
} PROC;
```

The TSS defines the process interrupt stack and the LDT descriptors define the user mode code and data segments of a process. In kernel mode, the code and data segments are in the GDT, which are full 4 GB segments. If the system has less than 4 GB physical memory, the kernel segment size can be set to the actual amount of physical memory. In user mode, each process has a fixed size Umode image. The MTX kernel runs at 1 MB. Currently, the run-time size of the MTX.32.1 kernel is less than 1 MB. Assume that the maximum run-time kernel size is 1 MB. Then the memory area above 2 MB is free. We shall allocate process user mode images above 2 MB. User mode images can be generated as either flat binary or ELF executable files. Flat binary executables do not have separate code, data and bss size information. Without the size information, we can only assume a fixed image size, e.g. 2 MB for every Umode image. ELF executable files have size information if they are generated with separate code, data and bss sections. To simplify memory management, we shall assume a fixed image size of 2 MB for ELF files also. The actual image size is much smaller, but allocating a larger memory area causes no harm. Specifically, we shall assume that the Umode image of a process is allocated at pid*2 MB, e.g. P1 at 2 MB, P2 at 4 MB, etc. Since the purpose here is to demonstrate segmentation, these assumptions are not important. If desired, the reader may experiment with different image size and memory layout. The startup sequence of MTX32.1 is as follows.

14.6.1   MTX32.1 Kernel Startup Sequence

(1). SETUP: It defines an initial GDT containing 5 entries. In the initial GDT, the kernel code is a non-conforming code segment, so that user mode processes can only execute kernel code through interrupt or trap gates in the IDT.

```
gdt: .quad  0x0000000000000000    # null descriptor
     .quad  0x00cF9A000000ffff    # kernel cs,0xA=nonconform segment
     .quad  0x00cF92000000ffff    # kernel ds, 0x2=R|W data segment
     .quad  0x0000000000000000    # task tss
     .quad  0x0000000000000000    # task ldt
gdt_desc: .word -gdt-1            #  gdt size 1
         .long  GDT_ADDR          # hard coded as 0x9F000
```

After loading SETUP to 0x90200, the booter jumps to 0x90200 to run SETUP, which begins execution in 16-bit real mode. As described in Sect. 14.5.1, SETUP uses the initial GDT to enter protected mode, move the MTX kernel to 1 MB and ljmp to [0x08:0x100000], which sends the CPU to the entry point, pmode_entry, of the MTX kernel.

(2). entry.s:

pmode_entry sets the stack pointer to P0's kstack high end and calls init() in init.c.

(3).

```
int init()
{
    vid_init();    // initialize display driver
    printf("MTX in 32-bit Protected Mode using Segmentation\n");
    kernel_init(); // initialize kernel, create and run P0
    remap IRQs; install IDT vectors
    initialize I/O buffers and device drivers
    fs_init();    // initialize file system and mount root device
    set P0's CWD to root directory;
    main();       // call main() in t.c
}
```

init() first initializes the display driver to make printf work. It calls kernel_init() to initialize kernel data structures, create and run the initial process P0. Then it remaps the IRQs and sets up the IDT by installing exception and interrupt vectors and handlers, as described in Sect. 14.3.

14.6.2 GDT for Segmentation

In protected mode MTX, the GDT is placed at the location GDT_ADDR=0x9F000, which is 4KB below the ROM area at 0xA0000. The CPU's GDTR is loaded with

$$\text{GDTR} = |\text{u16 limit}=(5*8-1)|\text{u32 GDT\_ADDR}=0x9F000|$$

In the GDT, only the kernel code and data segment descriptors are initialized as 4 GB segments. The TSS and LDT descriptors are initially 0. In kernel_init(), they are set to the TSS and LDT of the initial process P0. During task switch, we switch both TSS and LDT in the GDT to that of the next running process, and load the CPU's TR and LDTR registers with the modified TSS and LDT descriptors. Thus, the TSS and LDT in the GDT always refer to that of the current running process. Figure 14.11 shows the GDT and LDT contents of MTX32.1 during system operation.

The IDT is placed at 0x9F040, which is aligned to a 16-byte boundary for better CPU data cache efficiency. The choice of the GDT and IDT locations are quite arbitrary. If desired, the reader may experiment with other locations for the GDT and IDT. After initializing the system, init() calls main() in t.c. The logic of main() is

```
Index     CPU.GDPR ──────> GDT at 0x9F000

┌─────────────────────────────────────────────────┐
│ 0x00│ null descriptor (required)                  │
│ 0x08│ kernel code descriptor: 4GB segment         │          running PROC:
│ 0x10│ kernel data descriptor: 4GB segment         │     ┌──────────────────────────┐
│ 0x18│ task TSS descriptor    : TSS segment        │ ->  │ TSS.[ss0:esp0]->kstack   │
│ 0x20│ task LDT descriptor    : LDT segment        │ ->  │         LDT              │
└─────────────────────────────────────────────────┘     └──────────────────────────┘
                                                                    │
                                                        ┌───────────┴──────────────┐
                                                    0:  │  user code descriptor    │
                                                    1:  │  user data descriptor    │
                                                        └──────────────────────────┘

K_CODE=[1:T=0|pL=00]=0x08;                     U_CODE=[0:T=1|pL=11]=0x07
K_DATA=[2:T=0|pL=00]=0x10;                     U_DATA=[1:T=1|pL=11]=0x0F
```

Fig. 14.11 GDT and LDT contents of MTX32.1

```
/******************* t.c file logic ********************/
  PROC proc[NPROC+NTHREAD];
  PROC *freeList,*tfreeList,*running,*readyQueue,*sleepList;
  int kernel_init()
  {
     initialize procs,freeList,tfreeList,readyQueue,sleepList;
     create P0 as the initial running process;
     set P0's TSS.[ss0:esp0] = [kernel ds: p0stack high end]
              LDT.[user code, user data] to defaults
     switch_tss(running): set TSS and LDT descriptors in GDT to
                          P0's TSS and LDT; load TR and LDTR
  }
  int main()
  {
     kfork("/bin/init"); // kfork P1 as the INIT process
     unlock();           // allow interrupts
     while(1){           // P0 loops
        if (readyQueue)
             tswitch();  // switch to a ready proc in readyQueue
        else halt();     // hlt; waiting for interrupts
     }
  }
```

14.6.3 Process TSS and LDT

In kernel_init(), it initializes the TSS structure and LDT of P0. Since P0 only runs in
Kmode, it does not need a Umode image, so its LDT entries are set to defaults. Then
it calls switch_tss(), which sets the TSS descriptor in the GDT to point to P0's TSS.
This makes P0's kstack as the initial interrupt stack of the system. The TSS and
LDT of other processes are set up in fork1() when they are created, as shown below.

```
PROC *fork1()
{
    (1). create a new proc pointed by p as in real mode;
    (2). initialize new proc's TSS structure:
         p->tss.esp0 = (u32)&p->kstack[SSIZE];    //interrupt stack
         p->tss.ss0  = KDATA;                      // 0x10
         p->tss.(es, ds, ss, fs, gs) = USER_DATA;  // 0x07
         p->tss.cs   = USER_CODE;                   // 0x0F
         p->tss.ldt  = 0x20;                        // 0x20
         p->tss.iobitmap = 0;
    (3). /* allocate Umode image memory at pid*2MB */
         p->res->paddress = (p->pid)*0x200000;
    (4). set_ldt_entries(p); //set new proc's ldt[ ] entries
         return p;
}
```

The LDT entries of a new process are set up by set_ldt_entries(), as shown below.

```
int set_ldt_entries(PROC *p)
{   /* G = 1, size = 512*4K = 2MB */
    u64 ldt_code = 0x00c0fa00000001FFULL; // LDT code 2MB prototype
    u64 ldt_data = 0x00c0f200000001FFULL; // LDT data 2MB prototype
    u64 addr = p->res->paddress;          // fill in p's PA address
    ldt_code |= ((addr)<<16) & 0x000000ffffff0000ULL;
    ldt_code |= ((addr)<<32) & 0xff00000000000000ULL;
    p->ldt[0] = ldt_code;
    ldt_data |= ((addr)<<16) & 0x000000ffffff0000ULL;
    ldt_data |= ((addr)<<32) & 0xff00000000000000ULL;
    p->ldt[1] = ldt_data;
}
```

14.6.4 Switch TSS and LDT during Task Switch

During task switch, switch_tss() switches both TSS and LDT descriptors in the GDT to that of the next running process. It also loads the CPU's TR and LDTR registers with the new TSS and LDT. The code of switch_tss() is

```
int switch_tss(PROC *p)
{
    set_tss((int)&p->tss);              // GDT.tss points to p->tss
    set_ldt((int)&p->ldt);              // GDT.ldt points to p->ldt
    asm("ltrw %%ax\n\t"::"a"(TSS_SEL)); // load Task Register TR
    asm("lldt %%ax\n\t"::"a"(LDT_SEL)); // load LDT Register LDTR
}
int set_tss(u32 tss)
{
    u64 tss_entry = 0x0080890000000067ULL;  // TSS prototype
    u64 addr = (u64)tss;
    tss_entry |= (addr<<16) & 0xffffff0000; // fill in address
    tss_entry |= (addr<<32) & 0xff00000000000000ULL;
    gdt[GDT_TSS] = tss_entry;               // GDT_TSS=3
}
int set_ldt(u32 ldt)
{
    u64 ldt_entry = 0x0080820000000fULL;    // LDT prototype
    u64 addr = (u64)ldt;
    ldt_entry |= (addr<<16) & 0xffffff0000; // fill in address
    ldt_entry |= (addr<<32) & 0xff00000000000000ULL;
    gdt[GDT_LDT] = ldt_entry;               // GDT_LDT=4
}
```

14.6.5   Changes in MTX32.1 Kernel

Other changes in the MTX32.1 kernel are listed and explained below.

(1). kfork(): kfork() is only used by P0 to create the INIT process P1, which is the first process with a user mode image. kfork() first calls fork1() to create a new proc with a Umode memory area and initialize its TSS and LDT. Then it calls load() to load the image file,/bin/init, to P1's memory area and initializes P1's kstack for it to return to Umode. To do this, we pretend again that P1 had issued a system call from virtual address 0 and is about to return to Umode. In real mode, the saved syscall context is in the process user mode stack. In protected mode, it is in the process kernel mode stack. Besides memory management and exception processing, this is the only difference between real and protected modes. When a process does a syscall, it first saves the Umode CPU registers uSS, uSP,uflags, uCS,uPC in the proc's kstack by INT 0x80. Then it enters kernel to execute the syscall entry code int80h(), which saves other Umode CPU registers in kstack. In order for a new process to return to Umode, its kstack must contain such an interrupt stack frame, as shown in Fig. 14.12.

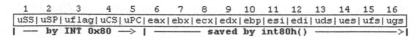

```
 1    2    3     4    5    6   7   8   9  10  11  12  13  14  15  16
|uSS|uSP|uflag|uCS|uPC|eax|ebx|ecx|edx|ebp|esi|edi|uds|ues|ufs|ugs|
| -- by INT 0x80 --> | ---------- saved by int80h() ------------->|
```

Fig. 14.12 Process kernel stack to goUmode

```
     17   18   19   20   21  22   23   24    25
    |kPC|kax|kbx|kcx|kdx|kbp|ksi|kdi|kflag|
    |<———— for RESUME in tswitch()————>|
```

Fig. 14.13 Process kernel stack to resume

In order for the new process to resume in Kmode when it is scheduled to run, its kstack must have a resume stack frame corresponding to the RESUME part of tswitch(), as shown in Fig. 14.13.

Accordingly, we initialize the various fields in the new proc's kstack as follows.

- [uSS|uSP]=[UDS|high end of user stack area=2 MB-4]
- saved Umode registers=[0x0200|UCS|uPC=0|eax to edi=0| uds to ugs=UDS]
- resume stack frame=[goUmode| 0 | 0 | 0 | 0 | 0 | 0 | 0 | 0]
- saved ksp points to kstack[SSIZE-25]: p->ksp=&p->kstack[SSIZE-25];

When the new proc is scheduled to run, it first resumes to goUmode (in ts.s), which pops the saved Umode registers, followed by iret, causing it to return to VA=0 in Umode.

(2). fork(): fork() first calls fork1() to create a new proc with a Umode memory area. It copies the parent's Umode image to child. In addition, it also copies the parent's kstack to child's kstack so that their "saved" Umode registers are identical. Then it fixes up the child's kstack for it to return to its own Umode image. Referring to the kstack diagram in Fig. 14.12, we see that in the child's kstack only entries 1 to 16 are relevant. Therefore, we only need to copy 16 entries from the bottom of the parent's kernel stack. The copied Umode segment selectors uCS, uSS, uds, ues, ufs and ugs do not need any change since they are the same for all Umode images. The actual memory area referred to by the selectors is determined by the process LDT. In order for the child process to resume when it is scheduled to run, its kstack must have a resume stack frame. Figure 14.14 shows the kstack contents of the child process.

Therefore, we fix up the child proc's kstack as follows.

- Append a resume stack frame=[goUmode| 0 | 0 | 0 | 0 | 0 | 0 | 0 | 0] to the copied kstack.
- Let child PROC.ksp point to kstack[SSIZE-25];
- Change saved eax (at index 6) to 0 for it to return pid=0 to Umode.

For the parent process, simply change the saved eax to child pid as the return value.

```
|<—————————— copied from parent's kstack ———————————>|
  1    2    3    4    5    6    7    8    9   10   11   12   13   14   15   16
|uSS|uSP|uflag|uCS|uPC|eax|ebx|ecx|edx|ebp|esi|edi|uds|ues|ufs|ugs|
|—— by INT 0x80 ——> |———— saved by int80h() ————————>|

   17   18   19   20   21   22   23   24   25
|kPC|kax|kbx|kcx|kdx|kbp|ksi|kdi|kflag|
|<———— for RESUME in tswitch()————>|
```

Fig. 14.14 Child process kstack in fork

(3). vfork(): vfork() is identical to fork(), except that it does not copy the parent's image, only the parent's LDT. This allows the child to share the same Umode image with the parent. In real mode, we had to create a Umode stack frame in the parent's ustack for the child to return to Umode. In protected mode, this is no longer necessary since the child process returns from its own kernel stack, which is the same as in fork(). However, in order not to interfere with the parent's ustack contents, a vforked child still needs a separate ustack area for it to return to Umode. For protection, we can mark the data segments shared by both parent and child as read-only (type=0) until the child exec to its own segments. While sharing the same data segment, if either process tries to write to the segment, it will generate a protection error. We can modify the exception handler to recognize such a trap, split the image and restore the write access to the separated data segments. However, this is not yet implemented in MTX32.1.

(4). Threads: Threads in protected mode are the same as they are in real mode, except that all threads in the same process share the same LDT of the hosting process. The resume stack frame of each thread is created in the thread's kstack, not in the caller's ustack as in real mode.

(5). Access Umode Space from Kmode: In 16-bit real mode, the Kmode and Umode spaces of a process are in different memory segments. It must use the intersegment copying functions to access the Umode space. In protected mode, a process in Kmode can access its Umode image directly. For example, to get syscall parameters at an offset from the top of ustack, the operation becomes a simple memory reference.

u32 parameter = *(u32 *)(running- > res- > paddress + uSP + offset);

Similarly, writing to Umode space becomes a simple memory reference also.

(6). Memory Management: When using segmentation, process images are allocated in contiguous memory. Memory management can use the same algorithm as in real mode, e.g. as variable-sized partitions.

(7). kexec(): In protected mode, kexec() is exactly the same as in real mode. The only changes are: the return stack frame is in the proc's kstack and the ustack TOP is at the virtual address 2 MB-4, which is an offset in the proc's Umode data segment.

(8). Exception Handling in Protected Mode: This is already explained in Sect. 14.5.

(9). I/O buffers: In real mode, MTX has only a few (4) block device I/O buffers due to limited space in the MTX kernel. In protected mode, this limitation no longer exists. The kernel may provide a large number of I/O buffers to improve I/O performance. In MTX32.1, we use some of the real mode memory as I/O buffers. With a large number of I/O buffers, the buffer hit ratio is constantly around or above 60 %.

(10). Device Drivers: In protected mode, all the device drivers do not need any change, except for the FD driver. This is because the FD controller, which uses channel 2 DMA of the ISA bus, can only accept 18-bit real-mode address. If all the block device I/O buffers reside in the low 1 MB real-mode memory, the FD driver does not need any change. Otherwise, we can use a 1KB area in real mode memory to transfer data between the FD and I/O buffers in high memory.

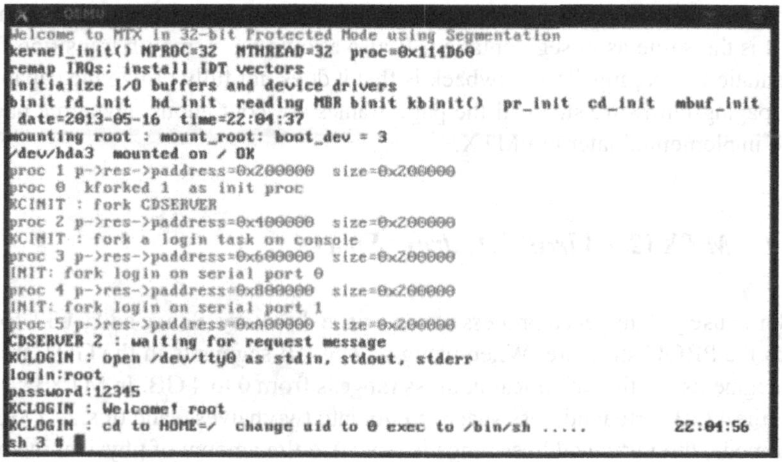

```
 QEMU
Welcome to MTX in 32-bit Protected Mode using Segmentation
kernel_init() MPROC=32  NTHREAD=32  proc=0x114D60
remap IRQs; install IDT vectors
initialize I/O buffers and device drivers
binit fd_init  hd_init  reading MBR binit kbinit()  pr_init  cd_init  mbuf_init
 date=2013-05-16  time=22:04:37
mounting root : mount_root: boot_dev = 3
/dev/hda3  mounted on / OK
proc 1 p->res->paddress=0x200000  size=0x200000
proc 0 kforked 1 as init proc
KCINIT : fork CDSERVER
proc 2 p->res->paddress=0x400000  size=0x200000
KCINIT : fork a login task on console
proc 3 p->res->paddress=0x600000  size=0x200000
INIT: fork login on serial port 0
proc 4 p->res->paddress=0x800000  size=0x200000
INIT: fork login on serial port 1
proc 5 p->res->paddress=0xA00000  size=0x200000
CDSERVER 2 : waiting for request message
KCLOGIN : open /dev/tty0 as stdin, stdout, stderr
login:root
password:12345
KCLOGIN : Welcome! root
KCLOGIN : cd to HOME=/ change uid to 0 exec to /bin/sh .....          22:04:56
sh 3 #
```

Fig. 14.15 Startup screen of MTX32.1

14.6.6   Summary on Segmentation

Segmentation is a unique feature of the Intel x86 processor architecture. Only a few real OS used segmentation. In the early days of PCs, IBM's OS2 used segmentation. Minix started in 16-bit real mode. Minix2 extended Minix to the Intel i386 architecture and used segmentation. Currently, Minix3 uses paging. We use MTX32.1 primarily as an introduction to protected mode operations. It also allows for a smooth transition from 16-bit real mode to 32-bit protected mode.

14.6.7   Demonstration System of MTX32.1

In the MTX install CD, MTX.images/mtx32.1 is a runnable image of MTX32.1. Figure 14.15 shows the startup screen of MTX32.1 running under QEMU. In the figure, each process displays its starting virtual address and image size. User interface and command executions are identical to that of RMTX in 16-bit real mode.

14.7   MTX32.2: 32-bit Protected Mode MTX using Static Paging

The second version of MTX in 32-bit protected mode is MTX32.2, which uses static paging. In MTX32.2, the user mode image of each process is allocated a piece of contiguous memory, which is aligned to a page boundary and consists of an integral number of pages. Then we set up the paging hardware in such a way that the image is accessed as contiguous pages. This simplifies memory management since it is the same as in segmentation. It also allows for a smooth transition from segmentation to paging. The drawback is that it does not fully utilize the capability of the paging hardware since all the page frames are contiguous. Dynamic paging will be implemented later in PMTX.

14.7.1   MTX32.2 Virtual Address Spaces

In order to use paging, each process needs a page directory. So we add a u32 *pgdir field to the PROC structure. When using paging, all segments in the GDT are flat 4 GB segments, so that the linear address range is from 0 to 4 GB. In MTX32.2, we divide the 4 GB virtual address space evenly into two halves, each of size 2 GB. In kernel mode, the virtual address range is from 0 to the amount of physical memory, which is identity mapped to PA=[0, size of physical memory]. In user mode, the virtual address range is from 2 GB to 2 GB+Umode image size. Thus, the kernel space is mapped low and the user space is mapped high. The virtual address spaces are set up as follows.

(1). SETUP: During booting, SETUP's GDT defines 6 segments, as shown below.

```
setup_gdt:
  .quad  0x0000000000000000  # null descriptor

  .quad  0x00cF9A000000FFFF  # kcs PpLS=9=1001, type=A,non-conform
  .quad  0x00cF92000000FFFF  # kds PpLS=9=1001, R|W data segment
  .quad  0x0000000000000000  # tss
  .quad  0x00cFFA000000FFFF  # ucs PpLS=F=1111, type=A,non-conform
  .quad  0x00cFF2000000FFFF  # uds PpLS=F=1111, R|W data segment
```

The initial GDT no longer has an LDT. Instead, it defines 2 user mode segments. All the code and data segments are flat 4 GB segments as required by paging. The actions of SETUP are exactly the same as that in MTX32.1. It moves the GDT to 0x9F000, enters protected mode, moves the MTX kernel to 1 MB and jumps to the MTX kernel entry point, pmode_entry, which sets the stack pointer to P0's kstack and calls init() in init.c.

(2). init.c: init() first initializes the display driver to make printf() work. Then it builds page tables to map kernel's virtual address space to physical memory. At this moment, the kernel can access all the available physical memory via segmentation. Although the kernel page directory and page tables can be located anywhere in memory, we shall place them directly above the kernel image. Assume 512 MB physical memory and the MTX kernel occupies the lowest 4 MB. We shall build the kernel page directory at 4 MB and the page tables at 4 MB+4 KB, 4 MB+8 KB, etc. as shown by the following code segments.

```
#define PASIZE    0x20000000      (ASSUME: PA size = 512MB)
#define KPGDIR    0x400000        (kpgdir at 4MB)
#define PAGSIZE   4096
#define KPGTABLE  (PGDIR + PGSIZE) (pgtables are next to kpgdir)
#define ENTRIES   (PASIZE>>22)     (number of page table needed)
int i,j;
u32 *kpgdir = (u32 *)KPGDIR;   // kernel pgdir at 4MB
u32  kpt = KPGDIR+0x3; // page table addr;3=011=Kpage,W,Present
for (i=0; i<ENTRIES; i++){     // fill kpgdir with 128 entries
    kpgdir[i] = kpt;           // each pointing at a page table
    kpt += PGSIZE;
}
// create 512/4=128 page tables starting at 4MB+4KB
kpg = (u32 *)KPGTABLE;
kpte = 0x3; // starting physical address=0,3=011=Kpage,W,Present
for (i=0; i<ENTRIES; i++){
    for (int j=0; j<1024; j++){
        kpg[i*1024+j] = kpte;   // page table entry
        kpte  += PGSIZE;
    }
}
```

14.7.2 MTX32.2 Kernel Page Directory and Page Tables

The kernel page directory and 128 page tables create an identity mapping of VA = [0, 512 MB] to PA = [0, 512 MB]. Once built, kpgdir plays two roles. First, it will be the page directory of the initial process P0, which runs in Kmode whenever no other process is runnable. Second, it will be the prototype of the page directories of all other processes. Each process has its own page directory and associated page tables. Since the kernel mode address space of all the processes are the same, the first 512 entries of their page directories are identical. When creating a new process we simply copy the first 512 entries of kpgdir into the process pgdir. The high (512 to 1023) entries of a process pgdir define the user mode page tables of that process. These entries will be set up when the process is created in fork1(). After setting up the kernel kpgdr and page tables, init() loads the control register CR3 with kpgdir and turns on paging. After these, all kernel addresses are mapped to physical addresses by the paging hardware. In this case, both addresses are the same due to the identity mapping of VA to PA.

14.7.3 MTX32.2 User Mode Page Directory and Page Tables

P0 runs only in Kmode, so it does not need a Umode image. Every other process has a Umode image. To simplify memory management, we assume that the Umode image of each process has a fixed size of 4 MB, which is allocated at (pid+1)*4 MB in physical memory. The choice of 4 MB image size is because it only needs one page table. For each process, we build a pgdir and its associated page table in the area between 6 and 7 MB, which has enough space for 128 processes. During task switch, we simply load CR3 with the pgdir of the next running process.

14.7.4   MTX32.2 Kernel Startup Sequence

After setting up kernel page tables and enabling paging, init() continues to initialize the MTX kernel by the following steps.

1. Call kernel_init() (in t.c file) to initialize kernel data structures and create the initial process P0. It sets P0's pgdir to kpgdir, GDT.tss to P0's TSS and loads CPU's TR register with GDT.tss, which makes P0's kstack as the initial interrupt stack. After these, the system is running P0.
2. Install IDT vectors and exception handlers (in traps.s and trapc.c) as described in Sect. 14.3. Install I/O interrupt and syscall vectors. These are exactly the same as in MTX32.1.
3. Initialize device drivers and file system. Mount the root device and set P0's CWD to the root directory.
4. Call main() in t.c. In main(), P0 calls kfork("/bin/init") to create the INIT process P1. kfork() calls fork1(), which is the beginning part of both kfork() and fork().

14.7.5   Process Page Directory and Page Table

To support paging, fork1() is modified to create a pgdir and page tables for a new process.

```
PROC *fork1()
{
       int i;   u32 *pgtable, pgt_entry;
(1). create a new proc p; initialize its TSS as in MTX32.1
(2). // simple memory allocation by pid
       p->res->paddress = (p->pid+1)*0x400000; // at 8MB, 12MB, etc.
(3). // allocate a pair of [pgidr, pgtable] in the area of 6MB
       p->res->pgdir = (u32 *)6MB + (p->pid-1)*2048; //6MB,6MB+8KB,etc.
       memset(p->res->pgdir, 0, 4096); // zero out pgidr

(4). // copy first 512 entries of kpgdir and create pgtable pointer
       for (i=0; i<512; i++) p->res->pgdir[i] = kpgdir[i];
       p->res->pgdir[512] = (u32)p->res->pgdir+4096+0x7; //7=111=UWP

(5). // create pgtable to map proc's VA=[0-4M] to PA at paddress
       pgtable = p->res->pgdir + 1024;
       pgt_entry = (u32)(p->res->paddress + 0x7); // PA|7=111=UWP
       for (i=0; i<1024; i++){
            pgtable[i] = pgt_entry;
            pgt_entry += 4096;
       }
       return p;
}
```

fork1() creates a new process and initialize its TSS. It constructs a pair of pgidr and pgtable for the new process in the area of 6 MB+(pid-1)*8KB. Since each process only needs 8KB for its pgdir and pgtable, the 1 MB area at 6 MB has enough space for 128 processes. The first 512 entries of every process pgdir are copied from kpgdir. The remaining pgdir entries are cleared to 0 except pgdir[512], which points to the process pgtable. Each pgtable contains 1024 entries, which map the virtual address space VA=[0x80000000, 0x80000000+4 MB] to the 4 MB PA of the process image.

14.7.6 Process Interrupt and Resume Stack Frames

After creating P1, kfork() loads the Umode image file,/etc/init, to the memory area of P1, sets up P1's kernel stack and enters it into the readyQueue. The initial kernel stack of a process consists of two sections; a RESUME stack frame for it to resume running in Kmode, preceded by an interrupt stack frame for it to return to Umode, as shown in Fig. 14.16.

The kstack frames of P1 are set up as follows.

```
memset(p->kstack, 0, 4*SSIZE);                  // zero out kstack
p->kstack[SSIZE-1]  = UDS;                       // uss = UDS
p->kstack[SSIZE-2]  = VA(4*1024*1024-4);         // usp = 4MB-4
p->kstack[SSIZE-3]  = UFLAG;                      // uflag=0x0200
p->kstack[SSIZE-4]  = UCS;                        // ucs = UCS
p->kstack[SSIZE-5]  = VA(0);                      // upc = VA(0)
p->kstack[SSIZE-13] to p->kstack[SSIZE-16] = UDS; // other segs
p->kstack[SSIZE-17] = (int)goUmode;              // RESUME to goUmode()
p->ksp = (int *)&(p->kstack[SSIZE-25]);          // PROC saved ksp
```

The only thing new here is the VA macro

$$\text{\#define VA(x) ((x) + 0x80000000)}$$

which converts an offset address in Umode to a virtual address. When P1 is scheduled to run, it first uses the resume stack frame to resume to goUmode, which restores saved CPU registers and iret back to VA(0) in Umode. After creating P1,

```
    1    2    3    4    5   6   7   8   9   10  11  12  13  14   15   16
  |uss|usp|flag|ucs|upc|ax|bx|cx|dx|bp|si|di|uds|ues|ufs|ugs|
  |<── int 0x80/iret──>|<── pushed by INTH/pop by goUmode ──>|

   17 18 19 20 21 22 23 24  25
  |PC|ax|bx|cx|dx|bp|si|di|flag|
  |<────── tswitch/RESUME──────>|
```

Fig. 14.16 Process interrupt and resume stack frames

P0 switches process to run P1. P1 forks one or more login processes and waits for ZOMBIE children. When the login processes start up, the system is ready for use.

14.7.7 Switch TSS and pgdir during Task Switch

During task switch, we switch TSS in the GDT and reload the CPU's TR and CR3 registers with the TSS and pgdir of the next running process. Reloading CR3 causes the CPU to flush its TLB and switch to the pgdir of the next running process.

14.7.8 Changes in MTX32.2 Kernel

(1). fork(): The only changes are in the interrupt and resume stack frames of the child process, both are in the child proc's kstack.

(2). Memory Management: When using static paging memory management is again trivial. Each process (except P0) has a Umode image of size 4 MB, which is allocated at (pid + 1)*4 MB. If desired, the reader may modify this simple scheme by using different image sizes and managing process images as variable-sized partitions.

(3). loader: Both MTX32.1 and MTX32.2 use the same simple memory management scheme as in real mode, i.e. as variable sized partitions. The image loader is the same as in real mode, except that it is modified to load either flat binary or ELF executables.

(4). kexec(): When using static paging, kexec() is exactly the same as in real mode. The only modification is that the TOP of ustack is at the virtual address 4 MB. After loading the new Umode image, the command line is copied to the high end of the Umode stack, and the long word at TOP-512 points to the command line in ustack. Then the PROC's Kmode stack is re-initialized as follows.

```
kstack[SSIZE-1]  = UDS;                    // uSS
kstack[SSIZE-2]  = VA(TOP - 512);          // usp=0x8000000+TOP-512
kstack[SSIZE-3]  = UFLAG;                   // uflag
kstack[SSIZE-4]  = UCS;                     // uCS
kstack[SSIZE-5]  = VA(0);                   // uPC=0x80000000 in Umode
kstack[SSIZE-13] to kstack[SSIZE-16] = UDS // other segments = UDS
kstack[SSIZE-17] = (int)goUmode;
running->ksp = (int *)&(running->kstack[SSIZE-25]);
```

When the process returns to Umode, it executes from VA(0) with the command line as parameter in ustack. Parsing the command line into argc and argv[ ] is done in Umode.

(5). Access Umode Space from Kmode: When a process executes in Kmode at privilege level 0, it can access all the pages in both Kmode and Umode. So a process in Kmode can access its Umode space directly.

```
Hi ┌══════════════════ protected mode kstack ══════════════════┐
   │uss|usp|uflag|ucs|upc|ax|bx|cx|dx|bp|si|di|uds|ues|ufs|ugs│
   └──────────────────────────────────────────────────────────┘
      1   2    3    4   5
```

Fig. 14.17 Process kernel stack due to interrupt

```
|oss|osp|flag|cs|upc|0/err#|nr|ax|cx|dx|bx|esp|bp|si|di|ds|es|fs|gs|ss|
|<──────── by exception ──────>|  |<────────── by trap_common pushal ──────>|
  1   2    3   4   5     6     7   8   9   10  11  12  13  14 15 16 17 18 19 20
```

Fig. 14.18 Process kernel stack due to exception

(6). Dispatching Signal Handlers: When a process is about to return to Umode, it checks for signals and handles any pending signal. For signals other than 9, a process may have installed a user mode signal catcher. If so, the process must return to execute the catcher in Umode. In protected mode, dispatching a process to execute a signal catcher is similar to that in real mode. If the process entered kernel via an interrupt or syscall, the process kstack must contain a regular interrupt/syscall stack frame, as shown in Fig. 14.17.

If the process entered kernel due to an exception, its kstack contains an exception stack frame, as shown in Fig. 14.18.

In both cases, dispatching a process to execute a user mode signal catcher is the same:

- save upc (at index 5) in kstack as oldPC
- replace upc in kstack by newPC, which points to catcher()in Umode
- create 2 slots in ustack to contain oldPC, sig#
- decrement usp (osp at index 2) by 2 slots for catcher(int sig#)
- when catcher() finishes, it returns by oldPC to where it lastly entered kernel.

(7). Device Drivers: In 32-bit protected mode, all device drivers remain the same, except for the FD driver, which is modified as follows. In MTX32.2, the data areas of I/O buffers are allocated in the memory area of 7 MB. Since the FD's DMA controller can only accept 18-bit real-mode address, we use a fixed 1KB area in real-mode memory at 0x90000 for data transfer between the FD driver and I/O buffers.

(8). User Mode Programs: In MTX32.2, user mode images begin from the virtual address 0x80000000 (2 GB). To comply with this, the initial virtual address of user mode images is set to 0x80000000 in the Makefile.

14.7.9   Demonstration System of MTX32.2.

In the MTX install CD, MTX.images/mtx32.2 is a runnable image of MTX32.2. Figure 14.19 shows the startup screen of MTX32.2 running under QEMU. In the figure, each process displays its starting virtual address. In addition to the console, the system also supports two login processes on serial ports, which are not shown.

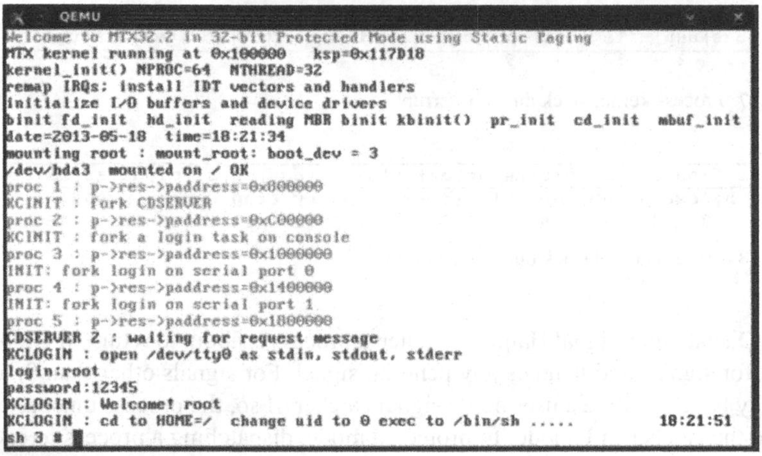

Fig. 14.19 Startup screen of MTX32.2

14.8   PMTX: 32-bit Protected Mode MTX Using Dynamic Paging

The third version of MTX in 32-bit protected mode is PMTX, which uses dynamic paging. It is the final version of MTX in 32-bit protected mode for uniprocessor systems.

14.8.1   PMTX Virtual Address Spaces

In PMTX, the 4 GB virtual address space is also divided into two equal halves, except that the kernel mode virtual address space is from 2 to 4 GB and user mode virtual address space is from 0 to Umode image size. Thus, the user space is mapped low and the kernel space is mapped high. This organization conforms to most other Unix-like systems, such as Linux and xv6. In Linux (Bovet and Cesati 2005), user space is from 0 to 3 GB and kernel space is from 3 to 4 GB. In xv6 (Cox et al. 2011), user space is from 0 to 2 GB and kernel space is from 2 to 4 GB, which is the same as in PMTX. The PMTX kernel is compiled with the starting virtual address 0x80100000 but it runs at the physical address 0x100000 (1 MB). This can no longer be achieved by segmentation. We must use paging when the kernel execution begins. Instead of setting up all the page tables in one step, the virtual address mapping is accomplished in two steps, which resemble that of multi-stage booting. The following describes the steps in detail.

14.8.2   PMTX Kernel Startup Sequence

SETUP: During booting, the booter loads SETUP to 0x90200 and the PMTX kernel
to 0x10000. Then it jumps to 0x90200 to run SETUP. The initial GDT in SETUP is

```
setup_gdt:
    .quad  0x0000000000000000  # null descriptor
    .quad  0x00cF9A000000FFFF  # kcs  PpLS=1001, type=non-conforming
    .quad  0x00cF92000000FFFF  # kds  PpLS=1001, R|W data segment
```

It defines only two 4 GB kernel code and data segments. SETUP moves the initial
GDT to 0x9F000 and loads the GDTR register to point at the initial GDT. Then it
enters protected mode, moves the MTX kernel to 1 MB and ljmp to the entry address of the MTX kernel at 1 MB. Unlike the previous versions of MTX in protected
mode, the initial GDT is only temporary. It provides the initial 4 GB flat segments
for the PMTX kernel to get started.

   entry.s: pm_entry is the entry point of the PMTX kernel. In order to let the kernel use virtual addresses from 0x80000000 by paging, entry.s defines an initial page
directory, ipgdir, two initial page tables, pg0 and pg1, a new GDT, an IDT and a
page directory, kpgdir, at offsets from 0x1000 to 0x8000, as shown below.

```
#-------------------- entry.s file ---------------------------
pm_entry: # entry.s beginning code in first 4KB of kernel
         .org 0x1000             # at offset 4KB
ipgdir:
         .long 0x00102007        # point to pg0 at 0x102000
         .long 0x00103007        # point to pg1 at 0x103000
         .fill 510,4,0           # 510 0 entries
         .long 0x00102007        # point at pg0 at 0x102000
         .long 0x00103007        # point at pg1 at 0x103000
         .fill 510,4,0           # 510 0 entries
.org 0x2000                      # at offset 8KB
pg0:       # 2 initial page tables pg0, pg1: to be set in entry.s
.org 0x3000
pg1:
.org 0x4000
kgdt:              # GDT
    .quad 0x0000000000000000 # null descriptor
    .quad 0x00cF9A000000FFFF # kcs  PpLS=9=1001,type=non-conform code
    .quad 0x00cF92000000FFFF # kds  PpLS=9=1001,type=R|W data segment
    .quad 0x0000000000000000 # tss
    .quad 0x00cFFA000000FFFF # ucs  PpLS=F=1111,type=non-conform code
    .quad 0x00cFF2000000FFFF # uds  PpLS=F=1111,type=R|W data segment
kgdt_desc: .word.-kgdt-1
           .long  kgdt
.org 0x5000
idt: .fill 1024,4,0             # 2KB IDT table at offset 0x5000
.org 0x6000
kpgdir: .fill 1024,4,0          # final kernel mode kpgdir at 0x6000
.org 0x8000                     # Other PMTX kernel code begins here
```

14.8.3   PMTX Kernel Virtual Address Mapping

In the initial page directory, ipgdir, entries 0 and 1 point to the two initial page tables pg0 and pg1. The two initial page tables are filled with page frames from 0 to 8 MB to create an identity mapping of the lowest 8 MB of physical memory. Entries 512 and 513 of ipgdir also point to pg0 and pg1, which map the virtual address range VA=[2 GB to 2 GB+8 MB] to [0 to 8 MB]. The new GDT, kgdt, defines 6 segments, in which tss, ucs and uds are the TSS, user mode code and data segments of the current running process. The actions of entry.s are as follows.

(1). Set up initial page tables pg0, pg1; map VA=[0,8 MB]-[2G,2G+8 MB] to [0,8 MB]:

```
        movl  $pg0   -KVA, %ebx     # KVA = 0x80000000
        movl  $0x07,    %eax     # page R|W and Present
        movl  $2*1024,  %ecx     # loop 2048 times
loop0:  movl  %eax,    0(%ebx)    # start with pageframe=0
        addl  $4,       %ebx
        addl  $4096,    %eax     # next pageframe
        loop  loop0              # loop 2048 times
```

(2). Load CR3 with physical address of ipgdir and turn on paging.

```
        movl  $ipgdir  -KVA,%eax   # physical address of ipgdir
        movl  %eax, %cr3          # load CR3 with PA(ipgdir)
        movl  %cr0, %eax          # enable paging
        orl   $0x80000000,%eax
        movl  %eax, %cr0
```

(3). Do a jmp to flush the instruction pipeline.

```
                       jmp 1f
                  1:
```

(4). Do another jmp to force the CPU to use virtual address.

```
                  movl  $2f,%eax
                  jmp  *%eax
             2:
```

The second jmp at step (4) is tricky but essential. Before the second jmp, the CPU was executing with real address in the range 0–8 MB. The second jmp uses PC relative addressing, which forces the CPU to switch to virtual addresses in the range of 0x80000000 to 0x80000000+8 MB.

(5). Load GDTR with the new kgdt descriptor.

        lgdt kgdt_desc   #load GDT at 0x8010400

The new GDT defines 2 kernel mode segments, a TSS and 2 user mode segments. All code and data segments are flat 4 GB segments as required by paging.

(6). initproc is a statically defined PROC structure for the initial process P0. entry.s sets the stack pointer to the high end of initproc's kstack. Then it calls init() to initialize the PMTX kernel.

(7). init.c file: init() first initializes the display driver to make printf() work. At this moment, the kernel's virtual address space is limited to 8 MB. The next step is to expand the virtual address range to the entire available physical memory. Assume 512 MB physical memory and the PMTX kernel occupies the lowest 4 MB. We shall build the new page directory at 0x8016000 and the page tables at 4 MB. This is done by the kpgtable() function shown below.

14.8.3.1   PMTX Kernel Page Directory and Page Tables

```
#define KPG_DIR    0x80106000  // at offset 0x6000 in kernel
#define KPG_TABLE 0x80400000   // begin from 4MB
#define PGSIZE     4096
void kpgtable(void)
{   u32 i, j, NPGTABLES = 128; // 512MB PA needs 512/4=128 pgtabels
    u32 *pgdir  = (u32 *)KPG_DIR;
    u32 *ptable = (u32 *)KPG_TABLE;
    u32 pte = (u32)(PA(KPG_TABLE)|0x3; // begin PA=0,0x3=|Kpage|W|P
    memset(pgdir, 0, 4096);             // zero out kpgdir
    for (i=512; i<512+NPGTABLE; i++){   // from kpgdir[512]
        pgdir[i] = pte;                 // pointing at pgtables.
        pte += PGSIZE;
    }
    pte = (u32)0 | 0x03;                // start with PA=0
    ptable  = (u32 *)KPG_TABLE;         // KPG_TABLE at 4MB
    for (i=0; i<NPGTABLES; i++){        // fill 128 pgtables
      for (j=0; j<1024; j++){           // pgtabe, 4KB each
          ptable[i*1024 + j] = pte;
          pte += PGSIZE;
      }
    }
}
```

(7).1. kpgtable() creates a kpgdir at 0x80160000, in which entries 512 to 639 point to 128 page tables, which map VA=[0x80000000, 0x80000000+512 MB] to [0, 512 MB]. As in MTX32.2, the kernel page directory, kpgdir, also plays two roles. First, it will be the pgdir of the initial process P0, which runs in Kmode whenever no other process is runnable. Second, it will be the prototype of the page directories of all other processes. Each process has its own page directory and page tables. Since the kernel mode address spaces of all processes are the same, the high 512 entries of all page directories are identical. When creating a new process we simply copy the high 512 entries of kpgdir to the process pgdir. The low (0 to 511) entries of a process pgdir define the user mode page tables of the process. These entries will be set up when the process is created.

(7).2. Switch CR3 to the new kernel page directory, kpgdir. This allows the kernel to access all the physical memory from 0 to 512 MB. Figure 14.20 shows the memory map of PMTX.

(7).3. kernel_init(): After setting up the kernel mode kpgdir and page tables, init() calls kernel_init() (in t.c file) to initialize the kernel data structures, such as free PROC lists, ready queue and sleepList, etc. In PMTX, only the initproc and its resource structure are statically defined. The other NPROC (1024) and NTHREAD (512) PROCs are constructed in the memory area of 5 MB. In kernel_init(), it uses initproc to create the initial process P0, which uses kpgdir as the page directory. It sets the privilege level-0 stack in P0's TSS to P0's kstack. Then it calls switch_tss(), which changes the TSS in GDT to P0's TSS and loads the CPU's task state register, TR, with the new TSS. These make P0's kstack as the interrupt stack. The system is now running the initial process P0.

(7).4. Remap IRQ vectors. Set up IDT and install exception/interrupt handlers, as described in Sect. 14.5. The IDT only needs 2KB space. It is constructed at 0x105000. init() proceeds to initialize the IDT and install exception and I/O interrupt vectors. Exception handler entry points are in traps.s. Exception handlers are in trapc.c. I/O interrupt entry points are defined in ts.s by calls to the INTH macro. I/O interrupt handler functions are in the various device drivers. Among the interrupts, vector 0x80 is for system calls.

(7).5. Initialize I/O buffers, device drivers and timer: After setting up the IDT and interrupt vectors, init() initializes I/O buffers. The PMTX kernel has 1024 I/O buffers, which are allocated at 7 MB. When initializing the HD driver P0 also reads the partition table to determine the start sector and size of other partitions, which are used to construct the block device table. Then it initializes the file system and mounts the MTX partition as the root file system.

Fig. 14.20 Memory map of PMTX

0 1MB	1MB real mode memory PMTX kernel in 1MB to 4MB 0x104000:GDT; 0x105000:IDT 0x106000:kpgdir
4MB	128 kernel mode ptables of P0
5MB	1024 process + 512 thread PROCs
6MB	unused, for expansion
7MB	data area of 1024 I/O buffers
8-512MB	free memory for process images

14.8.3.2 Manage Page Frames

PMTX uses a free page list, pfreeList, for allocation/deallocation of page frames. The pfreeList is constructed by the code segment shown below.

```
u32 *free_page_list(u32 startva, u32 endva)
{   u32 *p = (u32 *)startva;
    while(p < (endva-4096)){
      *p = (u32)(p + 1024);
       p += 1024;
    }
    *p = 0;
    return (u32 *)startva;
}
u32 *pfreelist = free_page_list(8MB, 512MB); // build free page list
```

The pfreeList threads all the free page frames from 8 to 512 MB in a link list. Each entry of pfreeList contains the address of the next page frame. As usual, the list ends with a 0 pointer. In order for the kernel to access the entries of pfreeList, the link pointers must use virtual addresses of the page frames. When allocating a page frame the virtual address of the page frame must be converted to physical address. Conversion between virtual address and physical address are by the PA/VA macros.

$$\text{\#define PA(x)} \quad ((u32)(x) - 0x80000000)$$

$$\text{\#define VA(x)} \quad (\quad (x) + 0x80000000)$$

With the pfreelist data structure, palloc() allocates a page frame and pdealloc(VA(page frame)) inserts a deallocated page frame to pfreeList. The simplest way to deallocate a page frame is to insert it to the front of pfreeList. Alternatively, we may also insert it to the end of pfreeList to ensure that all page frames are used effectively.

(7).6. Finally, init() calls main() in t.c. In main(), P0 calls kfork("/bin/init") to create the INIT process P1 and load/bin/init as its Umode image. Then P0 switches process to run P1. P1 forks one or more login processes and waits for ZOMBIE children. When the login processes start, the system is ready for use.

14.8.4 Changes in PMTX Kernel

(1). PROC kstack: In PMTX, the kstack of each PROC is a u32 pointer. The kstack is allocated a 4KB page dynamically only when it is used to create a process. The combined size of the PROC and PRES structures is less then 512 bytes. This allows us to define a large number of NPROC (1024) and NTHREAD (512) structures, which are constructed at 5 MB. The kstack of a ZOMBIE proc is deallocated by the parent in kwait().

(2). fork1(): fork1() is the beginning part of all other fork functions. It creates a new proc and allocates a kstack for it. When called from kfork() or fork(), it also allocates a pgdir for the new proc. When called from vfork(), it lets the new proc share the same pgdir of the parent. The page tables of a process are created by a separate makePage() function.

```
PROC *fork1(int HOW) // HOW = FORK or VFORK
{ PROC *p;
  if (!(p = get_proc(&freeList)))
     return 0;
  if (!(p->res->kstack = palloc())){
     free p; return 0
  }
  if (HOW==FORK)
     if (!(p->res->pgdir = palloc())){
        free p's kstack,
        free p; return 0
     }
  else                    // HOW = VFORK, share pgdir of parent
     p->res->pgdir = running>res->pgdir;
  p->res->size = running>res->size; // same image size as parent
  initialize p's kstack, tss, etc.
  return p;
}

int makePage(PROC *p, int HOW) // HOW=FORK or EXEC
{
  u32 i, j, pte, *pgtable;
  u32 *pgdir = (HOW==FORK)?->pres->pgdir : p->res->new_pgdir
  u32 npgdir = p>res->size/(1024*BSIZE); // number of pgdir entries
  u32 npages = npgdir/1024;    // number of pages needed
  u32 rpages = npages % 1024;  // number of pages in last pdgir
  for (i=0; i<1024; i++)       // copy kpgdir to pgdir
     pgdir[i] = kpgdir[i];
  for (i=0; i<npgdir; i++){    // for each npgdir entry
     pgtable = palloc(); // allocate a pgtable; return 0 if fails
     memset(pgtable, 0, PGSIZE);       // zero out pgtable
     pgdir[i] = PA((u32)pgtable) + 7; // record PA+7 in pgdir[i]
     for (j=0; j<1024; j++){ // allocate page frames for page table
        pte = palloc();       // allocate a pte; return 0 if fails
        pgtable[j] = PA(pte+7);    // 7 for USER R|W pages
     }
  }
  if (rpages){      // need one more pgdir entry forpages
     pgtable = (u32 *)palloc(); // allocate a pgtable;
     p->res->pgdir[i] = PA((u32)pgtable) + 7);
     memset(pgtable, 0, PGSIZE) // zero out pgtable entries
     for (j=0; j<rpages; j++){  // fill pgtable with rpages frames
        pte = palloc();         // allocate a pte; return 0 if fails
        pgtable[j] = PA(pte+7);
     }
  }
  return 1; // for SUCCESS
}
```

(2). kfork(): kfork() is only used by P0 to create the INIT process P1. Corresponding to the modified fork1() and makePage(), the algorithm of kfork() is

```
int kfork(char *filename)
{
    PROC *p = fork1(FORK);      // create a new proc p with a pgdir
    p->res->size = INITSIZE;    // INITSIZE=4MB in type.h
    makePage(p, FORK);          // create page tables for P1
    load(filename, p);          // load /etc/init as P1's Umode image
    set up p's kstack for it to return to VA=0 in Umode
    enter p into readyQueue;
}
```

The image size of P1 is defined as INITSIZE=4 MB mainly for convenience since
it only needs one page table. After creating a new proc by fork1(), P0 allocates page
frames for P1 and loads the image file. Then it creates an interrupt stack frame, followed by a RESUME stack frame, for P1 to return to VA=0 in Umode. The stack
frames of a new process are set up as follows.

```
/********* kstack of new proc contains: *********************
|uss|usp|flag|ucs|upc|ax|bx|cx|dx|bp|si|di|uds|ues|ufs|ugs|//INT frame
  1   2   3   4   5   6  7  8  9  10 11 12 13  14  15  16
|PC|ax|bx|cx|dx|bp|si|di|flag|                         // RESUME frame
 17 18 19 20 21 22 23 24  25
**************************************************************/
    for (int i=1; i<26; i++)                  // clear "saved registers" to 0
        p->kstack[SSIZE-i] = 0;               // p points at new PROC
    // fill in the needed entries in p's kstack
    p->kstack[SSIZE-1] = UDS;                 // uSS
    p->kstack[SSIZE-2] = p->res->size-4;      // uSP = imageSize-4
    p->kstack[SSIZE-3] = UFLAG;               // uflag
    p->kstack[SSIZE-4] = UCS;                 // uCS
    p->kstack[SSIZE-5] = 0;                   // eip = VA 0
    p->kstack[SSIZE-13] to p->kstack[SSIZE-16] = UDS; // other segments
    p->kstack[SSIZE-17] = (int)goUmode;       // resume point in Kmode
    p->ksp = (int *)&(p->kstack[SSIZE-25]);   // saved ksp in PROC
```

The interrupt stack frame of a new process is logically the same as that in real mode.
The only difference is that it is now in the proc's kstack, rather than in the user mode
stack.

(3). Loader: The loader is used in both kfork() and kexec() to load an image file.
Since the page frames may not be contiguous, the loader is modified accordingly.
Instead of loading the image file to a linear address, it loads 4KB blocks of the file
to the page frames of a process. Since the modifications are simple, they are not
shown here.

(4). fork(): with dynamic paging, the algorithm of fork() is modified as follows.

```
int fork()
{
  PROC *child;
  (1). if (child=fork1(FORK) fails) return -1;
  (2). if (makePage(child, FORK)==0)
            {free child's pages, pgdir, kstack and PROC; return -1}
  (3). copyImage(running, child);  // copy Umode image to child
  (4). copy parent kstack to child kstack; // only the bottom part
  (5). fix up child's kstack for return 0 to the same VA as parent;
  (6). enter child into readyQueue;
  (7). return child pid;
}

void copyImage(PROC *parent, PROC *child)
{ int i, j;
  int npgdirs = (parent->res->size + 4MB-1)/4MB; // # pgdir entries
  u32 *ppgtable, *cpgtable, *ppa, *cpa;
  for (i=0; i<npgdirs; i++){
    pgtable = VA(parent->res->pgdir[i]&0xFFFFF000); //VA(frame addr)
    cpgtable= VA( child->res->pgdir[i]&0xFFFFF000); //VA(frame addr)
    for (j=0; j<1024; j++){
       ppa = VA(ppgtable[j]&0xFFFFF000); // VA(20-bit frame addr)
       cpa = VA(cpgtable[j]&0xFFFFF000); // VA(20-bit frame addr)
       memcpy(cpa, ppa, PGSIZE);
    }
  }
}
```

After copying the Umode image, fork() copies the parent's kstack to that of the child. Then it fixes up the child's kstack frame for it to return to Umode. Similar to fork() in real mode, we do not care about the execution history of the parent in Kmode. All we need is to ensure that when the child runs, it returns a 0 to the same VA in Umode as the parent. Therefore, we only need to manipulate the bottom part of the child's kstack. The idea is exactly the same as in kfork(), i.e. to create a stack frame for the child to resume running in Kmode, preceded by an interrupt stack frame for it to return to Umode. The needed stack frames and operations are shown below.

```
|uss|usp|flag|ucs|upc|ax|bx|cx|dx|bp|si|di|uds|ues|ufs|ugs| //INT frame
  1    2    3    4    5    6  7  8  9  10 11 12 13   14   15   16
|PC|ax|bx|cx|dx|bp|si|di|flag|                            // RESUME frame
 17 18 19 20 21 22 23 24  25
```

```
  child->kstack[SSIZE-6] = 0;       // return value=saved AX = 0
  for (i=18; i<26; i++)
      child->kstack[SSIZE-i] = 0; // Kmode saved regs do not matter
  child->kstack[SSIZE-17] = (int)goUmode; // goUmode directly
  child->ksp = (int *)&child->kstack[SSIZE-25]; // saved ksp
  enqueue(&readyQueue, child);
```

When the child process starts to run, it first resumes to goUmode(), which restores the saved registers (ugs to ax), followed by iret, causing it to return to the same (ucs, upc) as the parent but in its own Umode image.

(5). vfork(): In PMTX, vfork() is implemented as follows.

```
int vfork()
{
(1). PROC *child = fork1(VFORK); // create child share same pgdir
(2). child->vforked = 1;         // mark child as VFROKED
(3). copy parent's kstack to child kstack
(4). fix up child's interrupt and resume stack frames as in fork();
(5). create a separate ustack area for child in parent's ustack
(6). child->kstack[SSIZE-2] = child usp in (5); // child saved usp
(7). change child saved AX to 0;                 // child return 0
(8). enter child into readyQueue;
(9). return child pid;
}
```

When a vforked child returns to Umode, it should use its own separate ustack area. However, it seems that GCC generated code always restores user mode esp from a fixed save area, causing both parent and child return to the same ustack frame. If either process makes a syscall, it would change the ustack contents, causing the other one to crash when it returns to Umode. To prevent this, we have to implement the user mode vfork() syscall in assembly directly. The x86 CPU's paging hardware supports Copy-On-Write (COW) pages, which can be used to implement vfork. Using COW pages, vfork can create a child to share the same Umode page frames with the parent. If either process tries to write to a shared COW page, the paging hardware will generate a page fault. The page fault handler can split the pages into separate images. As of now, PMTX does not yet implement this kind of vfork. It is left as an exercise.

(6). kexec(): In general, when a process changes image, it should determine the new image size by the file's loading size. Currently, all executable programs in PMTX are very small. If we use file size as image size, all process images would be very small also. For this reason, we choose to support different image sizes as follows. When PMTX starts, the INIT process image size is set to 4 MB. Under normal conditions, all processes would run with the same image size of 4 MB. To run programs with different image sizes, enter the command with an optional SIZE parameter.

command_line [–m SIZEm]

where SIZE is the new image size in MB. Accordingly, we modify kexec() with an additional size parameter, which is 0 if no SIZE is specified.

```
int kexec(char *command_line, int size) // size = 0 or SIZE
{
 (1). if (caller is not a PROCESS OR has other active THREADs)
         return -1;
 (2). get command_line from original image;
 (3). new_size = (size)? original image size : SIZE
 (4). save pgdir and size of original image;
         if (!(new_pgdir=palloc()))// allocate a new_pgdir
           return -1;
         if (!(makeImage(running, EXEC))){ // if can't alloc new image
           deallocate new image;
           return -1;
         }
         load CR3 with new_pgdir;        // switch pgdir to new image
 (5). if (load(cmd, running) < 0){    // if load image file fails
         load CR3 with origian pgdir; // restore original image
         deallocate new image;
         return -1;                    // return -1 to original image
       }
 (6). if (caller is NOT vforked)
         deallocate original image;
 (7). if (caller is vforked)
         turn off PROC's vforked flag;
 (8). set up kstack for return to VA=0 in Umode.
}
```

In kexec(), it sets mew_size to the original image size or SIZE, if specified. It saves the original image and allocates a pgdir and page tables for the new image. If the allocation fails due to out of memory, it releases the new image, switches back to the original image and returns −1. If the allocation succeeds, it tries to load the image file to the new image. If the loading fails, it restores the original image, releases the new image and returns −1. If the loading succeeds, it releases the original image if the caller is not vforked. Then it fills the ustack with command line parameters and turns off the process vforked flag. Finally, it re-initializes the kernel stack for it to return to VA=0 in Umode, as shown below.

```
/********* kexec(): kstack of proc contains: *************
|uss|usp|flag|ucs|upc|ax|bx|cx|dx|bp|si|di|uds|ues|ufs|ugs| //INT fra
 1   2   3    4   5   6  7  8  9  10 11 12 13  14  15  16
|goU|PC|ax|bx|cx|dx|bp|si|di|flag|                    // RESUME frame
17  18 19 20 21 22 23 24 25  26
*********************************************************/

  kstack[SSIZE-1] = UDS;
  kstack[SSIZE-2] = TOP-512;       // TOP=image size
  kstack[SSIZE-3] = UFLAG;
  kstack[SSIZE-4] = UCS;
  kstack[SSIZE-5] = 0x0;           // virtual address 0 in UCS
  kstack[SSIZE-13] to kstack[SSIZE-16] = UDS;
  kstack[SSIZE-17] = (int)goUmode;
  running->ksp = &(running->kstack[SSIZE-25]);
```

In addition, kexec() also clears the process signal and resets all the signal handlers to default, but it does not close opened file descriptors. Thus, opened files remain open in the new image.

(6). kexit(): When a process terminates, it releases the Umode image by freeImage() unless it's vforked. freeImage(pdgir) traverses the process pgdir to find the Umode page tables, from which to find the page frames. Then it deallocates the Umode page frames and page tables, but keeps both the pgdir and kstack since the process is still executing. The pgdir and kstack of a ZOMBIE process will be deallocated by the parent in kwait(). Note that in kexec() a vforked process always creates a new image, thereby detaching itself from the parent image. Then it tries to load the image file. If the loading succeeds, its vforked flag is turned off, in which case it will release its own image in kexit(). If the loading fails, it releases the new image and returns -1 to the original image, in which case it does not deallocate the shared image since its vforked flag is still on. Alternative schemes will be discussed in the Problem section.

(7). Expand User Mode Heap Size: In PMTX, the heap area of a process is above its Umode image. The sbrk() system call expands the heap size by adding a new page to the process image and returns the virtual address of the newly allocated page frame. In the sample PMTX, the sbrk command demonstrates the sbrk() system call. Assume that a process image has n pgdir entries. On the first call to sbrk(), it allocates a page directory entry, pgdir[n], and allocates a page frame for the page table. Each subsequent call to sbrk() allocates an additional page in the page table. After calling sbrk(), the process may access the expanded heap area for read/write. The reader may modify the sbrk syscall to reduce the heap size by deallocating heap pages.

(8). Device Drivers: When using paging in protected mode, only the FD driver needs a slight modification, as described in Sect. 14.7.8. All other device drivers remain the same as they are in real mode.

14.8.5 Page Faults and Demand-Paging

The current implementation of PMTX does not support demand-paging, mainly because we want to keep the system simple. In the current PMTX, all Umode programs need only a few pages to run, which also makes demand-paging unnecessary. Despite these simplifications, we can demonstrate the principle of demand-paging by simulating page faults and handling the page faults. In PMTX, a process in user mode may issue the system call page_out(n) to mark the nth ($n < 1024$) entry of its page table as not present. When the process attempts to access the missing page, it generates a page fault even though the page frame is already loaded with the image's code or data. When the process traps to Kmode, the page fault handler can determine whether the page fault is due to a missing page or an invalid page reference. If it is due to a missing page, the page fault handler simply marks the missing page as present and let the process continue. If it is due to an invalid page reference, it sends the process a SEGMENTATION FAULT (11) signal as usual. Assuming 4 MB image size, the following shows the algorithm of the page fault handler.

```
    void ehandler(u32 signal, ... u32 err_nr, ..) // err_nr=error number
    {
        u32 cr2, cr3, pgentry, *pgtable;
        if (exception occurred in Umode){   // i.e. running->inkmode==1
            if (err_nr==14){                 // page fault
                cr2 = CPU.CR2 register;        // get offending VA from CR2
                pgentry = cr2/4096;   // convert VA to pgtable entry number
                if (pgentry < 1024){  // if < 1024, it's a MISSING page
                    pgtable = VA(running->res->pgdir[0]&0xFFFFF000);
                    pgtable[pgentry] |= 0x1; // mark ptable entry PRESENT
                    load CPU.CR3 with PA(running->res->pgidr); // flush TLB
                    return;                 // return to Umode to continue
                }
                // page fault due to invalid address: send sig#11 to process
            }
        }
        else{ // page fault occurred in Kmode: PANIC and stop }
    }
```

In the above pseudo code, the page fault handler gets the virtual address (in CR2)
that caused the page fault and converts it to a pgtable entry index. If the index is
within the Umode VA, it means a missing page. The page fault handler marks the
missing page entry as present and reloads the CR3 register with the process pdgir to
flush the CPU's TLB cache. When the process returns to Umode, it re-executes the
instruction that caused the page fault earlier. Since the page table entry is now present, it will not cause any page fault again. If the page table entry index is outside of
the Umode VA range, it must be an invalid address, in which case the process gets
a regular page fault signal. In general, a missing page may be within the Umode
VA range but does not yet exist. In that case, the page fault handler must allocate a
page frame, load the needed page contents into the page frame and mark the page
entry present before letting the process continue. This is the basis of virtual memory
based on demand-paging. It is left as a programming project.

14.8.6 Page Replacement

In the page fault handler, if a new page must be allocated but there are no free page
frames, some existing pages must be evicted to make room for the needed page
frame. This is known as page replacement problem in virtual memory, which has
been discussed extensively in many OS books. The reader may consult such books
for more information. Since PMTX does not support demand-paging, the problem
of page replacement also does not exist. Nevertheless, it is still worth discussing the
principles of page replacement.

(1). Local Vs. Global: When trying to evict some existing pages, the first question is where to look for such pages? The search is local if we only try to evict pages
of the current process. It is global if we may evict pages of other processes in the
system. In the latter case, the candidates are usually non-runnable, i.e. blocked or
sleeping, processes.

(2). Least-Recently-Used (LRU) Page Replacement: The scheme is to replace a page that has not been referenced for the longest time. To support LRU, we may maintain all the pages in a link list with most recently used pages in front and least recently used pages at the end. During page replacement, choose pages from the end of the link list. Since the link list must be reordered on every memory reference, implementation of LRU by the link list method is feasible but very expensive. An alternative scheme is to assume a large global counter which is updated on every memory reference. Whenever a page is accessed, copy the current counter value as its access time. During page replacement, choose a page with the least access time to replace. However, the scheme is impractical since no such hardware support exists.

(2). Not-Recently-Used (NRU) Page Replacement: Each page frame has an A (access) bit and D (dirty) bit, which can be used to implement a simple NRU page replacement algorithm. In this scheme, the kernel periodically clears these bits (by timer interrupts). During page replacement, use the (A, D) bits to rank the pages and replace a page with the highest rank order.

Rank	(A,D)	Choice
3	(0,0):	Best candidate since page is not accessed and not modified
2	(0,1):	This may happen if (A,D) are not cleared at the same time
1	(1,0):	Third best, the page will probably be accessed again soon
0	(1,1):	Worst candidate, replace this page must write back first

14.8.7   Paging and I/O Buffer Management.

In many OS which support demand-paging, I/O buffers for files blocks may be treated as pages. When a process needs a file block, it maps the file block to a page in its virtual address space. The page is initially marked as not present. When the process attempts to access such a file block, it generates a page fault. The paging subsystem can allocate a page frame for the missing page, page-in the file block data, if necessary, and let the process continue. Once a file block is in the paged buffer cache, it can be reused to avoid physical I/O. This scheme unifies file I/O with demand-paging. It is used in Linux, and also in many other Unix-like systems. The main advantage of using a paged buffer cache is that it maximizes the use of physical memory. Almost all spare physical memory can be used for file system caching. The disadvantage is that, under intensive file I/O demands, it may cause thrashing (constantly swap pages in/out memory), which seriously degrades the system performance. For this reason, most OS sets a size limit on the paged buffer cache in order to prevent thrashing. In addition, they also use a separate internal buffer

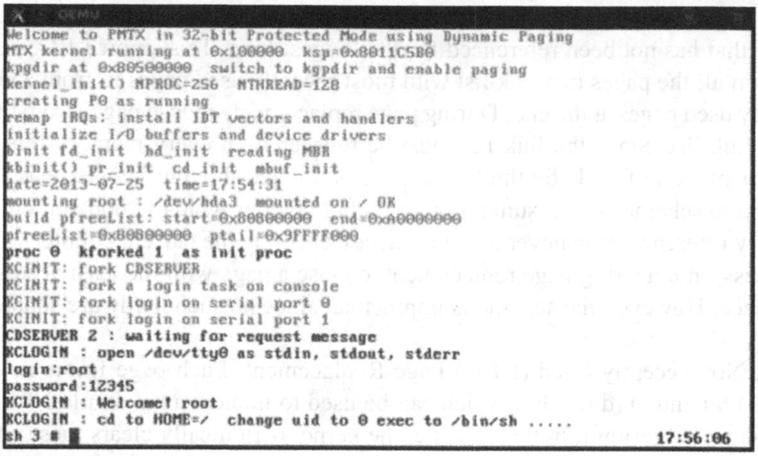

Fig. 14.21 Startup screen of PMTX

cache to maintain important system information, such as the superblock, bitmaps and directories, etc. Since PMTX does not yet support demand-paging, it only uses dedicated I/O buffers for block devices.

14.8.8   PMTX Demonstration System

In the MTX install CD, MTX.images/pmtx is a runnable image of PMTX. Figure 14.21 shows the startup screen of PMTX running under QEMU.

All executable user commands are in the /bin directory. In addition to regular commands, the user may run the following commands to test exception handling in PMTX:

Control_C key: kill process running on console or serial terminal
divide: handle divide error with or without a catcher
itimer: set interval timer and handle SIGALRM(14) signal
kill: kill process by pid, e.g. from console, kill a process running on serial terminal
pagefault: simulate page faults and page fault handling
segfault: handle segmentation fault with or without a catcher
signal: install signal catcher to IGNore or handle signal in user mode

14.9   Extensions of 32-bit Protected Mode MTX

The main advantage of 32-bit protected mode is that it opens the door for many possible extensions to the PMTX system. The following is a list of such areas.

1. EXT4 file system: Extend the file system to EXT3/EXT4 with 4KB block size.
2. Program development environment: port text editors and GCC to PMTX.
3. Dynamic linking: Support dynamic linking by shared and dynamic libraries.
4. Unix compatible sh: port or develop a Unix compatible sh.
5. Device drivers for PCI bus: Support SATA drives and USB devices.
6. Networking: Develop network drivers and port TCP/IP to support networking.
7. Other Unix software: port Unix utilities and X-Windows, etc. to PMTX.

These extensions would greatly enhance the capability of PMTX, making it a more useful system. However, before attempting such extensions, we should point out the following. So far, MTX has been a one-man's endeavor. Trying to do all the extensions is simply beyond the ability and time of any single person. More importantly, we should not lose focus on the original goal of MTX, which is intended as an educational system and should remain so. There is no need to create another PC based OS to compete with Linux (Bovet and Cesati 2005) or FreeBSD (McKusick and Neville-Neil 2004; McKusick and Bostic 1996). While some extensions are definitely needed and worthwhile, overdoing it may be counterproductive. I do not wish to see MTX end up in an awkward situation in which it is too complex for learning yet too primitive for practical use. Given the choice, I would prefer to see it remains simple and useful as an educational system.

14.9.1   64-bit Operating Systems

x86-64 refers to both AMD [AMD64 2011] and Intel 64-bit [Intel, Vol 3, 2014] processors. Currently, many OS, e.g. Linux and freeBSD, already have 64-bit versions. Although hard to justify the need, it is also possible to extend MTX to 64-bit mode. Interested readers may want to experiment with this. In that case, the following information on 64-bit x86-64 CPUs may be helpful.

14.9.2   x86-64 CPUs

AMD classifies the 64-bit environment of x86-64 CPUs into compatibility mode and long mode. In compatibility mode, a x86-64 CPU is the same as a x86 in 32-bit protected mode. In long mode, all registers and addresses are 64 bits, although the current implementation uses only 48-bit address. The startup sequence of a x86-64 CPU is as follows.

(1). Start in 16-bit real mode.

(2). Switch to 32-bit compatibility mode by setting up the GDT, LDT and IDT, page directory and page tables, then enter protected mode and/or enable paging. These are the same as x86 in 32-bit protected mode.

(3). Initialize long mode, which requires a 64-bit IDT containing 64-bit interrupt-gate descriptors and 64-bit interrupt handlers, a GDT, any LDT, if needed, and a single 64-bit TSS. The code segment descriptor must specify whether the CPU is executing in 64-bit or compatibility mode. The segment selectors DS, ES and SS are still used in compatibility mode but they are ignored in 64-bit mode. The segment selectors FS and GS are for 64-bit mode, which can be used by an OS. In 64-bit mode, paging is by 4 levels (or 3 levels of page tables). Page size is 4KB or 2 MB, super page size is 1 GB. Before entering long mode, paging must be disabled.

(4). Enable long mode by setting the long-mode enable control bit (EFER.LME) to 1. The long mode is activated only when paging is enabled. In 64-bit long mode, there is no segmentation, only paging.

(5). In 64-bit mode, interrupt processing is done by 64-bit IDT and 64-bit interrupt handler code. In compatibility mode, an interrupt pushes/pops [oldSS, oldesp] only if it involves a privilege level change. In 64-bit mode, an interrupt always pushes [oldSS, oldrsp], which is popped by iret.

(6). Hardware task switching is not supported in 64-bit mode. A 64-bit TSS in the GDT is still required to define the interrupt stack. (5) and (6) provide hints as how to set up the initial kernel stack of a process in 64-bit mode.

(7). The x86-64 CPU has additional control registers. The reader may consult AMD64 AMD64 2011 for more information.

14.9.3   Function Call Convention in 64-bit Mode

The x86-64 CPU has 8 more general registers. The registers are denoted as rip, rsp, rax, rbx, rcx, rdx, rbp, rsi, rdi and r8 to r15. During function calls, the first 6 parameters are passed in the registers rdi, rsi, rdx, rcx, r8 and r9, in that order. The called function must save and restore rbx, rbp and r13-15 if they are to be altered. On entry to a called function, the compiled code of GCC may allocate a fixed size stack area for all local variables and use rsp as the stack frame pointer. When developing a 64-bit OS kernel we must observe these function call conventions, especially when interfacing C with assembly code.

14.10   Summary

In this chapter, we presented 3 versions of MTX in 32-bit protected mode. MTX32.1 uses protected segments, MTX32.2 uses static paging and PMTX uses dynamic paging. It is shown that for protected mode operations we only need to add virtual address mapping and set up the IDT for exception and interrupt processing. Other than these, it requires only a few minor changes to the real mode RMTX kernel to make it also work in protected mode. This shows that when studying the principle of OS design, the actual memory management hardware is relatively unimportant. It also demonstrates that, despite the architectural differences between real mode and protected mode, the same design principle and implementation technique can be applied to all cases.

Problems

1. In MTX32.1, the LDT of each process defines only a code segment and a data segment. The data segment is used for both data and stack of the Umode image.

(a). Can we define a separate data and stack segments for each Umode image? Justify.

(b). Assume that the Umode image is an executable a.out or ELF file with size information, such as tsize, dsize and bsize. Show how to set up the LDT segments of a process to enforce proper access to the segments.

2. In MTX32.1, VA=PA in Kmode. In Umode, the VA range of every process is from 0 to 2 MB. Assume that we want the Umode VA begins at 1 MB.

(1). Show how to generate such Umode images. (2). Show how to set up the process LDTs.

3. The Intel x86 CPU supports super pages of 4 MB page size, which may be used when MTX32.2 and PMTX start. Describe the needed changes to entry.s and discuss the merit of using super pages.

4. In MTX32.2, page directories and page tables are constructed in the low end of physical memory. Assume 512 MB physical memory. Modify MTX32.2 to construct the page directories and page tables in the high end of physical memory. What is the disadvantage of this scheme?

5. In MTX32.2, we assume that every Umode image size is 4 MB. Modify fork1() for different image sizes, e.g. 8 MB, 64 MB, etc. Design an algorithm which builds the page tables for an image of size=SIZE in multiples of 4KB.

6. In MTX32.2, the process image is allocated as a piece of contiguous memory. Design a page frame management algorithm, which allocate/deallocate page frames dynamically. Manage the free page fames by (1). a bitmap. (2). a link list.

Discuss the advantages and disadvantages of each scheme.

7. In MTX32.2, the kernel virtual address space is mapped low and user virtual address space is mapped high. Try to reverse the the virtual address mappings, i.e. kernel space begins from 2 GB and user space begins at 0.

8. In PMTX, the physical memory area from 1 MB to 4 MB is dedicated to the PMTX kernel. Assume that PMTX kernel size=5 MB. Show

(1). How to boot up such a PMTX kernel? (Hint: consult booting bzImage of Linux in Chap. 3)

(2). Show how to modify enrty.s to set up the initial paging environment for such a PMTX kernel.

9. In PMTX, a process in kexit() keeps both its kstack and pgdir, which are eventually deallocated by its parent in kwait().

(1). Why are these necessary?

(2). What would happen if a process deallocates its pgdir or kstack in kexit()? How to handle such problems?

10. In PMTX, assume 512 MB physical memory and that the kernel's virtual address space is from 3 GB to 4G.

(1). Show how to set up the kernel mode page directory and page tables.

(2). Show how to set up the user mode page directory and page tables.

11. In PMTX, free page frames are managed by a pfreelist. Use a bit map to manage free page frames. Compare the advantages and disadvantages of the two schemes.

12. Null pointers: In PMTX, if a user mode program tries to dereference a null pointer, it should generate a page fault. Devise a scheme to implement this.

13. Modify PMTX to run processes with Umode images with the memory size option

cmd parameter-list -m SIZE k

where SIZE is a multiple of KB, e.g. –m 4096 k for 4096 KB, -m 7200 k for 7200 KB, etc.

14. In PMTX, kexec() always allocates a new image for the process. Modify it as follows.

(1). Allocate a new image only if the process is vforked or needs a image of different size. Otherwise, use the original image area to load the new file.

(2). Discuss the advantages and disadvantages of the new scheme.

15. In PMTX, the user mode program, demandpage, demonstrates demand-paging. The program issues a page_out(n) system call to mark the nth page of the process as not present. When the process attempts to reference the missing page, it generates a page fault. The kernel's page fault handler (ehandler() in trapc.c) uses page_in(n) to mark the missing page as present, allowing the process to continue.

(1). Modify page_out(n) to deallocate the nth page of a process.

(2). Modify page_in(n) to allocate a new page frame.

(3). The page fault handler assumes 4 MB image size. Modify it for different image sizes.

16. In PMTX without the –m SIZEm option, every Umode image size is 4 MB. The Umode page table of every process has 1024 entries, all of which have pre-allocated page frames. Show how to modify makePage() for the following cases.

(1). By actual image size, e.g. code + data + bss, is only 8KB. The Umode stack is at the high end of the VA with an initial stack size of 8KB. Pages that are not needed should have no page frames.

(2). Same assumptions as in (1), show how to expand the image's heap by page size.

(3). Same assumptions as in (1), except that the stack should be directly above the bss section. Show how to expand the image's heap by page size.

(4). In an ELF executable file, each program section has a virtual address, a memory size and a R|W|Ex flag. When loading an ELF file, allocate pages for the sections as needed and set code pages for RE(executable), rodata pages for RO, data and bss pages for RW.

17. In kexec() of PMTX, a vforked process first allocates a new image. Then it tries to load a image file. If the loading fails, e.g. due to an invalid file name, it release the new image and returns -1 to the original image. In this case, the vforked process should terminate since it cannot continue to execute in the shared image. Implement the following alternatives if loading file fails:

(1). load a default file, which issuses exit(1) to terminate.

(2). copy the binary code of exit(2) to the beginning of the new image and let it return to execute the new image. (HINT: write syscall(9, 2) in assembly and use as –ahls to see the binary code).

(3). call kexit(123) to terminate directly.

18. In PMTX, implement demand-paging by NRU.
19. In PMTX, implement block device I/O buffering by demand-paging.
20. Extend PMTX to 64-bit.

References

AMD64 Architecture Programmer's manual Volume 2: System Programming, 2011
Antonakos, J.L., "An introduction to the Intel Family of Microprocessors", Prentice Hall, 1999.
Bovet, D.P., Cesati, M., "Understanding the Linux Kernel, Third Edition", O'Reilly, 2005
Cox, R., Kaashoek, F., Morris, R. "xv6 a simple, Unix-like teaching operating system, xv6-book@ pdos.csail.mit.edu, Sept. 2011.
Intel 64 and IA-32 Architectures Software Developer's Manual, Volume 3, 2014
Intel i486 Processor Programmer's Reference Manual, 1990
McKusick, M.K., Bostic, K., "The Design and Implementation of the 4.4 BSD Operating System", Addison-Wesley, 1996
McKusick, M.K., Neville-Neil, G.,"The Design and Implementation of the FreeBSD Operating System", Addison-Wesley, 2004.
Tool Interface Standard (TIS) Executable and Linking Format (ELF) Specification Version 1.2 (May 1995)
Youngdale, E., "The ELF Object File Format: Introduction", Linux Journal, April, 1995.

Chapter 15
Symmetric Multiprocessing MTX

15.1 Multiprocessor Systems

A multiprocessor system consists of a multiple number of processors, which share
main memory and I/O devices. If the shared main memory is the only memory in
the system, it is called a Uniform Memory Access (UMA) system. If, in addition
to the shared memory, each processor also has private local memory, it is called a
Non-uniform Memory Access (NUMA) system. If the roles of the processors are
not the same, e.g. only some of the processors can execute kernel code while others
can not, it is called an Asymmetric MP (ASMP) system. If all the processors are
functionally identical, it is called a Symmetric MP (SMP) system. With the current
multicore processor technology, SMP has become virtually synonymous with MP.

15.2 SMP-Compliant Systems

A SMP system requires much more than just a multiple numbers of processors or
processor cores. In order to support SMP, the system architecture must have additional capabilities. Intel's Multiprocessor Specification (Intel Multiprocessor Specification 1997) defines SMP-compliant systems as PC/AT compatible systems with
the following capabilities.

1. Support interrupts routing and inter-processor interrupts. In a SMP-compliant
   system, interrupts from I/O devices can be routed to different processors to
   balance the interrupt processing load. Processors can interrupt each other by
   Inter-Processor Interrupts (IPIs) for communication and synchronization. In a
   SMP-compliant system, these are provided by a set of Advanced Programmable
   Interrupt Controllers (APICs). A SMP-compliant system usually has a system-
   wide IOAPIC and a set of local APICs of the individual processors. Together, the
   APICs implement an inter-processor communication protocol, which supports
   interrupts routing and IPIs.

© Springer International Publishing Switzerland 2015
K. C. Wang, *Design and Implementation of the MTX Operating System,*
DOI 10.1007/978-3-319-17575-1_15

2. An extended BIOS, which detects the system configuration and builds SMP data structures for the operating system to use.
3. When the system starts, one of the processors is designated as the Boot Processor (BSP), which executes the boot code to start up the system. All other processors are called Application Processors (APs), which are held in the idle state initially but can receive IPIs from the BSP to start up. After booting up, all processors are functionally identical.

15.3   SMP System Startup Sequence

15.3.1   SMP Data Structures

When a SMP system starts, BIOS detects the system hardware configuration and creates a set of SMP data structures for the operating system to use. The data structures include a Floating Pointer Structure (FPS), which is required, and a MP Configuration Table. If the FPS is absent, the system is not SMP-compliant. If the configuration table does not exist, the operating system may use a default MP configuration table, which is valid for only two processors. The FPS is in one of the following locations, which the BSP must search in order.

• first 1 KB of the extended BIOS data area.
• last 1 KB of real-mode base memory.
• BIOS read-only memory between 0xA0000 and 0xFFFFF.

The FPS is a 16-byte structure. It begins with a 4-byte signature "_MP_". The next field is a 4-byte pointer to the MP configuration table. The configuration table is divided into three parts: a header, a base section, and an extended section. The header begins with the four-byte signature "PCMP". It contains OEM information and the number of entries in the base section. The base section consists of a set of entries which describe processors, system buses, IOAPIC, I/O interrupt assignments and local APIC interrupt assignments. The first byte of each entry is the entry type. For processor entries, the type is 0 and the entry length is 20 bytes. All other entries are 8 bytes. The OS kernel must parse the MP configuration table to create OS specific data structures, such as the APIC ID, version and type of each processor, as well as the address of the system's IOAPIC.

As an example, MTX has a mp command, which scans the MP configuration table of a SMP-compliant PC. Figure 15.1 shows the sample outputs (with added comments) of running the mp program for a VMware virtual machine on a dual-core host PC. For other multicore PCs, the outputs vary but are similar.

Figure 15.1 shows that the virtual machine has only one IOAPIC at 0xFEC00000. Local APICs are at 0xFEE00000. These are memory-mapped addresses of processor registers. Each processor may use the same APIC address to access its own local APIC.

```
/************ Sample outputs of MTX's mp command ***********/
// Search for MP flopating pointer structure
Serach BIOS ROM area 0xF0000 to 0xFFFFF      (found the FPS)
signature = _MP_                     // MP table signature
mp_table_addr=0x9FD70                // MP configuration table address
signature = PCMP                     // signature
base_len=268 rev=0x4 cksum=0x6B      // length, MP version 1.4
0x49  0x4E  0x54  0x45  I N T E      // OEM information
0x4C  0x20  0x20  0x20  L            // INTEL 440BX
0x34  0x34  0x30  0x42  4 4 0 B
oemTablePtr=0x0 entryCount=25        // number of entries=25
localAPICAddr=0xFEE00000             // local APIC address
******* CPU #0 ********               // processor entries (type 0)
0x0  0x0  0x11  0x3                  // APICid=0; 0x3=BSP, enabled
cpu_signature=0x6F6 flags=0xFEBFBFF
******* CPU #1 ********
0x0  0x1  0x11  0x1                  // APICid=1; 0x1=AP, enabled
cpu_signature=0x6F6 flags=0xFEBFBFF
// bus entries (type 1)
0x02 PCI                             // bus ID, string
0x23 ISA                             // bus ID, string
// IOAPIC entry (type 2)
0x2 0x2 0x11 0x1 addr=0xFEC00000  // I/O APIC address
// IOAPIC Interrupts Assignment entries (type 3)
0x23  0x0  0x2  0x0                  // ISA IRQ0 routing
// Local APIC Interrupt Assignemnt entry (type 4)
0x23  0x0  0xFF  0x0        // ISA IRQ0 to Int0 of all local APICs
```

Fig. 15.1 MP table example

During booting of a SMP-compliant system, the BSP must initialize the system hardware for SMP operations. These include

- Configure IOAPIC to route interrupts to local APICs.
- Configure and enable BSP's local APIC.
- Send INIT and STARTUP IPIs to activate other APs.
- Continue to initialize the OS kernel until it is ready to run tasks.

The following sections describe these actions in detail.

15.3.2   Configure IOAPIC

1. Set up IOAPIC Interrupt Registers

A SMP system usually has only one IOAPIC. The IOAPIC has 24 (64-bit) registers, which specify how to route interrupts and map IRQs to interrupt vectors. The registers are accessed indirectly through a pair of IOREGSEL and IOWIN registers, which are located at 0xFEC00000 and 0xFEC00010, respectively. Other registers are byte offsets from the IOWIN register. All IOAPIC registers must be accessed by 32-bit reads/writes. To access an IOAPIC register, first select the register by writing its byte offset to IOREGSEL. Then read/write a 32-bit value from/to the IOWIN register. For each IOAPIC interrupt register, it takes two operations to read/write the two 32-bit halves of the register. Standard assignments of the IOAPIC interrupt registers are

```
IRQ 0-15  : IOAPIC registers  0-15
PCI A-D   : IOAPIC registers  16-19
```

For IRQ 0-15 interrupts, they must be set to edge-triggered and active high. For PCI A-D interrupts, they must be set to level-triggered and active low. In protected mode, the first 32 interrupt vectors are reserved. Each of the IOAPIC interrupt registers can be programmed with any of the remaining 224 vectors. The top four bits of an interrupt vector is the interrupt priority. Higher interrupt vector numbers have higher priorities. The standard PIC interrupt priorities are IRQ 0-2, 8-15, 3-7, where IRQ0 has the highest priority. If needed, the IRQs can be mapped by the IOAPIC interrupt registers to vectors that preserve their priorities. There are 16 different interrupt priorities, 0 to F. Since we cannot use the vectors 0x00-0x1F, it leaves only 14 available interrupt priorities. Thus, some of the IRQs must be mapped to vectors with the same priority. For example, if we remap IRQ0-15 to 0x21-0x2F and program the IOAPIC registers 0-15 for vectors 0x21-0x2F, then all the interrupts are of the same priority (2). Alternatively, we may choose vectors 0x20-0x9F for the PIC IRQs and assign two IRQs to each priority level, resulting in the following assignment.

```
PIC IRQs  : 0  1  2  8  9 10 11 12 13 14 15  3  4  5  6  7
vectors 0x:90 91 80 81 70 71 60 61 50 51 40 41 30 31 20 21
```

Similarly for the interrupt registers 16–19, which map PCI interrupts A–D. In addition to interrupt vectors, each IOAPIC interrupt register must also be programmed with interrupt delivery mode and destination. The delivery mode can be either physical or logical. The simplest way is to use logical delivery mode and route interrupts to APICs with the lowest priority. The priority of an APIC is in the APIC task priority register. Alternatively, we may also use physical delivery mode and program the IOAPIC registers to route interrupts to specific processors to balance the interrupt processing load.

2. Switch to Symmetric I/O Mode

In order to route interrupts to local APICs, the system must switch to symmetric I/O mode. For PCs with an Interrupt Mask Control Register (IMCR), this can be done by writing 0x01 to the IMCR's data register. Most virtual machines do not have an IMCR, so this step is optional.

```
. out_byte(0x22, 0x70);   // access IMCR
. out_byte(0x23, 0x01);   // force PIC IRQs to IOAPIC
```

3. Disable 8259 PICs

After setting up the IOAPIC to route interrupts, the 8259 PICs must be disabled to prevent multiple interrupts from the same source.

```
. out_byte(0x21, 0xFF);  // mask out master PIC
. out_byte(0xA1, 0xFF);  // mask out slave  PIC
```

15.3.3 Configure Local APICs

Each processor has a local APIC at the same base address 0xFEE00000. Local APIC registers are offsets from the APIC base address. The APIC registers can be accessed directly with 32-bit read/write. Some of the APIC registers and their usage are listed in Fig. 15.2. To enable the local APIC, write 0x010F to the spurious interrupt register (0x0F0). This also sets 0x0F as the default vector for spurious interrupts.

15.3.4 Send IPIs to Activate APs

After enabling the local APIC, the BSP must activate other APs by sending them INIT and STARTUP IPIs. This can be done by writing to the Interrupt Command Registers (0x310 = dest, 0x300 = IPI) to send IPIs to each individual AP or broadcast them to all the APs. In the latter case, the IPIs are issued as follows, where the delay is about 200 msec.

Register	Contents
0x020 :	ID register (unique ID; to be used as CPU ID)
0x080 :	task priority (as interrupt priority mask)
0x0B0 :	EOI (write 0 to signal end-of-interrupt)
0x0F0 :	spurious interrupt vector (also for enable APIC)
0x300 :	interrupt command register (generate IPIs)
0x310 :	destination ID of interrupt command
0x320 :	LVT timer (APCI timer: mask bit, mode and vector)
0x350 :	LVT LINT0 (INTR input)
0x360 :	LVT LINT1 (NMI input)
0x370 :	LVT error vector table
0x380 :	initial timer count
0x390 :	current timer count
0x3E0 :	timer divider

Fig. 15.2 APIC registers

```
.write 0x000C4500 to 0x300; delay; // broadcast INIT IPI to all APs
.write 0x000C4691 to 0x300; delay; // broadcast STARTUP IPI to all APs
```

15.3.5   Trampoline Code of APs

Each AP wakes up to execute a piece of trampoline code in 16-bit real mode. The
trampoline code must begin at a 4 KB page boundary in real-mode memory. The
location is determined by the vector number in the STARTUP IPI. In the above
example, the vector value is 0x91, which tells the APs to begin execution from
0x91000 in real-mode memory. Each AP must switch to protected mode, set up
page tables and configure local APIC before entering the OS kernel. In SMP, a
processor may use IPIs to synchronize with other processors, such as to flush their
TLBs and invalidate page table entries, etc.

15.4   From UP to SMP

Once a SMP system boots up, all the processors are functionally identical. In a SMP
system, processes may run in parallel on different processors. A SMP kernel must
be able to support parallel executions of multiple processes. Therefore, all kernel
data structures must be protected to prevent race conditions. Traditionally, most OS
kernels are designed for uniprocessor (UP) systems. Adapting a UP kernel for SMP
is usually done in three stages (Cox 1995).

15.4.1   Giant Lock Stage

Early Linux (Cox 1995) and FreeBSD (McKusick and Neville-Neil 2004) were
adapted to SMP by using a Giant Kernel Lock (GKL). In this scheme, the entire
kernel is treated as a critical region and protected by a single global lock, which is
usually a spinlock. In order to execute in kernel, a process must acquire the GKL
first. Only the process which holds the GKL can execute in kernel. The GKL is
not released until the process has completed the kernel mode operation. The main
advantage of this approach lies in its simplicity. It requires very little change to a UP
kernel to make it work in SMP. The disadvantage is that, while a process executes in
kernel, all other processes must either busily wait for the GKL or can only execute
in user mode. Such a system supports MP but does not realize the capabilities of a
SMP system.

15.4.2   Coarse Grain Locking Stage

To improve concurrency, a SMP kernel may use separate locks to protect different
subsystems or groups of closely related data structures. This allows for some degree
of concurrency but with only limited improvements in performance. For this reason,
most SMP kernels use coarse grain locking as a transitory stage.

15.4.3   Fine Grain Locking Stage

System V Unix, AIX and current versions of Linux (version 2.6 and later) all use
fine grain locking for SMP. In this scheme, small locks are used to protect individual kernel data structures, allowing parallel operations on different data structures. Although every SMP system strives for fine grain locking, there is no general
consensus as to what constitutes a fine grain lock. Currently, the approach used by
almost all SMP kernels is as follows.

- Identify the data structures in a UP kernel that need protection. Use locks to
  implement operations on the data structures as critical regions. Examples of such
  data structures include process table, process scheduling queue, page tables, in-
  memory inodes and I/O buffers, etc. This generally leads to concurrency at the
  individual data structure level in the original UP kernel.
- To further improve concurrency, try to decompose the data structures into separate parts. If the decomposed parts are logically related, devise ways to synchronize their operations. However, most existing SMP systems do not yet use this
  strategy.

As the lock grain size decreases, the overhead due to additional locking and synchronization will increase. Eventually, the process of reducing the lock grain size
must stop at some point when it no longer improves concurrency and overall speed.
The problem of designing SMP kernels is essentially the same as that of designing
parallel algorithms (Grama et al. 2003). Although the principle is simple, the dif-
ficulty is how to decompose the data structures to allow for maximal concurrency
yet with minimal interactions among the decomposed parts. So far, there are no
definitive answers.

Rather than discussing SMP in general terms, we shall consider the specific
problem of adapting MTX for SMP. In line with the evolutionary style of this book,
we shall develop the SMP system in two steps. In the first step, we extend the UP
PMTX to SMP_PMTX, which uses fine grain locks and modified UP sequential
algorithms for SMP. In the second step, we focus on the design and use of parallel
algorithms for SMP, and extend SMP_PMTX to the final version of SMP_MTX,
which uses parallel algorithms on decomposed kernel data structures to improve
both concurrency and efficiency. In addition, we shall also show an experimental
SMP MTX in 16-bit real mode.

15.5   SMP_PMTX in 32-bit Protected Mode

In this section, we shall extend the UP PMTX kernel to SMP_PMTX, which is the initial version of SMP_MTX. Although some of the discussions are SMP_PMTX specific, they may also be regarded as a general methodology for adapting UP kernels to SMP systematically.

15.5.1   Running PROCs and CPU Structures

In the PMTX kernel, running is a global pointer to the current running process. In SMP, a single running pointer is no longer adequate because each CPU may be executing a different process. We must be able to identify the process that's executing on each CPU. There are two possible ways to do this. The first one is to define NCPU PROC pointers, PROC *run[NCPU], and let run[i] point to the PROC that's currently executing on CPUi. The drawback of this scheme is that it is rather inconvenient to access run[cpuid] in assembly code unless we store the index in a CPU register. The second method is to use virtual memory. In SMP_PMTX, we represent each CPU by a cpu structure (defined in type.h) and map the cpu structure by a spare segment register, e.g. the gs register, to a virtual address. To every CPU its cpu structure is always at gs:0 and its current executing PROC pointer is always at gs:4, etc. Instead of gs, we may also use es or fs to map the cpu structure.

15.5.2   Spinlocks and Semaphores

In SMP, processes may run in parallel on different CPUs. All data structures in a SMP kernel must be protected to prevent corruptions from race conditions. Typical tools used to achieve this are spinlocks and semaphores. Spinlocks are suitable for CPUs to wait for critical regions of short durations in which task switch is either unnecessary or not permissible, e.g. in an interrupt handler. To access a critical region, a process must acquire the spinlock associated with the critical region first, as in

```
SPINLOCK s = 0;     // initial value = 0
slock(s);           // acquire spinlock
  // access critical region CR
sunlock(s);         // release spinlock
```

When a process exits the critical region CR, it releases the spinlock to allow other CPUs to acquire the spinlock. slock(s)/sunlock(s) are implemented in assembly because they rely on test_and_set like atomic instructions. For the x86 CPUs, the equivalent instruction is XCHG, which atomically exchanges the contents of a CPU register with a memory location.

For critical regions of longer durations, it is preferable to let the process wait by giving up the CPU. In such cases, semaphores are more suitable. In SMP, each semaphore must have a spinlock field to ensure that all operations on a semaphore can only be performed in the critical region of the semaphore's spinlock. Similar modifications are also needed for mutex and mutex operations, which are used for threads synchronization. Since PMTX already uses semaphores in file system and device drivers, in SMP_PMTX we shall use both spinlocks and semaphores to protect kernel data structures.

15.5.3 Use Sleep/Wakeup in SMP

As a synchronization mechanism, sleep/wakeup works well in UP but is unsuited to SMP. This is because an event is just a value, which does not have an associated memory location to record the occurrence of the event. When an event occurs, wakeup tries to wake up all processes sleeping on the event. If no process is sleeping on the event, wakeup has no effect. This requires a process to sleep first before another process tries to wake it up later. This sleep-first and wakeup-later order can always be achieved in UP but not in SMP. In a SMP system, processes may run in parallel on different CPUs. It is impossible to guarantee the process execution order. Therefore, in their original form, sleep/wakeup cannot be used in SMP. However, we can modify sleep/wakeup to make them workable in SMP.

Consider the case in which a parent process waits for a ZOMBIE child. In a UP kernel, if the parent calls wait() before the child has died, the parent would call sleep() to go to sleep since it cannot find a ZOMBIE child. In this case, the parent completes the sleep operation before the child can run. Later, when the child calls exit() to die, it tries to wake up the parent. Since the parent is already in the sleeping state, the child's wakeup call will find the parent. On the other hand, if the child terminates first, the child's wakeup call would miss the parent but it leaves behind a ZOMBIE PROC for the parent to find. When the parent calls wait() later, it will find the ZOMBIE child PROC and does not sleep. In either case, sleep and wakeup work well because in a UP kernel the actions of the parent in wait() and child in exit() are serialized, i.e. one at a time without interleaving. In a SMP kernel, the situation is different. When a parent calls wait(), the child may be running on a different CPU at the same time. Assume that the parent in wait() has just checked that there is no ZOMBIE child and is about to call sleep(). Right in this time gap, if the child running on a different CPU calls exit(), it would become a ZOMBIE and try to wake up the parent. Since the parent has not slept yet, the child's wakeup call would have no effect. Then the parent goes to sleep, but it already missed the child's wakeup call. Based on this analysis, it is immediately clear that, in order for the parent and child not to miss each other, the parent's sleep action and the child's exit action must be serialized. This can be achieved by requiring them to go through a common critical region, which serializes their actions even if they are executing in parallel. Therefore, we can modify sleep/wakeup as follows. For each event, define a spinlock sw=0, and impose the following restrictions on the usage of sleep/wakeup: when processes call sleep and wakeup on an event, they must execute in the same critical region of the sw spinlock. While holding the spinlock, if a process has to sleep, it must complete the sleep and release the spinlock in a single indivisible or atomic operation, as shown below.

1. For each event, define a SPINLOCK sw=0;
2. A process must acquire the sw spinlock before calling the modified sleep() function.

```
sleep(int event, SPINLOCK sw)
{  // caller holds the spinlock sw
   sleep on event;            // go to sleep as in UP kernel
   sunlock(sw);               // release spinlock
   tswitch();                 // switch process
}
```

3. When a process calls wakeup() for the same event, it must execute in the CR of the spinlock.

```
   slock(sw);                 // acquire spinlock
   change condition to OK;    // set condition inside CR
   wakeup(event);             // issue wakeup inside CR
   sunlock(sw);               // release spinlock
```

where the wakeup() function does not need any change but it must be issued inside the same critical region of a spinlock. With these modifications, we may use sleep/wakeup to implement wait and exit in a SMP kernel. The modified sleep/wakeup can also be used for general process synchronization. Assume that two processes Pi and Pj share some common data, e.g. a counter, which is modified by Pi and used by Pj to make decisions. To synchronize Pi and Pj, define a spinlock sw=0, and require Pi and Pj to obey the following rules.

```
        Process Pi:         |       Process Pj:
------------------------|--------------------------
{                       |   { while(1){
   acquire sw lock;     |      acquire sw lock;
   change counter value;|      if (counter value OK) break;
   wakeup(event);       |      sleep(event, sw);
   release sw lock;     |      }
                        |      release sw lock;
}                       |   }
--------------------------------------------------------
```

In the above pseudo-code, only one process can be inside the critical region at a time. If Pi and Pj obey these rules, there will be no race condition and hence no missing wakeup calls. This is the process synchronization mechanism used in xv6 (Cox et al. 2011). The modification amounts to putting the original sleep/wakeup on steroids since the shared variable inside a common critical region essentially makes up for the lack of memory location of an event. It is almost equivalent to the condition variable of Pthreads [Pthreads 2015], which relies on a mutex lock. The only difference is that in the modified sleep/wakeup, when a process resumes after sleep, it must acquire the spinlock again. In Pthreads, when a blocked process resumes inside a condition variable, the condition variable's mutex is automatically locked. Although it is possible to use only the modified sleep/wakeup for process synchronization in SMP, the drawback is that a process must retry after each sleep. In SMP_ PMTX, we use semaphore to implement wait and exit as follows. In each PROC structure, define a semaphore wchild=0. In kwait(), a process uses P(wchild) to wait for ZOMBIE children. In kexit(), a process uses V(parent $\rightarrow$ wchild) to unblock the parent. Using semaphores, there is no race condition between the parent and child.

15.5.4 *Protect Kernel Data Structures*

In a UP kernel, only one process executes at a time. So data structures in a UP kernel do not need any protection against concurrent process executions. When adapt a UP kernel for SMP, all kernel data structures must be protected to ensure that processes can only access them one at a time. The required modifications can be classified into two categories.

1. The first category includes kernel data structures which are used for allocation and deallocation of resources. These include
   free PROC list, free page frame list, pipe structures, message buffers, bitmaps for inodes and disk blocks, in-memory inodes, open file table, mount table, etc.

Each of these data structures can be protected by either a spinlock or a lock semaphore. Then modify the allocation/deallocation algorithms as critical regions of the form

```
allocate(resource)
{
    LOCK(resource_lock);
     // allocate resource from the resource data structure;
    UNLOCK(resource_lock);
    retrun allocated resource;
}
deallocate(resource)
{
    LOCK(resource_lock)
     // release resource to the resource data structure;
    UNLOCK(resource_lock);
}
```

where LOCK/UNLOCK denote either slock/sunlock on spinlocks or P/V on lock semaphores. Since P/V require implicit operations on the semaphore's spinlock, it is more efficient to use spinlocks directly. For example, in SMP_PMTX we define a spinlock sfreelist=0 to protect the free PROC list and modify get_proc()/put_proc() as follows.

```
PROC *get_proc()
{
    slock(sfreelist);
    // *p = get a PROC pointer from free PROC list;
    sunlock(sfreelist);
    return p;
}
void put_proc(PROC *p)
{
    slock(sfreelist);
    // enter p into free PROC list;
    sunlock(sfreelist);
}
```

where the operations on the free PROC list are exactly the same as that in a UP kernel. Similarly, we can use spinlocks to protect other resources. In short, this category includes all the kernel data structures for which the behavior of a process is to access the data structure without pausing.

2. The second category includes the cases in which a process must acquire a lock first in order to search for a needed item in a data structure. If the needed item already exists, the process must not create the same item again, but it may have to wait for the item. If so, it must release the lock to allow concurrency. However, this may lead to the following race condition. After releasing the lock but before the process has completed the wait operation, the item may be changed by other processes running on different CPUs, causing it to wait for the wrong item. This kind of race condition cannot occur in UP but is very likely in SMP. There are two possible ways to prevent such race conditions.

2.1. Set a reservation flag on the item before releasing the lock. Ensure that the reservation flag can only be manipulated inside the critical region of the lock. For example, in the iget() function of the MTX file system, which returns a locked minode, each minode has a refCount field, which represents the number of processes still using the minode. When a process executes iget(), it first acquires a lock and then searches for a needed minode. If the minode already exists, it increases the minode's refCount by 1 to reserve the minode. Then it releases the lock and tries to lock the minode. When a process releases a minode by iput(), it must execute in the same critical region as iget(). After decrementing the minode's refCount by 1, if the refCount is non-zero, meaning that the minode still has users, it does not free the minode. Since both iget() and iput() execute in the same critical region of a lock, race condition cannot occur.

2.2. Ensure that the process completes the wait operation on the needed item before releasing the lock, which eliminates the time gap. When using spinlocks this is the same technique as putting sleep/wakeup on steroids. When using semaphore locks we may use the PV(s1,s2) operation defined in Chap. 6, which atomically blocks a process on semaphore s1 before releasing semaphore s2. As an example, consider the iget()/iput() functions again. Assume that mlock is a lock semaphore for all the minodes in memory and each minode has a lock semaphore minode.sem = 1. We only need to modify iget()/iput() slightly as follows.

```
MINODE *iget(int dev, int ino) // return a locked minode=(dev,ino)
{
    P(mlock);                           // acquire minodes lock
    if (needed minode already exists){
        if (!CP(minode.sem)             // if minode is already locked
            PV(minode.sem, mlock);      // atomically (P(s1),V(s2))
        return minode;                  // return locked minode
    }
    // needed minode not in memory, still holds mlock
    allocate a free minode;
    P(minode.sem);                      // lock minode
    V(mlock);                           // release minodes lock
    load inode from disk into minode;
    return minode;
}
void iput(MINDOE minode)
{
    // caller already holds minode.sem lock
    P(mlock);
    // do release minode operations as in PMTX;
    V(minode.sem);
    V(mlock);
}
```

Note that, in iget() the locking order is to lock mlock first, then minode, which is opposite to that of iput(). Despite the opposite locking orders, deadlock cannot occur. This is because in iget() a process tries to lock an existing minode by CP(). If the minode is already locked, it waits for the minode and releases the mlock in a single atomic operation.

15.5.5 Adapt UP Algorithms for SMP

In addition to using locks to protect kernel data structures, many algorithms used in UP kernels must be modified to suit SMP. We illustrate this by examples.

15.5.5.1 Adapt UP Process Scheduling Algorithm for SMP

A UP kernel usually has only a single process scheduling queue. With a single process scheduling queue, we may adapt the UP process scheduling algorithm for SMP as follows. Define a spinlock, srQ, to protect the scheduling queue. During task switch, a process must acquire the srQ spinlock first, which is released by the next running process when it resumes.

15.5.5.2 Adapt UP Pipe Algorithm for SMP

In PMTX, pipes are implemented by the UP algorithm of Sect. 6.14.3, which uses the conventional sleep/wakeup for synchronization. We may adapt the UP pipe algorithm for SMP by adding a spinlock to each pipe and requiring pipe readers and writers to execute in the same critical region of the spinlock. While holding the spinlock, if a process has to sleep for data or room in the pipe, it must complete the sleep before releasing the spinlock, which can be done by replacing the conventional sleep(event) with the modified sleep(event, spinlock) operation.

15.5.5.3 Adapt UP I/O Buffer Management Algorithm for SMP

In Chap. 12, we showed several I/O buffer management algorithms for block devices. Again, the algorithms work only in UP because they all assume only one process runs at a time. We may adapt the algorithms for SMP by adding a spinlock and ensuring that both getblk() and brelse() are executed in the same critical region. While holding the spinlock, if a process has to wait, it must complete the wait and release the spinlock in a single atomic operation. The technique is exactly the same as that of adapting the UP pipe algorithm for SMP. Similarly, we may adapt other UP algorithms for SMP.

15.5.6 Device Driver and Interrupt Handlers for SMP

In an interrupt-driven device driver, process and interrupt handler usually share data buffer and control variables, which form a critical region between the process and interrupt handler. In a UP kernel, when a process executes a device driver, it can mask out interrupts to prevent interference from the interrupt handler. In SMP, masking out interrupts is no longer sufficient. This is because while a process executes a device driver, another CPU may execute the device interrupt handler at the same time. In order to serialize the executions of processes and interrupt handlers, device drivers in SMP must be modified also. Since interrupt handlers cannot sleep or block, they must use spinlock or equivalent mechanisms. In the following, we illustrate the principles of SMP driver design by specific examples in the SMP_ PMTX kernel.

1. The PC's console display is a memory-mapped device, which does not use interrupts. To ensure processes executes putc() one at a time, it suffices to protect the driver by a spinlock.
2. In the FD driver, only one process can execute the driver at a time. After issuing an I/O command, the process waits on a semaphore for interrupt. The interrupt handler only unblocks the process but does not access the driver's data structure. So the FD driver does not need any change.
3. In the HD and ATAPI driver, process and interrupt handler shared data structures. For such drivers, it suffices to use a spinlock to serializes the executions of process and interrupt handler.
4. In the timer driver, process and interrupt handler share timer service and process scheduling queues but the process never waits for timer interrupts. In this case, it suffices to protect each timer dependent data structure by a spinlock.

5. Char device drivers also use I/O buffers for better efficiency. In PMTX, all char device drivers use semaphores for synchronization. To adapt the derivers to SMP, each driver uses a spinlock to serialize the executions of process and interrupt handler. While holding the spinlock, if a process has to wait for data or room in the I/O buffer, it uses PV() or PU() to atomically wait and release the spinlock.
6. Process and interrupt handler in a SMP device driver must obey the following timing order.

```
        Process                      Interrupt Handler
    ----------------------------------------------------------
    (a). disable interrupts   |
    (b). acquire spinlock      |   (a). acquire spinlock
    (c). start I/O operation   |   (b). process the interrupt
                               |   (c). start next I/O, if needed
    (d). release spinlock      |   (d). release spinlock
    (e). enable interrupts     |   (e). issue EOI
    ----------------------------------------------------------
```

In both cases, the order of (d) and (e) must be strictly observed in order to prevent a process from locking itself out on the same spinlock.

15.5.7   SMP_PMTX Kernel Organization

Following the above principles, we have adapted the UP kernel of PMTX for SMP. The SMP_PMTX kernel consists of the following file tree, which is the same as in PMTX but with added features to support SMP.

```
SMP_PMTX--|-- Makefile and mk script
          |-- SETUP:  boot.s, setup.s, apentry.s
          |-- header: type.h, include.h     // added SMP types
          |-- kernel: kernel source files   // added files for SMP
          |-- fs:     file system files     // modified for SMP
          |-- driver: device driver files   // modified for SMP
```

The main features in support of SMP are in the following files.

type.h   define NCPU = 16 CPUs and CPU structure type
apentry.s startup code of APs in 16-bit real mode
mp.h   FP and MP structure types
mp.c   MP table scanning function
smp.h   SMP types and structures, e.g. APIC and IOAPIC structure types
smp.c   SMP configuration and startup code

15.5.8   Bootable SMP_PMTX Image

A bootable SMP_PMTX image consists of the following pieces.

```
Sector | 0  |  1  |  2     3   | 4 .......................|
       -------------------------------------------------------
       |BOOT|SETUP|  APentry  | 32-bit SMP_PMTX kernel ..|
       -------------------------------------------------------
```

During booting, the booter loads BOOT+SETUP in block 0 to 0x90000, APentry in block 1 to 0x91000 and the MTX kernel to 0x10000. For protected mode MTX kernels, the last word in the BOOT sector contains the boot signature 'PP'. When the booter detects this, it jumps to 0x90200 to run SETUP, which brings up the system in 32-bit protected mode. When the SMP_PMTX kernel starts, the boot processor (BSP) first calls findmp() to search for the FPS and MP table. It scans the MP table and returns the number of CPUs in the system. Currently, the SMP_PMTX kernel supports up to 16 CPUs. If desired, it can be extended easily for more CPUs. If the system has only one CPU, it falls back to UP mode. Otherwise, it calls smp() to configure the system for SMP operations and bring the system up in SMP mode. After initializing the kernel, the BSP broadcasts INIT and STARTUP IPIs to the APs with the vector 0x91, which corresponds to the loading address of APentry. Each AP begins by executing APentry in 16-bit real mode.

15.5.9   SMP_PMTX Kernel Startup Sequence

This section describes the startup sequence of the SMP_PMTX kernel. In addition to the subsection titles, we also use sequence numbers to show the logical order of the steps.

15.5.9.1   Enter 32-bit Protected Mode

(1). SETUP: SETUP defines an initial GDT to enter protected mode. The initial GDT defines both kernel CS and DS as 4 GB flat segments.

```
igdt:
  .quad 0x0000000000000000  # null descriptor
  .quad 0x00cF9A000000FFFF  # kcs: 9=PpLS=1001, A=non-conforming
  .quad 0x00cF92000000FFFF  # kds: 9=PpLS=1001, 2=R|W data segment
```

After moving the GDT to a known location (0x9F000), SETUP loads GDTR with the initial GDT and enters protected mode. Then it moves the MTX kernel from 0x10000 to 0x100000 (1 MB) and ljmp to pm_entry in entry.s to execute the kernel startup code.

15.5.9.2   Set up Initial Paging and GDTs

(2). entry.s sets up an initial paging environment, which allows the kernel to access the lowest 8 MB physical memory by either physical or virtual addresses. The initial ipgdir is defined at the offset address 0x1000 in the SMP_PMTX kernel.

```
        .org 0
pm_entry:
# entry.s code in 32-bit GCC assembly
# set up initial ipgdir and page tables; then call init()
        .org 0x1000          # at offset 4KB in kernel
ipgdir:
        .long 0x00102007     # point to pg0 at 0x102000
        .long 0x00103007     # point to pg1 at 0x103000
        .fill 510,4,0        # fill with 510 entries of 0
        .long 0x00102007     # point to pg0 at 0x102000 also
        .long 0x00103007     # point to pg1 at 0x103000 also
        .fill 510,4,0        # fill with 510 entries of 0
        .org 0x2000
pg0:                         # by entry.s code: for 0-4MB
        .org 0x3000
pg1:                         # by netry.s code: for 4-8MB
```

The two initial page tables, pg0 and pg1, are filled in entry.s to map the lowest 8 MB physical memory as real address and also as virtual address in the range of [2 GB, 2 GB + 8 MB]. Then it uses the initial ipgdir to turn on paging and forces the BSP to use virtual addresses starting from 0x80000000. So far, the startup actions are identical to that of PMTX. The SMP part begins here. At 0x4000 are NCPU = 16 GDTs, one per CPU, as shown below.

```
        .org 0x4000
kgdt: .rept  NCPU    # NCPU=16    #                        Index
        .quad 0x0000000000000000  # null descriptor        0x00
        .quad 0x00cF9A000000FFFF  # kcs 00cF PpLS=1001=9 0x08
        .quad 0x00cF92000000FFFF  # kds                     0x10
        .quad 0x0000000000000000  # tss                     0x18
        .quad 0x00cFFA000000FFFF  # ucs 00cF PpLS=1111=F 0x20
        .quad 0x00cFF2000000FFFF  # uds                     0x28
        .quad 0x80C0920000000027  # CPU struct=40 bytes   0x30
        .endr
gdt_desc: .word 56-1            # for CPU0's GDT
          .long kgdt           # GDT address of BSP
        .org 0x5000
idt:  .fill 1024,4,0           # 2KB IDT at 0x5000
        .org 0x6000
kpgdir:.fill 1024,4,0          # kernel mode kpgdir at 0x6000
        .org 0x8000            # other kernel code begins here
```

The first six segments of each GDT are the same as they are in PMTX. The last segment is used to map the CPU structure (defined below) by the gs segment, so that each CPU can access its own CPU structure by the same virtual address gs:0. Each GDT requires only 56 bytes. The 4 KB area at 0x4000 has enough space for a large number of GDTs or CPUs. The (2 KB) IDT at 0x5000 is common to all CPUs. The BSP uses the first GDT at 0x4000 and the initial ipgdir at 0x1000 to turn on paging. Then it sets the stack pointer to initproc[0]'s kstack and calls init() in init.c.

15.5.9.3   Find Number of CPUs in SMP

(3). init() calls findmp() (in mp.c) to get the SMP configuration of the system. It first finds the FPS and MP table. Then it scans the MP table to determine the number of CPU entries and returns the number of CPUs in the system. Each CPU is represented by a cpu structure.

```
struct cpu{
    struct cpu *cpu; // pointer to this cpu struct   at gs:0
    PROC  *proc;     // current running PROC on CPU at gs:4
    int   id;        // CPU ID number                at gs:8, etc.
    u32   *pgdir;    // pgdir pointer of CPU
    u32   *pgtable;  // pgtable pointer
    u32   *gdt;      // CPU GDT pointer
    PROC  *initial;  // initial PROC pointer of CPU
    // reserved fields for SMP_MTX, not used in SMP_PMTX
    int   srQ;       // spinlock during task switch on CPU
    int   sw;        // switch process flag of CPU
    int   rq;        // last ready queue used by CPU
} cpus[NCPU];        // NCPU=16, each of size=40 bytes
```

15.5.9.4   Initialize CPU Structures

(4). In SMP_PMTX, each CPU has an initial PROC, defined as IPROC initproc[NCPU], each with a statically allocated kstack. All the initial PROCs run in kernel mode only. They share the same pgdir and page tables of CPU0. Assume that the system has 512 MB physical memory and the SMP_MTX kernel occupies the lowest 4 MB. Then the memory area above 4 MB is free. As in PMTX, we shall build the kernel mode kpgdir at 0x106000 and the page tables at 4 MB. The cpu structures, their pgtables and gs segments are initialized by the following code segment.

```
// GDT_ADDR=0x80104000, KPG_DIR=0x80106000, KPG_TABLE=0x80400000
struct cpu *cp;
u32 myaddr,*mygdt,*gdt=GDT_ADDR; // NCPU GDTs at 0x80104000
for (int i=0; i<ncpu; i++){      // ncpu is the actual number of CPUs
    cp = &cpus[i];               // cp points to CPU structure
    cp->cpu = cp;                // cpu structure pointer
    cp->proc = 0;                // current running PROC pointer
    cp->id = i;                  // CPU ID
    cp->pgdir   = KPG_DIR;       // kpgdir at 0x80106000
    cp->pgtable = KPG_TABLE;     // pgtables begin at 4MB
    cp->initial = &initproc[i];  // CPU initial/idle PROC
    if (i==0) kpgtable();        // only CPU0 builds pgtables
    // fix up CPU's gs segment in GDT
    cp->gdt = gdt + i*2*NSEG;     // NSEG=7, pointer to this CPU's GDT
    mygdt  = (u32*)cp->gdt;  // fix up gs segment address in CPU GDT
    myaddr = (u32)&cp->cpu << 8;
    mygdt[13] |= (myaddr >> 24); // gs segment is 6th entry in GDT
    mygdt[12] |= (myaddr << 8);  // index 12=low, 13=high 4-byte
}
```

15.5.9.5   CPU Kernel Mode Page Table

(5). The function kpgtable() sets up the kernel mode kpgdir and page tables, which are shared by all the initial processes of the CPUs. In addition to regular pages, it also fills the last eight entries of kpgdir and their page tables to create an identity mapping of the address range [FE000000, 4 GB], which allows the CPUs to access IOAPIC and APIC register addresses above 0xFE000000.

```
// Assume 512MB; NPGTABLE=512/4=128 pgdir entries
void kpgtable()
{ u32 i, j, pte;
  u32 *pgdir   = cpus[0].pgdir;      // CPU0's pgdir
  u32 *pgtable = cpus[0].pgtable;    // CPU0's pgtable
  memset(pgdir, 0, 4096);            // clear pgdir
  // 128 regular pages for 512MB physical memory
  pte = (u32)0x3;                    // begin PA=0, 0x3=|Kpage|W|P
  for (i=512; i<512+NPGTABLE; i++){  // 128 entries from entry 512
      pgdir[i] = PA(pgtable) + 0x3;  // pointing to pgtables
      for (j=0; j<1024; j++){        // pgtabe, 4KB each
          pgtable[j] = pte;
          pte += 4096;               // pte is a u32
      }
      pgtable += 1024;               // pgtable is a u32 pointer
  }
  // LAST 8 pgtables : identity map [0xFE000000, 4GB]
  pte = 0xFE000000 + 0x3;            // begin PA=0xFE000000
  for (i=1016; i<1024; i++){         // pgdir entries 1016 to 1023
      pgdir[i] = PA(pgtable)+0x3;    // pointing to pgtables
      for (j=0; j<1024; j++){        // fill in pgtable 1024 entries
          pgtable[j] = pte;
          pte += 4096;
      }
      pgtable += 1024;
  }
}
```

Figure 15.3 shows the virtual address mapping of the CPUs in SMP_PMTX.

Figure 15.4 shows the memory map of SMP_PMTX, which is similar to that of PMTX. Instead of a single GDT, it has NCPU (16) GDTs, one per CPU beginning at 0x104000. The kernel mode kpgdir and page tables are shared by all the initial PROCs of the CPUs.

Entries	kpgdir: at VA=0x80106000
0-511	empty since all initial/idle PROCs run in Kmode
512-639	128+8 kernel mode page tables begin at PA=4MB 4KB pageTables: map VA=[2GB,2GB+512MB] to PA=[0,512MB]
640-1015	Empty space between 512MB and 0xFE000000
1016-1023	4KB pageTables: identity map [0xFE000000,4GB]

Fig. 15.3 Virtual address mapping of CPUs in SMP

```
0 to 1MB    1 MB real mode memory
1 MB        SMP_PMTX kernel in 1MB to 4MB
0x104000    NCPU(16) GDTs, one per CPU
0x105000    IDT for all CPUs
0x106000    kpgdir for all initial PROCs

4 MB        128 page tables for all initial PROCs

5 MB        1024 PROCESS + 512 THREAD PROC structures

6 MB        unused, for expansion

7 MB        data area of 1024 1KB I/O buffers

8-512 MB    free memory for process Umode images
```

Fig. 15.4 Memory map of SMP_PMTX

15.5.9.6 Load GDT and Enable Paging

(6). BSP loads GDT with cpus[0].gdt and sets gs=0x30, which refers to the last segment in the GDT. When an AP starts, it loads its own GDT at cpus[cpuid].gdt and sets gs=0x30 also. Thus, every CPU can access its CPU structure through the gs segment. In particular, the CPU structure is at gs:0 and the current PROC running on the CPU is at gs:4. To comply with these, we declare (in type.h)

```
extern struct cpu *cpu asm("%gs:0");    // &cpus[cpuid]
extern PROC *running   asm("%gs:4");    // cpus[cpuid].proc
```

The GCC compiler will use gs:0 for cpu, and gs:4 for PROC *running in the kernel's C code. In assembly code, we simply replace them with gs:0 and gs:4, respectively. Then the BSP switches pgdir to cpus[0].pgdir. It can now access all 512 MB physical memory, as well as the IOAPIC and APIC registers above 0xFE000000. When an AP starts, it first uses the ipgdir at 0x101000 to turn on paging. Then it switches pgdir to the same kpgdir and page tables of CPU0, allowing it to access the entire virtual address range directly.

15.5.9.7 Initialize SMP Kernel

(7). BSP: Continue to initialize the kernel. The actions are the same as in PMTX, i.e. initialize kernel data structures, create and run the initial process P0, remap IRQs, install IDT, initialize device drivers and mount the root file system, etc. In SMP_PMTX, the initial PROCs of the CPUs are statically allocated as IPROC initproc[NCPU]. The other NPROC=1024 process and NTHREAD=512 thread PROCs are constructed at 5 MB in init(). After initializing the kernel, P0 builds the free page frame list and calls main(ncpu) (in t.c) to create the INIT process P1. If the number of CPUs is 1, P0 brings the system up in UP mode. Otherwise, it calls smp() (in smp.c) to configure the system for SMP operations, which are described next.

```
byte 7        6         5         4         3         2         1         0
|--------|---------|---------|---------|---------|--------|---------|-------|
| DestID |<------------ reserved ----------------------> M| TRASPmmm| vector|
```

```
M=interrupt mask: 0=enabled, 1=masked off              (enable     0)
T=trigger mode:   0=edge, 1=level                      (edge       0)
R=Remote IRR:     undefined for edge, 1=level          (0          0)
A=active polarity: 0=high active, 1=low active         (high active: 0)
S=delivery status: 0=idle, 1=pending                   (status     0)
D=Destination Mode:0=physical, 1=logical               (physical   0)
mmm=delivery mode: fixed(0),pri(1),INIT(5),INT(7)      (fixed    000)
```

Fig. 15.5 IOAPIC register format

15.5.9.8 Configure IOAPIC to Route Interrupts

(8). Initialize IOAPIC to route interrupts: IOAPIC interrupt registers are set up in ioapic_init(). Figure 15.5 shows the IOAPIC register format.

For better control, we shall use physical delivery mode by processor ID. Therefore, we set each active IOAPIC interrupt register with

DestID=CPUid, M=0, TRASPmmm=0000000, byte0=vector

and mask out all inactive interrupt registers. In SMP, the PIC timer will be disabled. Each CPU uses its own local APIC timer and handles the timer interrupts.

15.5.9.9 Configure APIC and APIC timer

(9). Each CPU calls lapic_init(int cpuid) to configure the local APIC as follows.

- Disable logical interrupt lines: mask out LINT0, LINT1 registers;
- Disable performance register: mask out PCINT (0x340) register;
- Map error interrupts to an exception vector: lapicw(0x370, ERROR_VECTOR);
- Clear error status register: lapicw(0x280, 0);
- Acknowledge any outstanding interrupts: lapicw(0x0B0, 0);
- Configure APIC timer to generate periodic timer interrupts.

Figure 15.6 shows the APIC timer register format, which is configured by lapic_timer().

```
lapic_timer(int vector, u32 int_entry)
  {
     int_install(vector, int_entry);
     set timer register (0x320) to periodic, enabled, with vector
     set initial counter register (0x380) = 0x0010C000
     set current counter register (0x390) = 0x0010C000
     set timer divider register  (0x3E0) = 0x0000000B (divide by 1)
     enable APIC: write 0x010F to spurious interrupt register(0x0F0)
  }
```

Fig. 15.6 APIC timer register format

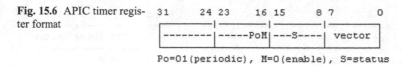

Po=01(periodic), M=0(enable), S=status

APIC timer interrupt vectors of the CPUs are 0x40 + cpuid and their interrupt handler entry points are defined as c0inth to c15inth (in ts.s). It is observed that for VMware virtual machines, the APIC timer count 0x0010C00 yields very close to 60 interrupts per second. For other SMP platforms, the APIC timer count may need to be adjusted to better match real time. For instance, the emulated bus frequency of QEMU is much higher than that of VMware. When running SMP MTX under QEMU, the APIC timer count should be increased by a factor of 16 or more.

15.5.9.10   Start up APs

(10). The last action of the BSP is to issue INIT and STARTUP IPIs to start up the APs. It uses the real-mode memory at 0x90000 as a communication area between the BSP and the APs. First, it writes the entry address of APstart() to 0x90000, followed by the initial stack pointers of initproc[i], (i = 1 to ncpu-1). Then it executes

```
int go_smp = 1                       // number of active CPUs so far
lapicw(0x0300, 0x00c4500); delay(); // broadcast INIT IPI to APs
lapicw(0x0300, 0x00c4691); delay(); // broadcast STARTUP IPI to APs
while(go_smp < ncpu);                // wait for all APs to be ready
run_task(); // enter scheduling loop to run tasks from readyQueue
```

In the STARTUP IPI, the vector number is 0x91, which corresponds to the loading address of APentry at 0x91000. When an AP starts, it executes the trampoline code APentry at 0x91000 in 16-bit real mode. First, it enters protected mode with 4 GB flat segments and reads the APIC ID register at 0xFEE00020 to get its cpuid number. It uses the ipgdir at 0x101000 to turn on paging. It uses cpuid to get the initial stack pointer at 0x90000 + 4*cpuid. Then it sets the stack pointer and calls APstart(cpuid) in smp.c.

15.5.9.11   APs Execute Startup Code APstart(cpuid)

(11). The actions of each AP in APstart(cpuid) are as follows.

- Load GDT in cpus[cpuid].gdt, switch pgdir to cpus[cpuid].pgdir;
- Configure local APIC by lapic_init(cpuid);
- Load IDTR with the same IDT at 0x105000 for exception and interrupt processing;
- Set gs = 0x30, cpu = &cpus[cpuid] and running = &initproc[cpuid];

- Initialize initproc[cpuid] with pid = 2000 + cpuid as the initial process running on AP;
- Set GDT.tss to initproc[cpuid].tss as the interrupt stack;
- Configure APIC timer, using the interrupt vector 0x40 + cpuid;
- Atomically increment go_smp by 1 to inform BSP that this AP is ready;
- run_task(): enter scheduling loop to run tasks.

(12). When all the APs are ready, the BSP enters scheduling loop to run task also.

After all the above steps (1) to (12), MTX is running in SMP mode. The SMP_PMTX kernel uses sequential UP algorithms adapted for SMP, as described in Sect. 15.5.5. Since most of the modifications are fairly simple and straightforward, we shall not show them here. The reader may consult the source code of SMP_PMTX for details. As in PMTX, it has only one readyQueue for process scheduling. All CPUs try to run tasks from the same readyQueue. The initial process of each CPU is also the idle process of that CPU. If a CPU finds the readyQueue empty, it runs the idle process, which puts the CPU in halt, waiting for interrupts. The idle processes are special in that they do not enter readyQueue for scheduling and they have no time limits. For this reason, they are assigned the special pid 0 and 2000 + cpuid for identification.

15.5.9.12 SMP_PMTX Demonstration System

On the MTX install CD, MTX.images/smp.pmtx is a runnable image of SMP_PMTX. Figure 15.7 show the startup screen of SMP_PMTX under QEMU with eight CPUs. After login, each process displays its pid and the CPU ID it is running on.

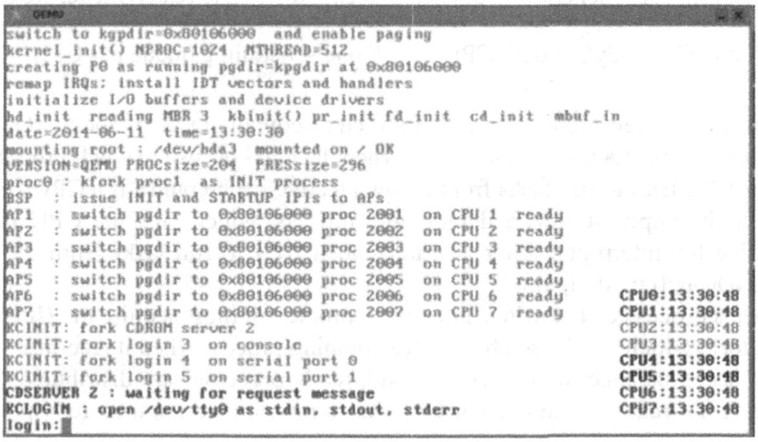

Fig. 15.7 Startup screen of SMP_PMTX

15.6   SMP_MTX using Parallel Algorithms

As a direct extension of PMTX to SMP, the SMP_PMTX kernel is very simple and easy to understand. However, it is not a good SMP system for the following reasons. Since all the kernel data structures have a single copy, processes can only access the same data structure one at a time, which severely limits the concurrency of the system. In particular, because of the single ready queue, process scheduling and switching can only be done by one process at a time, regardless of the number of CPUs, which does not fully utilize the capability of a SMP system. Therefore, simply using fine grained locks to protect UP kernel data structures and adapting UP algorithms for SMP is not the right approach to SMP. In order to truly support SMP, the algorithms must be redesigned to improve concurrency and efficiency. In the following, we shall apply the data partitioning principle of parallel computing (Grama et al., 2003) to design parallel algorithms for SMP. In this scheme, we decompose data structures in a SMP kernel into separate parts to allow parallel operations. If the decomposed parts are logically related, we devise ways to synchronize process executions on the various parts to ensure data consistency. Then we extend SMP_PMTX to the final version of SMP_MTX by using parallel algorithms.

15.6.1   Parallel Algorithms for Process Scheduling

In a UP kernel, it suffices to maintain a single process scheduling queue. In SMP, a single scheduling queue can be a serious bottleneck because it does not allow different CPUs to switch process at the same time, despite the fact that task switching on a CPU involves only the CPU itself. In order to improve concurrency, we shall use parallel algorithms operating on multiple scheduling queues. In SMP_MTX, the parallel process scheduling algorithm is as follows.

1. Multiple process scheduling queues: Instead of a single readyQueue, we define

    PROC *readyQueue[NCPU];   // one scheduling queue per CPU

2. Each CPU is represented by a cpu structure containing a spinlock, srQ, and a switch process flag, sw, which is set when the CPU needs to switch process.
3. Each CPU tries to run tasks from its own readyQueue[cpuid]. If a CPU's readyQueue is empty, it runs a default idle process, which puts the CPU in halt, waiting for interrupts. After an interrupt, it tries to run tasks from the same readyQueue[cpuid] again.
4. When a process calls tswitch() to switch process, it must acquire the CPU's srQ spinlock, which is released by the next running process when it resumes.
5. In order to balance the processing load, ready processes are distributed evenly among the ready queues. Each CPU has a next queue number, rq=cpuid ini-

tially. When a process executing on a CPU makes a process ready, e.g. by fork(), wakeup() or V() operations, it updates the CPU's rq number by rq=(rq+1)% ncpu and enters the ready process into readyQueue[rq].

6. When a new process is created by fork(), it is assigned a base priority of 128. When a process is unblocked from a semaphore queue, it is assigned the highest priority 256, which may set the CPU's switch task flag.

7. Each CPU uses its local APIC timer and handles its own timer interrupts. At each timer tick the timer interrupt handler updates the CPU usage time and time slice of the running process. Periodically, it adjusts the process priorities in the CPU's scheduling queue and sets the CPU's switch process flag if necessary.

8. In SMP, which has more CPUs to run tasks, dynamic process priority is less important than that in UP systems. If desired, process scheduling can be done by a short time slice only.

9. As in UP kernels, process switch takes place only when the running process exits kernel and is about to return to user mode. However, the SMP_MTX kernel supports preemptive process scheduling. Currently, the code (in APIC timer handlers) is commented out in order to avoid excessive process switch overhead in kernel mode. If desired, the reader may activate the code, recompile the system to observe preemptive process scheduling in the SMP_MTX kernel.

15.6.2   Parallel Algorithms for Resource Management

An OS kernel contains many data structures which are crucial to system operations. Examples of such data structures include free PROC list, in-memory minodes and free page frames, etc. When adapting a UP kernel for SMP it suffices to protect each of these data structures by a spinlock. Again, this simple approach has a major drawback in that it does not allow for any concurrency on the same data structure. In order to improve concurrency, we shall decompose such data structures into separate parts and manage them by parallel algorithms.

15.6.2.1   Manage PROC Structures by Parallel Algorithm

In an OS kernel, PROC structures are the focal points of process creation and termination. In a UP kernel, it suffices to maintain all free PROC structures in a single free list. In SMP, we divide free PROCs into separate free lists, each associated with a CPU. This allows processes executing on different CPUs to proceed in parallel during fork and wait for child termination. If a CPU's free PROC list becomes empty, we let it obtain PROCs from other free PROC lists dynamically. In the SMP_MTX kernel, free PROCs are managed by parallel algorithm as follows.

```
Define: PROC *free_proc_list[NCPU];    // free PROC lists, one per CPU
        int    procspin[NCPU]={0};     // spinlocks for PROC lists

PROC *get_proc()   // allocate a free PROC during fork/vfork;
{ int cpuid = cpu->id;                 // CPU id
   while(1){
   (1). slock(procspin[cpuid]);        // acquire CPU's spinlock
   (2). If (free_proc_list[cpuid]==0){// if CPU's free list is empty
   (3).     if (refill(cpuid)==0){     // refill CPU's free_proc_list
                sunlock(procspin[cpuid]);
                continue;              // retry
            }
        }
   (4). allocate a PROC *p from free_proc_list[cpuid];
   (5). sunlock(procspin[cpuid]);      // release CPU's spinlock;
   }
   return p;
}
int refill(int cpuid)                  // refill a CPU's free PROC list
{  int i, n = 0;
   for (i=0; i<ncpu && i!=cpuid; i++){ // try other CPU's free list
       if (!cslock(procspin[i]))       // if conditional lock fails
          continue;                    // try next free PROC list
       if (freeproclist[i]==0){        // if other free list empty
          sunlock(procspin[i])         // release spinlock
          continue;                    // try next CPU's free list
       }
       remove a PROC from free_proc_list[i];// get a free PROC
       insert into free_proc_list[cpuid];  // add to CPU's list
       n++;
       sunlock(procspin[i]);                // release spinlock
   }
   return n;
}
void put_proc(PROC *p) // release p into CPU's free PROC list
{ int cpuid = cpu->id;
   (1). slock(procspin[cpuid];         // acquire CPU's spinlock
   (2). enter p into free_proc_list[cpuid];
   (3). sunlock(procspin[cpuid]);      // release CPU's spinlock
}
```

The refill() operation tries to get a free PROC from every other free PROC list into the current CPU's free PROC list. Since the process already holds a CPU's spinlock, trying to acquire the spinlock of another CPU may lead to deadlock. So it uses the conditional cslock() instead. If the conditional locking fails, the process backs off to prevent any chance of deadlock. In get_proc(), if after refill the CPU's free PROC list is still empty, it releases the spinlock and retries the algorithm. This prevents self-deadlock on the same CPU.

Note that the PROC of a process may be allocated from the free list of one CPU but released to that of a different CPU. So the algorithm implicitly distributes PROCs among the CPUs. Under normal conditions, free PROCs should be evenly distributed among the CPUs. If a CPU's free list becomes empty, each refill operation may add ncpu-1 free PROCs to a CPU's free list. Since the number of processes can not exceed the total number of PROCs, the refill operation is guaranteed to succeed. Alternatively, we may add a cpuid field to each PROC structure and release a PROC to the same free list form which it is allocated. In that case, the need for refill operations would be greatly reduced. Other ways to further improve concurrency on the PROC structures include the following. Implement a process family tree to speed up exit and wait operations in kernel. For example, when searching for ZOMBIE child in wait(), a process only needs to lock its own children list, rather than the entire PROC table. Similarly, when a process terminates, it only needs to lock its own children list and that of the INIT process in order to dispose of orphaned children processes. Likewise, implement a process list on the same terminal to speed up signal delivery when an interrupt key is entered, etc.

15.6.2.2   Manage In-memory Inodes by Parallel Algorithm

In an OS kernel, in-memory inodes (minodes) are the focal points of file system operations. To improve concurrency, in SMP_PMTX we divide minodes into separate parts and manage them by parallel algorithms. When the system starts, we assign a fixed number of free minodes to each device and maintain them in a local free minodes list of the device, each protected by a spinlock. This allows processes to execute iget() and iput() on different devices in parallel. If a device's free minodes list becomes empty, we again let it obtain free minodes from other devices dynamically.

15.6.2.3   Manage Page Frames by Parallel Algorithm

In an OS kernel using dynamic paging, free page frames are the focal points of process image management during fork, exec and exit operations. In SMP_MTX, we divide free page frames into separate pfreelists, each associated with a CPU. Then we modify page frame management functions to support parallel operations on different pfreelists. Similar to PROC structures, a process image may be created from the pfreelist of one CPU but released to that of a different CPU, which necessitates the refill operation. For better efficiency, when refilling a pfreelist we try to transfer 1024 page frames at a time from each of the other pfreelists.

15.6.2.4   Manage Other Resources by Parallel Algorithms

We may apply the same data partitioning principle and technique to manage other resources in a SMP kernel. These include bitmaps of file systems, open file table entries, mount table entries, message buffers, etc. In order to keep the system simple, we have not used parallel algorithms for these data structures, which are suitable for programming projects.

15.6.3   Parallel Pipe Algorithm for SMP

In this section, we shall show the design of a parallel pipe algorithm for SMP. For each pipe, we decompose the pipe's data buffer into two separate parts; a read buffer for pipe readers and a write buffer for pipe writers. Then we redesign the pipe algorithm to allow a reader and a writer to execute in parallel on different buffers. Since the separate buffers are logically the same buffer, we must ensure that read/write of the separate buffers are synchronized properly. The SMP_MTX kernel implements such a parallel pipe algorithm, which is shown below.

```
/********************* Parallel Pipe Algorithm ************************/
Assume: each pipe has a rbuf for pipe readers and a wbuf for pipe writers.
(1). If rbuf has data and wbuf has room, a reader and a writer may proceed in parallel.
(2). If rbuf is empty and wbuf has data, swap the buffers.
(3). If wbuf is full, transfer data to rbuf until rbuf is full or wbuf is empty.

typedef truct pipe{
        char *rbuf, *wbuf;    // palloc() 4KB buffers during creation
        int  rhead = 0;       // read buffer index
        int  rdata = wdata = 0;   // counters
        int  rlock = wlock = 0;   // reader writer spinlocks
        int  nreader, nwriter;    // number of readers and writers
}PIPE;

PIPE pipe[NPIPE];                 // NPIPE pipe structures

int rswap(PIPE *p)    // called by pipe reader whenever rbuf is empty
{
   while(1){
      slock(p->wlock);           // acquire wlock
      if (p->wdata > 0){         // if wbuf has data:
         swap(p->rbuf, p->wbuf);  // swap the buffers
         p->rhead = 0;            // reset rbuf index
         p->rdata = p->wdata;     // adjust counters
         p->wdata = 0;
         wakeup(p->wdata);        // wakeup writer
         sunlock(p->wlock);       // release wlock
         return p->rdata;
      }
      if (p->nwriter){   // wbuf empty: if pipe still has writer
         wakeup(p->wdata);        // wakeup writer
        sleep(p->rdata, p->wlock); // sleep on rdata and release wlock
         continue;                // continue while loop
      }
      return 0;                   // no more writer
   }
}


int wswap(PIPE *p)    // called by pipe writer when wbuf is full
{
   if (!cslock(p->rlock))        // if can't get rlock, back off
      return 0;
   if (p->rdata == 0){           // rbuf empty: swap bufs
      swap(p->rbuf, p->wbuf);
      p->rhead = 0;              // reset read index
      p->rdata = p->wdata;       // adjust counters
      p->wdata = 0;
      wakeup(p->rdata);          // wakeup reader
      sunlock(p->rlock);         // release rlock
      return p->rdata;
   }
   // rbuf not empty: transfer data from wbuf to rbuf
   int count = PSIZE - p->rdata;                   // room in rbuf
   memcpy(p->rbuf, &p->rbuf[p->rhead], p->rdata); // compact rbuf
   memcpy(&p->rbuf[p->rdata], p->wbuf, count);    // transfer data
   memcpy(p->wbuf, &p->wbuf[count], PSIZE-count); // compact wbuf
   p->wdata -= count;            // adjust counters
```

```
        p->rdata = PSIZE;
        p->rhead = 0;
        wakeup(p->rdata);              // wakeup reader
        sunlock(p->rlock);             // release rlock
        return count;
}

int read_pipe(PIPE *p, char *buf, int n) // read_pipe() function
{ int r = 0;
   if (n<=0) return 0;
   while(n){
        slock(p->rlock);              // acquire rlock
        if (p->rdata == 0){           // if rbuf empty
           if (rswap(p) == 0){        // no data and no writer
               sunlock(p->rlock);
               return 0;
           }
        }
        while(p->rdata && n){         // read loop
           *buf++ = p->rbuf[p->rhead++]; // read a byte
           r++; p->rdata--; n--; // adjust counters
        }
        if (n==0 || r){               // has read some data
           sunlock(p->rlock);
           return r;
        }
        sunlock(p->rlock);            // unlock rlock, repeat read loop
   }
}

int write_pipe(PIPE *p, char *buf, int n) // write_pipe function
{ int r = 0;
   if (n<=0) return 0;
   while(n){
        slock(p->wlock);              // acquire wlock
        if (p->nreader == 0){         // no more readers
           sunlock(p->wlock);
           exit(BROKEN_PIPE);         // die by BROKEN PIPE
        }
        while(p->wdata<PSIZE && n){ // write loop
           p->wbuf[p->wdata++] = *buf++; // write a byte
           r++; n--;
        }
        wakeup(p->rdata);             // try to wakeup reader
        if (n<=0){                    // done with writing
           sunlock(p->wlock);
           return r;
        }
        // need space to write but wbuf is full
        if (p->wdata == PSIZE){
           if (wswap(p)==0){          // if did not transfer any data
               wakeup(p->rdata);      // try to wakeup reader
               sleep(p->wdata, p->wlock); //sleep on wdata,release wlock
               continue;
           }
        }
        sunlock(p->wlock);
   }
}
```

In the parallel pipe algorithm, the pipe reader plays the role of an initiator. Whenever the pipe's rbuf is empty, it calls rswap() to refill rbuf with data. In rswap(), it first acquires the wlock to ensure that it can swap the buffers without interference from any writer. It waits only if wbuf is also empty, in which case it will be woken up by the writer when wbuf has data. In contrast, the pipe writer's role is more passive. For better efficiency, the writer calls wswap() only if wbuf is full. While holding the wlock, if the writer tries to acquire the rlock also, it may lead to deadlock with the reader. So it uses conditional locking. If the locking fails, it backs off to prevent any possible deadlock. If the locking succeeds, it has acquired both wlock and rlock. Then it either swaps the buffers or transfers data without interference from the reader. Besides deadlock prevention, it is also worth noting the following. When the reader calls rswap(), it waits for rdata if wbuf is empty. Since the writer calls wswap() only when the wbuf is full, this may cause unnecessary delay of the reader. So it tries to wake up the reader whenever it writes data to wbuf. Since the writer only holds the wlock but not the rlock, its wakeup call may miss the reader if the latter is not yet sleeping. But this causes no harm since the reader will call rswap() when it finds the rbuf empty later.

In terms of parallel programming, pipes represent an extreme case in that the problem can not be parallelized easily. This is because pipe data must be FIFO. If we decompose a pipe's data buffer into more pieces to increase concurrency, additional synchronizations are needed, which may offset the gain in concurrency. However, there are many other problems which can be parallelized more easily. One example is the I/O buffer management problem for block devices.

15.6.4   Parallel I/O Buffer Management Algorithms

In the I/O buffer management problem, buffers are maintained in separate data structures, such as the free list and device lists, etc. These separate data structures lend themselves naturally to parallel operations. The basic principle of parallel buffer management is very simple. Since buffers are maintained in separate device lists, we may protect each device list by a lock and allow processes to access different device lists in parallel. The maximal degree of concurrency of such an algorithm would be the same as the number of devices. If we divide the buffers into more hash queues and protect each hash queue by a lock, the maximal degree of concurrency would be raised to the number of hash queues. Chapter 12 of Bach (Bach 1990) contains such a buffer management algorithm for MP Unix, which is as follows.

15.6.4.1   Unix MP Buffer Management Algorithm

1. Free buffers are maintained in a freelist. Assigned buffers are maintained in hash queues (HQs). An assigned buffer is in a unique HQ and also in the freelist if it is FREE.

2. The freelist has a lock semaphore, each HQ has a lock semaphore and each buffer has a lock semaphore.

3. As in UP Unix, ugetblk/ubrelse are the core of the MP buffer management algorithm.

```
BUFFER *ugetblk(dev,blk) // return a locked buffer for exclusive use
{
 while(buffer not found){
    P(HQ);                          // lock HQ of bp=(dev,blk)
    if (bp in HQ){
        if (!CP(bp)){               // if can't lock bp
           V(HQ);                    // release HQ lock
           P(bp);                    // wait for bp
           if (!CP(HQ)){             // if lock HQ fails
              V(bp); continue;       // retry the algorithm
           }
           else if (bp changed){
              V(bp);
              V(HQ); continue;      // retry
           }
        }
        // locked bp, which must be in freelist; HQ still locked
        while(!CP(freelist));       // spin lock freelist
          remove bp from freelist;
        V(freelist);                // unlock freelist
        V(HQ);                      // release HQ lock
        return bp;
    }
    /******** Part 2: buffer not in HQ ***********/
}
```

Although (Bach 1990) does not show the case when the needed buffer is not in the uffer cache, it is fairly easy to deduce its logic. With the HQ still locked, the process must

- Try to get a free buffer from freelist.
- If freelist is empty, unlock HQ, wait for free buffer; then retry the algorithm;
- If freelist is not empty but can not lock any free buffer, unlock HQ and retry the
- algorithm;
- If locked free buffer is dirty, ASYNC write it out and try freelist again;
- If locked free buffer is in a different hq, try to lock hq in order to get the buffer into HQ but must avoid any possible deadlock, retry the algorithm if necessary;
- With a locked free buffer in HQ, assign it to (dev, blk);
- Release the HQ lock and return the assigned buffer.

Some specific comments about the MP Unix algorithm follow.

1. Based on the single freelist data structure, it is essentially the same UP algorithm in Chap. 3 of (Bach 1990) adapted for MP. As in the UP algorithm, every released buffer is up for grabs, which may be reassigned, thereby reducing the buffer's cache effect.

2. In ugetblk(), when a process finds a needed buffer but the buffer is already locked, it releases the HQ lock to allow concurrency and waits for the buffer.

Once it releases the HQ lock, race condition may occur. For example, the buffer may be released by a process (on another CPU) as FREE, grabbed by yet another process and assigned to a different disk block, etc. When the process eventually acquires the buffer's semaphore lock, the buffer may be changed. If so, the process must give up the buffer and retry the algorithm again. This not only reduces the buffer's cache effect but also causes extra retry loops.

3. Because of the individual buffer lock, each buffer can only be used by one process at a time. In a real system, processes often access files in read-only mode, e.g. when search directories for pathnames, load executable files for execution and read file contents, etc. In a SMP kernel, such processes should be able to read from the same buffer concurrently.

4. The apparent degree of concurrency is equal to the number of HQs but the minimal degree of concurrency is only one due to the single freelist bottleneck.

15.6.4.2   New Parallel I/O Buffer Management Algorithm for SMP

In this section, we shall show a new parallel I/O buffer management algorithm, which does not have the above shortcomings. First, we assume that each allocated buffer is for exclusive use. Then we extend the algorithm to allow concurrent readers on the same buffer. To do these, we modify the buffer data structures as follows.

1. Instead of a single freelist, we distribute free buffers into the local freelists of different hash queues (HQs). Assume $n = NBUF/NHQ > 1$. Each HQ's local freelist begins with n free buffers.

2. Each HQ has a lock semaphore $= 1$, each buffer has a lock semaphore $rw = 1$ and a pcount, which is the number of processes on the buffer. Since each local freelist is associated with a HQ, there is no need for separate local freelist locks. They are the same as the HQ locks.

3. When read/write a disk block, the behavior of every process is

```
BUFFER *bp = mgetblk(dev,blk);    // return a reserved buffer
            P(bp.rw);             // lock buffer
               use the buffer bp; // use the buffer means R|W
            V(bp.rw);             // unlock buffer
            mbrelse(bp);          // release the buffer
```

The following shows the parallel algorithm of mgetblk() and mbrelse().

```
BUFFER *mgetblk(dev,blk)          // return a reserved bp
{
 while(1){
   P(HQ);                         // lock HQ of bp=(dev,blk)
   if (bp in HQ){
     bp.pcount++;                 // inc pcount to reserve the buffer
     if (bp.pcount==1)            // bp is free in HQ's local freelist
        remove bp from local freelist;  // bp in HQ, no need to lock
     V(HQ);                       // unlock HQ
     return bp;
   }
   Part2: // bp NOT in cache; HQ still locked
   if (empty(HQ.freelist)||(HQ.buffers all assigned && HQ.nbuf<NBUF))
      brefill(HQ);
   if (empty(HQ.freelist)){ // if after refill freelist still empty
      V(HQ); continue;            // unlock HQ, retry mgetblk()
   }
   // HQ's local freelist not empty
   allocate a bp from HQ's local freelist;
   if (bp dirty){
      P(bp.rw); awrite(bp); // write bp out ASYNC
      goto Part2;                 // try next buffer in local freelist
   }
   assign bp to (dev,blk);
   bp.pcount = 1;       // also, set bp data invalid, not dirty, etc.
   V(HQ);
   return bp;
 }
}

int brefill(HQ) //refill HQ's freelist with free bufs from other hq's
{ int n = 0;
   for each hash queue hq != HQ do{  // try every other hq
      if (!CP(hq))                 // if lock hq fails
         continue;                 // try next hq
      if (empty(hq freelist){      // if hq's freelist empty
         V(hq);                    // unlock hq
         continue;                 // try next hq
      }
      while (!empty(hq's freelist)){// locked hq has free buffers
         remove a bp from hq's freelist;
         if (bp dirty){
            P(bp.rw); awrite(bp);    // lock bp and write out ASYNC
            continue;
         }
         insert bp into HQ's local freelist;
         n++; break;
      }
      V(hq);                        // unlock hq
   }
   return n ;
}

void mbrelse(bp)                    // release a buffer
{
   while(!CP(HQ);                   // spin lock HQ
   if (--bp.pcount==0)              // if last user on bp
      release bp into (tail of) HQ's local freelist
   V(HQ)                            // unlock HQ
}
```

The brefill() operation of free buffers is similar to that of free PROCs and minodes, except that it must write out dirty buffers. Note that mgetblk() may call brefill() even if HQ's local freelist is not empty. This allows a HQ to keep its assigned buffers for as long as possible to improve the cache effect. Under normal conditions, free buffers should be evenly distributed among the local freelists. Each refill operation may add HQ-1 free buffers to a local freelist. Next, we show that the new algorithm is correct.

1. Buffer uniqueness: This is because every buffer is created inside a HQ critical region.
2. No race conditions: All operations are performed inside the critical regions of HQs. In particular, the pcount of every buffer is manipulated only inside the HQ critical region. This allows a process to return a reserved buffer even before locking it, which separates buffer allocation from buffer usage. Since each process does P(bp.rw) on an allocated buffer, each buffer is used exclusively.
3. Free of deadlocks: The only possible deadlock is in the refill operation, in which a process holding a HQ lock tries to lock another hq. Since the process backs off if it can not lock the other hq, deadlock cannot occur. The scheme is in fact overly conservative. In order to prevent potential deadlocks due to cross locking, it suffices to let only one side back off. The reader may try to improve the scheme by ranking the HQs.
4. Improved Cache effect: The pcount of each buffer acts as a reservation flag. Once a buffer is reserved, it is guaranteed to exist and do not change. A buffer is released as free only if its pcount is 0, i.e. when all processes have finished using it. This should enhance the buffer's cache effect.
5. If buffers are not always busy, the mgetblk() algorithm is guaranteed to terminate. A process retries only if after refill the local freelist is still empty. If buffers are not always busy, any process executing mgetblk() must eventually succeed.

The parallel buffer management algorithm eliminates the single freelist bottleneck. It raises the minimal degree of concurrency to greater than one. If we assume that each device has an I/O queue, the minimal degree of concurrency would be the same as the number of devices. Since I/O operations are needed only if a requested buffer is not in the buffer cache, the actual degree of concurrency should be higher. Assuming a buffer hit ratio of 50%, the minimal degree of concurrency is at least 50% of the number of HQs. In contrast, in the Unix MP algorithm, every buffer transaction must access the single freelist. The minimal degree of concurrency is only 1 regardless of the number of HQs.

Next, we extend the algorithm to support concurrent readers. For each buffer, we add the lock semaphores r = 1, w = 1 and a readers counter, which is the number of concurrent readers on the buffer. Define the code segments as shown in Fig. 15.8, which divide the classical reader-writer algorithm into separate parts. Then we rewrite reader and writer processes as shown in Fig. 15.9.

In readerEntry(), if the buffer's data are invalid, only the first reader issues start_io() and waits for I/O completion. Meanwhile, all other readers, which follow the first reader but before any writer, are blocked at P(bp.rw). When the buffer's data

```
readerEntry(bp)                      writerEntry(bp)
{                                    {
    P(bp.rw);                            P(bp.rw);
    P(bp.r);                             P(bp.w);
    if (++bp.readers==1){            }
        P(bp.w);
        if (bp data invalid){
            start_io(bp);
            P(bp.iodone);
        }
    }
    V(bp.r);
    V(bp.rw);
}
```

```
readerExit(bp)                       writerExit(bp)
{                                    {
    P(bp.r);                             V(bp.w);
    If (--bp.readers==0)                 V(bp.rw);
        V(bp.w);                    }
    V(bp.r);
}
```

Fig. 15.8 Decomposed reader/writer code

```
Reader Process:                      Writer Process:

bp = mgetblk(dev,blk);               bp = mgetblk(dev,blk);
readerEntry(bp);                     writerEntry(bp);
// concurrent read from bp           // exclusive write to bp;
readerExit(bp);                      writerExit(bp);
mbrelse(bp);                         mbrelse(bp);
```

Fig. 15.9 Reader/writer processes

are ready, the interrupt handler unblocks the first reader. Each reader unblocks a trailing reader, if any. This allows all readers in a batch to read from the same buffer concurrently. The rw semaphore also prevents reader/writer starvation since all processes access the buffer in FIFO order.

In a real system, processes often write only partial blocks. To accommodate this, we can modify the writer process to let it get a buffer as writer but use the buffer to read in data first. As in the Unix MP algorithm, if buffers are always busy, starvation for free buffer is still possible. Although this probably would never occur in a real system, an ideal algorithm should be perfect no matter how small the chances are. The reader may try to extend the algorithm to prevent starvation for free buffers.

The parallel buffer management algorithm assumes that all write operations are delay writes. When a delay write operation completes, the interrupt handler must release the buffer. As pointed out before, an interrupt handler cannot sleep or become blocked. On the other hand, it must lock the hash queue in order to release delay-write buffers. There are two possible ways to resolve this dilemma. The first one is to use a spinlock, which is nonblocking. The second one is to create a pseudo process to release delay-write buffers. A pseudo-process is logically an extension of the interrupt handler but it runs as a process ahead of all regular processes. Define a semaphore work=0 and let the pseudo process wait for work by P(work). When releasing a delay-write buffer the interrupt handler simply V(work) to unblock the pseudo-process. The parallel buffer management algorithm has been tested in a simulated SMP system (Wang 2002). The test results show that it indeed performs better than the Unix algorithm in both efficiency and cache performance.

15.6.4.3 I/O Buffer Management in SMP_MTX

The SMP_MTX kernel uses the above parallel algorithm for I/O buffer management but with some refinements to improve efficiency. It is implemented as follows.

1. Define NHQ=PRIME, NBUF=1024, where PRIME is a prime number used to implement the simple hash function: int hash(dev, blk){ return (dev*blk) % PRIME; }
2. Each HQ is assigned nbuf=NBUF/NHQ free buffers initially.
3. refill(HQ): insert buffers with dev=INVALID(-1) to the front of HQ's local freelist. Used buffers are released to the end of HQ's local freelist to honor the LRU principle.
4. BUFFER *getblk(dev, blk) returns a locked buffer by the buffer's rw semaphore, which eliminates the P(rw) line in both readerEntry() and writerEntry().
5. Modify bread(), bwrite(), awrite() and brelse() with an additional parameter

$$mode = EXCLUSIVE(0) \text{ or } READONLY(1) \text{ or } READWRITE(2),$$

which classifies the buffer usage as
5.1. EXCLUSIVE: If a buffer is used by only a single process, it suffices to lock the buffer's rw semaphore. For example, when writing to a new disk block the buffer is only used by the current process and there is no need to read in data. It only needs to get a locked buffer for the disk block, write to the buffer and release it for delay-write. In this case, the operations are

$$bp=getblk(dev,blk); \text{ write to buffer; } bwrite(bp,EXCLUSIVE);$$

Similarly, during system initialization, shut-down and sync operations, etc. data blocks may be read in first for possible modifications but the buffers are also used exclusively by a single process. In these cases, the operations are

$$bp=bread(dev, blk, EXCLUSIVE); \text{ use buffer; } brelse(bp, EXCLUSIVE);$$

5.2. READONLY: When traverse directories to resolve pathnames, load INODE into memory and read file contents, etc. disk blocks are read in but never modified. Such buffers should allow concurrent readers. In these cases, the operations are bp=bread(dev,blk, READONLY); concurrent reads; brelse(bp, READONLY);

5.3. READWRITE: When a process writes, it typically reads the disk block into a
   buffer, modifies the buffer and releases it for delay-write. If the buffer is not
   modified, it should be released without incurring a delay-write. In these cases,
   the operations are

> bp=bread(dev,blk, READWRITE);
>   use buffer; // may only use the buffer contents but not modify it
> if (buffer modified) bwrite(bp, READWRITE); // for delay-write
> else   brelse(bp, READWRITE); // no delay-write

6. DIRTY buffers are eventually written out by awrite(bp, READWRITE);

When the SMP_MTX kernel starts, it can only access 8 MB of physical memory
initially. The NBUF=1024 I/O buffers are defined in the kernel but their data areas
are allocated in the memory area of 7 MB. Each HQ is allocated nbuf=NBUF/
NHQ free buffers initially. While a HQ still has unassigned buffers, getblk() continues to use buffers in the HQ's local freelist. Otherwise, it tries to get more free
buffers form other HQs dynamically. Since the refill operation would increase the
execution time, it is desirable to reduce the number of such operations. We have
tested many different combinations of NHQ and nbuf values. The test results indicate that, for a fixed number of NBUF buffers, the algorithm performs better if we
keep NHQ small so that nbuf of each HQ is large. The test results also indicate that
the hit ratio depends only on the total number of buffers, not on the number of HQs.
Since the number of simultaneously executing processes cannot exceed the number
of CPUs, there is no need to choose NHQ much larger than NCPU. A large number
of HQs may reduce the search time but it also tends to incur more refill operations.
In order to maintain a proper balance between concurrency and overhead, for 16
CPUs we may choose NHQ=17, 19, 23, etc. In SMP_MTX, NHQ is chosen as
the Mersenne prime number $2**5-1=31$. It is well known that, for such numbers,
an optimizing compiler may generate code for faster modulo operation in the hash
function. With this scheme, the buffer hit ratio is around 40% when the system
starts. It increases quickly to over 80% after executing a few commands and there
are virtually no refill operations.

    In addition, we also tested the concurrency of the algorithm. In a conread com-
mand program, the main process forks many children processes and waits for all
the children to finish. Each child process opens the same file for read and reads
from the file in 512-byte chunks until it has read the entire file. In the SMP_MTX
kernel, we record the number of conflicts on the hash queues. Whenever a process
gets blocked on a hash queue, we count it as a conflict. In all the tested cases, the
conflict ratio is constantly at 0%, indicating that the processes are indeed executing in parallel on different HQs. The same program is also used to test concurrent
readers. In an OS kernel, when a process reads/writes an opened file (descriptor),
it usually locks the file's in-memory minode to ensure that each read or write operation is atomic, but this also prevents any chances of concurrent reads. So we

modify the read function in the SMP_MTX kernel as follows. Instead of locking the mionde, it locks the opened file instance (OFT). This allows concurrent reads on different opened instances of the same file, but not for inherited file descriptors, e.g. by fork(), which share the same OFT. In the conread program, each process opens the same file separately, so they may read concurrently. It is observed that, under normal conditions, the rate of concurrent reads is very low. In order to increase the chances of concurrent readers during testing, we add a small delay loop for the first reader in readerEntry() to simulate reading from a real disk. Under these conditions, the system shows a large number of concurrent readers, which increases as the delay time increases.

15.6.5 Parallel fork-exec Algorithms

In all Unix-like systems, fork and exec are probably the most frequently used system calls. It is therefore worthwhile to speed up these operations in kernel. The sequential fork algorithm for UP kernels consists of four major steps.

```
/************* Sequential fork() Algorithm ******************/
    (1). Create a child process PROC;
    (2). Allocate child user mode image space and copy parent image;
    (3). Copy parent kstack and fix up child's kstack contents;
    (4). Enter child PROC into ready queue; return child pid;
```

Step (2) and step (3) are independent, which can be executed in parallel. So we formulate a parallel fork algorithm as follows.

```
/**************** Parallel pfork() Algorithm *******************/
(1). Call fork1() to create a child PROC;
(2). Create a helper process to run in parallel, which
        copy parent kstack to child kstack;
        fix up child kstack for it to return to user mode;
        notify parent process of completion;
(3). Parent: allocate user mode space for the child and copy image.
(4). Wait for the helper process to finish;
(5). Enter child PROC into ready queue; return child pid;
```

Similarly, we can formulate a parallel exec algorithm.

```
/**************** Parallel pexec() Algorithm ******************/
(1). Fetch command line, verify command is an executable file;
(2). Create a helper process to run in parallel, which
        deallocate old image and fix up main process kstack as in exec;
        notify the main process of completion;
(3). Main process: allocate new image and load image file;
(4). Wait for the helper process to finish;
(5). Return to new image;
```

Since creating and starting up a helper process incur extra overhead, in each of the parallel algorithms we let the helper process perform the less time-consuming part of the parallelized work. If the helper process finishes before the main process waits, we have achieved a net gain in execution speed. Otherwise, the main process would have to wait for the helper process to finish, which may render the parallel algorithm ineffective. To further improve concurrency, we may create more helpers to share the processing load. For example, in the parallel exec algorithm, we may create another helper process to load one half of the image file, etc.

15.6.6 Parallel Algorithms for File System Functions

File system operations depend heavily on low-level supporting functions, such as management of in-memory inodes and I/O buffers, etc. Although the SMP_MTX kernel already uses parallel algorithms for these functions, it may be possible to further speed up file system operation by using parallel algorithms for the top-level functions. In this section, we investigate this possibility and discuss some of the preliminary test results. For the sake of brevity, we only consider parallel algorithms of mkdir and rmdir.

15.6.6.1 Parallel mkdir-rmdir Algorithms

The sequential mkdir algorithm for UP kernels consists of the following steps.

```
/********** Sequential Algorithm of mkdir **********/
(1). Preliminary checking, e.g. parent DIR exists and new directory
     name does not exist, etc.
(2). Allocate an inode number and a data block number for the new
     directory; Create inode and data block for the new directory.
(3). Enter new name into parent directory, update parent inode.
```

Steps (2) and (3) can be executed in parallel. So we formulate a parallel mkdir algorithm.

```
/*********** Parallel pmkdir Algorithm ***************/
(1). Preliminary checking; Allocate ino and bno for new directory;
(2). Create a helper process to run in parallel, which
         create inode and data block for the new directory;
         notify the main process of completion;
(3). Main process: enter new name into parent directory;
(4). Wait for the helper process to finish;
```

Likewise, we can formulate a parallel rmdir algorithm.

```
/*********** Parallel prmdir Algorithm ***************/
(1). Preliminary checking, e.g. directory empty and not BUSY;
(2). Create a helper process to run in parallel, which
         deallocate directory data block and inode;
         notify the main process of completion;
(3). Main process: remove dir entry from parent directory;
(4). Wait for the helper process to finish;
```

15.6.7   Performance of Parallel Algorithms

A parallel algorithm may be good in principle but useless if it does not improve the execution speed in a real system. The performance of a parallel algorithm depends on two key factors. First, the time needed to start up the helper process must be short. Second, the synchronization overhead between the main process and the helper process must also be a minimum. In order to test the practicality of the parallel fork-exec and mkdir-rmdir algorithms, we have implemented them in the SMP_ MTX kernel and conducted some tests as follows.

1. To minimize the helper process startup time, we set up a few (8) helper PROC structures ready to run in kernel. When creating a helper process we allocate a free helper PROC, initialize it to execute a function with parameters passed in on the kstack, and enter it into the readyQueue of the highest numbered CPU, which is dedicated to run only the helper process.
2. When a blocked process resumes, it may be rescheduled to run on different CPUs, whose current timer counts may differ. So we use the timer of the highest numbered CPU as the time base and set the timer count to 0x1000 (4096 bus cycles) for better resolution.
3. To reduce process synchronization overhead, we let the main process busily wait for a volatile flag variable until it is set by the helper process.
4. Implement the parallel algorithms as separate system calls, pfork-pexec and pmkdir-prmdir.
5. In a user mode program, we use pfork to fork many processes, each executes a different command by pexec. In a similar program, we use sequential fork-exec to do the same. Then we compare their execution time over a series of test runs. The following lists some samples of their comparative running time under QEMU.

```
pfork-pexec :  196608   188416 155648 147456 163840
fork-exec   :  200704   192512 167936 155648 204800
```

The test results show that on average the parallel pfork-pexec algorithms performed slightly better, but the difference is very small, with less than 5 % reduction in execution time. The rather miniscule improvement in performance is probably due to the small size of executable files and process images, which limit the effectiveness of the parallel algorithms. We expect the situation to improve for large executable files and process images.

In a similar way, we also tested the parallel pmkdir-prmdir algorithms but got opposite results. The parallel algorithms always ran slower than their sequential counterparts. This is probably due to the following reasons. First, both pmkdir and prmdir have rather lengthy preliminary checking phases, which are inherently sequential. By the time an algorithm has completed the checking phase, most information needed by the parallelizable parts, such as in-memory inodes and data blocks, are already in the I/O buffer cache. This would make the parallelized work essentially in memory operations. If the parallelized work can be executed in less time than creating and starting up a helper process, using parallel algorithms would not improve the overall execution speed. Second, QEMU supports SMP even on single CPU hosts. Its SMP environment appears to be simulated, in which the virtual CPUs may not be truly executing in parallel. Therefore, starting up a helper process always involves some extra time delay. Further analyses of the parallel pmkdir-prmdir algorithms reveal that, if they complete the checking phases successfully, steps (2) and (3) are also guaranteed to succeed. It is therefore unnecessary for the main process to wait for the helper process to finish. By taking full advantage of parallel executions, the entire operation may be considered as complete as soon as the main process finishes. Alternatively, we may redesign the parallel pmkdir algorithm as follows.

```
/******** Redesigned Parallel mkdir algorithm **********/
(1). Get dev and inode number (pino) of parent directory;
(2). Allocate an ino and bno for the new directory;
(3). Create a helper process, which uses dev, pino, ino, bno to
     construct inode and data block for the new directory;
(4). Main process: if (OK to create new directory)
     {enter new dir entry into parent directory; return 0;}
(5). deallocate ino and bno; return -1 for failed;
```

In the redesigned pmkdir algorithm, after steps (1) and (2), step (3) is guaranteed to succeed but its effect may be cancelled by the main process. In step (4) the main process performs the lengthy checking whether it's OK to create the new directory. If the checking succeeds, it completes the operation. Otherwise, it deallocates ino and bno, which nullifies the effect of the helper process. In either case, it is also unnecessary to wait for the helper to finish. With these modifications, the parallel algorithms indeed performed better than sequential algorithms. The following lists some samples of their running time under QEMU.

```
pmkdir-prmdir:  81920 77824 86016 57344 49152
mkdir-rmdir  :  86016 94208 90112 77824 94208
```

The test results show that we can make the parallel algorithms run faster only under very special conditions. Since it is unreasonable to use a dedicated CPU to run only the helper processes, we have to schedule them as ordinary processes in the SMP_MTX kernel. Under these conditions, pfork-pexec performs as well as fork-exec, but the sequential mkdir-rmdir algorithms are still faster. These seem to suggest that, in order to realize the full potential of parallel algorithms, we may need special hardware support, e.g. equip each main processor with dedicated co-processors which can be set up to execute the helper code directly, bypassing the usual process setup and scheduling in the SMP kernel. Unfortunately, this is beyond the capability of current SMP-compliant systems.

In summary, we believe that a SMP system should use parallel algorithms to improve both concurrency and efficiency. In SMP_MTX, we use parallel algorithms for process scheduling, resource management, pipes and I/O buffer management.

In order to keep the system simple, we only pointed out the principle and demonstrated some of the parallelization techniques but did not try to apply them to all data structures in the SMP_MTX kernel. Although our initial attempt of using parallel algorithms for fork-exec and mkdir-rmdir did not achieve the intended goal, we believe that the effort is worthwhile as it paves the way for further research. Unlike sequential algorithms, which can not be improved, parallel algorithms still have room for improvements. The algorithms could be redesigned and the implementation technique refined to improve their performance.

15.6.8 SMP_MTX Demonstration System

SMP_MTX is the final version of the MTX operating system. It uses parallel algorithms for SMP. The internal organization and startup sequence of SMP_MTX are identical to that of SMP_PMTX. So we shall not repeat them here. On the MTX install CD, MTX.images/smp is a runnable image of SMP_MTX. Figure 15.10 shows its startup screen with 16 CPUs. The reader may test the system as follows. Login in as root, password = 12345.

- Run commands as usual. Each process shows its pid and the CPU ID it is running on.
- Run pipe commands, e.g. cat f | grep line. The commands will run on different CPUs.
- Run thread commands, e.g. matrix, qsort, etc. The threads will run on different CPUs.
- Run segfault, divide and itimer commands to test exception and signal processing.

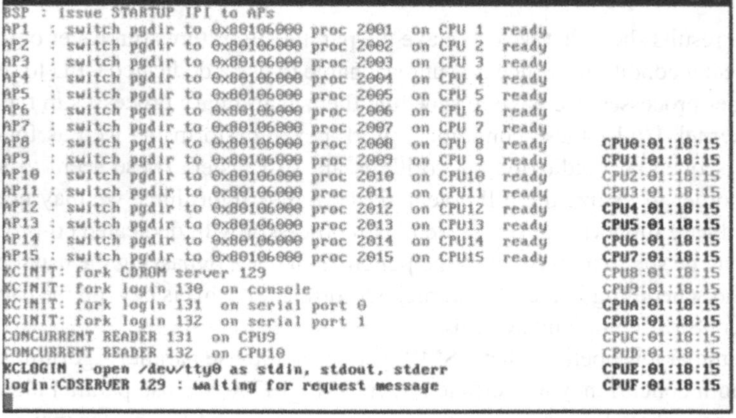

Fig. 15.10 SMP_MTX startup screen

SMP_MTX supports two different versions of file systems: fs.rw and fs.norw. The former supports concurrent readers but the latter does not, so it is much simpler. When compiled with fs.rw, the system usually shows a few concurrent readers during startup. This is because several login processes are trying to load and execute the same login file. Due to their experimental nature, parallel fork-exec and mkdir-rmdir are implemented in the SMP_MTX kernel for testing only. They are not used in regular command processing.

15.7 SMP and Real-time Operating Systems

A real-time operating system (Dietrich and Walker 2015) is an OS intended for real-time applications. Real-time applications usually have two very stringent timing requirements: fast response time and guaranteed completion time. Specifically, a real-time OS must be able to

- respond to interrupt requests of real-time events within a very short time limit.
- complete a requested service within a certain time limit, known as the task deadline.

If a system can always meet these critical timing requirements, it is called a hard real-time system. If it can only meet the requirements most of the time but not always, it is called a soft real-time system. In order to meet these critical timing requirements, a real-time OS is usually designed with the following capabilities.

- Minimum interrupt response latency and task switch time: A real-time OS kernel must not mask out interrupts for long periods of time. Code used to implement critical regions and task switching must be a minimum. All critical regions must be as short as possible.
- An advanced task scheduler: The scheduler must support preemptive task scheduling with a suitable deadline-based scheduling algorithm, such as the Earliest Deadline First (EDF) (Liu and Layland 1973) algorithm. Preemptive scheduling allows higher priority tasks to preempty lower priority tasks at any time. It is a necessary, though not sufficient, condition for real-time operations. Without preemptive scheduling, it would be impossible to meet task deadlines.
- To ensure fast response, tasks in a real-time OS usually do not have a separate user mode. All tasks run in the same address space of the OS kernel.

Due to their unique requirements and objectives, the design and implementation of real-time OS differ from that of general purpose OS. However, they also have many things in common, especially in the area of process synchronization, such as critical regions, protection of data structures to support concurrent executions, prevention of deadlocks and race conditions, etc. Therefore, some of the same design principles and implementation techniques of SMP kernels are also applicable to real-time OS kernels.

15.7.1 SMP_MTX for Real-time Processing

The SMP_MTX kernel supports preemptive task scheduling. We may adapt the SMP_MTX kernel for real-time operations as follows. Divide the processes into two classes; real-time and ordinary. Assign a fixed high priority, e.g. 256, to real-time processes, and lower priorities to ordinary processes. Modify the task scheduler to run real-time processes first with a short time slice by round-robin until there are no runnable real-time processes. Then run ordinary processes, which are scheduled by dynamic process priorities. Whenever a real-time process becomes ready, it preempties any ordinary process. Since the system only guarantees a quick start and a fair share of CPU time for real-time processes but not their completion deadlines, it is therefore only a soft real-time OS. This is the same approach used in (Dietrich and Walke) for real-time processing in Linux.

15.8 SMP in 16-bit Real Mode

Intel's MP Specification defines SMP-compliant systems as PCs with x486 and above processors, which seems to imply that SMP is intended for protected mode only. However, a PC in real mode also has the following capabilities.

- The x86 CPU in 16-bit real mode supports atomic instructions, such as xchg and locked inc/dec, etc. which are essential to SMP.
- If needed, IRQ0 to IRQ15 can also be remapped in real mode.
- In SMP, all the CPUs start in real mode. It should be easy to integrate the APs into a real mode kernel.
- Using BIOS INT15-87, a PC in real mode can read/write IOAPIC and APIC registers in the address range above 0xFEC00000.

Based on these, we have tried to extend the real mode RMTX to SMP. The result is a qualified success. In this section, we describe the adaptation of RMTX to SMP_RMTX and discuss some of the problems and possible remedies.

15.8.1 Real-mode SMP_RMTX startup sequence

1. During booting, CPU0 is the boot processor (BSP), which executes the booter code. As in RMTX, the real mode SMP_RMTX begins execution from the assembly code ts.s, which calls main() in t.c. While in main(), it first calls init() to initialize the kernel, create and run the initial process P0, which calls kfork("/bin/init") to create the INIT process P1 and enter it into the readyQueue of CPU0.
2. P0 calls findmp() to get the number of CPUs in the system. It scans the MP table and returns the number of CPUs in the system. If the number of CPUs is 1, it

falls back to UP mode. Otherwise, it calls smp() to configure the PC for SMP operations.

3. Read/write IOAPIC and APIC Registers: In real mode, we use BIOS INT15-87 to read/write high memory. The MTX kernel is loaded at 0x10000. We use the long word at 0x0F000 as an intermediate data area to read/write APIC registers by the functions

u32 apic_read(u8 apic_reg)   // read an APIC register
int apic_write(u32 w, u8 apic_reg) // write to an APIC register.

The function apic_read() sets up a GDT with source address = 0xFEE00000 + apic_reg and destination address = 0x0000F000. It issues an INT15-87 to read the 32-bit APIC register to 0x0F000 as the return value. Similarly for apic_write(), which writes a long word to 0x0F000 and then issues an INT15-87 to write it to an APIC register. By changing the high memory address to 0xFEC00000 and 0xFEC00010, these functions can also read/write IOAPIC registers.

4. Enable BSP's local APIC and start up APs: During booting, the boot processor is set up by BIOS to receive all interrupts from the 8259 PICs. For SMP in real mode, we do not remap the IRQs and configure the IOAPIC to route interrupts. Instead, we let the BSP handle all the PIC interrupts as in real mode. This helps reduce the needed changes in the RMTX kernel. When the BSP boots up, we enable its local APIC and broadcast INIT and STARTUP IPIs to other APs. When an AP starts, it begins to execute the trampoline code, which must be at a 4 KB page boundary in real mode memory corresponding to the vector number (0×11) in the STARTUP IPI. To comply with this, we append the following code segment to the assembly file ts.s. Since the SMP_RMTX kernel is loaded at 0x10000, the added code segment is at the 4 KB aligned page 0x11000. Instead of the actual assembly code, we only show the algorithm of APentry.

```
        .org 4096       ! aligned to 4KB boundary at 0x11000
        .globl _initproc,_APstart,_APspin,_APvmgdt,_APstack
(1). Set DS to MTX kernel DS
(2). Acquire APspin spinlock to ensure one AP at a time
(3). Set SS=DS, sp=APstack as a temporary stack
(4). Use APvmgdt to read APIC ID register at 0xFEE00020
(5). Get CPUID and store it in ES register
(6). Release the APspin spinlock
(7). Use CPUID to set sp to high end of initproc[CPUID]
(8). jmpi _APstart, 0x1000  ! jmp to APstart() in kernel
```

Prior to activating the APs, the BSP initializes the global APvmgdt for reading APIC ID register at 0xFEE00020 by BIOS INT15-87. When an AP starts, it first sets DS to the data segment of the SMP_RMTX kernel. Then it reads the APIC ID register to get its CPUID and stores it in the ES register. It uses initproc[CPUID]'s ksatck to enter APstart() in the RMTX kernel. The algorithm of APstart() is

```
int APstart()
{
      int cpuid = getes(); // ES of CPU contains the CPU ID number
(a). printf("============= CPU #%d starts ============\n", id);
      let run[cpuid] point to AP's initial PROC initproc[cpuid];
      initialize initproc[cpuid].pid with a unique PID, 123+cpuid;
(b). configure APIC timer with vector=0x40 + cpuid;
(c). enable local APIC;
(d). inform BSP that this AP is ready;
(e). enter scheduling loop to run tasks from AP's ready queue
}
```

5. Local APIC timer of APs: In the real mode SMP system, we need the AP's timer
   for the following reason. Since CPU0 receives and handles all the PIC interrupts,
   the APs do not have any interrupts. In order to run tasks, each AP must be able to
   examine its ready queue to do task scheduling. There are several possible ways
   to do this, such as

   - By IPI: CPU0 may issue IPIs to inform other APs to start an action.
   - By shared memory: the APs can monitor some memory contents that are
     changed by CPU0, but this requires polling by each AP.
   - By a local timer, which interrupts periodically, allowing each AP to look for
     work by itself.

Among these, a local timer is the simplest to implement. If a CPU finds no work to
do, it runs an idle process with interrupts enabled. A timer interrupt will cause it to
get up to handle the interrupt and then try to run task again.

6. After setting up the local timer, each AP increments a global variable go_smp by
   1 to inform the BSP that the AP is ready. Then it enters the scheduler to run tasks.
7. BSP waits until all the APs are ready. Then it enters the scheduler to run tasks
   also.

After all the above steps, RMTX is running SMP in 16-bit real mode. As in SMP_
MTX, each CPU tries to run tasks from its own ready queue. Ready processes are
distributed among the ready queues to balance the processing load of the CPUs.

15.8.2 SMP_RMTX Kernel

In order to support SMP, the RMTX kernel must be modified. The following describes the changes that are specific to the real mode RMTX kernel.

1. CPU ID and Running PROCs: In 16-bit real mode, we let the ES register carry
   the CPU ID number. In order to identify the PROCs running on different CPUs,
   we define PROC *run[NCPU] and let run[i] point to the PROC that's currently
   executing on CPUi. Then we define running as

#define running run[cpuid()]

This allows the running symbol to be used in the kernel's C code without any change. In assembly code, we simply use ES as an index to access the PROC running on the CPU.

2. Changes to the RMTX kernel for SMP

  2.1. tswitch() in ts.s file: In SMP, there may be several processes executing in parallel. When a PROC running on a CPU calls tswitch() to switch process, we must know the calling PROC in order to save its context. So we modify tswitch() to tswitch(running), passing as parameter the running PROC pointer. After saving its context, the process calls scheduler(), which returns a pointer to the next running PROC. Similar to SMP in protected mode, during task switch the current running process must acquire the CPU's spinlock, which is released by the next running PROC when it resumes.

  2.2. Interrupt entry and exit routines: CPU0 handles all the PIC interrupts. The interrupt entry and exit routines do not need any change for CPU0. Since PROCs running on APs also do syscalls and handle local timer interrupts, both the INTH macro and ireturn code are modified slightly by using the ES register to identify the PROC running on a CPU.

  2.3. Other Changes to the MTX Kernel: The above changes are specific to the real-mode RMTX kernel. Others changes to the RMTX kernel are exactly the same as those in protected mode. Therefore, we shall not repeat them here.

3. Due to the 64 KB code segment limit, the real mode SMP MTX kernel does not have enough room to use parallel algorithms. So it uses modified UP algorithms protected by spinlocks. Also, process scheduling is by time slice only.

15.8.3 SMP_RMTX Demonstration System

On the MTX install CD, SMP_RMTX is SMP MTX in 16-bit real mode. It runs on VMware virtual machines with multiple CPUs. Figure 15.11 shows the startup screen of SMP_RMTX on VMware with four CPUs.

15.8.4 Limitations and Future Work

The real mode SMP MTX seems to work but there are also some minor problems. We invite interested readers to explore these issues further.

1. In the system, CPU0 handles all the PIC interrupts. Each AP only handles its local APIC timer interrupts. Strictly speaking, it is not a SMP system in the true

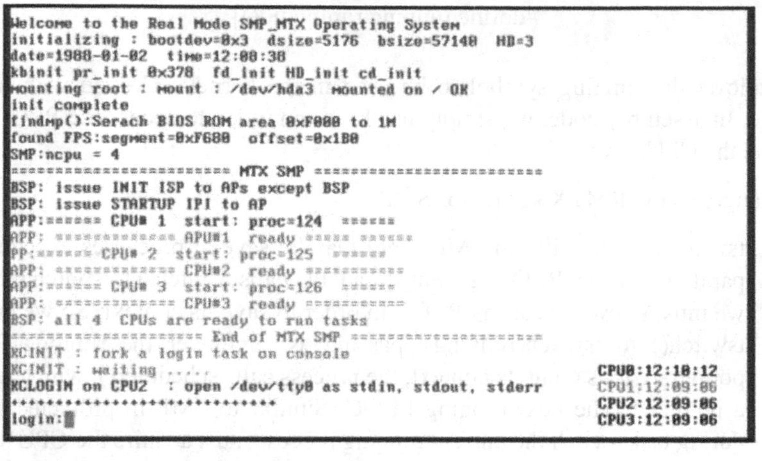

```
Welcome to the Real Mode SMP_MTX Operating System
initializing : bootdev=0x3  dsize=5176  bsize=57140  HB=3
date=1988-01-02  time=12:08:38
kbinit pr_init 0x378  fd_init HD_init cd_init
mounting root : mount : /dev/hda3 mounted on / OK
init complete
findmp():Serach BIOS ROM area 0xF000 to 1M
found FPS:segment=0xF600  offset=0x1B0
SMP:ncpu = 4
==================== MTX SMP ====================
BSP: issue INIT ISP to APs except BSP
BSP: issue STARTUP IPI to AP
APP:====== CPU# 1  start: proc=124  ======
APP: ============ APU#1  ready ===== ======
PP:====== CPU# 2  start: proc=125  ======
APP: ============ CPU#2  ready ===========
APP:====== CPU# 3  start: proc=126  ======
APP: ============ CPU#3  ready ===========
BSP: all 4  CPUs are ready to run tasks
==================== End of MTX SMP ====================
KCINIT : fork a login task on console
KCINIT : waiting .....                             CPU0:12:10:12
KCLOGIN on CPU2  : open /dev/tty0 as stdin, stdout, stderr   CPU1:12:09:06
+++++++++++++++++++++++++++++++                    CPU2:12:09:06
login:█                                            CPU3:12:09:06
```

Fig. 15.11 Startup screen of SMP_RMTX on VMware

sense. In order to let the APs handle other interrupts, we should configure the
IOAPIC to route interrupts to different CPUs. It is unclear whether this is possible in real mode.

2. Initially, the system had a puzzling problem of losing EOIs. After running for
a few minutes, all the APIC timers would stop, causing the system either to
hang or fall back to UP mode. The problem was eventually traced to the BIOS
INT15-87 routine. The SMP_RMTX kernel relies on the ES register for CPU
identification but INT15-87 also uses ES. Although we save ES before calling
INT15-87 and restore ES afterward, it seems that the INT15-87 routine enables
interrupts as soon as it finishes. If another APIC timer interrupt occurs before ES
is restores, the interrupt handler would fail, resulting in lost EOIs. So we try to
use CLI to disable interrupts immediately after calling INT15-87. In spite of this,
interrupts still occur, although very infrequently, in the time gap between the
end of INT15-87 routine and the CLI instruction. Since we can not control the
behavior of the BIOS INT15-87 routine, we have to use large APIC timer counter values and also check ES in the interrupt handler entry code. If the ES content
is not a valid CPU ID, it must be due to an APIC timer interrupt. In that case, we
simply issue an EOI but print an EOI_alert message. The system works normally
only after these patches. It can now run for days without losing any EOI. It may
be possible to avoid this problem by not using the BIOS routine. For instance, we
may switch the CPU to protected mode, write to APIC register and switch back
to real mode. But then the question is: if we switch the CPU to protected mode,
we could run SMP in protected mode, so why bother to switch it back?

3. The system runs quite well on VMware, most recently on VMware-player 6.0.2
under Slackware Linux 14.1. It should also run on multicore real PCs, but this is

unconfirmed since I can not find any multicore PC that still supports IDE drives. However, it does not run on QEMU. It seems that the APs in QEMU's SMP environment do not respond to any IPI if the BSP is in real mode, so the system just hangs.

Despite these minor problems, the SMP_RMTX system demonstrates that it is indeed possible to do SMP in 16-bit real mode. To the best of my knowledge, it is probably the only 16-bit real mode SMP system in existence. Whether it is useful or not remains to be seen.

15.9   Summary of PMTX and SMP_MTX

This section presents a comprehensive description of the PMTX and SMP_MTX systems.

15.9.1   PMTX and SMP_MTX Source File Tree

The source directories of all versions of MTX contain the following file tree.

```
MTX_VERSION
|-- SETUP : boot.s, setup.s, apentry.s
|-- type.h, include.h, Makefile and mk script
|-- kernel   : kernel source files
|-- fs       : file system files
|-- driver   : device driver files
|-- USER     : commands and user mode programs
```

SETUP   boot.s contains the signatures 'RR' for real mode and 'PP' for protected mode.

setup.s   is for transition from 16-bit real mode to 32-bit protected mode.

apentry.s is the startup trampoline code of the APs in SMP.

type.h   MTX kernel data structure types.

include.h constants and function prototypes.

Makefile top-level Makefile for recompiling MTX by the make utility.

mk   sh script for recompile MTX and install bootable image to HD partition.

15.9.2   PMTX and SMP_MTX Kernel Files

```
-------------- Kernel: Process Management Part -----------------
type.h    : kernel data structure types, such as PROC, resources, etc.
ts.s      : tswitch, interrupt mask, spinlocks, interrupt handler entry/exit code, etc.
io.c      :  kernel I/O functions; printf(), inter-segment copy in real mode, etc..
mtxlib    :  kernel library functions; memset, memcpy and string operations.
-------------- for MTX in protected mode -----------------------
entry.s   : 32-bit protect mode entry code
init.c    : paging and CPU initialization
traps.s   : low-level exception handler tables in assembly
trapc.c   : high-level exception and interrupt handlers in C
-------------- for SMP in protected mode -----------------------
mp.h      : SMP FP and MP structure types
mp.c      : FP and MP scanning functions
smp.h     : SMP types and structures
smp.c     : SMP configuration and startup code
--------------- Common to all MTX ----------------------------
queue.c   : enqueue, dequue, printQueue functions
wait.c    : ksleep, kwakeup, kwait, kexit functions
loader.c  : flat binary and ELF executable image loader
fork.c    :  kfork, fork, vfork functions
exec.c    :  kexec function
threads.c : threads and mutex functions
pipe.c    :  pipe creation and read/write functions
mes.c     :  message passing: send/recv functions
signal.c  : signals and signal processing
syscall.c :  syscall routing table and simple syscall functions
t.c       : main entry, initialization, parts of process scheduler
---------------- Device Drivers ---------------------------------
vid.c     : console display driver
timer.c   : timer and timer service functions (for UP MTX)
pv.c      : semaphore operations
kbd.c     : console keyboard driver
pr.c      : parallel printer driver
serial.c  : serial ports driver
fd.c      : floppy disk driver
hd.c      : IDE hard disk driver
atapi.c   : ATAPI CDROM driver
---------------- File system ---------------------------------
fs        : implementation of a simple EXT2 file system
-------------------------------------------------------------
```

PMTX and SMP_MTX are implemented mostly in C, with less than 3 % of assembly code. The total number of line count in the MTX kernel is approximately 14000 for PMTX and 18000 for SMP_MTX.

15.9.3   Process Management in PMTX and SMP_MTX

1. PROC Structure

Each process or thread is represented by a PROC structure consisting of three parts.

- fields for process management,
- a pointer to a process resource structure,
- kernel mode stack pointer to a dynamically allocated page for kstack.

In protected mode, the PROC structure is

```
typedef struct proc{
          struct  proc *next;// next PROC pointer
          int     *ksp;      // saved kstack pointer
          int     inkmode;   // in Kmode counter
          int     pid;       // process ID
          int     ppid;      // parent pid
          int     status;    // process status: FREE|READY|SLEEP, etc.
          int     priority;  // scheduling priority
          int     event;     // event to sleep on
          int     exitValue; // exit status
          int     vforked;   // proc is vforked
          int     time;      // time quantum
          int     cpu;       // CPU usage time in a reschedule interval
          int     pause;     // pause time
          int     type;      // PROCESS|THREAD type
      struct proc *parent;   // pointer to parent PROC
      struct proc *proc;     // process pointer for threads
      struct pres *res;      // process resource structure pointer
      struct semaphore *sem; // pointer to semaphore if proc is BLOCKed
      struct semaphore wchild;// semaphore for wait/exit using P/V
          TSS tss;           // TSS structure: PROTECTED MODE ONLY
      int* kstack;           // process kernel mode stack pointer
  }PROC;
```

In the PROC structure, the next field is used to link the PROCs in various link lists or queues. The ksp field is the saved kernel mode stack pointer of the process. When a process gives up CPU, it saves CPU registers in kstack and saves the stack pointer in ksp. When a process regains CPU, it resumes running from the stack frame pointed by ksp. In protected mode, when an interrupt or exception occurs, the CPU saves CPU registers in the process kernel mode stack. If a process enters kernel from user mode, the saved CPU registers include uss and usp, which are restored by iret when it returns to user mode. The inkmode field is a counter used to keep track of the number of times a process enters Kmode. When a process is created in kernel, its inkmode is set to one. It is decremented by one when a process exits Kmode and incremented by one when it enters Kmode. This allows the kernel to know whether an exception occurred in Umode or Kmode. In addition, it is used to determine whether a process is about to return to user mode, in which case it must handle any pending signals first, and it may also switch process. The fields pid, ppid, priority and status

are obvious. In most large OS, each process is assigned a unique pid from a range
of pid numbers. In MTX, we simply use the PROC index as the process pid, which
simplifies the kernel code and also makes it easier for discussion. When a process
terminates or exits, it must wakeup/unblock the parent. The parent pointer points
to the parent PROC, which allows a dying process to find its parent quickly. The
event field is the event value when a process goes to sleep. The exitValue field is
the exit status of a process. If a process terminates normally by exit(value) syscall,
the low byte is the exit value. If it terminates by a signal, the high byte is the signal
number. This allows the parent process to extract the exit status of a ZOMBIE child
to determine whether it terminated normally or abnormally. The time field is the
maximum run time quantum of a process and cpu is its CPU usage time. They are
used to compute the dynamic process scheduling priority. The pause field is for a
process to sleep for a number of seconds. In MTX, process and thread PROCs are
identical. The type field identifies whether a PROC is a PROCESS or THREAD.
PMTX is a uniprocessor (UP) system, which use sleep/wakeup for process management. SMP_MTX uses modified sleep/wakeup only in pipes. It uses semaphores for
process management. Device drivers and file system use semaphores for process
synchronization. When a process becomes blocked on a semaphore, the sem pointer
points to the semaphore. This allows the kernel to unblock a process from a semaphore queue, if necessary. For example, when a process waits for keyboard inputs, it
is blocked in the keyboard driver's input semaphore queue. A kill signal or an interrupt key should let the process continue. The sem pointer simplifies the unblocking
operation. Each PROC has a res pointer pointing to a resource structure, which is

```
typedef struct pres{
     int     uid, gid;              // user id and group id
     u32     *pgdir,size;           // pgdir and mage size
     u32     *newpgdir, newsize     // used in exec for new image size
     MINODE  *cwd;                  // Currnt Working Directory pointer
     char    tty[32];               // terminal special file name
     char    name[32];              // program name string
     int     vforked;               // process is vforked flag
     int     tcount;                // number of threads in process
     int     signal;                // 31 signals = bits 1 to 31
     int     sig[NSIG];             // signal handlers
     struct semaphore mlock;        // messageQ lock
     struct semaphore message;      // # of messages
     struct mbuf     *mqueue;       // message queue
     OFT     *fd[NFD];              // open file descriptors
}PRES;
```

The PRES structure contains process specific information. It includes the process
uid, gid, pgdir and image size, current working directory, terminal special file name,
program name, signal and signal handlers, message queue and file descriptors, etc.
In both PMTX and SMP_MTX, PROC and res structures are constructed in the
memory between 5 and 6 MB. The first NPROC=1024 PROCs are for processes
and the remaining NTHREAD=512 PROCs are for threads. Processes and threads
are independent execution units. Each process executes in a unique address space
but threads in a process execute in the same address space of the process. During

system initialization, each PROCESS PROC is assigned a unique PRES structure pointed by the res pointer. A process is also the main thread of the process. When create a new thread, its proc pointer points to the process PROC and its res pointer points to the same PRES structure of the process. Thus, all threads in a process share the same resources, such as opened file descriptors, signals and messages, etc. Some OS kernels allow individual threads to open files, which are private to the threads. In that case, each PROC must have its own file descriptor array. Similarly for signals and messages, etc. In the PROC structure, kstack is a process kernel mode stack pointer. The kstack of a process is dynamically allocated a 4 KB page only when needed. It is eventually released by the parent in wait(). In protected mode, PROCs are managed as follows.

PMTX: in PMTX, PROCs and resources are defined as

```
IPROC initproc; PROC *proc; PRES *pres;
```

where IPROC and PROC structures are identical except that IPROC contains a statically defined 4 KB kstack. initproc is the initial and idle process of the CPU. When PMTX starts, it can only access the first 8 MB of physical memory via paging. We assume that the kernel occupies the lowest 4 MB. Free PROCs and resources are constructed dynamically in the memory area of 5–6 MB. As in RMTX, free process and thread PROCs are maintained in separate free lists for allocation/deallocation. In PMTX, which is a UP system, there is only one readyQueue for process scheduling. In both PMTX and SMP, the kernel mode stack of each PROC in dynamically allocated a page frame only when needed. When a process terminates, it becomes a ZOMBIE but retains its pgdir and the kstack, which are eventually deallocated by the parent in kwait().

SMP: in SMP, PROC and resource structures are defined as

```
IPROC initproc[NCPU]; PROC *proc; PRES *pres;
```

where initproc[NCPU] are the initial and idle processes of the CPUs. As in PMTX, free PROCs and resources are constructed in the memory area of 5–6 MB but maintained in separate free lists, each associated with a CPU, for allocation/deallocation by parallel algorithms. Each CPU has a separate readyQueue [cpuid] for process scheduling in parallel.

2. ts.s: In protected mode, ts.s is in 32-bit GCC assembly.

PMTX: ts.s contains code for context switch, interrupt handler entry and exit routines, interrupt masking and port I/O, etc. As in real mode, interrupt handlers are installed by the INTH macro. In protected mode, the saved CPU registers include segment selectors.

SMP: to support SMP, ts.s contains the following new functions.

a. slock/sunlock for spinlock operations by the atomic instruction XCHG. It also implements conditional spinlock, which returns 0 if a process can not acquire a spinlock. The SMP kernel uses spinlocks to protect critical regions in which task switching is either unnecessary or not allowed, e.g. in interrupt handlers. It uses conditional locking and back-off to prevent deadlocks in concurrent algorithms.

b. In SMP, each CPU is represented by a CPU structure, which is mapped to a virtual address by the CPU's gs segment. In the CPU structure, the first three entries contain a pointer to the CPU structure itself, a pointer to the current PROC executing on the CPU and a spinlock for protecting the CPU's scheduling queue. In the SMP kernel, the symbol cpu (gs:0) points to the CPU structure and running (gs:4) points to the process executing on a CPU. When a process calls tswitch() to switch process, it first acquires the CPU's spinlock, which is released by the next running process on the same CPU when it resumes.

c. In SMP, the interrupt/exception entry and exit codes use gs:4 to access the PROC information of the interrupted process.

3. io.c: This file contains kernel I/O functions, such as printf(), which is based on kgetc()/kputc() in the terminal device driver.
4. mtxlib: This file contains precompiled utility functions, such as memset, memcpy and string operations, etc. which are the same for all versions of MTX.
5. entry.s: This file contains the entry code of MTX kernel in protected mode.

PMTX: In PMTX, the kernel is compiled with the starting virtual address 0x80000000 (2 GB) but it runs from the physical address 0x100000 (1 MB). entry.s sets up an initial paging environment to allow the kernel to access the lowest 8 MB physical memory when it starts. To do this, entry.s defines an initial page directory, ipgdir, at 0x101000, two initial page tables at 0x102000, a GDT at 0x104000 and an IDT at 0x105000. Upon entry, entry.s initializes the two page tables to the lowest 8 MB physical memory. It uses the ipgdir to turn on paging, allowing the kernel to access the lowest 8 MB as both real and virtual addresses. Then it forces the CPU to use virtual addresses starting from 0x80000000. It uses initproc's kstack to call init() in init.c to initialize the kernel.

SMP: In SMP, the initial paging environment is identical to that of PMTX, except that entry.s defines NCPU GDTs at 0x104000. Each GDT contains seven segment descriptors; null, kcs, kds, tss, ucs, uds and gs, where the gs segment is used to map the 40-byte CPU structure of each CPU. The 2 KB IDT at 0x105000 is common to all CPUs. The BSP uses the first GDT at 0x104000. It sets the stack pointer to initproc[0].kstack and calls init().

6. init.c: This file contains the initialization code of PMTX and SMP in protected mode.

PMTX: Upon entry to init(), the kernel can only access the lowest 8 MB physical memory through paging. It first initialize the display driver to make printf() work. Then it sets up a new page directory and the associated page tables to expand the virtual address range. Assume 512 MB physical memory and the kernel occupies the lowest 4 MB. The new page directory, kpgdir, is constructed at VA=0x80106000, in which entries 0–511 are 0's and entries 512–639 point to 128 page tables at 4 MB. Then it switches to the new kpgdir, allowing the kernel to access the entire 512 MB physical memory. The kpgdir will be the page directory of the initial process P0. The pgdir and page tables of other process are dynamically allocated. The last 512 entries of all page directories are identical since the kernel mode address spaces of all processes are the same. Then it calls kernel_init() to initialize kernel data structures. The NPROC (1024)+NTHREAD (512) PROC and resource structures are constructed in the memory area of 5 MB. Free process and thread PROCs are maintained in separate freeList and tfreeList for allocation/deallocation. Since PMTX is a UP system, all kernel resources are maintained in single data structures, which are managed by sequential algorithms. Then it creates and runs the initial process P0, which uses a statically defined PROC structure initproc. P0 continues to initialize the kernel. It remaps IRQs, installs exception and interrupt vectors in the IDT, initializes I/O buffers, device drivers and mounts the root file system. Then it initializes the free page frame list, pfreeList, from 8 to 512 MB for dynamic allocation/deallocation of page frames. Lastly, it calls main() to create and run the INIT process P1.

SMP: The init() function is SMP is slightly more complex. Its actions are as follow.

1. Initialize display driver to make printf() work;
2. Scan the SMP configuration data structures to determine the number of CPUs;
3. Initialize cpu structures: each CPU is represented by a cpus[NCPU] structure at the virtual address gs:0. It contains a pointer to the PROC running on the CPU at gs:4.
4. When start up, each CPU runs an initial PROC, which is also the idle process of the CPU. The initial PROCs are defined statically as initproc[NCPU]. All the initial PROCs run in kernel mode only. They share the same kpgdir and page tables of CPU0, which is the boot processor (BSP). As in PMTX, the BSP constructs the kpgdir at 0x80106000 and the page tables at 4 MB, for the virtual address range [2 GB, 2 GB+512 MB]. In addition, it also fills the kpgdir's last eight page tables to create an identity mapping of the address range [0xFE000000, 4 GB], allowing the CPUs to access the memory mapped locations of IOAPIC and APIC above 0xFE000000.
5. After building the kpgdir and page tables, the BSP switches to kpgdir, thereby expanding the virtual address range to [2 GB, 2 GB+512 MB] and [0xFE000000, 4 GB]. Then it calls kernel_init() to initialize the kernel data structures.
6. kernel_init(): in both PMTX and SMP, PROCs and their resource structures constructed in the 1 MB memory area from 5–6 MB. In SMP, free PROCs are divided into separate free lists, each associated with a CPU, which are managed by parallel algorithms.
7. After initializing the PROC lists, the BSP uses initproc[0] to create P0 as the initial running process. When the APs start, each AP uses an initproc[cpuid] as the initial process.

8. When kernel_init() returns, P0 remaps the IRQs, installs exception and interrupt vectors in the IDT, initializes I/O buffers, device drivers and mounts the root file system. The data area of (1024) I/O buffers for block devices are at 7 MB. In SMP, the I/O buffers are maintained in hash queues and managed by parallel algorithms.

9. In SMP, free page frames are divided into separate pfreeList[ncpu], each associated with a CPU and protected by a spinlock, for allocation/deallocation in parallel.

10. Then it calls main(ncpu) in t.c to configure the system for SMP operations.

7. traps.s and trapc.c: traps.s contains low-level exception handler tables in assembly. trapc.c implements high-level exception handlers in C. They are the same for all versions of MTX in protected mode.

8. mp.h, mp.c, smp.h, smp.c: These files are for SMP only. The header files contain SMP configuration, IOAPIC and APIC types. mp.c implements the MP table scanning function, which returns the number of CPUs in a SMP system. smp.c contains IOAPIC and APIC functions. It contains code to configure the system for SMP operations and start up the APs. It also contains the C code of APIC timer interrupt handlers and the startup code of the APs.

9. queue.c: This file implements get_proc()/put_proc() and enqueue()/dequeue() functions. get_proc() allocates a free PROC for a new process or thread. put_proc() returns a ZOMBIE PROC to a free PROC list. In PMTX, ready processes and threads are maintained in a single readyQueue by priority. enqueue() enters a PROC into the readyQueue by priority, and dequeue() returns a pointer to the highest priority PROC removed from the readyQueue. In addition, there are also other list/queue manipulation functions, e.g. enter/remove a sleeping process to/from the sleepList, etc. They are implemented in the relevant files for clarity.

SMP: In SMP, free PROC structures are maintained in separate free lists, each associated with a CPU and protected by a spinlock. They are managed by get_proc/put_proc using parallel algorithms.

10. wait.c: This file implements ksleep(), kwakeup(), kwait() and kexit() for process management.

PMTX: In PMTX, the functions are as follows.

1. ksleep()/kwakeup(): A process calls ksleep(event) to go to sleep on an event. An event is just a value which represents the sleep reason. When the awaited event occurs, another process or an interrupt handler calls kwakeup(event), which wakes up all the processes sleeping on the event. To ensure that processes are woken up in order, sleeping processes are maintained in a FIFO sleepList.

2. kwait(): kwait() allows a process to wait for a ZOMBIE child. If a process has children but no ZOMBIE child yet, it sleeps on its own PROC address. When a process terminates, it calls kexit() to becomes a ZOMBIE and wakes up the parent by kwakeup(). As in Unix, orphan processes become children of the INIT process P1, which repeatedly waits for and releases any ZOMBIE children.

3. kexit(): every process calls kexit(exitValue) to terminate. The actions of kexit()
   are:

   - give away children, if any, to P1;
   - release resources, e.g. free Umode image memory, dispose of cwd, close
     opened file descriptors and release message buffers in message queue.
   - record exitValue in PROC, become a ZOMBIE, wakeup parent and also P1 if
     it has sent any children to P1.
   - call tswitch() to give up CPU for the last time.

ZOMBIE PROCs are freed by their parents through kwait(). Orphaned ZOMBIEs
are freed by the INIT process P1.

SMP: The conventional sleep and wakeup are unsuited to SMP due to race conditions. In SMP, they are modified to execute in the same critical region of a spinlock. When a process calls the modified psleep(), it completes the sleep operation
before releasing the spinlock. The SMP kernel uses the modified psleep/wakeup
only in pipes. It uses a PORC.wchild semaphore to synchronize parent and children
processes in kwait() and kexit().

11. fork.c: This file contains fork1(), kfork(), fork() and vfork() functions for creat-
    ing new processes. They are implemented as follows. .

    1. kfork():

When the MTX kernel starts, it first initializes the kernel data structures and creates
a process P0 as the initial running process, which runs only in kernel mode and has
the lowest priority 0. When initialization completes, P0 calls kfork("/bin/init") to
create a child process P1. kfork() calls fork1(), which is the common code of creating new processes. fork1() creates a child process ready to run in kernel but without
a Umode image. When fork1() returns, kfork() allocates a Umode memory area for
P1, loads the/bin/init file as the Umode image and sets up the kstack of P1 for it to
resume. Then P0 switches to run P1, which returns to execute/bin/init in Umode.
P1 is the only process created by kfork(). After P1 runs, all other processes are created by fork() or vfork() as usual. The startup sequence of MTX is unique. In most
other Unix-like systems, the initial image of P1 is a piece of precompiled binary
executable code containing an exec("/etc/init") system call. After system initialization, P1 is sent to execute the exec() syscall code in Umode, which changes P1's
image to/etc/init. In MTX, when P1 starts to run, it returns to Umode to execute the
INIT image directly.

   In PMTX, P0 uses the statically allocated PROC structure initproc. In SMP, it
uses initproc[0]. In both cases, P0 sets up the kernel mode kpgdir and page tables,
which are shared by all the initial processes in SMP. In kfork(), the pgdir and page
tables of P1 are allocated dynamically.

    2. fork(): As in Unix/Linux, fork() creates a child process with an Umode image
       identical to that of the parent. If fork() succeeds, the parent returns the child's
       pid and the child returns 0. It is implemented as follows.

First, fork() calls fork1() to create a child process ready to run in Kmode. The child PROC inherits all the open file descriptors of the parent but without an Umode image. The child PROC is assigned the base priority of 127 and its resume point is set to goUmode, so that when the child is scheduled to run, it returns to Umode immediately. After fork1() returns, fork() allocates a Umode image area for the child of the same size as the parent and copies the parent's Umode image to the child. Then it copies the parent's kstack and fixes up the child's kstack for it to return to Umode. Finally, it returns the child's pid. When the child runs, it returns to its own Umode image with a 0. Because of the image copying, the child's Umode image is identical to that of the parent. The implementation of fork() in MTX is also unique. It only guarantees that the two Umode images are identical. The return paths of the parent and the child processes are very different.

PMTX: In protected mode, normal process image size is 4 MB but both PMTX and SMP support different image sizes. In fork(), the pgdir and page tables of the child process are allocated dynamically. The image copying function is modified to copy the page frames of the parent image. The stack frames for the child process to resume are all in the child's kernel mode stack. It consists of stack frame for the child to resume running in kernel, followed by an interrupt stack frame for it to return to user mode.

SMP: In SMP, free PROCs and page frames are maintained in separate free lists, each associated with a CPU, for allocation/deallocation in parallel. In addition, the SMP_MTX kernel also supports parallel fork() and exec() operations, which are implemented in the pforkexec.c file.

3. vfork(): After forking a child, the parent usually waits for the child to terminate and the child immediately does exec() to change its Umode image. In such cases, copying image in fork() would be a waste. For this reason, many OS kernels support vfork(), which forks a child process without copying the parent image. MTX also supports vfork(), which is implemented as follows.

PMTX and SMP: In protected mode, vfork() simply lets the child process share the same pgdir, hence the same page tables, with the parent. The resume stack frames of the child process are constructed in the kernel mode stack. A vforked child uses a separate user mode stack frame to return to user mode. The paging hardware supports COW (Copy-On-Write) pages, which can be used to protect shared images, but they are not yet implemented in either PMTX or SMP_MTX.

12. loader.c: This file implements the Umode image loader.

PMTX and SMP: In protected mode, the loader is modified to load either flat binary or ELF executables into the page frames of a process image. The image type is determined by a linker script, ld.script. Most user mode images are generated as statically linked ELF executables. The loader can load ELF executables with separate code, data and bss sections. MTX does not yet support dynamic linking.

13. exec.c: This file implements the kexec() system call. In MTX, the parameter to kexec() is the entire command line of the form "cmd argv1 argv2...argvn". It

uses the first token, cmd, to create the new image, and it passes the entire command line to the new image. Parsing the command line to argc and argv is done
in the new image in user mode. As of now, MTX does not support the PATH
environment variable. All executable commands are assumed to be in the/bin
directory. If the cmd file name does not begin with/, it is assumed in the/bin
directory by default.

PMTX and SMP: In protected mode, kexec() supports different image sizes
through an optional –m SIZE command-line parameter, in which case it creates a
new image of the specified SIZE. A vforked process always creates a new image,
thereby detaching it from the shared parent image. In addition, SMP_MTX also
supports parallel exec, which is implemented in the pforkexec.c file.

14. Memory Management: In protected mode, memory management is by dynamic
    paging.

PMTX: Each process has a pgdir and two sets of page tables. In the pgdir, entries
512 and above point to kernel mode page tables, which map the kernel virtual address space beginning from 0x80000000. The low 512 entries (0–511) point to user
mode page tables, which map the VA space of the Umode image. A process may
call sbrk()/rbrk() to expand/reduce its heap size. Each sbrk() call adds 4 KB to the
process image as the new heap space.

SMP: Memory management is identical to that of PMTX, except that free page
frames are maintained in separate free lists, each associated with a CPU and protected by a splinlock, for allocation/deallocation by parallel algorithms.

15. threads.c: This file implements threads [Pthreads 2015] support. In the MTX
    kernel, there are NTHREAD PROCs dedicated to threads. A process PROC is
    also the main thread of the process. Each process has a thread count, tcount,
    which is the number of active threads in the process. When a thread is created
    inside a process, it is allocated a THREAD PROC, which points to the process
    PROC. Threads in a process share the same resources of the process. They use
    tjoin and mutex for synchronization.

PMTX and SMP: In protected mode, the resume and interrupt stack frames of a
thread are all in its kernel mode stack. When the user mode thread function finishes,
it returns to the virtual address 5, which issues an exit(0) to terminate.

16. pipe.c: This file implement pipes. In MTX, pipes are in-memory IPC mecha-
    nisms for related processes, i.e. descendants of the same process which cre-
    ated the pipe. They are modeled after the classical producer-consumer problem.
    Instead of semaphores, they use sleep and wakeup for process synchronization,
    which are better suited to the semantics of pipes.

PMTX: In PMTX, the pipe structure is

```
typedef struct pipe{
        char  *buf;                     // pointer to a 4KB data buffer
        int   head, tail, data, room;
        int   nreader, nwriter;         // number of readers/writers
        int   busy;                     // FREE or in use
}PIPE;  PIPE pipe[NPIPE];               // NPIPE = 10
```

A PIPE contains a circular char buffer, buf[PSIZE=4 KB], with head and tail pointers. The pipe control variables are data, room, nreader and nwriter, where data=num-
ber of chars in the buffer, room=number of spaces in the buffer, nreader=number
of reader processes on the pipe and nwriter=number of writer processes on the pipe.
These variables are used for process synchronization during pipe read/write. When
PMTX starts, all the pipe structures are initialized as free. When a process creates
a pipe by the pipe(int pd[2]) system call, it executes kpipe() in kernel. kpipe() allocates a PIPE structure, initializes the pipe variables and allocates a 4 KB page frame
for the pipe's data buffer. Then it allocates two file descriptors, pd[0] and pd[1],
which point to the READ_PIPE and WRITE_PIPE OFT instances, which point to
the pipe structure. After creating a pipe, a process forks a child process to share the
pipe. During fork, the child inherits all the open file descriptors of the parent. If the
file descriptor is a pipe, fork increments the reference count of the OFT and also
the number of readers or writers in the PIPE structure by one. A process must be
either a reader or writer on the same pipe, but not both. Each process must close its
unwanted pipe descriptor. close_pipe() deallocates the PIPE structure if there are no
more reader and writer. Otherwise, it does the normal closing of the file descriptor
and wakes up any waiting reader/writer processes on the pipe. read_pipe() is for
reading from a pipe, and write_pipe() is for writing to a pipe. Pipe read/write are
synchronized by sleep/wakeup. A reader returns 0 if the pipe has no data and no
writer. Otherwise, it reads as much as it needs, up to the pipe size, and returns the
number of bytes read. It waits for data only if the pipe has no data but still has writers. After each read operation, the reader wakes up any sleeping writers. A writer
process detects a BORKEN_PIPE error and aborts if there are no readers on the
pipe. Otherwise, it writes as much as it can to the pipe. It may wait if there is no
room and the pipe still has readers. After each write operation, the writer wakes up
any sleeping readers.

SMP: The SMP kernel implements a parallel pipe algorithm to improve concurrency. The data buffer of each pipe is split into two separate buffers; a read buffer
for readers and a write buffer for writers. If the reader buffer has data and the write
buffer has room, a reader and a writer can proceed in parallel. Otherwise, they either
swap buffers or transfer data from the write buffer to the reader buffer. Reader and
writer processes are synchronized by modified sleep/wakeup operations. They use
conditional locking and back-off to prevent deadlocks.

17. mes.c: This file implements message passing as a general mechanism for IPC,
    which allows processes to send/receive messages through the kernel. It is used
    to implement a CDROM file server, which communicates with client processes
    by messages to provide iso9660 file system services.

18. signal.c: This file implements signals and signal processing. It contains the following functions, which are the same for all versions of MTX.

   1. kkill() implements the kill(sig, pid) syscall. It delivers a signal, sig, to the target process. To keep things simple, MTX does not enforce kill permissions. If desired, the reader may modify kkill() to enforce permission checking. As in Unix/Linux, MTX in protected mode supports 31 signals, each corresponds to a bit in PROC.res.signal. Delivering a signal i sets the i-th bit in the target PROC's res.signal to 1. In Unix/Linux, if a process is in the "uninterruptible sleep" state, it cannot be woken up by signals. In PMTX, processes only sleep for ZOMBIE children and when reading/writing pipes, so they are interruptible. Therefore, a signal always wakes up the target process if it is in the SLEEP state. If the target process is waiting for I/O, it is blocked on a semaphore in the device driver. Unblocking such a process may confuse the device driver. However, if the process is waiting for terminal inputs, it will be unblocked by signals. Since the unblocked process resumes running inside a device driver, the driver's I/O buffer must also be adjusted to ensure consistency.

   2. ksignal() implements the signal(sig, catcher) syscall. It installs a catcher function as the signal handler for the signal, except for signal number 9, which cannot be changed. When a process enters Kmode via a syscall and when it is about to return to Umode, it checks and handles outstanding signals by calling kpsig().

   3. kpsig() calls cksig(), which resets the signal bit of an outstanding signal and returns the signal number. For each outstanding signal number n, if the process signal handler function, sig[n], is 0, the process calls kexit($n<<8$) to die with an exit status$=n<<8$. If sig[n] is 1, it ignores the signal. Otherwise, kpsig() sets up the process interrupt ustack frame in such a way that, when the process returns to Umode, it first returns to the signal catcher function. When the catcher function finishes, it returns to the place where it lastly entered kernel. To keep the system simple, MTX dose not support signal masking.

   4. In addition to the Control-C key, which generates a SIGINT(2) signal to all processes on a terminal, several user mode programs, e.g. kill, divide, segcatcher, itimer, etc. are used to demonstrate the signal processing capability of PMTX and SMP.

19. syscall.c: This file implements the system call routing table. First, a function pointer table is set up to contain all the syscall function entry addresses.

        int (*f[ ])() = {getpid, getppid, getpri, ksetpri, getuid, ...};

When a process issues a syscall, e.g. syscall(a, b,c, d,e), it enters kernel to execute int80h, which calls kcinth(), which is

```
int kcinth(u32 parameters via kstack)
{
   int a,b,c,d,e,r;
   unlock();                    // handle syscall with interrupts on
   if (running->res->signal) // check and handle outstanding signals
       kpsig();
   // get syscall parameters a,b,c,d,e from ustack, a=syscall number
   r = (*f[a])(b,c,d,e);        // invokde the syscall function
   if (running->res->signal) // check and handle signal again
       kpsig();
   // change saved AX register to r for return value to Umode
   running->priority = 128-running->cpu;  // drop back to Umode priority
}
```

In kcinth(), the process checks and handles signals first. This is because, if the process already has a pending signal, which may cause it to terminate, processing the syscall would be a waste of time. Then it fetches the syscall parameters from the Umode stack, where a is the syscall number. Then it invokes the corresponding kernel function by

$$r = (*f[a])(b,c,d,e);$$

When the syscall function returns, it checks and handles signals again. Since syscall is only a special kind of interrupts, the second checking and handling signals are performed in the exit code of interrupt handlers. Each syscall function returns a value r, except kexit(), which never returns. Before returning to goUmode in assembly, it writes r to the saved AX register in the interrupt stack frame as the return value to Umode. In addition, syscall.c also contains simple kernel functions, such as getpid(), kps(), etc. Any additional syscall functions may also be added here.

20. t.c: This file contains the kernel initialization code, the main() function and parts of the process scheduler.

PMTX: In protected mode, pm_entry in entry.s is the entry point. It sets up the initial paging environment and calls init() in init.c. In init(), it sets up a new pgdir and page tables to expand kernel's virtual address space to the entire physical memory. Then it calls kernel_init() in t.c to initialize kernel data structures, creates and runs the initial process P0. P0 sets up the IDT for interrupt and exception processing, initializes I/O buffers, device drivers and mounts the root file system. Then it builds the free page frame list and calls main() to create and run the INIT process P1.

SMP: In SMP, the boot processor (BSP) executes init(), which creates and runs the initial process P0. P0 continues to initialize the kernel and eventually calls main(). In main(), P0 first creates the INIT process P1. Then it calls smp() in smp.c to configure the system for SMP operations and start up the APs. After these, P0 waits until all the APs are ready. Then it enters the scheduler to run tasks. Each AP wakes up to execute the same trampoline code, APstart(cpuid), in which it sets up the AP's execution environment to the SMP kernel, creates and run an initial process. Then it informs the BSP of being ready and enters the scheduler to run tasks also. In SMP, each CPU has a separate scheduling queue, readyQueue [cpuid], for process scheduling by parallel algorithms.

15.9.4   Process Scheduling in PMTX and SMP

Process scheduling in MTX is based on dynamic priority with time slice. The scheduling policy is aimed to achieve the following goals in order:

- quick response to interactive processes
- fast execution in kernel mode
- fairness to non-interactive processes

Process scheduling in MTX is implemented as follows.

PMTX: The system maintains a priority readyQueue and a global switch process flag, sw_flag, for process scheduling. Each process has a priority, a time slice and a CPU usage time field. Process priorities vary form 0, which is lowest and used only by the initial/idle process P0, to 256, which is the highest. When an ordinary process is created, it is assigned the base priority of 128. Process scheduling is implemented in the following functions.

1. scheduler(), schedule() and reschedule() in t.c file.

   - scheduler(): This function is called in tswitch() to pick the next running process during task switch. If readyQueue is empty, it runs the idle process P0, which does not have any time limit. Otherwise, it selects the next running process from the head of readyQueue, sets its time slice to SLICE=10 ticks and clears sw_flag to 0.
   - schedule(PROC *p): This function is called from kwakeup() and V() in device drivers and file system for an awakened or unblocked process. It enters p into readyQueue and sets sw_flag to 1 if p has higher priority than the current running process.
   - reschedule(): This function is called when the running process is about to return to user mode. It calls tswitch() to switch process if sw_flag is on.

2. V() in pv.c file: V() is called in device drivers and file system to unblock a process from a semaphore queue. It assigns a high priority of 256 to the unblocked process p and calls schedule(p).

3. Timer interrupt handler in timer.c file: At each timer tick, if the running process is in user mode, it decrements the process time slice by 1 and increments its CPU usage time by 1, with a maximum of 127. When the process time slice reaches 0, it sets a global switch process flag, sw_flag, to 1.

4. At each time interval of N*SLICE ticks ($N >= 2$), the timer interrupt handler recomputes the priority of each process in readyQueue by

$$priority = priority\text{-}CPU\ time$$

and reset its CPU time to 0. If a PROC's CPU time was 0, its priority is increased by a value between 1 and SLICE. This allows a process priority to rise if it has not run for a while.

5. Interrupt handler exit code: When a process exits kernel to return to user mode, it drops back to the user mode priority of 128-CPU time and calls reschedule(), which calls tswitch() to switch process if sw_flag is on

SMP: The process scheduling policy is the same as that of PMTX, except that it uses parallel algorithms for process scheduling.

1. Instead of single ready queue, the SMP kernel maintains ncpu ready queues, readyQueue[ncpu], each associated with a CPU and protected by a spinlock in the CPU structure.
2. Each CPU tries to run tasks from its own readyQueue[cpuid]. If the ready queue is empty, it runs the default idle process, which puts the CPU in halt, waiting for interrupts. Then it tries to run tasks from the same ready queue again.
3. Each CPU has a switch process flag, cpu.sw, in the CPU structure.
4. When a process calling tswitch(), it first acquires the CPU's pinlock, cpu→srQ, which is released by the next running process when it resumes on the same CPU.
5. In order to balance the processing load of the CPUs, ready processes are distributed evenly to different ready queues.
6. Each CPU uses the local APIC timer and handles its own timer interrupts.
7. In SMP, which has more CPUs to run tasks in parallel, the role of dynamic process priority is less important than that in UP systems. If desired, process scheduling in SMP can be done by a short time slice only, which is both simple and effective.
8. The SMP kernel is capable of supporting preemptive process scheduling, including process switch in kernel mode. The APIC timer interrupt handlers include code for preemptive process scheduling. It is commented out to avoid excessive process switch overhead in kernel mode.

15.9.5   Device Drivers

In MTX, all device drivers are interrupt-driven, except for the console display driver which does not use interrupts. Device interrupt handler entry points are installed in the assembly code file, ts.s, by INTH macro calls. Each INTH macro call is of the form

_xinth: INTH xhandler

All device drivers use semaphores for synchronization. Details of device driver design and implementation are discussed in Chap. 10. Device drivers in all versions of MTX are essentially the same, except for the timer, which is different in SMP. In the following, we only describe the timer and modifications to other device drivers for SMP operations.

1. Timer and Timer Service:

PMTX: Both RMTX and PMTX use the PC's channel 0 timer, which is programmed to generate 60 interrupts per second. During booting, the booter reads the BIOS time-of-day (TOD) and saves it at 0x90000. When a MTX kernel starts, it uses the saved TOD as the real time base. At each second, it displays a wall clock. Timer service is implemented by a timer queue, which is a list of interval timer requests (TQEs). Each TQE has a time field and an action function. When a TQE's time expires, the timer interrupt handler invokes the action function, which typically unblocks the process or sends an SIGALRM(14) signal to the process. Both RMTX and PMTX use the PIC timer interrupts for process scheduling by dynamic priority and time slice.

SMP: In SMP, the PIC timer is disabled. Each CPU uses the local APIC timer and handles its own timer interrupts using the interrupt vector 0x40+CPUID. The APIC timer can support very fine time resolutions. For the sake of simplicity, it is set to generate approximately 60 interrupts per second. The APIC timer interrupt handler entry points, denoted by c0inth to c15inth, are installed by the INTH macro in ts.s as usual. Each timer interrupt entry code calls a handler function in C, all of which call apictimerHandler(CPUID) in smp.c, where the parameter CPUID identifies the CPU. In apictimerHandler(), each CPU maintains its own tick count and a TOD clock. At each second, each CPU calls pr_clock() to display its wall clock on the console screen. Timer service functions, such as FD drive motor on/off control and interval timer requests, are provided by CPU0 only. In addition, each CPU supports process scheduling by dynamic priority and time slice.

2. Modifications to Other Device Drivers in SMP: In a SMP device driver, process and interrupt handler may execute on different CPUs in parallel. If the process and interrupt handler share data structures and control variables, their executions must be serialized to prevent race conditions. In SMP, such device drivers use a spinlock to serialize the executions of process and interrupt handler. While holding the spinlock, if a process has to wait for data or room in the driver's I/O buffer, it must complete the wait operation before releasing the spinlock. To prevent process self-deadlock, a process must release the spinlock before enabling device interrupts. Similarly, an interrupt handler must release the spinlock before issuing EOI.

15.9.6   File System

MTX implements a simple Linux compatible EXT2 file system, which is described in Chap. 12. The file system uses semaphores for process synchronization. In PMTX, all the file system resources, such as in memory inodes, free I/O buffers, etc. are maintained in single data structures and managed by sequential algorithms. In particular, the I/O buffer management algorithm for block devices is also sequential. In the following, we shall focus on modifications to the file system for SMP operations.

1. Resource Management by Parallel Algorithms

The SMP_MTX kernel uses parallel algorithms for resource management. In a file system, the most heavily contended resource is the in-memory inodes (minodes). To improve concurrency, the minodes are divided into separate lists associated with the devices and managed by parallel algorithms. When the SMP system starts, each device is allocated a fixed number of free minodes. To allocate a free minode for (dev, ino), it tries to allocate a minode from the device's local free list. If the device's local free list is empty, it refills the local free list by transferring minodes from the free lists of other devices. When a minode is no longer needed, it is released to the local free list of the current device for reuse. The same principle and technique can also be used to manage other resources, such as the blocks and inodes bitmaps, etc. but they are not yet implemented in the current SMP kernel.

2. Spinlocks

In SMP, most low-level functions in allocate_deallocate.c and util.c of the file system use spinlocks to protect critical regions. While holding a spinlock, if a process has to wait for a needed resource, it completes the wait operation before releasing the spinlock in order to prevent race conditions.

3. Block Device I/O Buffer Management

This is the most prominent modification to the file system. In SMP, block device I/O buffers are maintained in hash queues and managed by a parallel buffer management algorithm, which improves both concurrency and the performance of the buffer cache.

4. Parallel fork-exec and mkdir_rmdir Algorithms

SMP_MTX supports fork-exec and mkdir-rmdir by parallel algorithms. The ultimate goal is to replace all sequential algorithms by parallel algorithms in the SMP kernel. As of now, this work is still in an experimental stage. For this reason, parallel fork-exec and mkdir-rmdir functions are included for testing only. Further development is still needed and in progress.

15.9.7   PMTX and SMP Startup and login

In all versions of MTX, a bootable MTX image is composed of 4 contiguous pieces.

```
Sector:|  S0     S1     S3     S4  |  S5 ....................|
       |------|-----|-----|-----|------------------------|
       | BOOT |SETUP|  APentry  |<------ mtx kernel ----->|
```

where BOOT is for booting the (real mode only) image from a FD, SETUP is for transition from 16-bit real mode to 32-bit protected mode and APentry is the start-up code of the APs in SMP. The last two bytes of the BOOT sector contain the boot signature, which is PP for protected mode kernel or RR for real-mode kernel. When installed to a hard disk, a suitable HD booter is needed to boot up the MTX kernel. The HD booter used in MTX is MBR.ext4 developed in Chap. 3. It can boot MTX, Linux and Windows. During booting, the HD booter loads BOOT+SETUP to 0x90000, APentry to 0x91000 and the MTX kernel to 0x10000. It also writes the BIOS Time-of-Day (TOD) to 0x90000 and the boot partition number to 0x90508 in the BOOT sector. Then it checks the boot signature in the BOOT sector. If the word in RR, it jumps to 0x10000 to start the RMTX kernel in real mode. If the word is PP, it jumps to 0x90200 to run SETUP, which brings up the MTX kernel in protected mode.

15.9.7.1   PMTX Startup Sequence

In PMTX, which uses dynamic paging, the kernel virtual address space is from 2 GB to 2 GB+512 MB, and user mode virtual address space is from 0 to 4 MB. The PMTX kernel is compiled with the starting virtual address 0x80100000 but it runs from the physical address 1 MB. The PMTX kernel must set up the paging environment when it starts. This is done in two steps, which resembles that of multi-stage booting.

1. SETUP: During booting, the booter loads SETUP to 0x90200 and the PMTX kernel to 0x10000. Then it jumps to 0x90200 to run SETUP. SETUP contains an initial GDT, which is

```
setup_gdt: .quad   0x0000000000000000   # null descriptor
           .quad   0x00cF9a000000FFFF   # kcs 00cF 9=PpLS=1001
           .quad   0x00cF92000000FFFF   # kds
```

The initial GDT defines only two 4 GB kernel code and data segments. SETUP moves the initial GDT to 0x9F000 and loads the GDTR register to point at the initial GDT. Then it enters protected mode, moves the MTX kernel to 1 MB and ljmp to the entry address of the PMTX kernel at 1 MB. The initial GDT is only temporary. It provides the initial 4 GB flat segments for the PMTX kernel to get started.

2. Entry.s: pm_entry in entry.s is the entry point of the PMTX kernel. In order to let the kernel use virtual addresses from 0x80000000 by paging, entry.s defines an initial page directory, ipgdir, two initial page tables, pg0 and pg1, a new GDT, an IDT and a page directory, kpgdir, at offsets from 0x1000 to 0x8000. It fills the two initial page tables, pg0 and pg1, with page frames from 0 to 8 MB to create an identity mapping of VA=[0–8 MB] to PA=[0–8 MB]. Entries 512 and 513 of ipgdir, which point to pg0 and pg1 also, map the virtual address space VA=[2 GB to 2 GB+8 MB] to [0–8 MB]. The new GDT, kgdt,

defines six segments, in which tss is for the TSS in protected mode, ucs and uds are for user mode code and data segments of the current running process. After setting up the initial page tables, entry.s uses ipgdir to turn on paging. It then does a ljmp, using relative PC addressing, to force the CPU to switch to virtual address, allowing the kernel to access the virtual space [0x80000000, 0x80000000+8 MB].

3. Load GDTR with the new kgdt descriptor by lgdt kgdt_desc. The new GDT at 0x80104000 defines two kernel mode segments, a TSS and two user mode segments. All code and data segments are flat 4 GB segments, as required by paging.

4. initproc is a statically defined PROC structure for the initial process P0. entry.s sets the stack pointer to the high end of initproc's kstack. Then it calls init() to initialize the PMTX kernel.

5. init.c file: init() first initializes the display driver to make printf() work. At this moment, the kernel's virtual address space is limited to 8 MB. The next step is to expand kernel's virtual address range to the entire available physical memory. Assume 512 MB physical memory and the PMTX kernel occupies the lowest 4 MB. init() builds the new page directory at 0x80106000 and the 128 new page tables at 4 MB, 4 MB+4 KB, etc. which map the kernel's virtual address range to the entire physical memory.

6. kpgtable() creates a kpgdir at 0x80500000, in which entries 512–639 point to 128 page tables, which map VA=[0x80000000, 0x80000000+512 MB] to [0, 512 MB]. In PMTX, kpgdir plays two roles. First, it is the pgdir of the initial process P0, which runs in Kmode whenever no other process is runnable. Second, it is the prototype of the page directories of all other processes. Each process has its own page directory and associated page tables. Since the kernel mode address spaces of all processes are the same, the high 512 entries of all page directories are identical. When creating a new process we simply copy the high 512 entries of kpgdir into the process pgdir. The low (0–511) entries of a process pgdir define the user mode page tables of that process. These entries will be set up when the process is created.

7. Switch CR3 to the new kernel page directory, kpgdir. This allows the kernel to access all the physical memory from 0 to 512 MB.

8. kernel_init(): Then init() calls kernel_init() (in t.c) to initialize the MTX kernel data structures, such as free PROC lists, readyQueue and sleepList, etc. In PMTX, only initproc and its resource structure are statically defined. The other NPROC (256) and NTHREAD (128) PROCs are constructed in the memory area of 5 MB. It uses initproc to create the initial process P0, and sets the level-0 interrupt stack in P0's TSS to P0's kstack. Then it calls switch_tss(), which changes the TSS in GDT to P0's TSS and loads the CPU's task state register, TSR, with the new TSS. These make P0's kstack the interrupt/exception stack. The system is now running the initial process P0.

9. The IDT contains 256 8-byte entries, which requires only 2 KB space. It is constructed at 0x105000. init() continues to initialize the IDT and install exception and interrupt vectors in the IDT. Exception handler entry points are in traps.s.

Exception handlers are in trapc.c. I/O interrupt handler entry points are defined in ts.s by INTH macro calls. I/O interrupt handler functions are in the various device drivers. Among the interrupts, vector 0x80 is for system calls.

10. Initialize I/O buffers, device drivers and timer: After setting up the IDT and interrupt vectors, init() initializes I/O buffers. The PMTX kernel has 1024 I/O buffers. Their data areas are allocated at 7 MB. When booting from a hard disk, the hd-booter deposits the boot device number in 0x90508. Before initializing the HD driver, init() extracts the boot device number to set the global variable HD, which is used in both mount_root() and the HD driver. In addition, when initializing the HD driver, P0 also reads the HD's partition table to get the MTX partition's start sector and size. Then it initializes the file system and mounts the boot partition as the root file system.

11. PMTX uses a free page list, pfreeList, for allocation/deallocation of page frames. pfreeList threads all the free page frames from 8 to 512 MB in a link list. Each element of pfreeList contains the address of the next page frame. As usual, the list ends with a 0 pointer. In order for the kernel to access the entries of pfreeList, the link pointers must use virtual addresses of the page frames. When allocating a page frame, the virtual address of the page must be converted to physical address. Conversion between virtual address and physical address are done by the PA/VA macros. With the free page link list, palloc() allocates a free page from pfreeList, and pdealloc(VA(page frame)) inserts a deallocated page frame to pfreeList. In order to use all the available page frames, we add a pfreeTail, which points to the last element of pfreeList, and insert deallocated pages to the tail of pfreeList.

12. Call main() in t.c: In main(), P0 calls kfork("/bin/init") to create the INIT process P1 and switches process to run P1. P1 forks one or more login processes and waits for ZOMBIE children. When the login processes start, PMTX is ready for use. The startup screen of PMTX is shown in Fig. 14.21 in Chap. 14 of the book.

15.9.7.2   SMP_MTX Startup Sequence

SMP is based on PMTX. Its startup sequence is similar to that of PMTX. Therefore, we shall only focus on the SMP part. In SMP, initproc[NCPU] and their resource structures are statically defined. Each CPU uses an initproc[CPUID] as the initial and idle process, which has the special pid=0 for BSP and 2000+CPUID for APs. Each initial/idle process runs on a specific CPU. To prevent them from being grabbed by a wrong CPU, they do not enter ready queues for scheduling.

1. SETUP: When the SMP kernel starts, only the BSP (CPU0) is executing. SETUP defines an initial GDT for the BSP to enter protected mode. Then it moves the MTX kernel to 0x100000 (1 MB) and ljmp to pm_entry in entry.s to execute the SMP kernel startup code.

2. entry.s sets up an initial page environment, which allows the kernel to access
   the lowest 8 MB memory as either physical or virtual addresses. After setting up
   the initial page tables, entry.s uses the initial ipgdir to turn on paging and forces
   the BSP to use virtual addresses starting from 0x80000000. So far, the startup
   actions are identical to that of PMTX. The SMP part begins here. At 0x104000
   are NCPU (16) GDTs, one for each CPU, as shown below.

```
kgdt:  .rept  NCPU      # NCP=16   #                            Index
       .quad 0x0000000000000000    # null descriptor       0x00
       .quad 0x00cF9a000000FFFF    # kcs 00cF PpLS=1001=9 0x08
       .quad 0x00cF92000000FFFF    # kds                    0x10
       .quad 0x0000000000000000    # tss                    0x18
       .quad 0x00cFFa000000FFFF    # ucs 00cF PpLS=1111=F 0x20
       .quad 0x00cFF2000000FFFF    # uds                    0x28
       .quad 0x80C0920000000027    # CPU struct=40 bytes  0x30
       .endr
gdt_desc:   .word 56-1             # for CPU0's GDT
            .long kgdt             # hard coded GDT address of BSP
       .org 0x5000
idt:   .fill 1024,4,0              # 2KB IDT at 0x5000
       .org 0x8000                 # Other kernel code start here
```

The first six segments of each GDT are the same as they are in PMTX. The
last segment descriptor is used to map the 40-byte CPU structure by gs, so that
each CPU can access its CPU structure by the same virtual addresses in the
gs segment. The (2 KB) IDT is common to all CPUs. It will be constructed
at 0x105000.The BSP uses the first GDT at 0x104000 and the initial ipgdir at
0x101000 to turn on paging. Then it sets the stack pointer to the high end of
initproc[0]'s kstack and calls init().

3. The actions of init() are as follows.

3.1. Find Number of CPUs: init() first calls findmp() to get the SMP system con-
     figuration information. findsmp() tries to find the FPS and then the MP table. It
     scans the MP table for the number of processor entries and returns the number
     of CPUs in the system. Each CPU is represented by a cpu structure (in type.h).

```
struct cpu{
     struct cpu *cpu;    // pointer to this cpu struct
     PROC *proc;         // current running PROC on this CPU
     int   srQ;          // CPU spinlock
     int   sw;           // switch process flag
     int   rq;           // next ready queue to use
     int   id;           // cpu ID number
     u32 *pgdir;         // pgdir pointer of CPU
     u32 *pgtable;       // pgtable pointer
     u64 *gdt;           // per CPU GDT pointer
     PROC *initial;      // initial PROC pointer of CPU
} cpus[NCPU];            // NCPU=16, size = 40 bytes
```

3.2. Initialize CPU structures and gs segments: In SMP, each CPU has an initial
   PROC, initproc[cpuid]. Since all the initial PROCs run in Kmode only, they
   share the same pgdir and page tables of CPU0. Assume that the physical memory is 512 MB and the SMP kernel occupies the lowest 4 MB. Then the memory
   area above 4 MB is free. As in PMTX, the kgdir is at 0x80106000 and the 128
   page tables at 4 MB. The cpu structures and their pgdir's and pgtables are initialized by the following code segment.

```
//GDT_ADDR=0x80104000, KPG_DIR=0x80106000, KPG_TABLE=0x80400000
struct cpu *cp;
u32 *gdt = GDT_ADDR;             // NCPU GDTs at 0x80104000 in entry.s
u32 *mygdt, myaddr;
for (i=0; i<ncpu; i++){          // ncpu is the actual number of CPUs
    cp = &cpus[i];
    cp->cpu = &cpus[i];          // cpu structure pointer
    cp->proc = 0;                // current running PROC on this CPU
    cp->id = cp->rq = i;         // CPU ID and initial rq number
    cp->sw = 0;                  // switch process flag
    cp->pgdir   = KPG_DIR;       // kpgdir at 0x80106000
    cp->pgtable = KPG_TABLE;     // pgtables begin from 4MB
    cp->initial = &initproc[i];  // CPU's initial PROC
    if (i==0)
        kpgtable();              // only CPU0 builds kpgdir, pgtables
    cp->gdt = gdt + i*2*NSEG;    // NSEG=7, pointer to CPU's GDT
    mygdt   = (u32*)cp->gdt;     // fix up gs segment address in GDT
    myaddr  = (u32)&cp->cpu << 8;
    mygdt[13] |= (myaddr >> 24); // gs segment is 6th entry in GDT
    mygdt[12] |= (myaddr << 8);  // index 12=low, 13=high 4-byte
}
```

4. Kernel Mode Page Table: The function kpgtable() sets up the kernel mode kpgdir and page tables, which are shared by all the initial processes of the CPUs.
   In addition to regular pages, it also fills the last eight entries of kpgdir and their
   page tables to create an identity mapping of the address range [FE000000, 4 GB],
   allowing the CPUs to access IOAPIC and APIC addresses above 0xFE000000.
   The virtual address mapping of the CPUs is shown in Fig. 15.3. The memory
   map of SMP_MTX is shown in Fig. 15.4.
5. Load GDT and Enable Paging: The BSP loads GDT with cpus[0].gdt and sets
   gs = 0x30, which corresponds to the last segment in the GDT. Similarly, when an
   AP starts, it loads its own GDT at cpus[cpuid()].gdt and sets gs = 0x30 also. Thus,
   every CPU can access its own cpu structure and the current PROC running on the
   CPU using the same virtual address gs:0 and gs:4, respectively. To comply with
   these, the symbols cpu and running are defined in type.h as

```
extern struct cpu *cpu    asm("%gs:0");  // &cpus[cpuid()]
extern PROC *running      asm("%gs:4");  // cpus[cpuid()].proc
```

The GCC compiler will use gs:0 for cpu, and gs:4 for PROC *running. Therefore, in the SMP kernel's C code, the symbols cpu points to the CPU structure
and running points to the PROC that's currently executing on the CPU. In assem-

bly code, they are accessed as gs:0 and gs:4, respectively. Then the BSP switches pgdir to cpus[0].pgdir. The BSP can now access all 512 MB physical memory, as well as the IOAPIC and local APIC registers above 0xFE000000. When an AP starts, it first uses the initial igdt at 0x101000 to turn on paging. Then it switches to the same kernel mode kpgdir and page tables of BSP, allowing each AP to access the entire virtual address range directly.

6. BSP: Continue to initialize the SMP kernel. The actions are the same as in PMTX, i.e. initialize kernel data structures, create and run the initial process P0, remap IRQs, install IDT, initialize device drivers and mount the root file system, etc. As in PMTX, the NPROC=256 process and NTHREAD=128 thread PROCs are constructed at 5 MB. However, instead of a single free list, in SMP free PROCs are divided into separate free lists, each associated with a CPU and protected by a spinlock, for allocation/deallocation by parallel algorithms. After initializing the kernel, P0 sets up the free page frame list and calls main(ncpu) (in t.c) to create the INIT process P1. If the number of CPUs, ncpu, is 1, P0 brings the system up in UP mode. Otherwise, it calls smp() to configure the system for SMP operations by the following steps. The reader may consult Chap. 15 for more details

7. Initialize IOAPIC to route interrupts: Configure APIC and APIC timer:

8. Start up APs: The BSP issues INIT and STARTUP IPIs to start up the APs. The startup code of the APs is loaded at 0x91000. The BSP uses the memory area 0x90000 as a communication area for the APs to start up. First, the BSP writes the entry address of APstart() to 0x90000, followed by the initial stack pointers of initproc[i], (i=1 to ncpu-1). Then it executes

```
int go_smp = 1                            // number of active CPUs
lapicw(0x0300, 0x00c4500); smp_delay(); // broadcat INIT ISP to APs
lapicw(0x0300, 0x00c4691); smp_delay(); // broadcat STARTUP to APs
while(go_smp < ncpu);                     // wait for all APs ready
run_task();     // enter scheduling loop,run tasks from readyQueue[0]
```

When an AP starts, it executes the trampoline code, APentry, at 0x91000 in 16-bit real mode. After entering protected mode with 4 GB flat segments, each AP reads the APIC ID register at 0xFEE00020 to get its CPU ID number. It uses the CPU ID number to fetch the corresponding initial stack pointer deposited by BSP at 0x90000+4*ID. Then, it calls APstart(ID) in smp.c.

9. APs Execute Startup Code APstart(id): Each AP uses its CPU id number to access the cpus[id] structure, which was set up by the BSP in init(). In APstart(), the actions of each AP are as follows.

   - Load its own GDT in cpus[id].gdt, turn on paging and switch pgdir to cpus[id].pgdir;
   - Configure its local APIC by lapic_init(id);
   - Load the same IDT (at 0x105000 in entry.s) for exception and interrupt processing;

- Set gs = 0x30, cpu = &cpus[id] and running = &initproc[id];
- Initialize initproc[id] with pid = 1000 + id as the initial PROC running on AP;
- Set AP's GDT.tss to the initial PROC's tss as the interrupt stack;
- Configure APIC timer, each AP handles its own APIC timer interrupts, using the
- interrupt vector 0x40 + CPUID;
- Atomically increment go_smp by 1 to inform BSP that this AP is ready;
- call run_task() to enter scheduling loop to run tasks from readyQueue [cpuid].

10. When all the APs are ready, the BSP enters the scheduling loop to run task also.

After all the above steps, MTX is running in SMP mode. The initial process of each CPU is also the idle process of that CPU. Whenever a CPU finds its ready queue empty, it runs the idle process, which puts the CPU in halt, waiting for interrupts. The idle processes are special in that do not enter ready queues for scheduling and they do not have any time limit. For this reason, they are given the special pid 0 and 2000 + cpuid for identification. The startup screen of SMP_MTX for 16 CPUs is shown in Fig. 15.10.

15.9.8   User Interface and System Call Functions

User interface in PMTX and SMP_MTX is identical to that of RMTX in 16-bit real mode, which is covered in Chap. 13. In addition to the system call and user interface functions listed in Chap. 13, PMTX and SMP_MTX have a few additioanl system calls and user mode programs that are apecific to protected mode operations. The reader may consult the ucode.c file in the USER directory and also the syscall.c file in kernel for details.

15.9.9   Recompile PMTX and SMP_MTX

To recompile and install PMTX and SMP_MTX, cd to the source directory and run the mk script as

                    mk PARTITION qemu|vmware.

Examples:

mk 3 qemu   # recompile and install to P3 of a QEMU HD named vdisk
mk 4 vmware   # recompile and install to P4 of a VMware HD named Other.vmdk

The reader may examine and modify the dump script file to install to other locations.

Problems

1. When SMP_MTX starts, it can only access 8 MB physical memory via paging initially.

   1. Modify entry.s to let it access 20 MB physical memory via paging.
   2. For each CPU, build its kpgdir in the real mode memory 0x80000-0x90000, which has space for NCPU=16 kpgdir's.
   3. For each CPU, build its page table in the 1 MB area from 4 to 20 MB.
   4. Let the free page frames begin from 20 MB.

2. Extend SMP_MTX to more than 16 CPUs.

3. In SMP_MTX (also in xv6), the current running PROC pointer of a CPU is at the virtual address gs:4. Instead of using virtual memory, try to maintain the running PROC pointer in a CPU register. Compare the advantages and disadvantages of the two schemes.

4. Modify the UP Unix I/O buffer management algorithm of Chap. 12 for SMP. Implement and test it in SMP_PMTX.

5. Complete Part 2 of the MP Unix buffer management algorithm of Bach. Pay attention to the following cases.

   1. The free buffer list may be empty.
   2. Cross locking: If a process finds a needed buffer, it lock(buffer); lock(freelist); in order to take the buffer out of freelist. Meantime, another process may lock(freelist); lock(buffer) to get a free buffer from freelist;
   3. A locked free buffer is in a different hash queue.

6. Modify the parallel buffer management algorithm to raise its degree of concurrency to the number of hash queues.

7. SMP producer-consumer problem: Try to use signals to inform the producers and consumers of abnormal conditions. For example, when the last producer terminates, send a special SIG_PEND signal to all consumers, which unblocks the consumers if they are waiting for items. Similarly, when the last consumer terminates, send a special SIG_REND signal to all producers, which unblocks the producers if they are waiting for rooms.

   1. How to deliver such special signals?
   2. How does a process handle a special signal?

8. The parallel pipe algorithm allows only one reader and one writer to execute in parallel on the same pipe. In general, a pipe may have multiple readers and writers. Extend the parallel pipe algorithm to support multiple readers and writers on the same pipe.

9. In order to reduce system overhead, in SMP_MTX process switching in kernel mode is disabled. Verify that the SMP_MTX kernel supports preemptive scheduling in kernel mode.

10. It is well known that the problem of optimal task scheduling in MP systems is NP-hard.

1. Consult the literature to find out what NP-hard means and what does it imply?
2. In SMP_MTX, we only try to distribute ready processes to different ready queues evenly. Design other algorithms to balance the processing load of the CPUs.

11. In the SMP_MTX file system, in-memory minodes are maintained in separate devices. The in-memory minodes are not used as a cache memory. After using a minode, it is immediately released by iput(), which removes the minode from the device's minode_list if its refCount reaches zero. Modify iget() and iput() to use the in-memory minodes as a cache memory similar to block device I/O buffers.

12. Modify the SMP_MTX kernel to manage other resources, such as bitmaps and open file tables in the file system, by parallel algorithms.

13. Inter-Processor-Interrupts (IPIs): In SMP, CPUs may interact with one another by IPIs.

Part 1: Conduct IPI experiments in SMP. Modify the SMP_MTX kernel as follows.

1. int xhandler(){ printf("CPU %d in IPI handler\n", cpu->id); send_EOI() }
2. In ts.s: Install xinth and xhandler: xinth: INITH xhandler
3. In init(): Install a vector, e.g. 0x50 for xinth: int_install(0x50, xinth);
4. Add a syscall, sendIPI(int cpuid), which sends an IPI with vector 0x50 to the target CPU:

. lapicw(0x310, cpuid<<24);   // destination = cpuid
. lapicw(0x300, 0x00004050);   // physical deliver mode, interrupt IPI with vector 0x50

5. Add a user command, sendIPI cpuid, to test the sendIPI syscall. Verify that executing the command causes the target CPU to execute the xhandler function.

Part 2: Use IPI to implement parallel pfork-pexec and pmkdir-prmdir in the SMP_MTX kernel and compare their performances with sequential fork-exec and mkdir-rmdir algorithms.

14. Analyze other top-level file system algorithms, e.g. creat(), unlink(), etc. in the SMP_MTX kernel for parallelisms and design parallel algorithms for these functions.

15. Modify the real mode SMP_RMTX to do the following:

1. Remap IRQ0-15 to 0x20-0x2F. Verify that the system still works.
2. Use local APIC timers for all CPUs.
3. Try to configure the IOAPIC to route interrupts to different CPUs.
4. Run SMP_RMTX on other virtual machines.

References

Bach, M.J, "The Design of the Unix operating system", Prentice Hall, 1990

Cox, A., "An Implementation of Multiprocessor Linux", 1995

Cox, R., Kaashoek, F., Morris, R. "xv6 a simple, Unix-like teaching operating system, xv6-book@ pdos.csail.mit.edu", Sept. 2011.

Dietrich, S., Walker, D., "The evolution of Real-Time Linux", http://www.cse.nd.edu/courses/ cse60463/www/amatta2.pdf, 2015

Grama, A., Gupta, A., George Karypis, G., Kumar, V., "Introduction to Parallel Computing", 2nd Edition", Addison-Wesley, 2003

Intel MultiProcessor Specification, v1.4, 1997

Liu, C.L., Layland, J.W., "Scheduling Algorithm for Multi-programming in a Hard Real-Time Environment," J. ACM, Vol. 20, pp. 40–61, 1973.

McKusick, M.K., Neville-Neil, G., "The Design and Implementation of the FreeBSD Operating System", Addison-Wesley, 2004.

Pthreads: https://computing.llnl.gov/tutorials/pthreads/, 2015

Wang, X., "Improved I/O Buffer Management Algorithms for Unix Operating System", M.S. thesis, EECS, WSU, 2002

Chapter 16
Hybrid Operating Systems

16.1 Monolithic Kernel

In the beginning, computer systems were relatively simple. Most computer systems have only a single CPU, a small amount of memory and a few I/O devices. Therefore, operating systems for early computer systems were also fairly simple and small. Because of their small sizes, most early operating systems, e.g. VAX-11/VMS and Unix, etc. are based on monolithic kernels. A monolithic kernel consists of process management, memory management, device drivers and file systems, all in one integrated unit. A monolithic kernel is a complete kernel since it has all the functionalities of an operating system. As computer systems grew larger and more complex, additional device drivers, new file systems and other functionalities were added to the OS kernel. As a result, OS kernels also grew bigger and much more complex, making them more prone to errors and difficult to maintain. The concept of microkernel (Accetta et al. 1986) was conceived as an alternative approach to kernel design. It is aimed at addressing some of the issues of big kernels.

16.2 Microkernel

A microkernel is the minimum amount of software that can provide the mechanisms needed to implement an operating system. The mechanisms include low-level address space management, process scheduling, fetch and forward interrupts and Inter-Process Communication (IPC). In theory, all other functions of an OS, such as device drivers, memory manager, process manager, file systems and networking, etc. can all be implemented in user space outside of the microkernel. Each of the functions can be implemented as a server process. In a microkernel based OS, user processes do not execute kernel functions directly. Whenever a user process needs to do something, it sends a request message to a server process and waits for reply. The microkernel's IPC routes the request message to a server, which handles the

© Springer International Publishing Switzerland 2015   525
K. C. Wang, *Design and Implementation of the MTX Operating System,*
DOI 10.1007/978-3-319-17575-1_16

request and sends back a reply along with the results of the requested operation. The microkernel approach has many claimed advantages over monolithic kernels, such as

Because of their small size, microkernels can be made more reliable and portable to different computer hardware platforms.

Microkernel based OS are more modular because all OS functions, e.g. memory manager and file systems, etc. can be implemented as server processes in user space. Microkernel based systems are more reliable and available because errors in one server do not affect other parts of the system. The system can even be configured dynamically by replacing one server with another without recompiling and rebooting the system.

Microkernel based systems can support multiple operating systems.

Microkernel started in the late 80's. Active research and development continued through the 90's. Currently, both research and development seem to have slowed to a standstill. Microkernel based systems can be classified into three generations. The most famous first generation microkernel based system is Mach (Accetta et al. 1986) developed at Carnegie Mellon University. It implemented Unix on top of the Mach microkernel. However, the performances of first generation microkernel based systems were not good. The second generation microkernel based systems include MINIX (Tanenbaum and Woodhull 2006), L4 [L4 2015] and QNX [QNX 2014], etc. The most notable changes occurred in L4. It replaced the inefficient Remote Procedure Calls (RPC) in Mach with new IPCs. By using some clever shortcuts, such as passing message in processor registers, allowing sender-receiver to share address space to avoid message copying, automatic context switching in send-recv and lazy scheduling, etc. L4 was able to reduce the IPC overhead significantly. Despite these efforts, when running Linux on top of a L4 microkernel (Hartig et al. 1997), there is still a 5–10% overhead as compared with native Linux. Third generation microkernels focus mostly on the formal correctness proofs of microkernel, from specification to implementation.

16.3 Comparison of Monolithic and Microkernel Based OS

(1). Portability:

A well designed monolithic kernel can be ported to different computers just as easily as a microkernel. A good example is Linux, which has been ported to many computer platforms, including both CICS and RISC machines.

(2). Device drivers:

In Linux, most device drivers can be compiled as modules, which can be dynamically loaded into the kernel on demand. Although the loaded drivers still run in kernel space, their impact on the kernel size and security is also limited and isolated.

(3). Instead of running multiple OS on top of a microkernel, the current trend is to run multiple OS on virtual machines inside a hosting OS. Whether the hosting OS is microkernel based or monolithic kernel based makes little difference.

(4). Performance

A good example of microkernel based OS is MINIX, which has been a popular educational OS for many years. The microkernel of MINIX3 supports process scheduling, exchange of messages and low-level handling of interrupts. Device drivers are implemented as driver tasks, which have higher priority than regular processes. Process manager, memory manager and file system are implemented as server processes in user space. In MINIX3, when a user process tries to read a file block, it sends a message to the system task in the kernel and waits for a reply. The system task sends the request to the file server, which sends a request to the disk driver task, which starts I/O on the disk and waits for a reply message. When the read operation completes, the disk interrupt handler sends a reply message to the disk driver task, which sends a reply to the file server, which sends a reply to the system task, which finally sends a reply to the user process. As stated in (Tanenbaum and Woodhull 2006), to read a file block the best case requires 4 messages, the worst case requires 11 messages, each requires at least one context switch. For efficiency reasons, data are not transferred through messages. They are copied directly between address spaces. This is the typical way of how a microkernel based OS operates. In contrast, in a monolithic kernel based OS, a similar operation in the best case requires only one system call with no context switch, e.g. when the needed file block is in the buffer cache. Some additional comments on microkernel based OS follow.

(5). In a microkernel based OS, the kernel must schedule tasks/processes for execution. The process manager must manage process creation, process image, signal handling and process termination. The file server must serve process read/write requests by opened file descriptors. Since all the servers are in different address spaces, the process information must be duplicated or split into separate pieces residing in different servers. This adds complexity to the system design and requires more coordination during system operation.

(6). A major claim in support of microkernel is that file systems can be implemented as servers in user space. However, there are also reasons to counter such claims. Let us examine the problem of how to implement a file server in more detail. There are only a few options.

(6).1. As a stateless file server, like the Network File System (NFS) (Sandberg et al. 1985). In this case, the server does not maintain any state information about process file activities. It does not have any notion of opened file descriptors of processes, nor the current read/write position in an opened file. Each read/write request must specify the complete file name as well as the read/write position within the file. Such a file server would be very inefficient and difficult to use in an OS.

(6).2. As a stateless file server, which relies on a separate name server to provide additional information about each read/write request. For example, a stateless file server may use a Domain Name Server (DNS)-like protocol (Comer 1995; Comer and Stevens 1998) to map a process request in the form of a file descriptor to the file's state information. In a distributed system, relying on a separate name server is a must. In a system with shared memory, using a separate name server is not only hard to justify but also a source of inefficiency.

(6).3. As a stateful file server, which maintains state information of process requests. Since the file server and process manager are in different address spaces, the state information of every process must be split into separate pieces. Each server maintains only a part of the total state information, which means additional synchronization overhead and inefficiency.

(6).4. In a monolithic kernel, operations in the file system are inherently concurrent. For example, if two processes read/write different files, they can proceed independently. In MINIX3, the file server is single-threaded. It serves process requests by multiplexing its executions among different requests. While monolithic kernels strive for improved concurrency, using a single thread to simulate the concurrent operations in a file system is a giant step backward. Some file servers in microkernel based OS do support multi-threads. However, the problem of implementing a multi-threaded file server is exactly the same as that of implementing a file system in a monolithic kernel. In order to support concurrency, both require synchronization on shared data objects in the file system. For example, in a single-threaded file server, buffer management is trivial since there is no competition. In a multi-threaded file server, when a thread finds a buffer in the buffer cache, the buffer may already be locked by another thread. Thus, implementing a multi-threaded file server merely shifts the burden of the problem from the same address space of a monolithic kernel to the address space of a file server.

Based on these comparisons, it is fair to say that microkernel is more suited to distributed environment. Monolithic kernels are more suited to shared memory systems. To impose a microkernel on an OS of a shared memory SMP system would be like "cut off the toes to fit the shoes", a gross misfit.

16.4   Hybrid Operating Systems

MTX is a monolithic kernel based OS because it is designed for systems with shared memory. It is fairly easy to modify the MTX kernel to incorporate some of the microkernel features, making it a hybrid OS.

(1). Device drivers

In a strict microkernel based OS, all device drivers should be implemented in user space. But it is clearly unwise to do so. First, an OS cannot run without a root file system or a timer. To separate the root device and timer drivers from the kernel only slows down the system operation. Second, most PC based OS supports only one user, the sole owner of the PC or laptop, who expects fast console response. To separate the console driver from the kernel again makes little sense. On the other hand, in a PC based OS a user may never need to login remotely, and may only use the printer and CD/DVD drives occasionally. Such sparsely used device drivers can be implemented outside of the kernel without seriously impairing the system performance. In MTX, such drivers can be implemented as driver tasks, which run in user space with higher priority than ordinary processes. Communication between processes and driver tasks can be implemented by client-server message passing in the MTX kernel.

(2). File System Servers

MTX started in 16-bit real-mode. Due to the 128KB size limit of the RMTX kernel, it only implements an ATAPI driver but not the iso9660 file system in kernel. Support for CDROM file system is implemented in user mode. It has a cdserver command and a cdclient command. When MTX starts up, we may let the INIT process fork a cdserver daemon process. Alternatively, the server process may also be started up later. Then the user may run the cdclient command as a user process, which sends CDROM operations, such as ls, cd, cat, cp, etc. as request messages to the cdserver. The cdserver implements the iso9660 file system in user space. It handles user requests, allowing the user to access the CD/DVD contents. This makes MTX a hybrid OS since it includes features of both microkernel and monolithic kernel. Likewise, we may implement support for other file systems, e.g. DOS, MINIX and NTFS, etc. by server processes in user space. Examples of hybrid kernels are abundant, e.g. Microsoft NT (Solomon 1998), Mac OS X (Singh 2007), etc. Interested reader may consult the references for additional information.

In summary, microkernel and monolithic kernel represent two distinct approaches to OS design. Each has its strength and weakness. As usual, both sides have their strong advocates as well as critics. Occasionally, there has been heated debates as to which approach is better. To this end, it may be appropriate to quote the great pragmatic Chinese leader Deng Xiaoping: "It doesn't matter if a cat is black or white, so long as it catches mice". In OS design, a good cat may well be a zebra cat, part black and part white.

Problems

1. Implement other file systems, such a DOS, MINIX and NTFS, by server processes in MTX.

References

Accetta, M. et al., "Mach: A New Kernel Foundation for UNIX Development", Techical Conference—USENIX, 1986.

Comer, D.E., "Internetworking with TCP/IP: Principles, Protocols, and Architecture, 3/E", Prentice-Hall, 1995.

Comer, D.E., Stevens, D.L., "Internetworking With TCP/IP: Design, Implementation, and Internals, 3/E", Prentice-Hall, 1998.

Hartig, H., Hohmuth, M., Liedtke, J., Chhonberg, S., Wolter, J., "The Performance of u-Kernel-Based Systems", wiki.cs.unm.edu/ssl/lib/exe/fetch.php/papers:l4.pdf, 1997

L4: Microkernel Family: http://en.wikipedia.org/wiki/L4_microkernel_family, 2015

QNX: The QNX Neutrino Microkernel, http://www.qnx.com/developers/docs/6.3.2/neutrino/sys_arch/kernel.html, 2014

Sandberg, R., Goldberg, D., Kleiman, S., Wash, D., Lyon, B., "Design and Implementation or the Sun Network Filesystem", Sunmicrosystems, Inc. 1985

Singh, A., "Mac OS X Internals", Addison Wesley, 2007

Solomon, D., "Inside Windows NT, Second Edition", Microsoft Press, 1998.

Tanenbaum, A.S., Woodhul, A.S., "Operating Systems, Design and Implementation, third Edition", Prentice Hall, 2006

Appendix

How to Install MTX

MTX Install CD

The MTX install CD, MTXinstallCD.iso, contains the following file tree.
  MTXinstallCD

          |-- gen   : generate bootable iso image
          |-- isobooter : CD/DVD booter of the iso-booter in Chapter 3
          |-- vmlinuz   : Linux (2.6.27.7) kernel
          |-- initrd.gz : initial RAMdisk image of Linux
          |-- initrd-tree : initrd image files
          |-- hdbooter   : MTX/Linux HD booter of Chapter 3
          |-- MTX.images : rmtx,pmtx,smp,mtx32.1,mtx32.2, etc.
          |-- MTX.src   : MTX source files

The sh script gen is used to create a bootable CDROM image, which uses iso-booter as the no-emulation booter. The CDROM image can be burned to a CD/DVD disc or used as a virtual CD directly. During booting, the isobooter first boots up Linux on the RAMdisk image, initrd.gz, which is used to install MTX images form the MTX.images directory.

PC Platforms

MTX can be installed to a real or virtual PC with an IDE hard disk. There are several popular virtual PC platforms, such as QEMU, VMware, VirtualBox and Bochs, etc. MTX has been tested on the following virtual machines.

© Springer International Publishing Switzerland 2015   531
K. C. Wang, *Design and Implementation of the MTX Operating System*,
DOI 10.1007/ 978-3-319-17575-1

Slackware Linux 14.1 : QEMU and VMware-Player 6.02
Ubuntu   Linux 14.4 : QEMU-system-i386

This installation guide covers only QEMU and VMware.

Install and Run MTX Under QEMU

QEMU recognizes many virtual disk formats, including VMware's vmdk. It supports SMP on single CPU hosts, and it provides direct support for serial and parallel ports. Therefore, it is most convenient to run MTX under QEMU. The following examples show how to install and run MTX under QEMU.

Example 1. Use an existing regular virtual disk:
On the MTXinstallCD, vdisk is a flat virtual IDE disk image with 4 partitions. Each partition already contains a runnable version of MTX, which are
Partition 1: rmtx: MTX in 16-bit real mode.
Partition 2: pmtx: MTX in 32-bit protected mode using dynamic paging.
Partition 3: smp: SMP_MTX in 32-bit protected mode.
Partition 4: mtx32.1: MTX in 32-bit protected mode using segmentation.
The simplest way is to run QEMU on the vdisk image directly, as in
qemu –hda vdisk –m 512m –smp 8 –serial mon:stdio
Then boot up and run MTX from the various partitions. To run QEMU with more options, consult QEMU's user manual or the qq script on the MTXinstallCD.

Example 2: Install MTX to an existing virtual disk:
(1). Run QEMU on vdisk but boot up Linux from MTXinstallCD.iso, as in
qemu -hda vdisk –cdrom MTXinstallCD.iso –boot d # assume virtual CD
(2). When Linux comes up, it displays a help menu
MTX Setup: follow the following instructions

Example 3. Create a regular flat virtual disk and install MTX:
Alternatively, the reader may create a flat virtual disk and install MTX as follows.
(1) dd if=/dev/zero of=mydisk bs=1024 count=65536 # creat a file of 64 MB
(2) fdisk -C 8 mydisk # run fdisk on mydisk with 8 cylinders.
partition mydisk; the simplest way is to create only 1 partition.
change the partitions type to 90 for MTX.

(3). Run QEMU on mydisk but boot from MTXinstallCD.iso:
qemu -hda mydisk -cdrom MTXinstallCD.iso -boot d # virtual CD drive
Then install MTX images to the partitions of mydisk as in Example 2.
(4). After installing MTX, run QEMU on mydisk:
qemu -hda mydisk –m −512m –smp 8 -serial mon:stdio
Then boot up and run MTX from the partitions of mydisk.

Install and Run MTX Under VMware

Example 4. Run VMware-Player on an existing virtual machine:

(1). On the MTXinstallCD, the vmware directory contains a VMware-Player virtual machine. Mount the iso CD image and copy the vmware directory to/root, as in

> mount –o loop MTXinstallCD.iso /mnt
>
> cp –av /mnt/vmware /root/vmware
>
> umount /mnt

(2). Start VMware. Select "Open a Virtual Machine". From the prompt window, click on the directories and navigate to/root/vmware/Other/Other.vmdk.

(3). Start the virtual machine. Boot up and run MTX from the partitions of the virtual disk.

Example 5. Install MTX to a new VMware virtual machine:

1. Start VMware. Choose "Create a New Virtual Machine". In the following windows, choose "I will install operating system later" and Other for Guest Operating System. Then create a 0.1G IDE hard disk.
2. Configure the virtual machine's CDROM to boot from MTXinstallCD.iso
3. Start the virtual machine to boot up MTX install environment from the virtual CD.
4. Run fdisk to partition the hard disk and change the partition type to 90.
5. Enter install, choose a partition number and a MTX image to install.
6. Quit Linux. Then start the VM and boot up MTX from the installed partition.

When using VMware the reader should beware of the following limitations. VMware uses the vmdk virtual disk format, which can only be mounted by the vmware-mount utility program. VMware's serial ports are files or sockets. A serial port file can receive outputs but can not input. A socket serial port requires a suitable socket interface, such as socat, for I/O. VMware supports SMP but the number of CPUs cannot exceed that of the host machine.

Example 6: Access and convert regular virtual disks:

The main advantage of using a flat virtual disk is that it can be accessed directly under Linux, e.g. run fdisk to partition it. If a virtual disk has been partitioned and formatted as file systems, the partitions can be mounted as loop devices. Even if the partitions are not formatted, they can be mounted as follows.

> mount -o loop,offset=32256 mydisk /mnt   # 32256=63*512

QEMU's qemu-img program can convert virtual disks to different formats, including flat (raw) and vmdk. The reader may consult qemu-img for more detail.

MTX Source Code Files

In the MTXinstallCD.iso CDROM image, the MTX.src directory contains all the source code of this book. It is organized as follows.

MTX.src

|- BOOTERS: booter programs and demonstration systems of Chapter 3.

|- MTX.programs: demonstration sample systems of Chapters 4-10.

|- Source code of mtx32.1, mtx32.2, rmtx, pmtx, smp.mtx, smp.pmx, smp.rmtx.

It is highly recommended that the reader refers to the relevant source code when study the contents of this book.

Index

Printed in the United States
By Bookmasters